THE NEW A–Z OF THE MIDDLE EAST

Over there is where the destiny
of our century is bleeding.

LOUIS ARAGON

THE NEW A–Z
OF THE
MIDDLE EAST

Alain Gresh
and
Dominique Vidal

I.B. TAURIS
LONDON · NEW YORK

Published in 2004 by I. B. Tauris & Co Ltd
6 Salem Road, London W2 4BU
175 Fifth Avenue, New York NY 10010
Website: http://www.ibtauris.com

In the United States and Canada distributed by Palgrave Macmillan,
a division of St. Martin's Press, 175 Fifth Avenue, New York NY 10010

ISBN 1 86064 326 4
EAN 978 1 86064 326 2

A full CIP record for this book is available from the British Library
A full CIP record for this book is available from the Library of Congress
Library of Congress catalog card: available

Typeset in Stone by Dexter Haven Associates Ltd, London
Printed and bound in Great Britain by MPG Books Ltd, Bodmin

Contents

Map: the Middle East today   vii

Preface   ix

Brief chronology (1947–2003)   xv

List of articles   xxix

Articles A–Z   1

Appendices   348

Select bibliography   387

Index   393

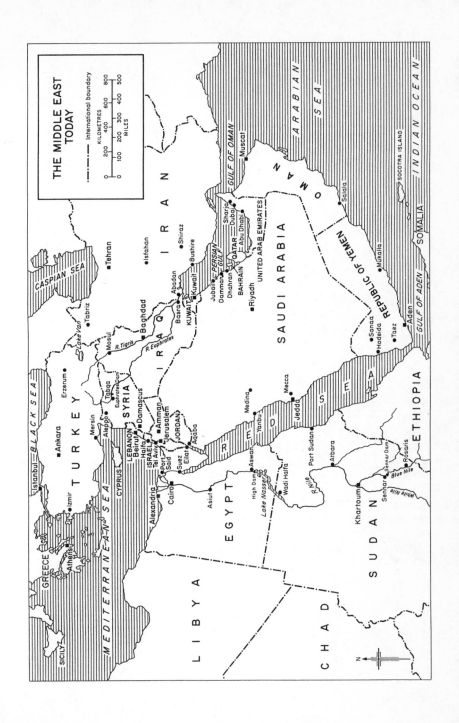

THE MIDDLE EAST
TODAY

International boundary

KILOMETRES
200   400   600   800
100   200 300   400   500
MILES
0

Preface
'From one Gulf War to another'

'We can say with confidence that the world is a better place today because the United States led a coalition of forces into action in Iraq.' On 9 July 2003, Donald Rumsfeld, US Secretary of State for Defence and one of the principal architects of US foreign policy, testified before a Senate committee and hammered home the refrain of neo-conservatives in Washington: in the war against terror, we are winging from victory to victory; the Taliban regime has collapsed; Afghanistan is in the process of reconstruction; the regime of **Saddam Hussein** is nothing more than a bad memory and Iraq is on the road to democracy. In a word, the offensive against al-Qaeda is a success.

Yet, despite these reassuring declarations, the toll of the 'war on terror' launched by President George W. Bush the day after the attacks on 11 September 2001 became more sombre by the day. Despite the blows it received, al-Qaeda continued to pursue its deadly activities. Over several months, the organisation (or the groups which claim to be affiliated with it) attacked in Riyadh on 12 May 2003 (35 deaths); in Casablanca on 16 May (over 40 dead); on 5 August in Jakarta (12 deaths); Riyadh again on 8 November (17 deaths); Istanbul on 15 November against two synagogues (25 deaths) and on 20 November against British interests (25 deaths). During the month of August 2003 in Iraq there were three attacks: one pulverised the Jordanian Embassy, another the UN headquarters in Baghdad and the third killed Ayatollah Baqr al-Hakim, one of the major **Shi'ite** leaders, as well as over 80 others. Every time Washington has blamed the long arm of al-Qaeda. The US denounced the influx of Islamic militants into Iraq, and there is no doubt that the American attacks in Afghanistan and Iraq, like the unwillingness of the White House to act over Palestine, has fuelled anti-American sentiments and played into the hands of al-Qaeda recruiters. America's difficulties bear witness to the crisis of American strategy in the Middle East but also to the differences between the war of 1990–91 and that of 2003.

On 17 January 1991, the President of the US, George Bush Senior, launched the first **Gulf War**, which began with a wave of bombings of extraordinary violence. Twelve years later, in March 2003, his son launched the second Gulf War and brought down Saddam Hussein and his regime.

They were both aiming for the same goals: to confirm US global leadership and to impose its order upon the Middle East; to defend US **oil** interests and to teach Iraq a lesson that would warn off anyone who tried to defy

Washington. It is, however, the differences rather than the similarities which distinguish these two wars.

To begin with, the motive for war. On 2 August 1990 Saddam Hussein had ordered his army to occupy **Kuwait** and bring about the end of a sovereign UN member state. In 2003, Washington had accused Iraq of having produced **weapons of mass destruction** (nuclear, chemical and biological), a dubious claim that was even more discredited later on by the occupying forces' failure to find any trace of the programme.

Second, the apparent objective. The first Gulf War was about liberating Kuwait, not toppling the Iraqi regime. However, during the second George W. Bush and his advisors fought a war for regime change – they were fighting their erstwhile ally of the **Iran–Iraq War**. It was after all Donald Rumsfeld who in December 1983 was sent to Baghdad to re-establish diplomatic relations.

Third, the difference between the countries involved in the operation. The first war spread across a broad coalition and was firmly backed by the UN. Twenty-five countries, comprising numerous Arab states such as **Saudi Arabia**, **Egypt**, the United Arab Emirates and **Syria** sent troops to the region. In 2003, not one government in the region participated directly in the conflict. With the exception of **Britain** and Australia, the Western countries abstained from participating in the venture, many indeed openly criticised it, notably **France** and Germany.

Finally, the context in which America has been operating. At the time of the first war, no one doubted the will of the US to affirm its leadership at the end of the Cold War. 'America must lead, and our people must understand that,' US Secretary of State James Baker bluntly stated. Some disbelieved the promise of 'a new world order', which they interpreted as an invitation to a multilateral management of the world that took account of the interests of the South as well as the East. They counted equally upon the former Soviet Union which, though historically defeated, had not yet entirely disappeared. The administration of Bill Clinton, who was more receptive towards multilateralism, encouraged this optimism. But in 2003, only the most incorrigible optimists could expect any real progress from the second war against Iraq – geopolitically, in the Middle East, or particularly in the continuing chaos of **Israel**–Palestine.

A multilateral leadership of the world? Taking up Paul Marie de la Gorce's forceful analysis: 'Beyond the hysteria of victory and triumphant conformism, we don't always live that which History gives birth to: the emergence of a single superpower of global dimensions'. From Pearl Harbor (1941) to the break-up of the USSR (1991), the US had progressively concentrated its economic, political, military, ideological and cultural assets. Superpower status, as was emphasised by the ex-French Minister for Foreign Affairs, Hubert Védrine, 'when it is without counterweight, as today, brings the temptation of unilateralism and the risk of hegemony'. Since his election, and above all since 11 September 2001, Bush took this unilateralism as a creed. He has displayed open contempt for multilateralism and advocates his right to wage 'preventative wars'.

Could the **Oslo Accords** put an end to a century of conflict, realise the Palestinian right to self-determination and reassure Israel of its security in the Middle East? One cannot rewrite history. In any case, the assassination of **Yitzhak Rabin** (1995) and the return to power of the Israeli right (1996) marked the beginning of the end of the dream. Israel's broken promises, accelerating settlement activity, and continued Palestinian terrorism did the rest. The election of the Labour party in Israel in 1999 did little to break the vicious circle. Five months after the failed Camp David negotiations (July 2000), the participants came close to an accord at Taba in January 2001. But while the Israeli army was busy brutally suppressing the burgeoning second Intifada, Ehud Barak had already embarked on a defamation campaign against Yasser Arafat, whose 'true face' he claimed to have discovered. Barak resigned, to confront Ariel Sharon in new elections, which he subsequently lost. Sharon, with the support of the Labour party and the increasingly obvious backing of the White House, set about destroying the Palestinian territories. Legislative elections on 28 January 2003 showed that most Israelis, caught between suicide bombings and military offensives, have retrenched, hiding their will to peace behind fear for safety.

In short, the Oslo Accords met with defeat, and the 'Road Map' launched in spring 2003 by the US and its 'Quartet' partners (the UN, the **EU** and **Russia**) hardly had a chance. The dream of peace of the 1990s had become a nightmare. The region plunged into an impasse the likes of which had not been seen for decades. A report in 2002 by the UN Programme for Development drew an uncompromising picture of the situation in the **Arab world**: poor economic development; breakdown in education; continuing inequalities between the sexes, absence of democracy etc. Despite its oil wealth, the region is trailing behind other parts of the world that are blessed with far fewer natural resources. While, since 1989 and the fall of the Berlin Wall, the world had seen undeniable advances towards democracy, multi-party elections and greater freedom of expression, the Middle East seemed paralysed – fixed in an earlier time. Monarchies are the norm and even republics are becoming hereditary, as for example in Syria, where **Hafez al-Assad** handed power to his son Bashar. Opposition parties are at best tolerated, citizens submit to an arbitrary state, its information services or the ruling party.

What is the cause of this backwardness? Many factors contribute to this, but primarily and most importantly the cause has been war, or rather wars. Of course, like other regions, the Arab world has seen several 'small wars', often very bloody: the Yemeni war (1962–70), conflicts between the two

Yemens, the **Lebanese Civil War** of 1958 and that of 1975–89. But, above all else, since the Second World War the Middle East has seen five Arab–Israeli wars (1948, 1956, 1967, 1973, 1982), the confrontation between Iraq and **Iran** (1980–88), the first conflagration in the Gulf (1990–91), and its successor in 2003. These conflicts of global dimension have been a heavy burden: they have drained the region's resources; they have justified foreign powers' intervention and the militarisation of regimes; they have killed civil society.

Thanks to this permanent state of war, Arab leaders have been able to keep an iron grip on their countries, crushing civil society with 'emergency measures', relying on the threat of the external enemy (Israel, the US) to stifle their people. That same regional instability paradoxically has also ensured them the support of Washington, desperate to maintain its supply of cheap oil. For, after war, oil is the region's second greatest malediction – prompting foreign intervention and ensuring that autocrats of all ilks have the resources to keep themselves in power.

The Arab regimes cannot be exonerated. But as long as the Arab–Israeli conflict continues, as long as the Palestinian problem is not resolved, it is unlikely that stability and democracy will advance in the Middle East. From this point of view, one can only remain sceptical when the Bush administration proclaims its will to 'democratise' the region.

Is this discourse sincere? Is the White House ready to accept free elections in a region where the overwhelming majority of the population is hostile to US policies, in the Palestinian areas as well as in Iraq? Can we suppose that these intentions are real? Who can believe that another war will further democracy? The experience of the occupation of Iraq does not bode well. If the US, with its armada, has the means of bringing about a military victory against Saddam Hussein, managing a country crushed by thirty years of dictatorship and ten years of **sanctions** will be a far greater challenge. Although happy to be rid of dictatorship, the Iraqi people do not accept the presence of American soldiers, who are incapable of re-establishing a semblance of order and rebuilding the infrastructure that they have destroyed.

Condemned by Muslim public opinion all over the world, Washington's wars against Afghanistan then against Iraq have fuelled the fires of **Islamist** extremism. In Pakistan, for example, the legislative elections in 2002, despite the electoral manipulations of General Pervez Musharraf, saw Taliban-inspired Islamist groups make considerable strides. On several occasions, the American President has rejected the identification of his 'war on terror' with a clash of civilisations or a crusade against **Islam**. However, a number of his administrative advisors have adopted a language that fits with this viewpoint, and a view which is reflected in the current US stance towards Muslim immigrants and its Muslim citizens. The fact that the targets of George W. Bush – from Afghanistan to Iraq, passing via Iran – have been predominantly Muslim countries only encourages this reading. It gives, in the opinion of the Arab and Muslim world, weight to the arguments of **Osama bin Laden** and all other fanatics who see in these policies a Judeo–Christian war against the Muslims. If the situation escalates, it may well bring about the clash of civilisations everyone fears.

Moreover, there are no signs of a solution to the Palestinian conflict, or even a scenario of the type which followed the 1990–91 Gulf War, with the opening of the Israeli–Arab conference in Madrid. The Bush administration has, on more than one occasion, declared that its vision of the Middle East includes a Palestinian state neighbouring Israel. But in the aftermath of the publication of the 'Road Map', it has become patently clear that Bush has neither the will nor the intention to press Sharon on the issue of settlements, which is a *sine qua non* of any peace deal in the region. If Bush himself tends towards the Israeli position as regards the conflict, the matter is not helped by the enormous political weight of two powerful Washington lobbies – one Zionist, the other fundamentalist Christian.

How to disentangle the entanglements of the Middle East, to decode its codes, to demystify its myths? By making use of the full ensemble of analyses: the national, the regional and the international; the economic, the social, the political, the ideological, the religious, the strategic, the military; the **minority**, the ethnic and the confessional; the geographical and the historical. The historical above all else: because the past, in the Middle East more than any other part of the world, is also the present. This is why we have opted for an A–Z, which we hope will let the reader find their own way through.

Brief chronology

1947
29 November: The UN General Assembly adopts the **Partition Plan** for Palestine by a majority of two thirds.

1948
9–10 April: Massacre at the village of **Deir Yassin** by Irgun and Lehi troops.
14 May: Declaration of the **independence** of the state of **Israel**. The Arab states reject the Partition Plan, and their armies enter Palestine on 15 May.

1948–49
The **1948–49 War** in Palestine finishes with the victory of the Jewish state. Armistice agreements are signed between Israel and its Arab neighbours.

1949
11 May: State of Israel becomes a member of the UN.

1950
24 April: Annexation of the **West Bank** by Transjordan. **Egypt** establishes its control over Gaza.
May: Anglo–French–American declaration on the Middle East.

1951
20 July: Assassination of King Abdullah of **Jordan**.
October: Israel rejects the UN peace plan accepted by Egypt, **Syria**, **Lebanon** and Jordan.

1952
23 July: Free Officers take power in Egypt. Two years later, **Gamal Abdel Nasser** becomes the unchallenged leader in Cairo.

1953
19 August: A CIA-provoked coup overthrows the Iranian Prime Minister Muhammad Mosaddeq, who was 'guilty' of having nationalised his country's petroleum industry.

1955
24 February: **Baghdad Pact** is signed.
28 February: Israeli attack on Gaza.

April: The Bandung Conference marking the birth of the Non-Aligned Movement voices its support for the 'rights of the Palestinian people'.

1956
March: Nationalist pressure in Jordan leads to the dismissal of British general Sir John Glubb ('Glubb Pasha').
26 July: Nasser nationalises the **Suez Canal** Company.
October–November: Tripartite aggression from Israel, **France** and **Britain** against Egypt.

1957
January: Presentation of the 'Eisenhower Doctrine'.

1958
1 February: Egypt and Syria join together to form a United Arab Republic (UAR).
14 July: The monarchy falls in **Iraq**, triggering 'pre-emptive' interventions by the British in Jordan and by the Americans in Lebanon.

1959
October: First Congress of Fatah, founded in **Kuwait**.

1961
29 September: Syria breaks away from Egypt and the UAR collapses.

1962
September: Revolution in North **Yemen**.

1963
March: Military coup brings the **Ba'th** party to power in Damascus.
June: Levy Eshkol succeeds **David Ben Gurion** as leader of the government of Israel.

1964
January: Bourguiba Plan for peace in Palestine/Israel is revealed.
13–17 January: First summit of the heads of Arab states is held in Cairo.
29 May: Creation of the **Palestine Liberation Organisation (PLO)**.

1965
1 January: Fatah undertakes its first military act against Israel.

1967

5 June: Israel attacks Egypt, Syria and Jordan. Following a lightning war of six days, Israel occupies the Sinai, the **Golan**, the West Bank, Gaza and East **Jerusalem**. **Settlements** begin later that summer.

22 November: **UN Security Council** adopts Resolution 242.

1968

21 March: Battle of Karameh in Jordan between Israeli troops and **Palestinians**.

10–17 July: Fourth meeting of the Palestinian National Council sees the amendment of the National Charter.

July: The **Ba'th** party comes to power in Baghdad.

1969

1–4 February: Fifth Palestinian National Council sees **Yasser Arafat** become chairman of the Executive Committee of the PLO.

25 May: Jaafar al-Nimeiri seizes power in Khartoum.

1–8 September: **Muammar Qadhaffi** seizes power in Tripoli.

November: The Cairo Accords between the Lebanese government and the PLO are made following several incidents in Lebanon.

1970

February: Severe clashes between the PLO and the Jordanian authorities.

July: Nasser and **King Hussein** of Jordan accept the Rogers Plan, which was to precede the implementation of UN Security Council Resolution 242.

September: Further clashes between the PLO and the Jordanian authorities in '**Black September**'.

29 September: Death of Nasser.

16 November: **Hafez al-Assad** comes to power in Damascus.

1970–71

PLO is expelled from Jordan. The leadership of the Palestinian resistance moves to Lebanon.

1972

5–6 September: Israeli athletes participating in the Munich Olympic Games are massacred by a **Black September** operative.

1973

April: Israeli operation in Beirut kills three major PLO leaders.

August: Palestinian National Front established in the West Bank and Gaza.

6 October: Egyptian and Syrian troops embark on an offensive against Israel, starting the **1973 War**, also known as the October or Yom Kippur War.

22 October: UN Security Council adopts Resolution 338. The war halts some days later.

26–28 October: Arab Summit at Algiers. The PLO is recognised as 'the sole representative of the Palestinian people'.

1974

1–9 June: Twelfth Palestinian National Council. The PLO accepts the idea of establishing a national authority on 'any liberated part of Palestine'. The Rejectionist Front is founded several months later.

26–29 October: Arab Summit at Rabat. Jordan follows mainstream opinion and recognises the PLO.

13 November: Speech by Arafat at the UN. The UN recognises the Palestinian right to independence and self-determination. The PLO is accorded observer status at the UN.

1975

April: Beginning of the **Lebanese Civil War**.

1976

30 March: Land Day sees sizeable demonstrations in the Galilee, repressed with violence. Six are killed.

13 April: Municipal elections in the occupied West Bank see a huge victory for candidates close to the PLO.

June: Huge intervention in Lebanon by Syrian troops against the PLO and the Lebanese National Movement.

12 August: Surrender of the Palestinian camp of Tel al-Za'atar in Lebanon after 57 days under Syrian siege.

6 September: PLO is admitted as a full member of the **Arab League**.

1977

12–20 March: Thirteenth Palestinian National Council in Cairo accepts the idea of an independent Palestinian state built on a portion of the original Palestine.

3–4 May: First official meeting of the PLO and Israeli Communist Party in Prague.

17 May: The Israeli right wins a general election for the first time. **Menachem Begin** becomes Prime Minister.

29 June: The European summit in London recognises the 'necessity for a homeland for the Palestinian people'.

19–21 November: Egyptian President **Anwar al-Sadat** travels to Jerusalem.

1–5 December: 'Front of Steadfastness' is created in Tripoli by **Libya**, Algeria, Syria, South Yemen and the PLO.

1978

14 March: Israel invades south Lebanon.

17 September: **Camp David Accords** are signed by Egypt, Israel and the **US**.

5 November: The Arab Summit in Baghdad closes by condemning the Camp David Accords.

1979

1 February: **Ayatollah Khomeini** returns to Tehran.

26 March: Israel–Egypt peace treaty is signed in Washington.

6 July: Meeting between Arafat, German Chancellor Willy Brandt and Austrian Chancellor Bruno Kreisky in Vienna.

1980

2 June: Assassination attempts are made against three Palestinian mayors: the mayors of Nablus and Ramallah are severely injured.

20 July: Israeli Knesset passes a Basic Law declaring 'reunified' Jerusalem the capital of Israel.

September: Beginning of the **Iran–Iraq War**.

1981

June: Israeli attack on the Osiraq nuclear reactor at Tammuz in Iraq.

July: Israeli–Palestinian war along the Lebanese border. Israel bombs Beirut.

7 August: Proposal of peace plan by Crown Prince Fahd of **Saudi Arabia**.

6 October: Assassination of President Sadat.

14 December: Israel annexes the Golan the day after a 'state of war' is declared in Poland.

1982

March–April: Palestinian insurrection in the Occupied Territories. Elected mayors are dismissed.

25 April: Israel completes its withdrawal from the Sinai.

6 June: Israel invades Lebanon. The siege of Beirut begins some days later.

21 August: PLO begins its withdrawal from Beirut under the protection of the Multinational Force.

1 September: Reagan Peace Plan is announced.

9 September: Final resolution of the Fez Summit is adopted.

14–18 September: Assassination of new Lebanese President Bashir Gemayel. Israel enters West Beirut. Massacres at **Sabra and Shatila**.

20 September: **King Hussein** proposes a 'Jordanian–Palestinian Confederation'.

21 September: Amin Gemayel is elected President of Lebanon.

1983

January: Arafat meets Israeli doves Uri Avnery and Matityahu Peled in Tunis.

April: Failure of negotiations between Arafat and King Hussein.

10 April: Assassination of **Issam Sartawi** at the International Socialist Congress held in Portugal.

17 May: Israeli–Lebanese peace accord.

25 May: Beginning of dissent within Fatah.

August–September: Civil war erupts again in Lebanon. The **Druze** take control of the Shuf.

November: Beginning of the siege of Tripoli by the Syrians and their 'rebel' Palestinian allies.

24 November: Six Israelis are exchanged for some 1500 Palestinian prisoners held by the state of Israel.

20 December: Arafat and 4000 loyalists leave Tripoli in Greek boats under French protection.

1984

February: Amin Gemayel debacle. The Wazzan government resigns. The Amal militia takes West Beirut. Walid Jumblatt's PSP militia surround Mount Lebanon.

5 March: 17 May 1983 peace accord between Israel and Lebanon is annulled by Amin Gemayel.

1 April: Multinational Force leaves Lebanon.

16 May: A government of National Unity is formed in Beirut.

23 July: Legislative elections in Israel. The two main parties form a government of National Unity after several weeks of negotiations.

1985

January: The Falasha **Jews** of Ethiopia are moved to Israel.

15 January: Staggered withdrawal of Israeli troops from Lebanon is announced.

11 February: King Hussein and Arafat issue a joint declaration in Amman known as the 'Jordanian–Palestinian Accord'.

Spring: New massacres at Sabra and Shatila and other Palestinian camps in Lebanon, this time by the **Shi'ite** militia of Amal.

June: Israel completes the withdrawal of troops from Lebanon, with the exception of a buffer zone in the south controlled by the South Lebanon Army.

1 October: Israeli air raid on the PLO headquarters in Tunis leaves 70 dead.

1986

15 April: US raids on Tripoli and Benghazi are followed by European **sanctions** on Libya, accused by Washington of organising anti-Western **terrorism**.

29 May: A new war of the camps is launched by the Shi'ite militia Amal against 'loyalist' Palestinians in Lebanon.

5 October: *Sunday Times* publishes claims by Israeli nuclear engineer Mordechai Vanunu that the Israel has a stockpile of 100–200 atomic bombs. Abducted and returned to Israel, Vanunu is sentenced to 18 years imprisonment.

1987

4 March: Reagan accepts that secret arms deliveries to **Iran** were a 'mistake' and promises increased co-operation with Congress at the beginning of the 'Irangate' scandal.

20–26 April: Eighteenth Palestinian National Council in Algiers reunites the PLO (Fatah, PFLP, DFLP, PCP).

31 July: 402 people are killed in clashes between Iranian pilgrims and Saudi police in Mecca.

December: The first '**Intifada**' begins in Gaza, then spreads to the West Bank.

1988

16 April: An Israeli commando assassinates Abu Jihad, number two in the PLO, in Tunis.

4 May: Marcel Canton, Marcel Fontaine and Jean-Paul Kauffmann are freed. The only French hostage left in Lebanon is Michel Seurat, who dies while held captive by Shi'ite radicals in Beirut.

31 July: King Hussein announces on television that he will sever 'legal and administrative ties' between Jordan and the West Bank, annexed by his grandfather King Abdullah in 1950 and occupied by Israel since 1967.

August: Ceasefire between Iran and Iraq after eight years of war.

12–15 November: Nineteenth Palestinian National Council is held in Algiers. The PLO declares the state of Palestine, recognises UN Security Council Resolutions 181, 242 and 338 and affirms its condemnation of terrorism.

15 December: US undertakes to engage in a 'substantial dialogue' with the PLO.

1989

14 March: General Aoun declares a 'war of liberation against Syria' in Lebanon.

2–4 May: Arafat visits Paris and declares the Palestinian National Charter 'null and void'.

1 June: Death of Ayatollah Khomeini.

30 June: Military coup by General Omar Hassan al-Bashir with the support of **Islamists** in **Sudan**.

1–24 October: Lebanese members of parliament meet at Taif in Saudi Arabia and come out with a document of national understanding which outlines constitutional reform.

1990

January: Sharp increase in the **immigration** of Jews from the USSR to Israel. The total number for the whole year reaches nearly 200,000 people.

1 April: In a speech given to the General Commandant of the armed forces, Iraqi President **Saddam Hussein** declares that his country has chemical weapons. He threatens to destroy half of Israel in flames if it tries anything against Iraq.

15 April: The first of 29 Aeroflot flights intended to deliver a million copies of the Qur'an from King Fahd of Saudi Arabia to Soviet Muslims.

22 May: The Republic of Yemen is declared, uniting North and South Yemen and taking Sana'a as its capital.

20 June: George Bush Senior suspends the US–Palestinian dialogue after a Palestinian commando attempts to enter Israel.

Gulf War

2 August: Iraq invades Kuwait. The UN Security Council demands the 'immediate and unconditional withdrawal of all Iraqi forces from Kuwait' in Resolution 660, adopted by 14 votes and one abstention (Yemen).

8 August: George Bush Senior announces he is sending thousands of US troops to the Gulf following the Iraqi annexation of Kuwait. The number of US soldiers in Saudi Arabia eventually reaches half a million – as many as were in Vietnam.

9 September: Following the US–Soviet summit in Helsinki, Bush and Gorbachev announce, 'We are united against Iraqi aggression as long as the crisis lasts … If the measures already taken fail, we are ready to consider supplementary measures in line with the Charter of the United Nations. We must demonstrate with no shadow of a doubt that aggression does not and will not pay.'

30 September: The USSR and Israel decide to re-establish consular relations and open a direct air connection.

8 October: Killings in the precinct of Jerusalem mosques (18 dead, 150 injured).

13 October: General Aoun seeks refuge at the French Embassy in Lebanon, after being forced out of his stronghold by the Syrian army.

29 November: The UN Security Council passes Resolution 678, authorising the use of force against Iraq from 15 January 1991.

1991

5 January: Assassination of PLO number two Abu Iyad in Tunis.

17 January: Day after the UN deadline for Iraq to withdraw from Kuwait,

intense bombing of Iraq and occupied Kuwait begins. The next day, Iraq responds by launching its first wave of Scud missiles.

24 February: Beginning of the land campaign against Iraq.

27 February: The Iraqi government says it will accept the 12 resolutions of the UN without conditions. Combat operations halt during the night of 27–28 February.

March: Popular uprisings in Iraq, first by Shi'ites in the south, then by **Kurds** in the north.

30 October: The Madrid Conference is opened by Bush and Gorbachev.

3 November: First bilateral negotiations between Israel and its Arab neighbours, including the Palestinians.

1992

24 February: US Secretary of State James Baker makes the guarantee of a $10m loan to Israel conditional upon a halt to Israeli settlements in the West Bank and Gaza.

9 March: Death of Begin.

7 April: Arafat escapes uninjured from an air accident in Libya.

15 April: UN Security Council imposes an air blockade on Libya.

23 June: **Yitzhak Rabin** and his Labour–Meretz coalition win the Israeli general election.

16 December: Following the abduction and assassination of an Israeli border guard by **Hamas**, the Rabin government expels 415 Palestinians suspected of Islamist sympathies into south Lebanon.

1993

January: Beginning of the secret Oslo negotiations between the PLO and Israel.

9–10 September: Mutual recognition of Israel and the PLO.

13 September: PLO and government of Israel sign the Declaration of Principals on Palestinian Autonomy at the White House, in the presence of Arafat, Rabin and Clinton.

30 December: Vatican and Israel agree a 'basic accord' leading to an exchange of ambassadors in January 1994.

1994

16 January: The US–Syria summit restarts Israeli–Syrian negotiations on the basis of an Israeli withdrawal from the Golan.

25 February: Massacre at the Cave of the Patriarchs in Hebron. The settler Baruch Goldstein kills 29 Palestinians.

29 February: Paris Accord between Israel and the PLO over economic issues.

May–July: Civil war in Yemen.

4 May: Cairo Accord between Rabin and Arafat on the implementation of the Israeli–Palestinian Declaration of Principles.

1 July: Arafat returns to Gaza.

26 October: Peace treaty signed between Israel and Jordan.

1995

24 July: Closure of the West Bank and Gaza following an attack on a bus in Jerusalem, claimed by Hamas, the preceding day.

28 September: Oslo II Accord on the extension of **autonomy**.

4 November: Assassination of Rabin by Yigal Amir, a far-right student. Rabin is replaced by **Shimon Peres**.

13 November: Attack in Riyadh against a National Guard station. Five US soldiers are killed.

November–December: Israel completes its withdrawal from all Palestinian towns, with the exception of Hebron.

24 December: Necmettin Erbakan, leader of the Islamist Refah party, wins the general election in **Turkey**.

1996

20 January: Arafat is elected President of the **Palestinian Authority**. His supporters win two thirds of the 80 seats on the Legislative Council.

March: Following the assassination of terrorist Yahya Ayash by the Israeli secret service on 5 January, Hamas responds by orchestrating a series of bloody attacks in Jerusalem, Tel Aviv and Ashkelon.

April: Following **Hezbollah** rocket attacks on northern Israel, Shimon Peres gives a green light to 'Operation Grapes of Wrath' against Lebanon. On 18 April, 98 civilian refugees in the UN camp at Qana in south Lebanon are killed by Israeli bombs. A ceasefire takes place on 27 April.

24 April: Held for the first time on territory that was Palestine, the Palestinian National Council in Gaza eliminates from its Charter all references to the destruction of the state of Israel.

26 April: The UN Security Council imposes sanctions on Sudan, accused of supporting terrorism.

May: Agreement is reached over the implementation of UN Security Council Resolution 986 on Iraq, the 'Oil for Food Programme', passed in 1995.

29 May: **Benyamin Netanyahu** and his coalition of the right, far right and religious parties win the Israeli general elections.

25 June: A car bomb explodes at al-Khobar, near the major military base at Dhahran in Saudi Arabia, costing the lives of 18 US soldiers.

5 August: President Clinton signs the executive order imposing sanctions on foreign companies investing in the Iranian or Libyan **oil** sector.

September: Clashes in Iraqi Kurdistan. The Iraqi army intervenes. The US conducts an aerial bombing campaign.

27–29 September: Jewish municipality in Jerusalem opens a tunnel underneath the Haram al-Sharif, provoking the most serious wave of violence in the West Bank and Gaza since the Intifada. Seventy-six are killed.

1997
15 January: Agreement over the Israeli redeployment from Hebron and the transfer of some powers to the Palestinian Authority.

25 February: Israel announces its intention to build a Jewish settlement on Har Homa, a hill in the occupied Arab part of Jerusalem.

1998
23 October: Wye River Memorandum. The Palestinian Authority is scheduled to be given control over a further 13 per cent of the West Bank within three months.

1999
7 February: Death of King Hussein of Jordan, who is succeeded by his son, who becomes King Abdullah II.

25 March: Heads of State of the EU reaffirm the 'lasting and unrestricted right of the Palestinian people to self-determination, including the possibility of a state' at their meeting in Berlin.

4 May: End of the period of Palestinian self-rule laid out in the Declaration of Principles of 13 September 1993. The Central Council of the PLO agrees to postpone the declaration of an independent Palestinian state.

17 May: Labour leader Ehud Barak wins the Israeli general elections.

15–16 December: Israeli–Syrian talks, stalled since 1996, begin once again in Washington.

2000
26 March: The Geneva summit between Clinton and Syrian President Assad fails, dashing hopes of a settlement between Israel and Syria.

May: The Israeli army withdraws from south Lebanon following an offensive by Hezbollah and the collapse of the South Lebanese Army.

10 June: Death of Assad, who is succeeded by his son Bashar.

11–24 June: **Camp David** negotiations between Clinton, Barak and Arafat.

28 September: **Ariel Sharon**, leader of the Israeli right, visits Temple Mount. The **second Intifada** begins the very next day.

21 December: Clinton announces his 'parameters' and resumes negotiations.

2001
21–27 January: Israeli–Palestinian negotiations in Taba, Egypt, allow an accord to be approached.

6 February: Sharon elected Prime Minister of Israel.

11 March: Israeli army imposes a complete blockade on Ramallah and sets up roadblocks on all access routes.

28 March: Israel launches a series of helicopter gunship raids on Gaza and the West Bank in response to the most recent bombings in Israel. The first Arab Summit held since the Gulf War concludes in Amman.

19 May: Representatives of the countries of the Arab League call on all Arab governments to sever all political contact with Israel until it ends its military operations against the Palestinians.

21 May: Mitchell Report proposes a freeze on the expansion of Jewish settlements in the West Bank and Gaza and the incarceration of Palestinian terrorists in an effort to stop eight months of violence.

End of May: 23 individuals (of whom 22 had escaped the massacres of Sabra and Shatila) file a collective legal suite in Brussels against Sharon for human-rights violations and war crimes.

1 June: The bombing of the Dolphinarium disco in Tel Aviv kills 21 young Israelis.

10 August: The day after a new bombing in Jerusalem which saw 17 killed and 90 injured, Israeli special forces seize Palestinian Authority offices in Orient House and nine local offices in East Jerusalem.

27 August: Abu Ali Mustafa, head of the PFLP, is killed by the Israeli army in Ramallah.

11 September: Attacks on the twin towers of the World Trade Center in New York and the Pentagon in Washington. The following day, the UN Security Council passes Resolution 1368, which recognises 'the inherent right of individual or collective self-defence in accordance with the Charter'.

2 October: George W. Bush declares 'the idea of a Palestinian state has always been a part of the vision, as long as Israel's right to exist is respected'.

7 October: The beginning of US–UK military operations in Afghanistan.

17 October: PFLP assassinates Israeli Minister of Tourism Rehavam Zeevi in Jerusalem.

23 November: Assassination of Mahmoud Abu Hannoud, one of the main military leaders of Hamas, near Nablus. Hamas responds by orchestrating three suicide bombings in West Jerusalem and Haifa on 1 and 2 December. On 4 December, Israel surrounds the headquarters of Arafat in Ramallah.

26 December: Benyamin Ben Eliezer, a notable hawk and Defence Minister in Sharon's cabinet, is elected head of the Israeli Labour party.

2002

3 January: The Israeli army announces that it has intercepted the *Karine A* in the Red Sea, laden with 50 tons of arms intended, according to the Israelis, for the Palestinian Authority.

18 February: Saudi Arabia proposes for the first time the normalisation of relations with Israel following a full Israeli withdrawal from all the Occupied Territories.

28 February–2 March: The Israeli army launches an operation in the refugee camps of Balata, near Nablus, and **Jenin** in the West Bank. Twenty-one Palestinians and two Israeli soldiers are killed.

13 March: The UN Security Council adopts Resolution 1397 by 14 votes and one abstention (Syria), which mentions for the first time 'two States, Israel and Palestine, live side by side within secure and recognised borders'.

27 March: The Arab Summit in Beirut adopts the Crown Prince Abdullah Peace Plan which offers Israel full normalisation of relations with the **Arab world** in exchange for a complete withdrawal from territories occupied in 1967. That evening, a suicide bomber in Netanya, Israel, kills 29 people. In the month of March alone, suicide bombers kill 80 Israelis. The next day the Israeli army launches Operation Defensive Shield: the re-occupation of the whole of the West Bank.

30 March: UN Security Council calls on Israel to withdraw from Ramallah in Resolution 1402, passed by 14 votes and one abstention (Syria).

3 April: The Israeli army enters the Jenin refugee camp. It withdraws on 24 April, with a total of 52 Palestinians and 23 Israelis dead. Thirty-five per cent of buildings in the camp are destroyed and some 8000 people are left homeless.

2 May: Arafat leaves his Ramallah compound after being besieged for over a month by the Israeli army.

10 May: The siege at the Church of the Nativity in Bethlehem ends with the exit of 123 Palestinians who have been there for 39 days.

19 June: Beginning of the Israeli Operation Firm Voice in the Palestinian territories. The day after a suicide bomber kills 19 Israelis, 55 Palestinian figures call for an end to attacks on civilians in Israel in a letter published in the *al-Quds* newspaper.

24 June: George W. Bush makes the creation of a Palestinian state conditional on the establishment of a new leadership and reformed political and economic institutions founded on democracy, a free-market economy and action against terrorism.

8 November: After two months of negotiation, the UN Security Council unanimously adopts Resolution 1441, which requires Iraq to destroy all its **weapons of mass destruction** programmes or face disarmament by force. UN weapons inspectors return to Iraq.

2003

28 January: Sharon is re-elected Prime Minister of Israel in the general election. The Likud party wins a significant majority of seats in the Knesset; Labour loses ground to the centrist Shinui party.

6 February: US Secretary of State Colin Powell presents US information on Iraq's weapons of mass destruction to the UN Security Council.

27 February: Britain and the US present a draft resolution to the UN Security Council to authorise military action against Iraq. The resolution is withdrawn on 17 March following the failure to win the support of France.

18 March: President Bush delivers a 48-hour ultimatum for Saddam Hussein and his two sons to leave Iraq or face a US-led military coalition. After a last-ditch effort to retain some of his power, Arafat signs legislation surrendering a part of his authority to new Palestinian Prime Minister Mahmoud Abbas. This paves the way for the release of the 'Road Map' peace plan.

20 March: President Bush announces the beginning of war on Iraq.

9 April: The US declares that the regime of Saddam Hussein has been overthrown.

30 April: The US releases the long-awaited 'Road Map' (elaborated with Russia, the EU and the UN) for peace to Israeli and Palestinian leaders hours after the new Palestinian Prime Minister Mahmoud Abbas and his cabinet are sworn in.

25 May: The Israeli cabinet reluctantly votes to accept the US-led 'Road Map'.

29 June: Hamas, Islamic Jihad and Arafat's Fatah movement formally announce a three-month ceasefire.

19 August: The UN compound in Baghdad is bombed by anti-US opposition.

21 August: Hamas announces an end to the ceasefire after Israeli helicopters kill their third most senior leader, Ismail Abu Shanab.

10 September: Ahmed Qorei replaces Mahmoud Abbas as Prime Minister.

11 September: The Israeli government officially declares its desire to expel Arafat from the Occupied Territories.

1 October: The Israeli government passes the extension of the 'security wall'.

12 October: A 'peace agreement' is adopted in Amman by the Palestinians and Israelis representing peace groups, to be officially signed in Geneva on 1 December.

List of articles

1948–49 War
1956 War
1967 War
1973 War
1982 War
Abu Nidal
Aliya
American aid
Arab League
Arab world
Arabian Peninsula
Arabs
Arafat, Yasser
Arms trade
Assad, Hafez al-
Autonomy
Baghdad Pact
Balfour Declaration
Barghouti, Marwan
Ba'th
Begin, Menachem
Ben Gurion, David
Bin Laden, Osama
Black September
Camp David Accords
Camp David and Taba
    Negotiations
Confessionalism
Curiel, Henri
Deir Yassin
Druze
Egypt
European Union
Expulsions
Final status negotiations
France
Gaza Strip
Genocide

Golan Heights
Great Britain
Gulf War 1990–91
Habash, George
Hamas
Hariri, Rafiq
Hawatmeh, Nayef
Herzl, Theodor
Hezbollah
Hussein, King
Hussein, Saddam
Immigration
Independence
Infitah
Intifada
Intifada, second
Iran
Iran–Iraq War
Iraq
Islam
Islamism
Israel
Israeli Arabs
Israeli political parties
Jenin
Jerusalem
Jews
Jordan
Khomeini, Ayatollah
    Ruhollah
Kurds
Kuwait
Lawrence, T.E.
Lebanese Civil War
Lebanon
Libya
Lobby
Maronites

Masada
Minorities
Mubarak, Hosni
Muslim Brotherhood
Nasser, Gamal Abdel
Netanyahu, Benyamin
Oil
Oriental Jews
Oslo Accords
Ottoman Empire
Palestine Liberation
    Organisation (PLO)
Palestinian Authority
Palestinians
Partition Plan
Peace conferences
Peres, Shimon
Qadhaffi, Muammar
Rabin, Yitzhak
Refugees
Right of return
Russia
Sabra and Shatila
Sadat, Anwar al-
Sanctions
Sartawi, Issam

Saud dynasty
Saudi Arabia
Settlements
Shamir, Yitzhak
Sharon, Ariel
Shi'ism
Sudan
Suez Canal
Sykes–Picot Agreement
Syria
Taif Accords
Terrorism
Trade patterns
Turkey
UNIFIL (UN Interim Force
    in Lebanon)
UN Security Council
    Resolutions
United States of America
US Centcom
Water
Weapons of mass destruction
West Bank
Yemen
Yishuv
Zionism

The first of the Arab–Israeli conflicts, this broke out immediately after the declaration of **independence** of the state of **Israel** on 14 May 1948. The armies of Transjordan, **Egypt** and **Syria**, backed up by Lebanese and Iraqi contingents, entered Palestine on the morning of 15 May.

Clashes had already begun at the end of 1947. Immediately after the UN General Assembly had adopted the **Partition Plan** for Palestine on 29 November, something tantamount to a civil war broke out between **Palestinians** and **Jews**. On the Palestinian side there was a rejection of the Partition Plan and therefore the creation of a Jewish state. On the Jewish side, if the UN's decision was accepted, there was the belief that it might be 'improved' to the advantage of Israel, which could occupy all or part of the Arab state, with anything left over going to Transjordan. This was also **Britain**'s aim, since it was relying on King Abdullah to maintain its influence in the region. London therefore gave a green light to the agreement negotiated between Golda Meir and King Abdullah.

Until March 1948 the fighting went largely in favour of the Palestinians and their reinforcements from the Arab armies. They cut communication lines, surrounded Jewish settlements and cut off the major towns, including **Jerusalem**. But at the end of March, with 2000 already dead, Jewish forces, helped in particular by Czechoslovakia, regained the offensive. Veritable massacres ensued, the most notorious of which steeped in blood the little village of **Deir Yassin**, where, on 9 April 1948, **Menachem Begin**'s men killed 250 of the inhabitants, creating a wave of panic that spread throughout the entire Palestinian Arab community. A Palestinian historian later suggested that the number of dead was 110. The Haganah, the Jewish armed force of the time, cleared the road to Jerusalem and seized Tiberias, Haifa and Safad. Jaffa fell on 12 May, two days before the declaration of Israel's independence.

The Arab armies' entry into the war on 15 May failed to turn the tide. Though hostilities continued, interrupted by truces, until 16 January 1949, from July onwards the conflict turned in Israel's favour. Having formed the Israeli Defence Forces (IDF or Tsahal, to use the Hebrew form), Jewish troops had the advantage of unusually capable commanders, with double the manpower thanks to exceptional mobilisation and a distinct advantage in heavy arms, coming mainly by airlift from the Czech base of Zatec. This is to say that the Soviet Union, which was in favour of the Partition Plan and which recognised Israel on 17 May 1948, contributed to its first military victory. At the time, Moscow's only concern was the expulsion of Britain from the entire region.

Soviet thinking was shrewd. Beaten and humiliated by the defeat, the **Arab world** was profoundly unsettled. And the price London had to pay over this crisis was all the greater because public opinion believed that the British were pushing for war. Since then, the publication of British archives has even revealed that in February 1948 a meeting took place in which Ernest Bevin, the British Secretary of State for Foreign Affairs, decided with the Jordanian Prime Minister to use the **Arab League** as a means of ensuring Hashemite control over the region assigned to the Arab state by the UN. Coupled with the limiting of the territory claimed by Israel and the strengthening of the British hold over the Negev, this was London's main objective.

Britain would pay dearly for the 'Nakba' (the Arabic word for 'catastrophe'). Its man in Egypt, Nokrashi Pasha, was assassinated in December 1948; the Wafd returned to the political arena in 1950; and then, on 23 July 1952, the Free Officers took power (see Egypt). In **Iraq** too, troubles were on the increase. In Syria coup d'état followed coup d'état. Even Transjordan, which had succeeded in annexing the **West Bank** to form the Kingdom of **Jordan**, was not spared: Abdullah, son of Sherif Hussein and great-grandfather of the present King Abdullah, was assassinated in 1951 in the al-Aqsa Mosque in Jerusalem.

But if Britain suffered as a result of the war, the real victims were the Palestinians. The armistice agreement signed by Israel and its various adversaries between 23 February and 20 July 1949, ratified the enlargement, by a third, of the Jewish state from the borders defined by the Partition Plan: from 14,000 to almost 21,000 sq. km, obtaining notably the Galilee, a strip near Jerusalem and the Negev as far as the port of Eilat on the Red Sea. The Arab state failed to materialise, Israel and Transjordan having divided the West Bank between them, while Gaza fell under the tutelage of Egypt. But above all, between 700,000 and 800,000 Palestinians had to leave their homes.

As the work of modern Israeli historians shows clearly (see **Expulsions**), this exodus was the result of a policy of expulsion of the Palestinian population. This determination continued after the war with the destruction of Arab villages or the establishment within them of new Jewish immigrant **settlements**, or with the division of their lands between the neighbouring *kibbutzim* (communes). The law on 'abandoned property' legalised this system. As for the refugees, the UN in April 1950 would record almost a million in Jordan, Gaza, **Lebanon** and Syria. In December 1948, the UN proclaimed their 'right to return', which Israeli leaders, however, had no intention of respecting: 'We must prevent their return at all cost,' declared Israeli Prime Minister **David Ben Gurion** on 16 June 1948.

With Israel already expanding, its Arab neighbours shaken and the Palestinians condemned to occupation or exile, the first Arab–Israeli conflict created the conditions of those that were to follow. It is here that we find the origins of the tragedy that has steeped the Middle East in blood ever since.

1956 WAR

The second Israeli–Arab conflict, the Suez operation, was marked by the participation of **Britain** and **France**, on **Israel's** side, in an attack against **Egypt**. This strange intervention had its roots in the evolving alliances between the parties involved in the **1948–49 War** and had profound consequences for the region.

The Soviet Union and the people's democracies, particularly Czechoslovakia, had played a significant role in the birth of the Jewish state and in its victory at the time of the first conflict with its neighbours. For a while, Israel had maintained good relations with the Eastern bloc within the framework of a policy of non-alignment, but this accord did not last (see **Russia**). The balance between East and West in Israeli policy was quickly discontinued in favour of an increasingly open rapprochement with the West. Ranging from Israeli's political support for the **US** in the Korean War of 1950, to making its army, ports and airports available (1951), followed by their military bases (1955), the escalation was such that, to Arab eyes, the Jewish state appeared to be a puppet of the West, which served as a cover for Israeli intransigence. In violation of UN decisions, Israel had prevented the return of any refugees, annexed the eastern part of **Jerusalem** and made it its capital, and stepped up reprisals after certain border incidents, at Qibya in **Jordan** in 1953 and Gaza in 1955.

By a process of opposition, due essentially to anti-British feelings strengthened by Israel's collusion with the West, Arab leaders drew closer to the communist countries. **Gamal Abdel Nasser**, one of the fathers of what was later called the Non-Aligned Movement, created in 1955 at Bandung, initiated this trend, which was a cause of concern to both Washington and London. Paris, moreover, had a personal score to settle with the Egyptian president, who it accused of actively supporting the Algerian rebellion, whose leaders had been made welcome in Cairo. This desire for revenge was coupled with the natural sympathy of the SFIO (the French section of the Workers' International), then in power, towards Israel, to such an extent that the French government, like that of Britain, dreamed of replicating against Nasser the operation successfully carried out in 1953 in **Iran** against Mosaddeq by the Americans.

A series of acts raised tensions higher. In February 1955 Israeli troops attacked Gaza, allegedly in response to attacks. In September 1955, having been refused arms by the West, Egypt announced that it would obtain supplies from Czechoslovakia. In October 1955, **Syria**, followed by **Saudi Arabia**, signed a military pact with Cairo, and the three countries' forces were united under the command of the Egyptian general Abdel Hakim Amer. In April 1956 **Yemen** joined the scheme. In July 1956, Nasser announced the nationalisation of the **Suez Canal** – the first time that a Third World country had successfully regained possession of one of its natural resources – while Paris and London set up a joint intervention general staff. October 1956 was the decisive month: on 23 October, at Sèvres, the British and French secretly prepared an offensive against Egypt, having supplied Israel with improved weapons; on 24 October the new Jordanian assembly joined the pact between Egypt, Syria, Yemen and Saudi Arabia; on 29 October war broke out. The operation was given the moniker Kadesh, recalling the wanderings of Moses and the **Jews** in the Sinai.

In six days the Israeli Defence Forces (IDF) occupied the Sinai, having captured 5000 soldiers and 10 Egyptian T-34 tanks. On 31 October London and Paris bombed Egyptian targets, Cairo having rejected their ultimatum calling for a retreat from the canal zone. Five days later, despite a ceasefire decreed by the UN on 1 November, French and British soldiers landed at Port Said and Ismailiya. They were not to leave until 22 December under the joint pressure of the US and the Soviet Union, which also insisted that Israel leave the Sinai and Gaza by 14 March 1957. The operation had proved to be a fiasco.

Admittedly, Israel had obtained, if not new conquests, the presence of UN observers at Gaza and Sharm el-Sheikh – hence free navigation in the Gulf of Aqaba and around the port of Eilat. But for Britain and France the situation had deteriorated: the canal was closed, **oil** supplies hindered and, above all, the standing of the two countries in the region had been irredeemably compromised. With the exception of **Lebanon**, the leaders of all Arab states had broken with Paris; and the Algerian uprising was strengthened by the failure of the landing at Suez, intended to cut it off from its vital bases. As for Britain, its treaties with Egypt and Jordan were repealed. The US had been shrewd enough to oppose the Anglo–French venture, although it had condemned the nationalisation of the Suez Canal: America's time had come.

Thus, the second Israeli–Arab conflict, like the first, had a boomerang effect. The intervention, intended to suppress the nationalist upsurge and re-establish the Franco–British order, heralded the downfall of the old colonial powers and accelerated the American takeover without in any way undermining Nasser's authority. There were other unintended effects: Syria strengthened its alliance with Moscow, soon to be followed by **Iraq** where, on 14 July 1958, a revolution cut the umbilical cord attaching it to London. Lebanon and Jordan only managed to escape a similar outcome due to the landing of American marines at Beirut and British forces at Amman.

1967 WAR

Commonly known as the Six Day War, the length of the military operations properly speaking, this was the third conflict between **Israel** and
its neighbours. Like its predecessors, it ended with a crushing victory for
the Israeli Defence Forces (IDF), but it also brought about a profound
alteration of frontiers: with the occupation of East **Jerusalem**, the **West
Bank**, the **Golan Heights** and Sinai, Israel quadrupled the area of its
territory.

At the time, each of the protagonists blamed the other for the outbreak
of war, the Western media, particularly the French, taking up the cudgels
on Israel's behalf against the **Arabs**, as though it were some David facing a
Goliath. The 1967 War was even presented as a thundering Israeli riposte
to Egyptian aggression. This theory now finds few defenders. Furthermore,
Israeli leaders of the period have since modified the statements they made
at the time. For example, General **Yitzhak Rabin**, who was the IDF Chief
of Staff in 1967, has since said, 'I do not think Nasser wanted war. The two
divisions he sent into the Sinai on May 14 would not have been sufficient
to launch an offensive against Israel. He knew it and we knew it.' In the
same vein, General Matityahu Peled has said, 'The thesis that claimed
genocide was suspended above our heads in June 1967, and that Israel was
fighting for its very existence, was only a bluff'.

Hostilities broke out, on the contrary, at the end of a real and disturbing
increase of tension, in which each side feared the other's intentions. The
climate was relatively calm when, in 1963, Israel decided unilaterally to
divert the course of the River Jordan. The Arab riposte came in January
1964: a Cairo summit also decided to divert two or three of the Jordan's
tributaries; concurrently, it gave birth to the **Palestine Liberation Organisation (PLO)**, which was formally established in Jerusalem in May, under
the presidency of Ahmad Shuqairi. In January 1965, Fatah sent its first
armed commandos into Israel, via Jordanian territory but with Syrian
backing. Israel reacted with retaliatory raids against the sites where the River
Jordan was being diverted by the Arabs, but also against the countries from
which **Yasser Arafat**'s men were infiltrating. More significantly, the general
staff was organising, according to **Egypt** and **Syria**, who publicly expressed
their anxiety in April, a large-scale offensive against the Arab countries.
Anxiety increased on 15 May 1967 with an Israeli military march-past in
Jerusalem, contrary to the armistice. So, on 17 May, Cairo had its troops
stand by, and on the next day called for the withdrawal of UN observers
from Sharm el-Sheikh and Gaza, which Egyptian troops took over on
21 May. On 22 May the Gulf of Aqaba was closed to Israeli ships or those
transporting strategic material for Israel. In Tel Aviv, where **Menachem
Begin** was entering into government for the first time, the rallying of

Jordan (31 May) and **Iraq** (4 June) to the Egyptian–Syrian military pact was seen as a *casus belli*.

This encircling led the next day to a lightning attack from the IDF: once the Arab air force had been annihilated (in just one morning), Israeli troops took only six days to secure the Egyptian Sinai, the Jordanian West Bank and, by means of a two-day refusal to accept the ceasefire decreed by the UN and accepted by the Arab belligerents, the Syrian Golan Heights. After five months of bargaining, the UN, with Security Council Resolution 242 (see Appendix 4), declared the need for an Israeli withdrawal from the Arab territories it was occupying, in exchange for the cessation of fighting, the recognition of all states in the region, freedom of navigation on the **Suez Canal** and in the Gulf of Aqaba, and the creation of demilitarised zones.

The crushing Israeli victory was, in many ways, destabilising, as the **Arab world** was the first to experience. This new 'Nakba' ('catastrophe'), far from fuelling nationalism, as in 1948, brought it into crisis. The wave of nationalism had of course continued into the early 1960s, notably with the **independence** of Algeria, the revolution in North **Yemen**, the armed struggle in Aden and the **Ba'th**–Communist coalition in Syria. It was to have certain other significant consequences: radicalisation in Iraq, the overthrow of the monarchy in **Libya**, British withdrawal and independence throughout the **Arabian Peninsula**. But already the trend was going into reverse. Discredited by their defeat at the hands of the IDF, the Egyptian and Syrian regimes were also experiencing the repercussions of their domestic failures, economic and political. Once its aims of securing independence had been achieved, the nationalist movement was naturally prey to conflicting interests, which expressed themselves in clashes over agricultural reform, social measures, methods of development, of democracy etc. The economic opening of the *infitah* that later emerged in Cairo and Damascus attested to the supremacy of the bureaucratic, agrarian and commercial bourgeoisie, whose preference was for opening up to the West. The event that symbolised the end of an era was the death of **Nasser**, struck down by a heart attack on 28 September 1970, and his replacement by **Anwar al-Sadat**.

But the tide of fate would also turn against Israel, which entered a qualitatively new period in 1967. Until then, the Jewish state had depended on the international legitimacy accorded it by the UN at its birth, in passing forgetting the extension of its territory as a result of the **1948–49 War** and the forced exodus of hundreds of thousands of **Palestinians**. However, the Egyptians (with Gaza) and the Jordanians (with the West Bank) had in fact possessed the means to create an Arab state with East Jerusalem as its capital. As of 10 June 1967, the tables were turned: Israel was now master of these territories, which it could exchange for peace. But not only did Tel Aviv's leaders reject any realisation, in whatever form, of Palestinian national rights, they took the first steps in the direction of colonisation, if not annexation: the seizure of the old city of Jerusalem, the refusal to allow the return of the 300,000 refugees newly created by the war, the first Jewish **settlements**, violent repression etc. The Palestinians felt the consequences of this choice immediately, the Israelis would do so later. The continued occupation of the West Bank and Gaza, the freezing of the Palestine problem and the resulting absence of peace were to be the sources of the crisis that shook Israeli society.

'It is not true,' said General Moshe Dayan at the time, 'that the Arabs hate the Jews for personal, religious or racial reasons. They see us, and rightly from their point of view, as Westerners, foreigners, even invaders who seized an Arab country to create a Jewish state. Since we are now obliged to achieve our aims against the wishes of the Arabs, we must live in a state of permanent war' (quoted by Eric Rouleau in *The Palestinians*).

1973 WAR

Variously called the Yom Kippur, the October or the Ramadan War, this was the fourth conflict between **Israel** and its neighbours. Its uniqueness stems from the fact that Egyptian and Syrian troops managed to break through Israeli lines, albeit temporarily. Although followed by an Israeli military success, this provisional victory was seen by the **Arabs** as revenge for the humiliations suffered in the 1948–49, 1956 and 1967 Wars.

'There is no longer any hope of a peaceful solution. Our decision is to fight,' announced **Anwar al-Sadat** in November 1971, having become President of **Egypt** a year earlier. This premature declaration of war, which nobody took seriously at the time, demonstrates Cairo's confusion following the failures of its diplomatic efforts. At the time, Israel still occupied all the territories conquered by the IDF during the Six Day **War of 1967**, notably Sinai. UN Resolution 242 (see **UN Security Council Resolutions**) which advocated the restitution of these territories to the Arab countries in exchange for peace, remained a dead letter.

The Rogers Plan, presented by the **US** in response to the war of attrition instigated by Egypt on the **Suez Canal** but with the aim of putting Resolution 242 into operation, had little more success; in September 1970, Tel Aviv suspended the negotiations initiated by the mediator, Gunnar Jarring, two months before. In December, a peace plan in which Sadat proposed a formal recognition of Israel in exchange for the Occupied Territories and the return of Palestinian refugees in return for freedom of navigation on the Suez Canal was also rejected. The Jewish state was equally unimpressed by the Nixon–Brezhnev communiqué of May 1972 which reaffirmed the 'commitment' of the US and the Soviet Union 'to a peaceful solution consistent with Resolution 242'.

The Egyptian head of state now believed that only the US was in a position to bring Israel to the negotiating table. But only another war, he added, would compel the great powers to apply the pressure at their disposal on Israel. At the same time, he could silence the rumbles of popular discontent then being voiced in Egypt, where the burden of defence was becoming increasingly intolerable the longer nothing happened. Such were the reasons, external and internal, that pushed Sadat to a 'limited confrontation' with Israel; it was with this aim, plainly stated, that in March 1973 he combined his office with that of Prime Minister.

Seven months later, on 6 October, the day of the Jewish holiday of Yom Kippur, Egyptian tanks crossed the canal, rushed the Bar Lev line and plunged into the Sinai, while Syrian soldiers advanced 5km into the **Golan Heights**. It took a week for the Israeli generals to pull themselves together, and for their tanks to regain the initiative on the two fronts. This was made all the easier since Sadat had halted his offensive. **General Ariel Sharon**, already exceeding orders, also crossed the canal and marched towards Suez. On the seventeenth two events took place: in the Sinai one of the major tank battles of history, and in **Kuwait** the decision to set up an embargo which heralded the **oil** war. On 22 October, Resolution 338 of the UN Security Council was accepted by Egypt and Israel – which nonetheless continued its counter-offensive on the ground. A Soviet threat to send in troops, American forces on red alert: the superpowers intervened with an iron hand, as Cairo had hoped, to make Israel, which had lost close to 2500 of its sons, see reason.

Imposing a ceasefire is one thing, constructing a lasting peace is quite another. However, conditions seemed favourable for serious negotiations. Unfortunately, they quickly degenerated. And what of the Soviet–American desire to work together for a solution to a conflict that was threatening the detente then making rapid progress? Washington once again opted for the 'Lone Ranger' approach, Henry Kissinger settling for a separate arrangement which excluded the USSR. What of the political and moral crisis set off in Israel by the surprise of the Yom Kippur War? It was to turn in favour not of the doves but of the hawks, even bringing **Menachem Begin**'s men into public life in 1977; until then they had always been excluded from power, and they proved to be the principal beneficiaries of the accusations levelled against the country's leaders over the great 'breakdown' of October. Perhaps a Europe (see **European Union**) goaded by the oil crisis would play a positive role? But the Old World, despite its show of intervention, would, as always, take a back seat to the White House. The pragmatism suggested to the Arabs by the avenging of their honour during the first days of the October War also raised hopes. But Egypt was not to be followed by its peers, most of whom, including the **Palestinians**, refused the conditions imposed by Israel.

Thus Sadat's hopes were dashed, at least those involving international discussions under the protection of the US and the USSR: in fact the Geneva Conference was no sooner inaugurated than adjourned. Cairo was to find another road to peace, opened by the White House, one that would lead the Egyptian President and his Israeli opposite number to the **Camp David Accords**. Even after the Yom Kippur War, Sadat was inclined, claimed **Colonel Qadhaffi** in 1977, to 'conclude any peace whatever with Israel, as long as he could regain the Sinai'.

1982 WAR

Called the **Lebanon** War, after the country in which the fighting took place, this was the fifth war in the history of the Middle East since World War II. It differed profoundly from those which preceded it on three main counts: it was more an Israeli–Palestinian than an Arab–Israeli conflict, it proved long-lasting and, finally, it did not end in a clear-cut victory for **Israel**.

Menachem Begin's launching of the invasion of Lebanon resembled **Anwar al-Sadat**'s initiation of the **1973 War** in that if the date chosen was a surprise, the opening of hostilities was far from unexpected. The **Camp David Accords** had led, as many observers had predicted, to a deadlock; for while the Israeli–Egyptian peace treaty was implemented, negotiations on Palestinian **autonomy** remained at the planning stage. The subject was of course bitterly discussed by **Egypt** and Israel, but **Jordan** and, more importantly, the **Palestine Liberation Organisation (PLO)**, were excluded from the talks. The assassination of Sadat in October 1981 also brought about a firmer attitude on the Palestine question in Cairo. Unable to solve the problem at the conference table, the Israelis tried to do so in the field: on the **West Bank** and in Gaza, where colonisation and repression intensified, and in Lebanon where the operations of the Israeli Defence Forces (IDF) were now stepped up. Aware that Egypt's only concern was not to compromise the regaining of the Sinai, that the **Arab world** was divided and the PLO relatively isolated, Israeli leaders felt they had a free hand. Throughout 1981 there was a noticeable rise in tension: the missile crisis with **Syria** in spring was followed on 7 June by a raid on the Iraqi nuclear centre of Tammuz and, in December, the annexation of the **Golan Heights**. But, above all, in June the IDF and PLO troops based in south Lebanon began shelling each other until the US negotiated a ceasefire.

Operation 'Peace in Galilee' was the unlikely name given on 6 June 1982 to the incidents of the summer of 1981 and the Israeli military operation in Lebanon – ignoring the fact that the ceasefire had been scrupulously observed by the PLO. Officially, the operation was merely to affirm control of a 40km strip from which **terrorists** would no longer be able to shell the north of the country. In practice, by way of this limited intervention the IDF found itself at the end of June at the gates of Beirut after the Syrian army had signed a ceasefire on the eleventh. Thus began the siege of West Beirut, where **Palestinians** and the Lebanese National Movement fought side by side, while the Phalangists lent support – but without taking part in the fighting – to the Israeli soldiers. There seemed no end to the phosphorus, napalm and scatter bombs that relentlessly poured down on the starving and parched western section of the city. On 7 August the American mediator Philip Habib declared an American–Lebanese–Palestinian agreement to allow the departure of the PLO militia under the protection of an international (Franco–Italian) contingent.

After one last wave of shelling it was all over. On 30 August **Yasser Arafat** and the last of his troops left Beirut, and on 15 September, the day after the assassination of Lebanese President Bashir Gemayel, **General Ariel Sharon**'s forces entered. On the sixteenth and seventeenth, under the gaze of these troops, the Phalangists massacred hundreds of men, women and children in the camps of **Sabra and Shatila**. Such was the tragic end of the first phase of the Lebanon War, that of full combat. A second phase now opened: that of Israel's occupation of south Lebanon, which provoked increasingly extensive armed popular resistance, to the point where, three years later, Tel Aviv would decide to withdraw its army, except for a 'security zone' which it only evacuated in 2000.

Such, in effect, was the major, most tangible result of the invasion of Lebanon, a shambles in which Israel floundered for months on end, at a cost of the lives of hundreds of its soldiers, thousands of wounded and hundreds of millions of dollars in occupation expenses, not to mention the virtually unanimous hostility of the primarily **Shi'ite** population, which had given the IDF a relatively good reception in June 1982, hoping it would get rid of the Palestinians for them. This was undoubtedly an exorbitant price to pay. Whether the benefits derived from the Lebanese affair were worth it from the Israeli perspective is far from clear.

The annihilation of the PLO was Ariel Sharon's publicly stated aim. 'We are here,' he declared on 12 June 1982, 'to destroy once and for all the PLO terrorists'. While the Palestinian resistance movement was not completely crushed in the vice and was able to get out of Beirut, it nonetheless suffered severe setbacks. But the resistance movement survived this new challenge, as it had previous ones.

A state in Lebanon that was strong, Christian and friendly to Israel had long been the dream of Israeli leaders. Clearly the operation had done little to bring it about. After a period that seemed promising for Tel Aviv, during which new President Amin Gemayel seemed to have taken the country in hand and set it on the path to peace with the Jewish state, the course of events was reversed. Beirut broke off contact, and Syria regained its influence and domination in Lebanon.

A final element, difficult to measure, nonetheless plays a considerable role in the negative assessment most observers make of the invasion of Lebanon: the damage to Israel's image. For the first time in its history, a military initiative undertaken by Israel did not appear legitimate in the West, since it was not necessary to either its defence or survival. An already shaken public opinion was further disturbed by the dreadful pictures transmitted by the media of the siege of Beirut, and especially Sabra and Shatila.

ABU NIDAL

Sabri al-Banna (whose *nom de guerre* was Abu Nidal) was born in Jaffa, Palestine, in 1937 into a wealthy family which owned several thousand hectares of land. After 1948 his parents took refuge in Gaza and later settled in Nablus. In 1960 he emigrated to **Saudi Arabia**, where he worked as a technician. It was in Saudi Arabia that he became involved in political activity, first with the **Ba'th** party, then with Fatah. His political work led to his arrest, torture and finally deportation from the country. After the **1967 War** he joined the *fedayeen* in Amman. In 1969 he was sent by Fatah to Khartoum and then in 1970 was made the Fatah and **Palestine Liberation Organisation (PLO)** representative in **Iraq**.

In 1974 Abu Nidal rejected the 'pragmatic' policy adopted by the PLO and came out in favour of pursuing an all-out struggle against **Israel**. He thus withdrew from the PLO and created the Fatah Revolutionary Council, which at that time had the support of Iraqi leaders. After that period his Arab alliances evolved according to circumstances; he was supported in turn by Iraq, **Syria** and **Libya**.

The influence of the Fatah Revolutionary Council was limited. It took part in several different loose-knit groupings hostile to **Arafat** and, of course, the **Oslo Accords**. But it was largely due to the effectiveness of its **terrorist** cells that Abu Nidal's group earned its international reputation. The organisation joined the Popular Front for the Liberation of Palestine, a Damascus-based amalgamation of opponents of Arafat. Its 'achievements' include the assassination of several senior members of the PLO, such as Said Hammami, Ezzedine Kalak and **Issam Sartawi**. In all likelihood it was also responsible for the killing of Abu Iyad, the second in command of the PLO in January 1991. Abu Nidal was sentenced to death by the PLO, and officials within Arafat's organisation have repeatedly accused the terrorist group of having been infiltrated by the Israeli security services.

Abu Nidal was also implicated in the 1982 Rue des Rosiers bombing and the attack on the Istanbul synagogue in September 1986. His group was also accused of the attack on the *City of Poros* on 11 July 1988 in Greece, in which some ten people died. At the end of 1989, violent internal conflicts weakened the organisation, and dozens of members were murdered, the victims of a 'purge' campaign ordered by its leader, who sought refuge in Libya in 1991. He was expelled by **Colonel Qadhaffi** (then seeking new legitimacy on the international scene) and went to **Egypt**, where he was treated for leukaemia and where, according to some sources, he assisted Cairo in its fight against **Islamist** movements. In December 1998 he fled to Iraq, where he was found dead in August 2002. Jalil al-Haboush, head of Iraqi intelligence at the time, said that Abu Nidal shot himself through the mouth when officials arrived to take him to court on charges of entering

the country illegally, and died eight hours later. Spokesmen for the Fatah
Revolutionary Council said that he was an unyielding believer who could not
have committed suicide. Following his death, one of his former spokesmen,
Atef Abu Baqr, who had defected from the Fatah Revolutionary Council
in late 1989, gave an interview to the newspaper *al-Hayat* in which he
extended the list of Abu Nidal's terrorist involvements. He had apparently
organised attacks involving a Gulf Air aircraft in 1983, the La Belle
discotheque in West Berlin in 1986, the Pan Am flight that was brought
down over Lockerbie, Scotland in December 1988, and the 1989 attempt
on the life of Egyptian President **Hosni Mubarak** in Addis Ababa.

ALIYA

The 'ascent' (literal translation from the Hebrew) of the **Jews** to Palestine.
After the dispersal following the Roman defeat of the Bar Kokhba Revolt
in AD135, the Jewish presence in Palestine remained marginal for many
centuries. Towards the end of the fifteenth century, its ranks were increased
by the many Jews expelled from the Iberian peninsula. Nevertheless, in
1835 only 10,000 Jews lived in Palestine. The tiny communities of **Jerusalem**,
Safad, Tiberias and Hebron survived on the charity (*halukah*) of the diaspora
Jews, especially from the eighteenth century onwards.

From being a religious idea, the renaissance of **Israel** gradually became
a political objective among diaspora Jews. After appeals from Napoleon,
the Saint-Simonians and Lord Byron, the idea was taken up by the **Zionist**
movement. Even before **Theodor Herzl**, the Russian Leon Pinsker imagined
and organised, with the Lovers of Zion, the new 'colonisation' of the
'biblical lands'. Several *aliyot* were to achieve this.

The first *aliya*, from 1882 to 1903, added 20–30,000 new people, virtually
all from Tsarist **Russia**, to the 25,000 Jews who lived in Palestine in 1880 –
mostly, as in the past, in Jerusalem, Hebron, Safad and Tiberias, among
almost half a million **Arabs**. The first agricultural enterprises came into
being during this *aliya* and, along with the 19 new **settlements** created by
Baron Edmond de Rothschild, were to harbour more than 5000 pioneers. At
the same time, the Jewish bourgeoisie began to invest capital in Palestine,
particularly in citrus-fruit production.

The second *aliya*, basically of Russians with a socialist background,
attracted 35–40,000 new immigrants between 1903 and 1914. Dozens of
additional settlements came into being. Tel Aviv was built, and Jerusalem
and Haifa expanded. Hebrew, once a literary and liturgical language, now
became an everyday one. These Central European Jews were joined by the
first Yemenis, who replaced the Arab *fellaheen* in the agricultural projects
because the *kibbutzim* (communes, the first founded in Degania in 1911)

were allowed to employ only Jewish workers. Thus on the eve of World War I there were about 80,000 Jews in Palestine. Two to three million left Russia and Poland at the same time for Western Europe and the Americas.

By the end of the war, in 1918, of the old Jewish communities and the first two *aliyot* only 60,000 remained in Palestine, that is to say 10 per cent of the total population. Over the next twenty years, however, the 'legalisation' of **immigration** by the **Balfour Declaration** brought this proportion to 30 per cent within twenty years.

The influx was slow at first. The third *aliya*, from 1919 to 1923, brought 35,000 Jews from the USSR, Poland and the Baltic countries, most of whom were socialists, workers and pioneers. In addition to these, the fourth *aliya*, from 1924 to 1931, with 82,000 participants, brought Jews from the Balkans and the Middle East who were, generally speaking, middle class. By the end of 1931, there were 175,000 Jews in the Holy Land, representing 17.7 per cent of the total population.

The triumph of Nazism in Germany stimulated further Jewish immigration to the **Yishuv**, and totally altered its characteristics. The fifth *aliya*, from 1932 to 1939, brought an additional 247,000 Jews, that is to say 30,000 a year – four times more than at any time since the end of World War I. Stemming less from Zionism than the threats of Nazism, this new wave of colonisation was mainly German and middle class, for the Zionist Organisation had concluded a treaty with Berlin in 1933 authorising the transfer of German Jewish capital.

By 1939, there were exactly 429,605 Jews in Palestine, 28 per cent of the total population. Despite the British blockade (see **Great Britain**), 118,338 others – this was the sixth *aliya* – joined them there before the declaration of **independence** on 14 May 1948. Among these were many survivors of the Holocaust, often travelling in secret to avoid the tragic fate of the Exodus. Thus when the state of Israel came into being it comprised 650,000 Jewish citizens, a third of the inhabitants of Palestine.

This number was to increase five-fold over the next twenty-five years, due to the additional numbers brought by numerous, and massive, *aliyot*. These influxes, however, differed greatly from the preceding ones, mainly in the origins of the new Israelis. Up until the 1970s the huge majority were Jews coming from Africa and Asia, with the last organised wave arriving from Ethiopia in the 1980s and 1990s (see **Oriental Jews**).

The Soviet–American detente also encouraged a new influx into Israel of Jews from the USSR. After reaching its peak in 1979, this stream of migration petered out until Mikhail Gorbachev took power in the years before the dissolution of the USSR. From 1986 to 2002 it brought to the Jewish state more than 900,000 new citizens. Although the integration of this mass of immigrants was not problem-free, in the end it was an undoubted success, although the state of Israel had to pay a high price – the aid given to the

Russians was markedly disproportionate to that given earlier to the **Oriental Jews**: a lump sum of nearly £4000 per person, reduced-rate mortgages and *de facto* priority in employment.

Finally, Israel also welcomed a non-Jewish *aliya*: upwards of 250,000 workers 'imported' from Asia, Eastern Europe and Africa from the late 1980s onwards, originally to replace the **Palestinians** who were being prevented from coming to work in Israel. This immigration, its participants subjected to terrible exploitation verging on slavery, is seen by the ultra-Orthodox as a threat to the Jewish majority.

Ariel Sharon's government raised additional funding in order to revive the process of immigration, which had fallen from nearly 200,000 new arrivals in 1990 to 43,500 in 2001 – this latter figure being a drop of 28 per cent compared with 2000. In addition to these financial incentives, Israeli leaders, with the Prime Minister in the lead, have made the most of anti-Jewish attacks in the world to depict an irresistible rise of antisemitism, with *aliya* as the only solution.

AMERICAN AID

The Middle East has always been a major recipient of American aid, both economic and military – a measure of the central role the region occupies in **US** strategy.

Official statistics (from the Statistical Abstract of the United States 1995–96, US Department of Commerce) show that from 1946 to 1993 the main beneficiaries of the funds disbursed to the region were **Israel** (about $54bn), with **Egypt** ($36bn) and **Turkey** ($14bn) some way behind. Together these sums represent approximately one quarter of all American aid, economic and military, over this long period.

The official statistics for 1999 indicate, among other things, an accentuation of these trends:

- Israel receives $2.9bn of military and economic aid ($1.86bn and $1.08bn respectively), making it the largest recipient of aid in the world;
- Egypt receives $2.1bn ($1.3bn and $0.86bn respectively), making it the world's second-largest aid recipient. However, after the 11 September 2001 attacks Washington blocked $120m of additional aid which was to have helped with Egypt's balance-of-payments problems.

These two countries are followed – much more modestly – by **Jordan** (with $290m, of which three quarters is economic aid), **Sudan** ($84m in economic aid), which was also thanked for its support during the struggle against **terrorism**, and the **West Bank** and Gaza ($80m of economic aid). Turkey, for its part, has seen a considerable reduction in the aid provided by the US; in 2000 Ankara received only $1.6m in economic and military aid (compared with $8.6m in 1998). **Lebanon**, on the other hand, received $27.5m (against $15m in 1998).

Thus Israel and Egypt between them, with a total of $5bn in direct aid (both military and economic), monopolise almost one third of all US foreign aid.

ARAB LEAGUE

The League of Arab States was created on 22 March 1945 in Alexandria. **Egypt, Iraq, Lebanon, Saudi Arabia, Syria**, Transjordan and North **Yemen** sponsored the infant organisation. As the era of colonial domination ended, the League was enlarged, and today has 20 members, including Palestine. Beyond the founder members it now includes **Sudan**, Tunisia, Morocco, **Kuwait**, Algeria, South Yemen, the United Arab Emirates, Bahrain, Oman, Mauritania, Somalia, Djibouti and the Comoros, **Libya** (which periodically threatens to withdraw from the League, as it did in April 2002) and the **Palestine Liberation Organisation (PLO)**, which has been a full member since 1976. In May 1979, the League's headquarters were transferred from Cairo to Tunis after the signing of the Egyptian–Israeli peace treaty. However, a decade later, with the re-integration of **Egypt** into the **Arab world** and the **Gulf War**, the organisation returned to Cairo on 31 October 1990.

The League has set up specialised standing committees (on the economy, culture etc.; the political committee is of particular importance). The Defence Council (made up of foreign and defence ministers) and the Economic Council (composed of ministers of finance) meet under the aegis of the League. Since 1964, the date when they were officially instituted, the summits of the heads of state have been the supreme authority, where conflicts are resolved and major decisions taken. The League has also created many specialised autonomous agencies, including the Arab Labour Organisation, the Postal Union and the Telecommunications Union.

The old idea of a federation of Arab countries resurfaced during the Second World War. On 29 May 1941, British Foreign Secretary Anthony Eden stated in the House of Commons of the Arab world, 'It seems to me both natural and just that not only natural and economic links but also political links be reinforced. For its part, His Majesty's Government will give the greatest support to any plan that receives general approbation.' In this way London sought to gain the sympathies of the Arab countries. Its Hashemite allies in **Jordan** and Iraq were at the time trying to set up a unified state in the Fertile Crescent (which would also incorporate Palestine and Syria). In opposition to this project and to the Hashemite hegemony, the Egyptian monarchy initiated counter-measures that led to the meeting in Alexandria.

Although expressing the aspiration for Arab unity, albeit in a distorted manner, the League has never been an instrument for implementing unity. Its statutes do not stipulate that it should make any effort in this direction, and the various concrete attempts at unity (such as the creation of the United Arab Republic in 1958) have taken place outside the League, which is governed by the rule of unanimity. The organisation has principally helped to co-ordinate the activities of Arab states, particularly on the Palestinian question. It is in this field that the most significant decisions have been taken: the creation of the PLO (1964); the recognition of the PLO as sole representative of the Palestinian people (1973–74); the adoption of the Fez Plan (1982). However, the Gulf War of 1990 split and potentially jeopardised the future of the organisation. The election of **Benyamin Netanyahu** as Prime Minister of **Israel** brought about a degree of consensus between member states; the first Arab Summit after the Gulf War finally took place in Cairo in June 1996. All member states participated in this summit, with the exception of Iraq, which was not invited.

Subsequently, regular meetings resumed, in the presence of representatives of Baghdad. The launching of the **second Intifada** in September 2000 and its repression led to the shutting down of all Israeli diplomatic representations in the Arab world – Morocco, Qatar, Oman etc. – and the withdrawal of the Jordanian ambassador to Israel, Egypt having already withdrawn its representative. Only Mauritania maintains diplomatic relations with the Jewish state.

At the Beirut Summit in March 2002, the League put forward for a second time (the first was the Fez Plan of 1982) a peace initiative based on suggestions by Saudi Crown Prince Abdullah bin Abdul Aziz. The member countries proposed to agree that 'conflict with Israel is at an end' and to establish 'normal relations with Israel', on three conditions: total Israeli withdrawal from the occupied Arab territories, including the Syrian **Golan Heights**; a 'just solution' of the problem of Palestinian refugees, in conformity with Resolution 194 of the UN General Assembly; the acceptance of an independent and sovereign Palestinian state on the Palestinian territory occupied in 1967, in the **West Bank** and Gaza, the capital of which would be East **Jerusalem**. But this plan came to nothing, and the League's inability to affect the Israeli–Palestinian conflict, as also in the Iraqi crisis, confirms the organisation's impotence.

In 2003 the Secretary-General of the Arab League was the Egyptian Amr Musa.

ARAB WORLD

What we know as the Arab world comprises the 22 member countries of the **Arab League**, including Palestine. Its population is majority Arab, but also includes **minorities**, particularly Kabyles and **Kurds**. In 2000 it had a total population of about 280 million, about a quarter the population of India and a fifth of that of China. **Egypt** is the largest country by far, with a population of almost 70 million. The **Arabs** represent 5 per cent of the world's population, double the numbers of fifty years ago; they have one of the youngest populations in the world, with 38 per cent under the age of 14. In all countries the demographic transition is underway, with a considerable decrease in the number of children per woman – although some countries, such as **Saudi Arabia**, are only at the start of this transition. Between now and 2020 the total population of the Arab world will rise to between 410 and 460 million. The rate of urbanisation, which stood at 25 per cent in 1950, exceeded 50 per cent by the end of the twentieth century, and stands at more than 80 per cent in countries such as Saudi Arabia, **Libya** and **Lebanon**.

A UN Development Programme (UNDP) report (2002) into human development in the region caused considerable controversy. Although its conclusions are debatable, it had the merit of highlighting the three main shortcomings of the Arab world.

The first concerns basic human liberties. The big movements of democratisation which took place in Latin America and East Asia in the 1980s, but also in Eastern Europe, Central Asia and Africa in the late 1980s and 1990s, did not affect the Arab world. In all countries executive power controls the legislative system and the judiciary. Regimes are characterised by autocracy and by a powerful influence of the military (and intelligence services) in political decision-making. Often there are tribal militias or militias belonging to the party in power, which operate parallel to the army in maintaining order. There have been no notable handovers of power (with the exception of **Sudan** in 1989, with the installation of an **Islamist** dictatorship, and Somalia, which disappeared as a state). The longevity of the region's leaders has no equivalent elsewhere. **King Hussein** of **Jordan** ruled for over forty-five years, and at his death he was replaced by his son; the same was true of **Hafez al-Assad**, who ruled **Syria** for over thirty years; **Saddam Hussein** was in control in **Iraq** from 1971 to 2003; **Qadhaffi** came to power in 1969. When these heads of state die, as we have seen, they pass power to their direct heirs, who maintain the status quo even in republican regimes such as Syria.

The second shortcoming is that the region suffers from massive sexual inequality. The education of women has developed faster than in any other region in the world, but the sexist thinking which assigns to women solely a reproductive role persists; half of all women are still illiterate. With the exception of South Asia, the Arab world is the only region in the world where educational inequalities between men and women remain so marked. The level of political discrimination is even more striking. Women represent only 3.7 per cent of members of parliament, compared with a world average of 12 per cent.

The third area of backwardness is that of education, culture and research. More than 65 million Arabs are illiterate, with levels of illiteracy higher than in many poorer countries. The rate of illiteracy fell from 60 per cent in 1980 to 43 per cent in the mid-1990s, but is still higher than the average for developing countries. The region has fewer students per inhabitant than the countries of Asia and Latin America. Investment in research appears very weak, the availability of translations of foreign texts is low, and the 'brain-drain' is ongoing.

How do we explain these failings? There is no single answer. We can set aside the 'culturalist' explanation, which sees 'Arab culture' as the reason for the Arabs' lack of success; after all, in their history they have built powerful and brilliant empires. Leaving aside the consequences of colonialism, one has to remember the wars that have ravaged the region for around fifty years: the Arab–Israeli conflicts (1948, 1956, 1967, 1973, 1982) and the **Iran–Iraq War** (1980–88) and the first **Gulf War** (1990–91), not to mention the latest war against Iraq. No other part of the world has known such a concentration of war and killing. **Israel**'s illegal occupation of Arab territories since 1967 and the Arab–Israeli conflict are still major obstacles to security and progress: they affect all areas of economic, political and social life, they divert the wealth that is produced, and they justify (in the name of defence against the external enemy) the repressive policies of authoritarian regimes. They also dominate all debate in society, maintaining a sense of permanent threat. And they create infinite feelings of frustration over what appears a double standard on the part of the international community and the West in particular. In the 1990s, military spending represented an average of 7.4 per cent of GNP, compared with a world average of 2.4 per cent.

In addition to a permanent state of war – and **sanctions** – there is, paradoxically, the curse of **oil**. The Arab world's total non-oil exports amount to only $40bn, less than the exports of Finland. As the UNDP report puts it, 'the Arab world is more cash rich than developed'. The specialisation in oil has prevented the development of other productive activities, while at the same time enabling social peace to be bought. **Immigration** has made it possible for non-producing countries to profit from the 'oil boom'. In addition, the explosion of oil prices in 1973–74 not only contributed to the consolidation of a conservative Islamism financed by Saudi Arabia, but also made it possible for the Gulf emirates to 'buy' the elites of the region, attracted by the mirage of oil and high wages. The massive financing of the **Palestine Liberation Organisation (PLO)**, for example, contributed to bureaucratisation and corruption in that organisation.

Finally, oil has been the main reason for Western interventions in the region, and also for the West's turning a blind eye to regimes which were seen as likely to guarantee the West's security of supplies. As Richard Haas, a leading official in the US State Department, said at the end of 2002, preceding administrations had not made the democratisation of the Arab world a sufficient priority. It is, however, not very likely that George W. Bush's administration, despite its fine words, will change this state of affairs: free elections would only bring to power parties opposed to Washington, given the prevailing level of hostility to the US.

However, contrary to general opinion, this hostility is not directly simply against 'Western values'. A study of public opinion in the Arab world (*International Herald Tribune*, 8 October 2002) showed that the people questioned had a positive vision of American political freedoms and values, but very negative views of US policy. On the other hand, views of **France**, Canada and Japan tended to be positive.

Such opinion polls confirm that Arab aspirations are the same as those of other people in the world: peace, development and democracy. While there have been positive signs in recent years, from Morocco to Bahrain, it is unlikely that the war against Iraq will encourage this development.

Some facts about the Arab world: between 1970 and 1997 life expectancy rose from 51 to 65. Fifty-four million people have no access to drinking **water**, and 29 million no access to healthcare. Of the 22 countries defined by the World Bank as below the poverty line in terms of water (less than 1000 cubic metres per person per year), 15 are Arab. Furthermore, the amount of cultivatable land per inhabitant fell from 0.4 hectares in 1970 to 0.24 in 1998. Twenty per cent of Arabs live on less than $2 a day. And during the past twenty years the figure for the growth of per-capita income has stood at a mere 0.5 per cent – less than in sub-Saharan Africa. Regional co-operation is very weak, despite the projected creation of a free-trade zone by 2005.

ARABIAN PENINSULA

The cradle of Arab–Islamic civilisation, the Arabian Peninsula is now the **oil**-producing epicentre of the modern world. It is divided into seven states, of which three – **Saudi Arabia**, **Kuwait** and **Yemen** – are dealt with in separate entries. This entry provides a brief overview of the remaining four: Bahrain, Qatar, the United Arab Emirates and Oman.

Before looking at each of these states individually, a few of their common features merit attention. First, they are all blessed with oil, albeit in varying quantities and qualities. In 2001, 21.5 per cent of the world's oil production and 44 per cent of its reserves were concentrated here. Despite a relative decline in its importance to the West, 20 per cent of the industrialised world's oil supplies still traverses the 800km-long Gulf (470km at its widest, but only 50km at the Straits of Hormuz, its narrowest point). Oil wealth was the cause of the boom enjoyed by the region's states from the mid-1970s (much earlier for Saudi Arabia and Kuwait) and the reason for the region's crucial importance in the eyes of the great powers, the US foremost among them.

Until recently, all the states of the peninsula, with the exception of Saudi Arabia and North Yemen, were colonies or protectorates of **Britain**, initiated in the nineteenth century to secure the routes to India. The 'security' the British imposed in the peninsula was based on the simple principle of discouraging any attempt on the part of a local power to establish supremacy by encouraging the peninsula's division into emirates – a series of fragile protectorates whose economic base and state structures were fashioned to serve British interests. A century later the collapse of its empire and its financial crisis led the UK to disengage from the area – a decision taken by a Labour government in 1968 and applied on 1 December 1971 by a Conservative government.

'The departure of the British,' wrote Raoul Delcorde in *La Sécurité et la stratégie dans le golfe Arabo-Persique*,

> caused disturbances in the balance of the Gulf. To fill the vacuum, two solutions presented themselves: either that one sufficiently strong state take it upon itself to maintain order in the region (implying the agreement of the other states) while itself being supported by a great power, or that each state equip itself with a military capacity and a degree of internal cohesion sufficient to guarantee its own security. But facts can prove obstinate: the divisions and troubles that arose on the Arab side of the Gulf and the Soviet presence in Iraq necessarily led to the emergence of Iran as a new centre of power.

In the early 1970s the US was bogged down in the Vietnam War, and rather than commit itself militarily elsewhere in the world it sought client regimes. The obvious candidate for this role in the Gulf was the Shah's. Unlike Saudi Arabia, the only other candidate for hegemony in the region, **Iran** possessed the human resources necessary to become the pivot of the American policy of containing the Soviet Union (see **Russia**) in a region whose importance to the economy of the West was underlined by the **1973 War**. There was, of course, a long-standing historical rivalry between the Persians and **Arabs** in the Gulf, and Iran took advantage of the situation to seize the upper hand. Although it accepted Bahrain's demand for **independence**, on the eve of the Britain's departure – and therefore with British complicity – it occupied the islands of Abu Musa and the two

Tunbs, the keys to the Straits of Hormuz. In addition, the Shah's army crushed the popular guerrilla movement in Oman. Despite the fears of **Egypt**, Kuwait, Saudi Arabia and **Iraq**, Iran set itself up as the policeman of the Gulf. Indeed, it was in response to Iranian expansionism that the federation of the United Arab Emirates (UAE) was formed, though Bahrain and Qatar both refused to join. For its own part, Saudi Arabia, while sharing the Shah's hostility towards the threat of both the Soviets and the Arab nationalists, concentrated on safeguarding its own interests.

Once it had extricated itself from the impasse in Vietnam, the US began to involve itself more directly in the region, increasing its imports of oil from the Gulf, attracting the main share of the region's petrodollars and selling fabulous quantities of arms to local states. Iran alone purchased over $10bn worth between 1972 and 1976. The Iranian Revolution of 1978–79, however, changed everything. The main pillar of American policy disappeared overnight, and Iranian hegemony acquired a revolutionary dimension. The sizeable Shi'ite (see **Shi'ism**) **minority** stepped up the unrest in the Emirates. Even the Saudi regime fell victim in 1979 to fundamentalist riots which it was able to put down mainly due to the help of French gendarmes. This situation persuaded the US to reorganise its military strategy in the region, notably through the creation of the Rapid Deployment Force.

In order to confront any 'attempt by an external power to take control of the Persian Gulf region', which President Carter considered to be 'an attack against vital American interests', the State Department guaranteed a chain of bases and military 'facilities' for the Pentagon in Morocco, **Turkey**, Egypt, Diego Garcia in the Indian Ocean, Oman, Somalia and Kenya. From 1980, the **Iran–Iraq War** tested the newly established system. While the US, like the USSR, was totally incapable of preventing the terrible bloodshed that marked that conflict, the emirates feared its possible extension. Iran, furthermore, did not hesitate to apply strong pressure on them, both from outside and – via the Shi'ite minority – from inside. Closely linked to Washington, whose growing intervention they encouraged – but with whom they could not openly ally themselves, given America's support of **Israel** – the region's leaders agreed to implement an old Saudi project long deferred: the Gulf Cooperation Council (GCC).

The organisation, officially established in May 1981 and composed of Saudi Arabia and the five other emirate states (but not the two Yemens), went beyond the idea of a mere Common Market envisaged in the 1970s. In economic terms, the GCC co-ordinates the industrial policies of its member countries by preparing them for the post-oil period; building sites have sprung up everywhere, and integration is advancing by leaps and bounds. Politically, it attempts to eliminate the principal factors tending to destabilise the region's regimes: the differences between member states, which it tries to resolve peacefully, the Israeli–Arab conflict, in which the GCC intervened in favour of a political solution to the Palestinian problem and, above all, the Iraq–Iran confrontation, on which it adopted a tougher position after the entry of Iranian forces into Iraqi territory during the summer of 1982. But the **Gulf War** illustrated the impotence of the organisation, which was incapable of preventing the Iraqi invasion of Kuwait on 2 August 1990.

In the wake of the allied victory in the Gulf, the impotence of the GCC presented an acute security problem as long as **Saddam Hussein** managed to maintain himself in power. The creation of a joint military force, known as the Shield, and the pact with Egypt and **Syria** – the two latter states maintained a military presence in the region in exchange for economic and financial aid – rapidly demonstrated its limitations. Very quickly, Kuwait, like Bahrain, Qatar and the UAE, came to prefer the protection of the US, which took up a long-term position in the region, notably in Saudi Arabia. The collapse of the Iraqi regime in 2003 has changed the demographics of US deployment in the region. In August 2003, US forces withdrew from Saudi Arabia – due mainly to the hostility of the population fomented by **Islamist** propaganda. But if it has changed the demographics, it has not changed US policy: the military is here to stay in the region.

Bahrain

Bahrain is formed of 33 islands with a total area of 711 sq. km, but its population (650,000 in 2001, of whom 245,000 were foreigners, representing two thirds of the workforce) inhabits only two of these: Bahrain itself and al-Muharraq. From its two centuries of Persian domination before British colonisation, it retains a sizeable minority of Iranian origin, which still speaks Farsi and is firmly attached to Shi'ism. In 1968, when Britain gave up its protectorate, Iran threatened to annex Bahrain, but a conference organised in 1970 under the auspices of the UN gave it independence, proclaimed in August 1971. The island's life has been characterised by chronic political agitation and the presence of both a leftist and an Islamist opposition. The dissolution of an elected assembly in 1975, set up only two years earlier (a sign, at the time, of a fumbling attempt to democratise an absolute monarchy), the discovery of an 'Iranian plot' in 1981, and an abortive coup d'état in 1985 have all strengthened the regime's repressive character. Political unrest has nevertheless continued, fuelled by economic problems, notably unemployment, which is especially high among the Shi'ites. In November 1992, the Emir decided to create a Consultative Council, but this did not satisfy the demand for a return to the 1973 constitution, for which thousands of citizens petitioned in October 1994. The following month witnessed a virtual *intifada*. Dozens were shot, hundreds were arrested, and torture was widely used.

In 1999, on the death of his father, the new Emir, Sheikh Hamad bin Isa al-Khalifa, paved the way for an increase in democratic freedoms: opposition figures were freed from prison; exiles were allowed to return to the emirate; there was a formal recognition of equality of its citizens (the majority Shi'ite population suffer various discriminations at the hand of the Sunni authorities); the abolition of emergency laws; the restoration of freedom of speech. A new National Charter, backed by a referendum in February 2001, set the seal on national reconciliation and guaranteed a return to parliamentary life. The Emir proclaimed himself King in February 2002, with the emirate becoming a constitutional monarchy. Municipal elections in May were followed by national elections in October, in which the turnout was no higher than 53 per cent – the opposition boycotted the elections to protest against the King's creation of a second non-elected chamber which, in the event of conflict between the two assemblies, would have the final word.

A decline in oil production, which began as early as the 1930s, led Bahrain to diversify its economy at an early stage. Traditional activities – fishing and pearls – aside, the country constructed a huge aluminium factory and a petrochemical complex. After the outbreak of the **1982 War** in **Lebanon**, the capital Manama became the region's principal financial centre. Bahrain also possesses an airport and a seaport equipped with a dry dock. But the Iran–Iraq War and then the 1991 **Gulf War** put an end to this boom, which was again threatened by the tension leading up to the war in Iraq in 2003.

Since 26 November 1986 Bahrain has been linked to Saudi Arabia by a causeway 25km long.

Qatar

Qatar, with an area of 11,400 sq. km, mostly desert, had a population in 2001 of 610,000, of whom 75 per cent were foreigners (Indians, Iranians, Pakistanis, Asians or people from other Arab countries). From being an economy based on animal husbandry, fishing and pearls, Qatar leapt to a high level of development following the exploitation of its oil reserves: refineries, petrochemicals, cement factories, steelworks, communication networks on both land and sea, health and education systems etc. The political life of the country, independent since 1971, has taken the form of internal struggles within the ruling al-Thani family. Ahmad Ibn Ali was supplanted in 1972 by his cousin, Prime Minister Khalifa Ibn Hamad, who in 1977 named his son Hamad Ibn Khalifa Crown Prince.

A serious territorial conflict pitted the emirate against Bahrain for several years, before being settled largely in favour of Bahrain by the International Court of Justice in March 2001. In September 1992, acute tension blew up between Qatar and Saudi Arabia over the question of their common border, and Qatar subsequently boycotted several GCC meetings. Driven by its Crown Prince, the country has to this day maintained its distance from its powerful neighbour, refusing to take a position over the civil war in Yemen in 1995, developing contacts with both Iraq and Iran as well as tentative relations with Israel. On 27 June 1995, profiting from his father's trip abroad, Crown Prince Hamad Ibn Khalifa seized power.

The ousted Emir took refuge abroad, and his son launched a wide-ranging programme of reforms, particularly in the realm of politics, with the first municipal elections in March 1999 and the presentation of a proposed constitution in July 2002 which would permit freedom of expression, association and religion and the election of a parliament in 2005, with the additional feature of women having the right to vote. The government also supported the emergence of the free-speaking satellite television channel al-Jazeera, which has a huge reputation in the Arab world, but which has led to tensions in relations between Qatar and each of the Arab regimes. The alliance with the US has a high priority, and in December 2002 Washington set up a high-technology command post in the emirate which could be used in the event of war with Iraq, a contingency plan which was put into action in March 2003.

United Arab Emirates

On the eve of its independence in 1971, the Federation of the United Arab Emirates was meant to combine all the emirates of the one-time 'Pirate Coast'. Qatar and Bahrain, however, declined the offer, and the federation therefore came to comprise only seven members: Abu Dhabi, Dubai, Sharjah, Ras al-Khaimah, Umm al-Qaywain, Ajman and Fujairah – a total of 77,700 sq. km and 3.1 million inhabitants in 2001, of whom almost 80 per cent are foreigners. The massive influx, not only of Arab immigrants, but also of Pakistanis and Indians, can be explained by the oil boom of the 1970s, which made the UAE one of the richest countries in the world.

The political life of the UAE is nonetheless troubled by power struggles between the emirates, notably between Abu Dhabi, whose Emir, Sheikh Zayid, is President of the Federation, and Dubai, whose Emir, Sheikh Rashid, occupies the post of Prime Minister. Thus its provisional constitution (from absolute monarchy) has regularly been extended since its adoption in 1971, as no agreement could be reached on a definitive text. Similarly, the dissolution of the armed forces of each emirate and their fusion into a single army, the cause of numerous crises, has not been accomplished. In June 1987, Sharjah was shaken by a coup d'état against the Emir, Sheikh Sultan, who was overthrown by his brother until pressure from the other emirates and Saudi Arabia reinstated him and made his brother Crown Prince and Vice-Governor. The UAE, like many other countries, has had a bone to pick with Iran, which in 1971 forcibly annexed the islands of Abu Musa and the Greater and Lesser Tunbs, which occupy a strategic position in the heart of the Gulf. In 1992 the problem was revived by Iran's decision to annex Abu Musa, provoking renewed tension. But the dialogue resumed in 2001. The great age of Sheikh Zayid places a question-mark over the future of the federation, because he has effectively been the cement holding it together.

Oman

Oman, the old Sultanate of Muscat and Oman, is located at the entrance of the Gulf and covers an area of 309,500 sq. km. It includes Dhofar, which was pacified in 1975 after lengthy fighting led by Omani forces, backed by Saudi Arabia and a strong contingent of Iranian troops, against the Popular Front for the Liberation of Oman, supported by South Yemen. The country is essentially desert, with mountains rising to over 3000m. Most of its 2.5 million inhabitants live in the coastal strip and the capital, Muscat. Twenty per cent of the population are Pakistanis, Indians and Iranians, though the number of foreigners has decreased as a result of the oil recession. From the beginning of the 1960s, oil has given Sultan Qabus – who came to power in 1970 after ousting his father Ibn Taimur – the means of modernising an extremely backward country through the development of petroleum-related industries, the construction of seaports and airports, and the establishment of an infrastructure and public services. In 1992 the Sultan set up a Consultative Council, although it has few powers. In August 1994 200 people were arrested and accused of perpetrating an 'Islamic plot'. In 1996 the Sultan gave the country its first constitution, which confirmed it as an absolute hereditary monarchy, but also provided for the setting up of a Consultative Council, elected in 1997 then again in 2000 and 2003.

At the regional level the demarcation of Oman's frontier with Yemen was settled in June 1995 and with Saudi Arabia in July 1996. Oman has been in contact with Israel since 1994, when in September **Yitzhak Rabin** made his first official visit to the Gulf. But Israel was to close its diplomatic representation following the outbreak of the **second Intifada**. The country's economy suffered from the effects of the 2001 collapse of the American company Enron, which had been a major customer.

Conflicts

Inter-state conflicts have weighed heavily on relations between the monarchies of the Gulf, largely because every square kilometre is rich in oil. It is important to distinguish between major conflicts and smaller, less important disputes that nonetheless lead to political splits.

To the first category belong the struggle between Iraq and Iran over the Shatt al-Arab, which led to the war between the two countries; Iraq's claims to Kuwait and the series of disputes over the Kuwaiti islands; Iran's claims to Bahrain, followed by the Iranian occupation of the three small islands belonging to the UAE in the Straits of Hormuz. This is not to mention the difficulties arising from the demarcation of frontiers between Iraq, Iran, Kuwait and Saudi Arabia, although these are now mostly settled or on the way to being settled. The major frontier dispute between Saudi Arabia and Yemen, which was settled in June 2002, could also be mentioned.

In the second category, a minor war in 1986 between Bahrain and Qatar concerned the control of the island of Fasht al-Dibel; the two countries also disputed the Hawar Islands, but the conflict was settled by the International Court of Justice at the Hague in 2001.

Abu Dhabi, Qatar and Saudi Arabia fought over the zone of Khawr al-Ubayd; more important was the UAE's claim to the Mussadam Cape, which controls the Straits of Hormuz and which belongs to Oman, although separated from it physically. Various territorial conflicts engage the rival monarchs of the UAE. Finally, mention should be made of the dispute over the Buraimi oasis between Saudi Arabia, Oman and Abu Dhabi, a conflict that goes back to the 1950s and was only partially resolved in 1974.

ARABS

The word designates an ethnic group (or a people) made up of individuals who speak one of the variations of the Arabic language, identify with the history and culture that have grown up since the emergence of the great Umayyad and Abbasid empires of the twelfth century – one of whose main characteristics is adherence to **Islam** – and possess a sense of their Arab identity. Though close links exist between Arabs and Islam, the terms are not synonymous. The overwhelming majority of Muslims are not Arabs (but Indians, Pakistanis, Indonesians etc.) and in **Egypt**, **Lebanon**, **Syria**, **Iraq** and other Arab countries there are Christian Arabs.

The Arabs were originally inhabitants of the **Arabian Peninsula**, from where they embarked on the conquest of the world in the name of Islam. Gradually, they were assimilated into the populations they conquered – large numbers of whom converted to the new faith – and from them borrowed many of the traits of what has come to be known as Arab–Islamic civilisation. Today, the zone peopled by Arabs is, roughly speaking, that occupied by member states of the **Arab League**. Arab **minorities** continue to exist on the fringes of this area (in **Turkey**, Black Africa, **Israel**), while Arabs have emigrated to Europe or America. Within Arab countries, pockets of non-Arabs remain: **Kurds**, Armenians, Berbers and so on.

The emergence of Arab nationalism is recent and has been greatly influenced by European ideas. Between the fifteenth and nineteenth centuries, Arabs were content to be subjects of the **Ottoman Empire**, which was predominantly Turkish but also Muslim. The decline of the Empire and the aggression of the Christian powers – who had conquered Arab countries such as Algeria and Egypt – provoked a crisis among Arab intellectuals. At the beginning of the twentieth century Abd al-Rahman al-Kawakibi, a Syrian Muslim, called for the restoration of an Arab caliphate. These ideas were later taken up by Neguib Azury, a Lebanese–Syrian Christian who created a League of the Arab Fatherland and founded a review, *Arab Independence*. Azury's disciple, Edmond Rabath, later wrote, 'The old, archaic ideal of the Muslim community will gradually be supplanted, under the pressure of events, by the magnificent notion of rediscovered Arab unity and greatness'. The tension between 'Muslim solidarity' and 'Arab solidarity' was already being felt, and explains why many of the original proponents of Arabism were Christians. It was not, however, until World War I that Arab elites rallied to this new doctrine. The great Arab Revolt of 1916, in which **T.E. Lawrence** (Lawrence of Arabia) won fame, allowed them to envisage in concrete terms the formation of a united Arab kingdom. Although **Britain** and **France** finally decided to divide the Middle East into separate states, the pan-Arab vision was to remain in the hearts of many nationalists. It must be stressed, however, that alongside this growing Arab nationalism (*qawmiyya*), a local patriotism (*wataniyya*) linked to specific states such as Egypt, Tunisia or Syria, remained strong.

After World War II, in the struggle against colonialism, Arab nationalism expressed itself with renewed vigour. It acquired a revolutionary character with the emergence of **Ba'thism** and Nasserism. The radio station Voice of the Arabs, broadcast from Cairo, mobilised Arab peoples from the Gulf to the Atlantic. The movement even resulted in Egypt and Syria forming a single state, the United Arab Republic (1958–61). But this experiment was, like that of various other federations, shortlived and without any future, undermined by differences that proved impossible to overcome.

The defeat of the **1967 War** marked the end of these great dreams of unity, and in its wake the ideology of Arab nationalism suffered a double attack. On the one hand, Palestinian nationalism (a local patriotism) and the exploits of the *fedayeen* were paradoxically able to mobilise the Arab masses for more than ten years. On the other hand, the Islamic 'thrust' that established itself from the late 1970s rejected all solidarity not founded on Islam.

Although organisations calling for pan-Arabism are today in decline, the idea nevertheless remains an indispensable point of reference in all political discussion from the Arab East (the Mashreq) to the Arab West (the Maghreb). One sign among others of the great hold it retains on Arab peoples was Arab mobilisation during the 1990–91 **Gulf War**. It should also be pointed out that some **Islamist** organisations – for example **Hamas** – have a political discourse which in many ways appropriates the discourse of Arab nationalism.

Although political Arabism seems to be on the retreat at the start of the new millennium, the era has witnessed the emergence of a shared

Arab culture which stretches from the Maghreb to the Mashreq, which is characterised by increasingly frequent human and cultural exchanges, the emergence of a common language – of the press and television, particularly the big television channels like al-Jazeera, which manage to escape censorship – alongside local dialects, and a multiplicity of informal economic exchanges. However, faced with a blockage that is both social and political the **Arab world** is currently going through the biggest crisis in its history.

ARAFAT, YASSER

Born on 24 August 1929 in Cairo, where most of his childhood was spent, Yasser Arafat is nonetheless Palestinian, and related, on his father's side, to the powerful al-Husseini family who played an important political role in **Jerusalem** during the period of the British Mandate. In 1948 Arafat gave up his studies at Cairo University to take part in the fighting in Palestine. He was disarmed by Arab troops who invaded the country after the proclamation of the state of **Israel**, a memory that has remained with him ever since. After the defeat, he took refuge in Gaza, then returned to Cairo in 1950 to continue university and qualify as a public works engineer.

While in Cairo he met Khalil al-Wazir (Abu Jihad) and Salah Khalaf (Abu Iyad), with whom he was to found Fatah, and who would become his right-hand men in the leadership of the **Palestine Liberation Organisation (PLO)**. Together the three young men were active in the Palestinian Students Union – Arafat was president from 1952 to 1956 – and edited a journal, *The Voice of Palestine*. Arafat was arrested and jailed for several days in October 1955, at the time of **Nasser**'s liquidation of the **Muslim Brotherhood** organisation (to which he was close, although not a member). During the Suez **War of 1956**, he fought as a sub-lieutenant in the Egyptian army.

Over these years in **Egypt** the foundation of what was to become the Fatah doctrine was shaped: a decided mistrust of Arab leaders, who refused to arm the **Palestinians** and hoped to keep them under strict control, and a profound belief in armed struggle, for which the guerrilla campaign mounted in Gaza in 1956–57 against Israeli troops (which Arafat helped to co-ordinate with Abu Jihad) served as a model.

Threatened again with arrest, Arafat (whose *nom de guerre* is Abu Ammar) – settled in **Kuwait**, one of the few countries where, despite the British protectorate that lasted until 1961, Palestinians enjoyed a certain freedom of action. It was there, in 1959, that he founded Fatah (a name made up of the Arabic initials for 'Movement for National Liberation') and published *Our Palestine*. Central to the doctrine of this new organisation was the firmly held notion that the liberation of Palestine was primarily the business of Palestinians, and should not be entrusted to Arab regimes or postponed until the achievement of an elusive Arab unity. This doctrine, in the era of all-conquering pan-Arabism, was tantamount to heresy. However, the failure of the United Arab Republic and the dissolution of the Syro–Egyptian union in 1961 strengthened Fatah's ideas.

The victory of the Algerian Revolution in 1962 confirmed Arafat's belief in the soundness of the principle 'rely on your own strength'. Preparations for armed struggle were accelerated, and on 1 January 1965 the first military operation against Israel took place. But Fatah, a movement without ideological references, had difficulty asserting its authority. It was condemned by virtually all the Arab governments. Even the **Ba'thist** Syrian regime, usually prompt to help the organisation, was quick to condemn its militants, and in May 1966 Arafat was imprisoned. It was not until after 1967, with the defeat of the Arab regimes in war, that the *fedayeen* became the focus of Palestinian mobilisation.

Two days after the end of hostilities, a Fatah congress was held in Damascus. After lengthy debate, it was decided, at Arafat's instigation, to take up armed struggle again. Subsequently he participated in several guerrilla raids into the occupied **West Bank**. He also established his first contacts with Nasser (November 1967), whose help was to prove decisive. On 21 March 1968 he took part in the Battle of Karameh in **Jordan**, where Palestinian commando units confronted the Israeli Defence Forces (IDF). This battle, which demonstrated the determination of the Palestinians and had repercussions throughout the Arab world, gave Arafat and Fatah the authority necessary to take over the reins of the old, ailing PLO. In February 1969 this organisation was revived, and a new executive committee elected. Arafat became President. From that moment, until the signing of the **Oslo Accords** in 1993, his life became inextricably linked with that of the PLO.

The implementation of the accords on Palestinian self-government marked an important turning point in Arafat's life. He returned to Gaza on 1 July 1994. On 20 January 1996 he was elected, by universal suffrage, President of the **Palestinian Authority**, retaining at the same time his position as president of the executive committee of the PLO. His aim is the creation of an independent state, the first in the history of the Palestinian people, with Jerusalem as its capital. This dream was to be shattered at the **Camp David** negotiations. Henceforth denounced by the Israeli authorities and by the **US** government as a **'terrorist'**, and under threat of expulsion, he lost much of his ability to control the Palestinian political scene. However, as Yossi Beilin, a former Israeli minister, has pointed out, it seems that there is no other leader capable of replacing him. In his view, in the place of Arafat, a leader may emerge from the ranks of Islamic fundamentalists who will not agree to negotiation with Israel, or a moderate who does not have the authority recognised in Arafat to be able to achieve a historic agreement and make the necessary concessions. Arafat was forced to appoint Mahmoud

Abbas (Abu Mazen) Prime Minister under US pressure in early 2003, and he assumed the position of interlocutor with the Israelis, but with Arafat retaining power behind the scenes as the father figure in the Palestinian nationalist movement. Abbas resigned as a result, and on the second anniversary of the 11 September attacks in the US, Israel made Arafat's expulsion a matter of policy.

ARMS TRADE

The Middle East has long been the top customer for global arms sales. After a long period of growth fuelled by the Arab–Israeli conflict and the other conflicts of which the region has been, and in some cases still is, the theatre, its position has declined noticeably in recent years. According to the *SIPRI Yearbook* 2002, published by the Stockholm International Peace Research Institute, whereas in 1992 the region absorbed almost 33.85 per cent of the main conventional weapons sold in the world, by 2001 this proportion had fallen to 13.28 per cent. The situation after the first **Gulf War**, the restrictions in **Saudi Arabia**, the stock-market crisis and the fluctuations in the **oil** market broadly explain the fall in orders from the Middle East, which have also been the main factor in the global fall of arms sales in the world. These went from $32.5bn in 2000 to $21.3bn in 2001, in other words a big fall compared with 1997.

Who buys these weapons, and how much do they spend? According to the International Institute of Strategic Studies (IISS), arms spending in the region stood at $69bn in 2001, compared with more than $80bn in 1985. Of the ten main world importers of conventional arms, four are to be found in the Middle East: Saudi Arabia, which was way out in front ($4.8bn, putting it first in the world, well ahead of second-place China with $2.2bn), **Egypt** ($700m, fifth), **Israel** ($600m, sixth) and **Kuwait** ($400m, eighth). SIPRI's study of the period 1997–2001 provided the following figures for world arms imports: Saudi Arabia (ranking third), **Turkey** (fourth) and Egypt (eighth), followed by Israel (eleventh), the United Arab Emirates (thirteenth), **Iran** (twentieth), Qatar (twenty-ninth), Kuwait (thirtieth), **Jordan** (thirty-third), **Syria** (forty-sixth), Bahrain (fiftieth), Oman (fifty-fifth), **Yemen** (fifty-ninth), **Sudan** (seventieth) and **Lebanon** (one hundred and third).

Statistics showing how the principle exporters of arms cut up the cake are less easy to come by. It is clear that there has been a marked reversal in the positions of **Russia**, whose share has declined, and the **US** whose share has increased. The US, which was hot on the heels of the USSR from 1986 to 1990, with 28 per cent of the Middle East arms market, now clearly has the upper hand. Operation Desert Storm provided a spectacular showcase for arms 'made in the USA'. In the three months that followed the victory, the

US arms industry took orders worth $30bn; nor did the rest of the decade disappoint. A similar outcome might be expected following the 2003 War in **Iraq**. Even if it does not, the US is well ahead in global arms sales, with $9.7bn, followed by the UK ($4bn), Russia ($3.6bn), **France** ($1bn) and China ($500m). But according to SIPRI, for the period 1997–2001 the US was also the main supplier in the Middle East, where it sold one half of all weapons imported into the region. Their customers include Saudi Arabia, way ahead of Egypt, which is followed by Turkey and Israel.

Washington has therefore broadly overtaken Moscow, which was formerly the main supplier of arms in the Middle East – with more than 29 per cent of the market between 1986 and 1990. Now Russia sits in fourth place. It is true that one of its main clients, **Libya**, has been the subject of international **sanctions**, and the other, Iraq, of an almost total embargo, and Syria is barely liquid. All of a sudden Iran has become Moscow's main customer, with arms deliveries of T-72 tanks, MiG-29 and MiG-31 fighters, SU-24 and TU-22M bombers (armed with cruise missiles), A-50 surveillance aircraft, SA-5 ground-to-air missiles etc. A long way behind Tehran, the United Arab Emirates and Egypt also buy arms from the Russians.

The second-biggest supplier in the region, the UK, supplies mainly Saudi Arabia, followed by Jordan, Qatar and Kuwait. As for France, the third supplier, it does its best business with the United Arab Emirates, Qatar, Turkey and Kuwait – the Middle East accounts for two thirds of French arms sales. Finally, Germany, in fifth place, deals mainly with Turkey. Then there are the new producers, including China, Argentina, North Korea and Brazil.

Among the main arms exporters in the Middle East, once again by 2001 figures, Israel is in the lead (and in sixth position globally) with $300m.

The diversity of procurement sources for most Middle East countries (with the exception of Israel, Syria and Egypt) stems also from the various trump cards held by each seller.

– Modern tanks: Russia offers the T-72, the AMX-30 and 30 B2 as well as the Leclerc, Germany the Leopard and the UK the Challenger and Chieftain. The US had re-entered the fray with the production of the M series, including the monstrous M-1 Abrams.

– Fighter planes: America dominates the field with the Skyhawk and the F family (notably the F-15 Eagle, F-16 Falcon, FA-18 Hornet and F-104 Starfighter); Russia offers the MiG series (in particular the MiG-29 Fulcrum and MiG-31 Foxhound) as well as the Sukhoi series (especially the Su-27); the French have the Mirage series (among which the highest performer is the 2000C); the British offer the Sea Harrier, the Hawk and the Tornado, China the F-7 (MiG-21) and F-8 Finback, and Taiwan the Ching-Kuo.

– Helicopters: a strong point for France, whose inventory is graced by the Gazelle, Puma, Super Puma, Dauphin, Alouette and Écureuil, and also includes the Cougar and the Franco–German Panther. Competition comes from the British Lynx and Scout, the American Stallion, Cobra and Sea Cobra, Eagle, Chinook, Apache, Black Hawk, Sea Hawk, Defender and S-70, the Anglo–American Wessex and Whirlwind, the Russian Mi-series, not to mention the Italian Hirundo and Mangusta, or the Brazilian Gaviao and Esquilo (manufactured with Aérospatiale).

– Naval equipment: the US, Russia, France, UK and Italy share the market.
– Medium and long-range missiles (see **Weapons of mass destruction**): there is a race to acquire these between Israel and the arrayed Syria, Iraq (before 1991), Iran, Egypt, Saudi Arabia and Libya.
– The equipping of armies with missiles is an equally bitterly contested affair. Russia offers the SAM (Surface-to-Air Missile) and the SA-2, 3, 5, 6, 7, 8, 9, 13, 16, 18 (portable) and 24. The US, for its part, has been able to sell throughout the region its Blowpipe, Chaparral, Hawk, Redeye, Tow, Walleye and Stinger portables, and of course the Patriot, billed as the incontestable star of the Gulf War until its relative ineffectiveness was demonstrated. The UK promotes the Blowpipe, Javelin, Rapier, Tigercat and Starburst (portable). France chips in with the Crotale and Mistral portables, and together with Germany produces the Hot, Milan and Roland. Germany has its SA-8b Gecko. For air forces, AAMs (Air-to-Air Missile) and ASMs (Air-to-Surface Missile) include the American Amraam, Harpoon, Hellfire, Hydra, Maverick, Penguin, Phoenix, Popeye, Rockeye, Shrike, Sidewinder, Skipper, Sparrow, Skyflash, Maverick and Walleye, the French Magic R-530 and R-550, MICA and Exocet, the Russian AA range (Atoll, Acrid, Apex, Aphid, Alamo and Archer) and the Swatter, the Israeli Python III and IV, the Shafrir and the Barak. For their SAMs (Surface-to-Air Missiles) and SSMs (Surface-to-Surface Missiles), navies can choose between the American Harpoon, Sea Lance, Sea Sparrow, Standard, Phoenix and Tomahawk, the French Exocet, Crotale, Aster and MM-15, the British Sea Cat, Seawolf and Sea Skua, the Russian Styx, Grail and Sunburn, the Chinese C-802 and the French–Italian Otomat, as well as the Italian Aspide and the Israeli Barak, Python III and IV, Gabriel and Popeye.
– Even chemical, biological and nuclear weapons feature in the arms race (see **Weapons of mass destruction**).

One of the factors that has contributed to the recent decline in sales of arms to the Middle East has been the development of independent local arms industries. This is particularly true of Israel, which manufactures, among other things, its own machine pistol (the Uzi), its own assault rifles (the Galil), its own tanks (Merkava), aircraft (Kfir, mainly helicopters and transport planes), missiles (AIM 9-L and AIM 7), patrol boats (OSA, Komar, Reshef and Alya) etc. Not only does Israel equip its own army, it also sells its arms to countries like South Africa, Argentina, Ecuador, Guatemala, Haiti, Honduras, Kenya, Liberia, Salvador and Venezuela.

ASSAD, HAFEZ AL-

Hafez al-Assad, who died on 10 June 2000, ruled unchallenged over Syria for almost thirty years, leading an austere life which contrasted radically with the corruption that was widely present in the corridors of power.

Assad was born on 6 October 1930 at Qordaha in northern Syria. He belonged to the Alawis – a sect of **Shi'ite** origin which is considered by many Sunni Muslims to be heterodox and whose members are to be found in **Lebanon** and, above all, Syria, where they represent slightly over 10 per cent of the population. Assad grew up in a family of well-to-do peasants and was educated at the *lycée* in Lattaqieh. During this period, he belonged to the **Ba'th** party, and took part in student demonstrations against the French occupation. In 1952 he entered the military college at Homs, where he met Mustafa Tlass, who is still Minister of Defence. A fighter pilot, he took several training courses in the Soviet Union and was later sent to **Egypt** during the period of the shortlived United Arab Republic (1958–61). There, along with several other Syrian officers, among them Salah Jadid, he formed the Ba'thist Military Committee, which was largely instrumental in bringing the Ba'th to power in Damascus in 1963.

Appointed Commander-in-Chief of the air force in 1965, the following year he helped Salah Jadid to eliminate the clique in power, who they judged to be too right-wing. But as head of the air force and Minister of Defence he was quick to oppose the radicalisation imposed by Jadid, as well as Jadid's adventurism. Thus, during the events of September 1970 (see **Black September**) in **Jordan**, he refused to supply air cover to Syrian tanks trying to give assistance to the **Palestine Liberation Organisation (PLO)**. Internal squabbles intensified, and on 16 November 1970 a coup d'état carried Assad to the presidency of the Council. In the months that followed, he was elected Secretary-General of the Ba'th party, then President of the republic.

Within a few years Assad consolidated his rule, which became authoritarian and depended on the army and the Defence Brigades – a Praetorian guard led by his brother Rifa'at. He has been behind all the major policy decisions taken in Syria since 1970: participation in the October **1973 War**, negotiations with Henry Kissinger in 1974–75, intervention in Lebanon in 1976, the rejection of the **Camp David Accords** in 1978, the bilateral negotiations with **Israel** on the convening of the Madrid Conference and many more. A formidable enemy, possessed of an iron will, he was able to be flexible when necessary, as the vicissitudes of his relations with his neighbours or with the White House show. On the domestic front he ruthlessly eliminated all opposition, including that within the Ba'th party and the army.

In November 1983, after a serious heart attack which kept him out of public life, a war of succession took place between his brother Rifa'at and

the generals of the army, among them Shafiq Fayyad. After a period of unrest and armed clashes, the return of Assad brought an end to the discord and he exiled the protagonists temporarily. Assad took advantage of the situation to reorganise the structures of power and undermine the position of his brother, who had meanwhile been appointed Vice-President alongside Abdul Halim Khaddam, the Minister of Foreign Affairs responsible for the Lebanese portfolio. Rifa'at was exiled for a second time, and Assad confirmed his own supremacy at the Eighth Party Congress in January 1985.

From the end of the 1980s, Assad began to groom his son Basel for power. But Basel's death on 21 January 1994, at the age of 32, forcefully revived the question of succession. The other son, Bashar, was put forward as successor: at the age of 29 he was appointed Commander of the Presidential Guard in 1995, and undertook various missions, notably in Lebanon. He began to build around himself a group of close associates. A few days after the death of his father, the Ba'th Party Congress appointed him to supreme power. The challenges that face him are enormous: crisis in the economy; the old guard's grip on power and the country's wealth; instability related to the war in **Iraq** and its aftermath; and the non-resolution of the Arab–Israeli conflict.

Before his death, the elder Assad made several efforts to sign a peace agreement with Israel, notably with **Yitzhak Rabin**, and then with Ehud Barak. While he was firm in his demand that Israel should return to the June 1967 borders and withdraw from the **Golan Heights**, he appeared to be very flexible on the conditions for peace (normalisation, security arrangements etc.). But despite American mediation, and despite some progress in the negotiations of 1999–2000, Ehud Barak rejected the proposed peace.

AUTONOMY

The concept of autonomy (or self-government) lay at the heart of the Israeli–Palestinian peace negotiations in the early 1990s. First put on the agenda in the Washington Declaration of 19 December 1993, and then put into operation by the **Oslo Accords** and the **Taba** agreements known as Oslo II, it is the term for the transitional status accorded to the **Gaza Strip** and **West Bank** – excluding **Jerusalem** – through until 1999. On that date, which was intended to mark the end of final negotiations, the intention was to settle a definitive status that would either extend in some shape or form the existing model of self-government or, as the **Palestinians** were hoping, lead to the creation of an independent state.

This schema drew its inspiration directly from the 1978 **Camp David Accords** which, in their second section, stated that, over a period of five years, 'full autonomy would be granted to the populations of the West Bank and Gaza'. Furthermore, 'the Israeli military government and the Israeli civil administration will cease to exercise their functions once an autonomous authority has been freely elected by the inhabitants of these regions'. Egypt, **Israel** and **Jordan** (which had not been consulted) were to reach an agreement on the 'modalities for the establishment of an elected self-governing authority'. Palestinians from the Occupied Territories would be able to join Arab delegations, subject to Israel's endorsement. Finally, at the end of the first three years of the transitional period, negotiations would begin on the future of the West Bank and Gaza, although the text was silent on the question of Jerusalem. In a letter of clarification to **Menachem Begin**, appended to the treaty, President Jimmy Carter stated that he had indeed been informed that everywhere that the words 'Palestinian' or 'Palestinian people' appeared, the Israeli Prime Minister 'understood Palestinian Arabs' – in other words that he rejected the notion of a 'Palestinian people'.

This project never saw the light of day. Jordan refused to involve itself in the negotiations, and the acceleration of Israeli **settlements** in the Occupied Territories from 1979 onwards contradicted the spirit if not the letter of the agreements. Interminable discussions between Cairo and Tel Aviv proved incapable of reaching a definition of the powers of a future autonomous Palestinian authority: in the face of Israel's obduracy, **President Anwar al-Sadat** himself, a man not known for extremist views, was to give up. The reasons for the Israeli intransigence are not hard to find. Any free election in the West Bank and Gaza would inevitably have ended in victory for supporters of the **Palestine Liberation Organisation (PLO)**, as had already been amply shown in the municipal elections of 1976. With such a scenario in mind, Israel's concept of the likely 'powers' of any future elected authority was extremely restrictive. In line with his principle that autonomy was to do with inhabitants and not territories, Begin's view was that the Jewish state would continue to maintain control of internal security, the totality of state land and **water** distribution; settlers and settlements would be totally under Israeli administration; and Israel would also supervise posts and telecommunications, imports and exports, travel to Arab countries, transfer of funds abroad etc. In addition, at the end of the five years of the transitional period, Israel would assert its sovereignty over the West Bank and Gaza.

Unlike the failed attempt of Camp David, the new-style autonomy actually saw the light of day on 4 May 1994, initially in Jericho and Gaza. Despite delays in the operational timetable of self-government, the Israeli army eventually withdrew from the greater part of the Gaza Strip, and then from seven large Arab towns in the West Bank: Jericho, Ramallah, Nablus, Qalqiliya, **Jenin**, Tulkarem and Bethlehem (the Israeli withdrawal from Hebron was postponed several times, and was only to take place in 1997, and then only in a partial fashion). A **Palestinian Authority** was set up, to which Israel transferred the basic administrative functions of law and order, the economy, education, health etc. It was legitimated on 20 January 1996 by the election of a Council and a President, an election which confirmed **Yasser Arafat** and his Fatah associates in their control of the new institutions. As for the Palestinian police, which was 27,000 strong in 1996, and the various rival security forces set up by Abu Ammar, their function has been to oversee law and order and the repression of violent activities hostile to the peace agreements, but they are also involved in the intimidation of anybody who puts up opposition to the ruling regime.

Curtailed in this way, the Oslo version of autonomy suffered from serious limitations which (leaving aside its transitional character and the absence of agreement on decisive questions such as Jerusalem, the settlements, water and refugees) threatened to sink the entire experiment.

The first has to do with the territorial framework chosen: in 2000, at the conclusion of seven years of negotiations, the zone of total Palestinian sovereignty, known as Zone A, represented only 17.2 per cent; Zone B (Palestinian Authority, with the Israeli army responsible for security) 23.8 per cent; Zone C (total Israeli control) 59 per cent. Note that the latter area contained resources essential for the Palestinian economy, such as ground water, and the agricultural land in the Jordan valley.

The second limitation is the issue of the Jewish settlements, which, far from being put on hold, continued to expand unabated after 13 September 1993, to the point where there were 150,000 settlers by 1995, in addition to those in 'Greater Jerusalem'. Although ten times less numerous than the Palestinians, they control twice the amount of land, enjoy proportionately higher benefits of water resources, and are answerable only to the Israeli authorities. 'Arafat was forced to sign at the White House an agreement which includes the *de facto* and *de jure* recognition of the totality of Jewish settlements in the territories.' This forthright observation came from Israeli Labour's Minister of Police, Moshe Shahal, following the signature of Oslo II on 28 September 1995.

The third obstacle is the question of balance in the Palestinians' unequal economic relations with Israel. The Palestinian economy has naturally emerged much weakened by the long years of Israeli occupation, during which the Jewish state, not content with having taken the majority of land and water resources, also appropriated something like 20 per cent of the GNP of the Territories, at the same time as putting 95.5 per cent of its investment into the Jewish settlements. In 1993 production in the West Bank was 2.5 per cent of that in Israel, with Gaza running at a mere 1 per cent, and GNP per inhabitant per annum stood at $2040 and $1250 respectively, as against $13,000 in Israel. The principal result of the underdevelopment of the Territories is their high degree of dependence on neighbouring Israel: 90 per cent of imports into Gaza and the West Bank come from Israel, which in return takes 75 per cent of their exports; the tens of thousands of jobs normally available in Israel account for 34 per cent of the waged population of the West Bank and a quarter of its GNP. The Palestinian economist Adel Samara explains, 'Israel has deliberately cut the links with other countries. It has transformed the Territories into a captive market, and prevented the creation of a self-sufficient economic centre.'

The economic agreements known as the Paris Accords, signed on 29 April 1994 and then slightly modified at the time of the signature of the Oslo II Accords, provide no means for the Palestinian Authority to escape this dependency. They provide for no central bank and no currency; despite the creation of a free-exchange zone between the two partners, they impose quotas on exports to the Jewish state of the principal Palestinian agricultural products and also impose quotas on imports into the West Bank and Gaza of produce coming from Arab countries and elsewhere. Palestinian fiscal policy is almost identical to that of Israel. The sealing of the Palestinian territories in the wake of the **Hamas** attacks in spring 1996 highlighted the extent of this terrible dependence: every day of total closure of the Israeli border to Palestinian workers and products represents, according to World Bank estimates, a major loss of revenue for the Palestinians – 30 per cent of normal revenue for Gaza and 25 per cent for the West Bank. This is not to mention the tragic consequences of shortages of food and medicine. In such a context, international aid becomes extremely important.

The period of Palestinian autonomy laid down in the Declaration of Principles of 13 September 1993 was to come to an end on 4 May 1999. The next day, in the light of President Bill Clinton's undertaking in a letter to Yasser Arafat to do everything in order that the negotiations on the final status of the West Bank and the Gaza Strip would be resolved 'within the space of a year', the Central Council of the PLO agreed to postpone the proclamation of the independent Palestinian state.

The failure of the Camp David Summit in July 2000 and the onset of the **second Intifada** in September led to the re-occupation of most of the West Bank. The Israeli army targeted and destroyed all the symbols seen by Israel as symbolising autonomy and the Palestinian Authority – Yasser Arafat's headquarters, television, radio, schools, roads, electrical supplies, the runways at Gaza Airport, the port of Gaza etc. The repeated closures and sieges of Palestinian towns, the destruction of infrastructures and agricultural land have strangled the economy of Gaza and the West Bank and have made daily life intolerable in the Territories.

The ideal of autonomy has been overtaken by events in the Palestinian area. On 13 March 2002 the **UN Security Council** adopted Resolution 1397 (see Appendix 14), which speaks of 'a vision of a region where two States, Israel and Palestine, live side-by-side within secure and recognized borders'. Only such a perspective can restore peace both in Palestine and in Israel.

This vision is endorsed by the 'Road Map' for peace adopted by the 'Quartet' (US–UN–EU–Russia) and released in early 2003.

The concept of autonomy has also played a role in **Iraq**, where, during the 1960s, the **Kurds** were fighting for the autonomy of Kurdistan, within a democratic state. They won a theoretical recognition of their cause in 1970, but the interpretation which **Saddam Hussein** was eventually to impose in the course of the 1970s and 1980s stripped the agreement of any meaning. In the wake of the **Gulf War**, Kurdish *peshmerga* fighters and Baghdad agreed to hold negotiations on the question of Kurdish autonomy. These ran into difficulties over the exact definition of the territories concerned, the allocation of economic resources to the Kurds and the central government, and finally the definition of the real powers which the Kurdistan regional council would have. The negotiations thus failed, and the Kurds, under Western protection, were to end up with *de facto* autonomy over the northern part of the country. Following the war in March 2003, the two main Kurdish parties (the Kurdistan Democratic Party and the Patriotic Union of Kurdistan) have remained committed to unity with the rest of Iraq, and participate in the US-sponsored Iraqi Governing Council, where they hope to persuade other Iraqis that a federal solution to the Kurdish question is preferable.

Finally, the notion of autonomy was also applied in **Sudan**, in an attempt to settle the southern question in that country. It was initially proposed by the Communist Party in the 1960s, was partly put into effect during the 1970s, but was then abrogated by Jaafar al-Nimeiri in 1983, a move which prompted a resumption of the civil war.

BAGHDAD PACT

The official name given to the Treaty of Mutual Co-operation between **Iraq** and **Turkey** on 24 February 1955, drawn up by **Britain**, Pakistan and **Iran**, and which collapsed after the republican revolution in Baghdad in 1958. Iraq formally withdrew in 1959.

In the escalating Cold War, the strategy of the **US** was to create a chain of regional defence organisations around the Soviet Union (see **Russia**), based on the model of NATO in the West. In the Middle East this strategy proved delicate for three reasons: first, Britain was seeking to protect its interests as a dominant Western power against the ambitions of the Americans; second, the Arab–Israeli conflict prevented the Arab nations from aligning themselves with Israeli allies; finally, any move towards a pro-Western regional structure added fuel to the very nationalist fervour that the West sought to curb at least as much as that of the 'Soviet threat'.

Initially, when faced with the hesitancy of the British government in creating regional pacts, Washington made do with Turkey's membership of NATO in May 1951. In May 1950 Turkey had also signed a mutual defence agreement with Pakistan. On 10 November 1951, the Americans, British, French and Turks formed the 'Supreme Allied Command in the Middle East', in which the countries of the region, notably **Egypt**, were invited to take part. But the dream disappeared with the revolution of the Free Officers, who took power in Cairo in July 1952. During the same period, the CIA, under the direction of Norman Schwarzkopf Senior, intervened in Iran to bring down the nationalist government of Dr Muhammad Mosaddeq in August 1953.

When Tehran fell back into line, the Americans turned their attention to other projects. In his speech of January 1953, President Eisenhower and his Secretary of State, John Foster Dulles, mooted the idea of a new type of agreement to the countries in the region. In exchange for their participation in a regional anti-Soviet structure, their national priorities would be better accommodated – the least they could expect would be a more 'objective' American attitude in the Arab–Israeli conflict.

The first step, taken to reinforce the 'Northern Tier', was an agreement between Turkey and Pakistan in April 1954, followed by a whole host of bilateral agreements for military aid between the US, Turkey, Iraq and Pakistan. The second step was decisive: four months after the signing of the treaty between Egypt and Britain, Turkey and Iraq ratified, on 24 February 1955, a defence treaty which was 'open to any member State of the **Arab League** or any other State that was truly committed to peace and security in the region'. Britain signed up in April, Pakistan in September and Iran in November. The first meeting was held in Baghdad on 21 and 22 November 1955, when a permanent Military Council and Committee were set up, with the participation of a representative from the US.

But the hope of expanding the pact to Arab countries beyond Iraq once again faltered on the attitude of Egypt, led by **Gamal Abdel Nasser**, who saw the treaty as the introduction of great-power rivalries in the region, a way of dividing the **Arab world** as well as a manoeuvre to outflank him. This rekindled the fears of the Soviet Union, which declared in April 1955 that it could not 'remain indifferent to the development of the situation in the Middle East since the formation of blocs and the installation of foreign military bases on the territory of the Near and Middle East directly affect the security of the USSR'.

Designed to challenge the communist and nationalist threat, the Baghdad Pact paradoxically reinforced them by accelerating the rapprochement between Egypt and the Soviet Union. As he had not received from Washington the weapons needed to counterbalance the Israeli threat, the Egyptian President turned to Moscow. On 27 September, the delivery of planes, tanks and weapons from Prague to Cairo was officially announced. Similarly, Damascus saw the pact as a threat and thus accelerated the rapprochement between **Syria** and Egypt, while internal troubles in **Lebanon** and **Jordan** prevented them from joining. Thus the American strategy backfired on them: the boomerang effect benefited the Soviet Union, which for two decades gained a foothold in an Arab world from which it had previously been isolated due to its unequivocal support of Jewish and then Israeli forces during the **1948–49 War**.

On 21 September 1959, after the Iraqi retreat, the Baghdad Pact became the Central Treaty Organisation (CENTO), with an emphasis on economic co-operation, and as of 1964 it was accompanied by a Regional Co-operation for Development (RCD) group. The **Khomeini** revolution struck a death-blow to this distant successor to the Baghdad Pact by provoking first the withdrawal of Iran and consequently of Turkey and Pakistan.

BALFOUR DECLARATION

The name given to a letter written on 2 November 1917 in which Lord Arthur James Balfour, British Foreign Secretary, made it known to Lord Walter Rothschild, a representative of British **Jews**, that 'His Majesty's Government view with favour the establishment in Palestine of a National Home for the Jewish people' (the full text can be found in Appendix 1). This document marks the reappearance of the idea of a Jewish state in the Holy Land for the first time since the Roman Empire crushed the last Jewish rebellion in AD135. Arthur Koestler later wrote that in the Balfour Declaration, 'One nation solemnly promised a second nation the territory of a third'.

Both long- and short-term factors brought **Britain** to make this commitment.

Britain, in the throes of a world war, hoped to improve its position by reconciling the **Zionist** movement which, since its creation in 1897, had grown in power and influence within the Jewish communities of Europe and America. British strategists thought that the promise of a 'national home' might turn the Jews into a trump card: in Palestine they would support the British army of occupation, in the **US** they would bring their weight to bear in favour of entering the war against the Central European empires, in Germany and Austro-Hungary they would break away from their government, and in **Russia** they would slow down the radicalisation of the revolution (many Bolshevik and Menshevik leaders were of Jewish origin) and prevent the country's defection from the alliance against Germany.

But Britain also had wider aims. Obsessed by the security of its colonial system, it feared the ascendancy of another major European power in Palestine – **France** – which 'so close to the Suez Canal would be a permanent and formidable threat to the Empire's essential lines of communication' (Sir Herbert Samuel, first British High Commissioner in Palestine). From that point onward, the skill used to present the Zionist project made it all the more attractive to Britain: 'A Jewish Palestine,' explained Chaim Weizmann, the Zionist Organisation's principal leader, 'would be a safeguard for England, particularly in matters concerning the Suez Canal'.

There were no illusions on either side about the Balfour Declaration: Britain did not act out of sympathy for the Zionist cause, but to defend its own interests in the Middle East, as several recent historical studies have underlined. The Israeli historian Mayir Verete demolishes the traditional interpretation that sees the **lobbying** of Chaim Weizmann in Balfour's letter; Weizmann, he stresses, had had no contact with British officials dealing with foreign policy in the two and a half years preceding the Declaration. Verete argues that the Declaration was a result of a British government policy designed to balance the concessions made by Mark Sykes to his counterpart François Georges-Picot in the negotiations over the future of the **Ottoman Empire** from 1916 onwards. Britain did not intend to internationalise Palestine, even if it did seek to secure a northern enclave around the cities of Haifa and Acre, and spheres of influence in Transjordan to the east and between Rafah and Aqaba in the south. To divide the Holy Land with France would be to lose control of a piece of land which was of vital strategic importance to the protection of British interests in **Egypt** on the one hand, and **Iran**, **Iraq** and the Gulf on the other. With the promise of a national home for the Jews, London sought to bring on side the Jewish community in its battle for Palestine over the long term, simultaneously lending its aspirations a veil of legitimacy. In the short term, it encouraged the Jews to engage in the world war already underway on the side of the Allies.

The Zionists were well aware of Britain's reasons for involving itself in their project, and of the need never to relax the pressure required to ensure that Britain kept its word. For its part, London was conscious that the Zionist movement had other ambitions. In the words of Lord Curzon, Balfour's successor: 'While Weizmann tells you one thing, and you are thinking in terms of a "national Jewish homeland", he has something quite different in mind. He envisages a Jewish state, and a subject Arab population governed by the Jews. He is trying to bring this about screened and protected by the British guarantee.'

But in winning the Jews it remained essential not to lose the **Arabs**, who still constituted the overwhelming majority of the Palestinian population, not to mention most of the countries of the Middle East colonised by the British, directly or indirectly. Did the Balfour Declaration ostensibly contradict the assurances given to Sherif Hussein and Ibn Saud? Diplomats thought so: the efforts undertaken by the British authorities to promote the 'National Home' of the Jews were tempered, in the text, by the need to do nothing 'that would prejudice the civil and religious rights of the non-Jewish communities in Palestine'. Such artistic licence was to prove expensive.

BARGHOUTI, MARWAN

Marwan Barghouti, born on 6 June 1959 in Kafr Kubr, a village to the north of Ramallah, was only eight years old when the **West Bank** was occupied by Israeli troops during the June **1967 War**. At the age of 15 he joined **Yasser Arafat**'s Fatah. In 1978, accused of 'belonging to an illegal organ-isation', he was sentenced to four and a half years in prison: he was only 19. There he met many key figures of the Palestinian national movement, including Jibril Rajoub, the future Palestinian head of security in the West Bank. By the time he left prison in 1983 he had learned Hebrew, which he speaks perfectly, and at Bir Zeit University he resumed the studies of history and political science which he had begun in prison. He became President of the University Student Union and was involved in setting up the Shabiba, the Fatah youth movement banned by **Israel**. He was again arrested in September 1985, but this time the authorities placed him in administrative detention for six months, thus avoiding putting him on trial. He was banned from his own country in 1987.

From exile in Amman, **Jordan**, he was involved in the launching of the first **Intifada**, playing an active role as a co-ordinator between the **Palestine Liberation Organisation (PLO)** (then based in Tunis) and the 'revolt of the stone-throwers'. He became a member of Fatah's Revolutionary Council. When he returned to the Palestinian territories in 1994, following the amnesty agreed after the **Oslo Accords**, he was elected Secretary-General of Fatah for the West Bank. He actively supported the peace process, and was one of its major proponents in the refugee camps and among ordinary

Palestinians. In 1996 he was elected to the Palestinian Legislative Council and stood out there for his denunciation of corruption and his fight for human rights – particularly on women's issues. He established strong links with the peace camp in Israel, and even with right-wing politicians.

However, it was not long before he changed his stance. In 1998 he called for an end to negotiations for as long as the **settlement** policy continued and the Israeli government refused total withdrawal from the Occupied Territories.

With the launching of the second Intifada, which he described as 'a legitimate resistance to an illegitimate occupation', he played a growing role in the resistance which, in his view, had to accompany the negotiations. 'We have tried seven years of intifada without negotiations, then seven years of negotiations without intifada, maybe now it's time to try both together,' he suggested. He organised self-defence groups, which also conducted offensive actions against the occupying army and the settlers. He was accused of leading the al-Aqsa Martyrs Brigades, a clandestine military group close to Fatah, which was also to conduct suicide operations against Israeli civilians. His stated positions, his organisational abilities and his integrity and charisma enabled Fatah to remain the main Palestinian organisation in the face of **Hamas**, and enabled the perspective that he defended – two states living side by side – to remain the option supported by the majority of Palestinians. He made the following point: 'Let us not forget that we Palestinians have recognized Israel on 78 per cent of the historic territory of Palestine. It is Israel which refuses to recognize the right of Palestine to exist on the remaining 22 per cent, the territories occupied in June 1967.' In August 2001 he was to expand on that: 'We are talking about the 1967 borders. We recognize Israel, and we repeat that constantly. The question is not whether we recognize Israel, but whether Israel recognizes us.'

Having tried – in vain – to assassinate him in August 2001, the following October Israel issued an arrest warrant for him. At that point he went into hiding, until his arrest on 15 April 2002 in the course of Operation Rampart, conducted by the Israeli army throughout the West Bank and particularly in **Jenin**. He was accused of **terrorism**, crimes against the state of Israel and crimes against the Jewish people, and appeared in court on 6 September 2002. His trial was to drag out over many months. He and his lawyers rejected the court's competence to judge him – an attitude which may also be adopted by the 5000 Palestinian political prisoners held by the occupation authorities.

Why did the **Sharon** government decide to put him on trial rather than assassinate him as it has done with dozens of other Palestinian activists? Presumably in order to put the **Palestinian Authority** itself on trial: Barghouti is the highest-ranking Palestinian leader imprisoned in

Israel and Ariel Sharon hoped, through him, to discredit Yasser Arafat and his colleagues, and beyond that, the very idea of a solution based on the equal coexistence of two peoples and two states. 'The crime of which I am accused,' retorted Barghouti before the court, 'is not "terrorism" – a term apparently used only to speak of Israeli civilian deaths, never of Palestinian civilian deaths. My crime is that I demand my freedom, and the freedom for the children, and freedom for the whole of the Palestinian people.'

The trial has begun to backfire on its organisers. The defence has achieved a number of spectacular coups, in particular obtaining support from Nelson Mandela, who compared the trial with his own trial by the South African authorities in 1964, and from the lawyer Gisèle Halimi, who is known for having defended imprisoned members of Algeria's National Liberation Front. The fact that he is being defended by the lawyer Shammai Leibowitz, the grandson of the famous Yeshayahu Leibowitz, an Orthodox Jew who, post-1967, was a powerful voice of conscience in Israel, represents another success. In his speeches, Leibowitz has compared Barghouti to a Moses leading his people towards the Promised Land.

Barghouti represents a generation which has grown up under foreign occupation, was involved in the first Intifada and is familiar with the insides of Israeli prisons. It is deeply nationalist, but in its struggle it has acquired experience and realism, in particular in learning to understand Israeli society. It has rallied to the idea of a compromise solution based on the coexistence of two states, but was moved to action by the stalemate in the Oslo Accords. The younger generation of Palestinians had its first experience of fighting with the second Intifada. It grew up in the ghettos of the big towns and camps, born out of the Oslo Accords and run by the Palestinian Authority, and the only contact they have had with Israel has been through its soldiers and settlers. This generation is more desperate and radical than the preceding generation, and risks turning long-term to violence and total rejection of compromise. However, it still identifies with the figure of Marwan Barghouti who, according to some observers, could become Palestine's Nelson Mandela.

BA'TH

The Ba'thist movement (from the Arabic word 'ba'th' meaning renaissance) was created in Damascus in the 1940s by an Orthodox Christian, Michel Aflaq, and a Sunni Muslim, Salah al-Din Bitar.

The party's first congress was held in 1947 in the Syrian capital. In 1953, it merged with Akram Hourani's Arab Socialist Party and took the name Arab Ba'th Socialist Party. The Ba'th was the first party to consider the **Arab world** as a whole as its theatre of activity, and regional sections were created in Transjordan (1948), **Lebanon** (1949–50) and **Iraq** (1951). But the Syrian region remained its stronghold. The movement was at its peak in the 1960s and became, along with Nasserism, one of the principal expressions of revolutionary Arab nationalism.

An extremely ideological party, the Ba'th adopted the slogan of 'Unity, Liberation, Socialism'. Arab unity lies at the heart of its doctrine, and has priority over all other aims. According to Aflaq, the Arab peoples form a single nation, aspiring to form a state and play a unique role in the world. Secular in orientation – it rejects the denominational or confessional division of seats in the Syrian parliament (see **Confessionalism**) – Ba'thism nonetheless accepts the role **Islam** has played as a constituent element of Arabism. The call to socialism in the 1950s remained vague, and at this stage the Ba'th was in favour of a pluralist democracy and free elections. The Palestinian question is far from being central to its ideology, if it concerns the Ba'th at all.

The Ba'th very quickly became prominent in the political life of **Syria**, where military and civilian leaders succeeded one another in power after **independence**. But the turning point in the party's history was 1958, when the United Arab Republic (UAR) was formed by **Egypt** and Syria. The Ba'th, which shared Nasser's analysis of Arab and international politics, agreed to dissolve its Syrian branch. Its members were involved in decision-making, but, increasingly marginalised, resigned from office at the end of 1959. The self-dissolution of the organisation, followed by the collapse of the UAR in September 1961, provoked a long internal crisis. This grew worse even when the party came to power in Iraq in February 1963 and in Syria in March of the same year.

Following long periods of clandestine existence, a change took place in the ideology and the very organisation of the party. It stepped up its attacks against liberal democracy, and the military element played an increasingly important role in the machinery of the organisation. Demands were put forward that were socialist in character. Above all, the failure of the UAR caused certain Ba'th officials to question the dogma of Arab unity. In Syria, those referred to as 'regionalists' – Dr Nureddin al-Atasi, **Hafez al-Assad**, Salah Jadid – as opposed to 'nationalists', those in favour of an Arab plan, increasingly affirmed their control following the Ba'th's seizure of power in 1963. In February 1966 they expelled their rivals within the party from government through a coup d'état. The Ba'th's founders, including Aflaq, were forced into exile. Two separate Pan-Arab leaderships, each with regional branches, were established: one in Damascus, the other in Baghdad (after the Ba'th took power in July 1968). The initial ideological differences became blurred and gradually gave way to bitter political rivalry. The two parties were now transformed into political instruments of the state, and during the first **Gulf War** the Syrian army fought alongside American troops against Iraq.

Paradoxically, it was at the height of its power, with the leadership of two major states, that Ba'thism began to decline as an ideology. The defeat of 1967 had exacerbated the crisis of Pan-Arabism, and there was a swing towards, first, supporting the Palestinian resistance, then towards Islamisation. The regional policies of Iraq and Syria, dictated by state interests, attracted no great following in the Arab world. However, Ba'thism has made its own mark on domestic politics, with the application of socialist measures (or rather the establishment of state capitalism), a degree of secularisation and violent police repression. While violence as a means of government continued to be the model in Syria and Iraq (until the collapse of the regime following US-led military action in 2003), the two countries gradually abandoned 'socialism' in favour of an economic opening to the West. The collapse of the Iraqi regime confirmed the end of Ba'thism.

BEGIN, MENACHEM

Leader of the Israeli right wing, which he brought to power for the first time in 1977, Menachem Begin held the post of Prime Minister until his resignation as a result of the **1982 War** in **Lebanon**.

Begin was born on 13 August 1913 at Brest-Litovsk in **Russia**, a town with a Jewish majority where the **Zionist** movement was already very active. From the age of 12 he was a militant member in the organisation, first on the left with Hashomer Hatzair, then on the right with Betar. A paramilitary youth organisation of an offshoot of Zionism that was ultra-nationalist, authoritarian, not to say fascist in character, Betar was created in the 1920s by Ze'ev Jabotinsky, who preached 'the transformation of "this country" (including Transjordan) into an independent state under the leadership of a well-established Jewish majority' (Ze'ev Jabotinsky, *Basic Principles of Revisionism*). Begin met Jabotinsky, nicknamed by his socialist adversaries 'Vladimir Hitler', when he was 16. A fervent Revisionist enthusiast, he became the leader of Betar while studying law in Warsaw and afterwards the organisation's permanent representative. With the German invasion, Begin fled to the east, where he was arrested by the Soviet secret police and interned in a labour camp in the Arctic Circle. He owed his release to an agreement signed by Stalin with the Polish government-in-exile (Brest-Litovsk came under Polish rule in the inter-war years).

Having enlisted into General Anders's Polish army, Begin rejoined his wife in Palestine in the spring of 1942, where he was appointed commissar of Betar and head of the Revisionists' secret army, the Irgun. With his troops, in 1944 he joined the secessionist group the Stern Gang (formed in 1943 and later renamed the Lehi) in an armed struggle against the British occupying forces. The attacks he organised led him into serious clashes with mainstream Zionist organisations, notably the Haganah, which he denounced for its 'wait-and-see policy'. From November 1944 to September 1945, the Haganah, under the name of Operation Season, conducted a veritable witch-hunt of Begin supporters. The alliance, however, triumphed (15 May 1948) when in its turn the Haganah turned to violence against the British representatives, and especially after 1947 as clashes escalated with the **Arabs** in Palestine (see **1948–49 War**).

During this period, Begin's Irgun was responsible for some of the operations most condemned by public opinion, Jewish included: the attack of 22 July 1946 on the King David Hotel in **Jerusalem**, headquarters of the British, that resulted in 200 dead and wounded, many of whom were **Jews**; the massacre in the Palestinian village of **Deir Yassin** on 9 April 1948, where 200 civilians lost their lives and which led to the massive flight of Arab populations; and the *Altalena* affair – named after a ship chartered by the Irgun to procure arms in large quantities – described by the Prime Minister, **Ben Gurion**, as 'an attempt to overburden the army and destroy the state'.

This reputation for adventurism, hysterical nationalism and distinctly factious tendencies counted heavily against the Irgun. When the war was over, Begin dissolved his military organisation to turn his attention to the political arena and founded the Herut ('Freedom' in Hebrew) party. In the spring of 1947, he moved into a flat in Tel Aviv. It was in this same flat that, 30 years later, he heard the news of his victory in the 1977 elections. Between these two events, Begin patiently conducted a long haul on four fronts: violent polemic – going as far as rioting in front of the Knesset – against the reopening of relations with West Germany; denunciation of the socialist grip on the state and the often scandalous failures of the Labour government; the unification of all discontented elements in the state of **Israel**, particularly the **Oriental Jews**; and the chauvinist discourse on the Jewish people's right to all land on both sides of the Jordan. But Begin's rise to power owed less to his own efforts than to the gifts that the Israeli Labour party kept handing him.

The best of these was undoubtedly the mentality of conflict and occupation in which socialist governments were caught up. 'Henceforth,' wrote Eytan Haber in his biography of Begin, 'anything Begin advocated no longer seemed to smack of extremism. The apparently unbridgeable gulf that had been opening up between Begin and his opponents no longer existed. The national consensus had broadened considerably, and Menachem Begin had pride of place within it.' Traumatised by the shock of the Yom Kippur War, which cast doubts on the policy followed for twenty-five years, and tired moreover of a Labour regime in power for as long, Israelis saw no other solution than to experiment. From being a pariah, the man whose name never passed the lips of Ben Gurion, Begin became respectable and respected and, what is more, was considered to be the best orator in Israel. Indeed, the socialist Prime Minister Levy Eshkol had offered him a ministerial portfolio on 1 June 1967. Ten years later, he was Prime Minister, the Likud party in 1977 having gained 33.4 per cent of votes, whereas the Herut of 1949 had collected barely 11.5 per cent.

The firm silence in which Begin wrapped himself after his departure from the political arena in 1983 until his death on 9 March 1992 said a great deal about his failure in power. After the success of **Camp David**, he launched into desperate action prompted by the double failure of the Israeli economy and of the Lebanese War. In 1938, during a congress, Begin had challenged his master, Jabotinsky, and obtained a modification of Betar's solemn oath. 'I shall make ready my weapons for the defence of my nation and I shall bear them only in its defence' had, at the request of the young Zionist from Brest-Litovsk, become 'I shall make ready my weapons for the defence of my nation and the conquest of my country'. This was more than just a different turn of phrase.

BEN GURION, DAVID

Born in Plonsk, Poland on 16 October 1886, David Grin emigrated in 1906 to Palestine where, under the name of Ben Gurion, he became leader of the Mapai party and president of the **Zionist** Executive. Forty-two years later, he proclaimed the **independence** of the state of **Israel**, whose prime minister he was to be for a considerable period.

The son of a founder of the Lovers of Zion, which organised the first Jewish *aliya* to Palestine, in 1905 Grin espoused the Zionist-socialist doctrine of the Poalei Zion (Workers of Zion). After his emigration to Palestine he worked as an agricultural labourer for four years before, in 1910, joining the editorial staff of the socialist journal *Ahdut* (*Unity*). He wrote his first articles in this journal under the pen-name Ben Gurion, after the leader of the independent Jewish government at the time of the revolt against Rome. Soon, however, the young man sailed to Salonika, then on to Constantinople. He hoped to achieve his objective, the renaissance of a Jewish state, by the 'Ottomanisation' of Palestine. World War I shattered this dream. Banished from the **Ottoman Empire**, Ben Gurion set out for the **US**.

After a vain attempt there to raise an army of Jewish pioneers, he published his first book, *Eretz Yisrael* (*The Land of Israel*). It was after his marriage to Paulina Mombaz that he heard, on 2 November 1917, of the famous **Balfour Declaration**. While most Zionists celebrated this as a victory, Ben Gurion warned, 'Only the Hebrew people can turn this right into a tangible reality and it alone must, by its body and soul, by its strength and its capital, construct its "national home"'. (This quotation, and others below, is drawn from Michel Bar-Zohar's remarkable biography, *Ben-Gurion*.)

On his return, at the end of 1918, to a Palestine liberated by the British, Ben Gurion resumed his struggle for the unification of socialists and, to avoid sectarian obstructions, he chose to work in the unions. Rising swiftly through the ranks of the Histadrut (the **Yishuv**'s labour federation), he proved to be a leader. Not only did he increase the membership of the Histadrut tenfold, but he considerably widened its sphere of influence, notably through the creation of a network of enterprises and services linked to it.

In 1929 the members of the various socialist parties approved unification. Ben Gurion became Secretary-General of Mapai (the Workers' Party), which gained 42.3 per cent of the Yishuv's votes in 1934, and half the votes of the Nineteenth Zionist World Congress in 1935. In this way Ben Gurion became president of both the Zionist Executive and the Jewish Agency.

From isolated incidents in 1920, 1921 and 1929, Arab resistance to the establishment of the Jewish national home escalated in 1936 to the level of generalised rebellion. **Britain** now back-tracked and proposed the partition of Palestine. The Yishuv unanimously rejected this, but Ben Gurion, for his own motives, accepted.

> A partial Hebrew state is not an end but merely a beginning. We shall take there all the Jews we possibly can. We shall create a diverse economy. We shall organize a modern national defence and then I am sure we shall not be prevented from settling in other parts of the country, either by agreement with our neighbours, or in any other way.

Three years later, this conception of the Jewish state would be imposed on the movement by the president of the Executive. The British White Paper of 1939 and the outbreak of World War II had helped persuade him that it was no longer on Britain, but on the US, that Zionists had to count. Having crossed the Atlantic at the end of 1941, Ben Gurion organised the Biltmore Conference which, in May 1942, recommended the constitution of a 'Jewish Commonwealth'. Within six months, all the Zionist authorities, even those in Palestine, had ratified the shift in policy, despite the influence of those who believed in a bi-national solution. Alternating between fundamentalists engaged in anti-British **terrorism** and opportunists ready to comply with conditions laid down by London, Ben Gurion imposed his person and his policy at the head of the movement, orchestrating acceptance for his partition proposal. Formulated in August 1946 by the Executive of the Jewish Agency, this proposal was the inspiration for the **Partition Plan** adopted by the UN on 29 November 1947.

Ben Gurion now held all the reins. As president of the Executive, he drafted and, on 14 May 1948, delivered the declaration of independence. As Prime Minister, he imposed the new state's authority, including the use of force when the Irgun became factious. As Defence Minister, he was in charge of the Jewish forces during the **1948–49 War**. With reinforcements of arms from Prague, he launched the counter-offensive of spring 1948, then created Tsahal, the Israeli Defence Forces (IDF), securing victory for it. His strategy, based on a tacit agreement with King Abdullah of **Jordan**, was to take advantage of the Arab attack to prevent the birth of the Palestinian Arab state, extend to its detriment the territory of the Jewish state and rid the latter of the majority of its Arab population. 'We liberated a very large territory, much more than we expected,' he confided in 1949. 'Now, we shall have to work for two or three generations. As for the rest, we shall see later.' The timing was to be altered, but not the agenda.

From 1949 to 1953, the Prime Minister therefore applied himself to the transformation of Israel: he doubled the population by organising the arrival of 700,000 new immigrants, set in motion a vigorous economic development, created an entire education system, and ensured the increase in numbers of **settlements**, including those in the Negev. Indeed, it was there, to the Sde Boker *kibbutz*, that Ben Gurion retired in 1953, having handed over authority to Moshe Sharett. But the Lavon Affair erupted soon after that: accused of masterminding a programme of provocation by simulating anti-British attacks in **Egypt** – which failed, causing several Israeli agents to lose their lives – Pinhas Lavon, the Minister to whom Ben Gurion had bequeathed the defence portfolio, submitted his resignation. The ensuing crisis provided an opportunity for the 'Old Man', as he was then called, to return to public life.

From 1955, he organised the **1956 War**, the Suez War. From 1949, Israel had abandoned its original position of neutrality and become involved in the nascent Cold War. 'We must explain,' admitted Ben Gurion in 1952, 'that the whole of Israel is available as a base for the free world'. But this time, the alliance with the West was sealed militarily. Tel Aviv directed its army against Egypt, symbolic vanguard of the Arab nationalist movement, against whom Britain and **France** also sent their forces.

Pressure from two sides – American and Soviet – forced the IDF to withdraw. Ben Gurion nevertheless took care to reinforce the IDF with valuable aid received from France, in particular, which even assisted the Jewish state in the construction of a nuclear reactor. For 'personal reasons' the Old Man resigned in 1963. On bad terms with his successor, Levy Eshkol, and the principal leaders of Mapai, in 1965 he went as far as to found the Rafi party, thus creating a schism in Labour ranks.

After the 1967 War, for which he criticised Israel for having taken the initiative, Ben Gurion held himself aloof from the reunification of Labour factions. He strongly recommended the return of all occupied Arab territories – except East **Jerusalem**. His final retirement to Sde Boker was made in 1970, where he died on 1 December 1973.

BIN LADEN, OSAMA

Born in Riyadh in 1957, Osama bin Laden comes from a very large family. He has 50 brothers, sisters, half-brothers and half-sisters. His father, originally from Hadramawt in **Yemen**, settled in **Saudi Arabia** in the 1920s. He developed close relations with King Saud, the founder of the country which was to bear his name. He became one of the biggest businessmen in the country, and the company which he created (which has its headquarters in Jeddah and carries his name) went on to employ 35,000 people. This company was involved in the monumental renovation of the holy cities of Mecca and Medina. In 2000 it built a skyscraper in Jeddah, called al-Faysaliya, and was also involved in building an airport in Kuala Lumpur, Malaysia.

When his father died, Osama bin Laden was only 11 years old. After completing his secondary schooling in Medina, he entered the King Abdul Aziz University in Jeddah, one of the best educational establishments in the country (1974–78), from where he graduated in engineering.

It is not known when his political involvement dates from, but it is said that in the 1970s he was involved in the struggle against the Marxist regime in South Yemen. The big turning point in his life came with the USSR's invasion of Afghanistan (see **Russia**) in December 1979. The **US** was at that time pushing Pakistan and Saudi Arabia to organise a movement of Muslim volunteers to fight the 'evil empire'. Bin Laden joined up, and he was to come under the influence of a Palestinian sheikh, Abdullah Yusuf Azzam, who was to play a critical role in his educational and political development. He became a hardened fighter, created a network of links with the thousands of Muslim volunteers – some of whom were to become his close lieutenants. He maintained close relations with the Pakistani security services and the CIA. As well as using his personal wealth in this fight, he also proved his organisational abilities by contributing to the establishment in Pakistan, in the mid-1980s, of the Maktab al-Khidmaat (Services Centre), which assisted in enrolling, training and sending thousands of fighters to Afghanistan. The organisational model established here was to be of use in the creation of al-Qaeda. After the withdrawal of the Soviets from Afghanistan in 1989 – it would take another three years for the Kabul regime to fall under the onslaught of the Mujahedin – and the assassination of Sheikh Azzam, bin Laden returned to Saudi Arabia.

He was there during **Iraq**'s invasion of **Kuwait**. He suggested to Prince Sultan, the Saudi Minister of Defence, the organisation of popular resistance to the invasion. His plan was not taken up, and the **Saud dynasty** preferred to appeal to the UN. Dick Cheney, at that time US Defence Secretary, promised that American troops would not stay 'a minute longer than necessary'. Their withdrawal was eventually announced in April 2003. This was another key moment in bin Laden's trajectory: as far as he was concerned the US now became the number one enemy, and the Saudi royal family deserved to be overthrown. This transition was one shared by many young Saudis: in the first half of the 1990s a wave of **Islamist** protest shook the kingdom.

The first text written by bin Laden, published in August 1996, was entitled 'Declaration of War against the Americans Occupying the Land of the Two Holy Places (Mecca and Medina)'. He called for the expulsion of the infidels from the **Arabian Peninsula**. He confirmed that his main concern, over-riding the issue of Palestine, was the withdrawal of American troops stationed in Saudi Arabia after the first **Gulf War**.

Taking advantage of the fact that Islamists were in power, bin Laden installed himself in **Sudan** between 1992 and 1996, whereupon he took refuge in Afghanistan, at that time under the rule of Commander Massoud and Burhanuddin Rabbani (according to some sources the Khartoum regime had at one point suggested handing him over to the Saudis). There he set up several training camps and forged an alliance with the Taliban, who took Kabul in 1996. Having been deprived of his Saudi nationality in 1994, he embarked on a broad-ranging programme of **terrorism**, with American targets first in line. His men apparently played a role in the fighting in Mogadishu which ended with the death of 18 US soldiers in October 1993. Among the main actions attributed to his group subsequently, in addition to the attack of 11 September 2001, are the attacks on US forces in Riyadh (1995), the bombings of the US embassies in Kenya and Tanzania (7 August 1998), the attack on the American warship USS *Cole* in the port of Aden (12 October 2000), the murderous bombing in Bali (12 October 2002), the attack on the French **oil** tanker *Limburg* off Yemen (6 October 2002), the attack on Israeli tourists in Mombasa (10 December 2002), the attacks in Riyadh (12 May 2003), in Casablanca (16 May), in Riyadh again (8 November), and in Istanbul (15 and 20 November). It is very rare for bin Laden directly to claim responsibility for a bombing. On 15 October 1999 the UN Security Council demanded that the Taliban government hand over bin Laden.

On 23 February 1998, together with four other leaders of Islamist groups (from **Egypt**, Pakistan and Bangladesh), bin Laden signed an appeal to create a 'World Islamic Front for Jihad against Jews and Crusaders'. This was a declaration of war on the US, which was accused – in this order – of occupying the Arabian Peninsula, crushing the Iraqi people, and finally of wanting to make people forget the occupation of Palestine. In the face of these aggressions it now became lawful to 'kill Americans and their allies, both civilian and military. This is a duty for every Muslim who can do it, in whatever country it may be.'

Bin Laden is the head of an organisation known as al-Qaeda ('The Base'), a decentralised co-ordination of various Islamist groups. He is the only figure of our time to have been capable of federating such differing groups and so many nationalities. The fact that his is a deterritorialised network makes it harder to fight. As well as the Pakistani and Saudi recruits the generation of the 'Afghans' is now being joined by young people coming out of the Islamic diaspora in the West, who have converted to a radical Islamism. The American intervention in Afghanistan following the 11 September 2001 attacks was the signal for him to disappear undercover. According to US officials, he is still alive and has taken refuge in the tribal zones bordering Afghanistan and Pakistan. Only a small number of the most important al-Qaeda figures have been killed or arrested since the New York and Washington attacks, and their organisational capacities have only in part been weakened. Bin Laden's second in command is Ayman al-Zawahiri, a former leader of the Egyptian Islamic Jihad.

Before 11 September 2001, bin Laden had been indicted by a federal jury in New York on 4 November 1998. He was accused of the murder and attempted murder of American citizens and attacks on American buildings, and also of having relations with **Iran** and a non-aggression pact with Iraq. The only action cited was the attack on US marines in Somalia.

BLACK SEPTEMBER

The name Black September is used to designate both the events of September 1970 that ended in the crushing of the **Palestine Liberation Organisation (PLO)** by the Jordanian army and a Palestinian organisation that was created as a result of those events.

After the Six Day **1967 War**, the *fedayeen* established their bases in **Jordan**, and from there conducted their operations against **Israel**. But very quickly the problem of relations between the Palestinian resistance and **King Hussein's** regime reared its head. Jordan had suffered harsh Israeli reprisals. The King disapprovingly watched the rise of an alternative centre of power which undermined his authority and opposed his attempts at political settlement. Confrontations between Jordanian and Palestinian forces increased; crisis was unavoidable. The pretext was to be the Rogers Plan – named after the US Secretary of State – which restated the broad outlines of **UN Security Council Resolution** 242. **Nasser** and King Hussein accepted it during the summer of 1970, the PLO unanimously rejected it. **George Habash's** Popular Front for the Liberation of Palestine (PFLP) thought confrontation should be hastened and Amman taken over. On 7 September 1970, PFLP commandos hijacked three planes from international airlines to the town of Zarka in north Jordan and declared the airport a liberated zone. Although the PFLP had been suspended from the PLO at **Yasser Arafat's** request, the trap closed on the entire organisation, which King

and Haganah were fighting for Qastel – Chief Abdel Qader al-Husseini was to fall in this fighting. Not only was the Revisionist initiative co-ordinated with those of the Haganah, it is clear that it got the green light – admittedly not without some reservations – from its commander, and was to benefit from support from its artillery, as formally testified by Meir Pail in the above article. For its part, the Irgun claimed at that time in a communiqué that 'the commander of the Haganah knowingly lied when he said, after the attack at Deir Yassin, that it was contrary to the "general plan". The truth of the matter is that the taking of Deir Yassin was part of his plan.' A communiqué from the Lehi even accuses the Haganah, which took over the village, of having allowed the men of the Solel Boneh, the Histadrut union public works company, to loot it systematically.

It was not simply that the villagers of Deir Yassin perished in the name of the 'freedom' of Jerusalem. They were deliberately sacrificed in order that the horror of the massacre would accelerate the exodus of **Palestinians**. The military aim of the **Zionist** general staff was to seize the largest possible proportion of Palestine, but also that part which was most ethnically pure. While mainstream Zionism could hardly celebrate a massacre of which it officially disapproved, the Revisionists had no such scruples. The Irgun communiqué explains: 'The conquest of Deir Yassin created terror and fear among the Arabs of the surrounding villages…A panic-stricken flight began which facilitated the restoration of communication between the capital and the rest of the country.' In the Hebrew version of his memoirs, Begin expanded on the phenomenon, which he attributed to 'Arab propaganda'. This, according to him, 'spread a legend of terror among the Arabs and the Arab troops, who were seized with panic when the soldiers of the Irgun were mentioned. This legend was worth half a dozen battalions of Israeli forces.' And he adds,

> Having been led to believe the wild stories about 'Irgun butchery', the Arabs throughout the country were seized by panic, and began to flee their villages. This mass exodus was to transform itself into a wild, uncontrollable stampede. Out of something like 800,000 Arabs who lived in the present territory of the state of Israel, only 160,000 are still there. The political and economic significance of this development cannot be overestimated.

DRUZE

Descended from one of the branches of **Shi'ism**, the origin of the Druze go back to the Fatimid caliphate established in Cairo in the tenth century. The Caliph al-Hakim, who reigned from 996 to 1021, sought to be accepted as divinity. After his disappearance, his followers were persecuted, but his vizier al-Darazi took refuge in **Syria** and managed to convince several tribes there of the divine nature of his late master. It is to him that the sect owes its name. Some years later, in 1043, the new preaching was declared 'complete', and proselytism and conversions forbidden: 'The veil is drawn, the door is closed, the ink is dry and the pen broken'. The doctrine, maintained by a small caste of initiates highly influenced by Greek and Hindu philosophy, is so esoteric that, unlike mainstream branches of Shi'ism, the Druze are considered by most other Muslims to be apostates.

There are Druze communities in **Lebanon**, Syria and **Israel**. In the last of these, they number around 70,000 and receive different treatment from other **Arabs**, Christian or Muslim. In particular, they are liable to military service, which gives them certain privileges. In the 1980s and 1990s, however, an upsurge of insubordination has developed among the Israeli Druze, accentuated by the **Intifada**. But it is mainly in Lebanon that the Druze play a political role.

The first Druze emirate was created in the twelfth century at Mount Lebanon. At the end of the sixteenth century, Fakhreddin II unified under his rule the territories of what is now modern Lebanon. From this date, **Maronites** and Druze were to assert their power over the Lebanese mountain.

The Druze community represents only about 7 per cent of the Lebanese population, but compensates for its numerical weakness by a high degree of unity, a strong territorial concentration in Mount Lebanon (the Shuf, Metn, Hasbaya) – which was accentuated in the period 1983–85 by the exodus of many Christians from the region – and considerable fighting ability. A long-standing split has set the Yazbaki clan (headed by the Arslan family) against the Jumblatts, who nevertheless maintained their supremacy. One man, Kamal Jumblatt, was from 1943 until his assassination by Syrian agents in 1977, both the most prominent Druze in Lebanon and the leader of the Lebanese left wing. He was succeeded by his son, Walid, as head of both the Jumblatt clan and the Progressive Socialist Party (PSP). Although the PSP has, since the 1980s, recruited members from other religious denominations, it is still mainly identified with its Druze base. The signing of the **Taif Accords** in 1989 and the assignment under this agreement of the three principal posts of state to a Maronite, a Sunni and a Shi'ite marked the weakened position of the Druze in the new political configuration. In order to preserve the role of his party in the 1996 elections, Walid Jumblatt managed to have the mountain divided into six small constituencies, while in the rest of the country the ballot took place on the basis of five main divisions. For several years he allied himself with Maronites in order to contest the role of the Syrians in Lebanon.

EGYPT

The history of modern Egypt began when, following the failure of Napoleon's famous expedition, Muhammad Ali, an Albanian officer in the Turkish army, seized power in Cairo. His descendants ruled the country for a century and a half. In the nineteenth century the strategic importance of Egypt's geographical situation, accentuated by the construction of the **Suez Canal** and the expansion of cotton growing, made what was still theoretically a province of the **Ottoman Empire** into a prime target for the European powers. In 1882, **Britain** occupied the country and, after the outbreak of World War I, established a protectorate over it.

At the end of the war a small group of nationalists, headed by Saad Zaghlul, formed a delegation (the Wafd) and travelled to London to negotiate **independence**. Britain's refusal of their request aroused great anger and violent demonstrations, prompting the British government to recognise Egypt as an independent sovereign state in a unilateral declaration of 21 February 1922. This was, however, a bogus independence, since real power remained in the hands of the British High Commission. Political life in the subsequent period revolved around three poles: the Palace, the British proconsul and the Wafd, which had become a political party with a popular membership but feudal leadership, and carried the day in all elections that were not heavily rigged. A treaty signed in 1936 by the Wafdist government of Nahas Pasha led to several minor concessions (such as the re-stationing of British troops in the Suez Canal Zone), but did not live up to the expectations of the nationalists. Nahas was dismissed by the Palace in 1937. In 1942, London foisted on King Faruq, who had been flirting with Nazi Germany, the reinstatement of a Wafd government; Nahas Pasha and his administration lost much of their prestige in the process.

After 1945 the anti-British movement became more radical, and in February 1946 a wave of demonstrations swept through Egypt. Despite the war in Palestine and the imposition of martial law at home, the movement gained strength and carried the Wafd to power again in 1950. Prompted by the radical mood in the country, Nahas Pasha unilaterally repealed the treaty of 1936 that he himself had signed. Guerrilla warfare was stepped up against British troops in the Canal Zone. The burning of Cairo in January 1952 was used as the pretext for a brutal 'return to order'. The Wafdist cabinet was dismissed by the King, and the Wafd, uncertain and divided, became a discredited force. The way was now open for the Free Officers, who seized power on 13 July 1952 and established a republic on 18 June 1953.

Gamal Abdel Nasser, the central figure of the new regime, refused to return to the multi-party system. He established single-party rule, embarked on agricultural reform and, above all, opened negotiations with London. On 19 October 1954 he signed a treaty under which British troops would withdraw from the zone over an 18-month period; in an emergency, however, their return was envisaged. The Suez expedition of 1956 rendered this clause null and void: after 75 years of foreign occupation, Egypt was once again free. It also became the centre of revolutionary Arab nationalism. The Voice of the Arabs, broadcast from Cairo, contributed to the upheavals that shook the Middle East between 1956 and 1967. But although traditional structures were swept away, greatly damaging the colonial presence, Nasser was not in the end able to realise the dream of unity. The United Arab Republic (UAR), made up of Egypt and **Syria**, only lasted for three years (1958–61). The beginning of the 1960s ushered in a new period of 'radical-isation': the nationalisation of industry, phase two of the agricultural reforms, and the creation of the Arab Socialist Union. The alliance with the USSR – symbolised by Nasser's and Khrushchev's inauguration of the Aswan Dam in 1964 – was strengthened. However, with the defeat of the **1967 War**, dreams of independent economic development were shattered against Israeli tanks. Egypt became a conquered nation, partially occupied and crushed by the burden of the war. The President tried to rally his country; refusing to accept the situation, he reconstructed his army with the help of the USSR and gave support to **Yasser Arafat** and the *fedayeen* organisations. Further-more, he conducted a war of attrition over the Suez Canal between 1969 and 1970, all the while claiming his readiness to negotiate a political solution (the Rogers Plan).

When **Anwar al-Sadat** succeeded Nasser in 1970, he had already chosen a radically different course to that of his predecessor. It was, however, not until after the October **1973 War** that he was able to pursue it. His policy consisted of *infitah* (an open economy) and an alliance with the **US** 'which holds 99 per cent of the cards' to resolve the Arab–Israeli conflict. The new direction followed by Sadat was vindicated by his trip to **Jerusalem** in November 1977 and the signing of the **Camp David Accords** the following year. With this agreement Egypt won peace, the Sinai and considerable **American aid**, but lost its relationship and credibility with virtually the entire **Arab world**. The population had enthusiastically welcomed the end of a painful war, but were soon disillusioned. The economic crisis, far from being resolved, worsened. Public liberties were under constant attack, and when in 1981 four men assassinated the President, few Egyptians mourned him.

After Sadat's death a new phase opened, marked by a more balanced policy. **Hosni Mubarak** consolidated the Camp David Accords, but made peace with **Jordan**, **Iraq** and the **Palestine Liberation Organisation (PLO)**, then renewed relations with the majority of Arab countries. He maintained preferential relations with the US in this period, but normalised those with the USSR. Under Mubarak the opposition enjoyed greater freedom, but the government party maintained its hold on the state apparatus. The *infitah* policy was maintained, but Mubarak tried to combat corruption and to extend productive activities.

Nine years into Mubarak's presidency, on the eve of the **Gulf War** of 1990–91, the results of his new policies were ambiguous. Along with other Arab countries, the struggle against **Islamism** served as a pretext for serious limitations on democracy. The rise in **terrorist** incidents, mainly in the form of attacks on the Coptic Christian **minority**, have justified the maintenance of a state of emergency. In the Arab world, however, Egypt had regained its diplomatic status. On the economic front, the situation was worsening. More than ever before, Egypt was dependent on American military and economic aid and the good will of international organisations such as the IMF and the World Bank.

In such a potentially explosive climate, the Gulf crisis seemed to threaten the entire edifice so laboriously constructed by Mubarak over the previous decade. The **Arab League**, which reconvened in Cairo on 10 August 1990, was seriously divided, with Egypt heading the anti-Iraq coalition. Nearly 35,000 Egyptian soldiers were deployed in the Gulf, although their role in the actual combat was extremely limited. The economic situation was, at this time, aggravated by the expulsion of hundreds of thousands of migrant workers from Iraq and the negative effect of the crisis on tourism. This was partially compensated for by a rise in international petrol prices and economic aid from the West, Japan and the Gulf states. Despite its clear alignment with America, Egypt emerged from the Gulf crisis relatively unscathed. It was one of only a few Arab countries in which popular opinion did not mobilise in support of **Saddam Hussein**, largely due to Iraq's treatment of Egyptian migrant workers.

President Mubarak seemed to emerge as a winner from the crisis: it confirmed the pre-eminence of his country within the Arab League, increased valuable support from the US and its allies, and served to isolate further opposition parties already partially discredited through their support for Saddam Hussein. As a result of all this, Egypt is the only country in the world – with the exception of Poland – to have obtained a substantial reduction of its foreign debt, primarily to the US.

Moreover, the 1990s were a difficult time for Egypt. At the regional level, the signing of the **Oslo Accords** partly marginalised Cairo, which was confronted with an alliance between Washington, Ankara, Amman and Tel Aviv. Despite its efforts to act as mediator during the Israeli–Palestinian crises of 1999–2001 and the Arab League summit which met in Egypt in November 2000 to offer support for the **second Intifada**, Cairo was caught between its alliance with Washington (which supplies it with $2bn of aid annually) and a public opinion angered by the images of Israeli repression in Palestinian areas carried by Arab satellite television channels, particularly al-Jazeera. Relations between Egypt and the US became more tense after

11 September 2001 since several Egyptians were either directly involved in the attacks – notably Muhammad Atta, leader of the 19 terrorists – or were suspected of being members of **Osama bin Laden**'s 'inner circle', for instance Ayman al-Zawahiri. Cairo criticised the US intervention in Afghanistan, and spoke out against attacks on Iraq, with which it had established a free-trade agreement in January 2001. These tensions, and the prison sentence imposed on the American-Egyptian human-rights activist Saad Eddin Ibrahim, led to a freeze on all supplementary US aid.

On the domestic front, Islamist violence has escalated in recent years, particularly since 1992, most notably in the form of attacks on tourists – in Cairo in April 1996 and September 1997, and in Luxor in November 1997, where 60 people were massacred, by which means the Islamists hope to damage one of the country's chief sources of revenue. As a result of this, repression has reached unprecedented levels, with tens of thousands of arrests, widespread use of systematic torture and numerous executions. By 1996 the levels of violence seemed to have dropped – six historic leaders of the Gama'a Islamiya movement called a ceasefire in July 1997, then going on to a radical self-criticism and apology to the people of Egypt. This victory led neither to the lifting of the state of emergency in force since 1981 nor to a liberalisation of the political system. The attacks on the non-violent wing of Islamism, the **Muslim Brotherhood**, intensified. A new and more restrictive law limited the activities of non-government organisations. The parliamentary elections of November 2000 signalled popular disaffection with the ruling party, Mubarak's National Democratic Party (NDP), and signalled the return of the Muslim Brotherhood which, with 17 MPs (elected as independents), became the main opposition. The NDP congress in September 2002 was obliged to react to this discontent by removing the more obviously corrupt elements. It also marked the growing status of Gamal Mubarak, the President's son, described as the 'beating heart' of the NDP. His promotion to number three in the party augurs ill for the future of democracy.

At the economic level the government proved incapable of meeting popular aspirations. The country's main income derives from **oil**, the Suez Canal, tourism and the remittances of millions of Egyptians working abroad. However, all these incomes are dependent on the international situation. For example, after the Luxor massacre in 1997 and the attacks of 11 September 2001 tourism collapsed. This has led to reduced levels of growth in recent years; a persistent balance-of-trade deficit – despite some successes in petrochemicals, natural gas and cement; a budget deficit of around 5.8 per cent of GNP; a huge public debt – with the inclusion of state enterprises, in 2001–2 this stood at nearly 70 per cent. In February 2002 Egypt received promises of loans of $10bn from the international organisations over a period of three years, but negotiations for a rapid disbursement of $2.1bn were stalemated. In a country where half the population is under 25, and where 900,000 young people enter the job market every year, the social situation remains explosive. In 2001 the country's GNP stood at $1370 per inhabitant.

Egypt is a country extending over millions of square kilometres, of which only a tiny proportion is cultivatable. With a population of nearly 68 million in 2001, it represents one third of the population of the Arab world. Egyptians are either Sunni Muslims or Coptic Christians (around 10 per cent). These latter, already the victims of discrimination, have been affected by inter-religious conflict – the bloodiest episode took place in December 1999 in the village of al-Khosheh, with the deaths of at least 20 Christians and one Muslim.

EUROPEAN UNION

The dialogue between Europe and the Arab countries, initiated after the **1973 War** and the ensuing **oil** crisis, made no progress until the end of the 1970s, with the period marked by the American 'Lone Ranger', which bore fruit in the talks at **Camp David**. The European Economic Community (EEC, forerunner of the EU) was expecting economic advantages, while their partners in the South were hoping for a political breakthrough, particularly over the question of Palestine. Conscious of this stalemate and its causes, the summit of statesmen and heads of government that met in Venice on 12 and 13 June 1980 formulated its very first common policy statement on the conflicts in the Middle East. In a special declaration (see Appendix 8) the nine representatives were at pains to stress that

> the time has come to promote the recognition and implementation of the two principles universally accepted by the international community: the right to existence and to security of all States in the region, including Israel, and justice for all the peoples, which implies the recognition of the legitimate rights of the Palestinian people.

Adopting a new tone over the issue of Palestine, they stated,

> A just solution must finally be found to the Palestinian problem, which is not simply one of refugees. The Palestinian people, which is conscious of existing as such, must be placed in a position, by an appropriate process defined within the framework of the comprehensive peace settlement, to exercise fully its right to self-determination.

And, in a move that contradicted the post-Camp David interpretation, they noted that the principles of peace 'are binding on all the parties concerned, and thus on the Palestinian people, and on the **Palestine Liberation Organisation (PLO)**, which will have to be associated with the negotiations'.

Having reaffirmed their rejection of any 'unilateral initiative designed to change the status of **Jerusalem** and that any agreement on the city's status should guarantee freedom of access for everyone to the Holy Places', the nine member states stressed

> the need for Israel to put an end to the territorial occupation which it has maintained since the conflict of 1967, as it has done for part of Sinai. They are deeply convinced that the Israeli settlements constitute a serious obstacle to the peace process in the Middle East. The Nine consider that these settlements, as well as modifications in population and property in the occupied Arab territories, are illegal under international law.

This was the line that the EEC adopted throughout the 1980s in a vain attempt to contribute to a global settlement of the conflicts in the region. The subsequent declarations of the European Councils made constant reference to it, and on occasion drew their inspiration from it. On 9 June 1982, the ten representatives 'strongly condemned the latest Israeli invasion of Lebanon', which they thought to be 'unjustifiable'. Reaffirming their 'commitment to the independence, the sovereignty, the territorial integrity and the national unity of Lebanon', they demanded that 'Israel withdraw all its military forces immediately and unconditionally'. They also insisted that the solution to the Lebanese question 'could not be found without a global, just and lasting peace being in place in the region'. The same line was taken during the **Intifada**: on 9 February 1988, just after the outbreak of the Palestinian uprising, the 12 Ministers for Foreign Affairs emphasised that 'the status quo in the occupied territories cannot continue'. Once again they said how convinced they were that 'the only solution lay in a comprehensive political solution' based on 'the Declaration of Venice of June 1980' and affirmed they were 'strongly in favour of an international **peace conference** being organized under the auspices of the United Nations'.

During the first **Gulf War**, Europe supported Washington's preparations for war, which it had imposed upon the UN. Throughout the build-up to the war, the European states alternated between pledges of solidarity for the 'allies of the coalition' to half-hearted attempts to find a negotiated solution. But, on 24 February 1991, in a short declaration after the war had been in progress for seven days, they stated that they 'deeply regret that Iraq has failed to positively respond to the international coalition's demands that it withdraw from **Kuwait** immediately and unconditionally' and went on to say, 'In this darkest of hours, the Community and its member states have joined forces with the Allied coalition'. The EU suffered all the disadvantages of this alignment without enjoying any benefits. In the aftermath of the Gulf War it was Washington that took all the glory, as it did during the peace process, while the EU found itself marginalised. The differences of analysis on the **Iraq** question, between the pro-American position taken by London, the more ambiguous position of Paris, which supported the Security Council resolutions while at the same time seeking a more active role in the region, and the position of the countries of the South, which were more favourable to peace, once again prevented the emergence of any common initiative in 1998. Tony Blair's alignment with the White House in Operation Desert Fox in December torpedoed any chance of European co-ordination.

The Community attempted to compensate for the political ground that it had lost to America by regaining the upper hand in the economic field. Since the 1970s, it had concluded bilateral co-operation agreements with (in chronological order) **Israel** (1975), Algeria, Tunisia, Morocco (1976), **Syria, Jordan, Egypt** and **Lebanon** (1977). At the European summits in Corfu (June 1994), Essen (December 1994) and Cannes (June 1995), the EU set itself a more ambitious goal: a partnership between the countries of Europe and the Mediterranean designed to turn the region into 'a zone of open exchange and dialogue guaranteeing peace, stability and well-being'. Considering that 'a policy of ambitious co-operation with the South is entirely in keeping with the policy of openness shown towards the East, while harmonizing the Union's geo-political foreign policy', the 15 member states defined their offer of a 'partnership' as a combination of 'a political dialogue, the development of balanced and lasting economic and social relations, the fight against poverty and the need for a better understanding between cultures which can only be achieved by human contact'.

This is to be the basis for 'the creation of a Euro–Mediterranean region by the year 2010', shared by the EU and its 12 partners in the South. **Libya** was initially excluded because of its links with '**terrorism**', but was subsequently included, as was Mauritania, with the status of observer.

On 27 November 1995, which, as we were reminded by the Spanish EU Commissioner Manuel Marin, was the nine-hundredth anniversary of the launch of the First Crusade by Pope Urban II, the first Euro–Mediterranean Conference opened in Barcelona. The 27 participating countries formally ratified the new strategy of the EU towards the South. Yet, behind the 'grand design' of the 15, there was a much less humanitarian motivation. Europe had lost its foothold in the region and was trying to re-establish itself by using its favourite formula: a free-trade zone. In the analysis that appeared in *Le Monde diplomatique*, Gérard Kebabdjian, wrote,

> There has been an in-depth revision of the policy of European co-operation, in that commercial exchanges must play strictly by the rules of the market which is completely dependent on the trends of the world economy. Agricultural products are not open to negotiation, so the Mediterranean countries have nothing to gain in the marketplace, and a zone of free exchange was created to put an end to the advantage they hold in the manufactured goods market. Some markets are going to be open to European exports and will receive nothing in return.

Association Agreements were signed at the end of 1995 with Tunisia and Israel, with Morocco at the start of 1996, followed by Jordan and the **Palestinian Authority** in 1997, Egypt in 2001 and Lebanon in 2002. Syria was still negotiating terms in 2002. Malta and Cyprus, which also have Association Agreements with the EU (dating from 1971 and 1973 respectively), were planned to join the Union in 2004. As for **Turkey**, a candidate since 1963, it joined the customs union in 1996 and was judged by the December 1996 European Council meeting in Helsinki to be a suitable candidate for joining the EU. But a section of the European political classes has been opposed to Turkey's membership. In the view of Valéry Giscard d'Estaing, President on the convention on the future of Europe, this would mean 'the end of the European Union'. As he stated at the start of November 2002, 'Turkey is a country close to Europe, an important country, which has a veritable elite, but it is not a European country'.

Despite the €4.4bn invested by the EU in 1995–99, the €5.35bn planned for 2000–6, and the rather higher sums placed at its disposal by the European Investment Bank, the Barcelona Process does not seem likely to make much difference to the North–South imbalances in the Mediterranean. The production of the non-European countries of the Mediterranean basin in 2000 was about 7.2 per cent of that of the EU. Again, in 2000 51 per cent of the exports of these countries were destined for the EU, which, however, sold them only 11.4 per cent of its exports. Only Turkey and Israel are likely to profit in real terms from this new 'space': the GDP of these two countries is the equivalent of all the other Mediterranean countries combined, and account for more than 40 per cent of the EU's exports to the region and almost a third of its imports from the region.

If there is one Mediterranean partner with which the EU has committed itself heavily, it is the Palestinian Authority. After having contributed to the budget of the UN Relief and Works Agency for Palestine Refugees (UNRWA) since 1971, the EU became the main funder of the Palestinian territories: the total of its aid for the period 1994–2001 amounted to €1.4bn. As the recognised banker of Palestinian **autonomy** it has also attempted – not without some difficulty – to become one of the political sponsors of the peace process.

Paradoxically, the blockage of the peace process by **Benyamin Netanyahu** revived the EU's political initiative, which, after the Maastricht Treaty, had a joint foreign and security policy. Thus 1996 saw the appointment of a special representative for the Middle East, Miguel Angel Moratinos, replaced in 2003 by the Belgian Marc Otte. He has since taken part in the majority of international meetings devoted to the conflict, and also in the commission headed by US Senator George Mitchell, and – officially – in the **Taba** negotiations of January 2001. Meanwhile, on 26 March 1999, the 15, in the declaration of the Berlin Summit, recognised 'the continuing and unqualified right' of the **Palestinians** to self-determination, 'including the option of a state'.

In December 2001 the EU asked the President of the Palestinian Authority to dismantle the 'terrorist networks of Hamas and Islamic Jihad', and asked Israel for a 'withdrawal of its military forces and a stop to extrajudicial executions, the lifting of closures' and 'a freeze on settlements'. In Barcelona in March 2002 the EU reaffirmed that

> on the Israeli–Palestinian conflict, the overall objective is two-fold: the creation of a democratic, viable and independent state of Palestine, bringing to an end the occupation of 1967, and the right of Israel to live within safe and secure boundaries, guaranteed by the commitment of the international community, and in particular the Arab countries.

The violence of the military offensives conducted by Israel in the Autonomous Territories under the cover of its response to terrorism led the 15 to stronger words. In particular they denounced the destruction of Palestinian buildings and infrastructures financed by Europe (losses amounting to more than €17m) and threatened Israel with a suspension of its Association Agreement with the EU. They also criticised the Palestinian Authority for the slowness of its realisation of programmes.

The 15 have an effective weapon: the Association Agreement, thanks to which it sells the EU 30 per cent of its exports and buys from it 50 per cent of its imports. The second article of the agreement specifies that it will be suspended in the event of major violations of human rights. On 10 April 2002, the European parliament voted a resolution calling on the Council to suspend it. Similarly, the EU could fight more determinedly for its proposal for an international buffer force – and could even take unilateral initiatives in this area.

If the EU is finding it hard to make its presence felt, this is because it no longer has the necessary consensus within its ranks. For the most part the elections that have taken place in member states in recent years have brought to power forces that are more Atlanticist. Suddenly certain governments, even if they are willing to approve the broad lines of Middle East policy established in recent years, are more interested in not upsetting Washington's policy in the region. This tendency obviously became more marked after 11 September 2001, which divided Europe not only on the Israeli–Palestinian question, but also on the Iraq question. While Paris could count on Berlin and Brussels, it failed to convince London, which is more than ever aligned with Washington, or Rome (under Silvio Berlusconi, freshly converted to the 'crusade against Islam'), not to mention Madrid (which also has a pro-US tendency) or the Hague etc.

Given the lack of independent initiatives, the EU tends to make its influence felt in the Middle East through the 'Quartet', where, with the US, **Russia** and the UN, it contributes to creating a certain framework for the peace process. But the 'Road Map' released in April 2003 – which envisages reforms to the Palestinian Authority, the proclamation of a Palestinian state in 2005 and free elections – seemed near dead only months after its inception.

EXPULSIONS

When, on 29 November 1947, the UN adopted the **Partition Plan** for Palestine, the country had 608,000 Jewish inhabitants and 1,237,000 **Arabs**. The proposed Jewish state was to have 498,000 **Jews** and 407,000 Arabs. Yet the Arabs, at the conclusion of the first Arab–Israeli conflict and in spite of the fact that Israeli territory had increased by a third, numbered only 160,000. Between 700,000 and 900,000 **Palestinians** have taken the road into exile. The overwhelming majority have settled in the surrounding Arab countries, in refugee camps run by the UN Relief and Works Agency for Palestine Refugees (UNRWA). In 1950 the organisation reckoned their number at about a million.

Flight or eviction? The debate, long and heated, as to the causes of the Palestinians' departure during the **1948–49 War** has recently acquired important new contributions, in particular from Israeli historians such as Benny Morris. Years of work spent burrowing among documents, including the declassified national archives of the state of **Israel**, led him to express grave doubts over hitherto accepted ideas in his book *The Birth of the Palestinian Refugee Problem*.

David Ben Gurion explained to the Knesset in 1961 that 'we have explicit documents testifying that they left Palestine following instructions by Arab leaders...under the assumption that the invasion of the Arab armies will destroy the Jewish state and push all the Jews into the sea'. Morris gives the lie to this, saying that at no time did the Palestinian or Arab leaders publish a general appeal to the Arabs of Palestine to leave their homes and villages; there was no campaign in the radio or in the press ordering Palestinians to flee. So if we write off the directives that are cited by traditional Israeli historiography, how are we to explain the Palestinian exodus?

In the territory conquered by Israeli troops at the time, 369 Arab towns and villages were emptied of their populations. Morris admits he does not know under what conditions in 45 cases. The inhabitants of 228 other towns left during attacks by Israeli troops; 41 of these were expelled by military force. In 90 cases, the Palestinians fled in panic following the fall of a neighbouring town or village, fearing an enemy attack or encouraged by rumours spread by the Israeli army. This was particularly true after the massacre, on 9 April 1948, of 250 inhabitants of **Deir Yassin** near **Jerusalem** by militiamen from fundamentalist groups, especially those of the Irgun of **Menachem Begin** and of the Lehi of **Yitzhak Shamir**, who was to admit in his memoirs, 'The legend of Deir Yassin helped us to save the towns of Tiberias and Haifa. The Arabs fled in panic, crying Deir Yassin! Deir Yassin!' Morris, in contrast, lists only six cases where the departure was precipitated by local Arab authorities.

For the early months of 1948, a report by the security services of the Haganah dated 30 June 1948 takes a similar line: 'At least 55 per cent of the total of the exodus was caused by our operations'. To this they add the operations of the Irgun and Lehi dissidents, 'which directly caused about 15 per cent of the emigration', and the effects of the psychological warfare of the Haganah: this brings us to 73 per cent of the departures having been caused directly by the Israelis. In 22 per cent of cases the report cites the 'fears' and the 'crisis of confidence' prevalent among the Palestinian population. As to local Arab appeals for people to flee, they are relevant in only 5 per cent of cases. And yet still Benny Morris concludes that on the Jewish side there was no plan for expelling the Palestinians.

Numerous documents nonetheless attest to the determination of the Prime Minister (and Defence Minister) of the young Israel to come out of the war with the Jewish state as large as possible and, in demographic terms, as homogeneous as possible. Ben Gurion was the author of the Dalet Plan implemented at the end of March 1948 which, according to Morris, already showed 'clear traces of a policy of eviction on both a local and national level'. In July 1948, Ben Gurion offered the following answer to Yigal Allon, who had asked him what to do with the 70,000 Palestinians who were in Lydda and Ramleh: 'Evict them!' Shortly afterwards, in Nazareth, discovering the Arab population still present, he exclaimed, 'What are they doing here?'

Morris's conclusion in his first book was that

> Ben-Gurion clearly wanted as few Arabs as possible to remain in the Jewish state. He hoped to see them flee. He said as much to his colleagues and aides in meetings in August, September and October. But no expulsion policy was ever enunciated and Ben-Gurion always refrained from issuing clear or written expulsion orders; he preferred that his generals 'understand' what he wanted done. He wished to avoid going down in history as the 'great expeller' and he did not want the Israeli government to be implicated in a morally questionable policy.

In the late 1990s, Morris's private political views would take him to the point of supporting the policies of the National Unity government led by **Ariel Sharon**, and even to argue for a new transfer of Palestinians. Paradoxically, as a historian Morris has restated and even consolidated the conclusion of his research.

Other Revisionist historians have re-examined the history of the expulsions, and their conclusions are sometimes more hard-hitting than Morris's. Professor Ilan Pappé at Haifa University dedicated a chapter to the subject in his *The Making of the Arab–Israeli Conflict, 1947–51*. Distancing himself from the cautious words of Morris, he concluded that

The Dalet Plan can in many regards be seen as a strategy of expulsion. The Plan was not an improvised tactic – expulsion was considered as one of several means to carry out reprisals following attacks on Jewish convoys and settlements. It was also seen as one of the best ways to ensure the domination of Jews in areas seized by the Israeli army.

In fact, the very text of the Dalet Plan leaves little ambiguity about the true intentions of the Jewish leadership. It orders

> operations against enemy population centres near or inside our lines of defence in order to prevent them being used as bases by active armed forces. These operations may be carried out in the following manner: the villages may be destroyed (by fire, explosives or laying mines in the debris) or search and control operations may be mounted by surrounding the village and closing the circle. Should resistance be met, the armed elements should be wiped out and the population expelled beyond the borders of the State.

Furthermore, it is undeniable that a policy was put into practice to prevent the return of refugees, which had been called for by the UN General Assembly on 11 December 1948 – a resolution which the Israeli government certainly recognised, in a protocol with its Arab neighbours signed on 12 May 1949 at the Lausanne Conference.

In his diary in 1940, Josef Weitz, the director of the Jewish National Fund, had written, 'It should be clear that, in this country, there is no room for two peoples...The only solution is an Israel without Arabs...There is no option other than transferring the Arabs from here to neighbouring countries.' It was he who in 1948 became responsible for the 'Transfer Committee'. Not only did Israel forbid the refugees to return, but their villages were either destroyed or filled with new Jewish immigrants, and some 300,000 hectares of their lands distributed among the neighbouring *kibbutzim* (communes). The law regarding 'abandoned property' – which makes possible the seizure of the possessions of any 'absent' person – legalised this wholesale confiscation. Almost 400 Arab towns and villages were thus wiped off the map or Judaicised, as were most of the Arab neighbourhoods of mixed towns.

Officially, the Israeli government of the time denied

> any responsibility for the creation of this problem. The accusation that these Arabs were forcefully removed by the Israeli authorities is completely false. On the contrary, everything possible was done to prevent this exodus. The question of return cannot be disentangled from the military context. While the state of war continues, refugees will endanger the maintenance of law and order at home and will provide a formidable fifth column for external enemies.

There followed five decades of controversy, fanned, after the Six Day 1967 War, by the influx of a further 250,000 refugees fleeing from the West Bank. The Arab regimes, claims Israel, must bear the responsibility for the fate of the Palestinian refugees, a fate they have done nothing to improve and have even exacerbated. Utterly at the mercy of those who hire them, this cheap, malleable workforce has, it must be said, met with a mixed reception from its Arab 'brothers', whose regimes are ready to repress all forms of organisation, even to the extent of massacre. But the **Arab world** would reply that it is not a question of refugees but a national problem. And indeed, the refugees themselves have always refused any resettlement. Caught between the two arguments, the Palestinian refugees are left to rot.

Fifty-four years after the great exodus, the UN Relief and Works Agency for Palestine Refugees (UNRWA) counted almost four million Palestinian refugees, a third of whom live in its camps. In Gaza the proportion is as high as 80 per cent. Without doubt it is they who would be most directly affected by the establishment of a Palestinian state alongside Israel. But how many of them are homesick, and always will be, for their family village, now in Israeli territory? The question of the **right of return** remains – as was confirmed in the **Camp David and Taba Negotiations** in 2000–1 – one of the main stumbling blocks in the negotiation of an overall peace settlement.

FINAL STATUS NEGOTIATIONS

In line with the timetable fixed by signature in Washington of the Declaration of Principles on Palestinian Autonomy on 13 September 1993, the second round of the peace process began on 5 May 1996 in the Egyptian resort of **Taba**. However, this second round was broken off after the initial ceremony while parliamentary elections took place in **Israel** to elect a new prime minister and a new Knesset. The outcome of these talks between Israel and the **Palestinian Authority**, which in theory should have been concluded by the end of May 1999, obviously depended to a large extent on the stance adopted by newly elected Prime Minister **Benyamin Netanyahu** and his coalition government.

The agenda envisioned by the Oslo negotiators comes under five principal headings, the details of which can be found in the corresponding entries in this volume.

The first relates to the final status of the Autonomous Territories. For the Palestinian Authority there can be only one solution: the setting up of an independent Palestinian state enjoying complete sovereignty over the totality of territories of the **West Bank** and the **Gaza Strip**, occupied by Israel on the occasion of the Six Day **1967 War**. If one is to believe its programme, the Netanyahu government declared it would 'oppose the establishment of a Palestinian state or any other foreign sovereignty east of the Jordan'. It thus limited itself to proposing 'to the Palestinians an arrangement in terms of which they will be able to conduct their lives freely within the framework of autonomy'. For their part, the Israeli Labour party had decided, following the revision of the Palestinian National Charter in April 1996, to modify their own programme by including reference to the possibility of an eventual Palestinian state.

The second heading, obviously related to the first, concerns the fate of **Jerusalem**. For **Yasser Arafat**, as for all the Palestinian leadership, there is no question but that the Palestinian state must have al-Quds (East Jerusalem) as its capital. From the Israeli side, with the exception of what are referred to as the Arab parties, the general consensus rejects any 'division' of Jerusalem. The Netanyahu government's programme stipulated that 'Jerusalem, the capital of Israel, one and indivisible, will always remain under Israeli sovereignty', and even goes on to specify that 'the government will prevent any action opposed to [this] exclusive sovereignty'. At ground level, this reunification has expressed itself by a **settlement** programme which has allowed **Jews** to form a majority not only in the city as a whole but also in East Jerusalem. Moreover, Netanyahu had made this point one of the strong points of his electoral campaign, reproaching **Shimon Peres** with being ready to 'sell off' Jerusalem cheaply and thus forcing him to take a harder line. In fact, according to leaks from the secret exchanges of views in winter

1995–96 between negotiators close to the Prime Minister and Yasser Arafat, the Israeli side only ever envisaged one outcome: a joint Jewish–Arab municipal council for dealing with the city's problems.

The third heading relates to Israeli settlements. Officially the Palestinian Authority is calling for them to be dismantled and for the departure of all their inhabitants. It has nevertheless established contacts with settlers' representatives in an attempt to define the conditions under which some of them might continue to live within an independent Palestinian state. Pursuing its interest in the creation of 'Greater Israel' (a long-standing concern of the Likud party, but one that seemed to have been forgotten for the moment), the Netanyahu government programme talked about 'the strengthening, enlargement and development' of Jewish settlements 'on the Golan Heights and in the Jordan Valley, Judea, Samaria and Gaza'; it said it would 'allocate, in these regions, the resources necessary for this undertaking'. For Israel's Labour party, there was never any question of terminating the settlements: the compromise envisaged by their 'secret' negotiators hinged rather on border modifications that might make it possible to reallocate to Israeli territory a large number of the highly populated settlements lying within reach of either the 'Green Line' or Jerusalem. A feasibility study looked into the possibility of annexing 11 per cent of the West Bank in order to concentrate 70 per cent of the settlements in that territory.

The fourth heading, inseparable from those cited above, relates to the borders of the Palestinian entity. Where the borders will eventually run depends both on the status of that entity and on whether it will be an independent state or an extended **autonomy**; also on whether or not the differentiated zones of autonomy set in place will be preserved by the Oslo II Accords, on the future of the settlements and, of course, Jerusalem. Security imperatives also affect the border issue, with Israel, for example, insisting on maintaining control of the Jordan valley, which divides the Jewish state from **Jordan**.

The fifth and final heading concerns the position of the Palestinian refugees. The negotiations on this front – which have been underway since 1992 within the framework of the multinational negotiations begun after the Madrid conference – have made very little progress. Essentially, discussion is still stalled on the issue of the principle adopted by the UN in 1948: the right to return or the right to compensation. Neither Shimon Peres nor his successors have shown the slightest flexibility on this point. Israeli negotiators may be willing to discuss the eventual return of the people 'displaced' in 1967, but they rule it out for the refugees created by the first Arab–Israeli war, and for their descendants. The Netanyahu government said that it would 'oppose the "right of return" of Arab populations to any part of Eretz ["Greater"] Israel to the west of the Jordan'. The Palestinian side is particularly insistent on this question because it is the precondition for the unity of the **Palestinians** of the 'interior' and the 'exterior'. The absence of any progress would signify the exclusion from the peace process of the totality of the Palestinian diaspora.

Parallel with the bilateral talks, multilateral negotiations were also decided on by the Madrid conference, on 1 November 1991. They were solemnly opened on 28 and 29 January 1992 in Moscow, in the presence of 36 countries, including all the countries party to the conflict, with the exception of **Syria** and **Lebanon**, who considered them (and still consider them) premature, and **Iraq**, **Iran** and **Libya**, who were excluded by the event's American and Russian sponsors. Five working groups were set up: **water** resources, environment, refugees, arms control and regional economic development. Moving at a rate of one or two meetings per year, and almost without media coverage, each of these has subsequently pursued its activity independently, with the total package being co-ordinated by a 'steering group' which has seen its role grow in the course of the proceedings. Since there is no majority voting, and since the process depends on consensus-building, results obviously vary from one group to another, depending on the stakes and therefore the obstacles likely to be encountered.

The group dealing with the environment has drawn up an 'environmental code of conduct for the Middle East', known as the Bahrain Code, after the country in which the resolution was adopted on 25 October 1994. This is accompanied by a series of concrete proposals regarding protection against maritime pollution, treatment of waste, the fight against desertification, and so on.

On the other hand, the group dealing with refugees has made no progress whatsoever, with the Palestinians struggling to win even a working acceptance of the principles established by the UN in 1948.

Without glossing over the thorny problems of sovereignty, the group dealing with water resources has reached agreement on a series of concrete projects (improvements in municipal systems, research into irrigation, treatment of used water, conservation, major works, public awareness programmes, the creation of a research centre on desalination, a training programme for personnel etc.).

The group set up to discuss arms control divided into two wings at the end of 1993, one 'conceptual' and the other 'operational'. The former decided on the creation of a centre of regional security in Amman, but has not yet succeeded in drawing up a consensus-based 'declaration of principles'. The second has made some progress on maritime issues, communications and exchanges of military information.

The group on regional economic development, having first served as a framework for the mobilisation of financial resources for the Occupied Territories, adopted a plan of action at the end of 1993 known as the

Copenhagen Plan. This envisaged a series of specific sessions on communications and transport, energy, tourism, agriculture, financial markets and investments, trade, education, networks and bibliography. In each of these sectors one country was charged with 'guiding' the thinking process. Unlike the other working groups, from which they found themselves excluded, the member countries of the EU play a major role. The whole is co-ordinated by a committee, which is subdivided into four sub-committees (finance, infrastructure, trade and tourism) placed respectively under the responsibility of **Egypt**, Jordan, Israel and the Palestinians. This proliferation of institutions has not so far achieved much in terms of concrete economic co-operation, but progress has been made on the creation of a 'climate' propitious to globalisation in the region, for which the signal was given by the economic conferences in Casablanca (October 1994) and Amman (October 1995).

FRANCE

France was the first Western power to entrench itself in the Middle East, and a long-standing rival of **Britain** in the fierce struggle for supremacy in the region. It was also the first power to be expelled from the Middle East, and it took General de Gaulle to restore the country's prestige and markets there.

In 1535 François I obtained certain privileges, known as 'capitulations', for France and its nationals within the **Ottoman Empire**. This first step was complemented by interventions in favour of Lebanese **Maronite** Christians, whose protector France officially became in 1639. The capture of **Jerusalem** by the Crusaders on 15 July 1099 and the later recognition of France as the protector of the Catholic holy places heralded the country's link with Palestine. A new era of French colonial interest in the Middle East began with Napoleon's Egyptian expedition (1798–99).

To **Egypt**, where the rise of French influence was to be spectacularly symbolised by the construction of the **Suez Canal** (1869), were added French conquests in North Africa: Algeria, beginning in 1830, then Tunisia, which became a French protectorate in 1881, and Morocco in 1912. At the other end of the Ottoman Empire, the territory of Obock, the future French Somaliland, was occupied from 1862. Paris even began to dream of a *pashalik* dependency stretching from Morocco to the Sinai, and of a Syro–Egyptian state.

Although such projects did not materialise, France's position on the eve of the First World War and the break-up of the Ottoman Empire was nonetheless very strong. Apart from the areas it had colonised or in which it had established supremacy, France was very influential in Ottoman economic, social and cultural life. Most of the foreign capital invested in the Empire was French, accounting for 11 per cent of French capital abroad (more than in its colonial empire proper). This domination was based on state loans as well as shares and bonds in private companies. French capital dominated the banking system, railways, ports, roads, urban public utilities and certain mining operations, not to mention the world of commerce. The principal creditor of the Ottoman Empire and of Egypt – in British hands after 1882 – the French state would see its control of their economic policies strengthened by the bankruptcy of 1875–76. Even in the cultural domain, French influence prevailed, primarily in education – French was the principal means of communication, after Turkish, from one end of the sultan's dominions to the other.

At the outbreak of the First World War, therefore, the situation in the Near East looked favourable for France, despite its weak military presence in the region during and after the war. This is clear from the **Sykes–Picot Agreement** and its implementation in the peace treaties and conventions of 1923 and 1924. Paris retained North Africa, obtained a Mandate for **Syria** (including **Lebanon**), Cilicia, the *vilayet* of Adana and the **oil** region of Mosul, which in 1918 Clemenceau ceded to the British in exchange for 25 per cent of the Turkish Petroleum Company.

For France, the decades which followed amounted to a futile attempt to combat the Arab nationalist movements on the one hand and British competition on the other. Division and repression was the French tactic during its Mandate. Faisal, elected king by the Syrian National Council on 8 March 1920, was forcibly expelled by the troops of General Gouraud, who, on 24 July, occupied Damascus. The first task of the mandatory power was to divide the country into six regions: a Greater Lebanon with a Christian majority, an Alawite state, the state of Aleppo, the state of Damascus, the Jebel **Druze** and the *sanjak* of Alexandretta. The states of Aleppo and Damascus were combined in 1925 to become the Syrian state. Then, in the Jebel Druze, insurrection broke out that spread to the whole mandated area. The dismantling of the country and the takeover of its government by a French high commissioner provoked insurrections among the overwhelming majority of the population. It took a year and a half – and the bombing of Damascus by General Sarrail – before the reinforced French expeditionary force finally put down the rebellious nationalists.

After repression came negotiations. In 1926 Lebanon was granted the status and constitution of a parliamentary republic attached to France. Ten years later, the French Popular Front drafted a treaty granting Lebanon **independence** in exchange for military bases and facilities for the French army. But the treaty, like that promised to Syria, was never signed because soon afterwards Paris underwent a change of heart. Obviously France's prestige among the people it was governing – and the people of the region in general – suffered as a result of such methods. The Arabs' aspirations for unity meant that they opposed the cantonisation that was being attempted by the occupying power, while their Islamic identity was outraged by the privileges reserved for Christians (and, to a lesser extent, the Druze). Their democratic aspirations were also trampled underfoot by brutal repression, and their hopes of independence mocked by French prevarication.

The final stroke came during the Second World War. Caught between the German offensive in **Libya** heading for Egypt, and that from the Caucasus towards **Iraq**, Britain had, at all costs, to defend its rear flank. The Vichy government had allowed the Germans to use Lebanon and Syria for their bases, with the result that Britain occupied both countries in July 1941 with the help of the Free French forces – following a series of short but bloody battles in which Moshe Dayan took part, losing his right eye in the process. In the name of de Gaulle, General Catroux declared independence. It was, however, too late. The nationalist movement turned against Catroux. The Lebanese (1943) and Syrian (1944) parliaments abolished French privileges. France's attempt to land troops was to no avail; furthermore, the British, backed up by American and Soviet guarantees, lost no time in accepting the two countries (with no regard whatever for France's position) into both the **Arab League** and the UN, of which they were founder members. On 31 December 1946 the last French soldiers left the Levant.

Did France hope that by forming an exclusive alliance with **Israel** that it would regain a footing in the Middle East? The fact is that Franco–Israeli ties became increasingly close, to the extent that French experts would pass on to their Israeli colleagues the secrets of nuclear power (including the atom bomb) and help them to make the Jewish state a major power in this field. The guilt felt by France, like the other Western states, after a **genocide** that it had allowed to take place, and the sense of brotherhood felt by the socialists who were then in power in both countries, no doubt had a bearing on this trend, which was intensified from 1954 onwards by the conflict between the French government and Algerian nationalists. In supporting Israel against its Arab adversaries, French leaders apparently thought they could win back in the Arab east the influence that was slipping away in North Africa. This was obviously one of the reasons for French involvement in the **1956 War**. The Suez fiasco had serious consequences in Algeria, where it aggravated the uprising, and in the Levant, where Paris (like London) was condemned to an irreversible decline by the hostility it had aroused in an Arab nationalist movement at the height of its power – and by the rivalry of the **US**.

France owed its return to influence in the Middle East to General de Gaulle. In the middle of the Six Day **1967 War**, for which he held Israel responsible, the President drastically altered the traditional viewpoint of the French Foreign Office. Having condemned the occupation of Arab territories and the annexation of Jerusalem by the Jewish state, he penalised the latter with an embargo on arms sales to the 'belligerent countries'. It is from this period that the controversial phrase 'a self-confident and dominant people' dates. But the prophetic conclusion to this phrase is often forgotten: 'a self-confident and dominant people which is organizing, in the territories which it has conquered, an occupation which cannot proceed without oppression, repression and expulsion. Should this occupation meet any resistance, it is called terrorism.' The General's successors – Georges Pompidou and Valéry Giscard d'Estaing – remained faithful to this realignment in Middle East policy – but not to the embargo on arms destined for Israel, which was modified in 1969 and abolished in 1974. The French diplomatic service agreed with its Arab counterparts over the conditions of a lasting peace, authorised the **Palestine Liberation Organisation (PLO)** to open an office in Paris, and pressured the EEC to recognise 'Palestinian national rights'. For their part, the Israelis took great pleasure in pointing out the economic perks of the Gaullist U-turn: fabulous contracts with Iraq, Egypt, **Saudi Arabia**, Libya and **Iran**, oil exchanged for arms and advanced technology (particularly civil nuclear technology) and many consumer goods.

The Mitterrand view maintained a continuity with its post-de Gaulle predecessors, while also taking on board the heritage of the SFIO (the French section of the Workers' International), whose friendship with Israel goes hand in hand with a pro-US stance. The **Arab world**, uneasy about the **Zionism** attributed to François Mitterrand, was at first reassured: the President supported the Fahd Plan and statements about the Palestinian state made by the French Foreign Minister, who even met with **Yasser Arafat**. There were mutterings about Mitterrand's presidential visit to Israel in March 1982 that allowed **Menachem Begin** to reduce his diplomatic isolation – aggravated by the annexation of the **Golan Heights**. The *tricolore* once again rose in Arab estimation when France made it possible for the PLO to leave Beirut in 1982, when the city was besieged by the Israeli Defence Forces (IDF). And it was France again that saved Arafat in Tripoli in 1983 – this time from the Syrian army.

On the other hand, as Iraq's principal arms supplier after the USSR, France was to become enmeshed in the **Iran–Iraq War** – which led to the kidnapping and lengthy imprisonment of a number of its citizens by **Hezbollah** in Lebanon. The tension that ensued ended in the breakdown of diplomatic relations between Paris and Tehran in August 1987. Negotiations were, however, eventually resumed, and the French hostages were dramatically freed in the spring of 1988, right in the middle of a presidential election, opening the way for the normalisation of relations between the two countries.

The **Gulf War** of 1990–91 if anything accelerated France's retreat from a central diplomatic role in Middle East politics. On two occasions during the crisis – 24 September 1990 in the General Assembly of the UN and 15 January 1991 in the Security Council – France made concerted efforts to open a dialogue between the US and Iraq. However, these appeals were unsuccessful as France was pushed more firmly into the coalition built by the US following the Iraqi attack on the French Embassy in **Kuwait** on 15 September 1990. France's forces in the immediate region – 15,000 men of the Daguet Division and the battleship *Clemenceau* – were, during the crisis, inexorably propelled from a role of embargo enforcement toward what Mitterrand called on 21 August 1990 the 'logic of war'.

'All sides respect and listen to France. I assure you that just as we were involved in the war, France will be involved at the meeting where a rapprochement finally takes place,' said President Mitterrand during the conflict. It should, however, be noted that French diplomacy played no role in developments in the Middle East. Admittedly, France prided itself on having established the 'right to intervene' in the case of the **Kurds**, but this was to control the flood of refugees rather than to prevent the massacre which had triggered the mass exodus. France allowed the US to deal with the Arab–Israeli problem. In Lebanon, it lent belated support to the **Taif Accords** once it had abandoned General Michel Aoun. In the Gulf, it received only a thin slice of the economic, political and military advantages granted to the 'victors'.

French representatives – indeed the European powers in general – were conspicuous by their absence at the Madrid **Peace Conference**, which opened on 30 October 1991, and in the bilateral and multilateral negotiations that followed. In 1993 France lost further ground through ignoring the negotiations in Oslo – which were also viewed with suspicion by the US State Department. That is why, when the diplomatic bandwagon began to roll over the mutual recognition of Israel and the PLO, and the declaration of the principle of **autonomy** secured in the **Oslo Accords**, France did not even pay a minor role in the process. In effect, de Gaulle's fear of American hegemony in the region had been made a reality.

Only after the neo-Gaullist Jacques Chirac was elected president in May 1995 did France begin to sketch out a new independent policy on the Middle East. This new approach was unveiled by Chirac during his visits to Lebanon and Egypt in April 1996, when he talked of a 'new dynamic' in 'France's Arab policy' (a policy described as 'a myth' by the socialist Minister of Foreign Affairs Roland Dumas). Addressing a group of students in Cairo, President Chirac spoke of Franco–Arab relations as forming 'an essential component' of France's foreign policy, and argued that in future the **EU** must play a more central role in the Middle East region – primarily to defend what he saw as the four main goals of the peace process: recognition of the Palestinian people's legitimate aspirations for a sovereign state of Palestine; Israel's right to live in security; an Israeli withdrawal from the Golan Heights within the context of a comprehensive Israeli–Syrian peace; the return of complete sovereignty over all its territory to the elected government of Lebanon.

A few days after this address, the Israelis launched the bloody and unjustified Grapes of Wrath operation in south Lebanon, which the US was seen to tacitly support (thus damaging irreparably its status as arbitrators in the region). This event helped to facilitate France's partial return to diplomatic centre stage in the region. At the request of the Lebanese government, the Foreign Minister, Hervé de Charette, undertook a 'shuttle-diplomacy' tour of Beirut, Tel Aviv, Damascus and Tehran, as a result of which – much to the annoyance of the US and Israel – France argued for a ceasefire which took greater account of the Syrian and Lebanese position. For the first time since the Gulf crisis, France became directly involved in a multinational initiative within the Middle East – joining with the US, Syria, Lebanon and Israel to monitor the implementation of the agreed accords.

It was in this context, in Jerusalem in February 2000, at just the time when the Israeli air force was bombing Lebanon, that Lionel Jospin made statements which created a wave of anger throughout the Arab world: he effectively described the Hezbollah attacks against Israeli soldiers as **'terrorist'** and said that 'the Israeli responses, which we can understand, strike civilian populations as little as possible'. The reception which the French Prime Minister received the following day from the students of Bir Zeit University in the **West Bank** made a severe dent in the 'statesmanlike' image that he was trying to cultivate.

This was particularly true later, even though Jospin abstained from using the term 'terrorist' again. For instance, he gave credence to the idea that Damascus was refusing to seek peace with Israel: 'The Israelis,' he explained, 'are willing to resume negotiations. The Syrians didn't want to. Those are the facts as I see them.' This analysis is heavily contradicted by the facts of the Israeli–American–Syrian negotiations of spring 2000 over the Golan Heights. Once again, after an understanding was reached between President Chirac and his Prime Minister, France at that time proclaimed that its policy in the region had not changed. But even in relation to the Iraq crisis unfolding in the late 1990s, Jospin felt moved to express his difference: while France had not taken part in Operation Desert Fox conducted by the US and the UK in 1998, the Prime Minister was not prepared to condemn the Anglo-American raids, stating that 'Baghdad bore the main responsibility for the crisis'. However, this ambiguity would not prevent France from seeking to use all its powers in the Security Council to get the embargo lifted and avoid a new Anglo–American war.

Is this an indirect consequence of French-style 'cohabitation'? The Quai d'Orsay (French Foreign Ministry) is institutionally close to both the Presidency and Prime Minister's office, and under Jospin followed its traditional Middle East policy. Far from following his Prime Minister in his detours, the socialist Minister of Foreign Affairs Hubert Védrine set about an active diplomacy, on both Israeli, Arab and Iraqi issues, intended to get the voice of France and Europe heard in the face of attempts by the American 'hyperpower' to get itself in position as the hegemonic power in the region.

But in the second part of the 1997–2002 term of office, Védrine's initiatives came to clash with increasing regularity with the political changes taking place both in the US and the EU. The election of George W. Bush and the establishment of the most imperialist administration since the Second World War effectively crowned and amplified a wave of elections within the EU that were won by forces that were Atlanticist above all else. Even though they were in agreement with Paris on the Middle East, London, Madrid, Rome and the Hague put themselves firmly in line with Washington's position and refused to go against the US, however marginally. This process of vassalisation considerably reduced the margins of manoeuvre for France and its few allies, most notably the Belgians, on this issue. Since the election of **Ariel Sharon**, and despite the escalating repression in Palestinian areas, France and its partners, in parallel with the diplomatic activity of the 'Quartet' (US–UN–EU–**Russia**), proved neither willing nor able to take effective measures to make Israel cease military operations, respect ceasefires and resume negotiations.

In this difficult context, Chirac – buoyed by his second presidential mandate, and following the surprise victory of Gerhardt Schröder in the German elections of September 2002 – undertook major diplomatic activity against any unilateral action against Iraq. It is a fact that, despite the pressure of the 'hawks' in his administration, Bush turned towards the UN, where he finally accepted **UN Security Council Resolution** 1441, which entrusted the Security Council with the conduct of disarming Iraq. With an impasse reached over the next step in disarming Iraq, the US and its allies interpreted that resolution as leaving the door open for more or less 'automatic' military reprisals against Baghdad without a new decision from the Security Council. France was the most prominent country opposed to the American-led war in Iraq in 2003, which won it great store in the Middle East and lost it great credibility in the US.

In 2001 the Middle East featured relatively insignificantly in French trade relations: France imported goods worth about €10.1bn from the region (3 per cent of its total imports) and exported goods worth €12bn (2.7 per cent of its exports). Nevertheless the balance of this trade (€1.9bn) represents nearly one half of France's trade surplus (48.7 per cent). The country's five main customers in the region were, in order, the United Arab Emirates (€2.6bn), **Turkey** (€2.2bn), Saudi Arabia (€1.5bn), Israel (€1.4bn) and Iran (€1.1bn). Its five main suppliers from the region were Turkey (€2.5bn), Saudi Arabia (€2.4bn), Iraq (€989m), Israel (€928m) and Iran (€799m).

GAZA STRIP

A strip of land measuring 370 sq. km which adjoins **Egypt**, the territory of Gaza was part of Palestine under the British Mandate. After the **1948–49 War**, Gaza came under the administration of Cairo but was not annexed, retaining autonomous status. It is a much poorer region than the **West Bank**, with only a few agricultural resources (citrus fruits, vegetables), and more than three quarters of the population is made up of refugees.

With the **1956 War**, Gaza experienced its first Israeli occupation. This was the only direct confrontation between Israelis and **Palestinians** during the period 1949–67. In this conflict Palestinians acquired experience of armed resistance. It was in Gaza that most of the Fatah leaders formed their ideas and the rebirth of Palestinian nationalism began.

Israeli forces withdrew from Gaza in 1957, but the area was once again occupied in June 1967. Unlike the West Bank, the population launched itself recklessly into armed struggle, despite possessing no rear bases. It was not until 1971, under the leadership of **General Ariel Sharon** – who used every means at his disposal – that the Israelis managed to put an end to the uprising.

The Israeli military victory led, as on the West Bank, to the establishment of Jewish **settlements** and the integration of Gaza into the Jewish economy: almost half the active population of the area crosses, every day, into the Jewish state to work in industry, building trades or services. The population, extremely young, is highly educated, thanks to the UN Relief and Works Agency for Palestine Refugees (UNRWA). But those with qualifications cannot find work and have to emigrate. This phenomenon, already perceptible on the West Bank, has assumed greater proportions in Gaza.

From 1972–73, contacts between the elites of the West Bank and Gaza increased and, after the October **1973 War**, they united in support of the **Palestine Liberation Organisation (PLO)** and the idea of a state constructed inside the Occupied Territories. In the Gaza Strip, however, the movement was less well organised (a result of the large number of refugees, an absence of traditions, a weak associative life etc.). The **Muslim Brothers**, whose roots in the region are long-standing, are powerful and were frequently used in the 1970s by the occupying authorities to counteract the influence of PLO partisans. It was in Gaza that, on 8 October 1987, the **Intifada**, or Palestinian uprising, began. Gaza is also the birthplace of the Islamic Resistance Movement, **Hamas**, which went on to acquire considerable influence and challenge the primacy of the PLO.

The **Oslo Accords** stipulated that Gaza, where **Yasser Arafat** returned on 1 July 1994, should fall under the control of the **Palestinian Authority**. But by the end of the theoretical period of **autonomy**, on 4 May 1999, the Palestinian Authority controlled only 70 per cent of the Gaza Strip with a million Palestinian inhabitants, the remaining 30 per cent having been taken over by 16 settlements inhabited by 7000 Israelis. The settlers have the best land, which they irrigate massively, at the risk of destroying underground **water** resources (see **Water**). On the pretext of guaranteeing the security of these settlements, the Israeli army has literally cut the zone, which was already surrounded by an electrified fence separating it from Israeli territory, into three parts. During the summer of 2002 **Israel** even began deporting the families of West Bank **'terrorists'** to Gaza. Gaza has become one huge prison – or, to use the words of an Israeli analyst quoted by journalist Nahum Barnea (*Yediot Aharonot*), 'Israel's Alcatraz'.

The repression of the **second Intifada** has involved the destruction of many parts of Palestinian infrastructure – for instance Gaza's port and airport, which were financed by the **EU**. According to Human Rights Watch, in the course of two years the soldiers have demolished more than 600 houses and damaged 600 others and, according to B'Tselem during the first year they also destroyed 7 per cent of the cultivatable land. As a result, in addition to the collective punishments inflicted by the army there has been a rapid worsening of the living conditions of the 1.2 million Palestinian population, and particularly of the 900,000 refugees. In June 2002, 65 per cent of the economically active population was unemployed, and more than 80 per cent of the population were living below the poverty line (less than $2 a day). As the co-ordinator of Israeli public action in the Occupied Territories stated, 'people are not dying of hunger, but there are now obvious signs of malnutrition in some regions'.

With one of the highest rates of population growth in the world (5.4 per cent), the Gaza Strip is a powder keg. As a bastion of Hamas and Islamic Jihad, it has already several times been the scene of 'hunger strikes' against the occupying forces, but also against the Palestinian government, which is accused of incompetence and corruption.

GENOCIDE

Antisemitic racism was from the outset an important element of Hitler's fascism, and permeates the Nazi 'bible', *Mein Kampf*. Until 1933 the Brown Shirts' antisemitism was mainly expressed verbally: the **Jew** served as scapegoat, depicted – to fuel the discontent of the population which it polarised – as the 'Judeo–Bolshevik' or the 'Judeo–plutocrat'. With Hitler's acquisition of power, the 'legalisation' of antisemitism began: the Law of 7 April 1933, then the Nuremberg Laws (15–16 September 1935), established strict segregation aimed at preventing all contact between 'Aryans' and **Jews** – particular emphasis was placed on banning mixed marriages and excluding Jews from a number of professions. At the same time, acts of violence increased – ranging from the compulsory boycott of Jewish businesses to the imprisonment of thousands of Jews – by way of the third-degree treatments that were a speciality of the SA and the SS.

The assassination in Paris of Ernest von Rath, a counsellor at the German Embassy, by a man named Grynspan in November 1938 served as a pretext for the unleashing of an antisemitic campaign of terror. A pogrom extended over the whole of Germany, organised by Goebbels and Himmler, with the help of the Gestapo. 'Kristallnacht', the 'Night of Broken Glass', 9 November, exacted a dreadful toll: 191 synagogues set alight, 50 of which were destroyed; 7500 Jewish shops demolished and pillaged; 91 Jews savagely murdered. 'We must arrest as many Jews, especially the rich ones, as existing prisons can hold. On their arrest, immediate contact must be made with the appropriate concentration camps, in order to intern them as quickly as possible,' specified the message sent by the SS number two, Reinhard Heydrich, to all high-ranking police officers. In actual fact, on 10–11 November 20,000 Jews were rounded up to join the communists, social democrats and Christians already imprisoned, some since 1933. Those who were not imprisoned were by no means let off: a collective fine of a billion marks was imposed on German Jews as punishment for their 'abominable crimes', not to mention the cost of their destroyed possessions – the insurance claims were confiscated by the government. On top of this, antisemitic legislation was intensified, and Jews were henceforth totally eliminated from the German economy, forced to make over their businesses and possessions to 'Aryans'.

'The main problem remains, it consists of chasing the Jews out of Germany,' Heydrich had declared. At first the solution resorted to was paid-for emigration. From 1933 to 31 October 1941, 537,000 Jews legally left Germany, Austria and Bohemia-Moravia at a cost of $9.5m, paid by their co-religionists abroad. After toying with the idea of deporting the Jews to Madagascar, then assembling them in Poland, and finally imagining a 'reserve' in Siberia, high-ranking Hitlerites progressively came round to the 'Final Solution' long prophesied by Hitler. No one was left in any doubt on the matter. Thus on 30 January 1939, the Chancellor once more stated before the Reichstag, 'I'll make a prophecy. If Jewish capital, in Europe and elsewhere, manages one more time to plunge peoples into a world war, the consequence will not be the bolshevizing of the world, and consequently a victory for the Jews, but on the contrary the destruction of the Jewish race in Europe.'

Prepared during the summer of 1941, which saw the Einsatzgruppen (mobile killing groups) massacring hundreds of thousands of Jews on the 'Eastern front', and accelerated at a meeting in Wannsee, Berlin, on 20 June 1942, the Final Solution involved the deportation of all the Jews of occupied Europe to existing concentration camps and, more especially, to new camps under construction: extermination centres. Thus were born, among others, Auschwitz, Treblinka, Belzec, Sobibor and Chelmno, where the installation of gas chambers allowed the daily annihilation of thousands of men, women and children. 'The definitive solution to the Jewish problem in Europe concerns approximately 11 million Jews,' Heydrich had estimated at Wannsee; if one includes the victims of the wholesale massacres on the Eastern Front, those of the ghettos and the death factories, he achieved more than half of his objective.

Several decades later, the murderers were joined by the 'Killers of Memory', to borrow the apt title of the book that Pierre Vidal-Naquet devoted to Revisionist histories of the Holocaust. Fewer in number, but vocal nonetheless, and buoyed by the mounting influence of the National Front and similar groups in different parts of the world, which generally endorse their ideas while not openly advocating them, hardliners of all varieties of this version of history concentrate their 'revision' on the gas chambers, an instrument and a symbol of the massacre whose existence and function they contest, despite all the evidence. Moreover, their avowed goal is to deny the genocide of the Jews, or at least to play it down. The Holocaust, according to French right-wing politician Jean Marie Le Pen, 'is a detail of the Second World War'. Furthermore, extreme right-wing professor Robert Faurisson assures us, 'Hitler never gave the order for a single person to be killed on account of their race or their religion,' adding 'I contest that the policy of the physical extermination of the Jews ever existed'.

Nothing would be more absurd than to isolate the fate of the Jews from that of the other victims of Nazism: engaged in a crusade against 'Judeo–Bolshevism', the Nazi leadership aimed to conquer and colonise Central and Eastern Europe, creating *Lebensraum* ('living space') and liquidating tens of millions of *Untermenschen* ('sub-human people') – Jews, gypsies, Slavs, the mentally ill. In the same way, the genocide of the Jews by the Nazis has its place in a long chain which runs through the history of humanity: the indigenous peoples of Latin and North America, the Armenians and, more recently, the Cambodians and the Tutsis are tragic proof of this. But the Holocaust has several specificities: the fact of having been announced for a long time previously, its sheer scale – more than half the targeted population; the extent of the technical means employed – from the transport wagons to the crematoriums; and its purely racial character, excluding all other motives (territorial gains, economic advantage, rise in social status etc.). Among the victims of Nazism, the Jews were the only ones whom their butchers intended to exterminate in their entirety. In the middle of a century seen as representing human progress, its effect was all the more devastating on communities who had seen their assimilation as a guarantee against any renewal of the persecution of the past. It was a wound that was never to heal.

For over half a century, the extermination of the Jews has continued to exert a crucial influence: decisively in 1947 in favour of the creation of the state of Israel; then, during the various Israeli–Arab conflicts, in the form of a 'natural' sympathy of Western opinion with Israel. One cannot, however, dispute the claims of the Arab peoples, **Palestinians** above all, when they complain of paying in the stead of Europeans for the crimes committed or tolerated by them against the Jews. 'We are,' wrote Marguerite Duras in *La Douleur*, 'from that part of the world where the dead are piled up in an inextricable charnel-house. This is happening in Europe. It is here that Jews are being burned, millions of them. Here they are being mourned.' Having said that, how can we not understand that Israelis live in the shadow of that horror, whose memory is entrenched in their institutions and whose return they legitimately ward off by an ongoing search for security. More generally, the memory of the Holocaust is an important element of Jewish identity throughout the world, whether or not they have once again been integrated into the nations where they live. Even when they do not feel involved in Israeli policy, the memory sustains among them a certain feeling for Israel which is seen as a refuge in the event of such persecution ever occurring again.

However much the genocide may have been used as an argument, or as a pretext for something else, it would be absurd to underestimate its political, ideological and cultural importance.

GOLAN HEIGHTS

The Golan Heights is the name given to the Syrian plateau situated to the northeast of the state of **Israel**, which occupied it in June 1967, on the eve of the **1967 War**, and annexed it in December 1981.

The Golan's importance has been appreciated since early times. The caravan route from Damascus and Baghdad to the Mediterranean, it was occupied by the Greeks, who named it Gaulanitide. The Romans incorporated it into the province of Peraea, whose governors had their headquarters at Quneitra, currently the plateau's principal town. Then, in the seventh century, the **Arabs** conquered the region and named it al-Joulan. In accordance with the **Sykes–Picot Agreement** of 1916, the treaties that concluded the First World War made the Golan an integral part of the Syrian Mandate accorded to **France**, a status that would be confirmed by the new regional situation resulting from the Second World War.

The plateau's importance is above all strategic: from an altitude of 1000m it dominates the Hauran Plain in **Syria** and the Galilee valley in Israel; on the Lebanese side, it overlooks the Anti-Lebanon Mountain range and Mount Hermon. Its fortress character is strengthened by mountainous terrain which the Syrians, after the creation of the state of Israel, would dot with bunkers, trenches and artillery deadly to the Israeli lines situated beneath them. Furthermore, the Golan is an important source of fresh **water**: the eastern tributaries of Lake Tiberias and the Upper Jordan rise in the Golan, supplying Israel with nearly 300 million square metres of water.

It was these strategic and natural assets that Israel coveted when on 9 June 1967, once the battles had ceased on the Egyptian and Jordanian fronts, the Israeli Defence Forces (IDF) attacked the Golan, which fell in two days. The area occupied increased by 510 sq. km at the end of the **1973 War**. This lasted until 31 May 1974, when the Syrian–Israeli withdrawal agreement, brought about by the **US** Secretary of State Henry Kissinger, allowed Syria to regain the area invaded during the Yom Kippur War and a small part of the Golan, including Quneitra. But the problem of the plateau remained, coupled with that of refugees, numbering 110,000 in 1967.

Once in the Golan, Israel intended to remain. The installations inherited from the Syrian army were augmented. **Settlements** multiplied (50 were constructed between 1967 and 1988). The occupiers – numbering 17,000 in 2002, in 33 settlements – took control of rich soil and water resources. The 15,000 **Druze** inhabitants who had remained after the exodus of the Six Day War had to resist Tel Aviv's wish to impose on them Israeli citizenship and laws. Unrest, already rife in the spring of 1981, was exacerbated when, on 14 December 1981 – one day after General Jaruzelski's coup d'état in Poland – **Menachem Begin** made the *de facto* annexation official by obtaining from the Knesset a vote 'applying Israeli law to the Golan Heights'. The affiliation of the Golan to Eretz ('Greater') Israel, the protection of Jewish settlers, and Damascus's refusal to negotiate were insufficient to justify the Israeli decision; it was declared 'null and void' by the UN General Assembly on 17 December 1981 in a vote that was unanimous apart from two voices (Israel and the US).

On 1 September 1975, US President Gerald Ford had declared in a letter addressed to **Yitzhak Rabin** that the US had not adopted a definitive position concerning the border between Israel and Syria. 'If it is possible, the United States will accord great weight to the Israeli position that peace with the Syrians should be on terms that allow Israel to remain in the Golan Heights.' In principle, this position was binding over Ford's successors at the White House.

The Golan lies at the heart of Israeli–Syrian negotiations, which intensified after the Madrid Conference and **Oslo Accords**. For Syria, the territory must be returned, and no compromise is possible over the sovereignty of the plateau. For Israel, strategic considerations combine with the attraction of conserving a zone rich in water and the electoral weight of numerous settlers, largely supporters of the Labour party. But the task of drawing a definitive frontier between Israel and Syria faces another difficulty – the demilitarised zone of 1949–50, which Damascus refuses to cede, demanding a return to the 4 June 1967 borders. Israel hoped to hold to the 1923 border; but between the two lines there would be a 'small' strip of barely 20 sq. km, which would give access to Lake Tiberias and the upper Jordan valley.

In 1992, Prime Minister Rabin accepted the principle of withdrawal from the Golan Heights. But President **Assad** requested a clarification: how far would the Israeli withdrawal extend? He obtained clarification a year later, as Uri Savir, one of the Israeli negotiators, explained that after having spoken 'with Rabin in May 1994, US Secretary of State Warren Christopher had explained to the Syrians that, according to the US, as long as all its needs were satisfied, Israel would be prepared to effect a total withdrawal, which would mean withdrawal to the 4 June 1967' border. The assassination of Rabin, plus the victory of the Right in 1996, put a freeze on negotiations.

When Ehud Barak was elected in May 1999, he decided to resume negotiations with Syria. Talks resumed in Washington. Israel insisted that, in addition to the question of borders, three other outstanding issues should be resolved: water (the Golan Heights represent one third of Israel's water reserves, and Israel was concerned that the flow should not be interrupted); security (an accord of May 1995 fixed the broad principles); normalisation (the two countries agreed to exchange ambassadors and open frontiers). The only real difficulty remained the question of where exactly the border was to be established. In line with Rabin's commitment Damascus insisted that the Israeli army should withdraw to its positions of 4 June 1967. In December 1999, at a point where Washington thought that agreement was within reach, Barak informed the US that, given the domestic situation, he could not sign an agreement involving a return to the June 1967 borders. As a result, a historic opportunity was lost. Following the outbreak of the **second Intifada**, attention has focused on the **West Bank** and Gaza; Syria complains that the 'Road Map' marginalises the importance of the return of the Golan. With the new Syrian President, Bashar al-Assad, unable to concede more ground than his father, a settlement over the Golan now looks impossible before Israel reaches an agreement with the **Palestinians**.

GREAT BRITAIN

For a long time Britain was the most influential Western power in the Middle East. The attraction of the region for Britain was based on economic, political and, above all, strategic considerations. In the age of empire, the region's land and sea routes (including, from the end of the nineteenth century, the **Suez Canal**) constituted a vital lifeline between London and India in particular. From 1800 onwards, British strategy sought to create what Fernand

L'Huilier has described as a 'zone of security to shelter the main routes to India' from first the **Ottoman Empire**, then, after its dismembering, from Palestine and its neighbours.

Britain established itself in the Middle East in the nineteenth century when it seized or imposed treaties on in succession Malta (1815), the 'Pirate Coast' and the emirates of the Gulf (1820), **Egypt** (1882) and the **Sudan** (1898). During the same period, it took over the Suez Canal Company (1875) and secured the protectorates of the south coast of Arabia (1886–1914). In Persia, a shared sphere of influence was negotiated with **Russia** (1907); following the Anglo–Persian Oil Company's acquisition of the first **oil** concession, extraction began in 1910.

From its position of strength, the British Empire was able to grab the largest slice of the Ottoman cake at the end of the First World War when the Germans and their Turkish allies were defeated. In accordance with the **Sykes–Picot Agreement**, the territories allocated to British administration, either directly or indirectly, comprised modern **Iran**, **Iraq** and **Jordan**, the ports of Haifa and Acre in Palestine as well as a Mandate for Palestine, to which must be added British possessions in Egypt, Sudan, the **Arabian Peninsula** and the Gulf.

But this extraordinary expansion was based on contradictory promises that London would find difficult to put into practice. 'Better to win and perjure oneself than to lose,' said **T.E. Lawrence** (Lawrence of Arabia). Once victory was achieved in the war, decisions had to be made. Britain had promised **Syria** and **Lebanon** to the French; it held to this agreement. But to the **Arabs**, to ensure their participation in the war against the Ottoman Empire, it had claimed it would 'recognize and support Arab independence'. This promise, given to both the Wahhabi Ibn Saud and the Hashemite **Hussein**, was not respected – neither in the case of Syria nor Lebanon, to whom Paris would refuse any real **independence** until 1941, nor in Palestine, where London had promised **Zionist** leaders to promote the creation of the 'Jewish national homeland' envisaged in 1917 by the **Balfour Declaration**, nor even in the other territories under British influence, whose leaders were to see their dream of a great independent Arab state fade away. Under cover of the Mandate – aimed, as a French high commissioner declared, 'at allowing populations who, in political terms, are still minors, to educate themselves so as to attain self-government one day' – the British government did its utmost to avert the mounting wave of Arab nationalism.

Roughly speaking, this policy worked, by different means in different countries, until the Second World War. In Iraq, faced with a powerful nationalist movement, Britain had to grant independence in 1930 – but meanwhile retained its economic, political and military influence. Jordan remained an emirate constitutionally linked to Britain. In Egypt, the game of chess played out between the King and the Wafd party guaranteed Britain the continuation of its interests, particularly in the Canal Zone – and this despite a formally recognised independence. In the Arabian Peninsula and the Gulf, British predominance remained undisputed, even if the **US**, through its oil concessions, was beginning to gain a footing in the region (particularly in **Saudi Arabia**).

The situation was more complex in Palestine, where Britain had to face both a Zionist movement that insisted the Balfour Agreement be honoured (a promise included in the text of its Mandate), and an Arab nationalist movement which opposed the influx of Jewish immigrants. The Palestinian revolt took the form of increasingly long and violent uprisings which the British authorities, while brutally suppressing, had to take into account. Hence the successive White Papers of 1922 and 1930, which modified, though only verbally, the promises given to the Zionist Executive, and in particular the White Paper of 1939, which drastically reduced Jewish **immigration** and land purchase. But this tardy revision was not enough to spare London from paying dearly for its double game.

From being a pawn of British power, Palestine became, in effect, after the Second World War the catalyst of its decline. Buffeted by the **terrorism** of extremist Zionist groups, Arab demands and the pressure of world opinion stunned by the Holocaust, Britain had to turn to the UN (see **Partition Plan**). The partition of Palestine was no sooner decided than London set out to sabotage it, but in vain. The state of **Israel** unilaterally declared its own independence on 14 May 1948, and the Arab states' military action against the new state, launched on the next day, failed. This humiliation was promptly turned against the instigator of the conflict; henceforth Britain would be the prime target of the Arab national movement, in whose eyes it was responsible for the Palestinian tragedy. Neither attempts to hide behind the cloak of pan-Arabism nor efforts to seek the support of regimes it controlled would spare it the bitter setbacks brought by the 1950s: the nationalisation of the Anglo–Iranian Oil Company by Mosaddeq in Iran (1951), the nationalisation of the Suez Canal (1956), revolution in Iraq (1958) etc.

The final straws for the British authorities – the Suez fiasco of 1956 and the withdrawal from Aden and the Gulf after 1967 – brought to an end more than a century and a half of predominance in the Near and Middle East. A victim of the Zionist movement, on which it had thought it could count, and of the Arab national movement, which, like Lawrence, it had hoped to coax into its camp, London had to bear the cost of competition – not from **France**, which was also being ousted from the region, but from the US; the latter's rise in power would be in inverse proportion to Britain's decline.

Over thirty years after the completion of British military withdrawal from 'East of Suez', Britain plays little more than a marginal role in the politics of the Middle East. Yet it retains a strong economic interest in the region, which has been highlighted most clearly by its arms sales. Between 1991 and 1993 London made $10.3bn in arms exports to the region, compared with $13.9bn for the US, $1.4bn for France and $1.1bn for Germany.

Like other countries, Britain has been shaken by scandals linked to the sale of arms, notably 'Iraqgate', which tarnished the reputations of Prime Ministers Margaret Thatcher and John Major, as well as several of their ministers. In spite of the arms embargo on Iraq and Iran declared by the UN in 1985, two British companies exported armament components (including items used in the manufacture of nuclear weapons) worth millions of pounds to Iraq between 1988 and 1990. One of them even allowed the Iraqi army to increase the range of its Scud missiles. However, when the Scott Report on this matter was finally published on 15 February 1996 it largely cleared the British government of any serious culpability in 'illegal' arms sales.

Far from reducing London's alignment with Washington policy, the election of 'New Labour' Prime Minister Tony Blair in 1997 accentuated it. The British joined with the Americans in defending the international order that they had contributed to founding. Thus Britain associated itself with the US in the December 1998 raids on Iraq and the subsequent bombings, and in the intransigence with which the two countries opposed Security Council calls for the embargo against Baghdad to be lifted. The 11 September 2001 attacks merely strengthened these links – George W. Bush himself, addressing the US Congress, said that 'America has no truer friend than Great Britain'. Blair risked the loss of considerable political support by supporting the US-led war in Iraq in 2003, a decision which was immensely unpopular with the British public.

Indeed London was at pains to provide military aid as well as the assistance of its intelligence services in the US intervention in Afghanistan. But Tony Blair was worried that he would also have to conduct a struggle against terrorism within the UK, a traditional place of residence for many **Islamist** militants and a source of finance for various of their organisations, some of which were now suspected of having links to **Osama bin Laden**'s network. As a result of British backing for the US in a unilateral war against Iraq, 'Londonistan' might have become one of the fronts of that war. That worry did not stop Tony Blair from offering his whole-hearted support to the Bush initiative in Iraq. The Prime Minister suffered considerably as a result, and his discomfort only increased with the apparent suicide of David Kelly, the arms inspector who spoke too candidly to the BBC about the manipulation of information in the official government dossier about Iraq's **weapons of mass destruction**. Paradoxically, the alignment with Bush over Iraq has not prevented Blair's government from openly criticising the policies of **Ariel Sharon** and firmly defending the perspective of an independent and viable Palestinian state.

GULF WAR 1990–91

Strictly speaking, the Gulf crisis began on 2 August 1990, when Iraqi troops entered **Kuwait**, seized the capital and installed a puppet government. From 17 January to 3 March 1991 the crisis developed into a war.

But the tension between Baghdad and its neighbours in the Gulf had been mounting for weeks before that. On 17 July **Saddam Hussein** accused 'certain' Gulf leaders of ganging up on **Iraq** by lowering the price of crude **oil**. The following day, in a speech to the **Arab League** in which he detailed his grievances, he went on to say that since 1980 Kuwait had been 'stealing' Iraqi oil by drilling in the Rumaila field and that Kuwait owed Iraq $2.4bn in compensation. On 27 July, OPEC set the base price of a barrel of oil at $21 and imposed a maximum limit on production in order to stabilise this price. On 31 July the Kuwaitis offered in Jeddah to lend Iraq $9bn and the Saudis added an extra billion to meet the $10bn demanded by the Iraqis. These, however, were hollow gestures, given that the number of Iraqi soldiers amassed on the Kuwaiti border rose from 30,000 on 23 July to 100,000 on 31 July.

The invasion of Kuwait was part of the strategy of the **Ba'thist** regime after its defeat in the war with **Iran**. After eight years of conflict, the country was exhausted. The few 'spoils of war' – a few hundred square kilometres of occupied land and several tens of thousands of prisoners – had cost Iraq hundreds of thousands of lives, destruction amounting to $70bn and a foreign debt that exceeded $80bn, its highest ever figures.

It was this situation that led Saddam, in the face of growing social unrest, to take his Kuwaiti gamble. The Iraqi leader had three objectives.

The first was economic: he wanted to hold the 'Bank of the Middle East' to ransom. Kuwait had invested $122bn of capital in the West, which earned $9bn in interest in 1989 – more than the revenue from oil. Saddam obviously did not anticipate that the West would freeze Kuwaiti assets, leaving the invaders with only the cash that remained in Kuwait's treasury.

The second was oil: Iraq wanted to add Kuwait's oil wealth to its own and take control of 19 per cent of the world's oil reserves and the benefits that they would bring, as well as to have an impact on OPEC policy. Again, he did not reckon on the Western embargo and the fact that Iraqi and Kuwaiti oil production would be replaced by other OPEC members, particularly **Saudi Arabia**.

The third was strategic: apart from the economic situation, Iraq was seeking greater access to the Gulf. The control of the islands of Warba and Bubian would afford Iraq a proper naval port and the chance to exploit the Shatt al-Basra as an alternative to the Shatt al-Arab, which had been destroyed during the war with Iran. Perhaps this is what April Glaspie, the **US** ambassador to Baghdad, was referring to when she later said in an interview in the *New York Times*, 'like everyone else, I didn't think that Iraq would take the whole of Kuwait'.

These three objectives were all part of the grand vision that the Iraqi leader had long expressed. With **Egypt** discredited after signing a peace agreement with **Israel**, and with Iraq's traditional rival, **Syria**, bogged down by events in **Lebanon**, Saddam wanted to assume the leadership of a divided **Arab world**. By embarking on this new venture, however, he made the same grave mistake that he had made in 1980: he under-estimated the opposition. He undoubtedly misinterpreted the extent of the change in Soviet policy in the Middle East. Perhaps he was counting on the US to remain neutral, as, it is true, America had not been exactly reluctant to support Iraq during the war with Iran, and because, on 25 July 1990, Glaspie had told him, 'we have no opinion about inter-Arab conflicts, such as your border dispute with Kuwait'. Saddam interpreted this as a green light. When he realised his mistake, it was already too late: Kuwait was too important to US strategic interests for it to remain neutral following its invasion.

The US was trying to re-establish itself as world leader. The Gulf provided a perfect opportunity to consolidate American power. Its energy reserves were crucial: 65 per cent of the planet's oil reserves are concentrated in the Gulf. It is economically significant because the Arab market offers huge opportunities for the American economy, just as petrodollars throw it a lifeline. It has political and military significance: the US has always dreamed of bringing the moderate Arab regimes and, if possible, Israel into a strategic alliance, a sort of NATO for the Middle East. It hoped that the reaction to the Iraqi aggression against Kuwait, a consensus buttressed by the invocation of international law and the support of the UN, might finally establish an environment where such a dream might be realised.

The shock of the American and Iraqi strategies, simultaneously opposed yet somehow complicit with one another, led to an irreversible situation. This was especially so because the forces that would have normally inter-vened could not or would not become involved. Due to its economic and social crisis, the USSR was increasingly dependent on Western aid, which prevented the Kremlin from openly opposing American policy. Indeed, despite the internal debates and some reservation, Moscow stuck to the agreement reached between George Bush Senior and Mikhail Gorbachev in Helsinki on 9 September 1990, while it did its utmost to make Saddam see reason and avoid the worst. For Beijing the crisis was a perfect opportunity to erase the memories of Tiananmen Square and to restore relations with the West; China sought refuge in a UN abstention on the issue. Europe, involved as the immediate neighbour of the Arab world, once again proved its irrelevance in issues where America was involved. Torn between **Britain**'s commitment to going ahead to the bitter end and Germany's introspective focus on unification, Europe proved incapable of deciding upon a common policy or initiating the necessary mediation.

Thus in a short period of time, the conditions for the escalation of the crisis were in place. Both Bush and Saddam (at least not until he realised he had lost) were aware that their publics would see the slightest concession as capitulation, which was incompatible with the type of leadership they embodied. The crisis was then divided into four stages: reaction, mobilisation, hesitation and, finally, war.

Although events had taken them by surprise, the Americans reacted swiftly. They rallied their allies in New York to organise the protest of the UN against the invasion of the emirate. On 2 August the Security Council passed Resolution 660 by 14 votes and one abstention (**Yemen**). It demanded 'the immediate and unconditional withdrawal of all Iraqi forces'. The US, then Britain and **France**, immediately froze all Iraqi and Kuwaiti assets on the international financial markets. On 3 August the Ministerial Council of the Arab League declared that it 'rejects the effects of this invasion and refuses to recognize its consequences, and calls on Iraq to effect an immediate and unconditional withdrawal of its troops'. The declaration was passed by a majority vote, with the **Palestine Liberation Organisation (PLO)**, **Jordan**, Yemen and **Sudan** voting against the motion, Mauritania abstaining, **Libya** absent and Iraq excluded.

While this was happening, the military build-up was taking shape. On 8 August, while Saddam was announcing the annexation of Kuwait, Bush was informing his people of the decision taken on 5 August to send tens of thousands of American troops into the region, supported by warplanes and tanks. In Saudi Arabia, Operation Desert Shield began.

The meticulous preparation of the political and military machine, drawn up in the White House, was in response to Saddam's excesses (such as the call to *jihad*, the taking of Western hostages, the proclamation of Kuwait as the nineteenth province of Iraq, attacks against embassies in Kuwait etc.). In the UN, American diplomacy had amassed a glut of Security Council resolutions: boycott (6 August), the illegality of the annexation (9 August), the release of hostages (18 August), the naval blockade (25 August), conditions for the provision of food and medical supplies to Iraq (14 September), and finally the use of force (29 November). In the West, Washington rallied significant support, not only in enforcing the embargo, but also in the deployment of armed forces in the area. Britain was first to send its troops, followed by Canada, France (on 15 September, after the attack on the embassy in Kuwait City) and Italy. On 10 August, 12 out of the 20 Arab leaders agreed to send a pan-Arab task force into Saudi Arabia. Iraq, Libya and the PLO voted against, Algeria and Yemen abstained, Jordan, Sudan and Mauritania expressed reservations, while Tunisia did not attend the vote. This vast coalition led to the formation of a powerful multinational army in Saudi Arabia. When the war broke out, Iraq was confronted by more than 700,000 men from 26 countries (of whom 515,000 were American). Finally, by 15 January, the American leaders had secured more than $40bn to finance Desert Shield, thanks to the donations of their Western and Arab allies.

The third phase, hesitation, began on 29 November, when the Security Council adopted Resolution 678. It was unanimously passed (with the exceptions of Yemen and Cuba, and the abstention of China) and authorised 'the member States co-operating with the Kuwaiti government…to use any means necessary to force Iraq to withdraw from Kuwait, if it has not already done so by 15 January 1991'. In a move that was designed as much to reassure public opinion as it was to give him time to put the final touches to the military build-up, George Bush, now armed with Resolution 678, invited Baghdad to enter into a 'dialogue'. Yet the meeting between James Baker and Tariq Aziz in Geneva on 9 January failed. From then on there was nothing to stop the Gulf crisis developing into the Gulf War.

Twenty-four hours after the UN ultimatum had expired, it was the turn of the weapons to speak. From 17 to 23 February, Iraq's military and economic targets and its troops in Kuwait were on the receiving end of a formidable aerial bombardment. In response, Saddam's army fired a number of Scud missiles at Israel, Saudi Arabia and Bahrain, and set the Kuwaiti oil wells alight.

On the night of 23 February, Allied forces penetrated Iraq and Kuwait. Six months later, it was revealed that Iraqi soldiers had been buried alive on the front lines. The resistance was so weak that within three days the Allied forces had occupied the whole of the emirate and had reached as far as Basra in Iraq. On 26 February, Saddam announced the withdrawal of Iraqi troops over the radio, and the following day, Aziz told the UN that he unconditionally accepted the 12 Security Council resolutions. The last of the fighting died out on 28 February. It was not until 27 March that Baghdad gave its agreement to the definitive ceasefire as laid out in Resolution 687, in which the Security Council imposed a number of conditions on Baghdad: the recognition of Kuwait within its 1963 borders, payment of war damages, the destruction of its chemical and biological arsenal, and the extension of the embargo on arms sales.

Meanwhile, the Republican Guard, which had been allowed to return home from Kuwait by the West, crushed the popular uprisings in the north and south of the country which began when word spread that the regime had been defeated. The Western armies, who stood by and watched as the **Shi'ite** revolts ended in massacres – under the pretext of avoiding an Islamic revolution – finally intervened so that the Kurdish refugees could return to their homes.

Those who believed in a 'legal crusade' or a 'new world order' were left disillusioned. The dictatorship of Saddam Hussein survived. More than that:

he once again stamped his ruthless authority on the Kurdish and Shi'ite populations.

The main victim of the Gulf War was Iraq. Operation Desert Storm cost its people dear. An estimated 50,000–150,000 Iraqis were killed, compared with 466 Allied servicemen. The infrastructure was almost completely destroyed, fulfilling Baker's warning to Aziz that Iraq would be 'bombed into the Stone Age'. An embargo lasting for over ten years effectively destroyed the country.

The only country to profit from the Gulf War was the US. Not only did it regain its control over the oil reserves in the region, emphasising its political hold on the Arab regimes, but it also used its 'triumph' to drive out its Western competitors from many Middle Eastern markets, whether military, which had just seen an impressive demonstration of cruise missiles, such as the Tomahawk, and the Patriot (despite its apparently limited effectiveness), or civilian, with the huge reconstruction contracts that were out to tender. Conversely, Washington's local allies also received favours: Egypt's participation in the coalition earned it forgiveness of its military debt ($6.7bn) and the extension of its civil debt. Syria, under **Hafez al-Assad**, was allowed a free hand in Lebanon. **Turkey**, its reputation as a pillar of NATO intact, made a small advance in its aspirations in Europe and the Middle East. Iran was to win on two levels: it retrieved the land that Iraq had occupied, and its prisoners were released, while the Algiers Accords of 1975 were revived. In fact it seemed that Iran had become a respectable partner of Washington – for a time at least.

HABASH, GEORGE

Born on 2 August 1926 in Lydda in Palestine, George Habash came from a family of Greek Orthodox merchants who were driven out from their home town in July 1948, during the **1948–49 War**. Habash settled in Beirut where he studied pediatrics at the American University, qualifying as a doctor in 1951. Already very active politically, in 1952 he founded the Arab Nationalist Movement (ANM), an organisation to which he was to devote all his energy in the coming years. The ANM's aim was defined as follows: 'As long as no united state exists, unifying **Iraq**, **Jordan** and **Syria** [as a first step], any confrontation with the **Jews** and the Western alliance will be virtually impossible'.

Habash at first led the movement from Amman, where, also in 1952, he opened a people's clinic. After his arrest in 1957, he took refuge in Damascus at the time of the formation of the United Arab Republic of **Egypt** and Syria. A convert to Nasserism, together with the ANM he evolved theories dissimilar to those of Fatah. According to the ANM, what was essential for the liberation of Palestine was not the mobilisation of the **Palestinians** themselves, but the intervention of Arab countries against **Israel**. The role of Palestinians would be confined to that of a 'catalyst'. In 1964, the ANM created a Palestinian section which operated out of Beirut, where Habash had by then settled. The section carried out its first armed operation in 1966.

The **1967 War**, which dealt a serious blow to **Nasser**'s prestige, devastated the ANM. It disappeared, dragged down by the wreck of the idea of Arab unity personified by the Egyptian President. The Movement did, however, give birth to various regional offshoots, the most famous of which were the South **Yemen** branch, which seized power at the end of 1967, and the Popular Front for the Liberation of Palestine (PFLP), led by Habash himself.

The PFLP established itself in Jordan with the other *fedayeen* organisations. It was extremely militant in the field, and attracted international attention by its hijacking of aircraft, the first of which involved, on 23 July 1968, an El Al plane. Weakened in February 1969 by a split instigated by **Nayef Hawatmeh**, the PFLP nonetheless continued to play a subversive role within Jordan, where it called for the overthrow of the regime. 'The liberation of Palestine will come through Amman,' it trumpeted, dragging the **Palestine Liberation Organisation (PLO)** into the confrontation of September 1970 (**Black September**), which saw the elimination of the resistance in Jordan.

After this serious defeat, the PFLP changed direction. In 1972, it renounced external operations, preferring to concentrate its attacks on Israel, but without establishing any distinction between military and civilian targets. It adopted Marxism-Leninism as its theory, and split with its more extreme elements, like Dr Wadih Haddad. Nevertheless, it remained at the heart of the opposition to new orientations within the PLO. Habash condemned the idea of a mini-state made up of the **West Bank** and Gaza; he was opposed to the holding of the Geneva Conference and to **Yasser Arafat**'s visit to the UN, and he violently criticised the USSR, guilty in his eyes of setting the PLO on the path to surrender. His only ally on the international scene at this time was Iraq.

After the signing of the **Camp David Accords**, Palestinian solidarity was re-established, but the PFLP, which had left the PLO Executive Committee in 1974, did not rejoin it until 1981. Having undergone a major brain operation at the end of 1980, Habash remained on the sidelines for many months. Differences between the PFLP and Fatah, however, remained critical, and came to a head after 1982. Habash once again found himself at the centre of an anti-Arafat coalition, the Palestine National Salvation Front, in which the dissidents of Fatah, al-Sa'iqa and the PFLP-General Command of Ahmed Jibril also took part. But, unlike these groups, Habash did not refuse to take part in the Algiers Palestine National Council (PNC) of April 1987– after which he rejoined the executive organs of the PLO – and those in November 1988 and September 1991. Although he rejected some of the decisions made in this last Council – in particular the acceptance of Resolution 242 – he claimed to be in favour of maintaining Palestinian solidarity.

The **Oslo Accords** wrong-footed Habash and the PFLP. Along with leftist Palestinian and Islamic groups, the organisation sought to create a united front of opposition, but did not meet with any real success. In the West Bank and Gaza, the PFLP saw its influence evaporate; many activists, even those opposed to Oslo, saw no benefit in a toothless opposition. Some went so far as to participate in the elections on 20 January 1996. The PFLP attended the PNC meeting in Gaza in April 1996. It took issue with the number of seats allocated to the PFLP, and its representatives boycotted the session which abrogated the Palestinian National Charter of 1968.

In 1998, adopting a pragmatic point of view and believing that the Oslo Accords had become an established fact, he responded positively to an offer of dialogue with the **Palestinian Authority** on the eve of what was scheduled to be the conclusion of **final status negotiations** for the Palestinian territories. The Palestinian Authority and the domestic opposition arrived at agreement on the 'Palestinian constants': the creation of an independent Palestinian state with **Jerusalem** as its capital; the dismantling of Israeli **settlements**; the return of refugees to their homes; the reactivation of the PLO 'as the framework of Palestinian political action'. Israel accepted the return of the PFLP and its personnel on condition that they renounced the armed struggle.

In July 2000, Mustafa al-Sibri, alias Ali Abu Mustafa, succeeded Habash as Secretary-General of the organisation. One year later, in August 2001, the new head of the PFLP became a victim of Israel's assassination policy. The organisation, which up until then had been relatively inactive in the **second Intifada**, embarked on a series of reprisals which included several bombings and the assassination in October of Rehavam Zeevi, the Israeli Minister of Tourism, who had called publicly for the transfer of Palestinians. The new head of the PFLP, Ahmed Saadat, representing the most radical wing of the movement, was arrested by the Palestinian Authority in January 2002.

An uncompromising leader, Habash still commands respect within the PLO, among both friends and enemies. He has been able, whatever his alliances with Arab regimes, notably Damascus, to preserve the independence of the PFLP, and retains influence in the refugee camps of **Lebanon**, Jordan and Syria.

HAMAS

The Movement of Islamic Resistance (the initials spell 'Hamas' in Arabic, meaning 'zeal') was created by the Society of **Muslim Brothers** shortly after the launching of the first **Intifada**. Up until that point, the Society's activities had involved it principally in social and religious activities, but its leaders – notably Sheikh Ahmed Yassin, who was to become the organisation's spiritual leader – decided that it was no longer possible to sit on the sidelines. Hamas developed first in Gaza, which was to remain its principal power base, and then extended its activities to the **West Bank**.

The Muslim Brotherhood has a long history in Palestine, which is linked to the development of the organisation in **Egypt**. In 1935, Abdul Rahman al-Banna, brother of the movement's founder, went to Palestine for the first time, where he met Hajj Amin al-Husseini, the Mufti of **Jerusalem**. Members of the Egyptian Muslim Brothers played a part in the great Palestinian revolt in 1936. In 1945, Said Ramadan created the first branch of the movement in Jerusalem; two years later, there were 25 branches, with a total membership of between 12,000 and 20,000. During the **1948–49 War** several hundred of the Arab volunteers involved in the fighting were members of the Muslim Brotherhood.

The Arab defeat was a serious setback for the organisation. In the West Bank and **Jordan** it was granted recognition by the Hashemite regime, which used it as a tool in its fight against **Nasser** and the Arab nationalists. In Gaza it laboured under the weight of Nasserite repression after 1954, but was able to regain influence during the **1956 War** by virtue of its stance against the Israeli army.

The occupation of the West Bank and Gaza by **Israel** in 1967 opened a new phase. In the mid-1970s, the movement reorganised itself and assumed the title of the Society of Muslim Brothers in Jordan and Palestine. As elsewhere in the **Arab world**, **Islam** was becoming a growing force. In the Occupied Territories, the Society built a tight-knit network of social institutions around the mosques, consisting of kindergartens, libraries, clinics, sports clubs etc. Between 1967 and 1987, the number of mosques in the West Bank rose from 400 to 750, and from 200 to 600 in Gaza. The Gaza Islamic Centre, set up in 1973 and led by Sheikh Ahmed Yassin, was to become the Society's organisational centre. The movement received considerable support from overseas, with **Saudi Arabia** proving particularly generous. Whereas Fatah used its resources to buy itself a clientele among the notables, the Muslim Brotherhood concentrated on helping the poorest sections of the population.

However, despite their substantial means and resources, the Muslim Brothers suffered throughout the 1970s and 1980s from their inactivity in relation to the occupation. While their final objective remained the liberation of Palestine, their activities prioritised social reform – hence their relative inertia in the nationalist struggle. The Israeli secret services understood this, and therefore adopted a low-key approach to the Brotherhood, which was seen as a useful counterweight to the **Palestine Liberation Organisation (PLO)**. In 1980, the movement underwent a split. Islamic Jihad accused the Muslim Brothers of excessive passivity, and quickly embarked on a path of violent action. Several of its key members were to be killed by the Israeli secret services, in particular the movement's founder and leader, Fathi al-Shaqaqi, who was killed in Nicosia on 26 October 1995.

The decision to create the Hamas movement and to take part in the Intifada testifies to a significant development within the Muslim Brotherhood, with the younger militants taking a greater share of responsibilities. Hamas was to come out very actively during the 'revolt of the stone-throwers', maintaining a deliberate distance from the unified leadership, which was identified with the PLO. The movement was very well organised, identified itself with the least privileged in society, and had a religious aura. It was a serious competitor to Fatah and the PLO. It created a military wing, the Izzedin al-Qassam Brigades, whose actions were to develop in parallel with the Israeli repression.

Yitzhak Rabin's December 1992 decision to expel 415 Islamic militants to **Lebanon** served only to increase the organisation's popularity. On 18 August 1988 it had adopted a charter, in which it stated that the soil of Palestine was a religious property (*waqf*), which could be neither negotiated nor ceded – but already certain of its leaders were formulating more moderate theses and were beginning to think in terms of compromise with Israel. Finally, despite rivalry, and occasional confrontations, Hamas 'sees the PLO as the organization most close to its positions, like a father, a brother, a close relation or a friend'. It is worth noting that it is basically at the political rather than the religious level that Hamas opposes the PLO.

Hamas took up a position against the Madrid Conference, and subsequently against the **Oslo Accords**. However, the installation of the **Palestinian Authority** in Gaza posed a new challenge to the organisation, caught as it was between its rhetoric of calling for the total liberation of Palestine, its desire not to provoke a civil war between **Palestinians**, and its determination to keep its organisational network intact. While the Hebron massacre in February 1994 was creating the political conditions for the first suicide bombings, the Hamas leadership was beginning a dialogue with **Yasser Arafat**. Arafat adopted a carrot-and-stick approach to the organisation, ordering arrests and intimidations while at the same time maintaining dialogue with it and authorising certain of its press organs. At the end of 1995 he even appeared to be on the point of obtaining the movement's participation in the elections of January 1996. But in the event negotiations broke down, even though Imad Faluji, a member of the Hamas leadership, agreed to stand as a candidate in the Fatah electoral list in a personal capacity – he was subsequently to become a member of the government set up after the elections.

The series of suicide bombings in Israel in February and March 1996 – which were presented as revenge for Yahya Ayash, who had been executed on 5 January – brought dialogue with the Palestinian Authority to an end. The Israeli government demanded and obtained from Arafat a crackdown on Hamas and Islamic Jihad, the arrest of their main leaderships and the dismantling of a large part of their organisational networks. In addition, the sealing of the Autonomous Territories, imposed by the Israeli army in response to **terrorist** operations, deprived tens of thousands of Palestinian workers of work. The effect of this was to alienate a substantial part of the population from the movement. Aware of these constraints, some Hamas leaders such as Dr Mahmoud al-Zahar called for an end to the armed struggle and for the transformation of the organisation into a political party. Others, particularly those outside the country such as Ibrahim Ghosheh, rejected this strategy.

This split between pragmatists and radicals combined with the repression conducted by the Palestinian Authority to weaken the movement. In September 1997 the Palestinian police closed 16 offices and associations linked to Hamas. In Jordan Mossad tried to assassinate Khaled Mishaal, the head of the Hamas's political bureau in exile. The clandestine military wing was weakened by the co-operation between the Palestinian police, the CIA and the Israeli secret services. But the movement remained popular, and Sheikh Yassin, was welcomed triumphantly in Gaza on 6 October 1997 when he was released from prison by Israel.

The launching of the **second Intifada**, in September 2000, lessened the weight of internal differences within the movement, as well as differences with Fatah. The suicide bombings in Israel launched by Hamas in spring 2001 enjoyed broad support among Palestinians and strengthened the movement. In reprisal, Israel embarked on a policy of targeted assassination of militants involved in these actions. The main military leaders have been assassinated, and a vicious circle of bombings followed by reprisals has ensued. Negotiations in autumn 2002 between Hamas and Fatah to stop bombings within Israel's 1967 borders came to nothing, but newly appointed Palestinian Authority Prime Minister Mahmoud Abbas was successful in brokering a three-month ceasefire agreed by Hamas, Islamic Jihad and Fatah in June 2003. Seven weeks into that ceasefire, the Israeli army resumed its targeting of senior Hamas leadership. Hamas announced an end to the ceasefire on 21 August 2003 when Israeli helicopters killed its third-most-senior leader, Ismail Abu Shanab.

The movement is led by a Consultative Council (Majlis al-Shura), whose best-known members in the West Bank and Gaza are Sheikh Yassin, Dr Abd al-Aziz Rantissi and Dr Mahmoud al-Zahar. Ibrahim Ghosheh, Muhammad Nazzal and Dr Muhammad Abu Marzouk are the best-known figures outside the Occupied Territories.

HARIRI, RAFIQ

Rafiq Hariri, a Sunni Muslim, was born in Sidon in southern **Lebanon** in 1944. He went on to become the richest man in the country, and was appointed Prime Minister in October 1992, in the wake of the Taif agreements. Having studied at the Arab University in Beirut, he emigrated to **Saudi Arabia** in 1966, where he taught mathematics. Four years later he set up his own construction company. Thanks to solid connections which he forged with the Saudi royal family (see **Saud dynasty**), his business developed, notably in **France**, and while still resident in Saudi Arabia he began to take an interest in his country of origin. In 1983 he set up a foundation which bears his name and which funds overseas study for young Lebanese; he also supports a number of projects in the town of his birth. His business empire includes banks, insurance, building and computer companies.

Partly as a result of the close relationship which he enjoys with King Fahd, in the late 1980s he sought to involve himself in the negotiations which were to ratify the end of the civil war in Lebanon. He was present in Taif during the negotiations which created the new agreement, and it is suggested that the scale of his largesse helped in winning over some of the politicians. His business relations with the ruling circles in **Syria** obviously facilitated his role in the proceedings.

His nomination to the post of Prime Minister created a wave of popular expectation. People believed that he was the person to turn round the country's devastated economy and put it back on the road to prosperity. However, Hariri's credibility suffered from the overlap between his political and private interests, as well as from the uncertainties deriving from the diplomatic differences between Syria and **Israel**. The project for rebuilding Beirut's city centre, undertaken by Solidere, a company controlled by Hariri, has also been the target of criticism, both in architectural terms – as to whether it was really necessary to destroy the old city centre – and in terms of its cost.

After a falling out with the head of state, Émile Lahoud, over his nomination in 1998 (with some people suspecting a Syrian manoeuvre to sideline him), the billionaire returned to power in the national elections of 2000. This was strange voting behaviour by the Lebanese, who signalled their farewell to the government of Selim Hoss, condemning him for his inability to get the country out of an economic crisis which had begun, however, under the previous government led by Hariri. Determined to initiate a series of radical liberal reforms and privatisations, Hariri was also counting on international aid to get his country out of its economic predicament. As for relations with Syria, although Beirut continues to maintain good contacts with Damascus, the presence of 36,000 Syrian soldiers in Lebanon lost its legitimacy after the Israeli withdrawal from the south in spring 2000. Syria subsequently undertook a series of four partial redeployments of its troops in Lebanon, bringing its troops there down to an estimated 15–20,000.

HAWATMEH, NAYEF

Born on 17 November 1935 in Salt, on the East Bank of the Jordan, into a Greek Catholic peasant family, Nayef Hawatmeh began his higher education in Cairo in 1954 and, the same year, joined **George Habash**'s Arab National Movement (ANM). Back in **Jordan** in 1956, his revolutionary activities resulted in his being condemned to death *in absentia*. In 1958 he took part in the Lebanese Civil War (see **Lebanon**) and then took refuge in **Iraq**, where he directed the ANM section for five months. From 1963 to 1967 he was in South **Yemen**, where he played a part in the anti-British liberation struggle. After the Six Day **1967 War**, he took advantage of an armistice and returned to Jordan, where he joined the Popular Front for the Liberation of Palestine (PFLP). He became the head of the organisation's left-wing faction, which had Marxist-Leninist leanings and was critical of the Arab *petit bourgeoisie*. The split was finalised in February 1969, and Hawatmeh formed the Popular Democratic Front for the Liberation of Palestine (PDFLP), which became the Democratic Front for the Liberation of Palestine (DFLP) in August 1974.

The DFLP adopted the same adventurist attitude that had characterised the PFLP in Jordan in the period 1969–70, but the political differences between the two could not have been more marked. As early as 1969, at Hawatmeh's instigation, it denounced chauvinist slogans of the 'force the Jews into the sea' kind. In 1970, it opened a dialogue with the Israeli far-left organisation, Matzpen. Furthermore, from 1973 it became – along with Fatah and the communists – one of the most ardent defenders of the idea of a Palestinian mini-state. On 22 March 1974, Hawatmeh gave an interview to the Israeli newspaper *Yediot Aharonot* that aroused wide interest: 'I believe,' he said,

> that it would be a very good thing if Israeli society, with all its different components, became aware of a revolutionary Palestinian position regarding the Arab–Israeli conflict. I do not see why we must accept that Arab reactionary forces conduct a dialogue with Israel's most extreme tendencies while forbidding progressive forces from doing the same with progressive Israeli forces. Admittedly, such a dialogue would represent a threat both for Zionism and Arab reactionaries.

This frank, restrained language is not in contradiction, at least in the eyes of the DFLP, with ruthless armed operations, such as that undertaken at Maalot in May 1974, which left 16 Israelis dead, many of them schoolboys. The period 1974–77 witnessed a strengthening of the alliance between the DFLP and the socialist camp, as well as its adoption of most of the traditional communist analyses. On the Arab front, its main support was South Yemen, with which Hawatmeh had retained important contacts.

From 1977 the DFLP dissociated itself from Fatah, which it accused of making compromises with 'Arab reactionaries'. Hawatmeh nonetheless tried to maintain a middle ground between **Arafat** and the Rejection Front. A fervent defender of the Fez Plan of 1982, he nonetheless condemned the **Palestine Liberation Organisation's (PLO)** rapprochement with **Egypt** and Jordan. In favour of alliance with **Syria**, he disagreed with the PLO on numerous occasions, and refused to join the Palestine National Salvation Front (PNSF). In April 1987, at the Palestine National Council (PNC) in Algiers, he and Arafat were reconciled. A year later, in November 1988, he gave his approval to the new direction taken by the PLO: proclamation of the Palestinian state; acceptance of Resolution 242, a fundamental resolution to create a provisional government when the time was ripe. In 1991 he rejected the Madrid negotiations, and in 1994 and 1995 rejected the **Oslo Accords**. He took part in the ill-fated efforts to establish an opposition front uniting the Palestinian left and the **Islamists**. Realising his failure, he accepted that the DFLP play a role in the April 1996 Palestinian National Council meeting in Gaza which abrogated the 1968 National Charter.

Negotiations took place for the return of Hawatmeh to the Palestinian territories, but they came to nothing. The Front was also involved in the **second Intifada**, claiming its first commando operation against an Israeli military position in the summer of 2001.

HERZL, THEODOR

The founder of **Zionism**. Born in Budapest in 1860, Herzl settled with his family in Vienna at the age of 18. Having completed law studies and become an attorney, he turned his attention to literature and the theatre. At the age of 31 he separated from his wife and, scarred by the suicide of his best friend, left for **France**, where he was appointed correspondent for the *Neue Freie Presse*, a new Austrian daily. It was in Paris that he first encountered the shock of antisemitism, which resurfaced with the Dreyfus Affair.

Until that time, Herzl, like most West European Jewish intellectuals, believed the solution to the Jewish problem lay in the assimilation of his co-religionists into the populations among which they were living. The emancipation of the **Jews** and the recognition of their equal rights, initiated by the French Revolution, seemed to him an irreversible historical trend. Jacob Samuel, the main character of Herzl's play, written in 1894, *The New Ghetto*, dies crying, 'I want to come out of the ghetto'.

But the martyrdom of Captain Alfred Dreyfus – himself a believer in assimilation – and the wave of antisemitism that accompanied it, changed Herzl's outlook entirely. Already in 1882 his ideological predecessor, Leon Pinsker, had in his *Auto-emancipation* summed up the **Jew** in this striking portrait: 'seen by the living as dead, by the indigenous population as a foreigner, by the settled as a tramp, by the wealthy as a beggar, by the poor as an exploiter, by patriots as a stateless person, and by all classes of society as a competitor to be hated'. Taking as starting point the existence of a Jewish people and the impossibility of its assimilation, Herzl saw as the only solution the creation of a Jewish state – if possible in Palestine. This was the subject of his 1896 book *The Jewish State*, and the motive of the meetings he sought and obtained with the German Emperor, the Turkish Sultan, Pope Pius X, the King of Italy, and British and Russian ministers (including one who had organised pogroms).

To each of these people he emphasised the far-reaching significance of his project: for the British, the strategic role of a Jewish Palestine that would protect the 'lifeline' of the Empire; for the Germans and Russians the possibility of bringing to an end their 'Jewish problem'; and for the Turks a chance to reduce the **Ottoman Empire**'s enormous debt for the concession of Palestine. At Basel on 29 and 30 August 1897, Herzl's plan for a Jewish state was adopted by the first Jewish World Congress, organised by Herzl, who in turn became its president.

'At Basel,' he wrote in his journals, 'I created the Jewish state. If I said that publicly today, it would be met by general laughter. Perhaps in five years, certainly in fifty, everyone will understand.' Indeed, 50 years and nine months later, the state of **Israel** saw the light of day. But Herzl was not to know the outcome of his 'vision'; after fighting in vain for the foundation of his Jewish state – whether in Argentina, the Sinai or Mozambique – he died on 3 July 1904.

HEZBOLLAH

This Lebanese organisation was created in 1982, a crucial year in the history of a **Lebanon** which was being torn apart by the **Lebanese Civil War**. The 'Party of God' had its roots in the **Shi'ite** community, federating several groups which were opposed to the majority movement represented by Amal under the leadership of Nabih Berri. Three factors contributed to the emergence and strengthening of Hezbollah: the radicalisation of the Shi'ite community; the Iranian Revolution; resistance to the Israeli invasion of Lebanon.

The birth of Amal had marked the awakening of the Shi'ite community in Lebanon, the largest community in the country and also the most marginalised. Created in 1974 by Imam Musa Sadr, who disappeared mysteriously four years later in **Libya**, the movement played the card of Shi'ite confessionalism against the mobilisation of the **Maronites**, but also against the groups of the Lebanese far left and the **Palestine Liberation Organisation (PLO)**, which were very influential among the Shi'ites. However, the organisation got itself too involved in local politicking and was not up to meeting the social aspirations of the disinherited. This opened the way for internal contest. As Walid Sharara and Marina da Silva noted in *Le Monde diplomatique*,

> the various groups that would subsequently make up Hezbollah appeared in the borderland between town and country formed by the southern suburbs of Beirut and part of its eastern suburbs (Nabaa, a Shi'i neighbourhood destroyed by the Phalangists in 1976). They later extended their influence to the villages where the suburban population originated, in peripheral areas abandoned by the central government (the Beqaa and South Lebanon), which had until then been bastions of the Pan-Arab and leftwing parties allied to the Palestinian resistance.

The influence of the organisation was rooted in its many networks of assistance to the population: the rebuilding of houses damaged or destroyed by Israeli bombing, the provision of schools, clinics and hospitals, donations to war victims etc.

The second factor in the growth of Hezbollah was the victory of the Islamic Republic in **Iran**, whose revolutionary message found a huge echo among the Shi'ite communities in the early 1980s. In the preceding period, Najaf, one of the holy towns of Shi'ism in **Iraq**, had played a key role in the formation of a generation of revolutionary cadres. It was there that figures such as **Ayatollah Khomeini**, Muhammad Baqr al-Sadr (the founder of the Da'wa party who was to be executed by **Saddam Hussein**), as well as Sheikh Muhammad Hussein Fadlallah (the future spiritual head of Hezbollah) taught and were in contact with each other. Hundreds of young Lebanese went there to study with these men, before the **Ba'th** regime expelled them in the 1980s: they were to form the backbone of Hezbollah. The Iranian Revolution was not only to increase the prestige of the radicals who argued for a revolutionary **Islamism**, but would also give them the financial and military means to assert themselves. With the aid of funds from Tehran, Hezbollah was able to reinforce its network of social solidarity. And the arrival, in the summer of 1982, of several hundred Iranian 'Revolutionary Guards' in the Beqaa made it possible to develop its military apparatus. All these advances would have been impossible without the alliance which had been forged in the early 1980s between Iran and **Syria**, which has survived all the ups and downs in the region for the past twenty years.

Finally, the third element in the growth of Hezbollah was the **1982 War** in Lebanon. The Israeli soldiers were initially welcomed during the summer by a Shi'ite population – in a majority in the south – which was exasperated with the behaviour of the Palestinian militias. But the soldiers soon came to be universally hated. The war ended with thousands of deaths and tens of thousands of refugees (mainly Shi'ite). The long occupation from 1982 to 1985 created a popular resistance that was strengthened every time the Israeli army embarked on harassment, arrests and reprisals. This resistance, launched in the summer of 1982 by the parties of the left, was to force the Israeli army to retreat in 1985 – except from southern Lebanon, where the occupation would continue through to May 2000. Hezbollah joined this resistance, and from 1985 onwards became its most dynamic element. It then became the sole element, following the **Taif Accords** of 1989 and the Syrian decision to disarm all the other militias. For many Lebanese, even those hostile to the movement's ideology, it won incontestable prestige as a result of its victory against the Israeli army.

During the 1980s Hezbollah became notorious for committing one of the first suicide bombings in the region, which earned it accusations of **terrorism**. On 11 November 1982, a young man drove a Mercedes into the headquarters of the Israeli occupying troops, killing 141 people; on 26 October 1983 there were two attacks on American and French contingents of the multinational force, with 100 Americans and 31 French killed. Also during the 1980s, Hezbollah was to embark on kidnapping foreigners – one of their victims would be the French researcher Michel Seurat. Hezbollah contributed to the abrogation of the peace treaty signed in May 1983 between President Amin Gemayel and the Israeli government, and to Syria's regaining of influence in Beirut.

The Taif Accords led to a development in the organisation which, while still pursuing its struggle against the Israeli military presence in the south, became increasingly involved in Lebanese politics, and renounced the project of creating an Islamic state. In 1992, in the first elections since the outbreak of civil war, Hezbollah won 12 seats out of a total of 128; although this number varied in the course of subsequent elections, as a result of factors that often had very little relation with the free choice of voters, Hezbollah remains one of the most influential parties in Lebanese political life. Its social network, its al-Manar television channel, its radio station and its publications, its effectiveness and courage in armed actions, have made it an organisation to be respected, whose prestige extends well beyond the borders of Lebanon.

The May 2000, withdrawal of the Israeli army from the whole of southern Lebanon – with the exception of the disputed farms of Sheba'a – seems not to have weakened Hezbollah: first because it can claim an unprecedented victory over the Israeli enemy; second because it continues its struggle – at least within certain limits, fixed by Syria – by calling for the liberation of the Sheba'a farms and its prisoners held by **Israel** (Hezbollah itself captured four Israeli soldiers, with whom it intended to barter); finally, because the outbreak of the **second Intifada** in September 2000 confirmed many **Arabs** in their view that the conflict with Israel was ongoing and that therefore they should not disarm.

The organisation's Secretary-General since 1992 has been Hassan Nasrallah. The **US** has put Hezbollah on its list of terrorist organisations and has called unsuccessfully for the Lebanese government to freeze its assets.

HUSSEIN, KING

The third king of **Jordan**, Hussein, was born in 1935 in Amman. He was given both a classical Arabic and modern Western education, which he completed at Sandhurst Military Academy in **Britain**. He was at the side of his grandfather King Abdullah when the latter was assassinated on 20 July 1951. His father Talal took the throne for a short while and adopted an anti-British policy before being forced to abdicate on grounds of insanity. Hussein was subsequently crowned king. By the time he came of age, on 2 May 1953, he had consolidated his power. King Hussein ruled for more than forty years, a reign unequalled in the Middle East.

The dynasty has, however, been through many crises, the first of which erupted in the mid-1950s. Nasserism was then in full swing and exerted a profound influence on the Palestinian population in Jordan. Hussein, committed to alliance with the West, was in favour of joining the **Baghdad Pact**. But the opposition of his people was too strong; he gave up the project and in March 1956 even had to dismiss 'Glubb Pasha', the English commander of his army. In October of the same year, a particularly bloody Israeli Defence Forces (IDF) raid on the village of Qalqiliya killed 48 people and further hardened the climate of public opinion. On 21 October, the nationalist parties won the elections and Suleiman Nabulsi was appointed Prime Minister. After the Suez **1956 War**, the King even denounced the alliance treaty with London, but, feeling his power threatened, reacted by turning to the army, composed of Bedouins loyal to the Hashemites. In April 1957, he dismissed the government, dissolved parliament and banned political parties. His authority restored, the King nonetheless felt constrained to bring in British paratroops in July 1958, following the collapse of the Hashemite monarchy in **Iraq**.

In 1964, following a rapprochement with **Nasser** and in the face of the Israeli decision to divert the flow of the River Jordan, Hussein sponsored the creation of the **Palestine Liberation Organisation (PLO)** in **Jerusalem**. However, its leader, Ahmad Shuqairi – supported by Nasser – was hostile to the Hashemite King: at the heart of the crisis lay the problem of controlling the **West Bank Palestinians**. After the **1967 War**, the conflict surfaced again, but this time with the *fedayeen* organisations, which the King eliminated with great brutality in 1970–71, during the events of **Black September**.

Hussein tried to regain the initiative in the Palestinian question and strengthen Palestinian loyalty to the crown. He also hoped, by an agreement with **Israel**, to regain the West Bank. On 15 March 1972 he set out his plan for a United Arab Republic, in other words the transformation of the kingdom into a federal state, composed of two regions: the West Bank which would be called Palestine, and the East Bank, which would retain the name of Jordan. But his proposals met with little success, and were rejected by Arab countries and the PLO as well as Israel.

Egypt and **Syria**'s **1973 War**, in which Jordan took no part, provided the prelude to the PLO's diplomatic breakthrough. A year later, in October 1974, at the Arab Summit in Rabat, the King concurred with the general consensus that made the PLO the sole representative of the Palestinian people, the only political actor entitled to negotiate the future of the West Bank and Gaza.

The King remained faithful to this commitment, and condemned the **Camp David** operation initiated by **Anwar al-Sadat** in 1977–78. The Israeli invasion of **Lebanon** and the departure of the PLO from Beirut in the summer of 1982 created conditions that were propitious for a new role for Hussein. The Sixteenth Palestinian National Council (PNC) in Algiers ratified the idea of a Jordanian–Palestinian federation in February 1983. But, under pressure from the Palestinian **Intifada**, on 31 July 1988, Hussein renounced all rights to the West Bank.

In the crisis that preceded the **Gulf War**, Hussein refused to side with the **US**, provoking much criticism in the West and retaliatory measures from the Gulf emirs. Yet after the end of the war he continued to make Washington aware of his role at every **peace conference**. After the **Oslo Accords** he decided on a radical change in policy, making an alliance with Washington in order to assure the survival of the monarchy. At the risk of undermining his popularity, on 26 October 1994 he signed a peace treaty with Israel accelerating the normalisation of relations with the Jewish state. Furthermore, he broke off relations with Iraq, notably after the defection of Saddam Hussein's two sons-in-law on 8 August 1995, who, once they arrived in Amman, called for the overthrow of the Iraqi regime. He also authorised several dozen US military aircraft to be stationed in Jordan in order to survey Iraq. This change of course, unpopular with the opposition as well as a large proportion of the population, was the riskiest gamble taken by the Hashemite sovereign during his long reign.

He did not live to see the new upheaval which would be introduced by the failure of the Oslo Accords and the growing crisis between the US and Iraq. Suffering from cancer, often absent from the country, he returned to Amman in January 1999, after a six-month convalescence, to announce the succession of his son rather than his brother, Prince Hassan. He died on 7 February, and his son ascended the throne, taking the name Abdullah II. The King was a determined and courageous ruler, safeguarding the Hashemite kingdom in extremely troubled circumstances. It remains to be seen whether his successor will be as successful.

HUSSEIN, SADDAM

A Sunni Muslim, Saddam was born on 28 April 1937 in Tikrit, a town to the north of Baghdad, into a peasant family. He ruled **Iraq** for over thirty years and, more than any other leader, left a mark on the contemporary history of his country, for better or for worse. Late in starting his education, he entered a Baghdad secondary school in 1955. He became politicised there and, in 1957, joined the **Ba'th** party. Shortly after the uprising of 14 July 1958 which brought the monarchy to an end, his party went into opposition. In October 1959 he took part in an abortive assassination attempt against General Qasim; wounded, he was forced to flee, first to **Syria**, then to **Egypt**, where he completed his secondary education. It was there that

he learned of the success of the coup d'état of February 1963 which overthrew Qasim and in which the Ba'th had participated. He therefore returned
to Baghdad and joined the party leadership. But the Ba'th was ousted from
power in November 1963, and Saddam went into hiding.

Arrested in October 1964, Saddam spent two years in prison. On his
release, he was elected Deputy Secretary-General of the party. On 17 July
1968, Ba'thist army officers, lead by Hassan al-Bakr, organised a coup d'état
against the government, then, on 30 July, went on to eliminate a number
of their allies. The inexorable rise of Saddam Hussein began on this date.
In alliance with al-Bakr, he developed the political wing of the Ba'th –
whose influence was reduced – and was particularly successful in Ba'thising
the armed forces, and by the end of 1970 had introduced 3000 political
commissars into the officer corps. In November 1969 Saddam became vice-
president of the Revolutionary Command Council (RCC), the real centre
of power. Through the elimination of their rivals, sometimes by political
assassination, the Hussein–al-Bakr duo were able give the RCC unchallenged
power by the end of 1971. Saddam Hussein stood out as the real man of
strength. Brutal but pragmatic, he took the major decisions that put a
stamp on Iraq, from the nationalisation of **oil** to the attack on **Iran** and
then the invasion of **Kuwait**.

Al-Bakr's function was above all to ensure the loyalty of the maximum
number of officers. Little by little, however, his usefulness declined. On
16 July 1979, he resigned from his position as President of the republic and
of the RCC, to be replaced immediately by Saddam, who constructed
around himself an increasingly grandiose cult of personality. A few days
later, several highly placed leaders were tried and executed on charges of
conspiracy and complicity with Syria. More than ever, the RCC became, for
Saddam, a dependable tool, dominated by Sunni elements from his home
town of Tikrit and members of his own family. After 1979, Saddam began
to steer Iraq towards the camp of moderate Arab states, and after the death
of **Sadat**, towards a treaty between Baghdad, Amman and Cairo.

The **Iran–Iraq War** paved the way for the full-scale rearmament of Iraq,
made possible by the complacency of Saddam's foreign patrons, particularly
in the West, a complacency that was not shaken when he deployed chemical
weapons against the Iranian army and against Kurdish rebels. After all,
Saddam was seen as the best defence against the 'Islamist threat'. The war
ended in 1988 leaving hundreds of thousands of victims and Iraq bled dry
and in ruins. In an attempt to escape the domestic crisis, Saddam Hussein
again ordered his troops into battle by invading Kuwait on 2 August 1990.

Without the benefit of hindsight, Saddam could not have anticipated
the strength of the American reaction, and he missed out on the numerous
opportunities to find a peaceful resolution to the crisis which was to
develop into war and a crushing defeat for his country. Western passivity

allowed him to quell the Kurdish and **Shi'ite** uprisings in spring 1991, and after a period of uncertainty he was able to consolidate his power once again. In order to survive, he increasingly relied on tribal and other primeval solidarities.

The defection of Saddam's two sons-in-law, who sought refuge in **Jordan** on 8 August 1995, was a serious blow to the regime. General Hussein Kamel al-Majid and his brother, Colonel Saddam Kamel, were part of the inner circle that held power. Hussein Kamel, who was responsible for Iraq's military operations, provided the UN with evidence which confirmed that the government had hidden numerous documents on Iraq's weapons-of-mass-destruction programme, making the prospect of the complete lifting of **sanctions** a remote one, although the UN had authorised the sale of a limited amount of oil under the UN Oil for Food Programme in spring 1996. The two brothers negotiated their return to Iraq; their subsequent assassination on 23 February 1996 provided a vivid illustration of the brutal methods employed by this dictator.

The whole of Saddam's domestic and foreign policy was geared to assuring the continued existence of the regime, within a climate of fear and suspicion. Like other 'republican' leaders in the **Arab world** (such as **Hafez al-Assad**, **Hosni Mubarak** and **Muammar Qadhaffi**), Saddam gave his children key responsibilities. The position of his elder son Uday was weakened after an assassination attempt in December 1996, which cost him several months of hospitalisation. Uday's sheer depravity also contributed to his being sidelined. Uday was the head of the Union of Journalists, and controlled a vast media empire which included numerous newspapers (such as the influential daily *Babel*, which occasionally tested the limits of permissible discourse and was even banned in November 2002) as well as radio and television channels. A member of the Iraqi parliament since 2000, Uday was the only MP to call for Iraq to approve **UN Security Council Resolution** 1441, which called for the disarming of the country, in November 2002. Saddam's second son Qusay co-ordinated the security services and the Republican Guard. He also commanded the Special Guard charged with guarding his father and other dignitaries of the regime. Many analysts saw him being groomed to be Saddam's successor.

Saddam's poor understanding of international politics and his failure to appreciate the new mood in Washington following the 11 September 2001 attacks eventually led to his downfall. The UN Security Council unanimously passed Resolution 1441 on 8 November 2002, giving Iraq one final opportunity to comply with the demands of the international community or face 'serious consequences'. Iraq accepted the Resolution, and UN weapons inspectors returned to the country on 18 November. Complying with the need to make a full and complete declaration of its **weapons of mass destruction** (WMD) programmes, Iraq provided a 12,000-page document to the UN in December 2002, which the UN Monitoring, Verification and Inspection Commission (UNMOVIC) said contained some new information, but was essentially a repetition of information already provided to them. Over the next few months, UN weapons inspectors reported back to the Security Council on several occasions, with each report being seized upon by both pro- and anti-war lobbies as proving the validity of their claims – but several months after the end of the war (1 May 2003), the US was unable, despite intensive efforts, to find any proof of an Iraqi programme of WMD. The US and its allies (primarily the UK and Spain) were unable to win enough support to pass a second UN resolution explicitly authorising the use of force, and US President George W. Bush issued a 48-hour ultimatum on 18 March 2003 for Saddam and his sons to step down from power and leave the country. Saddam did not oblige; war began two days later.

The regime of Saddam Hussein seemed to collapse as US and UK forces advanced into Iraq, despite meeting unexpected levels of irregular resistance. Bush declared on 9 April that the regime had been overthrown, on the same day that a giant statue of the dictator was toppled in eastern Baghdad – a symbolic victory for the US. Although many senior figures from the former regime were accounted for in the months following the main phase of the war, Saddam remained elusive. His two sons were killed in a protracted gun battle in the city of Mosul in northern Iraq on 22 July 2003; their bodies were shown to the sceptical Iraqi public. The fact that Saddam himself remained unaccounted for until 14 December 2003 has encouraged many to suggest that the resistance being faced by the US forces in Iraq on a daily basis is co-ordinated by the former dictator and members of his regime with nothing left to lose – despite the fact that most evidence seems to point to **Islamist** or nationalist groups of Sunni origin without links to the former regime.

IMMIGRATION

The Middle East has always been a region which has witnessed numerous waves of migration. But in recent decades the phenomenon has taken on a new dimension. These new patterns of migration are a result of the division of the region into countries which produce **oil**, therefore able to implement massive investment projects, but which are sparsely populated, and countries which are densely populated yet produce no (or very little) oil (with the exception of **Iraq** and **Iran**, which have both population and oil).

Large-scale immigration has come about from this division within the Middle East, exacerbating inequalities in local labour supply, particularly in the Arabian Gulf. At the beginning of this wave of labour migration, the new workers were from Arab countries: **Egypt**, **Jordan**, **Yemen**, **Syria**, **Lebanon** or Iraq and, of course, Palestine. But since 1970, the entrepreneurs of the Gulf have cast their net further afield into Asia. In more recent years an increasingly large percentage of this auxiliary labourforce has been recruited in India, the Philippines, South Korea and even China. Wages for migrant workers vary, some receiving up to three or four times as much as others, depending on whether they are Asians or **Arabs**.

Until the **Gulf War**, the roughly 380,000 **Palestinians** in **Kuwait** were relatively integrated into Kuwaiti society, and often occupied important positions. This is not the case for most of the Gulf's immigrant workers, who often have to forfeit several months' wages to the labour contractor to obtain work and a visa. They are isolated and live alone (only rarely do families follow; if they do, it is always much later); they are treated much worse than locals and they are always at the mercy of the 'sponsors' who brought them in the first place.

The result of an essentially political decision, this massive immigration has obviously had political consequences. Many Gulf regions prefer to call in Asian labour to avoid the risks that they say would result from Arab migrants more susceptible to democratic and nationalist undercurrents. Nevertheless, the wave of immigration has profoundly destabilised the traditional societies of the Gulf, striking a blow against tribal Arab culture and identity and, at the same time, giving rise to feelings calculated to stimulate the upsurge of fundamentalism. It has not, however, hindered the development of a more or less revolutionary opposition movement, local Arabs and foreigners even sometimes joining forces.

Curbs on immigration have, throughout the region, followed the decline in oil revenues in the **Arabian Peninsula**. The statistics (see in particular those analysed by André Bourgey in *Crise du Golfe: la logique des chercheurs*) demonstrate that labour migration accounted for the demographic explosion in the Gulf countries and a dramatic acceleration of urbanisation. For example, Kuwait City has grown from 100,000 inhabitants in 1950 to

1,500,000 in 1990, while Dubai, with 4000 inhabitants in 1970, had 600,000 by 1990. In total the number of foreigners in the emirates tripled between 1970 and 1980, increased in the 1980s by more than 80 per cent in Kuwait, 70–80 per cent in Qatar and in the United Arab Emirates (UAE), by 30–35 per cent in **Saudi Arabia**, and by 30 per cent in Bahrain and Oman. Over this period only Saudi Arabia and Kuwait have a majority of Arabs in their immigrant population; Asians comprised the majority of foreign workers in Bahrain, Qatar, the UAE and Oman. In Iraq, Saudi Arabia and the various emirates, the number of immigrants reached a total of some five to six million.

If these immigrants made a notable contribution to the development of their adopted countries, they also had a considerable impact in their country of origin, as the case of Egypt demonstrates. The main effects on Egyptian society of migration can be summed up in three ways: it has exacerbated processes that are already marginalising the countryside socially and economically; it has provided a safety net that has moderated the social impact of unemployment (two to three million workers have left the banks of the Nile in recent years), and finally it has had a very substantial impact on both domestic spending power and foreign exchange – for example, in 1987 Cairo is said to have received $2.7bn from this source.

This precipitate rise was followed by decline. The fall in oil prices during the 1980s, and particularly after 1986, triggered an important change: the number of foreigners in the Gulf decreased by at least a quarter, perhaps as much as a third in the 1980s. This trend accelerated more noticeably with the outbreak of the Gulf War, when one of the greatest migrations in the history of the Middle East took place. In the space of one month, one million refugees arrived in Jordan. After the invasion of Kuwait, 865,000 Egyptians were expelled from Iraq and Kuwait; 750,000 Yemenis left Saudi Arabia; 300,000 Palestinians abandoned Kuwait, and so on.

In the aftermath of the war, the Gulf again needed hundreds of thousands of foreign labourers, and a proportion of the foreigners who left after Desert Storm returned. There has been a growing influx of Asian workers, usually organised by specialist recruitment agencies. Ten years later, the number of immigrant workers in the Arabian Peninsula, including their families, was reckoned at between 10 and 12 million – almost 10 per cent of the total number of migrants in the world. As a percentage of the economically active population, they varied between 55 in Bahrain and 90 in Qatar, the UAE and Kuwait, and 65–70 per cent in Saudi Arabia and Oman. The proposed policy of 'nationalising' the workforce, particularly in Saudi Arabia, was still only in its early days.

Only their living and working conditions have barely changed. On 1 May 2000, Amnesty International sent a protest to the Saudi government which, unfortunately, could apply equally to the majority of foreign workers in the region: 'Asian migrant workers in Saudi Arabia are at risk of human rights violations such as floggings, amputations, torture and executions, and are denied basic protection by employers and the government'. They are, Amnesty International continued, 'particularly vulnerable. They suffer human rights abuses in silence and solitude with no one to turn to for help.' Many of them are

> employed as domestic help or manual workers and like other workers are not protected by any trade unions. Their sponsors often confiscate their passport and they are forbidden to change jobs or travel from where they work. Many suffer at the hands of their employers on whom they are completely dependent. Some are not paid and are vulnerable to abuse by employers.

Furthermore, 'once arrested they may be tricked or coerced into signing a statement in Arabic, which they don't understand. They are not informed of their rights, nor of the judicial process that awaits them. They have no access to a lawyer and are often denied consular access.' The result: between 1990 and March 2000, more than half of the 778 people executed in Saudi Arabia were foreigners.

INDEPENDENCE

Set in motion by the dismantling of the **Ottoman Empire** after World War I, the era of independence lasted in the Middle East into the 1970s. Needless to say, the process took place within the framework of the often arbitrary borders defined by the victors in the war.

The first country to win its independence was **Egypt**, one of the few 'old' nations in a region that had throughout history been carved up at the whim of colonisers. A powerful nationalist movement developed around the Egyptian Wafd party. Disturbances after 1918 were so violent that London chose, on 28 February 1922, to concede independence unilaterally. But the British reserved enormous privileges for themselves in matters of communications, defence and the protection of their foreign interests, as they did in **Sudan**. The same went for a new treaty which the British signed on 28 August 1936 following a long struggle with the Wafd. Under this agreement the British benefited in particular from facilities in the event of war, and the recognition of their interests in the **Suez Canal** Zone, where they maintained a force of 10,000 men. Admitted to the UN in 1937, Egypt did not gain real independence until 1954, when **Gamal Abdel Nasser**, succeeding General Neguib, managed to force the British to evacuate the Canal Zone before going on to nationalise the Suez Canal Company in 1956.

Iraq was also the scene of a vigorous campaign for independence. The announcement of the British Mandate in 1920 unleashed an uprising which was put down with great difficulty by British troops. The coronation of Faisal, chased out of **Syria** by the French army, did not bring the turbulence to an end. Constantly on the retreat and having failed to honour three different treaties, **Britain** finally acknowledged the treaty of 1930, which granted total independence to Iraq in exchange, here too, for military facilities, including bases. What was once Mesopotamia thus entered the League of Nations on 3 October 1932.

At that time what is now **Saudi Arabia** was already independent. In 1915 Ibn Saud and Sir Percy Cox, the British Resident in the Gulf, had concluded the first Anglo–Arab agreement, which exchanged the organisation of an anti-Ottoman revolt for British recognition of the independence of the Arab territories of the Ottoman Empire. Having failed after the war to keep its promise so far as the **Arab world** as a whole was concerned, Britain extended its recognition in 1926 to 'the King of Hedjaz and Sultan of Nedj and his dependencies'. Since the Wahhabi Ibn Saud had by this time triumphed over his Hashemite rival, Sherif Hussein, Arabia was considered his on condition that he recognise British positions in the Gulf to the south and Transjordan to the north.

In 1921, Britain detached the territory to the east of the River Jordan, part of its post-war Mandate over Palestine, from the rest of Palestinian territory to create the Emirate of Transjordan. Abdullah, the brother of Faisal and son of the Sherif Hussein, was made its ruler. The new state was, without doubt, the most artificial creation of the **Sykes–Picot Agreement**. Transjordan lacked a people with any consciousness of its own identity, and gave the British little trouble. Though its frontier was recognised in 1927 by Ibn Saud, and a constitution – along with a treaty securing Britain's influence – was adopted in 1928, the emirate was not given formal independence until 1946. In 1950, following the annexation of **Jerusalem** and the **West Bank**, the King adopted the name 'The Hashemite Kingdom of **Jordan**'.

Shortly before this, **Lebanon** and Syria had attained their independence from **France**, under whose Mandate they were placed by the Sykes–Picot Agreement, despite concerted French attempts to delay the matter. In 1920, Faisal had been proclaimed King of Greater Syria by the General Syrian Congress, but he was expelled from Damascus by the French. There followed a long series of territorial 'adjustments'. In 1920, the French Mandate was divided into four states: Greater Lebanon, Damascus, Aleppo and an Alawite state. The last three were federated in 1922, and the Jebel **Druze** became autonomous. In 1924, the *sanjak* of Alexandretta, ceded to **Turkey** in 1939, was created. A further round of territorial carving took place in 1925: Greater Lebanon, Syria and the Jebel Druze, where an uprising broke out that extended to the whole country before being put down by the French army. It was not until 1936 that independence, in exchange for a military alliance, bases and 'facilities', was promised to Lebanon and Syria in a treaty which, with the fall from power of the Popular Front in France, was never ratified. At the beginning of the Second World War, the Vichy government allowed the Axis powers to make military use of the two countries, with the result that Britain occupied them in July 1941 with Free French forces. General Catroux, the Free French leader in the field and de Gaulle's representative, proclaimed the independence of Lebanon and Syria. But it was too late in the eyes of the national movement, which obtained admission to the UN without the slightest reference to France's special position. The last French soldiers left the Levant on 31 December 1946.

Britain's enjoyment of its French rival's misfortunes was to prove short-lived. Thirty years after the **Balfour Declaration** and 25 years after the British Mandate was established in Palestine, Britain's Palestinian policy reached a dead end. The UN, to which Britain had referred the matter, decided on partition, and on 14 May 1948, Sir Allan Cunningham, the seventh and last British High Commissioner in Palestine, boarded ship at Haifa. That very day **Israel** declared its independence: 'On this day when the British Mandate ends and in virtue of the natural and historic right of the Jewish people and in compliance with the Resolution of the UN General Assembly, we proclaim the creation of a Jewish state on the soil of Israel'. The Arab state also provided for by the UN was never to see the light of day. The downward spiral of Israeli–Arab conflicts began.

Ousted from Palestine, then Egypt (1954–56), from Sudan (1956) and Iraq (1958), the British, for a while, held on in the **Arabian Peninsula**. Admittedly, Saudi Arabia was a sovereign state, as was North **Yemen**, which had managed to preserve its freedom by a skillful game of alliances. But the other emirates, sultanates and principalities were still British protectorates. **Kuwait** was the first to break free from London, in 1961. Six years later, it was the turn of the Federation of South Arabia, which became the People's Republic of Yemen in 1970. Oman achieved independence in 1970, Qatar and Bahrain in 1971, the same year as the United Arab Emirates, formerly the 'Pirate Coast'. But the key date was undoubtedly 1967: the year in which Britain decided to withdraw all its troops east of Suez.

Thus, the state structures born out of the dismantling of the Ottoman Empire led to the independence of most of the peoples it had governed in the Middle East, with two notable exceptions: the **Palestinians** and the **Kurds**.

INFITAH

An Arabic term meaning 'opening', *infitah* refers to the 'open door' or liberal economic policy that broke with the socialism of **Nasser** and the first Syrian **Ba'thist** leaders. This new approach was adopted by **Anwar al-Sadat** when he came to power in **Egypt** and also by President **Hafez al-Assad** of **Syria**, though on a more limited scale and under much stricter state control – and by **Iraq**, notably before the disastrous invasion of **Kuwait**.

Begun in Egypt after 1971, the policy of *infitah* got into full swing after October 1973. Sadat defined its major principles: encouragement of the private sector and foreign investment, opening up to non-Egyptian banks, liberalisation of foreign trade and curtailing the role of the public sector. A series of decrees and laws made possible the realisation of this new economic philosophy.

Twenty years later, the balance sheet remained inconclusive. Private and foreign capital invested primarily in the non-industrial and agricultural sectors, where profits are immediate and substantial: import–export, real estate, banks and tourism. Speculation and corruption reached hitherto unknown heights. Social inequalities were aggravated, and the insolent wealth of the *nouveaux riches* mocked the continual poverty of the Egyptian people. Egypt's dependence on external aid has increased (particularly in terms of agriculture and finance), and millions of its labourers, technicians and executives have gone to work in the **oil**-producing countries. But the public sector, which was to be reformed, has proved sacrosanct: for social reasons, but also because there is no enterprising private capital capable of assuming the management of crucial industries such as steel and arms. Under pressure from the IMF, the government seems poised to advance rapidly with the privatisation programme.

Admittedly, the overall picture is not so bleak, and certain successes have been achieved: Egypt has become an exporter of oil, and certain sectors of agriculture and industry have acquired a new efficiency. But Egypt's example has highlighted the difficulties of imposing a liberal model on an underdeveloped economy without giving rise to profound distortions and social upheavals. The January 1977 demonstrations in Cairo are still remembered as symbols of this.

INTIFADA

In Arabic the term 'intifada' refers to 'raising the head', and by extension 'uprising', the name given to the Palestinian revolt that broke out in Gaza and the **West Bank** early in December 1987. On a larger scale and more determined than any previous movement in the Occupied Territories, the 'revolt of the stone-throwers' profoundly altered the landscape of the Middle East.

On 7 December 1987 a traffic accident – a collision between an Israeli vehicle and a Palestinian shared taxi, two of whose occupants died – sparked things off. Two days later, the first confrontations took place between young

Palestinians and Israeli soldiers in the camp of Jabalya. Within a week, the uprising had spread to the whole of the **Gaza Strip** and the West Bank, despite the state of siege decreed by the occupying powers. Taken by surprise, the Israeli government, all tendencies united, adopted a single priority: 'crush the subversion', in the words of the Defence Minister, **Yitzhak Rabin**, whose membership of the Labour party did not prevent him from leading the repression of the Intifada with an iron hand.

The escalation of demonstrations, strikes and confrontations was met with a spiral of repression. The army announced repeated curfews, fired on teenagers who taunted them, employed torture, arrested tens of thousands of Palestinians and interned (often without trial) thousands more. They did not stop short at 'ill-treatment' during their raids against the villages and deported several scores of Palestinians. Openly flouting the stipulations of the Geneva Convention, this violent conduct shocked public opinion, Jewish included, the world over, which proved susceptible to the flood of pictures diffused by the mass media. The attempt to use bulldozers to bury alive four villagers in Salem, and the scene in which two youths from Nablus were battered during a live broadcast by CBS cameras had particular impact. A thousand days after the start of the uprising, the statistics were as follows: more than a thousand dead, tens of thousands wounded, nine thousand prisoners – which, with the four thousand already in detention, made a total of thirteen thousand detainees from a population of 1.7 million inhabitants.

However, this massive use of force did not deter the insurgents. The roots of their determination were deeper than the combination of historical events – such as the hope inspired in April 1987 by the reunification of the **Palestine Liberation Organisation (PLO)** at the Palestine National Council (PNC) in Algiers and the anger unleashed in November following the overlooking of the Palestine question at the Arab Summit held in Amman. Resistance to the occupation had of course been present since June 1967. The progressive expansion of the Israeli colonisation of the West Bank and Gaza, in particular the increase in Jewish **settlements**, had met with growing opposition, which found expression both in demonstrations and acts of violence, as well as in the municipal elections of 1976, where PLO supporters won hands down. But the Intifada represented the explosion of the pent-up frustrations of an entire generation, born under the occupation, which was surmounting the relatively resigned attitude of previous generations and dragging them into action for **independence**. Never, even in 1981 and 1982, had Palestinians who had not sought refuge elsewhere made their presence so vigorously felt.

In fact, the scale of the Intifada exceeded that of preceding uprisings in many respects. It lasted more than four years; it reached across the whole of the Occupied Territories, including **Jerusalem**, Bethlehem and the villages, traditionally quietest; it came in a variety of forms: mass rallies, general strikes and confrontations, as well as the will to an independent everyday life and acts of civil disobedience. Its participants were both young and old: refugees from 1947–49 mingled with those born in the West Bank and Gaza; labourers and peasants found themselves side by side with tradesmen, professionals and intellectuals.

Born spontaneously, as all observers (including Israelis) have pointed out, from an explosive mixture of ingredients – shanty-town poverty, massive unemployment, the humiliation of national feeling and daily repression – the revolt of the stone-throwers quickly organised itself. Local people's committees organised the street fighting (without firearms) against the Israeli army, but also supplied teaching, medical back-up and other basic services – to the extent that observers began to speak of 'liberated zones'. Autonomous local committees also met up in a United Patriotic Leadership, which included the recently 'reconciled' elements of the Palestinian leadership, **Yasser Arafat's** Fatah, **George Habash's** Popular Front, **Nayef Hawatmeh's** Democratic Front, the Palestinian Communist Party and the Islamic groups – excluding their most extreme fringe, the Islamic Resistance Movement, known by its initials as **Hamas**. Only this last movement remained outside the general consensus of the Intifada's purpose, which was the creation of an independent Palestinian state on the West Bank and in Gaza, and the withdrawal of **Israel** to the borders it possessed prior to the Six Day **1967 War**. These aims represented a resurrection, 40 years after its failure, of the **Partition Plan** voted by the UN General Assembly.

As Elias Sanbar wrote (in *Palestine, le pays à venir*),

> The principle force of the Intifada, the reason it has grabbed the world's attention, is that it never seems to pose a threat to the existence of Israel. We should therefore appreciate the stroke of genius shown by the people in their decision to take up stones instead of guns. Such restraint was to demonstrate to the world that the uprising was a threat to the occupying force rather than to Israel itself and its borders as they were in 1948–49. In this light we can understand better the completely different reactions provoked by the acts of terrorism that the Islamists were later to commit within the Green Line.

The uprising caused a reshuffling of power positions in the Middle East and challenged many of the principal players. The first to react was **King Hussein** of **Jordan**: on 31 July 1988 he announced the severing of Jordan's links with the West Bank. 'Jordan is not Palestine,' he declared, 'and the independent Palestinian state will be established on Palestinian land occupied after its liberation'. The 'Jordanian option' having been closed, the PLO now became Israel's inevitable partner in future peace negotiations. The political opportunity presented by the revolt and the conditions to be met in order to sit down at the negotiating table forced Arafat and those close to him – as the United Patriotic Leadership of the Intifada did not hesitate to point out – to define a concrete peace programme. The PLO found itself forced to recognise the state of Israel in order to obtain reciprocal acknowledgement. The Algiers Palestine National Council of November 1988 had in any case taken the first steps in this direction, by proclaiming an independent Palestinian state while accepting **UN Security Council Resolution** 181 (1947) as well as Resolutions 242 and 338, and by reaffirming its condemnation of **terrorism**.

But the first year of the Intifada did not produce the results that had been hoped for. The Israeli government doggedly and successfully opposed American pressure to enter into Israeli–Palestinian negotiations in 1989–90. This obstacle intensified the radicalisation, and indeed a certain degeneration of the revolt of the stone-throwers. Increasingly, old scores were settled with collaborators (or those suspected of collaboration); individual actions targeted Israeli civilians and tourists. Some groups, who were out of control, took the law into their own hands. Many young people, who had been kept out of the schools and universities for months and who were rebelling against their elders and traditional political traditions, turned to the burgeoning **Islamist** movement Hamas, which had always denounced diplomatic solutions and saw its popularity surge,

It was in this context that the **Gulf War** broke out. Many Palestinians in Gaza and the West Bank, who had been driven to desperation by merciless repression, economic and social despair and the lack of a political future, placed their hopes in **Saddam Hussein** and a new-found faith in violence to force the creation of a Palestinian state. The bloody failure of the Iraqi leader struck a blow for the compromisers. In a way, the Madrid Conference of October 1991, followed by the secret negotiations leading to the **Oslo Accords**, realised the long-awaited objective of the Intifada.

Nevertheless, the dream still remains far from reality. The Oslo Accords foundered on Israel's pursuit of its settlement policies and the failure of the **Camp David** negotiations. In July 2000, this breakdown led to the second Intifada, the characteristics of which differed radically from the first, most notably in the Palestinians' use of firearms and suicide bombings.

INTIFADA, SECOND

On 28 September 2000, the head of the Israeli right-wing opposition **Ariel Sharon** paid a visit to the Haram al-Sharif in **Jerusalem**. Defying warnings from the **Palestinian Authority**, he had a large police presence to protect him, provided by the government of Ehud Barak. The next day the first violent clashes broke out: over a period of three days Israeli forces killed 30 **Palestinians** and wounded five hundred. The Palestinians, without any central directive, rose up in revolt. At a moment when the stalemate in the **Camp David** negotiations was yet again postponing the prospect of **independence**, they called for the immediate ending of the Israeli occupation. During the following month, more than two hundred Palestinians were killed, one third under the age of 17. To respond to this incredible brutality, the Intifada militarised itself as of the start of November (although the first suicide bombings were not to start until the spring of 2000). The gulf between the two parties was so great that all attempts at mediation were to fail: the Palestinians called for an immediate end to the occupation, an end which the **Oslo Accords** had failed to bring about; in the view of the Israelis, who were insensitive to the extent of Palestinian exasperation, the Intifada could only be understood as a determination on the part of the Palestinian Authority to destroy the Jewish state.

This revolt differed from the first Intifada, as Nadine Picaudou has shown in an article in *Le Monde diplomatique*:

> even the geography of the confrontation is different. The previous uprising took place in the heart of towns and pitted an unarmed civilian population against the Israeli occupying forces. This time limited and violent clashes break out on the outskirts of the autonomous Palestinian zones, at the approaches to Jewish settlements, at army checkpoints, which appear as so many front lines between hostile territories. The withdrawal to territorial spaces thus sanctuarized explains the new violence of the Israeli repression, the systematic use of crack snipers and missiles launched from helicopters against carefully chosen targets…The new geography of the confrontation cannot be dissociated from a sociology of the present uprising, which is very clearly distinct from the first Intifada. A civil mass mobilization against the occupation has been replaced by an insurrection which relies on the active participation of a minority, even if it is assured of the support of the majority. Because the population of the Palestinian territories appears simultaneously exasperated and demobilised.

From the start it was Fatah that took the lead in the uprising, cutting the ground from under the feet of the more radical organisations, notably **Hamas**. A National and Islamic Committee was set up to co-ordinate the activity of all the groups. **Marwan Barghouti**, one of the younger Fatah leaders, came to play a decisive role in the organisation of the resistance.

Barak's government had already mobilised huge resources against the Intifada – including the use of the air force – but the arrival of Sharon to power in February 2001 intensified the repression considerably. The former general instituted a policy of assassination of Palestinian activists and of repeated incursions and raids into autonomous Palestinian areas. While the official aim of the Israeli government was 'the dismantling of terrorist infrastructures', the Israeli Prime Minister had other objectives.

From Ramallah to Bethlehem, from Nablus to **Jenin**, what the Israeli army has moved to destroy has been the Palestinian Authority, its leader, its operating systems and its symbols. To this end it has mobilised considerable resources – at the time of Operation Rampart in spring 2002 it was to deploy four divisions, one more than it took for **Israel** to conquer Sinai in June 1967. But for Sharon it is not enough merely to pulverise the Palestinian Authority and extract himself from the straitjacket of the Oslo Accords – 'the biggest catastrophe that ever happened to Israel,' as he puts it. His strategic objective has been the capitulation of the Palestinian community and its renunciation of any form of resistance. For this he had to strike – and strike hard – which is what the army has been doing on the ground: the systematic destruction of infrastructures, some of which are funded by the EU; indiscriminate bombings of refugee camps; demolition of houses; attacks on hospitals and restrictions on the movement of ambulances and medical staff; looting; theft; destruction of every aspect of material and social life of the Palestinians.

Sharon hopes that in this way, having reduced the Palestinian population to compliance, he will be able to force acceptance of the 'long-term solution' which he has been preaching since 1998: a few Palestinian 'bantustans' – which may eventually be given the name of 'state' – locked within a straitjacket of Jewish **settlements**.

By the start of March 2002 the number of Palestinian dead exceeded those killed in the first Intifada: 1442 deaths in only a quarter of the time. Israeli deaths numbered 400, but their proportion in relation to those of the Palestinians went from 1:6 at the start of the uprising to 1:4. The cycle of bombings and repression continues. According to Agence France Presse, by 10 December 2002 the number of people killed since the start of the Intifada had reached 2757, of whom 2029 were Palestinian and 678 Israeli. During the month of March 2002, more than 80 Israelis were killed, a figure unprecedented in the whole history of the country if one leaves aside wars with its Arab neighbours.

Over two years of fighting, the Israeli army has arrested and interrogated thousands of Palestinians; dozens of militants have been assassinated; hundreds of houses have been demolished; thousands of dunums of land have been confiscated; thousands of fruit trees uprooted. The blockade of towns and refugee camps has prevented all circulation of the population, of tankers, of food lorries, of ambulances, of doctors and humanitarian assistance, in violation of the Geneva Conventions. Education, work, economic development, the whole social and economic life of the territories has been blocked, but so too has political life, with the repeated periods of house arrest for the head of the Palestinian Authority, **Yasser Arafat**, and the destruction of his headquarters in Ramallah. Two million out of three million Palestinians live below the poverty level; 15 per cent of families have lost all sources of income, particularly in the **Gaza Strip**. Even more serious in the long term, the segmentation of the **West Bank** into cantons with no contact between them, the impossibility of moving from one place to another, and the disappearance of central government have reinforced clan relations at the local level and a form of anarchy in which justice is in the hands of individuals, where violence is privatised.

In the face of repeated violations of the rights of the Palestinian population, some voices have been raised, including those of **France**, calling for the establishment of an international protection force in the Palestinian areas. This, however, has been refused by the US. The repression and the occupation engender resistance, but also bring about hatred and madness. The suicide bombings, often targeting civilians in Israel, began in earnest in spring 2001 – for the most part they were carried out by Hamas or Islamic Jihad, but the al-Aqsa Martyrs Brigades, linked to Fatah, were also involved. They are seen by the majority of Palestinians as a way of re-establishing the balance of power in the face of the violence of Israeli repression. On the other hand, for Israeli public opinion, but also for Western governments, they are an unacceptable form of **terrorism**. They have contributed to the isolation of the Palestinian Authority, despite its regular condemnations of these acts. Since the summer of 2002, Palestinian society has been debating these kinds of actions. The percentage condemning suicide actions has been growing, but it is not likely that such actions will stop, particularly since the Authority has been deprived of all possibility of acting and since no political perspective is in sight locally. The appointment – under American pressure – of Mahmoud Abbas, also known as Abu Mazen, as Prime Minister of the Palestinian Authority in spring 2003 did pave the way for the publication of the 'Quartet' (US–UN–EU–**Russia**) 'Road Map' for peace on 30 April 2003, which provided a glimpse of a way out for both sides. This new plan foresaw the establishment of a Palestinian state before 2005, and therefore required as a first step: the Palestinians to declare the end of the armed Intifada, to cease any attack against Israel and to reform their institutions; the Israelis to cease any attack against the Palestinian population, to withdraw their forces to the positions of September 2000 and to freeze any growth – including 'natural' – of their settlements.

Abbas had always fought against the militarisation of the Intifada, and on 29 June 2003 he was even able to secure a three-month ceasefire agreement from Fatah, Hamas and Islamic Jihad. Unfortunately, Sharon's Likud government kept few of the promises it had made when it accepted the 'Road Map', and resumed its attacks against **Islamist** militants. These, in turn, responded – in particularly brutal fashion – killing 22 Orthodox **Jews** in a bus on their way to Jerusalem. In the autumn of 2003, after the formation of a new government led by Ahmed Qorei (Abu Ala'), there were some hints of a resumption of negotiations.

The second Intifada represents the Palestinians' rejection of an illegal occupation, in place for 35 years despite innumerable resolutions by the UN.

It has created a huge gulf between the people of Israel and the Palestinians. Any success in the negotiations will necessitate a strong commitment by the international community, whose action is co-ordinated by the 'Quartet'.

IRAN

The first Persian Empire, the Achaeminid, was founded by Cyrus the Great in the sixth century BC. The second, that of the Zoroastrian Sassanids, who ruled from the third century AD, lasted for over four hundred years. Weakened by incessant wars with the Byzantine Empire, the Sassanids were defeated by Arab armies in AD637 at the battle of Qadisiyya. Converted to **Islam**, the Iranians contributed greatly to the cultural glory of the Abbasid Empire. However, Iran did not re-emerge as an independent political entity until the sixteenth century.

It was at that time that the Safavid Empire was founded by Isma'il Safavi, who declared the **independence** of Persia from the **Ottoman Empire** and decreed **Shi'ism** to be the state religion, using it as a means to forge a national identity. The Empire began its long decline in the eighteenth century, when Persia was invaded by Afghanistan and threatened by **Russia** and **Turkey**, who conquered Tabriz in 1725.

At the end of the eighteenth century, **Britain**, whose influence in India was growing rapidly, established itself as a decisive actor on the Persian stage. At the same time, a new dynasty – the Qajars – came to power and remained there until 1925. Throughout the nineteenth century, Persia played on the rivalry between the great powers, even while withstanding attacks from Russia and the Ottoman Empire, not to mention Britain's meddling. Although Persia suffered several losses of territory, it remained independent. The discovery of **oil** increased the country's importance.

The constitutionalist movement which emerged in 1905–6 opposed the rule of the Shah: it was not eliminated until the eve of the First World War, and then only with Russian assistance. During the war Iran remained neutral, but sympathised with the Ottoman Empire. The Empire's collapse and the advent of Bolshevik power in Russia left the field open after the war for Britain, which turned the country into little more than a virtual protectorate for over forty years. The Qajar dynasty was overthrown in 1925 by an army officer, Reza Khan, who had made himself Minister of Defence four years earlier following a successful coup. The Pahlavi era had begun.

The new sovereign, who assumed the name Reza Shah, encouraged economic development and Westernisation – though at a slower pace than in Atatürk's Turkey, and never for a moment relinquishing his despotic power. There was repeated conflict with Britain, which still had a predominant influence in the region, particularly through the Anglo–Iranian Oil

Company, which extracted oil and operated the giant refinery of Abadan. In an attempt to rid himself of this oppressive custodian, in the 1930s the Shah developed cordial relations with the USSR and, to an even greater extent, with Germany, which took an active part in the country's economic development, by 1939 accounting for 41 per cent of Iranian trade.

At the outbreak of World War II, Tehran proclaimed its neutrality. But, after the Nazi attack against the Soviet Union was launched in June 1941, Iran became the only feasible land route by which Britain could send supplies to its new ally. Moscow and London now demanded that the Shah expel his German advisors. When he refused, Soviet and British troops were sent into the country and Reza Shah was forced to abdicate in favour of his son, Muhammad Reza.

After the conclusion of the World War II and the elimination of the Kurdish Republic of Mahabad in northern Iran, Britain became the favourite target of the nationalists. The refusal of the Anglo–Iranian Oil Company to even discuss the question of sharing its profits with the state led to a radicalisation of public opinion. It was this that brought about, on 28 April 1951, the appointment of Muhammad Mosaddeq as Prime Minister and the nationalisation of Iran's oil industry. 'Oil is our blood, oil is our freedom,' yelled demonstrators. In August 1953, a coup d'état, organised by the CIA in collaboration with Britain, brought an end to Mosaddeq's government. The Shah reaffirmed his dictatorial power and brutally eliminated all secular opposition. At this point the US replaced Britain as the tutelary power in Iran.

The 1960s and 1970s saw the confirmation of both the dictatorial character of Muhammad Reza Shah's regime and Iran's commitment to economic Westernisation. A series of reforms, including land reform and women's suffrage, known as the 'White Revolution', gave rise to widespread disturbances in 1963, in which **Ayatollah Ruhollah Khomeini** won fame. A number of major industrial projects were considerably helped by the rise in oil prices in 1973. The creation of a formidable military machine transformed Iran into the 'policeman of the Gulf'. Tehran intervened against the Dhofar, rebellion in Dhofar, and in November 1971 took forcible control of the three islands of Abu Musa and Greater and Lesser Tunb.

The Shah degenerated into megalomania; in October 1971 in Persepolis he celebrated 2500 years of the Persian Empire. In 1973, Prime Minister Hoveida declared that 'the last thing Iran needs is a Western-style democracy'. All secular opposition was hunted down by the secret police, Savak. As for the proposed 'modernisation', it took the form of an anarchic urbanisation, the unravelling of the rural economy and growing poverty. The presence of 30,000 American advisors and numerous foreign bases outraged the population's sense of nationalism.

The sole force to survive the dreadful political repression, the Shi'ite clergy, became the only channel for the people's aspirations towards dignity, sovereignty, liberty and **independence**. The whole of 1978 was marked by popular demonstrations and by dreadful repression. The latter proved futile; on 16 January 1979 the Shah was forced to leave the country and on 1 February Khomeini triumphantly returned to the capital. The Islamic Revolution triumphed 25 years after a secular and democratic revolution led by Muhammad Mosaddeq had been well on the way to success but was summarily crushed by the Western powers, thus clearing a path for the mullahs.

In February 1979, the liberal Mehdi Bazargan was appointed Prime Minister. He fell from power nine months later when the revolution took a radical swing. On 4 November 1979, students following 'the way of the Imam' occupied the US Embassy, whose staff were not released until 20 January 1981. A new constitution formalised the immense powers of the 'Leader', in other words Khomeini. In 1980 and 1981 the regime seemed to be on the brink of disaster, challenged successively by a Kurdish uprising, the move to armed opposition adopted by Massoud Rajavi's Mojahedin-e Khalq and the flight of president elect Bani Sadr, who took refuge in **France** in the summer of 1981. But the Iraqi invasion of September 1980 and the outbreak of the **Iran–Iraq War** inspired an outburst of patriotism. In 1983 Iran managed to force all Iraqi troops from its territory, and then invaded its neighbour. The war, thanks mainly to Khomeini's obduracy, was to last until August 1988.

This long conflict allowed Iranian leaders to disguise their differences and postpone certain crucial decisions. Iran was using its oil income to pay for imports, but no actual course of development had been decided on, whether liberal or etatist. A programme of intended reforms was paralysed by the supervisory Council of Guardians, responsible for ensuring that laws conformed to Islam. The economic and social situation was still disastrous: between 1978 and 1979, the GDP of Iran grew by a mere 10 per cent, while its population increased by 30 per cent.

Within a few months of the acceptance of **UN Security Council Resolution** 598, which brought war with **Iraq** to an end, Khomeini died (June 1989). His designated successor as imam, Ayatollah Montazeri, had been dismissed in March 1989. The new Leader, a simple *hojat ol-eslam*, Ali Khamenei, was appointed in contested circumstances. He had neither the authority nor the stature of his predecessor, and aligned himself with Hashemi Rafsanjani, the President of the Republic.

Over a period of ten years, Iran's problems had accumulated. There had been no process of reform, and Iran was crippled by nearly $30bn of debt. Social dissatisfaction led to several riots, which were brutally repressed. The support of at least some elements of the Iranian regime for **terrorist** actions against dissidents abroad had led to the isolation of Iran in diplomatic circles; there were also accusations that the country was seeking to obtain a nuclear capability. In July 1996, the US, which had already imposed a trade embargo on trade with Iran, adopted a law threatening to impose **sanctions** on any foreign country which helped the Iranian oil industry to develop, despite European opposition. Although the repression has to some extent softened, the political system seems incapable of dealing with the aspirations of a country changing rapidly under the Islamic rule.

The regime's initial policy of refusing birth control utterly transformed the demographic structure of the country: 65 per cent of Iranians are under the age of 24, and the voting age has been reduced to 16. The vigorous pursuit of literacy campaigns and the extension of free education cut the rate of illiteracy by a quarter (to about 15 per cent) and led to an explosion in the number of students (two million). Urbanisation accelerated, and the war against Iraq contributed to the strengthening of nationalist sentiment, to the detriment of religious identification. Even the introduction of the compulsory wearing of the *chador* in a sense helped the emancipation of women, enabling them to 'come out' from their traditional families under its protection: there were now more women in work, and they represented more than half of all students – as opposed to only a quarter in the time of the Shah. All these changes worked in favour of a liberation of society and a separation between the political and religious fields, which became even greater when the image of the clergy was tarnished by a number of financial scandals.

The elections were to reflect the realities of the new country. On 23 May 1997, Muhammad Khatami won the presidential election against the candidates supported by the government. With the vote of more than 70 per cent of the electorate, particularly women and young people, this intellectual, a former official at the Ministry of Culture and Islamic Guidance, had been obliged to resign in 1992, and had become spokesperson for the reform movement. He was propelled to power, carrying with him the hopes of the whole society. Subsequently an ongoing trial of strength brought him into conflict with the religious institutions, which monopolise numerous powers.

Under the terms of the constitution, Khamenei maintains exclusive control of the judiciary, the army forces, the Pasdaran (Revolutionary Guards) and the media (radio and television). He also controls the proceeds of charitable foundations (major holding companies set up in the wake of the Revolution, notably with goods confiscated from the Imperial family), which enabled him to finance the clergy and its institutions. This clergy, determined to hang onto power, increased its attacks on the reformists: repeated closures of newspapers, police harassment, arrests and assassinations of intellectuals and members of the opposition.

Despite these powerful elements of resistance, Khatami succeeded in expanding the area of civil liberties, extending the rule of law, political pluralism and changes of government. He was able to get his own people into position in the key ministries – communications and culture – and even succeeded in replacing the Security Minister, who had been responsible for the political bloodletting of autumn 1998. He organised the holding of new municipal elections in March 1999, and then national elections in February 2000 (again won by his tendency), and was then triumphally re-elected in June 2001. But for how long will the population continue to support a President whose real margins of manoeuvre are so narrow at a time when the social situation is worsening?

At the regional and international level, for a decade Iran has been seeking to emerge from its isolation. It first effected a reconciliation with the Gulf monarchies, in particular with **Saudi Arabia**. Its relations with Russia have been strengthened. Moscow has supplied it with weapons and expertise for its civil nuclear programme. The two countries also have a shared view on various regional conflicts: both opposed the Taliban regime in Afghanistan, and both support the present authorities in Kabul.

Iran still has no diplomatic relations with the US. Although the election of Khatami and his appeal for dialogue at the December 1997 summit of the Organisation of the Islamic Conference (OIC), followed by various American gestures of goodwill, led to a period of relaxed relations, the election of George W. Bush as US President has strained relations. Although the two countries had in fact co-operated to get rid of the Taliban regime in Afghanistan, there are many friction points. One of the main ones relates to the building of a nuclear power station at Bushehr, on the Persian Gulf, and Russia's construction of five nuclear reactors – despite Moscow's assurance that these were civil installations, supervision by the International Atomic Energy Agency (IAEA) and Tehran's signature of the Non-Proliferation Treaty. In 2003, US concerns about the Iranian nuclear programme were echoed by both the IAEA and the EU, and Tehran finally recognised in November 2003 that it had broken the treaty and decided to sign the additional protocol to the Non-Proliferation Treaty. Washington is opposed to the building of an oil pipeline between Kazakhstan and Iran. Furthermore, Bush included Iran in his 'axis of evil'.

Europe, which is already Iran's principal trading partner, does not share this US intransigence. It could thus become a substantial economic ally, all the more crucial for Iran because, while the democratisation of the country has made good progress, economic difficulties remain, and divide the reform camp between supporters of a strong state sector and supporters of privatisation of state enterprises and government monopolies in transportation, telecommunications, energy etc.

Iran, with an area of 1.63 million sq. km, is three times larger than France. In 2000 it had a population of 64 million. Aside from Persians, who speak Farsi and represent around half the inhabitants, the principal ethnic groups are Turks, **Kurds**, Baluchs and **Arabs**; there are also slightly over a million nomads. Iran accommodates around two million foreigners: 1.5 million Afghans – mainly refugees who fled the Soviet intervention of 1979 – and 500,000 Iraqis, expelled from their country because of their Iranian origins. The country's main resource is oil, with production in 2001 reaching 3.7 million barrels per day, compared with 3.17 in 1979 and 1.32 in 1981. Oil accounts for around 90 per cent of exports, the rest being made up of agricultural produce, minerals and carpets.

IRAN–IRAQ WAR

The war fought between **Iran** and **Iraq** from 1980 to 1988 threatened the **oil** lifeline provided by the Gulf and, more generally, peace in the region and in the world.

According to the *Guardian*, it was 'the most expensive and the most futile war in the contemporary history of the Middle East'. The figures for the social and economic costs of the conflict speak for themselves. There were at least a million victims on both sides, with Iran officially admitting 300,000 dead. If many of these were soldiers – including adolescents of 13 recruited into the Iranian army – many others were civilians killed in military operations aimed at towns and civilian populations. In economic terms the damage was no less enormous. According to the most realistic estimates, the two belligerents must each have spent between a third and a half of their national budgets.

In all, additional military expenditure, losses in GDP and non-invested capital would reach $500bn between the two countries. Iran officially (over)estimated the cost of reconstructing its economy at $300bn. Iraq evaluated its reconstruction at $50–60bn. On top of this, Tehran emerged $10bn in debt, Baghdad $60bn. Close to seven hundred ships were damaged or destroyed – amounting to $2bn – in the zone where 25 per cent of Western oil supplies were in transit, and in which 30 per cent of Iraq's hydrocarbon resources and 90 per cent of Iran's was concentrated.

For all that, was the Iran–Iraq War 'futile', as the *Guardian* put it? History can be used to provide justification for the war, if not the real motive. From the sixteenth century, the **Shi'ite** Safavid dynasty, which had restored the Persian Empire, coveted Mesopotamia, then a province of the **Ottoman Empire**. This rivalry between the two empires, complicated by the intervention of the colonial powers, led to clash after clash. Already the control of certain territories was at stake, particularly the 200km Shatt al-Arab waterway, the meeting place of the Tigris and the Euphrates, which flows into the Gulf. Numerous treaties have interrupted this battle, the most recent having been signed in 1913 and 1937. The conflict was resurrected following the Iraqi revolution in 1958. The paths of the two regimes split: Iran under the Shah established itself firmly in the Western camp, while **Ba'thist** Iraq gradually forged links with the Soviet Union. Aggravated by the question of the **Kurds**, the dispute had to wait until 1975 before a temporary solution was reached. On the initiative of the Algerian President, Houari Boumedienne, the Shah and **Saddam Hussein** made their peace. Both relinquished their demands: the Shatt al-Arab was shared between them, free navigation in the Gulf was guaranteed, and the Kurdish uprising was cut off from its bases.

But the peace was shortlived. In 1979 the Islamic Revolution triumphed in Iran. The ayatollahs and mullahs succeeded the Shah, toppled from the throne by a formidable popular movement. Tehran's new leaders did not hide their ambition to overthrow the Baghdad regime by supporting Iraq's Shi'ites, who formed the majority of the population. The Ba'th party, for its part, made no bones about its desire to see the last of **Khomeini**. In September 1980, after months of border incidents, Saddam abandoned the 1975 treaty and launched an attack on Iran. Tehran not only repulsed the attack, but carried the war into Iraqi territory from 1982.

The absurdity of the war became all the more apparent when deadlock set in. The Orwellian logic of the conflict then became clear. In *Nineteen Eighty-Four* George Orwell envisages a situation where 'war is a purely domestic affair'. In the three empires he describes, war is waged by each group in power against its own subjects. The object of the war is not to make or prevent territorial conquests, but to keep the structure of society intact. This prophetic vision is singularly apt when applied to Iraq and Iran.

Why, in 1980, did Baghdad's Ba'thist regime take military action? Clearly, its aims were multiple. No doubt it wanted to regain the Shatt al-Arab and the territory of Khuzistan. It also hoped to deal a definitive blow to the Islamic Revolution, which it believed was ready to fall. Furthermore, it aimed to break its own regional isolation, even hoping – in the light of **Egypt's** isolation following **Camp David** – to gain supremacy in the **Arab world**. So much is clear from its sudden defection from the 'Rejectionist Front', of which it had been the centre, to its alliance with **Saudi Arabia** and the emirates of the **Arabian Peninsula**.

However, Saddam's decision was almost certainly based on motivations internal to Iraq. In 1980, his regime was in difficulties. A powerful opposition was arrayed against him, composed of communists excluded from the National Front and harshly repressed, Kurds once again in revolt, and fundamentalist Shi'ites encouraged by the victory of their co-religionists in Tehran. A real guerrilla force was taking shape. It was to break this eruption of opposition by welding the population together in battle against the 'hereditary enemy' that Baghdad embarked on its military expedition. Ironically, it was when the battle turned against Iraq that it met with some success. The enthusiasm of the 'defenders of the fatherland' allowed the Ba'th to split the opposition.

The same calculation was made in Tehran. The need to face up to the Iraqi attack remobilised a disillusioned population and put a worried army back on its feet. The priority given to national defence was used to justify breaches of civil liberties and the halt to social reforms. It served as a pretext for reactionary clergy to take control of the country. Promised reforms were bogged down in parliamentary commissions. The argument is strengthened by the fact that in 1982, although Iran had repulsed Baghdad's troops, Khomeini decided to continue the hostilities. He rejected both the ceasefire proposals from Iraq and the countless mediations (UN, Non-Aligned, Islamic Conference, Algerian, Saudi Arabian etc.).

The final and no less curious aspect of the Iran–Iraq conflict was the role played by the superpowers. This war did not fit into the East-versus-West framework of the Cold War: each of the belligerents had allies and enemies in both camps. Paris and Moscow found themselves side by side as Baghdad's principal arms suppliers. Irangate revealed that Washington, humiliated by Tehran over the embassy hostages, was still delivering to the Islamic Republic many of the arms it needed. At the same time, and in full awareness of the use by Saddam's troops of **weapons of mass destruction** (notably chemical weapons, the use of which is banned by international conventions), American military advisors assisted the Iraqi military hierarchy in ways such as supplying them with satellite photos indicating Iranian positions etc. Furthermore, **Israel**, which was supposedly taking a stand against radical **Islam**, was the first to supply Iran, with the aim of weakening its Iraqi Arab enemy. No doubt the 'exceptional' nature of the Iran–Iraq War, which clearly did not obey the traditional laws of the form, also explains the protracted length of the conflict.

Why then did it end when it did? Tehran's decision, after refusing for six years, to accept the UN's ceasefire proposal, was based on a combination of four factors. First, the military defeats it had undergone. On all fronts, particularly in the south, with Iraq's recapture of the Fao Peninsula, the mullahs' army had been forced to relinquish the territory it had conquered since 1982. Then there were the effects on morale on the home front – particularly that of the capital, hitherto spared the fighting – caused by the new armaments employed by Baghdad: missiles and chemical weapons. There is no doubt that the 'war of towns' was a significant factor in the Ayatollah's about-face. Furthermore, the tragic shooting down of an Iranian Airbus by an American ship in July 1988 must also be mentioned. The fourth and probably decisive factor was the evolution of the political balance of power within the Iranian leadership and the rise of political actors with whom the West might be able to deal with, notably in the person of President Hashemi Rafsanjani.

In an unexpected twist, the apparent victory of Iraq quickly turned to defeat. Baghdad was also suffering the catastrophic cost of the war, with $80bn of external debt and a similar amount needed to rebuild the country. Iraq was on its knees. This was undoubtedly a motivating factor in the decision to invade **Kuwait**. The ultimate paradox is the fact that on 15 August 1990, Saddam had to surrender voluntarily the few 'prizes of war' that had been won in the long conflict with Iran in order to win Tehran's favour. He then agreed to release Iranian prisoners of war, to retreat from the territory Iraq had occupied, and in particular to respect the terms of the 1975 Algiers Accords. So, after going full circle, hundreds of thousands died for nothing.

IRAQ

Baghdad was the capital of the Abbasid Empire between the eighth and thirteenth centuries. Present-day Iraq was part of the **Ottoman Empire** until the outbreak of the First World War. Unlike other populations in the Middle East, the future peoples of Iraq – **Shi'ites** (the majority) and Sunnis alike – did not take part in the Arab revolt led by Sherif Hussein of Mecca. They united with the Ottoman Sultan against the British. However, on 23 August 1921, London imposed as king Emir Faisal, son of Sherif Hussein, who had been driven out of **Syria** by French troops in 1920. The Mandate which **Britain** obtained from the League of Nations in 1920 was to last for more than ten years, but would come up against the opposition of a population that was angered by this 'imposed' power. An uprising took place in 1919–20, but was broken, mainly through the British use of chemical weapons. In 1925, the League of Nations recognised the inclusion of the *vilayet* of Mosul (Kurdistan) into Iraq, to the detriment of **Turkey**. The country achieved **independence** in 1932, albeit at the expense of having to sign a treaty of alliance with Britain, which kept its military bases and a controlling hand in the key decisions. During the Second World War, a coup d'état was carried out by General Ali al-Kailani; it expressed nationalist sentiments, but having tried to get support from Nazi Germany it was crushed by British intervention.

The end of the war saw the growth of a national movement that was both anti-monarchist and anti-British. Attempts in 1948 by the regime's leading figure, Prime Minister Nuri Said, to sign a new treaty with London resulted in massive popular demonstrations. The **1948–49 War** allowed the authorities to put their house in order, Iraqi contingents taking part in the fighting and the defeat of the Arab armies.

After **Nasser** came to power in **Egypt**, King Faisal II and Nuri Said took the leadership of the pro-Western Arab coalition. Iraq joined the **Baghdad**

Pact in 1955 then, in 1958, formed a federation with **Jordan** to counter that of the United Arab Republic.

But it was too late: on 14 July 1958 a group of officers led by General Qasim overthrew the monarchy and established a republic. Qasim opposed the Arab nationalists who favoured union with Egypt, undertook progressive reforms and sought the backing, at first, of the powerful Iraqi Communist Party (ICP). Nevertheless, his regime's hesitancy, the increasingly personal character of his leadership, and the renewal of the Kurdish uprising brought Qasim down on 8 February 1963. After a relatively uneventful reign by the Aref brothers, who had Nasserist tendencies, the **Ba'th** party seized power in July 1968, and held it until 2003.

It took the Ba'th another ten years to consolidate its power. At the time it was a relatively small party torn by rival currents and lacking experience in government. It had to deal with the Kurdish national movement and various other competing nationalist organisations. It gained respect and revenue from a daring **oil** policy. In 1972 it nationalised the bulk of the Iraq Petroleum Company – a first in those days – and it managed to survive the Western blockade thanks to aid from the USSR, with whom Baghdad had signed a peace and friendship treaty. This policy paved the way for the creation of a National Front with the Communist Party in 1973, which allowed the Ba'th to turn its attention to the Kurdish movement, which was defeated in 1975, although the **Kurds** did win a certain **autonomy**, giving them extensive cultural rights.

The swelling oil coffers facilitated a series of profound changes for the country and also reinforced the authority of its leaders. Between 1972 and 1974 oil revenue climbed from $575m to $5.7bn. The government also introduced social measures which were designed to boost its popularity. In part these consisted of generous salary rises and a reduction in taxes, but there was also very substantial investment in infrastructure, heavy industry and the petrochemical industry. The Iraqi economy was fast becoming a state economy. Between 1972 and 1978 the number of state employees, excluding soldiers and officers, went from 400,000 to 650,000, of whom 100,000 worked in public-sector industry and 150,000 in the Interior Ministry. However, the government took a gamble on development which it lost when, after the outbreak of the war with **Iran**, Iraq depended on oil for 99 per cent of its exports. Nevertheless there were undeniable breakthroughs in three areas: education, health and the position of women.

In July 1979 **Saddam Hussein** assumed power, although he had previously been little more than the 'strong man' of President Hassan al-Baqr's regime. The already strong element of terror in Iraq now reached unprecedented levels. Saddam created a cult of personality without parallel in the **Arab world**. He also initiated a shift from the hardline policy that characterised the first ten years of Ba'thist rule to a search for reconciliation with the Gulf monarchies. The alliance with the USSR was torn up and the Ba'th party outlawed the Communist Party. Finally, Saddam kept a cautious eye on the troubles that had gripped Iran and which had a strong impact on the Shi'ites that made up 50–60 per cent of the Iraqi population. Demonstrations, which had already broken out in the Shi'ite holy cities of Karbala and Najaf in 1977, now spread because of the actions of Muhammad Baqr al-Sadr, who had grown close to **Ayatollah Khomeini** during his exile in Iraq. The regime reacted ferociously to this agitation. Mosques were placed under strict control, and in 1980 Sadr and dozens of members of his family were arrested and later executed. When he ordered his troops to attack Iran in September 1980, Saddam was hoping to put an end to the 'Islamic Revolution' once and for all.

Despite its powerful arsenal, the reticence of the international community towards its aggression (which even the UN failed to condemn), and some initial success, the Iraqi army was eventually forced to retreat. The **Iran–Iraq War** ended in 1988 leaving the two protagonists on their knees. Hundreds of thousands of Iraqis had been killed or wounded, the country lay in ruins – in particular in the area around Basra – and was in debt to the tune of several tens of billions of dollars. Baghdad's massive use of chemical weapons against Iran, and then against the Kurds, at the time aroused no serious criticism from the US, the USSR or the West generally.

The invasion of **Kuwait** on 2 August 1990 was **Saddam's** only hope of finding the money to finance his grand vision, yet the result was catastrophic. The war with Iran and then the **Gulf War** were disastrous for Iraq. The bulk of its infrastructure and industry was destroyed. For the Iraqi people this was a worst-case scenario: not only had their country regressed several decades, but the Ba'thist dictatorship was still in place. After its defeat in Kuwait in spring 1991, the Iraqi army crushed the mainly Shi'ite uprising in the south, while Kurdish militias were able to take control of the main towns of the north, primarily due to Western intervention. Despite these warnings, Saddam managed to reassert his power in a country starved by **sanctions** and whose total diplomatic isolation was strictly enforced by the international community.

After long negotiations, in May 1996 Baghdad and the UN reached an agreement on the application of **UN Security Council Resolution** 986, passed in 1995. Iraq was allowed to export $2bn worth of oil every six months, and could buy food with the sum that was left once the various UN agencies had taken their cut and the victims of the Gulf had been reimbursed via the UN Compensation Commission. Both the functioning and the legality of this institution – which, until the 2003 war, collected 25 per cent of the income from oil exports – seem more than dubious.

The total lifting of the embargo should, in principle, have been confirmed if and when Baghdad met the disarmament conditions imposed by the UN.

Between 1991 and 1998, despite obstructive manoeuvres by the Iraqi government, the UN inspectors carried out an impressive programme of work, involving the destruction of the nuclear programme, almost all the missiles, and a substantial proportion of the chemical weapons. A long-term control was also set in place, with a system of surveillance cameras at dozens of sites. But Washington, which had been hoping for a coup d'état to get rid of Saddam, now had regime change as its objective. On 31 October 1998, President Bill Clinton signed the Iraq Liberation Act, which provided for material assistance to the Iraqi opposition.

Rolf Ekeus, who led the UN inspectors in Iraq between 1991 and 1997, has revealed that not only had the US used the inspectors for spying purposes, but they had also 'pressured' the UN Special Commission (UNSCOM) 'to undertake controversial missions – at least inspections that the Iraqis thought were controversial – and thereby cause a stalemate which could form the basis for direct military intervention'. This was the attitude which, after the withdrawal of the UN inspectors, led to a series of raids carried out by the US and Britain (Operation Desert Fox) on the night of 16–17 December 1998 on targets in Iraq. The effectiveness of this action was highly debatable, even leaving aside the fact that it took place without the support of the UN, particularly because it would leave the regime free of all control for the next four years.

On 8 November 2002, UN Security Council Resolution 1441 (see Appendix 15), which had been negotiated over a long period between Paris and Washington, ordered Baghdad to destroy all its programmes for **weapons of mass destruction**, under threat of force. But the inspectors' return to Iraq, accepted unconditionally by Saddam, did not disarm the George W. Bush administration.

Following reports by UN weapons inspectors from UN Monitoring, Verification and Inspection Commission (UNMOVIC) and the International Atomic Energy Agency (IAEA) on 19 December 2002, 14 February 2003 and 7 March 2003, the international community failed to reach a unanimous decision on the next step. The US, UK and Spain introduced a new draft resolution to the UN on 27 February, but withdrew it on 17 March when it became apparent there was no chance of consensus. On 19 March 2003, President Bush gave Saddam a 48-hour deadline to leave Iraq with his sons or face military action. The war began on 20 March and continued until 9 April, when Bush declared the main phase of military activity over. It was on that day that Saddam's regime was declared ended following the toppling of a giant statue of the former President in Paradise Square in eastern Baghdad.

The Iraq which the US and its coalition allies went to war with in 2003 was a country which had been profoundly transformed by its isolation throughout the 1990s, thrown back decades and unable to rebuild its industrial infrastructure. Subjected to a murderous system of sanctions, Iraqi society collapsed, the education and health systems fell into disarray, illiteracy increased, and the regime's control over the population was strengthened. These problems were worsened in the post-war situation.

The Iraqi opposition, primarily based in exile, was traditionally fragmented and divided among itself. The Kurdistan Democratic Party and the Patriotic Union of Kurdistan dominated the Kurdish region of northern Iraq, where they retain control; the Supreme Council for the Islamic Revolution in Iraq (SCIRI), presided over by Ayatollah Muhammad Baqr al-Hakim – who would be killed in August 2003 – and the Da'wa party, based in Tehran, represent the Shi'ite **Islamist** current; the Iraqi National Congress (INC), founded in 1992 and presided over by Ahmed Chalabi, which saw itself as the opposition parliament, lost credibility in the late 1990s by falling into the American (and particularly Pentagon) orbit; and there are dozens of other groupings, such as the Movement for Constitutional Monarchy, the Iraqi Communist Party etc. Most of these groupings, with the exception of the Kurds, were based abroad, so it was difficult to estimate their influence among indigenous Iraqis prior to the collapse of Saddam's regime.

It was predictable that the US would begin its administration of post-war Iraq by setting up a military administration, in a throwback to the good old days of colonialism. Retired general Jay Garner was initially brought in to head the Coalition Provisional Authority established to run the country, but was soon replaced by Ambassador Paul Bremer, whose approach was more direct and authoritative. Bremer cancelled the *loya jirga*-style national conference due to be held in July with the intention of electing an interim Iraqi government, deciding instead to appoint a 25-member Iraqi Governing Council. The Council brought together representatives of the main exiled opposition groups (such as Chalabi's INC) in addition to Kurdish and Shi'ite parties and non-aligned figures who had remained in Iraq under Saddam. The Council faces much scepticism from Iraqis, who see it as a puppet of the US. Since then chaos has prevailed. The killing of Baqr al-Hakim on 29 August 2003 in a car-bomb explosion outside the shrine of Imam Ali in Najaf after Friday prayers only added to the difficulties of the Council. This followed the bombing of the UN compound in Baghdad on 19 August 2003, which had revealed the extent and level of organisation of the anti-US opposition to be far greater than previously anticipated. With the growing armed resistance, President Bush decided to accelerate the transfer of power to the Iraqis, but this decision will be very difficult to implement.

In a land area of 438,000 sq. km, Iraq had an estimated 24.6 million inhabitants in 2003, one third of whom were Kurds. Shi'ites represent more than half of the Arab population, and the country also has a small Christian **minority**. The real progress made in the 1970s was wiped out by the conflict with Iran and the Gulf War. The country's main resource is oil, the production of which was resumed with the application of the 'oil for food' programme, and rose from 740,000 barrels per day in 1996 to 2.3 million in 2001. The level of production after 2003 remains very low due to the anarchy and armed resistance.

ISLAM

Islam (in Arabic, 'submission to God') is one of the three great monotheistic religions. Followers are called Muslims. Islam also designates a civilisation and a culture established over the centuries – one to which the Christians of the Middle East also see themselves as belonging.

The Prophet Muhammad preached in Arabia in the seventh century of our era. He unified a large part of the **Arabian Peninsula** by word and sword. After his death in Mecca in 632, his successors, the caliphs, were endowed with both a political and a spiritual mission. They were the guides of the faithful and the leaders of conquests. This overlapping of religion and state was to weigh heavily throughout the history of Islam, though of course it also characterised Christianity over a long period. A crisis in the succession to the Prophet brought about the two great Islamic schisms: **Shi'ism** and Kharijism. The 'mainstream' of Muslims, who accepted the Umayyad succession, are designated 'Sunni'.

Within a century, the Muslim **Arabs** extended their rule to the borders of China and Spain. Two great empires organised the administration, control and conversion of the conquered populations: the Umayyad Empire, which fell in 750, and the Abbasid Empire, which succeeded it and ended under the onslaught of the Mongols in 1254. Arab domination was replaced by that of the Turks and the **Ottoman Empire**, which survived until World War I. The constitution of Mustafa Kemal's Turkish republic brought to an end the institution of the caliphate, a symbol, at times precarious and disputed, of the unity of the *umma*, the community of Muslims. Today there are more than 1.2 billion Muslims in the world, of whom around 250 million are Arabs. The majority are to be found in Asia (Pakistan, Bangladesh, Indonesia, India). An extremely dynamic black Islam has also been solidly established in Africa.

For its followers, the Islamic religion is the natural continuation of Judaism and Christianity, from which it borrowed various elements. Thus it reveres Moses and Jesus, but teaches that Muhammad brought to a close the chain of prophets, that he is 'the seal of the prophets'. The word of God, contained in the sacred book, the Qur'an, was imparted to Muhammad by the Archangel Gabriel. The Sunna, a collected deeds of the Prophet and his close companions, is the second source of law. Using these texts as a basis, juridical schools were created – four for the Sunnis – which established (though not without some confusion) the social and religious duties of all good Muslims. Five ritual obligations, called the 'pillars of religion', are the basis of religious life: the profession of faith ('I testify that there is no God but God and that Muhammad is His Prophet'); the five daily prayers; fasting during the month of Ramadan; institutionalised charity (*zakat*); the pilgrimage to Mecca. Islam has no clergy as such and thus no official 'church'; no one intercedes between God and his creature. But a special task is allotted to the doctors of law, who must define the manner in which the principles defined in the Qur'an are to be applied.

Islam is not a fixed doctrine, and has witnessed many modifications throughout the course of history. As the Italian Islamic scholar Biancamaria Scarcia has written:

> Just as in the past, where it was used to achieve extremely contradictory ends, Islam today can as easily justify a progressive policy as a reactionary one. Today, no more than in the past, there is no one political Islam, in the sense that there is no single ideology or single Islamic vision of things.

One cannot therefore find in Islam or in the Qur'an an 'analytical grid' or keys allowing one to understand the situation in **Saudi Arabia**, **Libya** or **Iran**. There is no sura in the Qur'an that explains the action of the hijackers on 11 September 2001. In the course of its long history Islam has adapted itself to all kinds of changes in the world. To borrow another of Scarcia's ideas, civil society 'reserves...the possibility of elevating to the level of religion rules and solutions that have been imposed on it by circumstances and not by principles'.

The widespread adherence to religion in the most Islamic countries is a vitally important phenomenon. The religious disaffection that has marked the West 'was checked in Islam in the 11th century by vigorous efforts on the part of the Sunnis; the success of these efforts was made easier by internal evolution within societies and changes in their situation vis-a-vis the exterior' (Maxime Rodinson). Among these changes were the Crusades, colonisation and confrontation with an increasingly dominant West. Islam then became 'the driving force of resistance to colonial violence'. In Europe, the struggle against the church constituted one of the rallying points of those who fought for civil liberties in the nineteenth century; but the colonised masses rose up against oppression in the name of Islam, in which intellectuals and thinkers such as Jamal al-Din al-Afghani (1838–97) and Muhammad Abduh (1849–1905) sought answers to the immense trauma that colonisation had come to represent. Islam's presence remained strong up to **independence**; from then on it tended to become blurred in the political sphere. It was not until the 1970s – with the emergence of what came to be called **Islamism** – that the Arab and Muslim masses to were raise Islam as the standard of their revolt and their rejection of an unjust world order.

After the fall of the Berlin Wall in 1989 and the subsequent collapse of the Soviet Union, a number of strategists and thinkers, notably in the US, attempted to designate Islam as a new enemy. For example, in the *New York Times* one could read that Islamic fundamentalism was rapidly becoming the principal threat to world peace and security, similar to that of Nazism and Fascism during the 1930s and Communism in the 1950s. Again, on 21 January 1996, the *New York Times* had a headline 'The Red Menace is Gone. But Here's Islam'. Others – particularly after 11 September 2001 – claimed that the Third World War had begun. One might characterise this current as 'Islamophobic'. Not because it criticises one or other of Islam's teachings or its interpretations, but because it considers Islam to be a 'whole', with an intrinsically evil character deriving from the Qur'an. Thus one does not have a variety of Islams with different and contradictory tendencies but one single Islam. By the same token, Muslims are seen as hostile by nature. And because they are now also resident in the West they come to be seen as an 'enemy within'. Thus, for example, Jean-François Revel wrote in his pamphlet *L'Obsession anti-americaine* that one should not be blind 'to the hatred for the West of the majority of the Muslims who live among us'. Fortunately he did not conclude from this – at least not yet – that they should be expelled.

In conclusion it would be reasonable to ask whether it would not be better to talk about 'the Muslims' rather than 'Islam'. This would make it possible to appreciate their diversity today, scattered as they are in dozens of countries around the world, living, apart from their religion, in conditions of great diversity. This would also enable us to take on board the historical dimension: Muslims have known brilliant empires and ugly dictatorships, moments of openness and periods of introversion, great intellectuals such as Ibn Khaldun, Avicenna and Averroes, and periods of decadence. Can all this really be summed up in the one single term, 'Islam'?

ISLAMISM

The term Islamism, the meaning of which is contested by many of the leading figures involved in it – is used to describe movements which have **Islam** as the main focus of their political activity and which seek to establish an Islamic state. The term is one imposed upon them, but is ambiguous: it has contributed to the identification of Islam in Western minds with extremism and **terrorist** violence. It has also diverted the real debate: books are written in an attempt to understand the 'essence' of Islam in narrowly religious terms, instead of analyzing the concrete realities of Muslim countries. From the early 1990s onwards, certain American foundations have seen in Islamism the new global threat to replace the 'red peril'. After the 11 September 2001 attacks on New York and Washington by **Osama bin Laden**'s al-Qaeda group, such analysis has undoubtedly gained more support in Western public opinion. For regimes in the Middle East, the growth of Islamism has provided a convenient pretext for the rejection of demands for political reform and the merciless repression which they mete out to their own people. This line of argument tends to receive a sympathetic hearing in the West.

Islamism is a key phenomenon of our age, which one cannot afford to ignore: the political mobilisation of tens of millions of men and women in the name of religion. In the nineteenth century, Islam was a motor of resistance to colonial violence. Later, when young national states were beginning to see the light of day, the economic and political models adopted tended to model themselves on Western societies or, subsequently, on the model of the socialist countries. In that period Islam functioned as a rather vague political reference point, particularly at the level of the state. However – and this went broadly unnoticed among observers – it was making very deep inroads within civil society and at the level of the individual citizen.

Without giving a detailed picture of the **Arab world** in the period from the end of the Second World War to the early 1970s, two broad character-istics can be discerned: the consolidation of political **independence** and the failure of attempts at modernisation. The basic problems of poverty, illiteracy, sexual inequality and the lack of political freedom were a long way from being solved. At the same time, people's lives were undergoing major upheavals. How is one to measure the impact of the region's anarchic urbanisation on the hundreds of peasants who were being uprooted from their villages? And what can one say about **President Anwar al-Sadat**'s 'modernisation' in the 1970s, which saw the population of Cairo rise to 15–17 million (nobody knows the real figure), with an accompanying increase in inequality and a collapse of community life? The pre-existing fabric of society was being torn apart. In a world and a society marked by local conflicts (such as the Arab–Israeli confrontation and the Gulf), where the responsibility for setbacks is all too easily attributed to imported ideologies, whether Western or socialist, and Western interference, people see Islam as a final resort. They look to religion for political answers to their problems. It is here that we have to look for the true meaning of the 'Islamic revival'. The revival often gives an Islamic expression to old demands, as **Hamas** takes up the old line of the **Palestine Liberation Organisation (PLO)**.

In the view of François Burgat, this movement marks a 'further distancing of the ex-colonial power'. Having first been expressed at the political and economic level, this distancing now expresses itself on 'terrains that are ideological, symbolic and more broadly speaking cultural, where the shock of colonialism was at its most traumatic'. Burgat goes on to suggest,

At the same time as supplying a language which is its own, the categories of local culture and history confer on the dynamic of independence movements what they had long lacked: the precious attributes of a kind of ideological 'autonomy' which gives them an aura of completeness, and the right for those who are mobilizing it once again to approach a certain universality (without however reneging on the structuring elements of their 'specificity').

A way, in fact, of opposing the modern world and a globalisation which reduces cultural diversity to a Western monoculture.

The resurgence of Islamist movements is also linked to the political void which was created in the Arab world as a result of the wide-ranging political repression in the 1950s and 1960s: political parties were banned, trade unions broken, and popular organisations emptied of any substance. In such a situation the mosque became the last place where one might still meet, discuss and engage in politics. The use of religion – and of certain groups such as the **Muslim Brotherhood** – by 'moderate' regimes in their struggle against the left, and against Nasserism and **Ba'thism**, is a further factor, albeit not decisive. Thus it was Sadat himself who encouraged the re-establishment of the Muslim Brothers, freed their leaders from prison, and gave them a freedom of action and expression that was denied to other components of **Egypt**'s political scene. Moreover, the **US** policy of aiding the Afghan Mujahedin in the 1980s, along with Pakistan and **Saudi Arabia**, allowed a new level of solidarity to emerge which would come to be a breeding ground for the al-Qaeda network.

In schematic terms, three successive phases have developed since the 1970s. First, there is an Islamism which can be characterised as 'traditional', whose objective is 'the foundation of an Islamic state and not just by implementation of the *shari'a*. From Mawdudi to Sayyid Qutb, via Hassan al-Banna, politics and the state are at the core of their thinking' (Olivier Roy). Its political expression can most notably be found in the various movements of the Muslim Brotherhood, but also in the Turkish Refah party or the Party of Islamic Renewal in Tajikistan. Funding from Pakistan, the Gulf states (especially Saudi Arabia and **Kuwait**) permit the construction of vast welfare networks of schools, clinics and charitable organisations, without which their influence would be minimal. It is a reformist trend, and has recourse to violence only in exceptional circumstances.

According to Olivier Roy in *L'Islam mondialisé*, three signs point to the decline of this legalist trend. First, the re-Islamisation of society, usually in a conservative fashion, has taken place everywhere. Of course, it has been done under pressure from Islamist movements, but it is more a case of the state itself which has sought to win religious legitimacy; this re-Islamisation has escaped the Islamist organisations and 'has been achieved without the prospect of a change in those in power'. Second, these groups have been 'nationalised', with agendas which reflect local struggles, whether in Egypt or Palestinian areas. They have subsequently lost their 'trans-national' perspective, and therefore some of the attraction they had for the young has also been lost. Finally, they have been contested by the emergence of a second wave of movements with a more radical plan of action.

Most of its devotees look to the doctrine of Sayyid Qutb, one of the historic leaders of the Egyptian Muslim Brothers, although they tend to interpret his writings with meanings that were not necessarily his. They call for a fight to the death with the governments of the countries of Islam, on the grounds that they are irreligious. These movements have been the object of particular attention in the West since the victory of the Islamic Revolution in **Iran**. Many of its militants fought in Afghanistan. However, by the end of the 1990s, their scope was limited and their audiences reduced. More than twenty years since the victory of **Ayatollah Khomeini** in Iran, they have failed to win power in any single state. Egyptian militants, for example, have come to the end of what could in the 1990s be described as a state of guerrilla warfare which momentarily caused the state to tremble. There is a new tendency for these movements to renounce violence, as in Egypt.

This defeat has been accompanied by the emergence of a third category of Islamism: the deterritorialised Islamism of al-Qaeda, whose influence remains at the margins of the Arab world (with the possible exception of Saudi Arabia). It is stronger in Afghanistan, Pakistan and the West. Roy notes, moreover, that Osama bin Laden echoes 'the recent manifestations of a profoundly secular and often Western terrorism, not just in his tactics, but in his target of American imperialism too'. The profile of members of the second generation of al-Qaeda, who have replaced the 'Afghans', can be characterised exactly by 'that rupture with the Muslim world which they nevertheless purport to represent': they left their home countries, settled in the West, have no previous involvement with Islamic militancy. Most of them underwent their re-Islamisation in the West itself. If their deeds are spec-tacular, their local roots are weak and the prospect of them seizing power is slim in the extreme. Nevertheless, al-Qaeda has come to embody terrorism, and represents the insatiable enemy upon which the US has declared war.

The global downswing for political Islamist movements is by no means accompanied by a decline of religion. On the contrary, Roy describes a neo-fundamentalism characterised as 'post-Islamist', as it no longer raises the issue of the state. It calls for the 'privatisation of re-Islamisation'. All over the Arab and Muslim world, the signs of an Islamic revival are evident. Paradoxically, this 'privatisation' will contribute to the secularisation of society, the separation of religion and state, but under forms very different from those which developed in the West.

As Burgat observes, 'the resurgence of the categories of Islamic culture thus creates not just one, but an infinite variety of political attitudes, not just one, but a thousand-and-one ways of being Islamist'. A failure to understand this diversity prevents an understanding of the reality of the Muslim world and reduces it to a monolithic and threatening entity.

ISRAEL

'On this day that sees the end of the British Mandate and in virtue of the natural and historic right of the Jewish people and in accordance with the Resolution of the UN General Assembly, we proclaim the creation of a Jewish State in Palestine.' These were the words with which, at four o'clock on 14 May 1948, **David Ben Gurion** announced the birth of Israel to the world from the foyer of the Museum of Tel Aviv. In a single phrase he stated the new state's double claim to legitimacy: that of the Jewish people's right, according to **Zionism**, to Palestine – based on the promise made almost four thousand years before by Jehovah to Abraham (Genesis IX, 18) – and that of the international law decreed by the UN following Hitler's **genocide**.

No sooner was it created than Israel found itself at war with its neighbours, whose armies invaded Palestinian territory the very next day. The Arab–Israeli **1948–49 War** was to be the first in a long series of conflicts which came to punctuate Israel's history. Ben Gurion was Prime Minister from 1948 to 1963, with a brief interlude between 1953 and 1955, when he went into retirement, only to have it interrupted by the Lavon affair (see **Ben Gurion, David**). The Old Man's long term in office was characterised by the country's demographic, economic and social expansion, by Israel's shift from its early policy of non-alignment to an increasingly open pro-Western commitment, but also by the preparation and realisation, in 1956 and together with **Britain** and **France**, of the intervention against **Nasser's Egypt**.

On the other hand, Ben Gurion, having resigned in 1963, did not sanction the **1967 War**, launched much against his will by his successor Levy Eshkol, supported by a government of National Unity. After Eshkol's death in 1969, Golda Meir presided over the coalition until 1970, the date of the retreat of the right. It was to be a Religious–Labour coalition – like all Israeli governments from 1948 to 1967 – that suffered the full shock of the 'surprise' of the **1973 War**. The consequences of the latter would lead Labour to its downfall. After one final **Rabin** government, in 1976, the right, reformed into Likud, won the general elections of 1977 for the first time in Israel's political history. After the **Lebanon 1982 War**, **Menachem Begin** was forced to hand over the leadership of the government to **Yitzhak Shamir**. The elections of 1984 having not produced a victory for either of the major parties, a government of National Unity was forced, with **Shimon Peres** and Shamir taking turns as premier until the elections of November

1988, which took place at the height of the Palestinian **Intifada**. The Shamir governments were to bury the Baker plan for Israeli–Egyptian–Palestinian negotiation, before being obliged to take part, after the **Gulf War**, in the regional conference called in Madrid under the sponsorship of the **US** and **Russia**.

As if by a boomerang effect, it was General Yitzhak Rabin who emerged victorious from the elections of June 1992, at the head of a left coalition. One year later, the secret Oslo negotiations were finally, on 13 September 1993, to conclude with the Israeli–Palestinian declaration of principles on **autonomy**, and then, in 1994 and 1995, in the Oslo I and Oslo II Accords. Israel left the autonomous towns to the **Palestinian Authority**, of which **Yasser Arafat** was to be triumphantly elected President. But after the assassination of the Israeli Prime Minister on 4 November 1995 and the interim government of Peres, the right returned to power on 29 May 1996 with **Benyamin Netanyahu**, who refused – except in Hebron – any further Israeli withdrawal. Three years later he was to give way to the leftist Ehud Barak, who privileged the Syrian option for a year, then withdrew Israel from south Lebanon, and finally went for participation in the **Camp David** summit. However, failure on this front and **Ariel Sharon**'s 28 September 2000 visit to the al-Aqsa Mosque led to the **second Intifada**. The right-wing Sharon, elected on 6 February 2001, embarked on a military escalation which, with the alternation of Palestinian suicide bombings and Israeli repression, was to lead to the re-occupation of most of the autonomous towns. This brief summary gives some idea of how much the development of the Jewish state has been marked by that first conflict with the **Palestinians** and, as a result, with the **Arab world**.

Admittedly Israel's balance sheet, 55 years after its foundation, appears impressive in many respects. Its population rose from 805,000 in 1948 to more than 6.5 million in 2002, with its Jewish element (77.2 per cent, or just over 5 million people) representing 38 per cent of the 13.3 million **Jews** reckoned to exist in the world. This growth owes much to the organisation of *aliya*, which, with almost 3 million immigrants over the course of 53 years, has contributed to a 41.5 per cent growth of the population – although many hundreds of thousands of them never settled, and moved on. The economic statistics are also impressive: GNP, which was less than $1bn in 1948, in 2000 exceeded $10bn; in per-capita terms, it rose from $1500 to more than $16,500. Among the capital invested in expansion, substantial payments have been made by the diaspora, $1bn was paid out by the German Federal Republic in reparations and, above all, more than $97bn of aid has been received by Tel Aviv from the US government since 1948.

After the Madrid Conference, and even more after the **Oslo Accords**, hopes for peace fed growth, which reached 6 per cent per annum on average during the 1990s. Foreign investment went up 15-fold: encouraged by the peace negotiations, reassured by the weakening of the Arab boycott, given confidence by the guarantee of $10bn from the US government, encouraged by the current privatisation of most of the public sector, and stimulated by the free-trade agreements between Israel and the US and Europe, multi-national capital saw Israel as the 'dragon' of the Middle East. But the breakdown of negotiations with the Palestinians and the subsequent escalation of conflict led to an economic downturn which combined with the crisis of the world economy, and particularly that of the new tech-nologies. A flight of foreign capital, a 50 per cent reduction in tourism and a falling off of immigration, plus a restrictive fiscal and monetary policy, was the cocktail which led the economy into recession for the first time since 1952. In 2001, Israel's GNP (which had risen by 6.4 per cent in 2000) fell back by 0.5 per cent, per-capita GDP fell by 2.9 per cent, fixed capital investment by 8.9 per cent and the export of goods and services by 13.1 per cent. The new-technology sector alone, representing half of the country's exports, registered a drop of 10 per cent, with the number of start-ups falling in the course of one year from 4000 to 2500.

Despite the black clouds gathering at the start of the twenty-first century, Israel testifies to the vitality of the Jews who chose Israel as the place to rebuild their lives after the tragedy of World War II. But this should not conceal the effects of the Israeli–Palestinian conflict on all aspects of the country's life. It is, in fact, the decisive element that has structured the young Jewish state, whose economy, social and political life, culture, ideology and, of course, defence have been organised around this continuous struggle. This, in turn, has fanned all the contradictions of Israeli society, sometimes stretching them to breaking point and even giving rise to new, still more dangerous ones. If the Israel of 2003 is generally agreed to bear little resemblance to the ideal dreamed of by the pioneers or the society visualised by **Theodor Herzl**, it is first and foremost because of the inevitable state of war between Zionism and Palestinian nationalism. The founder of the Zionist movement and his successors chose to ignore Palestinian national rights, just as, until the 1970s, the Palestinian movement denied Israeli identity. The contrast between project and reality could not be more striking.

'We wish to be in the vanguard of all that is in the interest of humanity, and represent, as a new country, a country of experimentation,' wrote Herzl. The socialist Zionists, adopting this conception and 'Marxifying' it, were able to give free rein to the most generous of utopias, thanks to their over-whelming influence in the **Yishuv** and subsequently in the young Israel: collective ownership of land, a system of communes (*kibbutzim*, accounting for around 30 per cent of the Jewish rural population and 3 per cent of Israelis in general) and co-operatives (*moshavim*, accounting for 70 per cent of agricultural production). Furthermore, there is a trade-union economy which represents up to 28 per cent of the GNP, 66 per cent of agricultural employment and 66 per cent of salaried employment. These achievements stem from an Israeli socialism which was nevertheless unable to influence the capitalist nature of the system and could not resist Likud once in power or the onslaught of globalisation. Crippled by debts which ran up to several billion dollars, the national *kibbutz* movement found itself hard pressed to enforce the changes which would allow it to retain its achievements: the commercial enterprises of the Histadrut trade union did not escape the widespread privatisation of the public sector; the minimum wage of Israeli workers was undermined by competition from Palestinian workers and Israel's new underclass, the 250,000 non-Jewish immigrants brought in to replace the Palestinians, as well as individuals contracted to work in Israel's budding high-tech industries. As Ze'ev Sternhell said in *The Origins of Israel: Between Nationalism and Socialism*, far from being a 'successful synthesis between socialism and the idea of the nation', socialist Zionism has submitted to 'the primacy of the nation'. Furthermore, 'the call of socialist Zionism to revolutionary nationalism has silenced all other such cries'.

'We will seek to bestow the moral salvation of work on men of every age and of every class, and thus our people will find their strength again in the land of the seven-hour day,' wrote Herzl. Israel has long since stopped seeing this as a social priority. The state of war has long served as justification for austerity: how is the rise in the standard of living to be maintained and important social needs satisfied when more than a third of the state budget is being devoted to defence, to 'maintaining law and order' in the **West Bank** and Gaza and to colonising them? The accelerated growth of the Israeli economy during the 1990s did not reduce social inequalities – far from it. On the one hand there are the managers, business lawyers and government experts who monopolise the profits of progress; on the other there are the immigrants from Eastern Europe, Africa and Asia treated like slaves, the **Arabs** exploited, the **Oriental Jews** discriminated against and old people marginalised. The end of the peace process translated into a fall in standards of living: in 2001, per-capita income fell by nearly 3 per cent. But this was a lot more marked among the less fortunate strata. A report by the National Insurance and the Ministry of Labour and Social Affairs reveals that 20 per cent of Israelis – 1.17 million – and 30 per cent of children – 531,000 – were living below the poverty line in 2001. In the meantime the government had ordered an austerity cure, and the same report estimated that the lower five tenths of society were bearing the weight of 70 per cent of the budget cuts, while the top two tenths suffered only 9 per cent. Now, a household belonging to the top tenth was already receiving 12 times the monthly income of a family in the lowest tenth. Not to mention the average income of company directors, which occasionally represented four times the figure of the minimum wage. A scandalous situation in a country with a tradition of egalitarianism.

'We are a people, an indivisible people,' claimed Herzl. In fact, Herzl's people are now profoundly divided along lines of ethnicity, at least in Israel. Roughly speaking, the dividing line between the haves and the have-nots follows the dividing line between Western and Oriental Jews. Forming the majority of the Israeli population between the 1950s and the mid-1980s, Jews from Arab countries make up – after the **Israeli Arabs** – the main body of the poor, the unemployed, the illiterate and criminal offenders. Contrary to expectations, these discriminations have been reproduced, even intensified, from generation to generation, with political repercussions that the (Western) Labour leaders in power since 1948 did not foresee. In an act of revenge for more than three decades of injustice, the Oriental Jews went over to Likud *en masse*, enabling it to come to power and stay there – in November 1988 70 per cent of them again voted for Shamir's party. The tensions were not eased by the far more generous welcome reserved for the hundreds of thousands of Soviet Jews, most of them Ashkenazim.

The elections of May 1999, with 33 parties, 15 of which would end up being represented in the Knesset, reflected the growth of antagonisms within a mosaic prey to centrifugal forces. As the Zionist ideals of the pioneers and the dream of a socialist society were on the decline, many Israelis fell back on their ethnic groupings. Communitarian ambitions thus progressively took over from collective struggle. Some communities, for example the Oriental Jews, led a defensive struggle in order to improve their status. Others were particularly fighting to escape from a pariah situation: for example the Jews 'imported' from Ethiopia, known as the Falasha, or non-Jewish immigrant workers from Africa, Asia and Eastern Europe. Palestinians were also fighting for equal rights. But the Russians wanted more: they nurtured hopes of exercising hegemonic influence, challenging the traditional Ashkenazi bourgeoisie. This communitarian segmentation went alongside a growing antagonism between secular and religious forces. Proof of this was the composition of the fifteenth assembly: the 'mainly ethnic' formations took almost a third of the 120 seats, the religious groups 27, and parties which had put the struggle against 'religious oppression' at the heart of their campaigns took 16.

'I cannot believe that the Jewish state I envisage will be narrow-minded, orthodox and reactionary,' affirmed Herzl. After more than a half century since the proclamation of the Jewish state, then dominated by the social democrats and flanked by a powerful left wing made up of Zionists and communists, in November 1988 the right, the extreme right and the religious groups picked up almost 53 per cent of the vote. Whereas Ben Gurion and his friends had attacked and marginalised the 'Jewish fascists', the far right continued to make headway, going from 2.6 per cent of the vote and three members of Knesset in 1981 to 10 per cent and 11 members in 1992. In 1996 one of the far-right groups, Tsomet, allied itself with Likud.

In 2002–3, under a government now reduced to the right and the far right, the idea of 'transfer' – in other words the ethnic cleansing of Eretz ('Greater') Israel – previously limited to the far right – unfolded like a wave over Palestinian society. The media were weighing the pros and cons, normally moderate public figures found sense in the idea, 46 per cent of Israelis in an opinion poll said that they were favourable, while on the ground, in the West Bank, settlers and soldiers were harassing the inhabitants of some villages to the point that they left.

'Will we, in the long run, become a theocracy? No! We will not allow the theocratic tendencies of our religious leaders to intensify. We will confine them to their temples.' In fact, they did not stay there very long. With a percentage of votes varying from 10 to 15 per cent, they succeeded in gradually imposing their agenda by acquiring a pivotal role and applying skillful pressure on the **Israeli political parties**. Already, Ben Gurion had yielded to them in 1948–49, when he renounced the idea of endowing the Jewish state with a constitution – the only law a **Jew** must obey, explained the religious authorities, is divine law – and accepted a compromise, a so-called status quo, in matters of education. Not only were the rabbinical tribunals to reign as masters over the personal life of Israelis – Jewish identity, marriage, divorce and inheritance depend entirely on them: 'It is legally impossible,' explained the Israeli jurist Claude Klein, 'to contract in Israel a marriage between a Jewish person and a non-Jewish one' – but the synagogue managed to have its own education system recognised and financed, while obtaining control of the religious education given by state schools.

The rabbis would squeeze still more from Begin, and then from Shamir, who both needed them in order to defeat their adversaries. New subsidies to religious schools followed and, more importantly, a stricter application by all state agencies of the Shabbat, the religious law by which Saturday is a day of rest, and the religious code governing the preparation of food. The ultra-Orthodox also turned their attention to autopsies and excavations. They called for a revision of the law regarding 'Who is a Jew' – which, along with the 'Law of Return', forms the basis for the attribution of Israeli nationality – in order to reduce the possibility of conversion to Judaism. Thus they set up an obstacle to the implantation into Israel of the reformist and liberal Judaism very powerful in the US and newly in vogue in Europe. Their most important mobilisation took place on 14 February 1999, when a demonstration brought together 250,000 ultra-Orthodox Jews in **Jerusalem** against three decisions of the Supreme Court: recognition of the representativity of liberal Judaism, the right for *kibbutzim* to open their shops on the Sabbath, and the requirement that students at religious schools hitherto exempted should do military service.

'The collective Israeli body has never managed to decide whether Judaism is a religion, a sort of nationalism, or both,' says sociologist Baruch Kimmerling of the Hebrew University of Jerusalem.

> Colonizers and immigrants, to be here we need legitimacy. The Jewish religion provides one form of legitimacy. This is why secular Zionism borrowed its central themes and even its terminology. Today, the ideological hegemony of Zionism is threatened by the uncoupling of the bond between religion and nation. *Kulturkampf* has begun. But, in order for Israel to become truly secular, it must accept that it is no longer the Jewish State, but a state of its citizens. In the final analysis, the status of Arabs in Israel is the best indication of how civilized our society actually is.

Otherwise, as the joke goes, even atheist Israelis are forced to believe that God promised them the Holy Land.

'The barracks is the place for professional soldiers', who, like the 'ministers of the faith,' said Herzl, 'have no right to interfere in affairs of state, for their meddling would provoke internal and external problems'. In defiance of this judicious advice, Israeli political life swarms with generals, from Sharon (in Likud) to the far-right Raphael Eitan (Tsomet), but also in the centre, with Amnon Lipkin-Shahak, and on the left with, after Barak, Amram Mitzna (Labour), as well as the pacifists Matityahu Peled and Yehoshafat Harkabi. Whereas its place had begun to be reduced with the prospects for peace, falling to 8.5 per cent of GDP in the 1990s, the defence budget, standing at $10.3bn in 2001, went up to 9.5 per cent of GDP. After a halving, over ten years, of the numbers employed in its public sector, and several restructurings, the Israeli arms industry is once again 'competitive' and has refound its place in the country's foreign trade. In total, in the period 1997–2001, Israel had eleventh place on the list of buyers of conventional arms in the world (with $2.8bn of imports), and twelfth place on the list of the biggest sellers (exports of $1bn).

The major budgetary outlay and principal economic power (after the Histadrut trade-union empire), the Israeli Defence Forces (IDF) is also a major ideological force, given the time at its disposal to train young Israelis, who undergo three years of military service and often spend months of duty as reservists in the West Bank and Gaza. Since autumn 2000, however, army chiefs of staff have been confronted with a growth in conscientious objection. Already at the time of the Lebanon War, the Yesh Gvul ('There is a Limit') movement had brought together dozens of young soldiers who refused military service in Lebanon. Twenty years later, Seruv ('Refusal') has been mobilising hundreds of young people and reservists. They braved the authorities and risked prison in order not to take part in repression of the Intifada. By autumn 2002 there were more than 1000 of them.

'We shall be an outpost of civilization against barbarism,' Herzl used to argue before the great powers to whom he presented his Palestinian project. On this point, his successors, at the time of the Yishuv and since the birth of Israel, have scrupulously abided by his ideas. One of the keys to the Israeli impasse no doubt lies here, a result of the very logic of the venture. By exclusively seeking its security in alliance with the great powers, especially the US (after a brief 'honeymoon' with the Soviet Union), the Jewish state has sacrificed its chances of peace with the Palestinians and the Arab world. How can Israel fully take its place among the nations of the Middle East, rather than remaining a North American outpost in the region? Furthermore, what state would safeguard its very sovereignty – 'the first aim is sovereignty,' Herzl used to say – by depending each year on $3bn (more than $800 per Israeli, man, woman and child) of economic and military aid paid out by the US, to whom it also owes a large part of the $19bn (more than 60 per cent of the GNP for one year) of Israel's foreign debt?

'In adversity, we shall remain united and we shall suddenly discover our strength. And it is that strength that will allow us to form a state, even a model state,' wrote Herzl. And indeed, the Zionist movement owes much of its success to the extremely strong motivation, political, ideological and moral, of its members. Many Israeli veterans nostalgically recall this, as the crisis of Israel gathers force and begins to affect the values upon which the Zionist movement was founded – which is perhaps its most threatening aspect. 'When they hear the word "values", they get out their cheque books,' says one of Rachel Mizrahi's characters. Another adds, 'What oppresses me in this country is not the fear of dying in the next war, it is the lack of any quality of life. Everything is false. Lies, rackets, speculations, fraud, string pulling, theft. Everybody does it and everybody thinks it's normal. It's pathetic. Do you remember, when we used to talk about morals and integrity?' The majority point of view? Certainly not. But since the **Lebanese Civil War**, and especially since the first Intifada, many eyes have been opened. Liberating in the eyes of the ghetto Jews and the survivors of the death camps, Zionism has become an occupier. Pacifist in its declared intentions, it has become an aggressor. The promised equality is nothing but a red herring in the eyes of the misfits of Israeli society, those blacks despised by the whites. The austerity of the pioneers has been tainted by all sorts of scandals. The much-vaunted democracy, for and by the Jewish citizens, is showing its limitations. The cult of money and the worship of new technology have not replaced the discarded values of socialist Zionism. Israelis find it difficult to admit to themselves, as Professor Leibovitz underlined, that 'there is one fundamental fact, which transcends ideology, theory or faith: this land belongs to two peoples. Each of them believes in its deepest soul that this land is theirs. In other words, there is a choice between co-existence and all-out war.'

Within its borders as they stood before the 1967 War, the so-called 'Green Line', in 2002 Israel had a population of 6.5 million, including more than a million Arabs, in an area of 21,000 sq. km. It had also annexed the Syrian **Golan Heights** (2000 sq. km) and East Jerusalem (143 sq. km). It had occupied the West Bank (5440 sq. km) as well as the **Gaza Strip** (330 sq. km). On the other hand, in May 2000 it had withdrawn from the 'security belt' which it had occupied in southern Lebanon since 1978. Its GDP amounted to $104bn in 2000. In 2001, exports of goods and services had fallen to $38.7bn, while imports stood at $43.4bn; the budget deficit had risen to $4.7bn, which was to be added to an external debt of $42.8bn (41 per cent of GNP), while internal debt stood at $70bn (67 per cent). Israel possesses few natural resources: no **oil**, some phosphates and potash. Part of the country's development lies in agriculture, whose success is due to the ultra-modern techniques employed, and in industries that import raw materials and export products of greatly added value, like diamonds, electronics, arms, chemical products etc. Since the late 1980s, high technology represents a growing part of the economic activity and exports of the country: tele-communications, semiconductors, network management, software, medical, pharmaceutical and biotechnology. More than half the country is taken up by the Negev Desert, which receives only 100–200mm of rainfall.

ISRAELI ARABS

Israeli Arabs are those **Palestinians** who were not part of the forced exodus during the **1948–49 War**. At that time they numbered 160,000; by 2002 they numbered a million, some 20 per cent of the population of Israel. For the most part they are to be found in three regions: the Galilee, 'the Triangle' around Umm al-Fahm, and 'the Little Triangle' around Taibeh. In 1949, Israel annexed these zones, which the **Partition Plan** had allocated to the Arab state, and their inhabitants became Israeli citizens (of second-class status) in a state that wanted above all to be Jewish. Up until 1966, Israeli Arabs lived under a military government that subjected them to carrying passes, to curfews and to house arrest, and which furthered Jewish colonisation by confiscating Arab land.

The population's social structure has undergone drastic changes in the last thirty years. More than 75 per cent rural in 1960, it was largely urban by the late 1980s. More than 50 per cent of the Palestinian workforce is employed in the construction industry. Over 13 per cent of Israeli Arabs are Christian and around 10 per cent **Druze**. The latter enjoy special treatment, since, alone among the **Arabs**, they are obliged to do military service. The Israeli government has always exploited religious divisions. But this has not been enough to halt the development of Palestinian national feeling, which gained strength after 1967 and asserted itself dramatically on 30 March 1976, 'Land Day', during which tens of thousands of Palestinians demonstrated. Bloody reprisals followed, leaving six dead and dozens wounded.

The Israeli Communist Party has gradually become the mouthpiece of this national **minority** fighting for its rights. Indeed 40 per cent of the Arab population has voted for its candidates in the various elections, and it controls most of the major Arab towns, including Nazareth. The Communist Party also came to symbolise the cultural renaissance of the Palestinians through its Arab language press (*al-Ittihad*, *al-Jadid*) and its intellectuals (Émile Habibi, Émile Touma, Tawfiq Ziyyad). Another less powerful force that expressed this nationalism was Muhammad Miari and Matityahu Peled's Progressive List for Peace. The influence of the **Islamist** movement increased during the course of the 1980s. In the municipal elections of 1989 they made huge gains, notably by seizing control of the second-largest Israeli Arab city, Umm al-Fahm.

In the 1990s, however, many observers remarked upon the 'Israelisation' of the Arabs, characterised by a desire to integrate and a demand for equal status with the Jewish population. A UN report in 1998 found 17 laws which were discriminatory against Arab citizens. The Arab population is discriminated against in public services, access to education, health, employment and housing. The funding of Arab municipalities is much lower than that allocated to Jewish towns.

The situation deteriorated rapidly in October 2000, when Israeli repression of solidarity demonstrations of Israeli Arabs with the Palestinian **second Intifada**, which had just begun, resulted in 13 deaths and more than 700 wounded in a week. Ehud Barak deprived himself of his Arab electorate who, in reaction, abstained massively in the elections of February 2001. The independent inquiry into the circumstances of the repression dragged out, but ended three years later by highlighting the responsibility of the law-and-order agencies – as well as the responsibility of former Prime Minister Barak and former Minister for Internal Security Shlomo Ben Ami. On 9 September 2001, for the first time, in Netanya a suicide bombing was carried out by an Israeli Arab. The Minister of the Interior proposed withdrawing Israeli citizenship from Palestinians accused of 'endangering state security'.

ISRAELI POLITICAL PARTIES

Israeli political life has always been characterised by the existence of a multiplicity of groupings which reflect the innumerable currents within **Zionism**, to which they all claim to belong, with the exception of the Communist Party. It is a framework that lends itself to diversity, a tendency which became more marked in the 1990s as the big parties, Likud and Labour, lost ground to the smaller ones. This was a result of divisions within the electorate and society at large, particularly between secular and religious tendencies, but also between Sephardim and Ashkenazim. But temporary modifications to the electoral system also played their part: from 1996 to 2001 voters could choose their 'camp' (by voting for the prime minister of their choice) while still remaining in their 'tent' (choosing MPs). Thus in the last two national elections there were 30 parties contesting the Knesset's 120 seats.

The principal party of the **Yishuv** between the two world wars, and of **Israel** until 1977, was Labour, created in 1930 under the name of Mapai (the Labour party of Eretz ['Greater'] Israel) from an amalgamation of two Zionist socialist groups. Reformist by nature and advocating alliances with **Britain** and the Zionist right, its share of the vote increased from 42.3 per cent in 1931 to 59.1 per cent in 1944. After the creation of Israel, Labour leaders held the posts of both president and prime minister. However, its position over the years deteriorated – along with that of its allies – from 53.4 per cent of the vote in 1949 to 26 per cent in 1977 when, for the first time, Labour had to cede power to the right.

This reversal was all the more striking because after 1969 Labour benefited from the backing of Mapam, within the Maarakh Labour alignment. Heir to the Hashomer Hatzair (the Young Guard) and the Poalei Zion Smole (Left Workers of Zion), Mapam maintained its original principles after the war. These included the project of a bi-national state, friendship with the Soviet Union and a commitment to *kibbutzim* (communes). But its entry into government in 1967 and the Maarakh in 1969 distanced it from these principles.

It took many years for the left to recover from this setback. Labour won a respectable 36.6 per cent of the vote in 1981, but in 1984 this fell again to 34.9 per cent – which did not prevent it from participating in the government of National Unity – and in 1988 to 30 per cent. Four years later it was able to win the election with 34.6 per cent of the vote, thanks to the contribution of the parties now united under the banner of Meretz – Mapam, Ratz (the civil-rights movement) and the centrist Shinui party – which took 9.6 per cent of the vote. On 29 May 1996, this coalition – whose leader, **Shimon Peres**, saw the post of prime minister snatched from his grasp by **Benyamin Netanyahu**, who had attracted less than 30,000 votes more – found itself once more in opposition, with 26.8 per cent and 7.4 per cent of the vote, producing 34 and 9 Knesset members.

Its return to power came with the following elections and the victory of Ehud Barak in May 1999, with 56 per cent of the vote compared with 44 per cent for the outgoing Prime Minister. But in parliament Labour and its affiliates had eight fewer seats (26 compared with 34). The early election called by Barak on 6 February 2001 after the failure of the **Camp David** summit was virtually suicidal: **Ariel Sharon** crushed him with 62.5 per cent of the vote, against 37.5 per cent – a rout which was accentuated by the mass abstention of Arab voters. Moreover, Benyamin Ben Eliezer, who replaced Barak as the party's leader, Shimon Peres and five other Labourist politicians joined the government of National Unity. Despite the opposition of a large number of party notables and militants, they remained there for 20 months, effectively giving backing to Sharon's intransigence. During this dark period, Meretz would be the only opposition party of any appreciable size. The socialist left went from 12 seats in 1992 to 9 in 1996, rising to 10 in 1999. Meretz suffered considerably in the 2003 general election, winning a mere 6 seats.

There are other minority tendencies on the left which have broken with the mainstream, notably the far left and the only organisation bringing together both **Arabs** and **Jews**, the Communist Party, created in 1922. It underwent numerous splits, of which the last, in 1965, considerably weakened it among the Jewish population. Anti-Zionists in a Zionist nation, pro-Soviets in an anti-Soviet country, advocates of a Palestinian state rejected by their fellow citizens, Israeli communists have yet to achieve more than 5 per cent of the vote, most of which comes from the Arab electorate. The Democratic Front for Peace and Equality (Hadash), which the Communists led, saw an upturn in its fortunes on 29 May 1996, with five deputies being elected, but it lost two seats in the 1999 elections. 2003 saw it retain its three members of Knesset.

The Communist Party, which had long been dominant among Arab Israelis, had for long been experiencing increasing competition from the new political movements. But these, more than any of the others, suffered from the big abstention of their electorate in the 2001 elections, a popular response to the repression of October 2000. However, the alliance between the Democratic Arab Party and one of the factions of the **Islamist** movement had made possible a breakthrough in 1996, giving it four members of the Knesset (an increase of two). This unified Arab list made further progress in 1999, with five members. Azmi Bishara's Democratic National Alliance (Balad) won two seats in 1999.

Electorally marginal, the parties of the far left were nonetheless able to contribute to a a powerful pacifist movement formed by Shalom Achshav ('Peace Now'), the Committee Against the War in **Lebanon** and the soldiers' organisation Yesh Gvul ('There is a Limit') during the **1982 War**, which saw the Israeli invasion of Lebanon. Inactive after the Israeli withdrawal from Lebanon, the pacifist movement once again emerged to express solidarity with the Palestinian **Intifada**. But the victory of **Yitzhak Rabin** dealt a fatal blow to this current of opinion: in the face of the Oslo negotiations and despite the threats posed to its development, Israeli pacifists were no longer in a position to mobilise, or at least not until the night of 4 November 1995, when Rabin was assassinated. 'Where were you when the far Right was insulting us? Where were you to support the peace process which was the only thing that would lead Israel to well-being?' his wife asked them. Things would be even worse after the failure of the Camp David summit and the outbreak of the **second Intifada**.

The second Intifada and Israeli military operations revived the peace faction, which was temporarily stunned by the failure of the Camp David summit and the outbreak of the second Intifada. In the framework of the 'seruv' ('refusal'), hundreds of young people, but also reservists, refused to carry out their military obligations in occupied Palestinian territory, running the risk of imprisonment. Militants from the Taayush ('For Existence') movement organised many caravans of cars to besiege Palestinian villages, taking them blankets, clothing, medicine, even food. Embodied in the figure of the seasoned protestor Uri Avnery, Gush Shalom ('Peace Bloc') was also extremely active. And all these mobilisations, together with others, progressively led the leadership of Shalom Achshav, which was close to the Labour party, to give the pacifists the opportunity for big mass demonstrations such as the one which, on the seventh and eighth anniversaries of the assassination of Rabin, brought 100,000 people onto the streets. But this upsurge of movement failed to find a framework of political representation.

The Israeli right has two main components. There is a current of Revisionist Zionism founded by Ze'ev Jabotinsky and personified by **Menachem Begin**, and a liberal movement, which before the war and as late as 1961 was composed of mainstream Zionists who later divided into liberals and independent liberals. Long opposed to each other – a faction of liberals even participated in the coalition government headed by Labour – these two wings achieved a spectacular rise when they united, first in 1965 within Gahal (Herut–liberal bloc), then in 1973 within Likud (coalition). Their combined vote rose from 16.7 per cent in 1949 to 35.3 per cent in 1977. Thus on 20 June 1977, Menachem Begin became Israel's first non-Labour prime minister, followed by **Yitzhak Shamir** in 1983. After the brief tenure of Labour's Shimon Peres at the head of a bipartisan cabinet, Shamir remained Prime Minister, at first of the government of National Unity, then of the right after the November 1988 election, then of the right and the extreme right from June 1990. In 1992, when its vote fell to 24.9 per cent and its seats in the Knesset to 32 Likud went into opposition, from which it had emerged 15 years before. Despite a further decline of its vote, it came to power – with the help of the religious parties – just after the election of 29 May 1996.

After three years in power, Likud was to collapse in 1999, losing more than a third of its representation (13 seats) and finding itself pressured on its right by extremist parties, notably Shas. Netanyahu left the party's leadership. But under the leadership of Sharon, resoundingly elected as Prime Minister with 62.5 per cent of the vote, the party returned to the political scene in 2001 with 19 Knesset seats and 8 ministerial portfolios, including finance, internal security and education. This revival was consolidated in the 2003 general election, when Sharon's Likud won 38 seats in the Knesset. In comparison, Labour lagged far behind with a mere 18 seats.

From the end of the 1970s Israel witnessed the rise of an increasingly active extreme right, born of the rejection of the Camp David Accords and nourished by the colonisation of the **West Bank**, the prevailing chauvinism, the severe economic, social and moral crises, all taking place against a background of religious fundamentalism. The best-known figure in all this is Rabbi Kahane, member of the Knesset from 1984 to 1988 – the Supreme Court then banned his candidature. His Kach movement has as its aim 'the expulsion of all Arabs from Greater Israel'. Kahane was assassinated in New York in November 1990; Kach was banned in Israel after the Hebron massacre of 25 February 1994.

But other groups are equally influential. Apart from their common background, Gush Emunim ('Bloc of the Faithful'), firmly entrenched in the West Bank **settlements**, shares with Kach a two-fold demand: the annexation of the Occupied Territories and, to a greater or lesser extent, the **expulsion** of their Palestinian inhabitants. Dubbed 'transfer', this project was once defended only by Kahane. But fear of the Intifada, and from 1993 the prospect of a Palestinian state, have brought a considerable section of public opinion round to the idea of expelling the **Palestinians** – supported by movements such as Tehiya ('Renaissance') and Moledet ('Fatherland') but not by Tsomet ('Zionist Revival'), a party run by General Raphael Eitan which presents itself as an advocate of secularism. Emerging on the electoral scene after 1981, these parties have experienced a worryingly consistent growth in popularity, increasing from 2.6 per cent of the vote and 3 Knesset seats at the time to 10 per cent and 11 seats in 1992. The alliance between Tsomet and Likud partly reshaped the terrain – and marginalised this movement (0.1 per cent in 1999). Moledet, for its part, was to get 2.4 per cent of the vote, with two members in 1996, but, along with Tsomet, was to join in 1999, a new far-right grouping, the National Union, which had four seats. Rehavam Zeevi, who took over as its leader from Benny Begin, had very radical views, openly preaching the transfer of Palestinians out of the West Bank and Gaza. Having become Minister of Tourism in the Sharon government, he was assassinated on 17 October 2001 by a Popular Front for the Liberation of Palestine (PFLP) commando unit.

The existence of relatively powerful religious parties is another feature of the Israeli political scene. Some of these are Zionist: the pre-1948 Mizrahi

('Orient', founded in 1902) gave birth to the Mafdal ('National Religious Party') which has since been in almost all government coalitions. Others are are non-Zionist: there is the Agudat Yisrael ('Community of Israel'), founded in 1911, and the Poalei Agudat Yisrael ('Workers of the Community of Israel'). Agudat has undergone three splits: the **Oriental Jews** regrouped in 1984 within the Shas party, from which the Yemenis formed Yahad Shivtei Yisrael in 1988; in the same year, the anti-Hassidic Ashkenazim of the Agudat founded Degel Tora. And Agudat itself was henceforth to be known as Yahdut Hatorah ('Unified Torah Judaism').

With a number of members of Knesset varying between 11 (in 1951) and 27 in 1999 (out of 120), the religious parties, with between 13 and 18 deputies (out of 120), form a formidable lobby. They made the Likud pay a heavy price for their support in 1977, without which Begin would not have been able to govern. While Israel has never been a secular state, in recent times it has become a theocratic state, where religious law is imposed on all citizens in their daily life, and where rabbis decide on a person's nationality, approve marriages and divorces, and even have a say in the educational curriculum. The surge in the popularity of the religious parties in 1988 led to the imposition of stricter obligations on the whole society: a strictly observed Sabbath, subsidies for religious institutions, exemption from military service for pupils of the *yeshivot* (rabbinical schools), even a re-examination of the 'Law of Return'. After a slight dip in 1992 (two seats lost), the religious parties experienced an upsurge in their fortunes in 1996, winning 20.1 per cent of the vote and ten seats in the Knesset (ten for Shas, four for Agudat, which is allied to Degel and nine for the National Religious Party). While the latter ran out of steam and in 1999 won 'only' five seats, the Unified Torah Judaism won one seat (making five in all), and Shas in particular made advances, gaining 17 seats. But its leader, Arie Deri, was sentenced to four years in prison for corruption and was removed from the party, and hence had to leave the post of Minister of the Interior, which he had held for the past 15 years. In the 2003 election, Shas gained 11 seats, United Torah Judaism 5.

Another force now came very much to the fore: the parties representing the Russian community, which had been considerably enlarged by the arrival of hundreds of thousands of Jews – and often non-Jews – from the Soviet Union, whose emigration Mikhail Gorbachev had authorised in the second half of the 1980s. The former Soviet dissident Natan Sharansky formed the first, Israel be-Aliya ('Israel in Immigration'), a moderate grouping which won seven seats in 1996, but then lost one in 1999. This was because it was being challenged on its right by a new and more extremist party: Israel Beitenu ('Israel Our Home'), set up by Avigdor Liberman, notorious for having proposed the bombing of the Aswan Dam, which entered parliament in 1999 with four seats, and there set up an alliance with the National Union.

The latest arrival on the Israeli political scene has been the centrist groupings, namely Shinui ('Change') and the Centre Party, which won six seats between them in the 1999 elections. Unlike the religious parties, Shinui refused to enter Sharon's National Unity government at first, though the Centre Party, made up of those who had abandoned Likud, did take a turn to the right. Shinui was a surprise winner in the 2003 general elections, profiting from the decline in fortunes of Labour and gaining a total of 15 seats in the Knesset.

JENIN

Was the Jenin refugee camp the victim of a 'massacre' in early April 2002? The **Palestinians** say yes, the Israelis no. Once again we would need to specify what the term 'massacre' means. Should the number of deaths have reached a threshold to justify the use of the term, and if so what threshold? Does the tragedy of Jenin, with a 'contested' total of 52 Palestinian dead, warrant the use of the term? International law defines 'war crimes' and 'crimes against humanity'. These are the starting concepts for any attempt to understand what happened in Jenin.

On 3 April 2002 the Israeli army attacked Jenin, which it had already re-occupied the previous year, and then at the end of February 2002, when Operation Jenin had led to dozens of deaths in the Palestinian communities. This re-occupation followed the carnage committed by a **terrorist** on 27 March in Netanya, on the same evening as the adoption of the Saudi peace plan by the Arab Summit in Beirut. The 29 dead, killed at a Pesach celebration, were in addition to more than 50 other Israelis killed in bombings during the month of March alone. Although **Hamas** claimed the Netanya bombing, Israeli reprisals were to target the **Palestinian Authority**, its institutions, and above all its security forces in the **West Bank**. Code-named Operation Rampart, the most massive operation since the **1967 War** targeted principally towns in the north of the West Bank, which were presented as 'capitals of terrorism': Nablus, Tulkarem, Qalqiliya and Jenin.

The soldiers made their way through the Jenin refugee camp neighbour-hood by neighbourhood, street by street, demolishing party walls to get from one house to another and avoid Palestinian gunfire. The Palestinian fighters resisted and mined several buildings. Already Israeli Apache and Cobra helicopters were attacking. The operation took a new turn on the ninth when 13 Israeli soldiers died in a Palestinian ambush. Loudspeakers then gave the order to evacuate the centre of the refugee camp, which the Israeli government had decided to destroy with tanks, bulldozers and missiles. Several thousand inhabitants left the area, but 4000 remained, without **water**, electricity or food. The Israeli soldiers dynamited the houses, both occupied and unoccupied. By 11 April all resistance had ceased. On 23 April, **Israel** ended the operation. The army withdrew from the camp, although continuing to surround it.

How many victims were there? According to the assessment of the Israeli Defence Forces (IDF), there were 48 on the Palestinian side and 23 Israelis; according to a UN report published in August 2002, 52 Palestinians. But the inhabitants spoke of at least 200 dead. Presumably the exact numbers will remain buried under the razed buildings of Hawashin Square, the ruins of the destroyed houses and the graves dug by the Israeli army in the vicinity – or further away: the Israeli press reported bodies being carried away in military lorries to cemeteries in Israel. In Jenin itself tanks and bulldozers flattened the debris, making any search for bodies very difficult.

Israel has thus done nothing for the true figures to be established with certainty. At first **Ariel Sharon** had accepted the arrival of an international fact-finding commission scheduled for 19 April by **UN Security Council Resolution** 1405. But then he changed his mind: he demanded that its composition be changed, and then called for impunity for Israeli officers and soldiers, and then finally simply refused to allow the researchers to come. UN Secretary-General Kofi Annan then decided not to send his fact-finding team. By default, we have to rely on inquiries conducted by several NGOs.

The most complete was carried out by Human Rights Watch (HRW), which was on the spot from 19 to 28 April 2002. The text stresses that the resistance of the Palestinian fighters should not 'obscure the basic fact: the refugee camp was the place of residence of 14,000 Palestinian civilians. In line with international humanitarian law, the IDF was obliged to take all necessary precautions to prevent their military incursion from having disproportionate repercussions on civilians.' This was in no sense the case, in fact quite the contrary. Of the 52 recorded dead, 22 'were civilians, including children, the physically handicapped and old people'. While the researchers 'found no proof of systematic summary executions', they reported 'cases of illegal and deliberate executions, as well as killings or wounds inflicted as the result of an excessive or disproportionate use of force (which) violates international humanitarian law, which bans "voluntary homicide" against non-combatants'.

The report went so far as to say, 'There are *prima facie* serious violations of the Geneva Conventions and war crimes'. And in particular it noted, in addition to executions, the 'lethal use of force against civilians who did not comply with the curfew'; the use of civilians as 'human shields' in order to 'carry out the extremely dangerous task of going first into buildings to inspect them'; the firing by 'helicopters' on the morning of 6 April, of missiles which 'at that hour of the morning, found many civilians asleep'; the use, in the Hawashin neighbourhood, after 'the majority of the fighting', of bulldozers which 'entirely destroyed the zone, from the first house to the last'; a ban on ambulances entering the camp 'for 11 days', and shooting at Jenin's own ambulances, with the report recalling that 'direct attacks on medical personnel and the refusal of the wounded's access to medical care constitute serious violations of the laws of war'.

It took a further two weeks for the Israeli army to withdraw from the autonomous zone of Jenin, on 24 April. In total, Israeli soldiers destroyed 35 per cent of the refugee camp and had rendered homeless about 8000 people, devastating the agricultural land, causing serious damage to water and electricity infrastructures, and finally reducing virtually all of the population of the camp to unemployment. In Nablus too the destructive ardour of the Israeli army went so far as to raze the historic centre, one of UNESCO's world heritage sites. It seriously damaged or ruined the thousand-year-old al-Khadra mosque, the sixteenth-century Greek Orthodox church, the old soap-works, the Turkish baths and the Roman springs. To deal with this situation the Conference of International Aid Donors – which brings together the UN, **US**, **EU**, Israel, the Palestinian Authority, Norway and the World Bank – in Oslo on 25 April promised exceptional aid of $1.2bn to the Palestinian Authority, $300m to deal with the humanitarian crisis in the West Bank and $900m to initiate the rebuilding of infrastructure. On 22 November 2002, Israeli soldiers killed Ian John Hook with two bullets to the head. He was the UN Relief and Works Agency for Palestine Refugees (UNRWA) official in charge of rebuilding the centre of the Jenin refugee camp.

For their part, the criminals are still free. Some show not the slightest remorse, such as Moshe Nissim, a 40-year-old Israeli reservist who confided to the daily *Yediot Aharonot*,

> No one refused an order to take down a house. When they told me to destroy a house I exploited that in order to destroy a few more homes. On the loudspeaker [the Palestinian residents] were warned to get out before I came in. But I didn't give a chance to anyone. I didn't wait. I'm sure that people died inside those houses. From my perspective we left them a football field, they should play there. The 100x100 was our present to the camp. Jenin will not return to be what it was.

JERUSALEM

Capital of the state of **Israel** according to Israelis and of the future state of Palestine according to the **Palestinians**, Jerusalem was founded in the third millennium BC by a Canaanite tribe which had settled on one of its hills. Over more than four thousand years the city has experienced numerous changes of rule: from Jewish (around 1000BC), to Egyptian (925BC), to Roman (63BC), to Byzantine (AD629), to Muslim (AD638), to Christian (AD1099), to Arab once more (AD1187), then Ottoman (AD1517) and, four centuries later – from 1917 to 1948 – to **Britain**. According to the Israeli archaeologist, Meir Ben Dov, in the course of its long history Jerusalem has been destroyed and rebuilt more than twenty-five times through the ages from Solomon to Suleiman the Magnificent.

Yerushalayim ('City of Peace') to some, and al-Quds ('Sacred') to others, Jerusalem is a holy city for all three great monotheistic religions. For **Jews**, it was here that God stopped Abraham from sacrificing his son and where the first and second temples were built and destroyed in 587BC and AD70 respectively. The sacred sites of Judaism are the tombs of King David, Absalon and Rachel, the Wailing Wall and several synagogues. For Christians it is the city of the Passion where Jesus preached, was arrested, crucified and rose again from the dead. The Christian sacred sites are the Basilica of the Holy Sepulchre, the church of Saint Ann, the tomb of the Virgin Mary, the Cenacle, the Garden of Gethsemane and the place of Ascension. For Muslims, Jerusalem is sacred because Muhammad ascended to Heaven from the rock. Containing the Dome of the Rock, the Mosque of Omar and the al-Aqsa Mosque, Jerusalem is the third city of **Islam** after Mecca and Medina. The holy city has been the heart of the stormy history of the Middle East for over four thousand years.

The city's status in the modern era has been a positive minefield. According to the UN **Partition Plan** adopted on 29 November 1947, Jerusalem was to constitute a *corpus separatum* under a special international regime, demilitarised and administered by a trusteeship council and a governor who could not be a citizen of either of the two specified states and who would guarantee the interests of the sacred sites of the three religions and peace between them, eventually to be included in the Palestinian Economic Union. But the **1948–49 War** ended with Jerusalem being effectively divided between **Jordan**, which occupied the eastern part, and Israel, which annexed the western part, declaring it, contrary to the armistice conditions, capital of their state. The decision taken by the UN on 19 December 1949 to internationalise Jerusalem was never put into practice.

This situation lasted until the **1967 War**, during which the Israeli army took from Hashemite troops the Arab Old City. Several days later, the Israeli Knesset extended 'the law, administration and jurisdiction of the State of Israel' to East Jerusalem and declared it the 'reunified eternal capital of Israel'. Finally, on 30 June 1980, the Knesset adopted a fundamental law claiming the whole of Jerusalem 'capital of the State of Israel', which was immediately condemned by the UN. Two years later the Arab Fez Plan adopted the slogan 'independent Palestinian state with Jerusalem as its capital'. A few days earlier, President Ronald Reagan, in a speech delivered on 1 September, had referred only to the 'indivisible' nature of Jerusalem, leaving the rest to the negotiators. Although his successors, George Bush and Bill Clinton, officially maintained this line, more pressure was exerted following a vote in Congress in favour of transferring the US embassy from Tel Aviv to Jerusalem, a move that has not yet been translated into reality. It was actually George W. Bush who was the first President to declare the move would take place.

The Israelis were determined to make Jerusalem the 'eternal capital of Israel' mentioned in their law. Successive governments undertook a stream of measures to change the face of the city, primarily to ensure a clear Jewish majority. The demolition of Arab districts began after the Six Days War, when hundreds of buildings near the Wailing Wall were knocked down, followed by the sacking of eighteenth-century areas, such as the Moroccan Quarter. Tens of thousands of **Arabs** were subsequently expelled from the area and their land and houses appropriated for Jews. The change in the city's population also extended its boundaries. In the space of 28 years, it almost tripled in size, with the annexation of districts such as Atarot, Neveh Ya'acov, Pisgat Ze'ev, Ramot Allon, Ramat Shufat, French Hill, Ramat Eshkol, Har Homa, Talpiot and Gilo.

To deal with this greater area, Israel has implemented a complex strategy. The confiscation or expropriation of the annexed Arab zones and the lack of any investment in the districts that have remained Palestinian has meant that the Jewish population has been squeezed into massive housing projects designed to turn former Arab districts into Jewish districts. Every effort has been made to force the Palestinians out: a ban on construction in 17 of their 30 districts, increasingly restricted access to 'resident' status and a miserable standard of living forcing them to move to the suburbs. The result is that, since 1994, Jews have been in the majority, even in the Arab districts of Jerusalem. There are 175,000 Jews to 170,000 Arabs out of a total population of 580,000 (410,000 are Jewish). This figure does not include the peripheral colonies, such as Givat Ze'ev, Gush Adumi, Ma'ale Adumim, Quedar, Betar, Gush Etzion and Efrat, which will one day link up with 'metropolitan Jerusalem', which would cover almost a fifth of the **West Bank**.

A sacred city for the Mosaic, Muslim and Christian religions, Jerusalem, in the eyes of believers, is difficult to split up, especially since, as experience has proved, the right to visit the shrines – the UN has recorded over a hundred – of one's faith in the divided city is often restricted, or even completely flouted. But the unification of Jerusalem would mean dashed hopes for either Israelis or Palestinians – or both of them – who see it as the capital of their state. It was this contradiction that was to cause the most problems during the second round of negotiations between Israel and the Palestinians. **Benyamin Netanyahu**'s government programme, launched on 19 June 1996, stipulated that 'Jerusalem, the capital of Israel, one and indivisible, will always remain under Israeli sovereignty'. It also stated that 'the government will prevent any action opposed to [this] exclusive sovereignty'. In the Geneva peace project, signed on 1 December 2003, Jerusalem is to be placed under joint sovereignty: the Jewish quarters – including in the East – will become Israeli; the Arab, Muslim and Christian ones will become Palestinian. In the Old City, the Wailing Wall and the Jewish quarters are to remain Israeli, but the rest – including the Temple Mount – will remain Palestinian.

JEWS

A noun whose definition has long been the object of extremely complex debates, so abundant and often contradictory are the conceptions of 'Jewishness'. The question 'What is a Jew?' elicits many responses. Lengthy controversial discussions have naturally developed on this theme in **Israel**. There, the 'Law of Return', adopted in 1950, stipulates that 'every Jew has the right to come to Israel'. This right was complemented by the Law on Nationality, voted in 1952, which automatically grants Israeli nationality to any immigrant taking advantage of the Law of Return, thus making them Jewish. But who is to be considered a Jew? 'Anyone born of a Jewish mother or who has converted to Judaism,' replies Talmudic law, and the ultra-Orthodox insist (so far in vain) that the converts in question must have done so in accordance with the most rigorous requirements of Jewish law.

Several famous affairs have brought the legal aspect of the question to the public eye. Thus the case of Daniel Rufeisen, a Polish Jew converted to Catholicism, who asked the Ministry of the Interior to enter him in the register of the Israeli population as Catholic under the category of religion, but as Jewish under 'ethnic group'. The Ministry, and the Supreme Court to which he subsequently appealed, refused him the **right of return**, considering that his conversion made him a non-Jew. On the other hand, in 1970 Benjamin Shalit, whose wife was not Jewish, managed to have their children registered as **Jews** under the 'ethnic group' heading. Following these affairs, the religious parties imposed a modification of Article 4(b) of the Law of Return: 'A Jew,' reads the final version 'is a person born of a Jewish mother or converted to Judaism and who does not belong to any other religion'. Clearly, in matters of religion and ethnicity, a certain ambiguity remains.

The religious criterion is certainly indisputable. The first major monotheistic religion, the Mosaic faith – with its sacred texts, its law and rites – unites millions of believers across the world. Its influence is all the greater in that, after the diaspora, it was religious faith that 'took up the idea of the survival of the people outside of the state-based political forms of national existence' (Ilan Halevi). But the Jewish religion, like many others, has not been spared, in Israel and especially elsewhere in the world, the phenomenon of religious disaffection. Many of those one calls – or who call themselves – Jews are atheists or agnostics. Even more numerous are those who are apparently still attached to their faith but do not practise its rituals. Except at major holidays and festivals, synagogues are as poorly attended as churches and temples. Religion is therefore not broad enough a term to define all Jews.

The alleged common origin – the Hebrews – is no more conclusive. True, in ancient Palestine a Jewish nation or people had emerged. But the collapse of the Jewish kingdoms under the successive blows of the Assyrians and the Babylonians, the Roman conquest and, above all, the crushing of the Bar Kokhba Revolt in AD135, caused its dispersal. While a small nucleus remained in the Holy Land, the main body of the Jewish population was scattered all over the Mediterranean, often assimilating into its host country. Others, with a profound sense of their own identity, even managed to convert their hosts, sometimes *en masse*. Thus the work of historians indicates that, contrary to the thesis that the Jewish religion does not proselytise – one cannot, it says, 'join' a 'chosen people' – the Jewish state of Southern Arabia, in the sixth century, or again the Jewish state of the Khazars in southwest **Russia** in the eighth century, were established by winning over the sovereigns and their subjects. Arthur Koestler, in *The Thirteenth Tribe*, thus claims that most of the Jews of Central Europe are descended from the Khazars, therefore from converted Turco-Mongols then dispersed into Slav territory. The same goes for North Africa, Spain, Gaul, Germany, Asia and elsewhere. The majority of modern Jews have therefore, apparently, no direct links with the Hebrews. Nevertheless, the song of the Hatikvah continues to assert that 'our dream of two thousand years is not lost, to return to the country of our fathers, the land of Zion, Jerusalem'.

All of which goes to show how much appeals to the concept of 'race' are open to question. The old anecdote of the French Jew who goes off to China in search of his 'brothers' reflects, on a humorous level, this pseudo-theory. Arriving at last in Shanghai, our man, in a dark sidestreet, discovers the synagogue and enters. The Chinese Jews, at prayer there, are at first astonished, then gradually turn threatening. Finally he calls out to them, 'But I'm a Jew, like you'. And they, showing him their slanted eyes, retort, 'Well you certainly don't look like one!' A simple visit to Israel will convince the most doubtful reader of the extraordinary diversity of Jewish 'types', as extensive as those of the hundred and fifty odd countries from which Israelis have come.

The very concept of the 'Jewish people' is, in this respect, ambiguous. If this concept has no ethnic reality and limited religious significance, on what basis can it be grounded? It may be true that, up to World War II, Central European Jews formed a sort of coherent national **minority** (territory, language, culture, organisations, demands) – in *The Jewish Question*, Ilan Halevi speaks of 'material conditions of nationalistic existence', echoing Zvi Graetz who, in his *Histoire des Juifs*, shows how conditions in Poland, for instance, 'led the Jews to live as a state within a state, with their own religious, administrative and legal institutions'. All this, however, is no longer true today. The Shtetl, Central Europe's Jewish 'little town', disappeared in the crematoriums after having endured the pogroms. Scattered into dozens of countries, the majority of post-Holocaust Jews no longer speak Hebrew, Yiddish or Ladino, and little is left of their common culture. The assimilation initiated on a large scale in the West in the nineteenth century was once again underway.

However, this assimilation was not universally reaffirmed after the Holocaust in every country. The **US**, with its powerful Jewish **lobby**, and **France**, with its Jewish community extremely deep-rooted in the population, offer two examples at either extreme. In France, in fact, notes Richard Marienstras,

> the prestige of the French revolution was such that the only desirable fate one could envisage, for the millions of Yiddish speaking Jews of East Europe, was assimilation. Very quickly, French Jews became an example to the world, and the value of this example was not diminished for them after the Dreyfus Affair. The 'solution' to the 'Jewish question' had to be integration. They therefore vehemently rejected the national or nationalistic dimensions of Jewish existence.

And one is familiar with the letter in which Léon Blum, in 1950, endorsed the 'admirable effort' of Israel, which 'henceforth guarantees a homeland worthy of all those Jews who have not had like me the good fortune to find it in the land of their birth'. In their book *France and the Talmud,* published in 1991, Frank Eskenazi and Edouard Waintrop observed that 'at a deeper level, the Jewish community is now demanding assimilation'. These demands, be they religious (they are often made by ultra-Orthodox Jews) or historical, based upon recollections of the Holocaust and the Vichy regime, or cultural (around the revival of Jewish languages) or the demands of philosophers and artists affirming their Jewishness, are becoming increasingly visible. But many French Jews are not turning back to communitarian identities. Only 100,000 – one in six or seven – take part, in one form or other, in the activity of the Comité representatif des institutions juives de France (CRIF) and of the organisations which are its members. Furthermore, when its president commented favourably on Jean-Marie Le Pen's election result as 'a message to the Muslims to keep quiet', can the CRIF really claim to speak in the name of the Jews of France?

Even when assimilated, however, the Jews exist, whether they are designated as such by others (as Jean-Paul Sartre noted, 'It is anti-Semitism that creates the Jew') or whether they are themselves conscious of being Jewish. It is, perhaps, best to say that, 'anyone who feels Jewish is Jewish', for whatever reasons of their own. For many, it is a long history of persecution culminating with the Holocaust, whose tragedy even the most assimilated of Jews remember, whether they were directly affected or not. The life of the Jewish man, explained Andre Neher in *Existence juive*, is 'that of the persecuted man'. For some, as we have seen, it is having the same faith, with the ways of life it still implies, to varying degrees, including a basic understanding of Hebrew. For others, it is the practice of one of the Jewish languages of the diaspora, insertion into one of the Jewish cultures which are themselves very varied. For yet other Jews, it is a certain affinity with the state of Israel. Without wishing to settle there (the great failure of **Zionism** lies in having attracted to Israel only one Jew in three) and without necessarily supporting its policies, they nonetheless see Israel as a last resort, 'just in case'.

At the beginning of the twenty-first century, Jewish identity undoubtedly draws on these four elements, which even assimilation has not completely eradicated. As Marienstras notes in his afterword to Jean Liberman's *Choosing to be Jewish*,

> the very notion of the Jewish people has become problematic after the Holocaust. At the end of the second millennium, there is no real historical continuity between the Judaisms of those killed during the Second World War, the people of Israel and the Jewish diasporas in France, Britain, the United States and Argentina, despite the Jewish ideologues who proclaim the contrary.

'I envy him,' wrote Maxime Rodinson, one of his most virulent critics,

> for having straightaway found the definitions and terms necessary to designate an entity that at the same time brings together King David, Einstein, Jesus of Nazareth, Maimonides, Moses, Mendelssohn, Karl Marx, Menachem Begin, Jacques Offenbach, Benjamin Disraeli, Michel Debré and Tristan Bernard, not to mention him and me...'

JORDAN

In 1922 the territories under the British Mandate situated to the east of the River Jordan were established as a semi-autonomous principality under the leadership of Emir Abdullah. He was a son of the Sherif Hussein of Mecca, of the powerful Hashemite family, who had raised the standard of the Arab revolt against the **Ottoman Empire** during World War I. In 1930 the Arab Legion was created, the backbone of the emirate's armed forces; it was commanded by a British officer, Sir John Glubb, or 'Glubb Pasha', until 1956.

A founding member of the **Arab League** in 1945, Transjordan gained **independence** in March 1946. However, **Britain**'s influence there remained predominant. Immediately after World War II, the question of Palestine galvanised the Hashemite sovereign into action. Making no bones of his territorial ambitions, Abdullah, encouraged by Britain, ordered his troops into Palestine alongside other Arab forces on 15 May 1948. When, in April 1949, Transjordan and **Israel** signed an armistice, the Hashemite King was well satisfied with the results. He had conquered rich territories – which became known as the **West Bank** – as well as East **Jerusalem** and the al-Aqsa Mosque, holy site of **Islam**. He owed this result to the efficiency of the

Arab League and to secret negotiations undertaken with **Zionist** leaders, which led to accusations of treachery by his Arab opponents.

The **1948–49 War** profoundly altered the contours of the state. The population, scarcely 500,000 at the outset of the war, tripled in a few months: 500,000 refugees and the 500,000 **Palestinians** of the West Bank. A destabilising element was introduced into a hitherto conservative state with a Bedouin majority. In December 1948, Abdullah took the title of King of Jordan; in April 1949 the country's name became the Hashemite Kingdom of Jordan (a name already adopted at independence in 1946 but not used before then). In April 1950, elections held in the West Bank and Transjordan effectively confirmed the annexation of the West Bank. On 20 July 1951, Abdullah was assassinated by a Palestinian at the al-Aqsa Mosque in Jerusalem. He was succeeded by his son Talal, who lost no time in abdicating in favour of his own heir, Hussein, who, once proclaimed king, effectively acceded to the throne on his coming of age on 2 May 1953. The Middle East was at the time in a state of turbulence, with the growth of Arab nationalism and the emergence of the new leader of **Egypt**, **Gamal Abdel Nasser**. Hussein, who had chosen the Western camp, survived various crises: particularly in 1956–57 and in 1965–66, when he found himself in opposition to the **Palestine Liberation Organisation (PLO)**. He made his peace with Nasser on the eve of the **1967 War**, and his army took part in the fighting, during which the kingdom lost the territories it had conquered in 1948–49: the West Bank and East Jerusalem.

Threatened by the *fedayeen* between 1967 and 1970, the authorities liquidated the Palestinian armed presence in September 1970 and June 1971. Since then, the Hashemite dynasty has experienced no serious crisis. Jordan did not take part in the **1973 War**. Its political leaders were split into two camps. One was in favour of retreat into Transjordan, the other retained more extensive ambitions. The decision was all the harder in that the territorial designs harboured by a section of the Israeli right regarding the East Bank of the Jordan were well known, and the deadlock could only lead to renewed fighting. On 31 July 1988, in a historic speech, **King Hussein** settled the matter by withdrawing all claims to the West Bank. But this decision, mainly due to the Palestinian **Intifada**, did not mean that Jordan had renounced a part in the attempts to find a solution to the Middle Eastern conflict, as was demonstrated by the delegation of Jordanians and Palestinians it sent to the **peace conference** which opened in Madrid on 30 October 1991. For the Hashemite sovereign, the very survival of his kingdom is at stake. As long as the Palestinian problem remains unresolved there is a great risk that Jordan will be 'Palestinianised' and that the most fragile state in the Middle East will be destabilised.

Although Jordan is considered a moderate Arab regime allied with Washington, the monarchy nevertheless took a stand against the **Camp**

David Accords. It also supported **Iraq** in its conflict with **Iran** and then during the **Gulf War**, which led to frosty relations with Washington and to an effective split with the Gulf monarchies. For this Jordan paid a heavy price, particularly when the hundreds of thousands of Palestinians who had been thrown out of **Kuwait** sought refuge there.

The new deal that came out of the **Oslo Accords** involved the King in a spectacular U-turn. When he signed the peace deal with Israel on 26 October 1994, he broke off relations with the Iraqi government, effected a rapprochement with the **US** and participated in the Israeli–Turkish military alliance which was denounced by other Arab states. Jordan managed to keep close relations with Iraq, its main trading partner, even while reconciling itself with **Saudi Arabia** and the Gulf monarchies in the hope of reaping the dividends of the Middle East peace process. This hope was shattered by the beginning of the **second Intifada**.

Despite Washington writing off some $700m of debt, Jordan's social difficulties, which sparked off bread riots in April 1989, have intensified. The structural adjustment imposed by the IMF has meant that subsidies for basic staple products have dried up. Apart from tourism, there is little foreign investment. The riots of August 1996, after the IMF had doubled the price of bread, are a good indication of the fragility of the situation.

Politically, the mid-1990s were a time of consolidating power. The constitution grants almost unlimited power to the King, but a democratic experiment was implemented after the hunger riots in April 1989. Freedom of the press was extended and the elections of November 1989 were relatively free, with the **Muslim Brotherhood**'s candidates forming the majority parliamentary group. However, in the first multi-party elections, held in November 1993, the climate changed and the regime imposed new electoral regulations, which favoured those already in power. The **Islamist** opposition, under the wing of the Islamic Action Front (IAF), lost half its deputies and the left was weakened. The parliament, whose powers had already been reduced, ceased to be of any significance. The peace, to which the population was strongly opposed, pushed the King to restrict freedom and to slow the march towards democracy. The succession of governments in power demonstrated the difficulty for them of the public support for the King, thanks to decisions made in foreign policy. The legislative elections of November 1997 were boycotted by some of the opposition, notably the Islamists. Since then, elections have been postponed on a regular basis.

King Hussein's January 1999 decision to pass over his brother Prince Hassan and declare his son next in line to the throne put the politics within the royal family on full public view. When Hussein died on 7 February 1999, the US and the Gulf states were swift to express their support for King Abdullah II. He has shown himself to be in favour of peace with Israel, and has expelled **Hamas** leaders after having closed down the Islamic movement's offices in Jordan. But the new King has yet to respond to the demands for political openings called for by the opposition.

Open to the outside world, Abdullah is much less open internally, saying himself that 'ultimately, the national interest provides the basis for freedom'. The opposition has attacked the rampant corruption and the growing restrictions on civil liberties enforced since the 2001 adoption of an amendment of the Penal Code which clamps down on activity which is 'defamatory, false, damaging to national unity or the reputation of the state, which encourages crime, strikes, illegal gatherings or which disturbs public order'.

Demonstrations in support of Iraq in 1998, then in solidarity with the Palestinians in autumn 2000, have been interpreted as warning signals. More than half of Jordan's population is of Palestinian origin and, although enjoying Jordanian nationality, they are faced with other forms of discrimination. Amman is therefore concerned that the Intifada might overflow, not to mention a new wave of Palestinian **immigration**, which would further tip the scales of the demographic equation between Palestinians and Jordanians. The Israeli Prime Minister did say after his election in 2001, after all, that 'the 1948 war is not ended'. Jordan, which **Ariel Sharon** considers a Palestinian state, would constitute a 'natural' destination for the Arab population of the West Bank. The idea was given slightly more credibility in the run-up to the 2003 war in Iraq, which some analysts saw as a pretext to change the map of the region, with a single Hashemite Kingdom possibly being created from Jordan and Iraq.

Spread over nearly 90,000 sq. km, Jordan counted 5.2 million inhabitants in 2001. Ninety per cent of inhabitants are Sunni Muslims, but there are also a number of Christians. Profoundly affected by the crisis, the country has not reaped the peace dividend. Its economic relations with Iraq suffered immensely as a result of **sanctions** imposed in 1990; economic ties with Israel have never taken off, and the economy remains dependent on American and Arab aid, in addition to expatriate remittances and tourist receipts, which have plummeted since the attacks of 11 September 2001. Jordan hopes its accession to the World Trade Organisation on 11 April 2000 will revivify its commercial and economic life. Jordan exports phosphate and derives significant revenue from tourism.

KHOMEINI, AYATOLLAH RUHOLLAH

Ruhollah Khomeini was born on 24 September 1902 into a religious family in Khomein, near Isfahan. He was educated at Qum, one of the centres of **Shi'ism**, the majority religion in **Iran** and the state religion since the sixteenth century. A theologian, he attained the rank first of *mujtahid* (one skilled in the interpretation of Islamic Law), then the title of ayatollah ('sign of God'), which made him one of the elite religious leaders. Very early, he showed an interest in political affairs, and in the 1940s published a polemic against secularism; but it was not until 1962 that he really became involved in politics.

An opponent of the agricultural reform and of votes for women and **minorities**, both significant elements of the 'White Revolution' initiated by the Shah which encroached on the interests of the Shi'ite dignitaries, he was involved in disturbances that took place in the major cities of Iran on 4 June 1963, and was imprisoned as a result. Released after he had agreed to curb his criticisms, he came to public attention once again through his condemnation of military relations with the **US** and the granting of diplomatic status and thus legal immunity to American military advisors. In November 1964 he was exiled from Iran, and took refuge first in **Turkey** and then in Najaf, a Shi'ite holy city in **Iraq**. By this time the death in 1961 of Muhammad Borujerdi, the supreme religious leader of the Shi'ites, and that of the religious dignitary and political activist Abol Qasim Kashani had opened the path to spiritual and political leadership of the religious community for him.

He remained in Iraq until October 1978, when the **Ba'thist** government in Baghdad declared him *persona non grata*. Exiled again, this time to **France**, Khomeini became the symbol for the Iranian militants who had risen against the Shah's dictatorship. Through his speeches – relayed to Iran by cassette – he fuelled the 1978 uprising against the regime. On 1 February 1979 he returned in triumph to Tehran; the Iranian Empire had collapsed, to be replaced by an Islamic Republic.

Khomeini's reasoning hinged on the question of power, which is a central issue in 'Twelver' Shi'ism. According to tradition, after his death the Prophet Muhammad was succeeded in turn by twelve imams ('guides'), the last of whom disappeared in the year 874. After communicating with the world through messengers, the twelfth imam definitively withdrew from life, though remaining alive. Thus began the Great Occultation, the era in which Shi'ites await the end of time and the return of the 'hidden Imam', who will return to restore a reign of justice on earth. The question for Shi'ites is who, in the absence of the hidden Imam, is to guide the faithful? There have been a number of answers to this question, but for Khomeini the role falls to the *faqih* (religious jurist), the scholar, the vicar of the hidden Imam, and delegate of divine sovereignty. This doctrine of the 'guardianship of the jurisprudent' (*velayat-e faqih*), which accords enormous power to the ruling religious dignitary, has been – and still is – contested by many other ayatollahs.

However, it was to become accepted as the basis for the new Iranian constitution. But not without difficulty, for the alliance that had overthrown the Shah was very broad, and included liberals, religious groups, the Mojahedin-e Khalq – a revolutionary Islamic organisation led by Massoud Rajavi – Kurdish nationalists, radical leftists, communists etc. The war launched by Iraq in September 1980 and the first Iraqi victories provoked an outburst of patriotism, which Khomeini took advantage of to crush pitilessly his erstwhile allies. In 1983 Iran launched a counter-offensive at the front, and all opposition – with the exception of the **Kurds** – was simultaneously crushed. Khomeini's position as absolute ruler of the country was confirmed, but the regime's base had shrunk. The prolongation of the **Iran–Iraq War**, due to the Ayatollah's obstinacy, alienated many who had sympathised with him, and the agreement, made in August 1988, for a ceasefire constituted a bitter personal defeat. He died on 3 June 1989.

The implementing of the war with Baghdad, the paralysis of the machinery of government under the constant condemnation of the religious community, led Khomeini, at the end of 1987, to make an important revision in his doctrine. 'To claim that the powers of the state are limited to the framework of divine principles is in total contradiction of what I said,' he wrote. 'Government action that is a part of the absolute sovereignty of the Prophet is a basic imperative of **Islam**, which takes precedence over all others, even prayer, the pilgrimage to Mecca, etc.' In thus wishing to guarantee the government a certain freedom of action, the Ayatollah was acknowledging that all internal reforms had been sabotaged, in the name of Islam, by the mullahs and that it was necessary – even more so now the war was over – to respond to the formidable economic and social challenges facing the country.

KURDS

Spread between **Iran**, **Turkey** and **Iraq**, the Kurds have a long history. According to legend, the birth of this people goes back to 21 March 612BC. Speaking an Indo–European language and for the most part Sunni Muslims, they inhabit inaccessible mountain regions and have never constituted a unified political entity. Their numbers are the subject of lively controversy, a debate in which political considerations are obvious: look at Turkey, for example, where their existence as a **minority** has only recently begun to be acknowledged. It is estimated that there are some 15 million Kurds in Turkey, 7 million in Iran and 5 million in Iraq, to which must be added the communities of **Syria** (approximately 1 million) and the former Soviet Union (350,000).

Following World War I and the dismantling of the **Ottoman Empire**, the Allies considered creating an independent Kurdistan. On 10 August 1920, the Treaty of Sèvres, signed with Turkey, provided for the creation of an autonomous Kurdistan in western Anatolia and the province of Mosul. But the rebellion and subsequent victory of Mustafa Kemal led to the Treaty of Lausanne in 1923 and the denial of Kurdish rights. Only the new Iraqi state, under British Mandate and in accordance with the decisions of the UN, was to grant a certain **autonomy** to Kurds. This promise too was broken. Kurdish revolts broke out, particularly in Turkey (in 1925, 1930 and 1937), only to be ruthlessly crushed. Furthermore, on 8 July 1937, the Saadabad Pact between Turkey, Iraq, Iran and Afghanistan stipulated, among other things, a co-ordinated struggle against Kurdish subversion and irredentism.

After World War II, and with the support of the USSR, the Kurdish Republic of Mahabad was created in Iran in January 1946. But, in December, Iranian troops put an end to the experiment. Until the late 1970s, Kurdish rebellion would primarily be concentrated in Iraq.

The man who was to symbolise this rebellion was Mustafa Barzani. Born in 1903 in the village of Barzan in Iraq to a family of religious leaders, Barzani was involved in the abortive experiment of the Republic of Mahabad. A refugee in the Soviet Union for more than ten years, he returned to Iraq after the declaration of the republic in 1958. When the Qasim regime failed to respect the promises of Kurdish autonomy, he launched, in September 1961, a rebellion in the north of the country whose slogan was 'Autonomy for Kurdistan, Democracy for Iraq'.

Truces, negotiations and guerrilla operations alternated without interruption until 1975. In 1970, an agreement seemed on the cards. The **Ba'th** conceded the creation of an autonomous Kurdish region, recognised that the Kurds constituted one of Iraq's two nations and granted them certain rights – one of which was the use of their language, which became the second national language. However, significant disagreements remained, both over the delimitation of Kurdistan – the **oil** town of Mosul was excluded from it – and the real power of the local elected representatives. In March 1974, **Saddam Hussein** decided on the unilateral application of autonomy. Spurred on by the Shah of Iran and by the **US**, who were alarmed by the pro-Soviet tendencies of the Ba'thist regime, Barzani resumed the uprising. It collapsed following the Algiers Accords of 6 March 1975 between Tehran and Baghdad which ended their dispute over frontiers and brought to a halt all Iranian aid to the Kurdish rebellion.

The outbreak of the **Iran–Iraq War** in September 1980 sparked Kurdish protest once again, this time on a larger scale. In Iran, after the fall of the

Shah, Dr Abdul Rahman Ghassemlou's Kurdish Democratic Party of Iran (KDPI) took control of Kurdistan; but the Islamic Republic's offensive led the KDPI to form an alliance with Saddam Hussein's regime. In Iraq too, difficulties created by the war against the 'Persians' encouraged Kurdish irredentism. But unity did not result as a consequence of all this. The KDP, headed since 1976 by Massoud Barzani, Mustafa's son, Jalal Talabani's Patriotic Union of Kurdistan (PUK) and the Iraqi Communist Party entered a cycle of alliances, splits and reconciliation.

The Kurdish revival has been equally apparent in Turkey. Since August 1984 the Kurdistan Workers Party (known as the PKK) has carried out guerrilla operations in the eastern provinces of the country. But if the organisation's **terrorism** has aroused many reservations, it has permitted a new debate, hitherto taboo, in Turkey on the Kurdish question.

The end of the Iran–Iraq War allowed the various governments of the region to turn on their own Kurds. Iraq, with particular brutality – including the use of chemical gas, notably against the village of Halabja in March 1988 – regained control of the north of the country, provoking the exodus of close to 100,000 Kurds into Turkey. Likewise in Iran, less successful offensives were mounted against the KDPI. Nevertheless, the assassination of Ghassemlou in Vienna on 13 July 1989 was a serious blow to the organisation.

During the **Gulf War** of 1991, the Kurdish question took on an international dimension not seen since World War I. The defeat of Saddam Hussein in spring 1991 triggered an uprising in Kurdistan in which the *peshmerga* militiamen laid siege to the main towns, but were soon overcome by the Iraqi army's elite units; Saddam's international opponents did nothing to stop them. Horrified by the spectre of chemical weapons being used again, nearly two million Kurds once again took to the road, seeking exile in Iran and Turkey. The Western armies put in place a 'safe haven' in the north of Iraq, allowing the refugees to return and ensuring that Kurdish organisations were in control of the region. But despite the fact that relatively free elections were held in Iraqi Kurdistan on 19 May 1992, the region was unstable for several years. The KDP controls the west of the region as far as the Turkish border, the PUK the east, up to the border with Iran. Violent skirmishes broke out between the two organisations from May 1994. The growing influence of Iran, and its alliance with the PUK, led to new confrontations in the summer of 1996. For the first time the KDP asked for help from Saddam's troops, who intervened briefly in September.

But since no party had the upper hand militarily, a ceasefire was concluded in November 1997. Protected by Western forces, Iraqi Kurds set up two decentralised administrations, one in the north, close to Turkey, led by the KDP, the other in the south, led by the PUK and close to Iran. Autonomous Kurdistan became a huge building site of roads, infrastructures and projects in healthcare, education, housing etc., all of which were partly funded by **UN Security Council Resolution** 986 on 'oil for food', which provided Iraqi Kurds with 13 per cent of the income from the sale of Iraqi oil. The relative prosperity of the region derives also from income from customs charges levied on goods being transported between Iraq, Turkey and Iran, and also from cross-border trade.

Although the benefits they had won since the Gulf War might have been lost following the US-led war on Iraq in 2003, the two main Kurdish groups were nevertheless generally supportive of US policy, hoping that Washington's intervention and the fall of Saddam's regime would lead to a more solid and democratic autonomy status. This optimism explains the new agreement signed by the KDP and PUK on 8 September 2002 to reactivate their unified parliament, set up between 1992 and 1994. Neither party has been foolish enough to raise the idea of an independent Kurdish state – an idea which Ankara, in common with Baghdad and Tehran, would violently oppose. Even before the 2003 war, the Kurds were keen proponents of the notion of a federal or confederated Iraq, made up of several autonomous regions, one of which would be Kurdish.

Following the collapse of Saddam's regime officially declared by President Bush on 9 April 2003, the Iraqi Kurds maintained their commitment to a united Iraq. Both the KDP and PUK are now represented on the US-appointed Iraqi Governing Council. It is this Council which will lay the framework for the future constitution of Iraq – which the Kurds hope will guarantee a federal status to the Kurdistan region.

Ankara has a long memory. The 1990–91 Gulf War and the weakening of central government in Iraq made it easier for the PKK to embark on actions in Turkey. They increased the number of their military actions while at the same time extending their political influence in towns in the southeast of the country, particularly Diyarbakir. Since they have been incapable of handling the Kurds' desire for a national identity, successive Turkish governments have sought to impose a 'military solution' marked notably by the mass transfer of populations and increasing numbers of incursions into Iraq against 'terrorists bases'. The kidnapping in Kenya, in January 1999, of PKK leader Abdullah Öçalan by the Turkish secret services with the aid of the CIA, and then his sentencing to death at the end of a charade of a trial, struck his party a serious blow.

However, a combination of the PKK's renunciation of armed struggle and European pressures encouraged the Ankara authorities to show greater flexibility. In 2002 the state of emergency which had been in place in the southeast of the country for decades was lifted. And in early August 2002 Turkish MPs finally voted a law permitting the learning of minority languages.

The situation of the Kurds remains equally uncertain in the neighbouring countries, none of which is willing to guarantee them the cultural rights and autonomy which they are seeking. Iran intervened on the side of Talabani in his struggle against Barzani, in an attempt to put an end to the activities of the KDPI (which had also renounced the armed struggle). Finally, Syria, which has about a million Kurds, does not recognise them as a national or ethnic minority. However, they are represented in parliament, may speak their language, and coexist peacefully with the **Arabs**. But Damascus's alleged support for the PKK has for several years poisoned relations with its Turkish neighbour.

KUWAIT

In 1756 the al-Sabah dynasty took control of a patch of desert and a few oases on the borders of the Gulf. It has survived as the ruling family of Kuwait until the present day despite all the vicissitudes of regional and international politics. Kuwait's relations with the **Ottoman Empire** were always loose, and in 1899 the ruling sheikh signed a treaty with the regional superpower **Britain** which delegated part of his powers – notably foreign relations – to the British government.

The discovery of **oil** on the eve of World War II totally transformed this traditional nomadic society. From the beginning of the 1950s, the ruler used the oil revenue to finance a programme of public works and improvement in education and medicine – an event unusual enough to warrant mention. On 19 June 1961, Kuwait gained **independence**, the sheikh was transformed into an emir, and the country was admitted into the **Arab League** – despite the claims of Qasim's **Iraq** (supported by most Iraqis) to what it considered to be a lost province of the mother country.

Kuwait enjoys an economic and social prosperity based on oil and immigrant labour. However, the population in 1990 included barely 40 per cent nationals; the rest were from other Arab countries – including 400,000 **Palestinians**. From the mid-1970s Kuwait has tended to replace these Arab migrants, at least as far as unskilled work is concerned, with an Asian labourforce obliged to undertake everything and anything, and is little concerned with the unrest of the **Arab world**.

In a troubled environment, the royal family has always tried to remain aloof from inter-Arab conflicts, even to assume the role of mediator. From 1967 it made a considerable financial contribution to the frontline countries and the Palestinian cause. In 1981 Kuwait was a founder member of the Gulf Cooperation Council (GCC), along with the United Arab Emirates, **Saudi Arabia**, Oman, Qatar and Bahrain. It has tended to oppose the hegemony of Riyadh. Until the **Gulf War** its relations with the **Palestine Liberation Organisation (PLO)** – in particular with Fatah – were solid because the Palestinian community was rich and influential. In 1964 a Soviet embassy was opened in Kuwait City, for twenty years the only one in the Gulf – apart from Iraq.

The government has also increased its foreign investments, and manages a portfolio estimated at $40bn, with an annual return of $5–8bn. Among the companies in which Kuwait owns shares are DaimlerChrysler (14 per cent), the German chemical group Hoechst (20 per cent), General Motors, General Electric, AT&T and various Spanish banking and oil groups. The purchase in 1988 of 20 per cent of BP shares aroused fierce opposition from the British government. Through this manoeuvre, plus the purchase in 1987 of the European distribution network of Gulf, one of the oil giants, Kuwait itself disposes of a quarter of its oil production. The scandal of Suq al-Manakh – the collapse of Kuwait's informal financial market in 1983 – seems largely forgotten today. Oil is the principal source of the wealth and importance of this small emirate, where 10 per cent of world reserves are located. Kuwait, an active member of the Organisation of Oil Exporting Countries (OPEC), took control of its own natural resources in 1975.

The victory of the Iranian Revolution and the **Iran–Iraq War** threw Kuwait, which had sided with **Saddam Hussein**, into a state of turbulence. Relations between the Sunni and **Shi'ite** communities deteriorated, and Shi'ites were banned from all sensitive posts. In 1983 the country was shaken by a number of political disturbances. The authorities took advantage of this, in July 1986, to dissolve the Assembly elected in February, which had contained representatives from across the political spectrum, from the left to Muslim groups. Freedom of the press was, however, more widespread in 1990 than in most Arab countries.

Yet until 2 August 1990 what were undeniably genuine rights were limited by several factors. First, most of the population – including Palestinians who had been living in the country for decades – had no political rights. Through all the years that the Palestinian community was established in Kuwait, the Emir granted naturalisation to a mere fifty families. Nationals, who numbered around 800,000 in 1990, are split into two categories: the only people who can vote are first-class citizens who can prove that their family was living in Kuwait before 1920; second-class citizens are denied the right to vote, except for Bedouins of Saudi origin, who were given the right to vote in 1967 because the government hoped through this move to block the path to nationalists and the left. Women do not have the right to vote.

Despite these restrictions, the vast majority of the citizens who remained in the country after 2 August 1991 (350,000 were abroad on holiday or had fled when Iraqi troops arrived) resisted the occupation. Even the opposition, which had organised meetings in the months leading up to the invasion to demand the restoration of the elected parliament and the restoration of the 1962 Constitution, refused to heed Saddam's call to collaborate, and took an active role in both civil and military resistance.

The occupation lasted seven months, but it left deep scars: the country, now annexed as the 'nineteenth province of Iraq', was pillaged. Thousands of Kuwaitis were arrested, deported, tortured or executed. Furthermore, the Coalition bombardment and the sabotage caused by the Iraqi army – hundreds of oil wells were set alight – destroyed much crucial infrastructure.

Liberation was also marred by atrocities. There was an open witch-hunt for Palestinians and foreigners who were suspected, often wrongly, of having collaborated with the Iraqis. Thousands were killed or went missing, and 300,000 Palestinians were expelled. Nor were the promises of political liberalisation made by Emir Jaber al-Ahmad al-Sabah kept. The first elections took place on 5 October 1992, but only 80,000 first-class male citizens (around 15 per cent of adults) were allowed to vote. Even so, candidates who were critical of the status quo – mainly left-wing nationalists who had been members of the parliament that was dissolved in 1986 – were extremely successful. The various Islamic movements, one Shi'ite and two Sunni (notably the Islamic Constitutional Movement, affiliated to the **Muslim Brothers** before severing ties during the 1990–91) gained three seats each. In total, even if the **Islamists** could not agree on a common policy towards the regime, around 30 of the 50 seats were won by opposition candidates and, for the first time ever, the opposition took part in government.

New elections took place in 1996, and then in 1999. The Islamists continued to advance politically, and became the main presence in the parliament elected in July 1999 and through that also the main force of opposition. But the Islamists are split between Shi'ites and Sunnis, and also by different political approaches. They were also shaken by the involvement of their members in the 11 September 2001 attacks and in the al-Qaeda network. The **US** thus succeeded in obtaining the closing down of the sources of finance for **Osama bin Laden**'s network in the emirate: the authorities put an end to the activities of the offices which collect money in the name of **Islam**. Government commissions now vet any funds destined for overseas very strictly. Women have once again seen the right to vote rejected: the Emir's decree which gave them full political rights in May 1999 was rejected by two thirds of members of parliament; an identical law failed by a narrower margin of 30 votes to 32.

On a regional and international scale, Kuwait signed a ten-year defence pact with the US on 19 September 1991 which provided port facilities to the American fleet and agreed army training, joint manoeuvres and so on. On several occasions between 1992 and 1994 the US deployed troops in the emirate, citing 'Iraqi threats' as justification. In April 1992 the border with Iraq was moved 600m further north by the UN, a move which cut a part of the port of Umm Qasr off from Baghdad and which is likely to be a bone of contention in the future. On 10 November 1994 Baghdad was pressurised into recognising the sovereignty of Kuwait, its territorial integrity and the new border. Relations with the PLO and the countries which supported Iraq – **Jordan** and **Yemen** – are gradually being normalised, and at the Arab Summit in Beirut at the end of March 2002 Kuwait for the first time restored relations with Baghdad. The confrontation between the US and Iraq which finally culminated in war in 2003 has meant the continuation of privileged links between the US and the emirate, with the US army reinforcing its military presence in the run up to the war. Although the US military presence in Kuwait looks set to continue as long as it remains in Iraq, in the long term Kuwait risks losing its special relationship with Washington as its strategic value diminishes.

In addition to the destruction it suffered in 1990–91, Kuwait had to spend $16bn to finance the intervention of the Coalition forces in the war. This meant that it had to draw on its investments abroad, whose value was halved. Moreover, the Kuwait Investment Office was implicated in a series of financial scandals. The deployment of American troops, notably in 1994, also proved very expensive. The reconstruction programme has been delayed by the policy of expelling Arab migrant labour from the emirate, thus depriving Kuwait of many sorely needed skills. To meet this expenditure the regime has been forced to reduce welfare spending, controversial in a country where the constitution guarantees income, free education and healthcare.

The territory of Kuwait covers 18,000 sq. km, and had a population of 2.2 million in 2000, around a third of whom are Shi'ites. Oil production, which was 1.5 million barrels per day in 1980 and 1 million in 1990, reached almost 2 million in 2000.

But the question which monopolises the attention of the ruling family is who will succeed Emir Jaber, whose health at the end of 2002 was decidedly fragile.

LAWRENCE, T.E.

Known to history as Lawrence of Arabia, during the First World War T.E. Lawrence championed the Arab Revolt against the Turks, as immortalised in his book *The Seven Pillars of Wisdom* and the film adapted from it by David Lean.

British intelligence recruited Thomas Edward Lawrence in Cairo in 1914. He was at the time fresh from Oxford but familiar with the **Arab world,** where archaeological digs had already taken him; he had a passion for literature, young boys and adventure.

The adventure proposed to him by the heads of British intelligence was a strategic one. In 1914 London feared that **Turkey**, allied to the Axis powers, would carry the **Arabs** in its wake; the Sultan, Commander of the Faithful, had declared a holy war (*jihad*). Negotiations were underway, on the one hand between Sir Percy Cox, British resident in the Gulf, and the Wahhabi Ibn Saud, and on the other between Sir Henry MacMahon, British High Commissioner in Cairo, and the Hashemite Sherif Hussein, descended from the tribe of the Prophet and leader of the Hejaz. The latter agreed, during the summer of 1915, to take up arms against the **Ottoman Empire** in exchange for the promise made by the British to 'recognize and support Arab independence'.

Sent to Hussein to help him organise the revolt, Lawrence worked with his sons, particularly the youngest, Faisal. As Faisal's liaison officer, he took part in the mobilisation of the Bedouins, in battles against the Turks and in the capture of important towns, particularly Aqaba in July 1917. Then Lawrence and the Arab troops backed General Allenby's offensive in Palestine (see **Palestinians**) and **Syria**. Lawrence's dream seemed about to materialise: a great pro-British Arab empire, with Hussein at its head controlling the Hejaz, Faisal controlling Syria and **Iraq**, and Abdullah Palestine and Transjordan.

But **Britain** was bound by other, contradictory promises made to the French, the **Zionist** movement and even to Hussein's Wahhabi rivals. Before ever seeing the light of day, the Arab Empire was dismembered and the scraps shared out between **France** and Britain. Hussein had to make do with the Hejaz, which Ibn Saud later seized from him; Faisal was chased out of Syria by the French, to be given the throne of Iraq, and Abdullah was made Emir of Transjordan. As for Lawrence of Arabia, he had had enough of this 'epic'; on 4 July 1922 he resigned from the Office of Colonial Affairs.

He then pursued a new career as a writer. According to some, he also became involved with the British fascist Sir Oswald Mosley, but his latest biographer, Jeremy Wilson, contests this: he had apparently turned down two invitations to join the movement. Lawrence was killed in a motorbike accident on 19 May 1935. As for the meeting which he was supposed to have had a few days later with Chancellor Hitler, this is apparently unfounded rumour.

LEBANESE CIVIL WAR

The second Lebanese Civil War (for the first, in 1958, see **Lebanon**) began on 13 April 1975 when a bus returning **Palestinians** and Lebanese civilians from the **Sabra** camp was fired upon while crossing the Ain al-Rummaneh area of Beirut controlled by the Phalangists. Twenty-seven passengers were killed. Reprisals and counter-reprisals followed, and fighting spread throughout the country. No one imagined at the time that 14 years later it would still be going on, though officially the war ended in September 1976.

The war grew out of a combination of three factors. First, an economic and social crisis had given rise to numerous protest movements against the confessional system (see **Confessionalism**) and an upsurge of left-wing organisations. Second, the **Palestine Liberation Organisation (PLO)** presence in Lebanon had become permanent – it had taken control of the refugee camps after 1967, and the Palestinian resistance had found sanctuary in Lebanon after its expulsion from **Jordan** in 1971. Finally, despite its neutrality, Lebanon had been dragged into the Arab–Israeli June **1967 War**; the Israeli army's raids in the south of the country made Lebanon a frontline country.

Two coalitions, far from homogeneous, confronted each other during the war's active phase, which lasted for eighteen months: the Lebanese Front and the Lebanese National Movement (LNM). Between these two fluctuated a galaxy of forces and personalities, some neutral, some aligned.

The Lebanese Front, which assumed a formal existence nine months after the outbreak of hostilities, was comprised of four groups, all predominantly **Maronite**: the faction of the President of the republic, Suleiman Franjieh, whose fiefdom was Zghorta in the north; the faction of the former president Camille Chamoun, with his 3500 militiamen known as the Tigers; the congress of monastic orders led by Father Kassis; and, finally, Pierre Gemayel's Phalangist party, whose 15,000 men made up the backbone of the right-wing coalition.

The LNM was an amalgamation of about fifteen parties, ranging from centrist to extreme left. Multi-denominational, it had a bedrock of Christian members, particularly Greek Orthodox. Its undisputed leader was Kamal Jumblatt, whose party, the PSP (Parti socialiste populaire), and 3000 militiamen made up the central force of the LNM. Among the other components were the Lebanese Communist Party (LCP), the Syrian National Social Party, the **Ba'th**, and the Murabitun – an essentially Sunni Nasserist movement.

To the extent that it is possible to rationalise the respective goals of the two coalitions, the Lebanese Front sought to drive out the Palestinians and maintain the **Maronite** bourgeoisie's hegemony over the state, whereas the LNM sought to form an alliance with the PLO and secularise the state. Many Lebanese hesitated between the two camps – the traditional Sunni

Muslim leaders, who would have been content with a redistribution of constitutional powers, certain Maronite leaders like Raymond Eddé, and parties representing other Christian denominations (such as the Armenians and the Greek Orthodox). Lastly, special mention must be made of the **Shi'ites** and the Movement of the Dispossessed, the future Amal, which fought at the side of the LNM until the Syrian intervention in the summer of 1976.

The outcome of the first phase of the war, which lasted until January 1976, was a stalemate, although the Lebanese Front had achieved a slight edge on its rivals. The PLO – with the exception of organisations belonging to the Rejectionist Front – had until then avoided committing itself. However, at the beginning of the new year, Maronite forces launched a major offensive against the Palestinian camps. The PLO no longer had a choice. It threw all its weight into the conflict and turned the balance in favour of the LNM. It was then that **Syria** intervened, at first politically, then militarily, against its former Palestinian allies. The Syrian leadership, which was at the time negotiating with **US** Secretary of State Henry Kissinger, hoped to reach a compromise with Washington and regain the **Golan Heights**. It also feared the advent of a revolutionary regime in Lebanon, which acts as a security zone for Syria, and dreamt, for this and for economic reasons, of strengthening Syrian hegemony over the land of cedars. On 1 June 1976 Syrian troops invaded Lebanon in large numbers and, with the help of the Phalangists, crushed the PLO and the LNM. An Arab mini-summit called in Riyadh by **Saudi Arabia** in October imposed a truce on all belligerents. Officially the Civil War was over. It left behind an enfeebled country – 30,000 dead, more than twice that number wounded, and 600,000 refugees – and did grave damage to Lebanon's economic potential.

But Lebanon had not only been more seriously tested than in 1958; the repercussions of the war effectively undermined the country. The army had not borne up well. It had split into rival factions which none of the successive presidents was able to gather into a new consensus. Confessionalism was reinforced by the war, by its horrors and by its massacres, gathering speed even after the events of 1982. Each community tended to close ranks to protect itself and retreated into its own geographical strongholds. Finally, the war continued in the south, where Israeli intervention became increasingly overt until the Israeli army finally pulled out of the region in May 2000. It was not until the **Taif Accords** in 1989 that the continual skirmishes petered out.

LEBANON

The unique characteristics of Mount Lebanon have been dictated from ancient times by its geography. This chain of mountains offers ecological conditions perfectly adapted for human habitation, particularly abundant water. Moreover, because access to it is difficult, Mount Lebanon has on various occasions served as a natural refuge for different persecuted minorities. In the sixteenth century, with the advent of the **Druze** Maan dynasty, and especially the reign of Fakhreddin II (1590–1633), the territory of present-day Lebanon was unified for the first time.

It was to be so again during the reign of Bashir II, descended from the great Chehab family, from 1788 to 1840. Only in this period did the conditions that would make Lebanon a specific entity in the **Arab world** begin to take shape: a Christian community in the mountains possessing strong links with Europe; a community of Druze highlanders sufficiently confident in its tribal structures to accept increasing numbers of Christians in its villages; a port, Beirut, which links the mountains to the West, has a Sunni Muslim presence and in the nineteenth century, and became the centre of Western learning and ideas for the whole of the **Ottoman Empire**; a missionary presence, at first Catholic and then Protestant; a silk industry concentrated in the mountains that promoted exchanges between the hinterland and Beirut.

The dual Druze and **Maronite** hegemony over the mountain led in 1843 to a system of double *qa'imaqamats* or lieutenancies. Two provinces were demarcated in Mount Lebanon, Maronite in the north and Druze in the south. They remained under the authority of the Ottoman Empire – which had exercised its suzerainty over Lebanon since the sixteenth century – even though European powers had already arrogated to themselves a right of inspection, which encouraged the expansion of **confessionalism**.

The year 1860 was important for Lebanon. It began with a peasant revolt led by a blacksmith named Tanios Shahine and ended, as the peasant uprising degenerated into religious war, with inter-denominational massacres. On the pretext of defending the Christian Maronites, Napoleon III despatched a French expeditionary force. A comprehensive settlement followed, negotiated between the European powers and the Sublime Porte (the Ottoman administration). This settlement, which recognised Lebanese 'uniqueness' by providing political representation for the various religious communities, remained in force until World War I.

After the Allied victory in 1918, Lebanon was one of the territories ceded to **France** under the terms of the **Sykes–Picot Agreement**. In the course of establishing its Mandate over Greater Lebanon (with its present-day frontiers), the French government institutionalised confessionalism and the Maronite hegemony. This domination was, however, shortlived. The

Vichy regime allowed the Axis powers to use bases in Lebanon and **Syria**, and **Britain** – backed by the Free French forces – occupied both countries in July 1941. A progression towards **independence** was now inevitable. Despite troop landings in 1945, Paris never regained its authority, and independent Lebanon went on to become a founder member of the UN and the **Arab League**.

But independence, proclaimed on 22 March 1943, did not come about simply because of the ebb of French power or the upsurge of the nationalist movement. An unwritten agreement had also been necessary, the National Pact, a compromise agreed between leading Sunni and Maronite families. By two central clauses in this deal, the Christians renounced French protection and accepted independence, while the Muslims abjured Arab unity and, above all, the dream of a Greater Syria. Another precondition for the birth of the new state was the maintenance of confessionalism.

This precarious balance was frequently shaken. The first serious jolt, in 1958, arose from a crisis both regional and national in nature. The Lebanese President, Camille Chamoun, took up the cudgels against **Nasser** in his war against the West, and in 1955 supported the creation of the **Baghdad Pact**. He could therefore only feel threatened by the establishment of the United Arab Republic (UAR), formed between **Egypt** and Syria on 1 February 1958. On the other hand, the UAR galvanised the progressive parties as well as Muslims in Lebanon. Disappointed by the lack of reforms – which Chamoun had nonetheless undertaken to put into practice – they could not accept that the President, contrary to the constitution, should run for a second term in office. From May 1958 clashes increased. On 14 July 1958, **Iraq**'s pro-Western monarchy collapsed and Chamoun called on the **US** to save his regime. The next day American marines landed in Beirut. Fighting went on for several more weeks and ended in a compromise: General Chehab, commander-in-chief of the army, succeeded Chamoun, and the pact of 1943 was renewed. Chehab and his successor, Charles Helou, tried, albeit unsuccessfully, to strengthen the state's authority and eliminate extreme inequalities, whether social or sectarian.

During the twenty years leading to the explosion of 1975, Lebanon experienced a transformation. Its role as a bridge between the Western European and American economies and the Arab world was galvanised by the **oil** boom. Lebanon, where the crudest form of liberalism reigned, attracted capital coming from the Gulf states or fleeing the 'socialist yoke' of Egypt, Syria and Iraq. In 1970, the services sector (finance and banks, commerce, tourism) represented over 70 per cent of GDP, one of the highest rates in the world. Within this context, the banking sector occupied a central and hegemonic place. The prosperity brought about by this boom was not, however, equally shared. The absence of the state – most obvious in the economic field – prevented any attempt at social welfare. Disparities and inequalities intensified, corresponding with denominational divisions to some extent.

These domestic tensions were heightened by the impact of the **1967 War** and the Palestinian presence in Lebanon. Commando units strengthened the resolve of the several hundred thousand refugees who had settled in Lebanon. In October 1969 the first serious crisis broke out between the state and the resistance forces. Backed by a Lebanese popular movement which mixed social and nationalist demands, the *fedayeen* succeeded in bringing about the Cairo Agreement, which legalised their presence in the camps in the south. After the elimination of the **Palestine Liberation Organisation (PLO)** in **Jordan**, in 1970–71, Lebanon became the last Palestinian base. **Israel**, in response, stepped up its reprisal raids.

Tel Aviv was less concerned with destroying the resistance movement – Israel's targets were mostly civilian and Lebanese – than with forcing the Beirut government itself to subjugate the Palestinians. But this tactic, successful in Jordan, was to fail in Lebanon. Its only result was to hasten the process of disintegration of the state and precipitate the **Lebanese Civil War**, which broke out on 13 April 1975.

When in June 1982 the Israeli Defence Forces (IDF) swept over Lebanon, the country's strength was already sapped, and no central authority was able to assert itself. Worse was to come. The next two years saw the failure of attempts by the Phalangists, backed by Tel Aviv, to impose their hegemony on Lebanon. President Amin Gemayel's regime suffered defeat after defeat: in the Shuf in September 1983, in West Beirut in February 1984. The opposition front (Amal, Walid Jumblatt's Parti Socialist Populaire [PSP], Suleiman Franjieh, Rashid Karameh etc.) extended the zones under its control, while the Multinational Force with American marines at its head hurriedly left the Lebanese capital. Meanwhile, in the south, resistance to Israeli occupation was spreading; initiated mainly by left-wing parties, it spread and became a mass movement when the Muslim groups joined it. Israel speeded up its withdrawal, which was completed in June 1985, apart from the buffer zone controlled with the help of the South Lebanese Army. Gemayel overturned his alliances, repealed the treaty he had signed with Israel in 1983, and on 30 April 1984 formed a government of National Unity under the leadership of Karameh.

In December 1985 a tripartite agreement between Amal, the Lebanese Forces and Jumblatt's PSP seemed to open the way for a lasting agreement. But it was not to be, and divisions again took the upper hand, without Damascus – which, with 35,000 soldiers, controlled 60 per cent of the territory – being able to impose its point of view. In September 1988, after the failure of attempts to find a successor to Amin Gemayel, Lebanon found itself with no president and two governments – one Christian, led by General Michel Aoun, commander-in-chief of the army, the other Muslim, led by Selim Hoss, who had succeeded Karameh following his assassination on 1 June 1987.

On 14 March 1989 Aoun declared a war of liberation against Syria. Despite the undoubted popularity that this move brought him, its main result was the ending of a bloody civil war between the Christians in the army and those of the Lebanese Forces led by Samir Geagea, both of whom agreed to accept the peace process initiated in Taif in **Saudi Arabia**. On 22 October 1989, a session of the Lebanese parliament was convened by a tripartite committee of the Arab League (Algeria, Saudi Arabia, Morocco), where 62 representatives unanimously agreed a plan of reforms that would reduce the powers of the Maronite president and pass them to the Council of Ministers and more particularly to the Sunni prime minister and the **Shi'ite** President of the National Assembly. Henceforth there would be an equal mix of Muslims and Christians in parliament. Since the election of the new President and the formation of a government of National Unity, the militia groups have begun to disarm and the authority of the state has been re-established.

On 5 November 1989, parliament met and, despite the protests of Aoun, elected René Moawad as President. Moawad was assassinated on 22 November and replaced by Elias Hrawi. Amazingly, the agreement was finally applied. Taking advantage of the Gulf crisis, during which he sided with the 'good guys', in October 1990 **Hafez al-Assad** launched an attack against Aoun's troops: at last Beirut was unified under a single power. The militias – except for **Hezbollah** – called a ceasefire and the army regained control; civil peace returned, although the situation in the south was still very tense. On 22 May 1991 a Treaty of Friendship and Co-operation between the Syrian Republic and the Lebanese Republic was signed in Damascus, indicating the grip that Syria still maintained on life in Lebanon.

The first parliamentary elections since 1972 were held in August and September 1992, but were boycotted by many of the Christian parties and leading figures, such as the Phalangist party, the Lebanese Forces, supporters of Aoun, Chamoun, Eddé, as well as by the head of the Maronites, Nasrallah Sfeir. The turnout was low, except in the south, where it bordered on 50 per cent. Hezbollah recorded a notable success, with eight members elected, which promoted it to the position of leading party in the country, as the other 120 seats had mainly been won by the gentry or by pro-Syrian candidates. Nabih Berri, leader of the Amal movement, was elected President of the assembly, while **Rafiq Hariri** became Prime Minister. In spite of the questionable manner in which the election was conducted, Syria had succeeded in its plan, while the Maronites appear to have lost most from the election.

The appointment of Saudi–Lebanese millionaire **Hariri** to the government raised hopes for reconstruction and a return to economic prosperity.

But the ultra-liberalism and the racketeering that were then to plague Lebanon, as well as a ridiculous plan to rebuild Beirut, soon wore down the optimism of the people. Although investment has picked up, the fate of the population is still in the balance. The aggression of the Israeli army in spring 1996 against the south, followed by the victory of the right in the Israeli elections highlighted the fragility of the peace upon which leaders were relying. Finally, the decision taken in October 1995 to extend President Hrawi's term by three years, without precedent in the country's history, merely confirmed that nothing happens in Beirut without the prior consent of Damascus. However, the elections in summer 1996, in which some of the Maronite forces took part, proved that there was no way other than the proposal made by Syria at Taif. Moreover, in August 1996, it was to the Syrian authorities rather than the Lebanese that **Benyamin Netanyahu** presented his 'Lebanon First' plan, which Damascus rejected without even consulting Beirut: **Assad** had expected to negotiate the withdrawal of Israel from the **Golan**, not from south Lebanon.

Ehud Barak eventually withdrew his army from south Lebanon in May 2000, a withdrawal hastened by the repeated attacks by Hezbollah and the collapse of the South Lebanon Army (SLA), Israel's ally. This withdrawal brought to an end a 22-year occupation, which no longer guaranteed the security of the north of the Jewish state and had also become unpopular with Israeli public opinion. Nevertheless, it left several issues unresolved: the mandate of the UN Interim Force in Lebanon (**UNIFIL**) in the region; land-mine clearance; the fate of the SLA troops; the compensation demanded by Lebanon for the years of occupation; the future of the 350,000 Palestinian refugees in the country who are subject to a high level of discrimination; the freeing of prisoners demanded by Hezbollah; and the establishment of recognised borders between Lebanon, Israel and Syria. UN Resolution 425 speaks of 'internationally recognized borders', referring to those of 1923 separating Lebanon from Palestine under the British Mandate. But Israel continued to occupy the Sheba'a Farms, on the flanks of the Syrian Golan, and established a large security base there. This zone, which is also claimed by Lebanon, remains the scene of repeated clashes with Hezbollah. Fears of Hezbollah 'taking advantage' of the US-led war in Iraq in 2003 to open a front against Israel proved unfounded, with the border remaining relatively quiet.

The other issue with which the new Lebanese President Émile Lahoud (elected in 1998) had to deal was the economic crisis. The return to power of Hariri in November 2000 raised new hopes among the population. Having inherited a disastrous economic situation – which began under his first term as Prime Minister and continued under Selim Hoss, the outcome of years of war and regional stalemate – the Hariri government embarked on a policy of trade liberalisation and privatisation. The signature of an Association Agreement with the **EU** on 10 January 2002, as an extension of the Barcelona process initiated in 1995 (which was designed to set up, with 27 Mediterranean countries, an economic and financial partnership and the installation of a 'common zone of peace and stability'), raised hopes in Beirut of a manna of investment much needed in a country which is the second most indebted in the world after Zimbabwe. For the EU the accord was the reward for having maintained a vigorous diplomatic presence in the region.

But economic openness was not translated into political openness. In a regional climate of generalised disorder, the regime, like its neighbours, became hardline and militarised, embarking on brutal round-ups of political opponents, an authoritarian tightening of the Penal Code, and the repression of all opposition to the Syrian occupation. Because while the Lahoud regime shows fewer signs of servility than its predecessors, it still remains Damascus's faithful partner. Although Syria has undertaken four partial troop redeployments in Lebanon, this does not mean it has any less influence in the country: the cabinet reshuffle in April 2003 was widely perceived as bringing in the most pro-Syrian government since Taif.

Lebanon is a country of 10,500 sq. km and had a population of four million in 1999. Since it has no natural resources, for a long time it has owed its exceptional development to its role as a bridgehead between East and West, between Arab capitals and the Northern banks. Leaving aside the necessity of rebuilding an economy that has been ravaged by years of war, it will also have to find a new place for itself in a Middle East that has been profoundly transformed since 1975, a region in which, under the combined pressure of liberalisation and the end of Arab socialism, new competitors have appeared.

LIBYA

A part of the **Ottoman Empire** since the sixteenth century, the territory of present-day Libya was subjected to the increasing intrusion of European colonialism in the nineteenth century, along with the other countries of North Africa. With the acquiescence of the other European powers, in September 1911 Italy began the conquest of the provinces of Tripolitania and Cyrenaica. Local resistance was particularly fierce, orchestrated by the religious Sanussi Brotherhood, a reformist movement created in the middle of the nineteenth century. The rebellion lasted right through World War I, at the end of which the socialist Italian government granted greater autonomy to the various regions. Idris al-Sanussi, leader of the brotherhood, was even put in charge of Cyrenaica; but the agreement was shortlived and he had to flee to **Egypt**.

Mussolini's accession to power in 1922 led to a renewal of hostilities and a new outbreak of resistance to colonialism, under the command of the

Sanussis and Omar al-Mukhtar. The fighting lasted nine months. In 1934 Italy unified the provinces of Cyrenaica and Tripolitania, to which it added the province of Fezzan, to constitute an entity named Libya. A wave of over 120,000 Italian colonists flowed into the newly formed country before 1940.

During World War II, Idris al-Sanussi raised forces against the Axis powers from his base in Cairo. At the end of the war, Cyrenaica and Tripolitania were occupied by **Britain**, and Fezzan by Free French troops. After long debates at the UN on the future of the Italian colonies, Libya gained **independence** on 24 December 1951 and Idris was proclaimed King.

The new regime committed itself to a pro-Western policy. In 1953 and 1954, treaties were signed confirming access to important military bases for the British and Americans. Within the **Arab League**, which it joined in March 1953, Libya championed the conservative bloc against **Nasser**'s Egypt. From the economic point of view, the discovery and exploitation of **oil** in 1959 gave the country the resources it had lacked. The boom that followed helped to promote urbanisation and the development of education and a middle class. In the climate of frustrated nationalist demands prevalent throughout the Middle East, especially after the **1967 War**, the ageing sovereign's despotic regime proved quite unable to cope. On 1 September 1969 a group of young officers, led by **Muammar Qadhaffi**, who was 31 at the time, seized power and proclaimed a republic.

Strongly influenced by Nasser, whose disciple he considered himself, Qadhaffi set his country on the 'path of socialism': he nationalised foreign banks, increased pressure on the oil companies, confiscated the properties of Italian colonists and established a single political party, the Arab Socialist Union. In December 1969 agreements were signed for the evacuation, the following year, of the Wheelus bases by the **US** and of Tobruk and al-Adem by Britain. Relations with Moscow proved difficult in these early years and Qadhaffi showed signs of being decidedly anti-Soviet.

As François Burgat and André Laronde have noted, the classical strain of Arab nationalism developed in Libya did demonstrate

> some distinctly specific traits. In the transition from the current of Nasserist Arabism prevalent in the 1960s to the resurgent Islamism of the 1980s, Qaddafi can be said to occupy something of an intermediate position...Even if he distrusted the conservatism of the traditional keepers of religious law, his worldview was closer to that of the Islamists than was Nasser's.

Once in power, he quite rapidly introduced measures to re-Islamise the legal system.

From 1975 the regime became more radical, and began to diverge from the Nasserist model. This was the year that saw the publication of the first part of *The Green Book*, subtitled 'Solution to the problem of democracy'. In 1976 Qadhaffi proclaimed the 'power of the people' and set up a system of direct democracy through popular committees. On 2 March 1977, the Peoples' Socialist Jamahiriyya – a neologism coined by combining the Arabic words for 'republic' and 'masses' – was born. After the nationalisation of oil, most of the economy passed into the control of the producers. Development was based on the import of foreign labour. There were great achievements on the social level, with the introduction of free medical care and compulsory primary education. The regime's creation of revolutionary committees in 1977 attests to the need to repress opposition at home, even if that opposition was divided.

In the international arena, Tripoli drew closer to Moscow, which helped it raise a powerfully equipped army; but the Soviet Union distrusted its embarrassing ally and, in October 1985, refused to sign a treaty of friendship and co-operation with Libya. Qadhaffi had developed a violently anti-American policy, extending support equally to revolutionary movements and regimes (South Africa's African National Congress, the Sandinistas of Nicaragua) and **terrorist** organisations, particularly that of **Abu Nidal**. In March 1982, the US imposed a commercial boycott on Libya, and on the night of 14 April 1986 launched an air raid against Tripoli and Benghazi, aiming to liquidate the Colonel; a hundred civilians were killed.

Libya observed a policy of Arab unity that fluctuated with changing circumstances. Attempts at unification with other countries have been as numerous as they have been shortlived: Egypt (1972–73), Tunisia (1974), **Syria** (1980) and even Morocco (1984). Radical in the extreme, Libya has not hesitated to support the militant Palestinian groups, and its relations with the **Palestine Liberation Organisation (PLO)** and **Arafat** have had their ups and downs. In 1987, the country redirected its efforts towards the Maghreb, particularly Tunisia, and normalised its relations with the PLO and, in 1989, with Cairo.

Qadhaffi has also become interested in his African environment, which he has almost come to consider as being part of the 'Arab space'. This attitude was spectacularly demonstrated in Chad, where he intervened directly in 1980 – after occupying, in 1973, then annexing, in 1975, the Aouzou Strip, claimed by both countries. This adventure ended in fiasco, Tripoli withdrawing its troops from Chad and, in October 1988, establishing diplomatic relations with Hissene Habre's government. In February 1994, the Court of International Justice in The Hague found in favour of Chad over the question of the Aouzou Strip; Qadhaffi subsequently accepted that he withdraw from the area.

The new-found moderation of Libyan foreign policy, noticeable since 1987 and the result of both external setbacks and economic difficulties (between 1985 and 1988 the value of exports dropped by half as a result of the fall in oil prices) have forced Qadhaffi to soften his domestic options. The authorities attempted to develop industry other than oil by encouraging the formation of agricultural and industrial co-operatives and small family businesses, whether agricultural or commercial. They sought to facilitate consumerism by opening the frontiers with Libya's neighbours. In 1992, the 'Popular Socialist' Jamahiriyya was renamed the 'Arab' Jamahiriyya.

But this shift has been at odds with the intransigence of the US, which considers Qadhaffi as one of the 'renegades' of international politics, along with **Saddam Hussein** and Fidel Castro. The implication of Libya in two bombings (of a Pan Am flight in December 1988 and a UTA flight in September 1989) resulted in the UN Security Council imposing an embargo in 1992 and 1993. Furthermore, in 1996 Washington accused Qadhaffi of building a chemical-weapons factory at Tarhuna and took unilateral measures against Libya and **Iran**. On 10 July 1999 the UN 'suspended' its **sanctions** (they would be 'lifted as soon as possible'), following Libya's delivery to the Scottish judicial authorities of two agents for the Lockerbie bombing (see **Qadhaffi, Muammar**). Over the course of August and September 2003, Tripoli reached an agreement with both Washington and Paris over the compensation of the victims of the terrorist attacks against the Pan Am and UTA flights. This opened up the road to an end to the sanctions imposed by the UN Security Council.

In that period Libya embarked on intensive diplomatic activity in order to emerge from its isolation. First it effected a return to the scene in Africa, giving itself a role as the continent's leader and main support. Its claims on the Aouzou Strip in Chad and its support for the Tuaregs and Toubous were forgotten. In February 1998, Qadhaffi proposed the creation of a community of Sahel-Saharan states (COMESSA) in which African countries would join forces with the Jamahiriyya, which was ready to finance their projects. Libyan capital provided three quarters of the funding for the African Trade and Development Bank. Libya also played a mediating role in several regional conflicts: Sierra Leone, Somalia, **Sudan**, Burundi, the Democratic Republic of Congo and the Central African Republic. The conditions were ripe for the calling of a special summit of the Organisation of African Unity (OAU) in Sirte, in September 1999, an organisation which Qadhaffi was proposing to transform into an African Union modelled on the EU. Adopted at the Lomé Summit in July 2000, this project was to have been financed entirely by Libya.

Beyond Africa, Tripoli also made a return to the international stage. This return was marked by three events in the course of 2000: in April, Libya's participation at the Cairo European African Summit; in September, its con- tribution to the freeing of Western hostages held on the island of Jolo; in November, the invitation to attend the Euro–Mediterranean Conference in Marseille as an observer. Criticising the lack of activity of the Arab League in the Palestinian conflict, it threatened to withdraw from that organisation in 2002. On another front, with the arrival on the scene of President Putin, relations between **Russia** and Libya have been strengthened, notably in Moscow's arming of the Libyan army.

Oil, which has long been Qadhaffi's miracle weapon both at home and abroad (accounting for more than three quarters of Libyan exports), must henceforth be used more prudently. Although, at a rate of one million barrels per day, reserves are estimated at more than fifty years, production decreased to a rate of 1.6 million barrels per day in 2001, half the figure for 1970. This has led to a marked fall in export income, which, along with the sanctions, has had an effect. In this context there had to be a reduction in public spending, and in particular in wages, which had already been eroded by inflation. Unemployment affects 27 per cent of the economically active population. Social services have been deteriorating, and crime levels have been rising.

The huge investments of the 1970s have produced relatively insignificant results. The 'Great Artificial River' – with a capacity to transport two million cubic metres of **water** per year from an underground reserve in the southern desert to the north to overcome water shortages and develop agriculture – has still not been completed.

All these difficulties have heightened instability in the country. Since the attempted coup d'état at Beni Walid in October 1993, the opposition, which is dominated by **Islamists**, has on several occasions seized the opportunity to attack. The response of the governing power has been particularly brutal, yet this has accelerated the process of the 'Islamisation' of society. The two million foreigners (compared with 5.6 million 'nationals') effectively serve as scapegoats for popular discontent.

Libya covers an area of 1.7 million sq. km. Its GNP stands at $34.1bn, of which 35.6 per cent is provided by the export of goods and services (2000 figures).

LOBBY

The name given in the **US** to pressure groups which seek to influence the country's policies at both congressional and a presidential level to protect particular interests. The best known and certainly the most powerful is the Jewish lobby, whose pressure on the White House has been pointed out by, for instance, President Harry Truman, in his *Memoirs*.

The impact of the Jewish lobby stems primarily from the sheer size of the Jewish community in America, the result of massive **immigration**, notably following the pogroms of the late nineteenth and early twentieth centuries: nearly six million, in other words a little more than in **Israel** itself – which saw only 86,000 **Jews** coming from the US in the course of 54 years. Since then, this substantial **minority** has enjoyed a considerable electoral influence, particularly in the states in which it is concentrated: in percentage terms Jews represent over 3 per cent of the population in California and Connecticut, almost 4 per cent in Pennsylvania and Massachusetts, over 4 per cent in Maryland, more than 5 per cent in New Jersey and 14 per cent in the state of New York. Furthermore, since the participation of Jewish Americans in elections is generally higher than that of their compatriots, their influence is larger in relation to their numbers. But this influence, already highly significant, is magnified ten-fold by the tight organisation of the majority of this population, whose voting discipline makes them a force to be reckoned with. However, as is also happening elsewhere in the world, Jews, despite the spectacular return to religion of a minority among them, are becoming increasingly integrated: the number of mixed marriages went from 7 per cent before World War II to 30 per cent in the 1960s, and then 50 per cent in the 1990s.

American Jews are represented by a large number of religious, political and community organisations. The conference of presidents of the principal Jewish organisations plays an active role, notably in regard to the White House and the State Department. Among other equally influential organisations mention should be made of the American **Zionist** Council, the B'nai Brith and the famous Jewish Defence League founded by Rabbi Kahane. Each of the big Israeli parties has a sister organisation in the US, in particular the right, which has links with the Zionist Organisation of America.

Since 1954, the interventions of the lobby have been co-ordinated, officially, by the American Israel Public Affairs Committee (AIPAC). Membership is a minimum of $50, and it has 65,000 members active in 50 states, with about 60 permanently present on Capitol Hill. Between 1978 and 2000 the pro-Israeli Political Action Committees (PAC) distributed $34,607,182 to 1732 candidates for Congress, in relation to their positions on Israel and the conflict in the Middle East. In total it has been suggested that the lobby has about 50 senators and more than 200 members of Congress on board. The aim of AIPAC is to get 100 pro-Israeli bills per annum passed through Congress. As one American journalist has joked, 'If Israel were ever to become an American state, it would have to make do with just two Senators instead of the fifty who represent it at the moment'. In overall terms, American Jews contribute 60 per cent of funding for the Democratic Party and 40 per cent for the Republicans. Traditionally they have voted 70 per cent Democrat and 30 per cent Republican. The exception was Ronald Reagan, whose pro-Israeli position brought him 40 per cent of the Jewish vote. The Democrat Bill Clinton, whose attachment to Israel could be described as quasi-religious, beat all records in 1992. According to analysts, he brought in 85 per cent of his Jewish fellow Americans – although it has to be said that he was up against George Bush, who had spoken of the lobby in disparaging terms as 'very powerful and effective groups which are against us'.

The organisation of trips to Israel, briefings, press campaigns, a network of government personalities and members of Congress, party funding plus vigorous and sometimes decisive voting patterns are all factors which come together to put pressure on the American presidency, particularly when it is at odds with Israel. Already effective in the US in the defence of the interests of the **Yishuv** prior to World War II, then during and following the war in the winning over of Roosevelt and Truman to the idea of the creation of a Jewish state, the lobby regularly intervened against the supply of sophisticated weapons to Arab countries – including those friendly to the US. It was against the prospect of negotiations that included the **Palestine Liberation Organisation (PLO)** and the Soviet Union, and often sought the support of Soviet Jews for the USSR–US detente agenda. More obviously, it sought to mobilise the massive support given to Israel during its wars against its Arab neighbours and an increase in American civil and military aid to the Jewish state.

The power of the pro-Israeli lobby can also be related to the weakness of the pro-Arab lobby, despite the recent creation of the National Association of Arab Americans and the American-Arab Anti-Discrimination Committee. But only 100,000 of the 2,500,000 Americans of Arab origin are involved in these organisations, compared with 2,000,000 American Jews active, out of a community of 5,800,000.

But the lobby's rigorous organisation is not proof against political crises. Already shaken during the **Lebanon 1982 War**, the American Jewish community was again divided by the Palestinian **Intifada**. So much so, in fact, that after the **Gulf War**, the famous handshake in Washington and the **Oslo Accords** raised the hopes of American Jews – undoubtedly infused with uncertainty, but the element of hope was stronger. Understandably, this new direction wasn't entirely to the liking of the lobby movement, which was admittedly a minority, but an active minority. It mobilised right-wing and far-right Zionist organisations, along with ultra-Orthodox groups. If only 1.5 per cent of Israelis are of American origin, it is interesting to note that 15 per cent of settlers in the **West Bank** and Gaza come from there.

AIPAC played a role in the defeat of George Bush Senior, but the consecutive victories of Bill Clinton and **Yitzhak Rabin** knocked it off balance. Under pressure from the new Israeli Prime Minister, the Committee agreed not to campaign against the new approach of the Jewish state, but it found itself outflanked by other, more extreme groups hostile to the very idea of compromise with the **Palestinians**. Some Jewish groups sought to delay the Congress vote on US aid to the **Palestinian Authority**, others attacked the policy of returning the territories to the Palestinians, while others (such as the American Zionist Organisation, with Likudnik tendencies) set up a 'peace process follow up committee'. Even worse, the funding traditionally raised for Israel fell from $1bn in 1991 to less than $500m in

1995. Some of these funds were even diverted to supporting **settlements** on the West Bank.

The failure of the **Camp David** negotiations, the outbreak of the **second Intifada** and the escalation of violence in the Middle East profoundly altered the positioning both of American Jews and of their fellow citizens. According to a public-opinion poll of October 2002, 85 per cent of Jews supported Israel and its 'anti-**terrorist**' policy, as did 54 per cent of Americans. And Republicans were markedly more inclined to support the Jewish state (67 per cent) than Democrats (46 per cent). This reversal was explained largely by a big rallying of the Christian right, beginning with the 'Bible Belt' in the southern US, which had run out of steam in fighting Evil (divorce, abortion, pornography, homosexuality, cinema violence etc.) and which found a new lease of life in fighting for a right-wing Israel battling against 'terrorism'. Supporters of the Christian right declared themselves 62 per cent in solidarity with the **Sharon** government. In addition to the reasons common to all supporters of Israel, 35 per cent of Evangelical Christians invoke the New Testament prophesy whereby the establishment of the Jews in their own country is the precondition for the return of the Messiah, and 59 per cent of the Christian right invoked the biblical promise made to the Jewish people. Finally, while only 38 per cent of Americans blame solely the Palestinians for the present conflict, the figure rises to 47 per cent among supporters of the Christian right (and 67 per cent among Jews).

The attacks of 11 September 2001 and the 'war on terror' declared by the Bush administration have again heightened feelings of a shared destiny: four out of five Americans believe that the enemies of the US, such as **Osama bin Laden** and **Saddam Hussein**, are also those of Israel. The Christian Republican activist Gary Bauer says the Bible is very clear on the country of the alliance: God promised this land to the Jews. But he has also said he thinks that Israel and the US are natural and mutual allies in the conflict between Islamic fundamentalism and Western democracies. In return, George W. Bush has won the sympathy of Jews: four fifths of them see him as a great defender of Israel. This convergence between the traditional Jewish lobby and 'Christian Zionists' is a substantial plus in the offensive strategy of the present US administration, and it threatens to weigh heavily if the search for peace in the Middle East should at some point require radical decisions to be taken.

MARONITES

The earliest reference to **Lebanon**'s most prominent Christian community is to be found in the writings of Muslim historians of the tenth century. The Maronites, probably of Arab origin, were at that time concentrated in the Orontes Valley, in **Syria**. Since the seventh century they had professed one of the many heresies that divided Christianity – monothelitism. To escape the persecution of the Byzantines they migrated to Mount Lebanon towards the end of the tenth century. In the twelfth century, while the Crusaders were still in the East, they returned to the bosom of Rome. In the sixteenth, they settled in Kesruan (where **Shi'ites** were in the majority) and in the seventeenth and eighteenth in the Shuf (where the **Druze** were in the majority).

The emergence of modern Lebanon owes much to them, and they established a pre-eminent position there from 1920, thanks to **France** and the **confessional** system. The bourgeoisie and the great Maronite families have developed a strong sense of community, reinforced by ideological references (Phoenician origins, non-membership of the **Arab world**), geographic concentration – particularly in Mount Lebanon – and a system of private education. The Church, the religious hierarchy and the monastic orders play an important role, both economic and political, as do a certain number of great families, whose power stems from the possession of extensive landed property, wealth, relations of 'clientelism' (a system of patronage), and the 'historic heritage' to which they lay claim. Examples are the Franjiehs in Zghorta and the Eddés in Jheilet in the Beqaa Valley. But the real distinguishing feature of the Maronites lies in the early existence of the Phalangist party, a party that is both communal and modern, transcending traditional divisions. Finally, it should be noted that the Maronite community was far from united in the 1970s and that it supplied left-wing parties with many of their cadres. Since 1978 something resembling a vendetta has existed between the Maronites of the north, allied to Franjieh, and the Phalangists.

The Maronites were the main losers in the civil war and the **Taif Accords**. Their domination over Lebanon came to an end, as was evident in the failure of the boycott of the elections of 1992 by their principal leaders. Some of them eventually agreed to take part in various elections. After the death of President **Hafez al-Assad** of Syria in June 2000, there was an intensified mobilisation of a section of the Maronites against the Syrian presence in Lebanon.

MASADA

A Jewish stronghold near the Dead Sea, southeast of Hebron, where in AD72 (or AD73), **Jews** chose to kill one another in ritual fashion rather than surrender to the Romans who were besieging them.

Charged with putting down a Jewish revolt, on 28 September AD70 Roman troops captured **Jerusalem**. As Flavius Josephus recounted in *The Jewish War*, 'The army having no one else to kill and nothing left to pillage, Caesar gave orders to destroy the City and the Temple from top to bottom without further ado, leaving only the highest towers standing'. Bit by bit, the whole country was reconquered. Only one stronghold remained rebellious: Masada. It was held by the Zealots, led by Eleazar, a descendant, it is said, of Judas. Flavius Silva, the Roman Governor of **Syria**, laid siege to the fortress. A wall was even erected around the fortress to prevent escape. But the place had formidable natural defences: the fortress stood on an immense V-shaped rock, surrounded on all sides by deep ravines. Only two narrow paths traversed the precipices. Ramparts and towers completed the defence. Moreover, behind these impregnable walls, the Zealots possessed large quantities of arms and provisions.

Having been reinforced in this way by King Herod, the site was ideally suited to lengthy resistance. But the Roman soldiers built scaffolds from which they were able to breach the walls using battering rams and fire. 'We are sure to be taken,' Eleazar announced, 'but we can choose, beforehand, to die nobly with those we most love'. There followed a long exhortation that ended, 'Let us therefore make haste to bequeath them, in place of the pleasure they hope to gain from our capture, amazement at our death and admiration for our courage'. Thus perished, according to the account of Flavius Josephus, 960 men, women and children whose throats were cut by Zealots chosen by lot, the last of whom committed suicide during the great fire lit to annihilate Masada.

This mass suicide made a lasting impression on the Romans and, long after, on other civilisations. The suicide of the besieged of Masada also symbolised that of the entire Jewish people, abandoned by God. In his first disquisition on death, Eleazar had regretted his companions' inability to 'penetrate the thoughts of God and realise that the Jewish people, that he had once loved, had been condemned by Him'.

The traditional interpretation of Masada sees in it the sign and symbol of the suicidal tendency of the Jewish 'people'. Pushing the historical analysis further and projecting it onto the destiny of the Jews, certain authors see this collective suicide as the result of the forward charge led by the 'war party' formed by the occupants of Masada.

However, others, even by that time, had chosen peace. In *Le Monde* of 4–5 June 1967, on the eve of the Six Day **1967 War**, Maxime Rodinson wrote,

If there is a tradition in Jewish history, it is that of collective suicide. Pure aesthetes can admire its savage beauty. Perhaps, like Jeremiah to those whose policies ended in the destruction of the first Temple, like Yohanan ben Zakai to those who caused the ruin of the second, one might remind ourselves that there is another way, as narrow as history has made it. Might we hope that those who proclaim themselves to be builders and planters will choose the path of life?

MINORITIES

A permanent component of the history of the Middle East, religious and ethnic minorities still occupy a central place in the confrontations shaking the region.

The origin of minority groups is explained by the geographical position of the Middle East at the crossroad of three continents. It is a thoroughfare of innumerable migrations, where some of the greatest civilisations of antiquity flourished. The Middle East was also the cradle of monotheism, which found expression in Judaism, then Christianity and finally **Islam**.

The spread and ultimate triumph of Islam did not, however, mark the end of the mosaic character of the region. On the contrary, Islam, which saw itself as the continuation of Christianity and Judaism, happily coexisted with the 'People of the Book'. This led in the **Ottoman Empire** to a loose, decentralised political system – the *millet* – a sort of 'aggregation of ghettos', as described by Laurent and Annie Chabry in their book *Politique et minorités au Proche-Orient*. They explain that 'This institutional pluralism had the effect of reallocating social roles within each community according to a virtually complete hierarchical pyramid scheme. In theory, this meant that all social activities were concentrated within the circle of the community.'

This coexistence, not always without conflict, survived the dismantling of the Ottoman Empire. The mandatory powers which came into existence as a result of the **Sykes–Picot Agreement** at the end of World War I respected the role of the old *millet* communities in society. Far from bringing the system to an end, they reinforced it by supporting the national demands of certain minorities. Divide and rule was, admittedly, hardly a new precept for Europeans in the Middle East. **France** had always invoked the 'defence of Christians' to justify its interventions in the Levant. And it backed the **Druze** and the Alawites, just as **Britain** backed the Hashemites, the **Kurds** and many more.

In fact there was always a great temptation to manipulate the contra-dictions accumulated during centuries of more or less repressed aspirations. The national aspirations of the Armenians, the Assyrians, the Kurds and the **Palestinians** have always been under attack and have never been fully satisfied. The same can be said of the religious aspirations of Jewish and

Christian minorities in a world dominated by Islam. Within Christianity there are various sects, the Catholic Melchites or Greek Catholics, the Syriac or Syrian Catholics, the **Maronites**, the Chaldeans, the Catholic Copts, the Catholic Armenians and the Roman Catholics, as well as – separate from Rome – the Greek Orthodox or Byzantine Church, the Syrian Monophysites, the Nestorians, the Copts, the Apostolic or Gregorian Armenians and, of course, the reformed churches. Within Islam there are minorities, including the **Shi'ites** and their dissident sub-sects, the Zaidis, Ismailis, Druze, Alawite, Baha'is and Yezidis.

Such are the distinguishing features of a region where, as Salah Bechir notes in *Revue d'études palestiniennes* (no 8), the community

> cannot push its autonomy to the point of identifying with a state. It is either dominant or dominated, allied to the dominant or allied to the dominated. The balance of power maintains this balance that is constantly imposed and constantly questioned, but always negotiated. Hence a state of internal conflict that is sometimes veiled, sometimes overt, but always present. In this perspective, an 'international frontier' is indispensable: it establishes the limits of the closed field, of the area where the conflicting forces coexist, where balance is negotiated.

This old equilibrium has been shattered – as witnessed spectacularly in **Lebanon**, but also in the region in general. An obvious cause of this was the Arab–Israeli conflict which has destabilised the Levant. The creation for the first time of a **confessional** state, the dispossession and dispersion of an Arab people and a succession of bloody wars have all contributed to the resurgence of minority protests. Inevitably, this resurgence has been manipulated by the regional powers, particularly **Israel**. This was the objective of the balkanisation of the Middle East denounced by some but endorsed by others. Among the former we find the old Lebanese leader Raymond Eddé condemning, behind the 'partition' of Lebanon, 'the creation, alongside Israel, of several states of a confessional character, buffer states that would contribute to the security of the State of Israel' (*Le Monde*, 16 November 1975). In addition, Prince Hassan of **Jordan** has pointed out that 'The prospect of a sharing out of Greater **Syria** between Druze, Maronites, Sunni and Shi'ite fundamentalists coincides with the development of Greater Israel' (*Times*, 3 September 1983). Indeed, Israeli extremist Oded Yinon readily admitted this in *Stratégie pour Israel dans les années 80*, where he advocates the dismantling of Tel Aviv's neighbours, including **Egypt**, into an endless string of tiny confessional states.

Twenty years later, Washington's war against Baghdad looks likely to shake the whole region and revive antagonisms aggravated by the policies of minority governments (Alawi in Syria, Sunni in **Iraq**), particularly because the Bush administration might end up following the sorcerer's apprentices who are advising him to seize the opportunity to 'redraw the borders of the

Middle East'. An American protectorate might be created through a reunification of Jordan and Iraq via the restoration of the Hashemite monarchy
– in the person of the maternal cousin of King Faisal, who had been
assassinated at the time of the revolution of 14 July 1958, or of King
Abdullah II of Jordan, or indeed of his uncle Hassan, who was removed
from the succession by **King Hussein** shortly before his death. Is this
nostalgia for **Lawrence** of Arabia, or science fiction, or simply kite-flying?

Peace between Israelis and Palestinians is therefore a necessary precondition for a new balance between minorities in the Middle East –
necessary, but not sufficient in itself. After the Palestinians there will remain
other national identities to be promoted – beginning with the Kurds – and
the tide of the various fundamentalist movements, fuelled by the failure
of external models, will only ebb within the framework of **autonomy**,
democracy and pluralism in the region.

MUBARAK, HOSNI

Anwar al-Sadat's successor was born in a peasant family in 1928 in Lower
Egypt. Mubarak finished his studies at the Military Academy in 1949, then
became a fighter pilot, undertaking further training in the USSR. Following
the defeat in the **1967 War** and the reshuffle that took place in the army
high command, he was appointed Chief of Staff of the air force in 1969,
three years later its Commander-in-Chief. The more than respectable results
obtained in the **1973 War** led to his promotion to the rank of general. In
April 1975, Sadat appointed him Vice-President of the republic, thus
confirming the confidence he felt in him and in the abiding role of the
army in the political life of Egypt.

During the six years following his appointment, Mubarak was closely
associated with the actions of Sadat. In particular, he supported the
developments which led to the **Camp David Accords**, though he took
no active part in the Egyptian–Israeli negotiations. The day after Sadat's
death on 6 October 1981, he received the necessary vote of confidence
from parliament and, a few days later, was elected President of the
Egyptian Republic. He has maintained the continuity of Egyptian policy,
attempting to modify it without ever really breaking with the legacy left
by Sadat.

On the political front, Mubarak has introduced a state of emergency in
the struggle against groups of Islamic extremists, but has defused the situation
by freeing political prisoners and engaging in a debate with the opposition,
which has acquired greater autonomy. But there is still no question of undermining the hegemony of the ruling National Democratic Party. In the
economic sphere he has placed the emphasis on productive activities and

the struggle against corruption, but without altering the basic foundations of the *infitah* policy.

At the regional level a 'cold peace' has been established between Cairo and Tel Aviv since the **1982 War**. Concurrently Mubarak initiated a rapprochement with the **Arab world**, renewed diplomatic relations with most Arab countries, met with **Yasser Arafat** and gave his support to **Iraq** against **Iran**.

In August 1990, the **Gulf War** forced the Egyptian President to side with the **US**, albeit reluctantly; he took the helm of the anti-Iraqi Arab coalition and sent more than 30,000 troops to **Saudi Arabia**. He used this situation to ensure that his country maintained the leading role in the **Arab League**. Mubarak secured large financial gains for Egypt as a result of this role – in particular a substantial reduction of its debt.

However, all the regime's defects would assert themselves in the years that followed, and the autocratic nature of the system became more marked. The political system seized up and corruption was rife everywhere. The President was re-elected in September 1999 for a fourth term, with almost 94 per cent of the vote. Despite the collapse of the armed Islamic groups and their renunciation of violence, the state of emergency was maintained. The **Muslim Brothers** were subjected to a regime of harassment and arrests. In the national elections of 2000, Mubarak's National Democratic Party (NDP), having obtained only 39 per cent of seats (compared with 71 per cent in 1995), was saved by the support of independent candidates. No real place was left for the opposition. At the same time, while the country was foundering in economic crisis, Mubarak showed himself incapable of having any effect on the Israeli–Palestinian conflict, marked by the failure of the Oslo process. Furthermore, the election of George W. Bush introduced a chill into relations with the US.

At the end of his mandate in 2005, Mubarak will be 77 years old and a doyen among leaders in the region. No Egyptian leader will have ruled as long as him since Muhammad Ali. Since he always refused to name a vice-president, his death (he suffered a period of illness in November 2003) will pose a serious constitutional problem. The appointment of his elder son, Gamal, as General Secretary of the NDP appears to be an attempt to deal with the problem, but it is also a sign of weakness.

MUSLIM BROTHERHOOD

The Organisation of the Muslim Brothers was created in **Egypt** in March 1928 by Hassan al-Banna. He was born in 1906, near Alexandria, and studied at high school before going on to the Dar al-Ulum in Cairo, an institution that had been established with the aim of training modern teachers. He became a teacher in 1927, in Ismailiya on the **Suez Canal**. His organisation soon succeeded in attracting funding from the Suez Canal Company and was given copious publicity in the official press. It has been suggested that the Brotherhood was encouraged by the King and even by the British. Whatever the case, the movement mushroomed; it went from four sections in 1929 to fifteen in 1932, three hundred in 1938 and two thousand in 1948. By 1946 the movement could claim a million members in Egypt.

The Organisation is structured around the General Guide, a charismatic leader to whom each member owes unconditional obedience.

> I swear before God the Highest, the Almighty, to stand firm by the message of the Muslim Brothers, to fight for them, to live according to the Brotherhood's rules of membership, to have complete confidence in its leader and to be totally obedient in all circumstances, whether fortunate or unfortunate.

Such was the oath that members were required to swear in 1945. Supporting the Guide there is a General Office of Orientation, a kind of political office chosen by him and confirmed by a general consultative assembly of between 100 and 150 members. At the time there was also a special unit overseeing clandestine and violent operations.

Al-Banna may initially have attempted, within the confines of an extremely fluctuating situation, to collaborate both with King Faruq and occasionally with the British, but he found himself overtaken by the development of the situation in Palestine and also in Egypt. The demonstrations of February 1946 in Cairo, and those of November 1948 and the events of the **1948–49 War**, in which militants of the Muslim Brotherhood took part, led to the organisation being banned in 1948. The author of the decree, Nokrashi Pasha, was assassinated a few days later, and on 12 February 1945 al-Banna was himself killed, probably by police bullets.

How can one best summarise the ideas of the Muslim Brotherhood? Olivier Carré writes, 'The Muslim Brothers have seen their role as innovators, not by inventing a new Islam, but in creating a living, present-day Islam in the wake of a wave of Islamic reformism' which began in the nineteenth century with Jamal al-Din al-Afghani, Muhammad Abduh and Rashid Rida. Al-Banna's main contribution was at the political level. By his vehement attacks on the secularist movement that was developing, particularly in Egypt under the influence of the Wafd, he created a situation in which, as Carré observes, 'there was no viable organization of societies without **Islam**, in other words, without Muslim courts, Muslim schools, and a Muslim executive government, putting into effect the injunctions of the law of God'. The Muslim Brothers claim to be opposed to Arab nationalism – in which they see even a kind of racism – and, particularly from the 1950s onwards, they preached broad principles of justice, and even came – after the taking of power by **Gamal Abdel Nasser** and the Free Officers on 23 July 1952 – to support agrarian reform.

Despite their participation in the revolution of 1952 and the support which they initially gave it, the Muslim Brothers were weakened by divisions that emerged after the death of al-Banna, and swung round to a position of opposing Nasser and his attempt to control the whole of political life. On 12 January 1954 the organisation was dissolved, on the basis that it was operating as a political party. In October of the same year, following an assassination attempt against the Egyptian President, thousands of members of the Brotherhood were caught up in a wave of repression. This long night was to last until Nasser's death in September 1970. A whole generation came to be radicalised by torture, prison camps and executions, especially under the influence of Sayyid Qutb, executed on 26 August 1966 after a false charge of conspiracy.

Qutb, like al-Banna, was born in 1906 and, like him, was trained at the Dar al-Ulum. A teacher and a man of letters, he did not join the Brotherhood until 1951. He soon took over responsibility for the organisation's propaganda. His was a message of social justice, even socialism, justifying nationalisation, agrarian reform and economic planning. However, it was in prison that he developed a thesis that was to have a strong appeal. For Qutb, 'the contemporary world is divided into two opposing camps: Islam on the one hand and the *jahiliyya* on the other'. This term, taken from the Qur'an (meaning literally the 'ignorance' of God), denounces the alleged 'barbarism' of non-Islamic societies.

In Qutb's view, 'In the aftermath of decolonization, there are no truly Islamic societies: in the independent states of the Muslim world, Westernised autocrats are taking up a modern form of "idolatry", be it socialist or capitalist'. In order to establish the Islamic state, 'it is necessary to break with the logic and customs of existing society, and build a prototype of a future Islamic society with "true believers", and then, at the right moment, go into battle with the jahiliyya' (Gilles Kepel). This thesis, which views the established governments in Islamic countries as non-Muslim, takes issue with the more passive perspective of the majority of the Brotherhood, which preaches compromise with governing regimes. Pushing Qutb's interpretation to the limit, from the 1970s numbers of militants began calling for *jihad* against impious Muslim governments, and later embraced the politics of violence.

In 1971, **Anwar al-Sadat** began releasing the Brothers from prison, and used them in his struggle against the Nasserists and the left. They achieved a certain legality. Since it was now tolerated, their organisation was once again able to grow, but it suffered competition from the Islamic groups that were inclined to violence. This situation was to last for more than twenty years, creating conditions that tended to favour the growth of the Brotherhood's influence, particularly within professional organisations (lawyers, engineers, teachers etc.). However, the growing violence of the 1990s prompted President **Hosni Mubarak** to crush a number of the Muslim extremist groups and to turn against the Brotherhood, whose Supreme Guide, elected at the end of 2002, is the 83-year-old Maamun al-Hudaibi. From 1994, the government launched a wave of arrests, took over control of the professional associations controlled by the Brotherhood, and sentenced members of the movement to heavy terms of imprisonment. Weakened by the repression, the organisation was also shaken by a revolt of younger leadership figures who wanted a more open organisation. Some of them attempted to create a party, al-Wasat ('The Centre'), in collaboration with Copts, but their request was rejected by the authorities. By depriving them of any possibility of legal political activity, President Mubarak has taken the risk of driving numbers of militants back into violence. While the Brotherhood settled into a social conservatism, mobilising mainly on social issues or to condemn allegedly impious authors, a new generation is emerging which favours an Islam which is more open and tolerant, and which looks to the experience of **Turkey**, where a moderate Muslim party won the national elections of November 2002.

However, the Muslim Brotherhood is not solely an Egyptian organisation. The influence of the Brothers spread very quickly into the rest of the **Arab world**. They play an important role in Palestinian areas, through **Hamas**, in **Jordan**, in the **Sudan**, in **Yemen** – where they are in government – and in **Kuwait**. In Jordan the organisation has been weakened. On the one hand King Abdullah II has ended the policy of co-operation pursued by his father **King Hussein**; on the other hand an internal split has developed, over questions of the movement's participation in government and its relations with Hamas. The hardliners, rejecting participation in the governing apparatus, were thus involved in the movement to boycott the elections in 1997. In **Syria** the Brothers were the driving force of the opposition in the 1980s, but they subsequently split, with some of their people returning to Syria. Since they are ideologically close to the Saudis, the Muslim Brothers have never attempted to create a branch in that country. In November 2002 they came under attack from Prince Nayef, Minister of the Interior, when he accused them of being the cause of all the problems in the Islamic and Arab world.

They have also formed links with organisations in the Maghreb and other areas of the Muslim world, as well as in Europe, where there are substantial Muslim **minorities**. While Egyptian Muslim Brothers have, in principle, a determining influence within the organisation, their organisation is by no means an international. There is a distinct lack of unity in their methods, their doctrines (for instance the theses of Islamic socialism have been strongly contested by certain sections) and their strategy: the Brothers were unable to arrive at a common shared position in 1990–91 during the **Gulf War**.

NASSER, GAMAL ABDEL

Born on 15 January 1918 at Beni Mor in the province of Asyut in Upper Egypt, Gamal Abdel Nasser was the son of a post-office official from a peasant background. He completed his secondary education in 1934, began to study law, and took part in the massive demonstrations of 1935 against the British occupying forces and the monarchy. The Wafd party's return to power in 1936 opened the doors of the Military Academy to lower-middle-class children, an opportunity which the young Nasser promptly seized. As **Anwar al-Sadat**, one of his companions, would later write, 'To successfully complete the work of renovation, we needed a solid, disciplined force which, prompted by a single desire, would be capable of palliating the absence of authority and of reconstructing the shattered nation. It was the army that furnished this body.' As a sub-lieutenant, Nasser received his first posting, Mukabad, near his birthplace. There he met Sadat and sketched out, in long, passionate talks on Egypt's future, the idea of creating an organisation of 'free officers'.

The road that led to the seizure of power was a long one, marked at every stage by humiliation. In February 1942, British tanks surrounded the royal palace and forced the King to appoint a new, pro-British government. When the **1948–49 War** broke out in Palestine, Nasser took part in the fighting – he won fame at the Battle of Falujah – and returned from the front with the bitter taste of treachery in his mouth. In 1951, armed struggle developed along the **Suez Canal** against the colonial presence; thousands of young volunteers – trained and armed by the Free Officers – went off to fight. But in January 1952 the King proclaimed martial law. Nasser's organisation numbered at that time about a hundred officers, with an executive committee made up of 14 members – a broad spectrum ranging from communists to those in sympathy with the **Muslim Brothers**, united by a hatred of colonialism, corruption and feudalism. The moment of truth arrived on 23 July 1952 when a coup d'état carried them to power. General Neguib, a patriotic, elderly officer who was much respected, served as the movement's figurehead, but Nasser, not yet 34, was its real leader.

As yet he had neither a clear idea of his role nor of his aims. In 1952, the Third World was not yet born and the Arab peoples lived under the tutelage of **Britain** or **France**. The Free Officers decreed the first agricultural reform and, on 18 June 1953, proclaimed the republic, bringing to a close a dynasty that had lasted a century and a half. What kind of republic it would be was initially unclear. After hesitations and clashes, Nasser removed the popular Neguib in the spring of 1954: there was to be no multi-party system in Egypt, and the army did not return to its barracks. A similar pragmatism prevailed in foreign policy. On 19 October 1954, a treaty signed with Britain stipulated the withdrawal of all British troops, but certain clauses – particularly regarding the return of these same troops should fighting arise – were badly received by nationalists. Nasser looked to the West for allies. He was fascinated by the US, a power with no colonial past. But Washington could not understand the refusal of Egypt's new master to participate in anti-Soviet pacts. Events then speeded up. In April 1955 Nasser took part in the foundation of the Non-Aligned Movement in Bandung. He bought from Czechoslovakia the arms the US had refused him. On 26 July 1956 he nationalised the Suez Canal, and emerged politically victorious from the resulting war. A new leader was born: for Egyptians, free at last, and for **Arabs**, whose struggle against colonialism he would galvanise.

After the failure of the United Arab Republic (the union between Egypt and Syria from 1958 to 1961), Nasser's domestic policy became more radical: the nationalisation of much of the private sector, a new phase of agricultural reform, the adoption of a National Charter, staunchly socialist, and the creation of a new political front, the Arab Socialist Union (ASU). A massive effort in economic development was undertaken with undeniable success. The reverberations of these measures contributed to a mobilisation of progressive forces in the **Arab world**.

The **1967 War** served to demonstrate the weaknesses of the Nasserist experiment. The collapse of the army reflected the treachery of those nicknamed the 'new class': senior officers, technocrats, newly rich peasants, state bourgeoisie, all those who had benefited from the revolution and who wanted to see the end of socialism. It was they who dug the grave of Nasserism and supplied the social foundations that allowed Sadat to achieve the 'counter-revolution'. Nasser's fear of all autonomous mass organisations (trade-union or political) and the bureaucratic nature of the ASU encouraged the new class. Having resigned after the defeat, Nasser was called back by popular demand on 9 June; nonetheless he was a broken man. When he died on 28 September 1970, Egypt gave him a grandiose state funeral. Whatever his mistakes, the people mourned the man who had given them back their dignity. 'Hold your head high, brother,' exhorted the streamers hoisted above Egyptian villages after 23 July 1952. The Nasser myth still remains very powerful, as is shown by the incredible success of Muhammad Fadel's 1996 film *Nasser 56*, which was shown in every cinema in Egypt, pulling in audiences of several million.

NETANYAHU, BENYAMIN

The man who beat **Shimon Peres** in the May 1996 Israeli elections was young and fairly inexperienced in politics. Narrowly elected Prime Minister by universal suffrage, used for the first time in the history of the Jewish state, Netanyahu had previously been ambassador to the UN from 1984 to

1988, Deputy Minister for Foreign Affairs from 1988 to 1991, and Deputy Minister in the Prime Minister's cabinet in 1991 and 1992, when he participated in the Madrid Conference and the negotiations in Washington. He had no parliamentary seat until 1988, and only became head of the Likud in 1993, profiting from the clan warfare opened by the retirement of **Yitzhak Shamir**, which pitted the Herut loyalists (Benny Begin, Dan Meridor, Roni Milo) against the supporters of **Ariel Sharon** and the group around David Levy.

'I am someone with whom you can work, who knows you and who admires you.' According to David A. Harris, director of the American Jewish Committee, this was Netanyahu's message to the Americans during his first visit to the US as head of the Israeli government in July 1996. The formula was in no way overstated. 'Bibi,' who was brought to power by the votes of **Oriental Jews**, nevertheless embodied – to the point of caricature – the profile of the Ashkenazi Jews who see the US as the model to which they aspire. Born in Tel Aviv in 1949, he arrived in America 14 years later with his family: his father, a professor of Jewish history and for a long time personal secretary to Ze'ev Jabotinsky, never took to **Israel**, which he saw as too socialist. He obtained a post at the University of Philadelphia. Reckoning the name Netanyahu to be 'unpronounceable' on that side of the Atlantic, Benyamin chose Ben Nitai as the surname under which he became a citizen of the US, initiating himself in the delights of American football, studying architecture and economics at the famous Massachusetts Institute of Technology and ardently defending the policies of the Jewish state.

In 1967, the Israeli army summoned Netanyahu to fulfil his military obligations. This he did in an elite anti-**terrorist** unit, where he got himself a reputation as a bold operator – he was wounded during an operation to rescue passengers from a Sabena airliner. His brother Jonathan was killed in 1976 in the operation to free the 106 hostages from an Air France aircraft at Entebbe in Uganda.

After a spell in Israel, where he was sales manager for a furniture company, he returned to the US in 1982. Moshe Arens, a friend of his father and the Israeli ambassador in Washington, called him back to act as Minister without portfolio. In the atmosphere of the **1982 War** in **Lebanon**, alarming for the Jewish state, the young diplomat (who had by this time renounced American citizenship) learned the techniques of using the media. Feted by the stars of American television, adulated by the **lobby**, he defended the indefensible.

Netanyahu is not only American by nationality, by virtue of having spent a good portion of his life in the US, or by the excellent Boston accent with which he speaks transatlantic English. Above all else, he embodies the great ideological inclinations of Reaganite America. He is a devotee of the liberal policies of Milton Friedman, whom his principal economic advisors happily plundered. His programme was to speed up the privatisation of state enterprises, reduce customs duties and abolish exchange controls, reduce the budget deficit by cutting public services and social programmes, reduce the higher rates of income tax and of company tax. The economic programme adopted on 2 July 1996 was broadly inspired by this philosophy.

Netanyahu also shares the White House's obsession – from Reagan to George W. Bush – with the crusade against terrorism, and has written no less than three books on the subject. He represents himself as the forerunner of the fight against this monster, whose ugly heads once reared in the USSR, but are today more likely to be seen across **Iran**, **Libya**, **Syria**, Lebanon, **Iraq** and **Sudan**, as well as in democratic countries, where the struggle has to pass through restriction of freedoms and suffer attacks from 'pernicious intellectuals such as Jean-Paul Sartre and Frantz Fanon who are eager to justify and legitimize subversive activity, bestowing an ephemeral veneer of respectability upon nascent terrorism'. He went on to write, 'I feel that the United States should lead the war on terrorism to stop this scourge and act in such a way that the free world rallies to American authority, like carriages hitched onto the back of a powerful locomotive engine'.

A fine project, but one which he believes was unfortunately undermined by Clinton's active support for the implementation of Palestinian **autonomy**. He explains that the reason for this is that in Gaza 'the terrorists have nothing to fear. They can make their plans, arm their killers, send them to Israel and welcome those who return without fear of Israeli reprisals... In the same way as free trade zones stimulate commerce, the creation of a "free terrorist zone" can only encourage the phenomenon.'

Netanyahu does not conceal his cherished dream behind this militant language: that, with the aid of globalisation, Israel will harvest the fruits of peace without ever having to go one step further down the road which leads to it, and might even go backwards. This would allow no prevarication, and ignores the fact that Israel does not exist in a vacuum. But voluntarism has long been a characteristic of Revisionist **Zionist** thought. As Netanyahu explained during his 1996 electoral campaign,

> Israel may be one of the 15 most advanced economies in the world. We may double our GNP per capita in less than a decade and may double our population, thanks to immigration and rising birth rates, in less than 15 years. We could have an economy worth a quarter of a trillion dollars. Our most valuable resource is a population with a solid technological base, able to keep its place in the competitive global market of tomorrow.

Narrowly elected in May 1996 by an electorate traumatised by Islamic suicide bombers, the champion of 'peace within security' pursued overall policies that were intransigent and arrogant. In September 1996 he opened the 'tunnel' in the old town of **Jerusalem**, an action which led to the most violent clashes since the first **Intifada** (with 83 deaths); he continued building **settlements**, particularly in Jerusalem (including, as of February 1997, the announcement of the building of the Har Homa settlement, on the hill of Abu Ghneim); encouraged unofficial settlements; gave the orders for the killing of a **Hamas** leader in **Jordan** – the failure of which obliged him to free Sheikh Ahmed Yassin, who was then permitted to return to Gaza. While, on 15 January 1997, he signed an agreement on Israeli withdrawal from four fifths of Hebron, for months on end he obstinately refused to enact the reassignment of the additional 13.1 per cent of the **West Bank** which the US was requesting. He would only cede on this at the end of the summit called by Bill Clinton at Wye River, on 23 October 1998. But he was not to keep this promise, any more than earlier promises: two months later parliament voted to dissolve itself – at his request.

This was because Netanyahu had no other choice. His right rejected the 'compromise' snatched by the US administration. He was compromised in various scandals, which had led to the resignation of the Minister of Justice, but also resignations of the 'centrists' Dan Meridor and David Levy. It was therefore an isolated Prime Minister who went to the polls on 17 May 1999. And one reason was that his systematic sabotage of the **Oslo Accords** had led not only to increasingly active tension with the **Palestinians**, but also to a standstill in the normalisation underway with Israel's Arab neighbours. At the same time, the economy, which had experienced an unprecedented boom during the first five years of the decade, with an average annual growth rate of 6 per cent, saw growth decline (2 per cent in 1998) and unemployment rise (8 per cent of the active population in the same year). Ehud Barak, promising peace both at home and abroad, was able to inflict a substantial defeat on his rival.

The failure of Barak was to lead to Ariel Sharon's victory in February 2001. With the former general now in the post of prime minister, Netanyahu headed for the hardline wing of Likud. The role fitted him like a glove. He systematically took a counter-position to the leader of the government of National Unity, criticising every concession, however minimal, to its Labour party ministers or to the US administration. He favoured the option of outright repression, the expulsion of **Yasser Arafat** and intransigent opposition to any perspective of a Palestinian state. He was building a right-wing launch pad from which he hoped to become prime minister again. In early November 2002 he accepted the portfolio of Foreign Affairs, hoping thereby to pave the way for his return to the position of prime minister. But he was defeated in the Likud primaries, which chose Sharon to head the party's list for the elections of January 2003.

OIL

The principal source of wealth in the Middle East – sometimes called 'black gold' – oil plays a key part in the power struggles in a region which, in 2001, produced 35.04 per cent of the world's oil and holds 68.16 per cent of the world's reserves (these figures and most of those that follow come from the *Arab Oil and Gas Directory* 2002).

Oil was discovered in the Middle East at the beginning of the twentieth century, and the first extraction operations started in 1909 in **Iran**. It played a part in the bargaining over the former **Ottoman Empire** that followed World War I with the British (75 per cent) and the French (25 per cent) sharing Mosul between them. It was also through oil that American penetration of the region took place: Standard Oil of California took a share in Turkish Petroleum in 1927, and was granted a concession by Ibn Saud in 1933. From 1938 to 1948, the **US** share in Middle Eastern oil production climbed from 13.9 to 55.2 per cent – which tripled over the same period. Three years later, Mosaddeq nationalised the Anglo–Iranian Oil Company, gaining worldwide renown but at the same time signing the death warrant of this initiative: in 1953 the intervention of the CIA brought his sacrilegious venture to an end.

Oil was not something to be trifled with. The West and its companies, which came to be known as the 'Seven Sisters' – Standard Oil of California (SOCAL), Standard Oil of New York (Mobil Oil), Standard Oil of New Jersey (Exxon), Gulf and Texas Oil Company (Texaco), all five of them American, plus one British (British Petroleum) and one Anglo–Dutch (Royal Dutch Shell) – dominated the market. This was the time of easy profits: massive concessions granted for periods of 60 to 94 years, total control of operations, royalties accorded like charity – around 12 per cent. Scarcely touched by the idea of 50–50 sharing, a Venezuelan innovation introduced into the Middle East in 1948, the profits were still colossal, at least for the oil companies. The local economies, on the other hand, gained little benefit. Extremely low-cost energy and high profits from oil became the number one ingredient of Western growth.

This evolution was not without its consequences. It brought in its wake a rapid increase in oil extraction: from 500 million tons at the end of the 1940s, world production had reached 2300 million tons by the end of the 1960s. At the same time, the dependence of Europe, Japan and, to a lesser extent, the US on the Middle East was increasing: the region's share in this production went from 17 to 30 per cent. More vulnerable than before, the West was also confronting an increasingly active nationalist movement, which made the recovery of its natural resources one of its prime targets. Such were the ingredients that, with the Arab–Israeli conflict as background, led to the explosion of the oil-motivated **1973 War**. There was, however, nothing surprising in this: the West had long since confronted opposition from the producers for sovereignty of their own subsoil, supervision of production and control of prices and taxation.

The means employed to maintain control of oil were diverse, from partial restitution by the companies – to avoid nationalisation – to nationalisation itself. An example of the first – participation – pattern is the agreement of 1972 by which the Sisters sold a 25 per cent share to the Gulf emirates, raising the national stake to 51 per cent. The various competitors had been thinking along these lines for years: thus in 1958 the Irano–Italian association allowed Iran a 75 per cent share in its venture, and a Japanese–Saudi–Kuwaiti agreement accorded 57 per cent to the producers. The same was true of contracts signed by Elf-ERAP with Iran (1966), **Iraq** and **Libya** (1968). The wave of nationalisation launched by Mosaddeq was resumed in 1961 when Iraq took back from the Iraq Petroleum Company (IPC) 99 per cent of its concession. The following year **Kuwait** followed suit, nationalising 60 per cent of the concession. The movement gathered speed in the 1970s. In 1970, **Muammar Qadhaffi** was the first to combine successfully nationalisation with control of production and prices. A year later Algeria did the same with the French companies. In 1972, Iraq nationalised British, but not French, oil companies. The trend continued with takeovers, mostly 100 per cent, in Iran (1973), Kuwait (1975), Qatar (1976), Bahrain (1978) and lastly **Saudi Arabia** (1980).

But ownership is nothing without control of production and prices, the principal goal of the Organisation of Petroleum Exporting Countries (OPEC), created in 1961. OPEC's first victory came in 1964. Royalties were added to tax on profits, and the state's share went from 50 per cent to 56.25 per cent. Prices, however, continued to fall, to such an extent that in **Syria** in 1970 one of the two pipelines carrying Saudi oil to the Lebanese port of Sidon was closed: a market depleted by the closure of the **Suez Canal** since the Six Day **1967 War** was the perfect opportunity for Algeria and Libya to raise their prices. Agreements made in Tehran in January 1971 raised the tax on profits from 50 to 55 per cent. And again in Tehran, then in Geneva, posted prices were pegged to rise in line with the dollar and the world monetary situation: in three years, the Gulf's gross takings from oil increased by 70 per cent. This record was to be smashed during the Yom Kippur 1973 War.

On 6 October 1973, Egyptian troops crossed the Suez Canal, and broke through the Bar Lev Line. Arab honour was avenged, but the Israeli army recovered. It was in the midst of Israeli counter-attacks that the Arab oil-producing countries, meeting in Kuwait on 17 October, decided on both a new price increase of 75 per cent and an embargo against allies of **Israel**. An additional increase of 115 per cent was decided in Tehran in December. In total the price of crude oil was quadrupled: from $3 to $11.5 a barrel. But this huge hike was in fact simply a correction of the real value of crude, the price of which had fallen disastrously over the preceding decades. Thus the main event of 1973 was less the actual increase in the price of oil itself than the simultaneous takeover, by the producers, of tariffs and the rate of extraction, a step towards the 'new international economic order' that, at the time, was the slogan of the Non-Aligned countries. Both the producers and the consumers were now under an obligation to be more parsimonious: the age of squandering was over, the Arab countries having thus protected the heritage of humanity itself as well as their own. It was the same story with the new readjustments in the late 1970s, which entailed both price reassessments and changes in the economy.

Yet the oil weapon was no longer what it had been. The Arab producers were encountering competition from newcomers, whose share in the market had increased (notably Mexico, **Britain**, Norway, Asia, Central Africa and **Russia**). OPEC's share in production thus went from 45 per cent in 1980 to 29.3 per cent in 2000. The Middle East's share fell from 30.7 per cent in 1980 to 27.25 per cent in 1990, but picked up to 30.7 per cent in 1995 and stabilised at that level. In terms of exports, the region saw its percentage rise from 54.5 per cent in 1980 to 44.5 per cent in 2000.

The war between OPEC and non-OPEC producers is accompanied by OPEC's own inability to maintain a concerted policy on quantity and prices – it is divided between radical countries such as Iraq and Iran, who wanted to finance their wars, or Algeria, whose concern was to gain rapid benefits from their reserves, and patient moderates guided by a desire not to upset Washington. Hence there was an abrupt fall in prices: a barrel of oil went from $34 in 1981 to less than $10 in 1986, and subsequently hovered between $10 and $15. Even after the crisis of the **Gulf War**, which at one point saw it go through the ceiling of $40 a barrel, it was to fall again to about $20, and would fall again in 1998. Following the initiative of Saudi Arabia, the world's biggest producer, Venezuela and Mexico (not a member of the cartel), the OPEC countries finally reached an agreement in March 1999 to reduce their production. The price per barrel thus rose from $10 to more than $32 in August 2000, its highest level for ten years, only to fall back to $23.12 in 2001 – in constant dollars, in other words corrected for variations in exchange rates and inflation, it went from $3.57 in 1998 to $8.60 in 2000 and $7.12 in 2001.

Now more than half of oil transactions are made on the free market, known as the spot market. Up to 80 per cent of prices are set according to 'spot' prices, based on NYMEX, the essentially speculative market in New York, whose contracts doubled between 1984 and 1990. As Pierre Terzian wrote in *Le Monde diplomatique*: 'OPEC's price-fixing role has been taken over by thousands of agents, most of whom deal with oil as if they were speculating on any other financial instrument or investment'. The oil-producing countries themselves resorted to the principle of national ownership of their oil wealth, following the example of Algeria, which limited the amount of foreign capital it allowed in its oil industry. Saudi Arabia, for its part, decided to open its gas sector to foreign companies, but the agreement was delayed. Once again, the oil crisis highlighted the need to find alternative sources of energy, primarily nuclear power, which would reduce the crucial role played by oil. But the Middle East nations have also cast off their illusions regarding the automatically positive nature of striking oil. In many cases, their petrodollars have been spent on arms (which accounted for 38 per cent of oil revenue in the 1980s), or on lining the pockets of the ruling classes, or on spectacular projects that serve little purpose. Only a small proportion was dedicated to aid, whether public or not, and to development. In addition, huge amounts of money have been invested in the West: in 1990, the Union of Arab and French banks valued the sum of Arab deposits invested abroad, from both the public and private sector, at $670bn. The debt under which the most populated countries in the **Arab world** are collapsing has risen to $250bn.

A sign of the economic mobilisation of the Arab world, and of the developing world more generally, in both 1956 and 1973, could oil, which was once symbolic of **independence**, come to be a factor of dependence? Many people suspect this is the case. In his book *Le Proche Orient*, George Corm attacks not only the social, political and economic effects of the 'torrential flow' of petrodollars which 'undermine the most fundamental structures of society' in the Arab world, but also the foolish projects sold to 'petro-monarchs who only accelerate the decay of the social fabric of societies made increasingly fragile by decades of abortive attempts at modernisation'. He attacks the 'various modes of blackmail employed by the West, the crude pressure which is exerted upon these countries whose apparent economic strength is simply the reflection of the sheer depth of their under-development'.

In 2000 Asia became – by far – the biggest buyer of Middle East oil (a total of $117.5bn in 2000), beginning with Japan, with imports of $47.5bn. Next came the EU (imports of $28.2bn) and the US ($23.7bn).

But the attacks of 11 September 2001 and their consequences once again shook the oil industry. In four months the average price per barrel fell by 28.3 per cent, with the price going from $24.46 in August to $17.53 in December. This fall was explained by fears of a world recession, but also by the continued existence of surplus production among the OPEC countries. As of January 2002, however, falling stocks in the industrial countries, signs of renewed growth in the American economy, and speculation on an eventual American intervention in Iraq, were to push the price of oil up again: in autumn 2002 it once again passed the $30-per-barrel barrier.

The rise in tensions resulted in renewed anxiety among countries that were consumers of Middle Eastern oil over security of supply and the renewal of production capacities to meet the growth in demand, which the

International Atomic Energy Agency (IAEA) estimated at 1.9 per cent per year. World demand for oil was expected to reach 95.8 million barrels per day in 2010, and 114.7 million in 2020. And (again according to the IAEA) non-OPEC supplies were expected to stabilise at about 46 million barrels per day until 2010, and would then begin to decline. Chronic instability in Iraq following the US invasion has kept oil prices high.

In these conditions, five OPEC nations in the Middle East – Saudi Arabia, the United Arab Emirates, Kuwait, Iran and Iraq – would have to boost their output from 1997's total of 19.5 million barrels per day to 30.5 million in 2010 and 46.7 million in 2020. These countries' contribution to global output should climb from 26 per cent in 1997 to 32 per cent in 2010 and 41 per cent in 2020 (article by Nikos Sarkis in *Le Monde diplomatique*).

> But to boost output they must avoid sanctions, while providing the stability needed to attract foreign investment and maintaining oil prices at appropriate levels. Adjusted for inflation, an oil price of $25 a barrel today represents only $7.20 in 1973 dollars and is less than half the level it was in the early 1980s. The real problem is not available resources but price levels and political stability in the Middle East. That region will remain the nerve centre of the world's oil industry for decades to come.

ORIENTAL JEWS

Oriental Jews are those of African and Asian origin (Mizrahim), as opposed to Jews from Europe and America (Ashkenazim). Since the 1960s, the problem of this group, called the 'black problem' in a somewhat racist fashion, has weighed heavily on Israeli society.

This 'problem' first attracted attention in **Israel** – sensationally – in 1959, when clashes occurred in the Wadi Salib district of Haifa. They were followed by a series of wildcat strikes in the 1960s and the creation of the Black Panther movement. An issue that could no longer be avoided, the 'Second Israel' was in 1974 the subject of a government inquiry, whose report exposed a scandalous system of discrimination. In 1977, as a direct result of their situation in society, the Orientals were a decisive factor in the electoral victory of the right-wing coalition led by **Menachem Begin**. In less than twenty years Israel had discovered that it had an underclass no longer willing to accept its position, to the extent that it would risk over-turning the traditional balance of political power.

The Oriental Jews are often, wrongly, confused with the Sephardim; but the Hebrew word *sepharad* means Spain, and its adjective therefore refers only to the descendants of the Jews expelled *en masse* from Spain (1492) and Portugal (1496) and scattered all over the Mediterranean basin, Northern Europe and even America. In many ways the Sephardim are closer to the

Ashkenazim, the Jews of Europe and America, than to Oriental Jews. In fact, Orientals are distinct from all Western Jews, whether Sephardim or Ashkenazim: by the feudal, traditional character of the African or Asian countries from which they come; by their essentially artisan and commercial tradition; by their lack of a national consciousness and a *fortiori* of a class consciousness; by the striking insularity evident in their customs and culture; by the Orthodoxy of their religious practices; and finally by the relatively lenient fate they experienced in their adopted countries as *dhimma*, permitted **minorities**. The status of *dhimma*, though humiliating, was, however, a far cry from the Holocaust, or even the pogroms, at least until 1948, when the creation of the Jewish state in Palestine and the **1948–49 War** with the Arab states unleashed antisemitic riots throughout much of the region. Oriental Jews were forced by this outburst of hostility to opt for Israel, and were transported there in planes specially chartered by the Israeli government. Sometimes the Israeli secret services accelerated the process of migration by hatching schemes that acted as provocations, like the dyna-miting in 1950 of the Shem Tov synagogue in Baghdad.

On their arrival in Israel, the Orientals suddenly found themselves thrust into a Western nation, historically constituted, peopled and run by Western Jews along Western lines – to a **Jew** from **Yemen** or **Iraq**, both the socialist and the liberal versions of **Zionism** are still basically Western. 'Israel,' explains Elie Cohen, the head of social services in Dimona, 'wanted to live in the Western way, think like the West, have a Western education system. But, with the massive immigrations, what Israel acquired was a majority which was not Western, which did not live in the Western style, did not think like Europeans.' This is particularly true of the latest arrivals, the Ethiopian Jews or Falashas.

Obviously the Orientals are not a homogeneous bloc: the Iraqis were integrated fairly rapidly, the Moroccans and Yemenis a lot more slowly, and the Ethiopians are still waiting. But each of these groups has in its collective memory, to varying degrees, humiliations past and present. In the late 1950s, families arriving from Yemen lost their children, who were declared dead but in reality had been given to childless well-to-do Ashkenazi families: behind their good intentions, the people responsible for this crime were expressing the appalling sense of superiority of the Ashkenazim over the Orientals. Forty years later would come the turn of the Falashas, the Ethiopians who were transferred *en masse* to Israel from 1984, where they met unemployment, exclusion from education, wretched ghettos and the distrust of the ultra-Orthodox, who even imposed a second circumcision on them. Even worse: the authorities were to destroy blood given by them in donor sessions, on the pretext of the danger of AIDS. Young people in Netanya, under a portrait of Bob Marley, say, 'Here we suffer because we're black'. On a wall they have spray-painted 'Death to Whites'.

The Oriental Jews were even less willing to put up with this culture clash when they rapidly became a majority in Israeli society. And this had consequences in all areas of life. Official statistics show that Orientals are concentrated on the lowest rungs of the professional ladder, receive the lowest wages, the poorest housing, have the highest petty-crime rate and experience harsh segregation in the education system. Until the 1980s they were not to be found, or were present only in token numbers, in the management of large companies, political parties or unions, in the Knesset or in other corridors of power.

So, who runs this nation that remains foreign to them? Who wielded this 'Ashkenazi power' which, since 1948, has victimised them? Until 1977 the answer was simple: the Labour party was pro-Ashkenazim, therefore the Likud equals the Orientals – an innuendo the right used in its election campaigns with great success. Admittedly, Begin and his colleagues were no less Western than their socialist rivals, but they had not borne the burden of the responsibility of heading the state since 1948. And, just as at the time of **independence**, Zionist envoys had led the Orientals to believe that the Messiah had come in order to convince them to return to the Holy Land, in order to gain Oriental votes in 1977 and 1981 the rumour was put about that Begin was Moroccan. The paradox is that after seven years of Likud rule, during which the Orientals saw little change in their lives, the 'miracle' happened again and again – until 1992, when the majority of Oriental Jews voted Labour. This resurgence in popularity did not last.

Meanwhile, the massive **immigration** of Jews from the Soviet Union has reopened a wound that has hardly had time to heal. This was because, unlike the majority of the Oriental *olim* ('new immigrants'), these Ashkenazi Russians, 30–40 per cent of whom, according to the Grand Rabbi of Israel, were not Jews, were welcomed with open arms by the state and provided with housing, benefits and education. After a shaky start, most of them found a job, which was admittedly not always in keeping with the qualifications that they had gained in the USSR. Nevertheless, the high level of education of many of the new immigrants was crucial to Israel's search for new technologies.

In 1997, the new Labour leader Ehud Barak, in a historic *mea culpa*, publicly apologised in the name of his party to the Oriental communities for what they had suffered. Was it out of gratitude to him, or was it out of exasperation with the continuation of social inequalities under the government of **Benyamin Netanyahu** that in the 1999 elections the Oriental Jews once again voted for Barak, and in the Knesset left Likud for the ultra-Orthodox Sephardi party Shas, the Gesher of the 'Moroccan' David Levy and the centrist party of the 'Iraqi' Yitzhak Mordechai. However, two years later this did not stop them voting *en masse* for **Ariel Sharon**.

In addition to reasons shared by more than 60 per cent of Israelis, among the Oriental Jews there was a specific explanation for this vote: the sense that they had been betrayed, yet again, by the Labour party. Studies carried out by the Adva Centre in 2001 and 2002 speak for themselves: in tertiary education, only 16.5 per cent of Oriental Jews completing high school entered university, compared with 30.1 per cent of Ashkenazim (and 10.6 per cent of **Arabs**). In employment, 54.7 per cent of Ashkenazim, compared with 28.9 per cent of Oriental Jews, are in managerial, professional or university jobs; 32.1 per cent of Ashkenazim and 44.4 per cent of Oriental Jews are in state employment or work in commerce; 13.2 per cent of Ashkenazim are industrial or agricultural workers, compared with 26.6 per cent of Orientals. As for wages, urban Oriental workers earn on average 31 per cent less than their Ashkenazi peers (while Arabs earn 49 per cent less).

The 'black problem' has therefore become – and remains – a central theme in Israel. 'Just as there are Christian Arabs and Muslim Arabs, I am an Arab Jew,' said Charlie Biton, a Black Panther leader, in a 1979 issue of *Les Temps Modernes* devoted to the 'Second Israel'. He went on,

> It is a fact that, since its creation, the State of Israel has tried to be a bastion of the West, of the US, in the Middle East. Hence the loss of our roots. But this is not a choice. After the signing of the peace, Israel will have to be an integral part of the Middle East, and all the travails and tricks of the Ashkenazim will change nothing.

This is precisely the attitude **David Ben Gurion** was arguing against when, a quarter of a century ago, he said, 'We do not want Israelis to turn into Arabs. We must fight the Levantine spirit which corrupts men and societies so that we may preserve the authentic Jewish values that evolved in the Diaspora.' His authentic Jewish values were presumably those of the Ashkenazim.

OSLO ACCORDS

The term 'Oslo Accords' refers to a group of accords arrived at between **Israel** and the **Palestinians** in order to set the ground rules for the establishment of **autonomy** in the **West Bank** and Gaza, and then the conditions in which final status negotiations were to unfold. They followed an exchange of letters between **Yasser Arafat** and **Yitzhak Rabin** on 9 and 10 September 1993: the **Palestine Liberation Organisation (PLO)** 'recognized the right of the state of Israel to live in peace and security', while Israel chose to recognise the PLO 'as the representative of the Palestinian people', without, however, any reference to the Palestinians' right to a state of their own.

The Oslo Accords fall into three main groupings.

- The text negotiated in secret in Norway between the Israeli government and the PLO and signed on 13 September 1993; it came into effect on 13 October. It consists of three parts: a Declaration of Principles on the interim 'self-government' or 'autonomy' arrangements, accompanied by four Annexes and minutes which clarify various points (see Appendix 11). The Declaration states the immediate aim of the two protagonists, namely 'to establish a Palestinian Interim Self-Government Authority, the elected Council (the "Council"), for the Palestinian people in the West Bank and the **Gaza Strip**, for a transitional period not exceeding five years, leading to a permanent settlement based on UN Security Council Resolutions 242 and 338'.

    It was intended that an agreement would be signed on 13 December 1993 on the withdrawal of Israeli troops from Gaza and the area around Jericho, which was to have taken place by 13 April 1994. A certain number of powers (education, health, social affairs etc.) were to be transferred to the Palestinians, who would begin 'to set up a police force'. By 13 July 1994 at the latest, and after a withdrawal of Israeli troops from populated areas, elections would take place for a Palestinian Council, which 'will have legislative powers' and a 'powerful police force'. The jurisdiction of this Council would extend over the West Bank and Gaza, but with the exclusion of areas to be carried over into the final negotiations: **Jerusalem**, Jewish **settlements**, military sites and the position of Israelis living in the areas concerned.

    By the start of the third year of the transition period, negotiations would begin on the final status. In addition to the above issues, these were to deal with the problems of refugees and frontiers.

- There were to be significant delays in the implementation of the so-called Oslo I Accord. On 9 February 1994 an initial text was signed covering security issues, and in particular the crossing-points between the self-governing zones and neighbouring countries, which remained under Israeli control. It was only on 4 May 1994, in Cairo, that Arafat and Rabin finally signed a text on the operational framework of the Declaration of 13 September 1993, in particular on the deadline and conditions for Israeli withdrawal from Gaza and Jericho. This date of 4 May thus marks the beginning of the period of autonomy which was supposed to come to completion on 4 May 1999. On 1 July 1994, Arafat arrived in Gaza and a provisional **Palestinian Authority** was set up.

- The third phase of the Israeli–Palestinian agreement, the **Taba** Accord, also known as Oslo II, was signed in Washington on 28 September 1995. It consists of a principal text, seven appendices and eight maps. It defines the timetable and conditions for the implementation of self-government for the majority of Palestinians. Its principal provisions were as follows:

- The election of an 82-member Palestinian Council (a number eventually to rise to 88) which would have legislative and executive powers, and the election of a president of the council. The election was actually held on 20 January 1996.
- The division of the West Bank (excluding Jerusalem) into three zones: A, B and C. The first comprises the six principal towns (**Jenin**, Nablus, Tulkarem, Qalqiliya, Ramallah and Bethlehem), with the addition of Jericho, which was already self-governing. It covered 3 per cent of the territory of the West Bank and 20 per cent of its population. These towns were evacuated by the Israeli army by the end of 1995 and then came under the control of the Palestinian Authority. The case of Hebron, where 300 Jewish settlers were living, was left to one side; the town was to be divided in early 1997, with the Israeli army continuing to control 25–30 per cent of the town's area and 20 per cent of its 120,000 inhabitants. Zone B covered 27 per cent of the territory and the majority of the 450 Palestinian villages: together, Zones A and B (if one includes Hebron) covered 90 per cent of the population of the West Bank. Zone B passed partially under Palestinian Authority, but the Israeli government continued to maintain responsibility for security and the struggle against **terrorism** in the zone. Finally, the Israeli authorities remained totally in control of Zone C, which covers 70 per cent of the West Bank but includes very few Palestinians; it contains principally all the Jewish civilian and military settlements, which are linked by a network of 'by-pass' roads. During the coming years, this process of partition was to develop further, and by 2000, on the eve of the outbreak of the **second Intifada**, the division was as follows: Zone A, 17.2 per cent; Zone B, 23.8 per cent; Zone C, 59 per cent.
- Economic relations between Israel and the Palestinians were the subject of a protocol signed in Paris on 29 February 1994 and were then included, in slightly amended form, in the accord.
- The question of **water** was not settled and was held over for discussion as part of the final negotiations. The Israeli government has thus been able to continue appropriating the majority of this resource.
- The undertaking by the PLO that, in the two months following the election of the Palestinian Council, they would delete the articles in the Palestinian National Charter calling for the destruction of the state of Israel – an undertaking fulfilled in April 1996.
- The setting of 5 May 1996 as the starting date for **final status negotiations**. A formal inaugural session did indeed take place, but the victory of Israel's right in the elections was to block the process. Final negotiations were only to begin four years later, a year after Ehud Barak's victory in May 1999. They would culminate, and collapse, at the **Camp David and Taba Negotiations**.

OTTOMAN EMPIRE

Encompassing all the countries under Turkish rule, the Ottoman Empire emerged as a result of the westward expansion of Turkic peoples in the thirteenth and fourteenth centuries, and came to an end in 1920, when it was dismembered at the conclusion of World War I, in which it had allied itself with the Axis powers.

The Ottomans made their presence felt on the regional stage with the fall of Constantinople, the capital of the Byzantine Empire, in 1453. They had held Greece, Serbia and Bulgaria since the beginning of the fifteenth century, and had achieved complete control of Asia Minor by the third decade. Selim I added the **Arab world** – Mesopotamia, **Egypt**, **Syria** and the **Arabian Peninsula** – to the Ottoman domains in the sixteenth century, and his successor, Suleiman the Magnificent, seized what is now modern Yugoslavia and most of Hungary and Transylvania. At the time of Suleiman's death in 1566, the Empire stretched from Vienna to Aden, from the Caspian to Algiers, encompassed the Mediterranean, the Black Sea and the Red Sea, controlled major lines of communication and governed fifty million people of over twenty different nationalities.

The decline of the Ottoman Empire stemmed from a number of factors. Some came from within the system itself: the often incompetent sultans, the inefficient and corrupt administration, the fact that the elite military body of Janissaries had become a destructive, hereditary caste. Others flowed from the reaction of sections of the peoples they oppressed, among whom nationalist ideas gained strength in the early twentieth century, not just in the **Arab world** but also among **Kurds** and Armenians. Finally, the Empire no longer derived the same benefits from its conquests, increasingly blocked from the eighteenth century by the strength of the great Western powers, which made no effort to hide their appetites. Each of them had its eye on the legacy of the 'sick man of Europe' – as Tsar Nicholas I called the Sublime Porte (the Ottoman administration) – and had earmarked its share.

To see this clearly, one has only to consult a map. To the west, **France** had grabbed North Africa, having since the time of François I benefited from the 'Capitulations' and the excuse of the defence of Lebanese Christians or the protection of Catholic sacred sites. In chronological order, **Britain** seized Malta, the 'Pirate Coast' and Gulf Emirates, Aden, Oman, Cyprus, Suez and Egypt, **Sudan** and southern Arabia. **Russia** had meanwhile achieved only a single zone of influence, Persia, and even this was shared with Britain, which also controlled Afghanistan. Germany's influence in the region was essentially economic and military.

But the West's designs on the Ottoman Empire were not confined to merely planting a flag in one or another of its territories: what Paris, London, Berlin and the others were after was raw materials at low prices, profitable investments for their capital, markets for their products and the guarantee of safe lines of communication. Hence the influx of foreign capital: nine billion francs in 1914, 54 per cent of which was French, 25 per cent British, 9.3 per cent German, the rest mainly Belgian, Swiss or Italian. In Egypt, for example, it is estimated that 70 per cent of shares and debentures were held by foreigners. Through this invasion of capital, Europe controlled banking, the means of transport and communication (railways, ports, roads), the main services (**water**, gas, electricity, telephone), mining enterprises and, of course, **oil**. It took care, at the same time, not to foster the emergence of local industry which would hamper its own exports to the Empire. Lastly, through their nationals, their missionary societies and educational establishments, all the colonial powers struggled to become the dominant cultural influence. At the beginning of World War I, for example, France counted more than 100,000 students in its schools, colleges and universities in the Ottoman Empire.

The Ottoman Empire was by this time ripe for division. The war, in which it took the side of Germany and Austro-Hungary, served as a pretext, and made the informal colonialism of the previous period official, a task completed in the **Sykes–Picot Agreement** and the Sèvres peace treaty signed on 10 August 1920.

PALESTINE LIBERATION ORGANISATION (PLO)

After the declaration of **independence** of the state of **Israel** in 1948 and the non-establishment of a Palestinian state, the Palestinian national movement, which had been powerful in the 1930s, disappeared from the political scene. It was around 1960 that the Palestine question came to the fore again. A new political elite was in the process of formation, one which compensated for the frustration of exile by high levels of education and an active participation in the movements then rocking the Middle East. The Arab regimes were forced to accept this reality, and in 1964, by a decision of the **Arab League**, the PLO was created in **Jerusalem**.

Presided over by Ahmad Shuqairi, it was in Arab tutelage, in particular that of **Nasser's Egypt**, that **Palestinians** placed their hopes for the liberation of Palestine. Other organisations developed concurrently, including Fatah, created in 1958 by a young Palestinian engineer, **Yasser Arafat**. Taking a more radical stance, he wanted to be independent of the Arab countries and to rely primarily on the Palestinian people themselves. On 1 January 1965, al-'Asifa, the military wing of Fatah, undertook its first military operation against Israel. Its aim at the time was the destruction of the 'Zionist entity', the creation of a Palestinian state and the **right of return** of the millions of refugees who had been victims of the **expulsion** in 1948–50.

The **1967 War** and the defeat of Egypt, **Syria** and **Jordan** caused a crisis within the PLO. The organisation became more extreme, adopting a new National Charter (July 1968) and integrating the various armed organisations, the *fedayeen*. In January 1969, Arafat became president of the PLO Executive Committee. The structures of the renewed PLO gradually fell into place. The first of these was a Palestine National Council (PNC), a kind of parliament that sits approximately every two years. A third of the delegates represent armed organisations; the other two thirds represent mass organisations (students, women, writers, trade unions), independent personalities and the various exiled Palestinian communities, from **Kuwait** to Brazil. The PNC elects the Executive Committee that runs the organisation. Over the years, especially in **Lebanon**, the PLO succeeded in building a virtual state machine (with ministers, research centres, a healthcare and industrial infrastructure) whose power was at its peak on the eve of the **1982 War**.

But one should not be misled by this huge bureaucracy. While the PLO has become accepted as the 'unifying framework' of the Palestinian resistance, each of the *fedayeen* organisations nonetheless retains considerable autonomy. They number around a dozen: Fatah; **George Habash's** Popular Front for the Liberation of Palestine (PFLP); **Nayef Hawatmeh's** Democratic Front for the Liberation of Palestine (DFLP); al-Sa'iqa, tied to Damascus; the Arab Liberation Front, formerly under the thumb of Baghdad; the PFLP-General Command of Ahmed Jibril, to mention only the most important.

Each of these groups had its own armed forces, and has often received support from one or other of the Arab regimes. The PLO is therefore a non-integrated organisation where the unity of the various components is constantly in question.

After the defeat of the Arab armies in 1967, the strategy of armed popular struggle advocated by Fatah took over. Falling back into safe bases in Jordan, the Palestinian resistance movement launched operations against Israeli economic and military targets backed by underground cells in the **West Bank** and Gaza. But the problem of relations between the PLO and **King Hussein** came to the fore with a vengeance. It was resolved in September 1970 (see **Black September**), and the resistance movement was expelled from Jordan. These events were to have profound consequences. The PLO withdrew to Lebanon, which became the last Arab country where it possessed military, and therefore political, autonomy. It reconsidered its position that made armed struggle 'the only road towards the liberation of Palestine', and committed itself to both political (especially on the West Bank) and diplomatic action. Finally, partly so as not to disappear from the military scene and partly out of despair, it launched itself into international **terrorism**, as symbolised by the Black September organisation.

The October **1973 War** changed the situation and the balance of power. The Arab countries, at the summits of Rabat (1973) and Algiers (1974), recognised the PLO as the sole representative of the Palestinian people. The Non-Aligned countries rallied to this position and accentuated the isolation of Israel (diplomatic relations between virtually all African states and Israel were broken off). Relations between the Palestinian resistance and the Soviet Union, which had had their ups and downs, improved. Moscow would henceforth put all its weight behind Arafat. This breakthrough by the PLO was consolidated by the visit of its leader to the UN General Assembly in November 1974, and its admission as an observer member of the UN. Within this framework the PLO renounced international terrorism, concentrated its military presence in Lebanon, and established a new political strategy after a long internal struggle between the 'realists' and the 'extremists'.

Up until 1973, the PLO had stood by 'the liberation of the whole of Palestine' (proclaimed by the National Charter) and the 'creation of a democratic state where Muslims, Christians and Jews will coexist', which presupposed the destruction of the state structures of Israel and the integration of its Jewish population into the new state. From 1974, at the triple prompting of Fatah, the DFLP and the Palestinians of the Occupied Territories, the PLO proposed the creation of a state based on the West Bank and Gaza. Without entailing the *de jure* recognition of the state of Israel, which the PLO refused (seeing this as its only card in any eventual negotiations), this new aim presupposed the effective coexistence of two states. The PFLP refused this course, walked out of the Central Committee and, along with a few smaller organisations, created the Rejection Front. The confrontation lasted three years and ended, in 1977, in victory for the 'realists'.

But the situation changed. In Lebanon, the Palestinians, engaged in the **Lebanese Civil War** of 1975–76, came out of it weakened after Syrian military intervention. This episode, symbolised by the siege of Tel al-Za'atar camp, was a perfect illustration of the ambiguous relations established between the PLO and the various Arab regimes: when their interests were at risk the latter had no hesitation in massacring their Palestinian brothers. The international background had also changed. Between 1974 and 1977 there had been a real possibility of convening a **peace conference** on the Middle East, co-sponsored by the US and the USSR, and even of finding a global solution to the Arab–Israeli conflict. This had helped the 'realists' to carry the day within the PLO.

But **Anwar al-Sadat**'s visit to Jerusalem, in November 1977, followed by the signing of the **Camp David Accords**, destroyed this process in favour of that of a separate peace. While Egypt was to regain Sinai, the Palestinians were to obtain autonomy only under occupation – massively rejected by the Palestinians of the West Bank and Gaza, despite their reputed 'realism'. The dynamics of the 1974–77 situation were destroyed. Despite massive mobilisation of the 'Palestinians of the interior', despite political initiatives, of which the contacts between the PLO and left-wing Israeli **Zionists** (the **Sartawi**–Peled–Avnery encounters) were hardly the least spectacular, and despite its breakthrough in Western Europe, the Palestinian resistance movement had lost the initiative. On 6 June 1982 Israel, liberated on its southern front, launched Operation Peace in Galilee.

While the conquest of south Lebanon by the Israeli army took only a few days, the siege of Beirut was to last almost three months. These terrible days were to be widely reported by the international press and, like the massacres of **Sabra and Shatila**, would contribute to the tarnishing of Israel's image. Despite fierce resistance, Arafat and his followers were forced to leave the Lebanese capital. A page had been turned in the history of the PLO. Losses were heavy. The resistance movement's politico-administrative machinery, concentrated in Beirut, was destroyed, and the PLO lost the 'capital' from which it had been able to deploy an intense political, diplomatic and military activity. A more serious problem was that the leadership of the resistance movement was henceforth effectively cut off from the main body of the Palestinian people. It no longer had contact with the last sizeable group of Palestinians which had supplied it with a large proportion of its soldiers and many of its cadres. Lastly, with the departure of its fighters from Lebanon, the very idea of armed struggle, one of the PLO's key traditions, was affected.

For the first time since the Six Day 1967 War, the PLO was no longer present on the enemy's borders. Far from the battlefield, it ran the risk of seeing a reduction in its political clout and autonomy, and of losing the attraction it exercised for the younger generation, particularly those in the camps.

It was against this background of crisis and uncertainty that the debates on strategic choices for the PLO resurfaced. For several years the factions of the PLO would tear themselves apart in search of a strategy that seemed impossible to find. The signing, on 11 February 1985, of an agreement between King Hussein and Arafat revived tensions. It was fervently denounced by almost all factions of the PLO, with the exception of Fatah. The Palestinian National Salvation Front, combining Habash's PFLP, Jibril's PFLP-General Command, the Fatah dissidents, al-Sa'iqa and **Abu Nidal**'s group, with the full support of Syria, tried to set up an alternative to the PLO. But clashes between Amal and the Palestinians in Lebanon and Hussein's repeal, in February 1986, of the Jordanian–Palestinian agreement, combined with to the efforts of the Soviet Union, ended in reconciliation. In April 1987, in Algiers, the Eighteenth Palestinian National Council met, with the participation of Fatah, the PFLP, DFLP and the Communist Party (a member of which was elected to the Executive Committee for the first time).

But, above all, the crisis provoked by the departure from Beirut remained. It would take the first **Intifada** to shake the PLO from its state of paralysis. While the organisation was not directly responsible for the outbreak of the rebellion on the West Bank and in Gaza, all the demonstrators nonetheless unequivocally identified with it; the PLO thus acquired a stronger legitimacy, and the power to make the radical diplomatic and political decisions necessary. From 12 to 15 November 1988 Algiers was the scene of the Nineteenth National Council, involving Fatah, the PFLP, DFLP, Communist Party and a few other smaller organisations; only the PFLP-General Command, al-Sa'iqa, the Fatah dissidents and Abu Nidal's group refused to participate, and later condemned the Council's conclusions.

The most spectacular decision was the proclamation, made on 15 November, of the establishing of a Palestinian state, which was quickly recognised by more than 90 countries, including Egypt. More important, perhaps, was the reference made in the declaration of independence (see Appendix 3) to UN Resolution 181, the famous **Partition Plan**. For the first time, the PLO ratified this UN decision to partition Palestine into two states, one Jewish, the other Arab.

In its political statement the PLO called for the convening of an international conference at which it would be a full member, based on Resolutions 242 and 338 of the UN Security Council (see **UN Security Council Resolutions**), and the guarantee of legitimate national rights for the Palestinians. This acceptance, for the first time, of Resolution 242, which does not even mention Palestinians but refers simply to the 'refugee' problem, was a spectacular gesture for the benefit of Western opinion, above all in the US. It nonetheless aroused fierce internal debates; some, particularly the PFLP, voted against the resolution or abstained. But there was another innovation: the **minority** agreed to abide by the majority decisions; the sacrosanct system of consensus that had for so long paralysed the PLO was 'forgotten'.

Strengthened by these decisions, and its confidence in the continuation of the Intifada, the PLO launched a diplomatic offensive. It even achieved the beginnings of a dialogue with Washington. But all these openings were to come up against the intransigence of the Israelis.

It was in this context that the Gulf crisis erupted, to be followed by the **Gulf War**. Many Palestinians and some among the PLO leadership hoped that **Saddam Hussein** would succeed in reversing the balance of forces in the region and forcing a solution to their problem. This was a tragic illusion which cost them dearly: the PLO lost the support of the Gulf states and isolated itself internationally. It seemed to have been virtually swept off the political scene when, in March 1991, following the defeat of **Iraq**, President Bush's administration relaunched the peace negotiations. The PLO also, for the first time, experienced competition from another political movement, **Hamas**, which refused to join its ranks.

However, there was still a decisive factor in the PLO's favour: its support among Palestinians, particularly those of the West Bank and Gaza. Thus when the time came to choose Palestinian representatives for a peace conference, which was the central point of negotiations for many months, the choice could not be made without reference to Arafat. The Palestinian delegation that was finally chosen – including its president, Haydar Abdel Shafi – and its various 'advisors' – Faisal Husseini, Hanan Ashrawi etc. – made no secret of the fact. In September 1991, the Palestinian National Council, despite powerful internal opposition, agreed to American proposals for the holding of a peace conference. This acceptance was confirmed by a majority on the organisation's Central Council – Fatah, the Communist Party (later to become the Popular Party) and independents – despite the opposition of the PFLP and DFLP. The PLO made major concessions: the peace conference would not be 'international' (the UN was kept out; Europe was marginalised) and its remit was circumscribed; there would be no Palestinian delegates representing the millions of exiles, or the Palestinians of Jerusalem, and the PLO was kept out in the corridor; the Palestinians' right to self-determination was not recognised; at least for the first period, they would have to content themselves with simple autonomy.

However, the opening of negotiations in Madrid on 30 October 1991 signalled an international recognition of the Palestinian cause. For the first time since 1948 the Palestinians were able to make their voices heard in a Middle East peace conference. But once again the negotiations ran aground on the intransigence of the **Yitzhak Shamir** government. After months of

U-turns, the Labour victory in 1992 made possible the opening of a 'secret channel' of negotiations, which resulted in the **Oslo Accords**.

The reasons which led the PLO to sign a document that was manifestly a step backwards in relation to the legitimate demands of the Palestinians were many. The organisation had been weakened by the position it took up during the Gulf War. Since the summer of 1982 it had lost a substantial part of its resources: many cadres had abandoned it, preferring to go into business; its armed forces were dispersed and no longer had a capacity for armed action; since the Gulf states refused to finance it, its financial resources were minimal and it could not meet the needs of its apparatus. Finally, nepotism and corruption were undermining its authority, particularly when one compares it to the moral rigour exhibited by the cadres of Hamas. Arafat, isolated since the assassinations of Abu Jihad and Abu Iyad, took all decisions upon himself. More than ever the PLO became identified with him.

Was he simply trying to maintain his power? Did he think that the Palestinians had no other choice? Whatever the case, his decision to base himself in Gaza radically changed the PLO's situation. For the first time in history, a **Palestinian Authority** was installed in the traditional land of Palestine. While the PLO continues to exist – if only because it is seen as representing the whole of the Palestinian people, including the refugees – it is progressively losing the little substance that remained to it. The majority of its institutions were repatriated to the Autonomous Territories, except the political department, which dealt with international relations, based in Tunis and led by Farouq Qaddoumi, who had turned dissident. Its institutions – the PNC, and the Central Council – have nevertheless served as a framework for dialogue with the organisations which rejected the Oslo Accords, notably the PFLP and the DFLP.

The Twenty-first Palestinian National Council was convened in April 1996 in Gaza to abrogate the National Charter, in line with Arafat's promise. By 504 votes out of 572 the PNC decided to abolish 'the articles of the Charter which rejected Israel's right to exist' – half of the 54 votes against came from members of the Legislative Council elected on 20 January 1996, in other words from people who had their legitimacy not from Arafat but from universal suffrage. This meeting also confirmed the 'return' to traditional Palestine of the leaders of the principal opposition organisations, notably those of the DFLP – with the exception of Nayef Hawatmeh – and the PFLP – with the exception of George Habash.

In 1999, on the eve of negotiations on the final status of the Palestinian territories, Arafat launched an offer of Palestinian dialogue with the opposition, to which the PFLP and the DFLP responded positively, in order to co-ordinate their position on the 'Palestinian constants': the creation of an independent Palestinian state with Jerusalem as its capital, the dismantling of Israeli **settlements**, the return of refugees to their homes and the reactivation of the PLO as the framework for Palestinian political action. But the blockage of the peace process, and the subsequent outbreak of the **second Intifada**, rendered these initiatives non-viable. Meanwhile the PNC met once again in December 1998, in the presence of President Bill Clinton, to confirmed the abrogation of the Charter.

Once repatriated, the PLO lost much of its substance, and in many ways became reduced to an instrument in the hands of Arafat as a counter-weight to the Palestinians of the interior. Its main, and historic, success was to have mobilised the Palestinian people and to have contributed to the Palestinian national renaissance post-1948. Its principal failure – and that of its President, Yasser Arafat – was its inability to create an independent state. Its impotence to stop, in time, the militarisation of the second Intifada has helped Ariel Sharon's strategy. At a time when the Authority is being pounded by the blows of the Israeli army, and the Palestinian refugees remain at the mercy of the goodwill of their host countries, the future of the Palestinian people will depend on their ability to maintain this framework of action, which the Palestine Liberation Organisation has represented for nearly forty years.

PALESTINIAN AUTHORITY

The Declaration of Principles on the interim arrangements for 'self-government' (or **autonomy**) signed in Washington on 13 September 1993, the first tranche of the **Oslo Accords**, states that the immediate aim of the **Palestine Liberation Organisation (PLO)** and **Israel** was to 'establish a Palestinian Interim Self-Government Authority, the elected Council (the 'Council'), for the Palestinian people in the **West Bank** and the **Gaza Strip**, for a transitional period not exceeding five years, leading to a permanent settlement based on UN Security Council Resolutions 242 and 338'.

The Palestinian Authority was to be set up in two stages. The first stage was intended to begin with the withdrawal of Israeli troops from Gaza and Jericho in May 1994 and the installation of limited self-government in those areas. The Authority set up here was a direct extension of the PLO – in fact, an extension of **Yasser Arafat** himself, who settled in Gaza on 1 July 1994, although his power was to extend over only a small fraction of the Palestinian population. The second phase began with the election of a legislative Council and its President on 20 January 1996 and the extension of self-government to the majority of the population of the West Bank. The intention was that, having initially been appointed by the Council, the national Authority would now have the credibility accorded by free elections.

Right from the start, the powers of the new Authority were drastically limited by the contents of the agreements signed with Israel. Not only are entire domains withheld from its jurisdiction – **settlements**, foreign relations, Israeli military installations etc. – but even in the sectors where it has power, the control exercised by the occupying authorities is still strong. What has happened is not so much a separation between the two sides as an institutionalisation of the dependence of the **Palestinians** on the Israelis.

In this very difficult context, further exacerbated by the difficulty of building an administration after more than twenty-five years of occupation, upon his return to Gaza Arafat set up an Authority consisting of 24 'ministries', headed by people originating from the interior and from exile. The principal failings of the PLO as an organisation were very soon to be reproduced in the new institutions: a concentration of power in the hands of one man, who maintains control of appointments and finances; a habitual practice of clientelism; a proliferation of police and security forces.

The achievements of the Authority can be looked at in three areas: the economy; the creation of a state based on human rights; the strengthening of Palestinian political society.

In the economic arena, the first year was marked by difficulties in establishing a balanced budget, the responsibility for which actually lay with all three of the principal protagonists: the Palestinians, the Israelis and international donor agencies. Right from the start, the rivalry between the Ministry for the Economy and the Ministry of Planning and the vague status of the Economic Council for Development and Reconstruction created difficulties for any attempt at a coherent development programme. At the same time, the delay in the implementation of the Declaration of 13 December 1993 deprived the Authority of numerous fiscal resources. Finally, the international donor agencies, which had reservations about funding current and recurring expenditure and were unable to co-ordinate their activities, took time to adapt. Finally, the performance of the Palestinian administration has improved and international aid – co-ordinated and delivered locally by structures run by the UN and the World Bank – has begun to arrive, notably from the EU, the prime donor, which, between 1994 and 2001, gave €1.4bn in aid.

But none of these things – a return to a balanced budget, international funding, or the efforts made for a strengthening of the private sector – will be sufficient to resolve two major outstanding problems:

– The dramatic reduction in the number of Palestinians authorised to work every day in Israel. Between 1992 and 1995 the figure fell from 120,000 to 30,000. The repeated closure of the West Bank and Gaza has reduced tens of thousands of Palestinians to poverty, which increased after the launching of the **second Intifada** in autumn 2000. In 2001, half of the economically active Palestinian population was unemployed.
– The impossible situation of having to operate within the framework laid down by the Oslo Accords, to manage a self-governing development of

'bantustans' which have no territorial continuity and which are totally dependent on Israel. The emergence of a class of *nouveaux riches* benefiting from their links to ruling elites and international aid does not mask the reality of life for the majority of Palestinians.

In 1996, the expenditure on police ($194 million) represented approximately 30 per cent of the Authority's expenditure. Such a level suggests that security had been set as a key priority from the very beginning by the Israeli government. Tel Aviv accepts, encourages and provides a framework for the establishment of an impressive apparatus of repression: in 2002 the Palestinian police forces numbered 29,000. Their action is limited by no legislation, and impunity seems to be the order of the day: arbitrary arrests, torture, deaths of detainees in suspicious circumstances. Furthermore, their violations of human rights are allowed to pass in silence by the international community in the name of the struggle against **Hamas**.

Repression within the Palestinian Authority is not directed solely at the **'terrorists'**. It is expressed in the systematic intimidation of all opposition and any attempt to criticise those in power, Yasser Arafat in particular. However, the elections for the Legislative Council and the presidency of the Authority on 20 January 1996 were indicative of the great diversity of Palestinian society and its desire to bring about democracy. The electoral turnout approached 80 per cent. It was only weak in **Jerusalem** as a result of Israeli pressure and in Hebron, which was still living under occupation. Even if Arafat won almost 88 per cent of the votes (albeit with almost 20 per cent spoiled ballot papers) and even if 51 candidates in the official Fatah list won seats (out of a total of 88 seats), several factors bear witness to the Palestinians' desire for democracy: the victory of a number of dissident Fatah candidates who enjoyed a legitimacy acquired during the **Intifada** and who had contested candidates imposed by Arafat; the election of several independent candidates known for their critical view of the Oslo Accords (Dr Haidar Abdul Shafi in Gaza, Hanan Ashrawi in Jerusalem, Abdel Jawad Saleh in Ramallah etc.); and the victory of other independent candidates associated with Hamas (notably in Gaza) and the PFLP.

Despite the numerous irregularities witnessed by the 1500 international observers, despite the presence of both direct and indirect pressure, and, in some instances, electoral fraud, the election on 20 January 1996 was taken wholeheartedly by the Palestinians as an opportunity to express their aspirations. This explains the failure of the boycott calls issued by Hamas, the Popular Front for the Liberation of Palestine (PFLP) and the Democratic Front for the Liberation of Palestine (DFLP) (despite advice to the contrary, in the case of the last two, by their militants inside the country). In the years that followed, however, the Council was not able to fulfil effectively its controlling role as an Authority, given that Arafat maintained his hold over it.

The launching of the second Intifada in autumn 2000 changed the situation radically. Security co-operation with Israel was suspended, and the Authority was accused of supporting terrorism. The Israeli army undertook large numbers of operations in Palestinian territory, destroying all the resources and symbols of the Authority: the Muqata'a, the headquarters of the Palestinian Authority, the buildings of the security forces, the prison, the Statistics Institute in Ramallah, the anti-terrorism centre in Gaza, the main security headquarters in the West Bank, Palestinian television and radio, many schools and roads, electricity networks, the runways at Gaza airport, the port of Gaza etc. The President of the Authority was himself several times besieged and effectively kept under house arrest in Ramallah. The Authority found itself with no financial resources. The income from customs taxes was no longer being paid by Israel, and its finances have been provided mainly by monthly payments from the Arab countries and the EU.

Now the Authority is being targeted by criticism from all sides, and its 'reform' is a key demand by Israel, the US and the international community. The formation of a new government in June 2002, changes within the security services, the promulgation of a Palestinian Basic Law and a law on the organisation of justice are gestures, responding to international demands as much as to internal criticism. These first steps were followed by the appointment of Mahmoud Abbas as Prime Minister of the Palestinian Authority in April 2003, a precondition for the implementation of the US-backed 'Road Map' for peace. He was succeeded by Ahmed Qorei some months later. But any attempt at serious reform is obviously impossible while the occupation continues. Moreover, the Palestinian Authority's ability to control the situation on the ground seems increasingly weak. Its inability to stop the suicide bombings has been one sign of this. However, the call for a change of regime within the Authority seems more likely to create anarchy than democracy.

PALESTINIANS

Since the end of the Second Jewish Revolt in AD135, the territory known as Palestine has had various masters (Rome, the Umayyads, the Abbasids, the **Ottoman Empire**) and a great mix of populations. At the beginning of the twentieth century it had around 500,000 inhabitants and relatively substantial economic activity, based mainly on agriculture (already harvesting up to thirty million oranges a year), an emergent industrial base and pilgrimages to the holy cities of **Jerusalem**, Bethlehem and Nazareth. The great majority of the population was Arab, both Muslim and Christian.

Like all the peoples of the region, they were to develop a nationalism, under the influence of European ideas and economic upheavals, although its precise borders were to vary with circumstance (sometimes Arab, some-times Greater Syrian etc.), but after the promises of the **Balfour Declaration** and the establishment of the British Mandate, this nationalism was defined as primarily Palestinian. This was the form that would assert itself over the years in the struggle against **Zionism**. It thus acquired all the forms of a modern nationalism, which even defeat in the **1948–49 War** was unable to destroy.

Today the Palestinian people number more than six million men and women scattered all over the world. Three major groupings can be dis-tinguished. Those who live in the territory of Mandate Palestine (**Israel**, the **West Bank** and Gaza); those living in **Jordan**; those settled – voluntarily or otherwise – in other Arab countries. To these should be added the diaspora which emigrated to Latin America, the **US** etc. Of these Palestinians, more than 3.3 million are refugees, according to figures drawn up by the UN Relief and Works Agency for Palestine Refugees (UNRWA). They fled their villages in 1948. More than a million of them still live in camps, on the West Bank, in Gaza, Jordan, **Syria** and **Lebanon**.

The Palestinians of Israel are discussed elsewhere (see **Israeli Arabs**), as are those of the West Bank and Gaza. The number of Palestinians in Jordan is reckoned at more than two million, but the figures are unreliable. In fact in Jordanian official statistics there is no differentiation between Palestinians (who have Jordanian passports) and the rest of the population. The only precise figures are for the refugees registered with UNRWA: over 1,670,000, in addition to the 350,000 who came from the West Bank and Gaza after 1967 – 250,000 of whom live in camps. Until 1970–71, it was there, in the camps, that Fatah and the **Palestine Liberation Organisation (PLO)** could count on the strongest support. Since **Black September** all activity that could be defined as Palestinian has been prohibited.

In Lebanon the economic, social and political life of the 387,000 Palestinians was closely linked to the PLO. The resistance movement had a network of mass organisations which kept its people involved. The latter furnished the PLO with its fighters, its political and administrative cadres, and the workers for the industries it had set up. For these people the PLO represented everything: national pride, physical and material security. The departure from Beirut in 1982, and then from Tripoli in 1983, left behind a population that was shattered and defenceless. It became a victim of ostracism and institutional racism.

In Syria there are close to 400,000 Palestinians, all refugees. Almost a third of them exist in camps, subject to very strict political control. But they enjoy the same social rights as Syrians.

Finally, more than 600,000 Palestinians settled in the Gulf states in the 1980s, half of them in **Kuwait**. This was a recent migration, going back for the most part to the 1960s, and following a classic pattern. The men leave to look for work, and the families follow a few years later. Palestinians held important positions as engineers, technicians, doctors, teachers, businessmen, journalists etc. Rich, very nationalistic, sending large subsidies to the families left behind, as well as giving financial aid to the PLO, the Gulf exiles were a significant segment of the Palestinian people. But the **Gulf War** and the expulsion of 300,000 Palestinians from Kuwait illustrated the precariousness of their situation.

All these groups possess a common trait: Palestinians have compensated for their frustrations by a high level of education, unequalled in the **Arab world**. The differences, sometimes considerable, from one host country to another, do not blur the common characteristics, however. Above all there is the deep feeling of belonging to one people, a feeling that unites the bourgeois of Kuwait with the West Bank peasant, the Lebanese refugee and the labourer working in Israel. They are bound to the same history. They recognise themselves in the same culture – that symbolised by the poet Mahmoud Darwish and writers such as Ghassan Kanafani and Émile Habibi. The PLO has been both the promoter and the symbol of this national pride.

The creation of the **Palestinian Authority** in 1994, following the **Oslo Accords**, was a moment of prime importance for the Palestinians. For the first time in their history they had a state institution of their own on part of their national territory.

PARTITION PLAN

UN Security Council Resolution 181, passed by the General Assembly on 29 November 1947, came to be known as the Partition Plan because it decided the partition of Palestine into a Jewish state, an Arab state and a zone under 'special international regime' (see Appendix 3).

Adopted by 33 votes (including the **US** and the Soviet Union) to 13, with 10 abstentions (including Britain), this text was the outcome of a protracted crisis and and would be the stimulus of an even longer one. In 1939, Britain, which had for a long time been in favour of **Zionism** in Palestine, somewhat reluctantly decided to alter its policy and issued a White Paper limiting Jewish **immigration** to 75,000 over the next five years and restricting land purchase. Anxious to win over the **Arabs** in the face of the impending war with Hitler's Germany, Britain also proposed, within a ten-year framework, a plan for a unitary state comprising at most a third of **Jews**.

But, after the war, this plan proved impracticable. The **genocide** gave a tragic legitimacy to the Jewish quest for a state. Many of the survivors having nowhere to go but Palestine, illegal immigration took place on a massive scale. The drama of the Exodus, and many similar incidents, shocked a public whose outrage was all the greater since it had been so notably absent during the Nazi extermination. To these factors, which made Britain's position untenable, were added the effects of Jewish **terrorism** in Palestine. From 1943 the Stern Gang, and from 1944 the Irgun, had attacked British soldiers and possessions. The terror culminated in an attack on the King David Hotel on 22 July 1946 which caused hundreds of deaths and stunned British public opinion. 'Bring our boys home!' yelled demonstrators, conscious of the fact that in two years close to 150 British soldiers had been killed and 350 severely wounded in Palestine.

Though anxious to maintain the British position, particularly since it was being threatened in **Egypt** and **Iraq**, the Labour government could no longer resist the pressure, particularly because it had already decided to give up the Indian part of the empire, the jewel in its crown. On 14 February 1947 it decided 'to take the problem in its entirety to the United Nations', which in May created a special commission, UNSCOP, to look at possible solutions. The notion of a unitary state controlled by one of the two communities was unrealistic given their relative sizes – 650,000 Jews, 1,333,000 Arabs. The option of a bi-national state proposed by the communists and the Zionist left was blocked by seemingly insurmountable differences between the two sides. A system of cantons was unrealisable in practical terms. The remaining option was partition.

The plan allocated 14,000 sq. km, with 558,000 Jews and 405,000 Arabs for a Jewish state, and 11,500 sq. km, with 804,000 Arabs and 10,000 Jews for an Arab state. The international zone, including the holy sites, **Jerusalem** and Bethlehem, would have 106,000 Arabs and 100,000 Jews. Between the two states an economic union was to be forged, jointly controlling currency, customs, railways and postal services, plus the ports of Haifa and Jaffa. Opponents of the project felt the Jews would have the best of the bargain: according to one observer, they would obtain 56.5 per cent of a territory of which they owned scarcely 7 per cent, and where they represented only 32 per cent of the population.

In any event, the Partition Plan was never put into practice. Zionist leaders, whose support for it had been purely tactical, had never given up the dream of a Greater **Israel**, and wanted more than the share allocated them by the UN. Arab leaders too demanded more, much more, and rejected the very idea of a Jewish state. Britain, at odds now with the UN and hoping to take advantage of the troubles to maintain its power, encouraged Arab leaders to attack the Zionists: after increasingly serious reciprocal attacks, Arab armies entered Palestine on 15 May 1948, triggering the **1948–49 War**, the first of the Arab–Israeli wars.

PEACE CONFERENCES

From the earliest beginnings of the Jewish settlement in Palestine through to the Madrid Conference of 1991, Israeli–Arab relations have developed with an aspect of confrontation – and, as we know, with five wars. However, in the belief that the integration of the Jewish state within its Middle Eastern environment was first and foremost a matter of military (and also economic and ideological) power relations, the leaders of the **Yishuv**, and subsequently of **Israel**, have not neglected the weapons of diplomacy. On several occasions, either by their own free will or because they were forced into it, they have embarked on negotiations with their Arab neighbours. However, history shows that they have always preferred to embark on such relations in a bilateral mode and have always opposed multilateral negotiations.

Despite this preference, the Jewish state has nevertheless been led to take part in negotiations that are multilateral in character. The first of this kind was the Lausanne Conference, an event often overlooked by historians. It was held, with interruptions, between 27 April and 14 September 1949, on the initiative of the Conciliation Commission for Palestine – the mediating organisation set up on 11 December 1948 by the UN General Assembly to take over the activities of Count Bernadotte, who had been assassinated by Lehi **terrorists** five months previously. On the basis of UN Security Council Resolutions – notably 181 (29 November 1947) and 194 (11 December 1948) – the Commission was mandated to encourage negotiations between the parties to the conflict, either directly or under its auspices, on issues such as the fate of the refugees (see **Expulsions**, **Palestinians** and **Right of return**), borders and the status of **Jerusalem**. After four months of consultations in the Middle East, where ceasefire negotiations were underway, the Commission invited the warring parties to Lausanne. They all responded favourably: the Palestinians and the Arab states in order to attempt to regain by means of negotiation a part of the terrain that had been lost during the war; and Israel for fear that boycotting the conference would compromise its chances of admission to the UN. For these same reasons the Israeli delegation was to sign, on 12 May, a protocol which was also ratified by the Arab representatives: all declared that they accepted the November 1947 **Partition Plan** and the December 1948 resolution on refugees as the basis for future negotiations. This was a major turning point, both for the **Arabs**, who were now in a position of having to recognise Israel *de facto* and negotiate with it, and for the Jewish state, whose territorial and demographic acquisitions at the end of the war would be brought into question: a return to the borders outlined by the UN; the repatriation of refugees; the internationalisation of Jerusalem; and even the eventual creation of a Palestinian state.

This level of consensus was exceptional, but was shortlived. Right to the end the Israeli leadership refused, as regards the repatriation of Palestinian refugees, to make the kind of gesture that the Arab states regarded as the precondition for all negotiation: the offer, in July 1949, to accept 100,000 exiles (out of a total of 750,000) was condemned as insufficient (including by the US). The offer had been intended to loosen the vice-like grip of the US, because at that time Washington was exerting an unprecedented pressure on Tel Aviv – a pressure not to be repeated in the future: in a note to the Israeli Prime Minister, President Harry Truman in June 1949 went so far as to threaten to consider a revision of its attitude to Israel as inevitable. Despite the (purely tactical) signing of the Lausanne Protocol, **David Ben Gurion** and the great majority of his government had no intention whatever of renouncing the sole peace which in their view was worth having – in other words the division of the rest of Palestine with King Abdullah of **Jordan**. Abba Eban, the representative of the Jewish state at the UN – before then becoming its unmovable Minister of Foreign Affairs – thought that his country 'sees no need to run after peace. The armistice is sufficient for us; if we run after peace the Arabs will demand a price of us – borders or refugees or both, Let us wait a few years.' As for the head of the Israeli delegation at the peace conferences, Eliahu Sasson, he would draw from all this a lesson which was to inspire his country's diplomacy in the longer term. As he wrote to Moshe Sharett,

> The twenty-five months of work which I spent at Lausanne taught me that all foreign mediation – even when it is the best, the most impartial, the most objective – will, even with the best of intentions, ask us to make concessions on refugees, borders and peace, which we must absolutely resist.

It would take 24 years – and three more military confrontations – for the Israelis to accept a modification of this position – and that for a mere two days! **Anwar al-Sadat** had made no secret of his view: in order to get the Middle East out of its impasse, the two superpowers would have to be stirred into action, and only a new conflict would bring that about. Hence the outbreak of the **1973 War**. Alarmed at the trial of strength into which their respective 'protegés' had dragged them, the two superpowers were obliged to take an initiative, in the form of an international conference. First proposed by US Secretary of State Henry Kissinger, and backed by his Soviet counterpart Andre Gromyko, the initiative soon ran into problems with the conditions set by both sides: **Egypt** wanted a conference under the auspices of the UN; Israel, on the other hand, preferred the US and the USSR, would not accept the presence of the **Palestine Liberation Organisation (PLO)**, and demanded as a precondition a list of its prisoners of war held by **Syria**; Jordan, for its part, proposed to represent the Palestinians; and Syria refused any fragmentation of negotiations, particularly on prisoners. The conference was finally called under the joint presidency of the US and USSR, and the UN Security Council contented itself with ratifying this formula; the PLO was kept out of negotiations; Damascus did not take part. What had started as a major project ended by not delivering very much at all. On 21 December 1973 there was a public session, addressed by Kurt Waldheim on behalf of the UN and by the five delegation heads (Egypt, the US, Israel, Jordan and the USSR); on the twenty-second a closed session was held. The conference then effectively went into hibernation, and was only to reawaken briefly in 1974, for a meeting between Kissinger and Gromyko, and for the signing of the Israeli–Syrian disengagement agreement.

On 30 October 1991, under the joint presidency of the US and the Soviet Union, the third multilateral conference in the history of the Middle East began in Madrid. Once **Kuwait** had been liberated, at the risk of being accused of double standards, how could the major powers not take action on other territories that had been occupied (for a period, moreover, of very many years)? Strengthened by its extraordinary gains from the **Gulf War**, Washington intended to consolidate them by eliminating the principal cause of instability in the region: the Arab–Israeli conflict. Moscow, for its part, had no particular problem following the Americans in this conference: as we have seen, it had always been arguing for such a conference. The Arab countries, for their part, had – as in 1949 and in 1973 – more to win than to lose from such a forum. This was particularly true for the Palestinians, and their National Council, aware of the eminently unfavourable balance of forces, nevertheless followed **Yasser Arafat** in thinking that it was better to be in the game than to stand outside as a spectator. As for Israel, despite its reluctance it knew it could neither prevent such a forum nor boycott it: it knew that the George Bush Senior administration would have no hesitations, if necessary, in imposing **sanctions** on Israel. And anyway Israel managed substantially to limit the damage. In the final event it was to be a regional rather than international forum, in which the UN was reduced to observer status, while Europe had to be satisfied with a walk-on role. The formal opening session served merely as an appetiser for the main meal of bilateral and multilateral negotiations. The Palestinian presence was part of a Jordanian–Palestinian delegation, and had no overseas representatives and nobody from East Jerusalem. **Yitzhak Shamir** was to win his gamble: having been transported to Washington for the bilateral talks, and to various other capitals for the multilateral ones, the negotiations initiated in Madrid simply petered out.

Without the 'Oslo miracle', a return to face-to-face secret negotiation over the Israeli–Palestinian sticking points, the mountain of Madrid would not even have given birth to a mouse. But given the prevailing conditions following the outbreak of the **second Intifada**, Oslo has ended up by leaving very little. One day there will presumably be a new international conference on the Middle East. When is a more difficult question to answer.

PERES, SHIMON

A child of the *shtetl*, the generic name given to the small Jewish towns in Poland and **Russia**, Shimon Persky spent his adolescence in Palestine. He was born in 1923 in Vishneva, a small town in what was then Polish Belorussia, and emigrated when he was 11 years old.

After studying business, he became addicted to politics at the Ben Shemen agricultural college, joining the Mapai Youth movement, of which he became secretary in 1943. At the time he chose the name Ben Amoz, but as another young man from Poland had already taken it he decided on Peres. Together with his group of young socialists, he got involved with the Geva *kibbutz* and then established the Poriyat *kibbutz* on the banks of Lake Tiberiad, which was later renamed Alumot. While on his way to Haifa by car, he met someone that would change his life, namely **David Ben Gurion**, who was soon to be Prime Minister of the new state of **Israel**. The 60-year-old Labour leader wanted to surround himself with a new generation of leaders. The 'Old Man' appreciated the qualities of this fresh young left-winger, who in 1947 joined the headquarters of the Haganah, the clandestine Jewish army. After Peres had refused an opportunity of promotion to the rank of major general – the same rank as **Yitzhak Rabin** and Moshe Dayan – in the new army, Ben Gurion put him in charge of acquiring the weapons that Israel needed to counter the Arab armies. After the war, this mission was to take him to the **US**.

From that moment, Shimon Peres's career was mapped out. He built up fruitful relationships in **France**, **Britain** and even, later on, in Germany. He thus arranged for the Israeli army to be armed, and to be reinforced after 1955 in order to counter the arms deliveries from Czechoslovakia to **Egypt**. There was further collusion with Guy Mollet and Maurice Bourgès-Maunoury, who in October 1956 met Peres in Sèvres to agree on the tripartite operation against **Nasser** and, during a break in the proceedings, to build a nuclear reactor in Dimona, southern Israel. This was Peres's finest hour, but paradoxically it was not something that he could ever brag about. He entered parliament and became Vice-Minister of Defence in 1959, and also supervised the perfection of the secret that would turn the regional balance of power on its head: the Israeli strikeforce. By 1966 Israel had the atomic bomb; the hydrogen bomb came in the 1970s.

By this time, Peres enjoyed considerable authority, even over his ageing mentor, who symbolised, and even inspired, many of his visions. Ben Gurion was for him the incarnation of his philosophy of the state – *mamlachtiyut*. In 1965, he resigned out of loyalty to Ben Gurion and supported him in his struggle against the Labour old guard: Peres even became general secretary of the Rafi party. The experience was a failure, and after the Six Day **1967 War** he rounded up the stray sheep. Golda Meir repaid him by re-appointing him as a minister in 1969, and he successively held the portfolios for the development of the Occupied Territories, refugees, the absorption of immigrants, transport and communications. Yet in 1974 it was the Israeli ambassador to the US who, on his return to Tel Aviv, would be promoted to leader of the party and then the country. The usurper was Yitzhak Rabin, who made Peres his Defence Minister but never trusted him, convinced that he was always plotting against him.

The rivalry between Peres and Rabin dominated Israeli politics for twenty years. The two men did not like each other: the military man did not trust the *apparatchik*, the intellectual mocked the simpleton, the showman scoffed at the grafter, and the father of the model family was, without any doubt, envious of the *bon viveur*. After he was humiliated in 1974, Peres got his revenge in the 1980s after his adversary was removed by the crushing defeat in 1977. Now in opposition, the Labour party appointed Peres as President; seven years later he became the leader of a government of National Unity. He rescued the economy from hyperinflation and, most notably, led the withdrawal of the Israeli army from **Lebanon**, which earned him a reputation as a peacekeeper. At that time, however, he was totally opposed to any negotiation with the **Palestine Liberation Organisation (PLO)**, preferring the 'Jordanian option', which **Yitzhak Shamir** soon invalidated. **Menachem Begin**'s successor became Prime Minister in 1986, by virtue of the 'rotatsia', and Peres was appointed Deputy Prime Minister and Minister for Foreign Affairs.

Peres suffered another humiliation in 1992 when, as before, the Labour militants chose Rabin. The victory reunited the two enemies, who pretended to be like brothers. As a political move, the new Prime Minister entrusted foreign affairs to his disgruntled challenger – even allowing him to engage in secret talks with the PLO in Oslo. The sponsor of the 'Jordanian option' had convinced himself of the irreversible nature of the Palestinian authority. Peres was at Rabin's side when he signed the Declaration on the principles of **autonomy** with **Yasser Arafat**, and again in Oslo to receive the Nobel Peace Prize alongside the Palestinian leader.

After the assassination of Rabin, Peres, at 72 years old, naturally became Prime Minister, but this time he was leader of a left-wing government. Although he continued the peace process with the **Palestinian Authority**, he became embroiled in two incidents that threatened his chances of re-election. Did he allow himself to become trapped by the commander-in-chief and the head of the information services? Did he commit an error of judgement? Whatever the case, the assassination of the **terrorist** Yahya Ayash pushed the extremists of the **Hamas** movement to end their ceasefire, which then unsettled public opinion and led to a strict blockade of the Occupied Territories. A few weeks later, **Hezbollah** fire into northern Israel served as the pretext for the Grapes of Wrath operation. Twenty-one years after he pulled Israel out of the chaos in Lebanon, Shimon Peres took the country back there when a bomb hit the middle of a UN camp on 18 April 1996, killing 98 civilian refugees.

Forty days later, he was beaten in the 1996 elections by the leader of the right, **Benyamin Netanyahu**. After several years, during which it seemed as if the unloved Peres had committed political suicide, he was re-elected leader of the Labour party in June 2003 following its overwhelming defeat by **Ariel Sharon**'s Likud in the January 2003 elections under the leadership of Amram Mitzna.

QADHAFFI, MUAMMAR

Qadhaffi was born in 1938 to a nomad family from the Serte region of **Libya**. He received a religious education, and at the age of ten was sent to school at Sabha in the Fezzan. As a teenager he became a militant Nasserite, and was even expelled from school in 1961 for having demonstrated against the Syrian secession from the United Arab Republic. Convinced that only the army could regenerate Libya, he joined the Benghazi Military Academy in 1964 and founded a secret organisation, the Free Officers.

He was the mastermind of the coup d'état of 1 September 1969, which ended the rule of the ageing monarch Idris al-Sanussi. Qadhaffi became president of the Command Council of the Revolution at the age of 31. A staunch nationalist and fervent partisan of Arab unity, at first he followed the line of **Gamal Abdel Nasser**, while at the same time being more open to Islamic tendencies. But after the death of the Egyptian leader in 1970 he distanced himself from the change of direction being imposed by **Anwar al-Sadat**, Nasser's successor. He then developed a new theory, chronicled in his *Green Book*, conceived as different to both capitalism and socialism. It advocated direct democracy and the rejection of representative democracy; an end to wage-earning (seen as a form of 'slavery'), with a new slogan of 'Partners, not wage earners'; and the return to the natural life, to natural socialism. The explicit ideal was old-style Islam as it was at its origins in the seventh century.

What factors influenced the Colonel's thinking? The journal *Hérodote* has some suggestions:

> His Bedouin origins linked him through his parentage to the great open spaces of the Sahara; there is also the influence of Nasser and, as a foil, the state of Libya under Idris I; there is what he has learnt from being in power and the various historic situations in which he has been obliged to take action; and his reading and his meetings with others, although it would be hard to unravel the intricacies of these; and finally there is Islam.

Although a devout Muslim, Qadhaffi is first and foremost an Arab nationalist, and his understanding of his religion is a very personal one, since he accepts only the Qur'an and rejects the Sunna (see **Islam**). This leads to a flexible interpretation of the injunctions. 'An important part of Islam, of Christianity and Judaism,' argues Qadhaffi,

> deals with the relations between God and Man, as well as the rites. Another part concerns the relations of men amongst themselves, what they may do and what they must avoid, but only general principles are given: work for good, prevent evil, establish good relations within the family, with neighbours, give fair treatment to strangers, orphans, the poor, prisoners etc. One can then go on to found a state or an empire, establish a republic or a monarchy, start a revolution, establish a *jamahiriyya*. In doing so, one has only to fear God, not steal and be tolerant.

From this to 'Render unto Caesar what is Caesar's and to God what is God's' is only a short step, but one that Qadhaffi is careful not to take; he has already been the object of numerous attacks from Islamic scholars. But his theories allow him to consign to oblivion certain precepts, such as those on women: 'It was not written that they [women] should be slaves, submissive, despised and that men should be the opposite. Oppression is the outcome of a social process.'

Since 1987, with the breakdown of his foreign policy (particularly in Chad) and the economic crisis caused by the slump in **oil** prices, Qadhaffi has modified his pronouncements in a more realistic sense. He has rebuilt relations with all his immediate neighbours, and also with countries in black Africa. 'I went to sleep beside four million Libyans, and I woke up beside 400 million Africans,' he stated, summing up the diplomatic operation which, in the space of a few years, transformed him from the aggressor of Chad and the *bête noire* of the Organisation of African Unity into the leader of the African Union, the new continent-wide organisation modelled on the **EU**.

Consolidated by his intervention in the freeing of the Western hostages on the Philippines island of Jolo in September 2000 (thanks to his long-standing relations with the Moro National Liberation Front), Qadhaffi's return to the international scene owes much to his April 1999 decision to hand over to Scottish judicial authorities two of the suspects for the December 1988 Lockerbie bombing (in which 259 died), one of whom would be sentenced to life imprisonment on 31 January 2001, the other acquitted. In March 2001 came a new success: the French appeal court rejected the case that had been brought against him related to the September 1989 bombing of UTA DC10 over Niger, which killed 170. The Lockerbie file looked set to be closed in 2003, when it was announced that a formula had been agreed for Libya to admit responsibility for the bombing, offer compensation to the victims' families and in return see the lifting of UN **sanctions**.

What will remain of these achievements in the new international landscape marked by the 'anti-**terrorist** crusade' launched by the **US** after the attacks of 11 September 2001? While Libya – unlike **Iraq**, **Iran** and North Korea – is not explicitly part of the 'axis of evil' as defined by George W. Bush, it is still seen as a state sponsor of terrorism, despite its firm condemnation of the 11 September attacks. In May 2002 Washington even went so far as to accuse Tripoli of pursuing the production of **weapons of mass destruction**.

Viewed as an international terrorist and madman by the US, and public enemy number one by the European press, Qadhaffi symbolises the frustration of those peoples oppressed by the international order and the problems of creating an independent path of development. He is grooming his eldest son from a second marriage, 30-year-old Saif al-Islam, to succeed him.

RABIN, YITZHAK

The first Israeli prime minister to have been born in Palestine (in 1922), Yitzhak Rabin was also the first important Israeli leader to be assassinated (by a Jewish extremist in 1995). Between these two dates his life was spent in the service of the Labour party, the state of **Israel** and, most particularly, the army.

The career of this 'Sabra' (a **Jew** born in Israel as opposed to a member of the diaspora) is effectively identified with the army. At the age of 18, having completed his studies at agricultural college, he enrolled in the Haganah, the Jewish underground army, and his activities against the British Mandate authorities earned him five months imprisonment in a military camp in Gaza in 1946. In 1947, at the age of 26, he became the youngest colonel in the Palmah, the vanguard of the Jewish army. He acquitted himself with distinction in the course of the **1948–49 War** in the battle for **Jerusalem**, but also – as he later explained in his autobiography – in the **expulsion** of the **Palestinians** from Lydda and Ramleh (in the territory intended for the Arab state). 'We were marching,' he wrote,

> at the side of Ben Gurion. Allon repeated the question: 'What are we to do with the population?' Ben Gurion moved his hand to say 'Expel them!' Allon and I conferred. I agreed with him that we needed to expel them. We set them walking on the road to Bet Horon...The population of Lod didn't go voluntarily. There was no other way except to use force and warning shots to make the inhabitants obey.

It might be added, massacring some 250 civilians in the process. But this 'detail', or even the above quotation, do not figure in the text published in either French or English version of Rabin's memoirs: the author has preferred to expurgate the whole of the account of this bloody episode, which preceded a paragraph dedicated to his marriage with Leah. Fortunately for historians, the original text did not escape the vigilance of the *New York Times*, which published it on 23 October 1979.

At the end of 1950, after the dissolution of the Palmah, Rabin was assigned to the general staff. Going up through the ranks, despite the opposition of **Shimon Peres**, he achieved in early 1964 the supreme position of head of the general staff, and thus, together with Moshe Dayan, who at that time was the Minister of Defence in the Levy Eshkol government, directed the lightning offensive of 1967. Despite one sign of weakness – the 23 May – for which he would for long be reproached, the stunning victory in the Six Day War earned Rabin a popularity which served as a launch pad for his political career.

After 1968 Rabin traded in his uniform for a diplomat's suit, which put him at the head of the most important embassy of all: he represented Israel in the **US**. He returned from five years spent in Washington convinced that the fate of the Jewish state would depend on alliance with America – and he benefited from not having been involved in any way in the disaster of October 1973. This enabled him to succeed Golda Meir on her resignation as Prime Minister in June 1974. There was then a brief and bitter experience: thirty months later a scandal – his wife Leah had kept an illegal bank account in the US – forced him to resign, and for the first time in the country's history the Labour party was obliged to cede power to the right, under **Menachem Begin.**

'Break their bones.' That eminently humanist formula marked Rabin's return to politics in 1982, his advice to **Ariel Sharon**, whose Lebanese operation he had approved, to deprive West Beirut of **water** and electricity. As Minister of Defence in the National Unity government set up in 1984, he co-ordinated Israel's withdrawal from **Lebanon**. But on 1 October 1995, he was responsible for the bombing of the **Palestine Liberation Organisation (PLO)** headquarters in Tunis: 60 bodies disappeared under the debris. Rabin declared, 'The time has come to hit the PLO at the top'. At the end of 1987 he was charged by **Yitzhak Shamir**, who was then Prime Minister again, in line with the 'rotation' agreement, to put down the **Intifada**. He was to do this with no scruples. Since he saw the movement simply as a 'fire of straw', which was to be broken 'with force and blows' – and all the resources of arbitrary behaviour of the emergency law inherited from the British Mandate. If in the long term shooting young unarmed Palestinians was politically ill-advised, one would simply break arms and legs instead. The method was immortalised on American television by CBS. Presented by Rabin's friends as a step backwards designed to avoid deaths by gunfire, it actually increased the number of deaths. One year after the beginning of the uprising, the insurgent Palestinians had suffered 400 dead and 25,000 wounded, including Khalil al-Wazir, known as Abu Jihad, **Arafat**'s right-hand man in charge of the Intifada, whom Rabin had had assassinated in Tunis on 14 April 1988.

This new and brutal confrontation with Palestinian nationalism event-ually convinced the general, who was chased out of government in June 1990, that 'the question has no military solution'. He saw in the **Gulf War** 'a formidable opportunity' for settling the Arab–Israeli conflict – because the collapse of the USSR, the re-establishment of American leadership and the weakening of the PLO had created the most favourable balance of power ever. Simultaneously hawk and dove, he was the man of the moment: the Labour party militants intuitively understood this, and chose him against his long-time rival, Peres, to lead them into the electoral battle of 1992. At the age of 70, Rabin became Prime Minister again. Over the period of a year he was to attempt, in vain, to outsmart the PLO: he left the negotiations begun in Madrid to dribble on in Washington, and seemed to give priority to peace with **Syria** and **Jordan**. Worse, in December 1992 the expulsion of

450 **Hamas** militants to Lebanon seemed to eliminate all hopes of peace. Now if ever was the time to move. With the Prime Minister's agreement, Yossi Beilin made secret contact with the PLO in Oslo. While Rabin refused to allow Peres to take the negotiations in hand, he allowed the Director General of the Ministry of Foreign Affairs, Uri Savir, to supervise them. Then he added his juridical advisor and associate, Yoel Singer. Against all expectations, and notably those of the Prime Minister, the two delegations arrived at an agreement on a formula for self-government inspired by the **Camp David Accords**.

The turning point came in September 1993: after mutual recognition between Israel and the PLO, Rabin and Arafat signed the Declaration of Principles on self-government which would lead on to the **Oslo Accords**. On the evening of his assassination on 4 November 1995, he had declared before a supportive crowd gathered in Tel Aviv, 'I fought for as long as there was no chance of peace'.

REFUGEES

Migrations have been a permanent feature of political geography in the Middle East: **Jews** from Spain in the fifteenth and sixteenth centuries, Muslims from the Balkans and the Caucasus in the nineteenth, Armenians and Assyrians from **Turkey** after World War I, not to mention Jewish **immigration** to Palestine.

If the fate of **Sudan**'s million refugees remains a major preoccupation, as does that of the hundreds of thousands of **Kurds** exiled from their divided country, it is nonetheless the problem of the Palestinian refugees created by the **1948–49 War** and the Six Day **1967 War** that has most abidingly marked the region. Indeed, for a considerable time the international community was to consider the question of **Palestinians** not as a national problem calling for a state solution, but uniquely from the point of view of the right of refugees to return to their homes.

RIGHT OF RETURN

According to the UN Relief and Works Agency for Palestine Refugees (UNRWA), a refugee is defined as a person who lived in Palestine between 1 June 1946 and 15 May 1948 and who lost his home as a result of the conflict and took refuge in one of the countries in which UNRWA operates. Estimated by UNRWA at about one million in 1950, by 30 June 2002 their numbers had risen to 3.9 million, not to mention the thousands of unaccounted refugees of the **Wars of 1948–49** and **1967**.

And yet these men, women and children, often crammed together into wretched camps, have had, in theory, for more than fifty years, the right to return to their homes, a right which is summed up in the formula of the 'right of return'. On 11 December 1948, while the first Arab–Israeli war was still in progress, the General Assembly of the UN in Paris voted Resolution 194, which stated,

> the refugees wishing to return to their homes and live at peace with their neighbours should be permitted to do so at the earliest practicable date, and that compensation should be paid for the property of those choosing not to return and for loss of or damage to property which, under principles of international law or in equity, should be made good by the Governments or authorities responsible.

Contrary to what Israeli leaders have stated subsequently, their government certainly recognised this resolution, specifically on 12 May 1949, in a protocol signed by **Israel** and its Arab neighbours on the occasion of the Lausanne **Peace Conference**. The text in question also sanctions the UN General Assembly's Resolution 181 (29 November 1947), which split Palestine into two states, one Jewish and the other Arab, as well as creating an international zone to cover **Jerusalem** and the holy places. This about-turn by Israel is easily explained: it was a precondition for its admission to the UN, which effectively happened on the same day. Already then, as Walter Eitan, General Co-Director of the Israeli Ministry of Foreign Affairs, was to confide, his 'main objective was to begin to undermine the protocol of 12 May, which Israel had been forced to sign within the framework of its battle to be admitted to the United Nations'.

Israel manifested its refusal of any return of the refugees in the diplomatic arena, but also on the ground. Having decided to prevent it 'at any price' – in the phrase used by **David Ben Gurion** in the Israeli cabinet – the government destroyed or equipped for the new Jewish immigrants more than 400 Arab villages, and shared out their land (30,000 hectares in all) to the surrounding *kibbutzim* (communes) and *moshavim* (co-operatives). The law on 'abandoned properties' – designed to make possible the seizure of the property of any person who was 'absent' – 'legalised' this generalised confiscation as of December 1948. The same thing would happen after 1967 in the Occupied Territories.

Even though Resolution 194 was re-voted every year in the UN, the issue of the Palestinian refugees was to be marginalised during the peace process which began in October 1991 in Madrid. It was discussed in three forums. The first, the Multilateral Group on Refugees, was created by the Madrid Conference, which opened on 30 October 1991. It had six delegations representing the Middle East: Israel, **Egypt**, **Jordan**, the **Palestinians**, **Syria** and **Lebanon**. The latter two boycotted the meetings. According to Israel

the agenda should have included all refugees in the region – including the
Kurds and those **Jews** who had emigrated from Arab countries. But the group
suspended work in December 1995. The second forum, the Quadripartite
Committee on Displaced Persons (the Palestinians, Israel, Jordan and Egypt),
created following the **Oslo Accords**, was supposed to resolve, during the
interim period of Palestinian **autonomy**, the problem of the people displaced in 1967. It made no serious progress. Finally, refugees were one of
the bilateral Israeli–Palestinian issues which the two parties began to
discuss within the framework of negotiations on the definitive status of the
Palestinian territories.

Leaving aside the vagaries which characterise each of these forums, the
fundamental blockage on this question has to do with the irreconcilability
of the principled positions of the **Palestine Liberation Organisation (PLO)**
and the Israeli government. For the **Palestinian Authority**, any definitive
agreement had to include: the recognition of the 'right to return', even if
only a symbolic number of refugees would actually have the possibility of
returning to Israel proper, with the others benefiting from compensation;
the recognition by Israel of its moral responsibility in the creation of the
drama of the refugees; the granting of a Palestinian passport to all refugees
who wanted one; their right to come and live in the future Palestinian state;
the granting, by host countries, of full civil rights to all refugees who decided
not to return. Although conceived as a temporary body at the time of its
creation, UNRWA would pursue its social, health and educational activities
during the enactment of this plan, which would take place over a period
of several years. For its part, the Israeli government initially rejected any
kind of right of return, saying that the refugees should settle in their host
countries, with the assistance of international aid.

This position, which remained unchanged at the **Camp David** negotiations in July 2000, saw a development for the first time during the
negotiations in **Taba** in January 2001. As the Israeli delegates wrote in a
document given to their Palestinian counterparts,

> The problem of Palestinian refugees is central in Israeli–Palestinian relations.
> Its overall and fair solution is essential to create a durable and morally
> irreproachable peace...The state of Israel expresses solemnly its sadness for
> the tragedy of the Palestinian refugees, their sufferings and their losses, and
> will be an active partner to close this terrible chapter opened 53 years
> ago...Despite its acceptance of Resolution 181 of the UN General Assembly
> of November 1947, the nascent state of Israel was caught up in the war and
> the bloodshed of 1948–9, which created victims and led to suffering on both
> sides, including the displacement and expropriation of the Palestinian civilian
> population, who thus became refugees...A fair settlement of the problem of
> Palestinian refugees, in accord with Resolution 242 of the UN Security Council,
> must lead to the application of Resolution 194 of the General Assembly of
> the United Nations.

On the basis of these principles, concrete solutions were placed on the table. Five possibilities would be offered to the refugees: return to Israel; return to the Israeli territories ceded by Israel to Palestine; return to the state of Palestine; settlement in their place of residence (Jordan, Syria etc.); departure for another country (several countries, including Canada, had already indicated that they were ready to accept **immigration** by sizeable contingents of Palestinians).

While insisting on the free choice of the refugees, the Palestinian representatives for their part reiterated that they did not intend to challenge the Jewish nature of the state of Israel, which they had recognised on the occasion of the Palestinian Declaration of **Independence** in 1988. As Laila Shahed, the Palestinian general delegate in **France**, stated, 'It is obvious that nobody is trying to alter the Jewish character of the Israeli state. It is obvious that the right of return cannot be applied to all refugees. We therefore have to discuss its application, but it is also equally evident that the principle must be recognised.' As of that time one obstacle remained: the number of Palestinians authorised to return to Israel itself. Although the Israelis agreed to the return of 40,000 refugees over a period of five years, plus people who would be allowed to rejoin their families, the Palestinians responded that any offer below 100,000 would not allow progress to be made. In any event, the two parties agreed to give priority to the refugees in Lebanon, who were suffering under Beirut's discriminatory policies. The Israeli text even said, 'The state of Israel recognises its moral duty in the rapid solution of the condition of the refugee populations in the camps of Sabra and Shatila'.

Furthermore, the Israelis and Palestinians proposed the rapid establishment, at the international level, of a commission and a fund to compensate the refugees. Finally, they reached agreement on the fact that the compensation for Jews who had left Arab countries to go and live in Israel was not a matter for bilateral discussion.

While it was undeniably real, this coming together of minds over the most difficult outstanding issue between the Israelis and the Palestinians led to nothing in the short term: Ehud Barak resigned, bringing on elections which were to give victory to **Ariel Sharon**. The eruption of the **second Intifada** would suggest it will be a long time before there can be a return to the principles defined in Taba. The Geneva proposal of December 2003 is also based, in its solutions to the refugee question, on the Taba proposals.

RUSSIA

Although one of the first acts of the Bolshevik Revolution was to renounce Tsarist designs on the Middle East, the USSR never abandoned the hope of playing a determining role in the region. It was a hope which was met with varying degrees of success over the years.

The objectives pursued by the Soviet Union in the Middle East were noticeably different from those which drove American policy, and British policy before it. For the USSR, **oil** was not the primary consideration, since the Soviet Union was itself an oil exporter. Nor was the relationship grounded in the prospect of substantial profits from economic relations with the countries in the region: from Moscow's point of view, economic relations between the USSR and **Egypt** or **Syria** were something of a bottom-less pit. The principal motivations of Soviet interest in the Middle East were rooted more in strategy and ideology: in its 'southern belt', the Kremlin's aim was simultaneously to favour the nationalist movement – which Lenin, in his time, had already pinpointed as a revolutionary factor – and to isolate, or at least sideline, the Western powers, which tended to respond in kind. In preceding centuries, the repeated hostilities between Russians and Turks were explained largely by the issue of Russian access to 'warm seas'. Subsequently the question came to be posed in terms of 'zones of influence', and the influence sought by the USSR was principally of a geopolitical character. Whenever conflict arose between some more or less 'anti-imperialist' government and the communist party of any given country, Moscow always tended to prioritise inter-state relations, to the detriment of 'proletarian internationalism'.

However, in the early days it was the spirit of internationalism that led the leaders of the emergent Soviet Russia to publish and denounce the **Sykes–Picot Agreement**. Thanks to minister Sergei Sazonov, who was associated with the negotiations preparing for the dismantling of the **Ottoman Empire**, the Tsar had succeeded in grabbing a sizeable slice of the cake. The northeast part of the Ottoman Empire was assigned to Russia, comprising Constantinople, the western shore of the Bosporus, the Sea of Marmara, the Dardanelles and part of the Asia Minor shore of the Black Sea. In the name of peoples' rights to self-determination, the Soviet communists abandoned all these claims. In fact, in a move designed to show their opposition to 'secret diplomacy', they made these arrange-ments public, along with other arrangements involving the major powers – thereby revealing things that had thus far been carefully hidden from the warring populations. This testimony of its commitment to the struggle against 'imperial plunder' was to win the USSR considerable prestige among the Arab nationalist movements that were developing in that period.

Building on this prestige, the (Bolshevik) Communist Party of the Soviet Union embarked on a twin project in the wake of the World War I. It created closer links with the Arab nationalist movement – with the aid of the Communist International, it assisted in the setting up of communist 'circles', or even parties, notably in Egypt, Syria–**Lebanon** and above all in Palestine. This Middle Eastern initiative was first put forward at the Baku Congress in September 1920. On a parallel track, the USSR also made efforts at closer contacts with the existing regimes, despite the double handicap represented by their relative 'control' by **Britain** and their '**Islamism**', which had little enthusiasm for dealing with an 'atheist' country. In both instances the principal objective was to strike the strongest possible blows against the principal enemy – London.

This was also the motivation which led, post-World War II, to Moscow's acceptance of the **Partition Plan** for Palestine. Andrei Gromyko declared before the UN on 14 May 1947 that 'the interests of both the **Jews** and **Arabs** of Palestine can only be protected as required by the creation of a demo-cratic, independent Judeo–Arab state which is double but homogeneous'. However, he continued, 'because of the increasingly tense relations between Jews and Arabs,' the partition of the country into two independent states was necessary. The USSR was to go even further. Not only was it one of the first countries in the world to recognise the state of **Israel**, but it also supplied it – via Czechoslovakia – with the weapons which enabled it to overcome the Arab armies which entered Palestine on 15 May 1948. For one or two years, relations between Israel and the USSR were excellent. But the Stalinist leadership of that period feared the influence of **Zionism** on Soviet Jews. In September 1948, Israel's ambassador to Moscow, Golda Meierson (later to become Golda Meir), received a massive and enthusiastic welcome at the Moscow synagogue. This was promptly followed by reprisals against Soviet Jews, in the form of a wave of antisemitism the like of which had not been seen since before the Revolution. A further downturn followed in 1949, which saw the beginning in Hungary of a series of trials which were to take place in the 'people's democracies' and in which anti-Zionism – in fact antisemitism pure and simple – was to emerge in all its brutality. **Jerusalem**, for its part, was flirting increasingly openly with Washington (see **1956 War**). In 1953, relations between Israel and the Soviet Union were broken off. Although they were re-established in the same year, after the death of Stalin and the denunciation of the affair of the 'white shirts' (Jewish physicians accused of attempting to kill Stalin), they would never again have the warmth of the early days.

After 1955, it was natural for the USSR to reverse its alliances and provide support for the Arab national movement and for countries which took up the cause – against Western imperialism (essentially the imperialism of the **US**, which had taken over from Britain and **France** in the region), and against Israel, which was viewed as imperialism's 'conduit' into the Middle East. Thus in the name of anti-imperialism and anti-Zionism Moscow opened its arms to the **Arab world,** and the Arabs found themselves driven into them by the attitude of the West – namely support for Israel, refusal to help the Arab countries (including militarily), obduracy in the face of their economic and political demands and determined attempts to sign them up into anti-Soviet military agreements.

With the September 1955 arms contract signed between Czechoslovakia and Egypt, there began two decades of 'success' for the USSR, which renounced the last remaining commercial agreement linking it to Israel. Gradually Egypt, followed by Syria, then **Iraq**, and subsequently South **Yemen**, turned more towards the Soviet Union. Substantive alliances were formed, involving co-operation in many fields (economic, social, cultural and, obviously, military). But success turned equally rapidly into failure. By the mid-1970s only South Yemen, Iraq (formally) and Syria remained tied to Moscow by treaty, and Cairo had gone quite the other way, having been seduced by the West. Soviet isolation in the Middle East seemed so extreme by the end of Israel's invasion of Lebanon in 1982 that many observers concluded that the USSR was now effectively excluded from the region.

Paradoxically, the Soviet Union's setback was due in no small measure to its success: Soviet aid had contributed greatly to the Arab national movement's accomplishment of its basic mission – the ending of the colonial presence and the winning of **independence** – and in so doing it had lost a large part of its *raison d'être*. At the same time Moscow did not allow its Arab allies to force Israel into respect for their rights and for those of the **Palestinians**. Finally, the 'Soviet model' of economic development (which, when exported, often became a caricature of itself) may have contributed to social progress, but it was not up to the level of popular expectations. The system's lack of adaptiveness, the absence of basic democratic reforms, the growing weight of the bureaucratic bourgeoisie and the weakness of the democratic movement were to lead, in the mid-1970s, to an opening up – *infitah* in Arabic – to the West. 'The United States,' as **Anwar al-Sadat** was inclined to say, 'holds 99 per cent of the cards' for resolving the Arab–Israeli conflict.

Taking advantage of America's lack of possibilities following the **1982 War** in Lebanon, Moscow was relatively successful in returning to the region, diversifying its alliances and opening new relations with **Saudi Arabia**, the Gulf emirates and Egypt. Strengthened by its progress in the Arab world, after Mikhail Gorbachev's accession to power Soviet diplomacy came to focus increasingly on the question of Israel. The 'secret' Paris meeting of July 1985 between ambassadors of the two countries soon translated into concrete action, ranging from an exchange of consular delegations in 1987–88, through to the establishment of diplomatic relations in 1991, and the green light increasingly given to the emigration of Soviet Jews to Israel – involving upwards of 900,000 people in the period from 1986 to 2002.

But Moscow's renewed presence in the Middle East did not survive the consequences of the systemic collapse of the USSR itself. Already during the **Gulf War** the USSR had given the impression of lining up behind the US: while applying pressure on **Saddam Hussein** in an attempt to avoid the worst, Soviet diplomacy never stepped outside the framework laid down by George Bush Senior and Mikhail Gorbachev at the Helsinki summit on 9 September 1990. Western aid was too crucial for the USSR to risk threatening it by expressing major differences, although a concern for the domestic and external security situation of the Islamic republics inclined them to prudence. This appears to explain the rapid decline of the Soviet Union's standing in the Arab world. A number of Arab voices were heard rejoicing – both noisily and prematurely – at the Moscow coup d'état of 19 August 1991. Yevgeni Primakov, Mikhail Gorbachev's special envoy, admitted that

> all our activity towards a settlement of the Kuwait crisis, by means of secret missions to Baghdad, was designed in order not to prejudice in any way the US and the Coalition as a whole at the moment when they were making major political, economic and military efforts in order to force Iraq to withdraw from Kuwait.

Not doing anything to upset the US: this was to be the basic tenet of post-Soviet Russia's foreign policy, at least during the first years of Boris Yeltsin's presidency. In the Middle East in particular, Andrei Rozyrev, Russia's Minister for Foreign Affairs, maintained a low profile. In relation to Baghdad, which had for long been one of the USSR's principal clients in the region, Russia limited itself to tentatively suggesting a relaxation of the UN **sanctions**, of which the principal victims were the Iraqi people. As co-president of the Madrid Conference, Moscow allowed the Americans to set out the basic framework of the Arab–Israeli peace process in line with US interests. It was symbolic that Russia's President was absent on 13 September 1993 for the Washington signature of the Declaration of Principles on Palestinian **autonomy**.

However, in the mid-1990s Russia's redefined foreign-policy objectives, which had been slowly emerging during the previous year in terms more suited to its position as a major world power, involved a radicalisation and a more marked distancing from Washington. As the *Washington Post* put it, 'the honeymoon is over'. From now on, in all sectors of policy, Moscow attempted to establish its difference. In fact on all issues, particularly on the Middle East, Washington tried to highlight its differences. Profiting from the growing anti-Americanism in the Gulf and freed from the ideological constraints which had previously conditioned its alliances, Russia was able to extend its contacts with all countries in the region, from Egypt to Saudi Arabia, and including Israel, where the hundreds of thousands of Russian immigrants originating from the former Soviet Union served as a bridge with the mother country.

It was on the question of **Iran** that Moscow chose most openly to challenge Washington. Already in the early 1990s the Americans had taken an extremely dim view of Russia's decision to supply dozens of MiG, Ilyushin and other SAM missile weapons to Tehran. When Russia announced its intention to deliver civil nuclear reactors to Iran, this proved too much. Claiming that the Islamic Republic was working towards the construction of a nuclear bomb, President Bill Clinton demanded that President Boris Yeltsin withdraw this project. Nothing would prevail on him, not even the blackmail exerted on the occasion of the two Russian–American summits. Citing the approval of the International Atomic Energy Agency (IAEA), and pointing out that the US was about to deliver the same kind of reactors to North Korea, Moscow went ahead and honoured the contract. The pursuit of these privileged relations – for example at the end of November 2000 Moscow lifted the moratorium on arms deliveries to Tehran – clearly disturbed Washington, particularly after the attacks of 11 September 2001 and President George W. Bush's crusade against the 'axis of evil', one of whose three pivots is none other than Iran.

Another area of friction with the US has been Iraq. Long Moscow's priority ally in the region, Baghdad continued to be the object of Russia's attentions. In February 1998, mediation by Vladimir Pasuvalyuk, Deputy Minister of Foreign Affairs in charge of Middle Eastern issues, saved Iraq from a US intervention. But this was a respite of only a few months: in December 1998, Washington and London were to conduct new bombing raids. Moscow, and also Paris, opposed them, particularly because Russia, which has 17 million practising Muslims, was fearful of the domestic repercussions of eventual operations in the Gulf. Russia voted in favour of **UN Security Council Resolution** 1441 in November 2002, which gave Iraq one final opportunity to disarm, but remained firmly opposed to the US-led war which brought down the regime of Saddam Hussein in March and April 2003.

On its frontiers, Moscow found itself in something of a trial of strength with Ankara, involving the use of both force and finesse to safeguard its interests. For a while Russia was threatened by Turkish designs on the Caucasus and the ex-Soviet republics of Central Asia, but with the passing of the years the Kremlin has succeeded in regaining ground in the name of *realpolitik*. It has managed to persuade both its former subjects and the heirs of the Ottomans that creating solid economic and political relations with Russia was worth more than vague notions of regional alignments. Despite the mobilisation of millions of citizens of Caucasian origin, Ankara will be extremely circumspect about supporting the Chechen 'rebels'. The most important question still remains to be settled: the route of the oil pipe-line planned to carry to the Mediterranean the massive oil wealth discovered in Azerbaijan – oil experts are seeing the Caspian as a new Gulf. On this crucially important point Moscow lost: in 1999 it was decided that the pipeline would not pass through Russian territory, but would go from Baku to the Turkish port of Ceyhan.

As regards relations between Israel and the Palestinians, Moscow is ob-viously having more difficulty in resuming its place in what, in the absence of Russia and the EU, has become an all-American show. With Vladimir Putin's arrival in power, Russia, given its limited options, confined itself to being one of the 'Quartet' on the Middle East (US–UN–EU–Russia). It was the Quartet which formulated the 'Road Map' for peace, released by Bush on 30 April 2003.

However, on the Israeli–Palestinian issue, as on the question of Iraq, the big puzzle for Russia relates to the complex nature of its relations with Washington. These took a notable turn in September 2001 when Putin im-mediately presented himself as a faithful ally of the US. There was a degree of quick thinking in this calculation. On the one hand it took account of the real state of the balance of power: Moscow, which had claimed military parity with the US at the time of Leonid Brezhnev and his successors, knew by now US superiority was overwhelming, and that its defence budget was only a tenth of that of its ex-rival. On the other hand, Russia, in order to carry through reforms and once again become a major modern state, badly needed reliable financial aid from the US and from the international financial institutions which are very much under the control of the US. However, it would be wrong to deduce from this change of direction that the Kremlin's number one has given up pursuing an independent policy that would defend what he considers to be the interests of his country, even if he avoids direct confrontation with the US. This could be seen, for example, in his use of 'anti-**terrorism**' as the justification for pursuing (with the complicity of the West) his 'dirty war' in Chechnya; or his pursuit of co-operation with Iran in arms supply and civilian nuclear energy; his refusal to join the US-led war in Iraq or, more importantly in the long term, his operation geared to making Russia America's principal oil supplier, which registered an initial success at the summit of October 2002.

SABRA AND SHATILA

Even before the end of the Palestine **1948–49 War**, refugee camps were created in **Lebanon**: some in the south of the country, others on the outskirts of Beirut. Sabra and Shatila were among the latter. Subjected to constant harassment by the Lebanese army, finding themselves forbidden all political or social activity, the **Palestinians** of the camps only began to achieve autonomy in the late 1960s with the increase in strength of the *fedayeen*. At the beginning of the 1980s the inhabitants of Shatila were estimated at 25,000, those of Sabra at 12,000.

On 2 September 1982, the last Palestinian fighters left Beirut. Bashir Gemayel, leader of the Lebanese Forces and an ally of **Israel**, was elected head of state. The departure of the Multinational Force (from the **US**, **France** and Italy), which had supervised the evacuation of the **Palestine Liberation Organisation (PLO)**, was completed on 14 September. The same day, a charge of 50kg of TNT destroyed the building containing the not yet inaugurated President Gemayel, who died in the incident. During the night of 14 September, the Israeli Defence Forces (IDF) surrounded East Beirut in violation of the commitments made to the PLO by the American envoy, Philip Habib. At 5pm on 16 September, at the instigation of the IDF, Lebanese forces belonging to right-wing militias entered the camps of Sabra and Shatila to 'exterminate terrorists'. On the morning of 17 September, Israeli soldiers, who had surrounded the camps, stood back while a massacre of civilians took place. It was to continue until the morning of the eighteenth. The toll: 800 dead, according to the Israeli commission of inquiry presided over by Judge Kahane; 1500, according to the PLO.

When the facts became known, emotions ran high around the world and in Israel. Though **Menachem Begin** denounced 'the bloodthirsty plot being hatched against Israel and its government' and refused any idea of an inquiry, on 25 September 400,000 demonstrators put the opposite viewpoint in Tel Aviv. They won their case, and on 28 September the Kahane Commission was set up to establish the truth of events.

The Commission's conclusions threw light on part of the development of the operation and relieved Begin of 'a certain degree of responsibility'. The report advocated the dismissal of Defence Minister **Ariel Sharon**, saying that he had 'responsibility for not having ordered adequate measures to be taken to prevent eventual massacres', and implicated several military leaders, including Raphael Eitan, the Chief of Staff. Despite the searching of consciences in Israel, the system effortlessly absorbed the revelations of the report, which had never examined the crux of the problem, namely the invasion of Lebanon, the IDF's entry into East Beirut and the alliance with the Lebanese Forces (which the Israeli newspaper *Yediot Aharonot* described as 'organised riff-raff'). If Begin ended by taking a back seat, Sharon remained a powerful minister, even under the National Unity governments. As for Raphael Eitan, he returned to politics and founded the far-right party Tsomet, which he represented in the Knesset. In 1996 he allied himself with Likud to bring to power **Benyamin Netanyahu**, who gave him the portfolio of agriculture and the environment. As for Sharon, he made a comeback at the head of a 'super-ministry' for infrastructure designed especially for him, which made it possible for him to resume the **settlement** of the Occupied Territories.

Twenty years later we have more information on the Sabra and Shatila massacres, as published in an article by Pierre Péan for *Le Monde diplomatique*.

> Israeli newspapers have published a number of articles confirming and rein-forcing those conclusions, in particular in 1994. Relying on official documents, Amir Oren wrote in *Davar* in July 1994 that the massacres were part of a plan decided upon between Sharon and Gemayel. They used the Israeli secret services, headed by Abraham Shalom, who was ordered to exterminate all terrorists. The Lebanese militiamen were simply agents in the chain of com-mand that led, via the secret services, to the Israeli authorities.
>
> The BBC's *Panorama* programme, 'The Accused', broadcast in June 2001, further illuminated the events, particularly the evidence of Morris Draper, Habib's assistant, which is hardly open to challenge. Reminded of Sharon's claims that he could not predict what was to happen in the camps, Draper commented that it was 'complete and utter nonsense'. He told of a meeting at the Ministry of Defence in Tel Aviv with Sharon and Arnos Yaron, his chief of staff, on the day when the Israelis had already entered West Beirut, despite their undertaking. Yaron justified that decision, citing the desire to prevent the Phalangists from turning on the Palestinians after the assassination of Gemayel. Draper said: 'The whole group of maybe 20 of us altogether fell silent. It was a dramatic moment.' He explained that the US had rejected the Israeli proposal to deploy the Phalangists in West Beirut 'because we knew it would be a massacre'. He added: 'There is no doubt whatsoever that Ariel Sharon was responsible. Well, more Israelis have to share in that responsibility.'

However, despite this responsibility, Sharon was elected premier of Israel in February 2001. But this was not the end of the story as regards the Sabra and Shatila massacres. Four months after his election he was accused on a charge of war crimes and **genocide** brought by 23 survivors in Brussels, on the basis of the Belgian law of 'universal competence'. But a year later the Belgian appeal court declared the application non-viable, dashing the plaintiffs' hopes. In the meantime, in January, a few days before his arrival in Brussels, Elie Hobeika, one of the main movers and presumed perpe-trator of the massacres, was killed in Beirut. His involvement had not prevented him becoming minister. The Lebanese judiciary was also the focus of charges arising out of the massacres, but the amnesty law in that country made any follow-up impossible. Similar obstacles still prevent the families of the victims from knowing the whole truth of what happened in the massacres and the identities of their various perpetrators, who were Lebanese and Israeli, but also American, French and Italian.

SADAT, ANWAR AL-

Born on 25 December 1918 in Lower **Egypt** into a peasant family of modest means, Sadat entered the Military Academy and graduated as an officer in 1938. In the first garrison town to which he was posted he met **Gamal Abdel Nasser** and some of those who were to become the Free Officers. A fervent nationalist, he saw in Nazi Germany a possible ally against the British occupation, and was arrested in October 1942 as a spy for the Axis powers. In contact with the **Muslim Brotherhood**, with whom he was to maintain close links for over ten years, he was implicated in a **terrorist** attack and spent three years in prison. Dismissed from the army in 1948, reinstated in 1950, he took part in the 1952 coup d'état that overthrew King Faruq.

During the Nasserist period, Sadat held a series of important posts: Secretary-General of the National Union (the sole party, which did not play a major role) in 1957, President of the National Assembly from 1960 to 1968, Vice-President of the republic in 1964, then again in December 1969. However, he remained an unobtrusive figure, seemingly little disposed to assume the mantle of 'rais' (president) after Nasser's death on 28 September 1970.

However, elected as the new President on 15 October 1970, Sadat ousted all his rivals and imposed a new direction on Egyptian policies. In May 1971 he eliminated Ali Sabri and the regime's pro-Soviet wing. The same year saw the beginning of the economic liberalisation that would culminate after October 1973 in the *infitah*. In July 1972 he expelled the 15,000 Soviet military advisors and initiated a rapprochement with the **US**. This change of direction was only possible because Sadat could depend on what was called the new class – middle-class bureaucrats, newly rich peasants, profiteers – which had emerged under Nasser (albeit with some difficulty) and which hoped to throw off the 'socialist yoke'. This change of direction came up against strong opposition, particularly from students and workers, and the diplomatic deadlock that, despite everything, left Cairo dependent on Moscow. On 6 October 1973, Sadat launched the fourth Arab–Israeli conflict with clearly defined aims: to get the US to unblock negotiations in the Middle East (see **1973 War**). After the ceasefire on 7 November 1973, the Egyptian President re-established diplomatic relations with Washington and undertook the 'one step at a time' policy so dear to US Secretary of State Henry Kissinger. The prestige he gained from the crossing of the **Suez**

Canal allowed the President to speed up his *infitah* policy, and in 1976 to liquidate the single-party system and establish a system of 'limited democracy', with several parties. The National Democratic Party, the official organisation, maintained its control of the state machinery.

But partial Israeli withdrawals from the Sinai were not peace, and Egypt was still at war. Its economic situation was deteriorating, and when, in January 1977, Sadat raised the price of basic necessities on the advice of the IMF, massive riots shook Cairo and most Egyptian towns. Sadat then decided on his other historic initiative: he went to **Jerusalem** in November and began the proceedings that would lead to the **Camp David Accords** and the Egyptian–Israeli separate peace. Although isolated from the rest of the **Arab world** – most countries broke off diplomatic relations with Cairo and the **Arab League** transferred its headquarters to Tunis – he maintained his policy, counting on the support of the Egyptian people exhausted by an interminable war and hoping that peace would bring an end to the economic crisis. Concurrently, he launched a major campaign against 'Soviet plots' in the Third World.

Despite massive economic aid from the US – up from $371m in 1973 to $1.135bn in 1981 – the social situation worsened, aggravated by the Arab boycott. It was all the more intolerable for the common people in that the *nouveaux riches*, the profiteers of the *infitah*, were flaunting their wealth. The deadlock in negotiations on Palestinian **autonomy** vindicated those who had predicted that the Camp David Accords were nothing more than a separate peace. The political opposition, although victimised and repressed, managed to make its voices heard. Finally, the upsurge of Muslim groups, which Sadat had greatly encouraged by granting amnesty to the leaders of the Muslim Brotherhood, by allowing them considerable freedom of expression, and by using them in his struggle against the left, but who rejected his alliance with **Israel**, led to sectarian problems of extreme gravity between Muslims and Copts. The President then staked his all in September 1981 by arresting 1500 opponents of all political shades: Muslims and liberals, nationalists and communists. He even dismissed the Coptic Pope, Shenuda III. A few days later, on 6 October, during a parade celebrating the victory of 1973, an armed squad of four men belonging to a Muslim group assassinated him.

His funeral was greeted with total indifference by the Egyptian people, an indifference in marked contrast to the place the Western media were to accord the death of the man of the Camp David Accords.

SANCTIONS

In looking at the imposition of sanctions on individual countries, a distinction needs to be made between unilateral measures and decisions taken by the UN. Article 41 of the UN Charter stipulates that

> The Security Council may decide what measures not involving the use of armed force are to be employed to give effect to its decisions, and it may call upon the Members of the UN to apply such measures. These may include complete or partial interruption of economic relations and of rail, sea, air, postal, telegraphic, radio, and other means of communication, and the severance of diplomatic relations.

Article 44 further provides, in the event that one of its members resorts to war, for the breaking of all relations with that country. UN Security Council decisions are binding on all members of the organisation.

During its history, the UN has several times taken recourse to sanctions: in 1966 against Southern Rhodesia; in 1977 against South Africa; in 1991 an embargo on arms for Yugoslavia, and then, in 1992, against Serbia, Montenegro etc. But sanctions have been applied most frequently against countries in the Middle East.

First against **Iraq**: on 6 August 1990 **UN Security Council Resolution** 661 imposed a trade embargo on Iraq and set up a sanctions committee. Once **Kuwait** had been evacuated by Baghdad, the UN should have lifted the sanctions. But then, through Resolution 687, they set a new objective: the elimination of Iraq's **weapons of mass destruction**. The continuation of these measures, well after the end of the **Gulf War**, had disastrous effects on the population, and according to some reports led to the deaths of hundreds of thousands of people and a deterioration in the country's education system. On 14 April 1995, Resolution 986 relaxed the embargo somewhat, setting in place the 'oil for food' programme, which allowed Iraq limited exports of oil (the ceiling was later raised) in order to buy food and medicine. Baghdad was able to resume its production of oil, but not to rebuild its infrastructure or develop its economy. The improvement in its humanitarian situation was extremely slow.

In March 1999, a commission appointed by the UN Security Council reported that in radical contrast to the pre-1990 situation, rates of infant mortality in Iraq were among the highest in the world, with 23 per cent of children being born underweight and malnutrition affecting four out of every five children. Only 41 per cent of the population had regular access to drinking **water**, and 83 per cent of schools were in need of repair. On 17 April 2000 UN Secretary-General Kofi Annan stated that the balance of the 'decade of sanctions' had raised serious doubts, not only on their effectiveness but also on their extent and severity, when innocent civilians often became victims not only of their own government but also of the actions of the international community. When vigorous and global economic sanctions are directed against authoritarian regimes, he suggested, then, tragically, it is generally the people who suffer, and not the political elites whose behaviour launched the sanctions in the first place. There is no doubt that the imposition of sanctions accelerated the collapse of the Iraqi state in 2003.

Another country affected by sanctions was **Libya**, which had allegedly been involved in the bombings of Pan Am Flight 103, otherwise known as the Lockerbie bombing (21 December 1988) and the bombing of UTA DC10 flight over Niger on 19 September 1989. In order to obtain the extradition of the Libyans responsible, Resolution 748 (1992) imposed an embargo on air traffic and the sale of arms; Resolution 883 (1993) reinforced the sanctions, froze Libya's overseas assets and banned the supply of oil equipment to the country. But once Tripoli had handed over two of its agents to the Scottish judicial authorities in 1999 (see **Qadhaffi, Muammar**), the UN suspended sanctions the same year. For its part, the **US** has continued to maintain its own unilateral sanctions. Following a multi-billion-dollar compensation deal with the families of the victims of the attacks, the UN Security Council finally lifted sanctions against Tripoli in September 2003.

Sudan was also subjected to an embargo on 26 April 1996, following a complaint by **Egypt** against Khartoum, which was accused of harbouring the people responsible for an assassination attempt against President **Hosni Mubarak** on 26 June 1995. Resolution 1054 mainly involved reductions of diplomatic personnel. On 16 August 1996, UN Security Council Resolution 1070 ordered an air-traffic embargo on Sudan Airways if the authorities did not give up the alleged culprits within three months. The abstention of **Russia** and China on this resolution illustrated the growing unease of the international community in the face of such an intensive use of sanctions – which has affected mainly Muslim countries. An additional source of concern is the fact that once sanctions have been imposed all it takes is an American veto for them to be prolonged indefinitely (as was the case with Iraq). This has intensified the unease, already running high because of Washington's unilateral recourse to embargo as a means of settling international differences. On 28 September 2001 the UN Security Council eventually lifted the sanctions against Sudan – with the US abstaining – as a way of thanking it for having ratified the international treaties against **terrorism** and for having complied with the Council's demand for the extradition of three suspects in the attempted assassination of the Egyptian President.

Since the end of World War II, on various occasions various countries have taken measures of retaliation or intimidation against other countries, outside of the framework of the UN. In 1951, the US and **Britain** imposed sanctions on **Iran**, in response to its nationalisation of the oil industry. In

1967, **France** imposed an embargo on its arms sales to the Middle East, a move which mostly affected **Israel**.

But it was after the Gulf War that Washington increased its resort to these kinds of measures in the Middle East, first against Libya and then against Iran. There was a new escalation in the US, with President Bill Clinton's signature of the D'Amato Act on 5 August 1996. In the same spirit as the Helms-Burton law directed against Cuba, it laid down measures against non-American companies which invested more than $40m in either Libya's or Iran's oil sector. This aroused strong international protests, particularly from Europe. Several Arab government even pointed out that Washington was thereby adopting 'secondary boycott' measures, the kinds of measures that were denounced when they were taken by Arab countries against Israel.

SARTAWI, ISSAM

Born in 1934 in the Palestinian town of Acre, Issam Sartawi and his family sought refuge in **Iraq** in 1948 as a result of the **1948–49 War**. He completed his medical studies there in 1960, and then went to the **US**, where he became one of the country's most distinguished cardiovascular specialists. On the declaration of the Six Day **1967 War**, he decided to leave the US, and devote himself to his people. On 10 January 1967, he arrived in the Middle East, where he joined the ranks of Fatah. However, as a convinced Nasserist and pan-Arabist he could not accept the organisation's regionalist theories, and in the autumn of 1968 created his own Action Organisation for the Liberation of Palestine.

After the expulsion of the **Palestine Liberation Organisation (PLO)** from **Jordan** in 1970–71, Sartawi dissolved his group and rejoined Fatah. In 1976 he was appointed by **Yasser Arafat** himself to undertake an important mission: to meet with representatives of the **Zionist** left. What were later called the Paris talks began in July 1976. On the one side Sartawi and Sabri Jirys, a Palestinian intellectual who had lived in **Israel** for a long time; on the other, General Matityahu Peled, Arie (Lova) Eliav, former Secretary-General of the Labour party, Meir Pail (member of the Knesset), Uri Avnery and Jacob Arnon. Serving as intermediary was **Henri Curiel**.

These conversations, which continued into the spring of 1977, were to have far-reaching effects. For **Palestinians** they marked one more step towards the recognition of the existence of Israel. For the Israelis they confirmed, and strengthened, the existence, alongside the Communist Party, of a Zionist peace camp ready to accept the PLO. But the limitations were equally obvious. The Israeli delegation had no official status (even though Prime Minister **Yitzhak Rabin** had been kept informed of the proceedings). And though the Palestinian group had Arafat's backing, the latter was unwilling (or rather unable, given the balance of power within the PLO) to make the matter public.

After **Menachem Begin** came to power in 1977, the contacts were maintained, thanks to Sartawi, despite violent attacks from the Rejectionist Front and the denunciations of Likud. Talks were reopened after the Palestinian departure from Beirut, and in January 1983, for the first time, Arafat met with a delegation composed of Peled, Avnery and Arnon. Some months later, Sartawi was to pay for his political courage with his life. On 10 April 1983, during the congress of the Socialist International (with whom he maintained contacts on behalf of the PLO), he was assassinated by **Abu Nidal**'s men.

SAUD DYNASTY

It is no accident that **Saudi Arabia** carries the name of its ruling family: since it came into being the country has been treated by the Saud dynasty as its private property. It was not until 1953, on the eve of his death, that King Abdul Aziz Ibn Saud accepted the creation of a Council of Ministers, which met for the first time on 7 March 1954. The state, in the Western sense of the term, has an ill-defined existence and real power rests with the al-Saud family – 10,000 princes and princesses – supported by the *ulama*, of whom the most prestigious come from the al-Sheikh family, the descendants of the founder of Wahhabism, Muhammad Ibn Abdul Wahhab.

The royal family plays an important role, and may even depose the king, as witnessed in 1964 in the case of Saud, the successor to Abdul Aziz. It has also had radical elements in the 1960s, when an organisation of Free Princes was created – a reference to the Free Officers who took power in Cairo in 1952 and rallied around **Nasser**.

The family is divided into clans, following the line of the three wives of Abdul Aziz Ibn Saud: the Sudairis, the Shammar (one of the most important tribal groups in northern Nejd) and the Jilouwi. The Sudairis (the strongest at the start of the 1990s) are the clan of the King and his brothers – notably Prince Sultan, the Minister of Defence, Prince Salman, the Governor of Riyadh, and Prince Nayef, the Minister of the Interior. The Shammar is the clan of the Crown Prince Abdullah, the King's half-brother and Commander of the National Guard. The Jilouwi clan counted King Khalid as a member, who was succeeded by Fahd in 1982.

At the end of 1995, the King's sickness resulted in Prince Abdullah bin Abdul Aziz effectively becoming regent. Although Abdullah's reputation as an 'Arab nationalist' is rather overstated – the National Guard was modernised by the **US**, and is still trained by numbers of American advisors – he has nonetheless distanced himself from Washington and established solid relationships with **Syria**. He has also set himself up as a mediator in the Israeli–Palestinian conflict, by getting the March 2002 Arab Summit in Beirut to adopt a proposed peace plan with **Israel**.

Abdullah has shown particular concern over the economic difficulties of his kingdom and the aspirations of the new middle classes. He has encouraged a growing freedom of the press, which now feels free to discuss societal problems – unemployment, drugs, the position of women etc. He paid a visit to the poorer areas of Riyadh in November 2002, thus officially recognising for the first time the existence of urban poverty. He is seen as a proponent of austerity, and tries to limit expenditure, and also corruption. He has also called on the clergy to defend a moderate reading of **Islam**. He is regarded with hostility by the King's brothers, notably Prince Sultan, the powerful Minister of Defence and number three in the succession.

The Crown Prince preaches liberalisation of the economy and membership of the World Trade Organisation. One major reform might be the opening up of the gas sector – negotiations have been started to allow foreign companies to invest in the gas industry in exchange for investment in the kingdom's infrastructures. But the negotiations have been dragging on.

Given that, like the King and Prince Sultan, he is around 80 years old, Abdullah must also take into account the aspirations of the new generation of princes, the grandsons of Ibn Saud, whose path to the throne was opened by the Basic Law adopted on 1 March 1992. This third generation is symbolised by Prince Bandar bin Sultan, son of the Minister of Defence and presently Saudi ambassador to Washington. An 'Americanized Bedouin' in the words of the transatlantic press, he is the prototype of the emirs educated in the best American universities, but more detached than their parents from their roots and from the aspirations of their people. The princes occupy major military positions and important Ministries, with the exception of the Ministries of Justice and Education, which go to the al-Sheikh family, along with the post of supreme Qadi, the chief judge, who delivers *fatwas* or juridical opinions.

The Saud dynasty now faces the most serious challenge since the Nasserist push of the 1960s. How is it to combine modernisation of society with respect for traditional values within a regional framework that has been rendered unstable by the aftermath of the Iraqi crisis at a time when the alliance with the US has become profoundly troubled?

SAUDI ARABIA

In 1744, Muhammad Ibn Saud, a local emir from the Nejd area of the **Arabian Peninsula**, signed a pact with a religious reformer to bring about, 'through force of arms if necessary, the reign of the word of God' (Henri

Laoust). Muhammad Ibn Abdul Wahhab had begun his preaching some years earlier. He aimed to restore Sunni **Islam** in its original purity at a time when the crumbling of the **Ottoman Empire** was accelerating and **Shi'ism** was gaining strength (in Persia and **Iraq**). He rejected all non-Sunni sects, condemning dangerous innovations and the worship of saints. His doctrine, Wahhabism, came to form the ideological basis for all the al-Saud family's attempts at constructing a state characterised by an alliance of the sword and the Qur'an.

The first Wahhabi state, which stretched as far as Iraq, was dismantled by Muhammad Ali, the Sultan of **Egypt**, in 1818. The second, less ambitious, ended in 1884. The third attempt succeeded. In 1901, Abdul Aziz (who was to become known under the name of Ibn Saud) conquered the oasis of Riyadh before taking control of the entire Nejd region and then al-Hasa in the east. After World War I he attacked his rival, Hussein, the Sherif of Mecca. The remainder of the Hejaz, including the two holy cities of Islam, Mecca and Medina, was won between 1924 and 1926. In 1932, Abdul Aziz assumed the title of King of Saudi Arabia, to which, after a war with **Yemen**, he added the province of Asir.

During the same period, the discovery of **oil** and the creation of the Saudi Arabian Oil Company (Saudi Aramco) changed the face of the new kingdom. These two facts secured for the Wahhabi state, which was floating on a veritable sea of oil (a quarter of the world's reserves), a substantial income and strengthened its alliance with the **US**, whose oil companies controlled Aramco (it was not until September 1980 that Saudi Arabia was able to assume complete control of its oil). A meeting between President Franklin D. Roosevelt and Abdul Aziz in 1945 consolidated the Washington–Riyadh axis, which was strengthened during the **Gulf War**, but was then shaken by the attacks of 11 September 2001.

On the King's death in 1953, Saudi Arabia experienced a period of instability, marked by strikes in the oil industry, clashes with the revolutionary Arab nationalist movement and power struggles within the reigning royal family that ended with the coronation of Faisal on 2 November 1964. The coup d'état that brought to an end the absolutist regime of Imam Ahmad Ben Yahya in North Yemen in 1962 and the intervention of **Nasser**'s Egyptian troops on the republican side dragged Saudi Arabia into a long conflict on its borders that would not be resolved until after **1967 War**.

With the weakening of the revolutionary nationalism that followed the war of 1967 and the defeat of Nasser, the Wahhabi kingdom's role in regional and international affairs grew more important. It possessed two trump cards: Islam and oil. After the October **1973 War**, oil receipts reached a level that enabled the kingdom – the third most important producer of oil in the world after **Russia** and the US – to embark on an ambitious development plan, to purchase ultra-modern armaments (almost 20 per cent of gross national income is spent on arms, by contrast, for example, with 4 per cent in **France**), while the investment of huge sums abroad has meant that, to all intents and purposes, the royal family has become an integral part of Western capitalism. Such wealth has allowed Saudi Arabia to 'buy' the security of the kingdom by financing **Syria** and, before the Gulf War, Iraq, the **Palestine Liberation Organisation (PLO)** and Fatah.

Islam is the second jewel in the dynasty's crown. In 1987, at the height of the **Iran–Iraq War**, King Fahd – who succeeded to the throne on 13 June 1982 – assumed the title of 'Servant of the Two Holy Places, Mecca and Medina'. The keys to Mecca and Medina afford the royal family unparalleled prestige. The *hajj* (or pilgrimage) is one of the five fundamental obligations of Islam that every Muslim must accomplish at least once in their life. In 1946, 60,000 foreign pilgrims fulfilled this rite; by 2002 they numbered more than 1.5 million. Jeddah is also the headquarters of the Organisation of the Islamic Conference, which has 40 member states. Finally, the World Islamic League, established in 1965, represents a forum of various Muslim communities, and also finances religious and preaching activities. This role as an 'Islamic power' goes together with proclamations that the Saudis will defend Palestine, and **Jerusalem** in particular, the third sacred city of Islam. However, the occupation of the Great Mosque of Mecca in 1979 and the bloody skirmishes and accidents that followed struck a blow against the prestige of the dynasty.

Without the alliance between the al-Saud family and the religious hierarchy – most of whom came from the al-Sheikh family, descendants of the founder of Wahhabism – King Fahd would not be able to maintain the stability of his reign. As the guardians of religious law – they opposed the education of women until 1960 – the *ulama* see that the King's decisions conform to religious law, and also serve to legitimise his power. It is for this reason that that in August 1990 they pronounced a *fatwa* approving the decision to ask for American help in August 1990. They are in charge of the feared *mutawwa'*, the religious police who 'enjoin good and forbid evil', forcing shops to close at the hour of prayer, hunting down people who drink alcohol or women who do not respect 'decency'. The *shari'a*, religious law, is strictly enforced, and amputations, public floggings and executions are commonplace. The development of Islamic universities, producing thousands of theology students into the labour market, the war in Afghanistan, and also a particular brand of religious teaching, fostered within the population the development of a radical current close to the positions of **Osama bin Laden**.

However, parallel to this ultra-conservatism, and as a result of its oil resources, the country underwent important changes. In 1970, a quarter of its inhabitants lived in towns; 30 years later the figure was more than 80 per cent. Infant mortality, which stood at nearly 170 per 1000 in the early

1960s, fell to 21 per 1000 in 1996. While only 4 per cent of girls went to school in 1960, in 1981 the figure had risen to 41 per cent, and by 1991 more than 80 per cent were in education. Women, indeed, by this time represented the majority of university graduates, although the job market was still largely out of bounds to them. The extent of their confinement in the family unit is virtually unparalleled in the Muslim world. But Crown Prince Abdullah, the half brother of King Fahd, who has effectively been the country's regent since the King's illness in 1995, has established himself as a reformer, stating, for instance, 'We will allow no one, whoever they are, to undermine [women] or marginalize her active role in serving her religion and country'.

The Crown Prince has also to maintain a delicate balancing act between his proclaimed solidarity with the **Arab world** and the historical alliance with the US. After the Gulf War, which involved more than 500,000 foreign soldiers in 'saving the country', around 5000 American soldiers remained stationed there, engendering active hostility and several bomb attacks in 1995 and 1996. The attacks of 11 September 2001 on the Twin Towers and the Pentagon were the starting point for a serious worsening of relations with Washington, which pointed to the presence of 15 Saudis among the 19 hijackers and the financing, by elements close to the Saudi throne, of Osama bin Laden's networks. It was announced by US Defence Secretary Donald Rumsfeld in April 2003 that the US would be withdrawing all its aircraft from Saudi Arabia, 'by mutual agreement', following the successfully prosecuted 2003 war in Iraq. Prior to the campaign in Iraq, US forces in the kingdom had doubled to some 10,000 troops.

The Crown Prince has also normalised his country's relations with its neighbours, notably with **Iran** – with which Saudi Arabia has been linked by a security treaty since 2001 – and Yemen, with which it signed a historic June 2000 agreement on border demarcation. In March 2002, Crown Prince Abdullah succeeded in getting the Arab Summit in Beirut to agree a peace offer which would consider the conflict with the state of **Israel** as 'at an end' and establish 'normal relations' with it in exchange for 'a total withdrawal [of Israel] from the occupied Arab territories' and the creation of a Palestinian state with its capital in East Jerusalem. This initiative goes beyond King Fahd's 1981 plan, which proposed only 'the recognition of the right of all countries in the region to live in peace'.

Furthermore, the unity of the four regions that make up the kingdom – Nejd, al-Hasa, Hejaz and Asir – is still precarious, as each has its own history and its own separatist tendencies. Thus al-Hasa has been hit by a series of workers' strikes, and the oppressed Shi'ite **minority** have revolted several times. Despite an agreement signed with the Shi'ite opposition at the end of 1993, signs of tension persist. Asir feels aligned to unified Yemen. Hejaz, which plays an active role in the modern economy and business world, has also reacted badly to the government's regressive policies.

Since the Gulf War the opposition has experienced a surge in popularity. In February 1991, 41 liberals appealed to the sovereign to introduce reform. In response to demands from a part of the population and under pressure from America, the King passed a Basic Law on 1 March 1992, as well as two laws defining the nature of the Majlis al-Shura (the Consultative Council) and the functioning of the regions. While confirming that the Qur'an and the Sunna (traditions of Islam) form the sole constitution of the kingdom, the Basic Law is an affirmation of the King's discretionary powers. He appoints and dismisses ministers, who report to him, he appoints and dismisses the 60 members of the Consultative Council, whose judgments he can ignore, and he appoints and dismisses the governors in charge of each province. More importantly for the future, the Basic Law lays out the rules of succession. Traditionally, it is one of Ibn Saud's sons who succeeds to the throne, usually the eldest. Henceforth the law states that 'the King chooses an heir that he can later change', and this power of nomination extends to the grandsons of Ibn Saud. King Fahd has decreed that Crown Prince Abdullah, the head of the National Guard, is his heir.

The **Islamist** opposition organised at the start of the 1990s around revolutionary demands: equality of all before the law, answerability of state officials, the elimination of corruption and usury, redistribution of wealth, strengthening of the army and of national **independence**, and restrictions on the power of the police. These demands were mixed with others, stamped with the rigour of Islam. With the 13 November 1995 bombing of a National Guard communications centre in Riyadh, which resulted in five American deaths, part of the opposition went over to violent struggle. The explosion of a booby-trapped lorry at al-Khobar on 25 June 1996, close to the huge Dhahran military base, with the deaths of 19 American soldiers, seems to have been carried out by Shi'ite elements. Efficient repression, combined with the co-optation of various 'turbulent' elements, made it possible for the royal family to reduce the levels of opposition. But the **terrorist** attacks in Riyadh on 12 May 2003, when more than 35 people were killed, then on 9 November, demonstrated the existence of proponents of terrorism in the kingdom. In July 1997, King Fahd appointed 16 new members to the Consultative Council, which now numbers 90. Although it has no real power, this admission of university figures and dissidents to the body created surprise.

The kingdom covers 2,240,000 sq. km, with nearly 23 million inhabitants (of whom around five million are foreigners). The army of 65,000 men is held in contempt, and its numbers are doubled by the White Guard and the National Guard, which is made up of the tribes most loyal to the al-Saud family. For the first time ever, in June 1988 Saudi Arabia had to take

out a government loan to counter the fall in the price of oil: the cost of the
Gulf War also drew heavily on the kingdom's reserves. The country's per-
capita GNP, consisting largely of its oil output (between seven and eight
million barrels per day on average in 2002), rose to $16,500 per inhabitant
in 1981, but had fallen by half 20 years later. The kingdom was obliged to
cut the level of subsidy given to consumption and agriculture, thereby
risking the social pact that had been created between the monarchy and
its subjects, particularly with 150,000 young people arriving onto the job
market every year. Proven oil reserves represent a quarter of the planet's
known resources, and the relatively high price of oil in 2002 gave the world's
prime exporter of oil substantial financial margins.

SETTLEMENTS

The settlement of the **West Bank**, Gaza, **Jerusalem** and other occupied Arab
territories was already underway by the end of the June **1967 War**. In July
the first settlement was set up on the **Golan Heights**; in September it was the
turn of the West Bank, with Kfar Etzion in the area of Hebron. At the same
time, the Labour-led government of Levy Eshkol set about the 'Judaisation' of
annexed Jerusalem. The central element in this strategy was the dispossession
of the **Palestinians** and the confiscation of their lands. Depending on the
situation, the Israelis were able to use 'security considerations' or laws dating
from the British Mandate – or even from the **Ottoman Empire** – and by
these means appropriated more than 65 per cent of the land available in the
West Bank, and more than 40 per cent in Gaza. In addition to a military role
(in relation to **Syria** or in the Jordan valley), the very tight enmeshing of
the West Bank and Gaza functions as a means of control and surveillance
of the Palestinian population. The armed settlers, who are sometimes
members of extreme right-wing organisations, have no hesitation about
using force to assist the occupation troops, or acting as police themselves.

There have been two phases in the settlement policy post-1967. The first
followed the lines of the Allon Plan – named after **Israel**'s Labour Deputy
Prime Minister of the time – which was put forward in July 1967. It stressed
the crucial importance of the River Jordan in the defence of the Jewish
state. It was here that the first settlements were set up: Israel did not make
a priority target of the highly populated Arab areas, although a number of
religious movements – acting with government support – were already
going beyond the formal framework of official policy. In 1997 the number
of settlers was relatively limited: five thousand for the whole of the West
Bank. A separate fate was reserved for Jerusalem, where the Arab part of the
city, broadly extended and then annexed, found itself being surrounded by
Jewish neighbourhoods whose population had reached 50,000 by 1977.

The year 1974 saw the creation of the Gush Emunim ('Bloc of the Faithful'), a movement demanding the right of Jews to settle in all parts of Eretz ('Greater') Israel. They embarked on violent confrontations and 'illegal' occupations in areas with large Arab populations. On the eve of **Menachem Begin**'s electoral victory in 1977, five settlements had already been set up in this manner, their existence endorsed by the government of **Yitzhak Rabin** and **Shimon Peres**. The arrival of the right in government gave the movement a powerful boost. Settlements were created in areas with large Arab populations, and by 1984 the number of settlers had climbed to 44,000.

But leaving aside a handful of zealots, the pioneering spirit of the 1930s and 1940s is now a thing of the past. By the 1980s there was already the question of how to 'fill' the settlements, and extensive use was made of Israel's housing crisis. Young couples who could not find affordable accommodation in Israel's big towns were offered the choice of going to live in urban settlements in the West Bank. Some of these are less than 30km from Tel Aviv, and prices there are two to three times lower. The formation of the National Unity government in 1984 led to restrictions being placed on the construction of new settlements. However, the number of settlements continued to grow: by this time, they were capable of accommodating up to a million people.

With the victory of the Labour party in the national elections of June 1992, there were expectations of a shift in Israeli policy. When Rabin became Prime Minister, he said that there should be a freeze on settlements. In fact there was nothing of the sort. By the end of 1995, the West Bank had 130 settlements, with a total of 150,000 inhabitants (compared with 112,000 in 1992); Gaza had 16 settlements, housing 6000 inhabitants; and the **Golan** had 33, with 16,000. In addition there were the 170,000-odd Jewish inhabitants of the nine settlements in East Jerusalem. As Rabin himself put it, 'the coming years will be marked by the extension of the building of Greater Jerusalem'.

The **Oslo Accords** have not altered the status of the settlements, which is only due to be discussed in the course of final negotiations. In order to prepare for the annexation of some of them, Israel's Labour government decided to build 26 new roads linking them directly to Israel. It also allowed existing settlements to pursue the annexation of land and undertake new construction. Even the massacre of 29 Hebron Palestinians by Baruch Goldstein on 25 February 1994 was not sufficient to convince the Prime Minister to take a hard line against the settlers – a weakness for which he subsequently paid with his life, on 4 November 1995.

The assassination achieved its objective: on 29 May 1996, the right and the extreme right were returned to power. This meant that settlement was once again on the agenda. The programme of **Benyamin Netanyahu**'s government proposed the 'strengthening, enlargement and development' of Jewish settlement 'on the Golan Heights and in the Jordan Valley, Judea, Samaria and Gaza'. And it added that it will 'allocate, in these regions, the resources necessary for this undertaking'. The man put in charge of the 'super-ministry' overseeing this renewed settlement programme was **Ariel Sharon**. Between the Oslo Accords of 1993 and autumn 2002, the number of settlers almost doubled, with the fastest growth taking place under the Labour governments of Rabin and Ehud Barak. Although it is hard to arrive at precise figures, given the duration of the building of housing in the settlements, the approximate number of settlement inhabitants in the West Bank and the **Gaza Strip** effectively rose by 49,000 in 40 months under Rabin (and Peres), by 30,000 in 36 months under Netanyahu, and by more than 20,000 in 20 months under Barak.

In addition to the confiscation and fragmentation of Palestinian land, the presence of the settlers has also intensified the presence of the army in the territories. The radicalisation of certain groups of settlers has fed the violence and aggravated the repression. Furthermore, the settlements create a discriminatory situation between the settlements – subject to Israeli civil law – and Palestinians, who are subject to military law.

However, there have been many calls, over a long period, for a freeze on the settlements, and their subsequent dismantling. As expressed in the Fourth Geneva Convention of 1949, and then the subject of condemnation in 1990 by **UN Security Council Resolution** 465, the direct or indirect transfer by the occupying power of a part of its own civil population into a territory which it occupies would be defined as a 'war crime' under the statutes of the International Court adopted in Rome in July 1998.

In July 2000, during the **Camp David** summit, the Palestinians accepted in principle Israel's annexation of the 'settlement bloc' where the majority of the settlers were grouped, but called for Israel to 'compensate' for the annexed territories by giving the Palestinian state an equivalent area of land.

In February 2001, Sharon was elected with more than 90 per cent of the settler vote, and he duly rewarded them for their support. As of 2001, the new government voted through a supplementary budget of $400m for the settlements. Parallel to the so-called 'legal' settlements (seen as such only by the Israeli government), the outposts which even the government viewed as 'illegal' were prospering. In November 2002, Benyamin Ben Eliezer and the three other Labour ministers resigned from the National Unity government in protest against the fact that the 2003 budget spared only the settlements from the austerity cure being inflicted on the rest of Israel.

In the course of the 1990s, the 'implantations' benefited from $1180 per head in subsidies per year, compared with $908 for the development towns and $522 for the local Arab communities in Israel. In all opinion polls, a majority, either relative or absolute, of Israelis have pronounced themselves in favour of the dismantling of most of the settlements, and where necessary compensation for the families thus 'repatriated'. Such a solution also matches the expectations of a majority of settlers, even if a **minority** has become radicalised. According to an inquiry by Shalom Achshav ('Peace Now') in July 2002, 68 per cent of settlers would obey a democratic decision to withdraw, with only 6 per cent stating that they were opposed to withdrawal, and 2 per cent saying they would oppose it 'by all means possible'.

The history of the conflict since 1967 speaks for itself: the annexation by Israel, within the framework drawn up at **Taba**, of most of the settlements now seems inevitable, but the dismantling of all the isolated settlements will be a *sine qua non* for any real peace agreement. Their continuation would make any idea of the construction of an independent and viable Palestinian state illusory. With hindsight we can also see the vagueness of the Israeli–Palestinian Declaration of Principles on 13 September 1993 as one of the major causes of the failure of Oslo.

SHAMIR, YITZHAK

Yitzhak Shamir became Prime Minister of the state of **Israel** after the elections of 1 November 1988, and represented the typical profile of the Israeli right.

Born in Poland in 1915, Yitzhak Yertsinski emigrated to Palestine. Like **Menachem Begin**, who was at that time still in Europe, he was a follower of Ze'ev Jabotinsky, the founder of the Revisionist movement, a **Zionist** faction at once radical and fascinated by Mussolini, dedicated to the cult of force and the leader and pledged to the Judaisation of Palestine on both banks of the Jordan. But even such ultra-nationalism was not enough for Shamir who, in 1940, founded his own group, the Fighters for the Freedom of Israel, known by its Hebrew acronym, Lehi. This group's hostility towards **Britain** pushed it to try to form an alliance with the Third Reich.

In the archives of the German Embassy in Ankara, after World War II, a letter dated 1940 was found from the Lehi, establishing a link between 'the evacuation of the Jewish masses living in Europe, one of the conditions on which the solution of the Jewish question depends' and the establishment of 'a Jewish state within its historic frontiers'. To these Hitlerite partners, the Lehi pointed out 'common interests between, on the one hand, the establishment of a new European order in conformation with German conceptions and, on the other, the national aspirations incarnated in the national military organization'. The letter pointed out that 'the creation of a Jewish state on a nationalist and totalitarian basis, linked by treaty to the

German Reich, would serve German interests and consolidate its future power in the Middle East'. The letter also contained an offer to 'take an active part in the war, on Germany's side', Jewish troops trained in Europe thus being able to 'participate in the conquest of Palestine'. The Lehi's fighting capacities, the letter continues, 'would not be inhibited by measures taken by the British administration in Palestine, nor by either its Arab population or Jewish socialists'.

The Lehi's offer was turned down by Berlin, and Shamir had to be satisfied with directing its anti-British **terrorist** activities in Palestine. Arrested in 1946, he was deported and only returned to Israel after **independence**. A group of which he was leader has been implicated in, among other things, the assassination of the UN mediator, the Swedish Count Folke Bernadotte, on 17 September 1948. In the 1970s Shamir played a major role: as president of the Herut party, he replaced Begin, who had resigned as Israel's Prime Minister, from September 1983 to July 1984, before becoming vice-premier, then Prime Minister again in 1986. The deadlock created by the elections of November 1988 allowed him to lead the Israeli government.

Shamir's second term as Prime Minister was marked by two major events: the **Gulf War**, in which he chose a policy of restraint following **Iraq**i Scud attacks on Israel; and the October 1991 Madrid **Peace Conference** that inaugurated direct talks between Israel and the neighbouring Arab states as well as multilateral regional talks. Shamir's premiership also witnessed the beginnings of huge social changes in Israel, with the huge upsurge in emigration from the former USSR from 1989 and the success of Operation Solomon, which saw 15,000 Ethiopian **Jews** (Falashas) airlifted to Israel in May 1991.

After his party lost the 1992 elections, Shamir stepped down from the party leadership, and in 1996 retired from the Knesset.

SHARON, ARIEL

His career began early. At the age of 14, Ariel Scheinerman, known as Sharon – born in 1928 in the Kfar Mahal *moshav* (co-operative), of a father originally from Brest-Litovsk and a Belorussian mother – joined the Haganah, the secret army of the **Yishuv**, and subsequently took part in the **1948–49 War**. Moshe Dayan noticed him during manoeuvres, and appointed him security chief for the Northern Region. In 1953 he was put in charge of setting up the new Unit 101, a commando unit designed to 'respond' to infiltrations by *fedayeen*.

Unit 101 was dissolved five months later and transformed into a paratroop battalion, but it was in existence long enough to carry out a massacre. As revenge for the deaths of a woman from Yehud and two of her children,

Sharon and his 'brothers in arms' crossed the border on the night of 14–15 October 1953 to dynamite one by one all the houses in the Jordanian village of Qibya, from where the murderers had allegedly originated. But there were about 60 civilians there, including many women and children, who were found dead in the rubble. In his memoirs, the perpetrator of this crime, who has been condemned unanimously by the UN Security Council, trumpeted, 'After Qibya, one might hope that the terrorists would think twice. They knew today that they risked paying dearly for each attack.' As the first massacre for which Sharon carries the entire responsibility, Qibya was not the last. Far from it: he would organise, order or cover up for plenty of others.

During the summer of 1995, several decades later, the history of atrocities committed by the Israeli army was the occasion of a controversy, in which the principal articles were published in the *Journal of Palestinian Studies*. For instance, the daily *Kol Hair* dated 30 June 1995 recounted in detail how a kind of death squad operated in the early 1970s, killing dozens of *fedayeen* in the **Gaza Strip**. The permission for these extra-judicial killings was given by Sharon. At the time he was commander of the southern front, and 'cleaned up' the refugee camps in the region with the aid of bulldozers. On 4 August, *Yerushalayim* and *Yediot Aharonot* published the evidence of reserve General Aryeh Biro, who admitted that, together with his men, during the **1956 War** he had killed between forty and fifty Egyptian prisoners after the Battle of Mutla, and then some *fedayeen* in Ras Sudar, and finally a whole Egyptian brigade between Ras Muhammad and Sharm el-Sheikh. 'If I am to be charged,' Biro said, 'then half the Israeli army should also be charged, because in similar circumstances they would have done as I did' (*Haaretz*, 17 August 1995).

On 8 August 1995, *Ma'ariv* reported evidence according to which Raphael Eitan, then commanding 890 Parachute Battalion, gave Biro the order to kill 49 Egyptian workers, guilty merely of having been on the spot where the Israeli paratroops were landing. At that moment, the paper explains, Sharon had taken command in the Mutla Pass. In his memoirs, Sharon says, 'I also ordered the transfer of troops into the defile, in sufficient number to eliminate in the morning the Egyptian soldiers who could still be there, and thus prevent any attack on our rear'. In the same article in *Ma'ariv*, Reserve Lieutenant Colonel Saul Ziv describes the scene that came to haunt him afterwards: the nightmarish massacre of about fifty defenceless *fedayeen*, murdered in their lorry at Ras Sudar. As for the execution of 168 Egyptian prisoners on the road to Sharm el-Sheikh, also ordered by Eitan, this was witnessed by Reserve Lieutenant Colonel Danny Wolf and Reserve Colonel Amos Ne'eman. Responding to denials by the chief of staff at that time, Moshe Levy, the historian Meir Pail retorts, 'The Israeli army was ashamed of publishing a communiqué recognising that its best elite unit had acted with such an absence of morality. Was not our national conscience founded on the comparison between our highly moral behaviour in battle and the barbarism of the adversary?'

Twenty-six years later, Sharon, as Defence Minister at the time of the **Lebanon 1982 War**, found himself at the heart of a new massacre: the one carried out between 16 and 18 September 1982 in the Palestinian camps in southern Beirut (see **Sabra and Shatila**). In Kings' Square in Tel Aviv, 400,000 Israelis demonstrated their horror. And for once the crime did not go (politically) unpunished: in February 1983 Sharon was obliged to resign as Defence Minister. But his purgatory would be of short duration: already by 1996 **Benyamin Netanyahu** was entrusting him with the infrastructure portfolio, which he transformed into a ministry of **settlements**. Another five years went by, and he popped up again in a move geared to furthering his career: his provocative visit to the Haram al-Sharif propelled him, via the elections of 6 February 2001, into the post of Prime Minister of **Israel**. Under cover of destroying the roots of **terrorism** the Prime Minister buried the **Oslo Accords**, smashed the **Palestinian Authority** and destroyed the infrastructures indispensable to the life of the Palestinian population.

An examination of Sharon's life could lead to the conclusion that he is hot-headed. That would be incorrect. The man is inspired by not one but two ideologies. First, he was raised in the tradition of **David Ben Gurion**'s Mapai; then he absorbed the heritage of Ze'ev Jabotinsky, in being involved in the foundation of Likud. From the neo-fascist on the one hand and the nationalist socialist on the other, Sharon created an original synthesis. From the former he has preserved the theory of the 'wall of steel': 'As long as there is the faintest spark of hope for the **Arabs** to impede us, they will not sell these hopes – not for any sweet words nor for any tasty morsel, because this is not a rabble but a people, a living people,' wrote Jabotinsky in 1923. But it was the socialist leader who taught Sharon how to use this military force: to impose the 'transfer' of the **Palestinians**.

After the electoral campaign of 2001, Sharon repeated untiringly, 'The 1948 war of independence is not yet over'. As the state of Israel exists and largely dominates its neighbours, this phrase can only have one meaning: a desire to carry through **expulsion**. The ideology of 'transfer', which at one time was limited to a small minority on the extreme right, is now running rampant through Israeli society. The media mention it regularly. Intellectuals sing its praises. And this agitation is working with a public opinion that has been traumatised by the bombings: in two years the percentage of Israelis favouring 'transfer' has gone from less than 10 per cent to more than 40 per cent. The settlers, for their part – operating on the ground and often with the army's complicity – are pushing the village Palestinians into leaving.

A regional conflict, into which Israel would be brought, could create conditions propitious for a completely new venture. Certainly, a mass 'transfer' would bring serious dangers both for the army and the government. In addition, the US, hoping to enlarge its circle of co-operation on Iraq, would be fearful of an operation liable to put a match to the powder keg of the Arab world. But the curriculum vitae of Ariel Sharon speaks for itself: from Unit 101 to the Ministry of Defence he has never hesitated in crossing red lines.

For a long-standing nationalist such as Sharon, the temptation of transfer becomes all the more pressing because the Jewish state finds itself in an untenable demographic situation. At some point between now and 2010, 'Greater Israel' will have an Arab majority within it. From the Israeli point of view there are only two ways out of this trap: either the creation of a Palestinian state side by side with Israel, or the expulsion of a maximum of Palestinians from 'Greater Israel', which would preserve the Jewish majority for a few more decades. Sharon, along with his friends, obviously excludes the first solution. Presumably he is counting on the second.

Everyone knows where he is thinking of sending the 'displaced' Palestinians: Jordan. Detached by Britain from its Mandate over Palestine, and populated in the majority by Palestinians, in his eyes the Hashemite Kingdom is the true Palestinian state. In 1970, at the time of the Black September clashes, the general, then commanding the southern front, was opposed to the support which Israel gave the 'little king' against the *fedayeen*: in his view, quite the contrary, they should have helped the Palestinians to take power in Amman and to put an end to the Palestinian question. Thirty-four years later, has he changed strategy?

SHI'ISM

Shi'ism is the main dissident branch of Islam, but its differences with the majority Sunni are less important than the elements they have in common, above all the belief in one God and in the message of Muhammad. Shi'ism developed around the crucial question of the succession to the Prophet Muhammad. The first caliphs after Muhammad's death were chosen from among those closely related to him. Ali, the Prophet's cousin and son-in-law, the fourth caliph, reigned from 656 to 661. Deposed by a revolt, he was subsequently assassinated. The Shi'a, the followers of Ali, defended his descendants' rights against the official caliphs. They were, to use an expression of Louis Massignon, 'Islam's legitimists'.

Shi'ism has evolved greatly in the course of history. It has split into several tendencies, which define themselves according to whichever imam, or successor of Ali, they support. The place of the imams is central to Shi'ism, since they continue the cycle of prophets who, for the Sunni, ended with Muhammad. Among these imams, Hussein, Ali's son and the third imam, occupies an important place. In October 680, he was pursued by Yazid, the Umayyad caliph, and surrounded at Karbala. He and his 72 companions held out for a long time, despite lack of **water**, but eventually he was killed. Hussein's martyrdom and his resistance to the 'evil' caliph play a crucial role in Shi'ite mythology, and were used as methods of political mobilisation in the struggle against the Shah of **Iran**. Every year, during the month of Muharram, spectacular ceremonies of mourning commemorate Hussein's actions.

The divisions within Shi'ism stem not only from the definition of the lineage of the imams, but also from their role. For the majority, particularly Iranian, Iraqi and Lebanese Shi'ites, called Imamis or Twelvers, there has been a succession of 12 imams, who derive their power from God, making them infallible. The last, Muhammad al-Muntazar, disappeared in 874. Having communicated with the outside world through messengers, he retired from view, but remained alive, beginning what is known as the Great Occultation, during which 'The community no longer has a visible absolute leader, until the end of time when the awaited Mahdi comes to establish a reign of truth and justice' (Yann Richard).

Another, more moderate, branch of Shi'ism is Zaidism. It recognises only five imams, whose authority stems largely from their personal qualities; it therefore does not maintain the rigid legitimism of the Twelvers, and rejects the dogma of the hidden Imam. Several Zaidi dynasties have ruled intermittently in history, mainly at Sana'a in **Yemen**, from 1592 to 1962.

A third Shi'ite sect, the Ismailis, seceded on the question of the succession of the sixth imam. They were the founders of the Carmathian states, the brilliant Fatimid dynasty in **Egypt** in the tenth century, the famous 'sect of the assassins' founded in the fortress of Alamut at the end of the eleventh century and, a deviant version of Ismailism, the **Druze** doctrine. Today, the Aga Khan is the leader of the main Ismaili communities, found in Iran, Afghanistan, India, Pakistan and Central Asia, as well as many other countries.

Shi'ism has played a major role in the history of Islam. Often in opposition, it has been the standard-bearer of numerous rebellions against caliphal power. But in many other cases it has not hesitated, in the name of this or that point of doctrine, to collude with the ruling powers.

Excluded from the decision-making centres of **Lebanon**, Pakistan and, for a long time, **Iraq**, today's Shi'ites still constitute turbulent communities. In Iran, where the Safavids made Shi'ism the state religion in the sixteenth century, the Shi'ite *ulama* have often in the past supported the reigning dynasties. But their involvement in opposition movements has been greater than that of Sunni religious leaders, in part because they enjoyed a relative economic **independence** vis-a-vis the state.

The Islamic Revolution in Iran and **Khomeini**'s coming to power represented an important victory for militant Shi'ism, but its rallying cry elicited little response in the long run in an Islamic world dominated by Sunnism. Khomeini imposed a theory of power, which has played a central role in Iran since 1979. On the question of who should guide the community of believers during the Great Occultation, his position was that this role would be played by the mullahs (theologians) and the *faqih* (scholars), viceroys of the 'concealed Imam' and earthly representatives of divine sovereignty. Khomeini was to be this *faqih* up until his death in 1989. He was then replaced in that position by Ali Khamenei. This doctrine of the 'guardian-ship of the jurisconsult' (*velayat-e faqih*), which gave the mullahs enormous powers, was – and remains – contested by numbers of other ayatollahs. The collapse of the Iraqi regime in April 2003 has given Iraqi Shi'ites a decisive say in the future of their country.

Today, Shi'ites number more than a hundred million, concentrated mainly in Iran, Pakistan, Iraq, Afghanistan, North Yemen, the Gulf, **Turkey** and the former Soviet Union. In **Syria**, the Alawites are sometimes classed as Shi'ites.

SUDAN

Muslim geographers of the Middle Ages designated the regions to the south of **Egypt** 'Bilad al-Sudan', the country of the Blacks. The Egyptian monarchs conquered them on two separate occasions in the nineteenth century: between 1820 and 1822, Muhammad Ali seized the northern part of present-day Sudan; forty years later, Khedive Ismail, having taken possession of the coastal region along the Red Sea, extended Cairo's authority in the south, which was then to be divided into three provinces: Upper Nile, Bahr al-Ghazal and Equatoria.

However, with the conquest barely achieved, a huge wave of rebellion spread throughout the country. Muhammad Ahmed bin Abdullah proclaimed himself Mahdi, messenger of God, raised an army of followers (the Ansar), and between 1881 and 1883 took control of virtually the entire country. At the time Egypt was under British occupation, and the retaking of Sudan by Anglo-Egyptian troops did not take place until 1898. This episode was a decisive element in the emergence of a Sudanese nationalist movement, giving birth to a huge religious brotherhood, the Mahdiyya, led by the Mahdi's descendants, which has remained a crucial factor in political life to this day.

In January 1899, Sudan passed under the control of an Anglo–Egyptian condominium, in which Cairo's role was largely fictitious. Nationalism began to impose itself after World War I, with the creation of the White Flag League. But it was mainly the two great religious brotherhoods, the Mahdiyya and the Khatmiyya (in favour of the union between Sudan and

Egypt), that animated the movement through which, on 1 January 1956, Sudan gained its **independence**. A parliamentary system along British lines was set up, dominated by two parties, the Umma and the National Unionist Party, offshoots of the Mahdiyya and the Khatmiyya respectively. But their inability to resolve the problem of the south and overcome the economic crisis led to the military coup d'état of General Ibrahim Abboud on 17 November 1958.

Abboud's dictatorship collapsed in October 1964, following an insurrectional general strike instigated by the powerful Communist Party. The parliamentary system was reinstated, but confronted the same difficulties as the military regime. And, on 25 May 1969, Jaafar al-Nimeiri and the Free Officers seized power. The new leader, a follower of **Nasser**, set the country on a radical path: nationalisation, close contacts with socialist countries, bloody confrontations with the brotherhoods. But, during the first two years of his presidency, Nimeiri also crossed swords with the Communist Party. On 19 July 1971, officers of the extreme left seized power for 72 hours: their movement was to be drowned in blood, the Communist Party dismantled, and its leaders, notably Secretary-General Abdel Khaliq Mahjub, hanged.

The revolt in the south

Southern Sudan, composed of the three provinces of Bahr al-Ghazal, Upper Nile and Equatoria, extends over an area of 650,000 sq. km, a territory larger than **France**. Far from constituting a unified whole, the south is divided into a multitude of ethnic groups: Dinkas, Nuers, Shilluks etc. Animists for the most part, the population is also 10–20 per cent Christian. Neglected, and for long isolated from the rest of the country by **Britain**, these provinces developed a certain feeling of solidarity against the Arab and Muslim north. On 18 August 1955, on the eve of independence, the Equatoria Corps mutinied in Juba, the principal town of the south. There then began a long war that was to last until 1972, made up of ceasefires, surprise attacks, massacres; and also of foreign interference: first **Israel**, then the **US** and, after Nimeiri's accession to power, Ethiopia supported the rebels. Finally, an agreement was reached in March 1972 in Addis Ababa: it stipulated the establishment within the republic of a self-governing southern region and of local legislative and executive bodies.

Peace lasted for ten years, but the central authority did nothing to consolidate it: the economic and social development of the south was neglected, and poverty remained the lot of most of its inhabitants. Nimeiri's decision, in October 1983, to apply *shari'a*, Islamic law, aroused disapproval that was all the stronger because the authorities had just taken the decision to repartition the south into three provinces, thus contravening both the letter and the spirit of the Addis Ababa agreement. This was the year that saw the outbreak of Colonel John Garang's uprising and the creation of the

Sudanese People's Liberation Army which, in a few months, was able to extend its influence and hold the army in check. This rebellion hastened the downfall of the dictatorship.

After the Addis Ababa agreement, Nimeiri had found himself alone at the helm. Several abortive coups stirred up by the right-wing opposition in 1975 and 1976, in particular by the Umma party and the **Muslim Brotherhood**, prompted him to attempt a national reconciliation in 1977. Sadiq al-Mahdi, the leader of the Mahdiyya Brotherhood, and Hassan al-Turabi, the head of the Muslim Brotherhood, returned to Khartoum. But the single-party system was maintained, and the Sudanese Socialist Union retained the monopoly of power.

At the regional and international levels the authorities allied themselves increasingly with American strategy, intervening in Chad on the side of Hissene Habre and in Ethiopia on the side of the Eritreans. But it was above all the economic crisis and the recommencement of the rebellion in the south that brought about the regime's downfall: famine, hidden from international public opinion, affected millions of people; the national debt rose to over $9bn; the price of basic necessities soared. At the end of March 1985 demonstrations broke out against the prohibitive cost of living. The main professional unions called for strikes, the outcome of which, on 6 April, was the constitution of a provisional Military Council that agreed to return the power to civilian hands after one year. Nimeiri sought refuge in **Egypt**.

In April 1986, the first free elections for almost twenty years took place. al-Mahdi's Umma party won, and set up a coalition government with the other major force, the Democratic Unionist Party, linked to the Khatmiyya Brotherhood. The Muslim Brotherhood won 51 seats, while the communists were marginalised.

But while parliament was re-established and Khartoum followed a more balanced foreign policy, the economic crisis worsened with the adoption of the structural-adjustment programme imposed by the IMF. Discontent grew. The war in the south spread, despite various mediations, because the government refused to negotiate with the People's Liberation Army. The shifts of tack by al-Mahdi, who had no hesitation in bringing the Muslim Brotherhood into government, aggravated the crisis. Once again, on 30 June 1989, the army seized power.

The Revolutionary Command Council for National Salvation, presided over by General Omar Hassan al-Bashir, was far from non-partisan. It suspended any semblance of democratic life, restricted individual liberties, but at the same time allowed and encouraged the activities of the National Islamic Front under the leadership of al-Turabi, who exercised a powerful influence on the new leaders. Khartoum, which supported **Iraq** during the **Gulf War**, became a crossroads for all the radical **Islamist** movements, and was to provide a haven for **Osama bin Laden** during the first half of the 1990s. Accused by Washington of supporting **terrorism**, the regime was also accused by Egypt on the occasion of an assassination attempt against its President, **Hosni Mubarak**, in Addis Ababa on 26 June 1995. In 1996, the UN Security Council imposed a number of **sanctions** on Khartoum. Neither the expulsion (to France) of the terrorist Carlos 'the Jackal', on 15 August 1994, nor the partial reconciliation between Cairo and Khartoum in June 1996, nor the measures taken against certain Arab dissidents (notably the expulsion of Osama bin Laden) were sufficient to counter the regime's international isolation.

Having muzzled the opposition, the Islamist authorities launched vigorous offensives in the south, achieving some successes and even succeeding in playing on differences within the People's Liberation Army, which split into several factions. This was a costly war, and had no decisive outcome. The various attempts at mediation resulted only in fragile ceasefires. With a debt of $17bn, galloping inflation and a sinking currency, Sudan experienced huge difficulties, which, in November 1995 and the summer of 1996, translated into violent demonstrations. Apart from its apparatuses of repression, the government's power rests basically on the divisions within the opposition, which is in principle united within a National Democratic Alliance, but which offers no alternative in terms of government.

There was a possibility of new developments with the elimination of al-Turabi in December 1999 (he was subsequently imprisoned). Sudan attempted to subdue clashes on its eastern and southern borders, and to bring the country out of its international isolation. In May 1999, it re-established links with the Eritrea of Issaias Feworki, who up until then had been accused of supporting the Sudanese opposition. In May 1999, it signed a co-operation agreement with Qatar. In December of that year peace talks began with Uganda, which had been accused of supporting the Popular Liberation Army of Sudan, while Sudan in turn was accused of giving support to the fundamentalist Christian movement in Uganda, Joseph Koni's Lord's Resistance Army (LRA).

Khartoum subsequently sought to re-establish diplomatic relations with Washington. However, on the pretext of the struggle against terrorism the US imposed a total embargo on the country. On 20 August 1998, the US bombed the El Shifa pharmaceutical factory in reprisal for the bombings of the American embassies in Nairobi and Dar es Salaam – the majority of local witnesses denied the allegations that the factory had been producing chemical weapons. Khartoum then resumed co-operation, allowing FBI and CIA teams to work on its territory and providing information which enabled them to arrest dozens of foreign extremists.

In this context, negotiations were resumed with the People's Liberation Army in Machakos, Kenya in October 2002. But these talks, which excluded the northern opposition, continued to run into difficulties, notably over the sharing of power, the sharing of **oil** wells and the Islamic nature of the Khartoum regime. Will America's powerful pressures be sufficient to restore peace to this divided country?

In 1997, a huge reform plan was launched to satisfy the requirements of the IMF, funding agencies and investors. It was designed to stabilise the currency – in 1996 inflation was running at 133 per cent – as well as guaranteeing foreign investments and privatising some state companies. The Great Nile oil project, involving local companies alongside Chinese, Malaysian and Indian companies, resulted in the building of an oil pipeline. This provided an outlet for six oilfields in the Abiye region to a refinery and export to the Red Sea at the port of Beshair, and made it possible to improve Sudan's financial situation.

Sudan extends over 2.5 million sq. km, and in 2001 had a population of 32.6 million, of which 15–20 per cent are southerners. The north is majority Muslim and Arab, but it also has non-Arabic-speaking **minorities** such as the Nubians, Beja and Fur. The south, on the other hand, is black and animist, with a Christian minority. To the Sudanese population must be added a large number of refugees – 600,000 – coming from Eritrea, Chad and Uganda. The country's main resources are agricultural: cotton, gum arabic, but there is also oil. This was discovered in the south, and Sudan officially became an oil-exporting country in August 1999. The civil war and famine have led to the deaths of two million people, and have turned four million into refugees in the space of the past eighteen years.

SUEZ CANAL

Linking the Mediterranean at Port Said to the Red Sea at Suez, this water-way has always been an economic and strategic pawn of the utmost importance.

The first canal to have cut the Suez isthmus dates from the year 2000BC, when Pharaoh Senustret III joined up the Bitter Lakes, which then formed a gulf on the Red Sea, to the Nile and from there to the Mediterranean. Abandoned and rebuilt several times, it silted up in the eighth century. During his Egyptian campaign, Napoleon once again conceived a water-way, this time direct, between the two seas. The project was realised under Napoleon III by Ferdinand de Lesseps: the Universal Company of the Maritime Suez Canal was created on 25 April 1859, and the inauguration of the canal took place on 17 November 1869.

For **Britain**, the Suez Canal was a vital link between London and its territories overseas, particularly in India – it cut in half the journey between British ports and Bombay. This is why in 1875 the British government took advantage of an Egyptian economic crisis to buy the 177,000 shares (out of 400,000) owned by the Khedive (the Turkish viceroy in Egypt). In addition to financial control, direct physical control was established from 1882, when the British army occupied **Egypt** and the Canal Zone. British soldiers remained in the Canal Zone until 1954; it was only then that an evacuation agreement was signed between Cairo and London. **Gamal Abdel Nasser** went further, and on 26 July 1956 nationalised the Canal Company.

A vital line of communication, the canal was naturally a pawn for the belligerents in Middle Eastern wars. It was closed for one day during World War I, following a Turkish raid, and for 76 days during World War II after German raids. The Battle of the Canal, which Egyptian nationalists launched against the British made it a dangerous place in 1951 and 1952. The Franco–Israeli–British operation in Suez led to its closure for five and a half months, from 29 October 1956 to 15 April 1957, after the withdrawal of the last Israeli army troops. But the canal's most significant closure was from 6 June 1967, at the outbreak of the Six Day War (see **1967 War**), to 5 June 1975. Its reopening to navigation only came about with the disengagement agreements reached by **Israel** and Egypt of January 1974, followed by more than a year of work to get the canal back into working order, mainly involving mine clearance; there were over 730,000 mines and explosives in the canal, and almost 690,000 anti-tank and anti-personnel mines along the banks. Reopened on 5 June 1975, for the first time the canal accepted Israeli ships, before they were given equal status with other users of the waterway with the signing of the Egyptian–Israeli peace treaty of 26 March 1979.

The canal's restoration also allowed improvements to its navigability to be carried out. Its width was increased to 160m and its draught to 16.2m, allowing 90 ships to pass through in a single day. The enlargement has also enabled ships of 370,000 tons laden and 260,000 unladen to sail the canal. There has since been a steady increase in the annual tonnage of shipping: from 274 million tons in 1966, it rose to 499 million tons in 2003. New work was undertaken to increase its depth to 18m, which would allow the passage of the larger ships which used the Cape of Good Hope route. General Ahmed Ali Fadel, appointed president of the Suez Canal Authority in January 1996, immediately decided to allow the giant ships a 20 per cent reduction, so that 'it remains the cheapest international sea route'. But traffic was hit by the economic crisis in Asia and the growing competition from pipelines as a means of transporting **oil**. In 1998 the Suez Canal Authority was placed under the authority of the Prime Minister in order to improve its efficiency. Revenue from the canal has begun to rise again, and 2002–3 brought in a record $2.6bn for Egypt. More than 14,500 ships used the canal in the course of the year.

Besides the alterations to the canal itself, Egypt has decided to develop its banks, and is constructing factories and holiday resorts along the

Mediterranean and the Red Sea, building new harbour installations at Port Said etc. It is planning to create a free-trade zone for Chinese exports destined for Europe and Africa. Finally, since 1980 a tunnel has passed 51m under the canal linking Egypt to the Sinai Peninsula, from which Israel withdrew in 1982 and where the government intends to settle during the coming two decades millions of people – but in 2000 the peninsula had only 350,000 inhabitants, and the province of Suez 452,000. The opening of a 2.9km suspension bridge over the canal in 2001 was expected to contribute to the region's development.

SYKES–PICOT AGREEMENT

A secret agreement reached in 1916 between **France** and **Britain**, and subsequently ratified by **Russia**, to divide the **Ottoman Empire**, an ally of Germany and Austro-Hungary in World War I. Complemented by the Saint Jean-de-Maurienne Agreement, which included Italy, it shared out zones of influence between the victorious powers as follows:
-   Russia retained the northeast of the Empire and, in the west, Constantinople, the west coast of the Bosporus, the Sea of Marmara, the Dardanelles, and part of the coast of Asia Minor and the Black Sea. But the port of Constantinople and the straits remained open to navigation for the allied fleets;
-   Greece obtained a small zone around Smyrna to the west of Anatolia; Italy, all the southern part of what was formerly **Turkey**;
-   France appropriated Cilicia and the *vilayet* of Adana, the Syrian–Lebanese coastal strip and a zone of influence corresponding to present-day **Syria**, as well as the **oil** region of Mosul that Clemenceau was to return to the British in 1918;
-   Britain took the eastern part of Mesopotamia, the western parts being included in its zone of influence as well as the territory of present-day **Jordan**, these two zones being intended to form a state or a confederation of Arab states;
-   Palestine was to be internationalised, only the ports of Haifa and Acre falling to Britain;
-   Only the **Arabian Peninsula** would be independent, under Hashemite rule.

Clearly, the Sykes–Picot Agreement contradicted the commitments made by Britain to the **Arabs**. But the Agreement's architect, Mark Sykes, had written to Lord Curzon, 'My aim is that the Arabs should be our first brown-skinned dominion – not our last colony. Arabs will react against one if one tries to lead them, and they are as stubborn as Jews, but one can lead them anywhere without the use of force if it is theoretically arm in arm.'

Like many a case of counting chickens before they are hatched, the Sykes–Picot Agreement would only ever be partially implemented. In 1917, Russian revolutionaries denounced the commitments undertaken by their predecessors in power. Between 1919 and 1922, Turkish nationalists, led by Mustafa Kemal, liberated Anatolia from its French, Italian and Greek occupiers after the armistice. But, for the rest, the map thus established supplied the backdrop for the inter-war clashes that 'gave birth to nations', a framework officially established by the Conference of San Remo (April 1920), the Treaty of Sèvres (August 1920) and ratified by the League of Nations (July 1922). It was *A Peace to End All Peace*, as in the title of a book by David Frokin dealing with the accords reached between the Allies in the period 1914–20.

SYRIA

On 3 October 1918, Emir Faisal, son of Sherif Hussein, entered Damascus at the head of his troops. Having defeated the Turkish army, he hoped to establish the independent Arab state promised him by the British. But on 24 July 1920, the French army put an end to this dream and drove him from Damascus: the French Mandate for Syria began. In addition to **Lebanon**, the territory was divided into four states (Damascus, Aleppo, an Alawite state and the Jebel **Druze**) which would not be reunited until December 1936. On the eve of World War II, to get into the good graces of **Turkey**, **France** ceded to it the *sanjak* of Alexandretta, something Syrian nationalists would never forgive. The French presence did not last long after the end of World War II, and in 1946 the last foreign troops left the country.

The early years of the new republic were far from peaceful. The defeat in Palestine and the failure of the Syrian troops who had intervened brought about the collapse of the parliamentary regime and the first military coup d'état, on 30 March 1949. For the next five years, military dictatorships were to succeed one another until the restoration of democracy and the holding of elections in 1954. They reflected the rise of new forces (**Ba'thist**, nationalist, communist) at the expense of traditional, conservative tendencies. The new power made approaches to **Nasser's Egypt** and the Soviet Union, and violently condemned the Anglo–French Suez expedition. Confronted with the pro-Western Hashemite axis between Amman and Baghdad, Syrian leaders came out in favour of total unity with Egypt. On 1 February 1958, a new state saw the light of day, the United Arab Republic, with Gamal Abdel Nasser as President and real master. But the experiment was to be shortlived: on 28 September 1961, the Syrian army put an end to it.

On 8 March 1963, a new coup d'état carried the Ba'th party to power. The first reforms (nationalisation, agricultural reform) shook the established social order, arousing fierce reaction from the middle classes. However, the existing regime was replaced on 23 February 1966, by another, still Ba'thist, but even more radical. The new leaders, Jamal Atassi and Salah Jadid, called for a harsh, uncompromising socialism and a hard line towards **Israel**. Syria took part in the **1967 War**: it lost the **Golan Heights**, occupied by the Israeli army. Despite this defeat, it maintained a radical attitude which isolated it from its Arab partners. This policy was opposed by General **Hafez al-Assad**, the powerful Defence Minister. After long internal struggles, he seized power on 13 November 1970.

Within a few years, the new President had established his authority and that of his Alawite co-religionists, as well as that of the army, by either integrating or liquidating the various elements of political life. On 7 March 1972, the Progressive National Front (PNF) was created, composed of the Ba'th party, the Communist Party and three Nasserite groups. This alliance guaranteed the Ba'th's hegemony and, over the years, the PNF lost all substance and influence. Political opposition, still represented by four elected deputies after the elections of 1973, disappeared from parliament during 1977. The small left-wing or liberal organisations could not stand up against the Ba'thist steamroller. The only radical and potentially threatening opposition came from Sunni Muslim groups, who called for a holy war against a power denounced as Alawite and accused of being atheist. Two huge waves swept over the country. In 1973, demonstrators succeeded in having an amendment made to the new constitution, stating that 'Islam is the religion of the Head of State'. From 1977, a broader movement, against a background of political and economic crisis caused by Syria's engulfment in Lebanon and backed by **terrorist** actions, shook the Ba'th hegemony. It ended in the uprising, steeped in blood, of the town of Hama, in February 1982. Since then, despite latent discontent, no force has been able to provide a coherent opposition. In the atmosphere of increasing openness adopted in the 1990s, the regime had the parliament pass a law of amnesty in late 1995. Several thousand opposition figures, including **Islamists**, were released from prison. The return to Syria of Sheikh Abdul Fatah Abu Ghoda, spiritual leader of the **Muslim Brotherhood**, after 13 years of exile demonstrated both the solid base of the regime and the rapprochement brokered with the Islamists, who recognised the firm position of Assad in negotiations with Israel.

Syria took part, on Egypt's side, in the **1973 War**. It won back part of the Golan and took advantage of this to normalise its relations with the US. In 1976, Syrian troops intervened on the side of the **Maronite** right in the **Lebanese Civil War**. Lebanon constitutes Syria's western flank and offers a channel of direct access to Homs and Hama. Moreover, Damascus sees it as a zone of influence, even part of 'natural Syria', snatched from the mother country by colonialism. After 1978–79, Assad took over the leadership of the anti-**Camp David Accords** Arab crusade and tried to assume the place left vacant after Egypt's ostracism by the **Arab world**. Despite its troops' pitiful performance against the Israeli army in June 1982, Syria was able to turn the situation to its favour, obtaining the Israeli evacuation of Lebanon and the alliance of the rival militias. But the limits to its power were illustrated in September 1988 by its inability to have a new Lebanese president elected. With Moscow's help, it reconstructed a military capacity that would make it a formidable adversary for Israel in the event of another war. An ally of **Iran**, but also of **Saudi Arabia**, hostile to the brother regime of Baghdad, it has tried to establish itself as principal interlocutor in any peace negotiations.

Damascus understood more quickly than others the significance of the changes set in motion when Mikhail Gorbachev came to power. Syria, linked with Moscow since a 1980 treaty of friendship, saw the decline of its firmest ally and principal source of armaments. Syria subsequently reduced its military spending from over 20 per cent of GNP in the 1980s to barely 10 per cent in the early 1990s. Its decision to join the Western camp during the 1990–91 **Gulf War** was therefore made without too much hesitation; Syria even sent a sizeable military force to join the coalition in Saudi Arabia. It soon reaped the rewards of making the right decision: its main rival, **Saddam Hussein**, was greatly weakened; it was given a free hand in Lebanon, where it was able to remove General Michel Aoun; it received significant subsidies from the Gulf and saw Europe lift the economic **sanctions** put in place in 1986 owing to Syrian implication in terrorism. But, even though it participated in the **peace conference** inaugurated in Madrid in autumn 1991, Syria reaffirmed its principles that a final settlement would require Israel to withdraw from all the Arab lands occupied in 1967, including the Golan, and full recognition of the national rights of the Palestinian people. Assad's attempts to conclude a peace with Israel a few months prior to his death came to nothing.

His death on 10 June 2000 brought to an end a rule that had lasted over thirty years. But the succession had been in preparation for several years. The son initially designated to succeed him, Basel, died in 1994 in a car accident. His brother Bashar, an ophthalmology student in London, was then recalled to Damascus. Over a period of six years he was initiated into the political issues and laid the foundations for his authority. He built up an inner circle based on loyalty to his father, Alawite solidarity and uncon-ditional support for his own positions. Since the real centre of power in Damascus was the army and the secret services, he rapidly built up his network. The formation of a new government (reshuffled in the spring of 2000) also illustrated his desire to fight corruption. The Ba'th party congress in June was marked by the entry of several of his associates and a strength-ening of the position of the military. He became the sole man in charge and commander in chief of the army. But hopes for a political liberalisation which had been aroused by his arrival, in a country which had been subjected to a state of emergency since the arrival of the Ba'th party in 1963, came to nothing. Despite the 'Damascus Spring' launched in September 2000 by the petition of 99 Syrian intellectuals and artists in favour of elementary civil rights, the increasing numbers of arrests of opposition figures in 2002 signalled a hardening of the regime and the difficulty of sidelining the old military, business and political circles.

On the regional and international scene, Bashar has continued the work of his father, maintaining the alliance with Iran, reinforcing Syria's hold over Lebanon (despite hostile demonstrations), normalising relations with **Iraq** – which meant mainly a resumption of diplomatic relations, the creation of a free-trade zone on the frontier and the reopening of the **oil** pipeline between the two countries. While the new President collaborated with the 'struggle against terrorism' of President George W. Bush, at the same time he maintained relations with **Hezbollah** and Palestinian opposition organisations.

Syria has an area of 185,000 sq. km, and in 2000 had a population of 16.3 million. As sectarian affiliations have been omitted from official records, only an estimated breakdown is available: Sunni 68 per cent, Alawite 12 per cent, Christians 10 per cent, **Kurds** 6 per cent, Druze 2 per cent, others 2 per cent. The economy has been affected drastically by the war effort. After a socialising policy and a significant agrarian reform in the 1960s, Syria, like Egypt, embarked on a policy of *infitah*. But Egypt continues to have the upper hand in all strategic decisions. As an agricultural country (with a sizeable output of cotton), it has a solid network of infrastructures and light industry. Production of oil (501,000 barrels per day in 2001) and imports of cut-price Iraqi oil, along with subsidies from the Gulf states, assure a relatively high standard of living. Lebanon, where more than half a million Syrians work, is a vital element in Syria's economy.

TAIF ACCORDS

On the initiative of the tripartite commission of the **Arab League** – consisting of Algeria, **Saudi Arabia** and Morocco – Lebanese members of parliament were called together at the end of September 1989 in Taif, Saudi Arabia, to discuss a project for a National Reconciliation Charter. Out of a total of 73 members of parliament (the survivors of the 99 elected in 1972), 62 were present: 31 Christians and 31 Muslims. The negotiations lasted for almost a month, and it was not until 22 October that an agreement, known as Taif Accords, was finally reached, thus bringing an end to the Lebanese Civil War.

The text paved the way for a reduction of the powers of the **Maronite** president, strengthening the cabinet and the positions of the Sunni Muslim prime minister and the **Shi'ite** speaker of parliament: henceforth the country would be run by a *troika*. In parliament the number of seats was increased to 128, to be shared equally between Christians and Muslims. Pending elections, the empty seats would be filled by co-optation. Once a new president had been elected and a government of National Unity formed, the country would set about disarming the militias and extending the authority of the state. The broader aim would be to replace the **confessional** basis of the state, but this was an objective for the longer term.

While there was unanimity on the need to end **Israel**'s occupation of south **Lebanon**, the Syrian presence aroused considerable debate. The final text stated that 'the Syrian forces present in Lebanon will terminate their security role within two years at the most [they would then be regrouped in the Beqaa]. The time during which the Syrian forces will remain in these regions will be specified in the agreement which will be established between the Lebanese and Syrian governments.'

The Lebanese parliament, which met on 5 November 1989, ratified the text – despite the opposition of General Michel Aoun, but with the support of the Christian leadership – and elected René Moawad as President. He was assassinated on 22 November, and was replaced a few days later by Elias Hrawi. The life of the assembly was extended until 1994, and on 7 June 1991 about forty new members of parliament were appointed. The elimination of Aoun in October 1990 made it possible to accelerate the process: Beirut was reunified and the militias – with the exception of **Hezbollah** – were disarmed. Civil peace returned, and the Lebanese were able to feel hope again, even though Syrian tutelage over the country had never been so strong, as was shown by the treaty of friendship and co-operation signed between the two countries on 22 May 1991. But the future of the country was also bound up with developments at the regional level. While the Israeli withdrawal from south Lebanon in 2000 enabled the country to re-establish its territorial integrity, developments in Palestinian areas and **Iraq** made the Lebanese understandably nervous, fearing that they might be drawn into fresh conflicts.

TERRORISM

On one of the most up-to-date search engines on the Internet, at the end of 2002 the word 'terrorism' brought up 317,000 documents, and the adjective 'terrorist' 159,000. This confirms what we already know: since the 11 September 2001 attacks in New York and Washington, the phenomenon has assumed a central position in international life. The operations attributed to **Osama bin Laden** and his al-Qaeda group even marked the birth of a transnational 'hyper-terrorism', a qualitatively new stage in the growing power of forms of action that have been around for a long time, but which have been seeing a spectacular re-emergence since the end of the bi-polar management of international relations by Washington and Moscow, in which both parties took the necessary steps to keep order in their own 'camp'. The fact that al-Qaeda's actions are no longer directly tied to precise conflicts – Palestinian, Kashmiri etc. – is a new feature compared with other movements that have used terrorism as a form of action, such as Palestinian, Northern Irish and Basque.

As Ignacio Ramonet wrote in *Le Monde diplomatique* (December 2001), the attacks on the World Trade Center invented

> a new terrorism – global in its organisation, also in its reach and its objectives. A terrorism with no demands, at least not in the sense of demanding the independence of a country, or concrete political concessions, or the installation of a particular regime. So far nobody has even claimed full responsibility for the attacks. This new terror manifests itself as punishment for the generic, unspecified behaviour of the US and the West. Both President George Bush, with his 'crusade' (before he retracted the offensive word), and Osama bin Laden have described this confrontation as a clash of civilisations, a war between religions. The world according to bin Laden is split into a camp under the banner of the cross (the crusade reference of Bush, the chief infidel), and another under the banner of Islam.

This desire to reduce the world's conflicts to a violent 'clash of civilisations' fits well with the Bush administration's desire to justify the new directions of US foreign policy. However, the parallel drawn between the fight against Nazism in the 1930s, that against communism in the 1950–80s, and terrorism today, does not hold up: terrorism is only, if one can define it as such, a 'form' of struggle, and definitely not an ideology capable of mobilising the peoples of the world. And so, whereas the former relied on countries as powerful as Germany, the Soviet Union or China, on which threatening governments do the terrorists of today rely?

In reply to the simple question 'What is terrorism?' it is hard to find an agreed definition, either in the statements by political leaders or in the specialist literature. Terrorism should not be confused with the use of violence. One of the first 'natural and inalienable' rights of the French Revolution and the Declaration of the Rights of Man was, after all, 'resistance to oppression'. From this point of view, who would dare to use the term 'terrorism' (except in very bad faith) to describe the armed combat of the French Resistance during the Second World War, as was done by the German occupying forces and their French accomplices?

International law has never succeeded in defining terrorism; it limits itself to listing specific crimes, such as the hijacking of, or attacks on, aircraft. More recently, international conventions have been drafted to combat bomb attacks (1997) and the financing of terrorism (1999). The 1999 convention defines it as an

> act intended to cause death or serious bodily injury to a civilian, or to any other person not taking an active part in the hostilities in a situation of armed conflict, when the purpose of such act, by its nature or context, is to intimidate a population, or to compel a government or an international organization to do or to abstain from doing any act.

Moreover, acts qualified as terrorist often have the quality of war crimes and come under the principles established by the Nuremberg court regarding

> violations of the laws or customs of war. Such violations shall include, but not be limited to, murder, ill-treatment or deportation to slave labor or for any other purpose of civilian population of or in occupied territory, murder or ill-treatment of prisoners of war or persons on the seas, killing of hostages, plunder of public or private property, wanton destruction of cities, towns or villages, or devastation not justified by military necessity.

The attempts at juridical definition of terrorism, particularly after 11 September 2001, carry risks of a threat to civil liberties both in Europe and in the US, just as they are used to justify oppressive policies in countries such as Algeria, Indonesia and **Russia**. This was the point underlined by John Fish, the Irish president of the EU's Bar Council, in April 2002, following the framework decision adopted by the European Council on 6 December 2001. He explained that the list of terrorist crimes was too broad. From this point of view the American experience offers a disturbing example.

Let us return to the definition of terrorism. It could be used to describe acts of violence that affect innocent civilian populations with a view to creating a climate of insecurity and to achieve certain political objectives. But how can you place within the same analytical category the gas attack by the Aoum sect in the Tokyo subway system and car bombings by IRA dissidents? Do the far-right American militias responsible for the deaths in the Oklahoma bombing fall in the same bracket as bombings by the Basque

ETA? And what do these actions have in common with the attack on the World Trade Center and the Pentagon? By having 'been applied to very different types of violence, some of which, particularly at the domestic level, have no political aim', the concept of terrorism has lost its meaning, as the South African expert Adrian Guelke explains in *The Age of Terrorism and the International Policy*. He goes on to claim that it has disintegrated. Finally, one should not forget that the term 'terrorism' was originally created to describe a state policy, that of the French Revolution. Now, this state terrorism, frequently used in the Middle East, is broadly ignored: indiscriminate bombings, deportations of populations and car bombs have been used by various governments, including the Israeli, Syrian, Iraqi and Iranian.

As the *Economist* put it, an honest government must admit that terrorism often highlights a legitimate grievance. History has amply proved this, with former 'terrorists' going on to become respected political leaders. In the 1940s **Menachem Begin** and **Yitzhak Shamir** were involved in murderous attacks on Arab civilians (and **Jews** too), as in the King David Hotel bombing, before going on to achieve high office in **Israel**. The 'FLN killers' denounced day after day by the French government and the majority of French newspapers went on to lead Algeria to **independence**, whatever the horrific nature of some of their methods. More recently we have other examples in confirmation. Even those who for a long time refused all compromise in order not to 'give in to the men of violence' eventually had to abandon their intransigence. The white government of South Africa ended up negotiating with the ANC. **Yitzhak Rabin** shook hands with **Yasser Arafat**, 'a man whose hands are stained with Jewish blood', and negotiated with the **Palestine Liberation Organisation (PLO)** in an attempt to break the deadlock of hatred in the Middle East.

Historically what has tended to mark terrorist action has been the spectacular nature of its methods. The hijacking of aircraft is one of these. Inaugurated by Guy Mollet's French government on 22 October 1956 – with the forced landing of the aircraft which was taking Ben Bella and various FLN leaders from Rabat to Tunis – this practice was revived after the Arab–Israeli **1967 War**. On 23 July 1968, the PFLP hijacked an El Al flight between Rome and Tel Aviv. Fatah only adopted this kind of action after **Jordan**'s **Black September**. In 1973 the PLO and its principal components decided to abandon it; only small dissident groups, including that of **Abu Nidal**, continued to use it. Security measures taken in airports and the PLO's condemnation of this kind of activity has led to a considerable reduction in the number of aircraft hijackings, which are now treated as local affairs.

The practice of kidnapping is as old as war itself. It is frequent in conflict zones, for example in Iraqi Kurdistan, where *peshmerga* groups on several occasions kidnapped foreign technicians during the 1980s. One country riven by conflict, **Lebanon**, was notorious for this kind of action during the 1980s – partly explained by the disappearance of the state. First used in the civil war, kidnappings extended – particularly after 1982 – to the foreign communities, driven particularly by **Hezbollah**. Without having disappeared, hostage-taking became rarer in the Middle East during the 1990s.

It is striking that the three big waves of non-state terrorism in the region corresponded to the periods of maximum frustration and political impasse for the Arab peoples: after 1970, after 1982, and in 2000. It is also obvious that the elimination of the 'objective causes' of terrorism will never eliminate the risk of action by fanatical individuals; on the other hand it reduces the numbers willing to support such action and among whom these individuals can develop, find support and complicity.

For some elements of Palestinian and Lebanese youth, any kind of action is seen as valid as a means of expressing its frustration. To forget this is to condemn oneself to never being able to fight the terrorist phenomenon in real terms. In emptying the **Oslo Accords** of all substance and in sabotaging all hope for a just peace, the Israeli governments which followed that of **Yitzhak Rabin** prepared the ground for the 'suicide bombings'. One might note, with Olivier Roy, that suicide attacks 'are completely absent from the orthodox Islamic tradition...they appeared during the 1980s, in **Shi'ite** movements such as Hezbollah, and then more recently spread to Sunni movements'. Suicide bombings have even extended this framework in the Occupied Territories, since all factions have used them and there have been very many 'volunteers' for suicide – a sign not of religious fanaticism but of infinite despair, accentuated by a lack of direction from the Palestinian leadership.

But to explain is not to justify. While the struggle in the **West Bank** and the **Gaza Strip** still maintains all its legitimacy, nevertheless, two years after the outbreak of the **second Intifada**, the majority of Palestinian public opinion now rejects the use of blind attacks on Israeli citizens – whether they are committed by the **Islamist** fighters of **Hamas** and Islamic Jihad, or by the al-Aqsa Martyrs Brigades close to Fatah. In so doing, the **Palestinians** have obviously drawn the lessons of these operations: so far from 'breaking' Israeli society, the suicide bombers have strengthened **Ariel Sharon** and his policy of force, since fear and anger have got the better of the continuing awareness of the necessity for a political solution. But the more lucid Palestinian leaders and militants go well beyond an analysis of the 'counterproductiveness' of these kinds of actions: they condemn terrorism because it tarnishes their cause, their ideals, and the future of the society that they hope to build.

Many international organisations have said exactly the same, in putting the actions of the Israeli state alongside those of the Palestinian suicide bombers. Human Rights Watch, which among other things gave us the most complete account of the 'war crimes' committed in April 2002 in the **Jenin** refugee camp by the Israeli army, also, on 1 November 2002, attacked the bombings in Israel, saying that the scale and systematic nature of these attacks differentiated them from other abuses committed in periods of conflict. It went on to say that they clearly came under the heading of crimes against humanity. Similarly, Amnesty International, in its report of 11 July 2002, pointed out that it had 'condemned for many years the violations of human rights and humanitarian law' carried out by Israel against the Palestinians in the Occupied Territories, of which 'the majority' constitute 'war crimes'. Amnesty added that no violation committed by the Israeli government, of any scale or severity, justified the killing of civilians. The obligation to protect civilians is absolute. Thus it described suicide attacks as crimes against humanity from the standpoint of international law and as war crimes from the legal characterisation of the conflict and the status of armed groups and Palestinian civilians. It concluded by noting that

> the UN General Assembly has recognized the legitimacy of the struggle of peoples against foreign occupation in the exercise of their right to self-determination and independence. However, international law requires all parties involved in a conflict to always distinguish between civilians and people actively taking part in the hostilities. They must make every effort to protect civilians from harm.

However, the simple 'moral' condemnation of crimes committed by the two parties is not sufficient. One cannot simply put the two protagonists back to back because both of them are violating humanitarian law, for two reasons. First because the violations committed by a government – a government which claims democratic principles – are always more serious than those committed by non-state groups, particularly because some of them are acting against the explicit orientation of the **Palestinian Authority**. And then for political reasons: the battle that the Palestinians are conducting is a legitimate resistance to an illegal occupation, whereas the Israeli government is developing a strategy to maintain an illegal occupation and colonisation. Comparisons can be overstated, and Israel is obviously neither the Third Reich nor colonial **France**. But to take one example, during the Second World War the Allies assuredly committed war crimes and crimes against humanity – notably in the bombing of Dresden, and even more so of Hiroshima and Nagasaki. The fight against Nazism was, however, nonetheless a just war, and nobody can stand the Allies and the Axis back to back. Similarly, during the Algerian war of liberation the FLN committed – as did the French army – war crimes, indeed crimes against humanity. However, its demand for independence was entirely justified. And here too symmetry is not applicable.

TRADE PATTERNS

As well as having a strategic and political importance, the Middle East also represents a considerable economic market with a combined population of over 250 million people. The needs of the region and its people are highlighted by the dependence of their economies, which are geared mainly towards the export of primary materials. They therefore have to import most of the manufactured goods they require. The vast majority of countries in the region have in recent decades had no problem in financing these imports due to their natural resources, principally **oil**. Furthermore, from the 1970s to the mid-1980s there was a huge trade surplus, which many countries invested abroad because they were unable or unwilling to invest it locally.

In order to discern the most important characteristics of the region's trade, we must look at some figures, most of which are taken from reports of the World Trade Organisation (WTO). In that year the total imports of **Saudi Arabia**, Bahrain, **Egypt**, the United Arab Emirates (UAE), **Iran**, **Iraq**, **Israel**, **Jordan**, **Kuwait**, **Lebanon**, **Libya**, Oman, Qatar, **Syria**, **Turkey** and **Yemen** exceeded $220bn, of which about 75 per cent was manufactured goods. The total of their exports increased to more than $290bn, two thirds of which was oil, an increase of 40 per cent on 1999. As well as oil, the following minerals can also be found in the region: gold, phosphates, sulphur, asbestos, coal, lignite, iron, chromate, copper, manganese, lead, zinc, antimony, nickel etc.

Oil and its derivatives, which are not available to Israel, Jordan, Lebanon and Turkey, represent around 37 per cent of exports in Egypt, 80 per cent in Iran, 61 per cent in the UAE, 62 per cent in Syria, 60 per cent in Qatar, 90 per cent in Kuwait, 76 per cent in Bahrain, 77 per cent in Oman, 92 per cent in Saudi Arabia, and 95 per cent in Libya. Up until 1982, revenue from oil had been steadily increasing: it stood at $2.8bn in 1966, $4.1bn in 1970, $13.5bn in 1973, $89bn in 1977, $177bn in 1981 and approximately $100bn in 1984. From 1974 to 1984, the region's trade surplus amounted to nearly $450bn, of which 5 per cent was reinvested in international financial institutions, 15 per cent in developing countries and 80 per cent in developed countries, particularly the **US**, which received 65–70 per cent of the total. The President of the Union of Arab and French Banks reported that, at the end of 1989, the amount of public and private money invested abroad by Arab banks had reached $670bn.

However, many illusions were shattered when the price of oil crashed and the oil market went into recession. The total exports of the countries of the Middle East, excluding Israel, tumbled from $159bn (oil accounted for $130bn) in 1982 to $79bn ($56bn worth of oil) in 1986 before recovering to $135bn in 1993 (oil exports earned in that year more than $100bn).

In 2000, the five main importers in the Middle East were Turkey ($54.5bn), Israel ($38.1bn), the UAE ($31.9bn), Saudi Arabia ($30.3bn) and Iran ($15.2bn). The five largest exporters were: Saudi Arabia ($84.1bn), the UAE ($39.9bn), Israel ($31.3bn), Iran ($30bn) and Turkey ($27.8bn).

As regards trading partners, Asia and the EU are now replacing the US as both customers and suppliers in the region. The EU is the principal supplier to the Middle East, accounting for almost 40 per cent of the region's imports, followed by Asia (28 per cent) and North America (13.5 per cent). Asia has become – by far – the main customer for Middle East oil ($117.5bn in 2000), led by Japan, which imported $47.5bn worth; next came the EU ($28.2bn) and the US ($23.7bn).

Although the 1990–91 **Gulf War** was a commercial victory for the US, subsequently competition from Europe and Japan in the region has increased. According to figures in the *Statistical Abstract of the US* 2001, Washington's biggest customers in the Middle East in 2000 were Israel ($7.7bn), Saudi Arabia ($6.2bn), Turkey ($3.7bn), Egypt ($3.3bn) and the UAE ($2.3bn). And its main suppliers from the region in that period were Saudi Arabia ($14.2), Israel ($13bn), Iraq ($6.1bn), Turkey ($3bn) and Kuwait ($2.7bn). There was a notable increase in trade between the US and Israel, following the free-trade agreement negotiated between the two countries.

Russia has failed to exert the same influence as the former Soviet Union did in the region, and does not have the same level of commercial interests in the Middle East. Although there are no reliable figures, it seems that Moscow is making it a priority to restore the markets that the Soviet Union had, namely Iraq, Iran, Syria, Egypt and Libya.

TURKEY

In a process that was far from smooth, modern Turkey emerged out of the dismantling of the **Ottoman Empire** in the wake of World War I. On 10 August 1920, the victorious powers imposed the Treaty of Sèvres on the defeated caliph with terms that were even harsher than those that had been signed with Germany. The country was to be dismembered. It lost its European territories, as well as substantial areas of Anatolia, where the plan was to set up states for the **Kurds** and Armenians. The straits (the Bosporus and the Dardanelles, the only maritime passage between the Black Sea and the Mediterranean), were placed under Allied jurisdiction. The Turkish military leader, Mustafa Kemal, raised the standard of revolt against this high-handed treatment. He enjoyed a series of military victories, notably against the Greeks, and in the Treaty of Lausanne signed on 21 July 1923 was eventually able to achieve real **independence** within the country's present borders (with the exception of the *sanjak* of Alexandretta, which **France** ceded to Turkey on the eve of World War II, despite opposition from Syrian nationalists). The straits became subject to Turkish sovereignty, but the conditions of their utilisation were to be governed by international regulations laid down in 1936 (the Montreux Convention).

The way was now open for political reforms. On 29 October 1923 the republic was proclaimed, and in March 1924 the caliphate was abolished. For the first time since Muhammad, **Islam** no longer had even a nominal religious figurehead. Kemal – who became 'Atatürk', the father of the nation – went on to commit his country to the path of modernisation, adopting the Latin alphabet to replace the Arabic script, affirming the secular nature of the Turkish state, introducing a new civil code and developing an economy based on active state intervention. The independence proposed for the Kurds in the Treaty of Sèvres was abandoned, and instead a programme of assimilation was pursued, despite a number of revolts. The Kurds became 'mountain Turks', and their language was banned. The government derived nominally from an elected parliament, but only one party was authorised, the Republican People's Party (RPP). At the international level, policy was built on non-intervention in the affairs of Turkey's neighbours (particularly the Arab countries), good neighbourliness and a degree of co-operation with the Soviet Union, which had assisted Kemal in his struggle 'against the imperialists'. In November 1938, Atatürk died, leaving a country that had been deeply transformed; he was succeeded by one of his associates, Ismet Inönü.

Turkey maintained neutrality during the period 1939–44, only declaring war on Germany on 23 February 1945. However, the Second World War resulted in two major upheavals. In November 1945, single-party government was abolished. The newly created Democratic Party won the elections of July 1946; Adnan Menderes was one of its leaders. The new government abandoned its policy of neutrality, and aligned itself resolutely with the West. From 1947 onwards, the **US** extended economic and military aid to the country, and, having participated in the Korean War, Turkey joined the North Atlantic Treaty Organisation (NATO) on 18 February 1952 and accepted the installation of a number of military bases on its territory. Seen as an outpost of the West in countering the 'Soviet threat', it thereby derived a comfortable financial income. It also played an active role in the attempts to set up anti-Soviet alliances in the Middle East, and in November 1955 joined the **Baghdad Pact**.

The army seized power on 27 May 1960, declaring its determination to preserve the principles of Kemalism. It was to do the same on two later occasions: 12 March 1971 and 11 September 1980. Each time the coup was made on the same pretext, namely the restoration of law and order and loyalty to the ideals of Atatürk. Turkey thus saw in this period an alternation of military and civilian governments. Its foreign policy was now characterised by membership of NATO and by a return to a policy of non-intervention in Middle East affairs, although the country's relations with **Israel** were fairly close. At the regional level, policy was marked by ongoing conflict with Greece and by the question of Cyprus, which achieved independence in 1960. The fate of the Turkish **minority** on Cyprus was a source of perpetual friction, which was eventually used to justify an invasion of the island in July 1974. The northern zone was occupied and transformed into a republic, recognised only by Ankara.

The military dictatorship set up in 1980 created a deep trauma in the country, such was the violence of the repression it introduced – particularly against the various Kurdish organisations that had been created during the 1970s. In 1984, a new organisation, the Kurdistan Workers' Party (PKK), Marxist-Leninist in orientation and led by Abdullah Öçalan, embarked on armed struggle in the southeastern provinces. With the active support of **Syria**, and under the benevolent eye of **Iraq**, **Iran** and Armenia, the PKK was able to extend its influence.

The return to democracy, which began in 1983, was effected under the leadership of Turgut Özal and his Motherland Party, which changed the face of Turkey in the space of a few years, most particularly in economic terms. Özal committed the country to liberal policies based on the development of exports. Between 1980 and 1990, these rose from $3bn to $13bn, and the share of industrial products in them climbed from 35 per cent to 80 per cent. Özal developed a dense infrastructure network (roads, airports, telephones etc.); competitive industrial companies, particularly in the field of construction, were operating in the markets of the Middle East and the USSR; the country experienced impressive growth, albeit at the expense of high inflation and dangerous social tensions.

At the regional level, Özal also broke with tradition. While stressing his determination to integrate Turkey into the European Economic Community, his plan was also to pursue active policies in the Middle East. He recognised the Palestinian state that was proclaimed in 1988; he dreamed of a giant aqueduct which would carry the **water** of the Seyhan and Ceyhan rivers down to **Jordan** and the Gulf; finally, despite criticisms from within the armed forces, he was to commit himself heavily in the **Gulf War**. As of August 1990, Turkey shut down the pipelines transporting Iraqi **oil** across Turkish territory. Özal authorised Coalition aircraft to use Turkish bases for bombing operations in Iraq; he even expressed regret that his country had not sent a military contingent to fight with the Coalition forces.

The early elections of 25 December 1995 were marked by a breakthrough by the Islamic Welfare Party (also known as Refah) of Necmettin Erbakan, which had already achieved striking victories in the municipal elections of 27 March 1994, having taken Istanbul, Ankara, Izmir and other major cities in Turkey. These victories were consolidated: with 21.3 per cent of the votes, Refah outstripped all the other major parties – the Motherland Party of Mesut Yilmaz (19.7 per cent), the True Path Party (DYP) of Tansu Çiller (19.2 per cent), the Party of the Democratic Left (DSP) of Bülent Ecevit (14.7 per cent) and the Republican People's Party (CHP) of Deniz Baykal (10.7 per cent).

The 1990s were marked by military and political offensives in Kurdistan. The army and its 'special units' were able to pursue a 'scorched-earth policy' in southeastern Anatolia with a free hand. Twelve years after its inception, the balance of the 'dirty war' in Kurdistan amounted to 16,000 dead, according to Ankara, and 35,000, according to the PKK; hundreds of thousands of exiles, not to mention the 2500 villages and thousands of hectares of forest destroyed. Even worse: under the pretext of cleaning out the guerrillas' support networks, the army several times invaded part of the security zone set up by the Allies in Iraqi Kurdistan at the end of the Gulf War.

Despite this brutal violation of Kurdish rights, as well as of international law, the government took a major step down the road to integration into the EU. On 13 December 1995, the European parliament ratified a customs-union agreement signed nine months earlier. In order to achieve this, Ankara had to make headway on human-rights issues, at least on paper. The Turkish parliament voted to revise the constitution which had been adopted in 1982 under the aegis of the military (this now gave the right to vote at 18, voting rights to Turks residing overseas, an end to the ban on unions taking up political positions, the right of teachers to take part in political life, the elimination of the paragraph approving of the army's intervention in 1980 etc.); but it also partially amended Article 8 of the anti-**terrorist** law, whereby the government was allowed to imprison citizens for simple crimes of opinion. These modifications are still to be fully introduced, and both their spirit and letter are yet to be translated into everyday life in Turkey. This could begin with an end to the systematic use of maltreatment, including torture, in police stations, to say nothing of Kurdistan.

Another important turning point was the rapprochement with Israel. Co-operation between the two countries was already long-standing. It was already a reality in the 1950s, and although it was weakened by Israel's occupation of the **West Bank** and Gaza and by Turkey's oil dependency, the rapprochement became more rapid after the Gulf War. Trading relations – now supported by a free-trade agreement – reached $1bn; 300,000 Israeli tourists visit Turkey each year, and Ankara abstained on the occasion of the UN Security Council vote against Israel's Grapes of Wrath operation. But the military accord signed in February 1996, on the occasion of the visit to Israel of the Turkish Chief of Staff, took things a step further. As of May 1996, under the terms of the accord, Turkish air bases and airspace were opened to the Israeli air force; the pilots of both countries began joint training programmes, and July saw the first joint naval manoeuvres. The Israeli Defence Forces (IDF) were also committed to training Turkish soldiers in methods of fighting cross-border infiltration. The accord also allows for exchanges between the two countries' secret services, particularly in dealing with Syria, Iraq and Iran and their 'support for terrorism'. In addition, several arms supply agreements were signed.

Running contrary to Turkey's tradition of neutrality in the Arab–Israeli conflict (which incidentally led to an **Islamist** attempt to assassinate President Demirel in May 1996), these developments came in the context of growing tensions between Ankara and Damascus. In addition to the dispute over the Hatay province (the former *sanjak* of Alexandretta, which the Syrians claimed that France had illegally handed over to Turkey), relations between Turkey and Syria were further poisoned by the Kurdish question. The dispute over the waters of the Euphrates, the flow of which is controlled by the Atatürk dam and thereby by Ankara, is also linked to the Kurdish question.

Leaving aside these bilateral issues, the Israel–Turkey agreement led to a modification in the geopolitics of the Middle East. As a member of NATO, and one which has increasingly played a frontline role since the Gulf War, Turkey has become an integral part of American–Israeli strategy, particularly because, turning its back on its costly friendship with Baghdad, Turkey offered its airfields as bases for American surveillance missions over Iraq. A new version of the Baghdad Pact was finalised in November 1995 at a meeting between Bill Clinton, **Shimon Peres**, **King Hussein** of Jordan and Çiller in a hotel in **Jerusalem** after the funeral of **Yitzhak Rabin**. The aim of this meeting was to form a Washington–Jerusalem–Ankara axis in conjunction with the 'moderate' Arab countries in order to oppose the 'radical' countries, whether secular or Islamist. An expert from the Jaffee Center for Strategic Studies in Tel Aviv concluded, 'It is possible that new blocs of power will be formed, but this time the United States will find that some of its important allies have swapped sides'.

During the summer and autumn of 1996, the first months of the government led by the Islamist Erbakan complicated the situation as regards regional alliances. While he backed the Turkey–Israel agreement, the new Prime Minister went on a visit to Tehran, thereby involving Ankara in a rapprochement with Iran which aroused anger in Washington. But at the end of June 1997, after a destabilisation campaign fuelled by the media, the military forced the Erbakan government to resign.

On 18 April 1999, the elections saw victory for the Nationalist Action party (MHP) and the DSP – the latter owing its success to the charisma of Ecevit, the 'conqueror of Cyprus' in 1974, but above all a man who had been a symbol of honesty throughout his political career. Among the meagre achievements of the government formed by the MHP and DSP there was at least the decision – historic for Ankara – of the European Council in Helsinki in December 1999 to give Turkey the official status of a candidate for EU membership.

Beyond the inner workings of Turkish political life, the central question was still the grip of the armed forces on all aspects of life in the country: the National Security Council, which every month holds a meeting with six military men in full uniform and five civilian figures, presents the government with 'opinions' on questions relating to national security. National security, as was pointed out in a circular of the military high command, 'covers virtually all matters of public interest', including economic affairs, which the military influences via its Oyak and TSKGV holding companies.

After a government crisis, new elections were held on 3 November 2002, which gave 363 of the 550 seats to the Justice and Development Party (AKP), the Islamist party which succeeded the Fazilet, excluded from the political arena because of its 'anti-secular activities'. Erbakan left leadership of the party to the former mayor of Istanbul, Recep Tayyip Erdogan. But the head of the AKP was also not electable immediately himself: he had been given a prison sentence in 1999 for having recited a poem which, in the courts' view, 'incited religious hatred'. Abdullah Gül was elected Prime Minister before ceding power to Erdogan some months later. They maintained a moderate line in internal and external policy, rejecting even the label 'Islamist'.

The new team found itself facing an economic and financial crisis which had already led to violent street demonstrations in February 2001. Worsening after the 11 September attacks, this crisis produced in the space of a year almost a million additional unemployed and an annual inflation rate of 80 per cent, and reduced 40 per cent of the population to living on $1.50 a day. The additional credit of $16bn given by the IMF in winter 2002 – after an earlier $20bn loan in 1999 – was supposed to help Ankara repay debts amounting to 100 per cent of its GDP.

This internal instability did not, however, prevent Turkey from becoming one of the main actors in the Middle East arena, strengthening its alliance with Israel and obtaining from Syria the expulsion of Öçalan. Ankara is also a powerful ally of the US, where it is seen as the most secular and moderate Islamic country in the region, but the relations worsened after Turkey's refusal to allow the US to open a northern front during the Iraq war in 2003. The Turks also renewed their links with the Central Asian countries of the former Soviet Union, particularly after the November 1999 agreement with Georgia, Azerbaijan and Kazakhstan on an oil pipeline linking Baku with the Turkish oil terminal at Ceyhan on the Mediterranean.

But the big ambition of Turkey – and of Erdogan – is its membership of the EU. Ever since the 15 judged it suitable for membership of the EU in December 1999, it has striven to meet their requirements on matters of human rights: in August 2002, parliament voted the abolition of the death penalty in times of peace – thereby saving Öçalan from execution – and granted linguistic and cultural rights to the Kurds. The problem of Cyprus remains a major obstacle to the integration of Ankara into the EU. UN Secretary-General Kofi Annan took a last-chance initiative in November 2002: he called on the two parties to accept the creation of one single country with a federal structure, a Greek Cypriot state and a Turkish Cypriot state which would have equal status, and which would exercise in sovereignty all the powers which the constitution does not delegate to the joint state.

The statement by Valéry Giscard d'Estaing on the future of Europe, in which he said that Turkey's membership would mean 'the end of the European Union', shows that the obstacles are also cultural, with some leaders within the EU seeing it as a 'Christian' entity.

Turkey has a surface area of 775,000 sq. km, and in 1999 it had a population of 64 million, of whom 12 million were Kurds, mostly living in the big cities of the West (particularly Istanbul, with two million). There are also Caucasians, Armenians, **Jews** (particularly in Istanbul) and **Arabs**. Most of the population are Sunni Muslims, but there are 12 million who are a **Shi'ite** sect (see **Shi'ism**). Their doctrine is particular to Turkey; they do not proselytise, nor do they have recruitment drives, and they practise their faith in secret. They have often been victimised by the pogroms of Orthodox Muslims, notably in 1993 and 1995. Consequently, they tend to be loyal to Kemalism, which has relegated religion to the private domain.

UNIFIL (UN INTERIM FORCE IN LEBANON)

UNIFIL was created in March 1978 as a result of Resolution 425 of the Security Council (see **UN Security Council Resolutions**) on the evacuation of south Lebanon after its invasion by **Israel**. Its mandate was to 're-establish peace and security' on the border and to 'help the Lebanese government to restore its authority in the region'. It has been regularly renewed since then, despite the equally regular abstention of **Russia**, which has nonetheless never invoked its right of veto.

In 1996, UNIFIL was comprised of six thousand men, of whom five thousand were soldiers. It consisted at that time of six battalions (from Fiji, Finland, Ghana, Ireland, Nepal and Norway) and four logistical detachments (from **France**, Italy, Poland and Norway). The force encountered serious difficulties in the field, and proved incapable of accomplishing the task assigned to it. The South Lebanese Army (SLA) of Saad Haddad and the Israelis opposed any deployment of UN soldiers in the zones under their control in the south. In addition, there were numerous clashes between the Palestinian Progressives and the SLA in which UNIFIL has been involved. Although the UN troops installed themselves in the north of 'Haddadland', they were unable to separate the SLA completely from its Palestinian-Progressive opponents because a gap remained in the narrow Litani Valley around the Beaufort Castle, allowing the two sides to cross swords. This gap was also one of the principal routes of Israeli penetration during Operation Peace in Galilee.

In June 1982, UNIFIL confirmed its impotence. The Israeli Defence Forces (IDF), in their march towards Beirut, crossed zones under UN control without impediment. During the three years of Israeli occupation, there was a great deal of friction, and UNIFIL tried to limit the effects of the 'iron fist' policy on the civilian population. Javier Perez de Cuellar, UN Secretary-General, explained the force's dilemma in the following way: 'For obvious reasons, UNIFIL does not have the right to prevent acts of Lebanese resistance against the occupying forces, any more than it has the mandate or the means to prevent [Israeli] counter-measures'. For their actions, UNIFIL and the UN's other soldiers of peace were awarded the Nobel Peace Prize in 1988.

Following the implementation of the **Taif Accords** in 1989, the Lebanese Army took over the role of UNIFIL in certain southern towns. However, on several occasions the army found itself caught up in the middle of battles in south Lebanon. In April 1996 in particular, during heavy Israeli bombardment, the UNIFIL camp at Qana, where many civilians had sought refuge, suffered a direct hit and a hundred Lebanese were killed. A report by the UN accused Israel of deliberately targeting the camp.

On 17 April 2000, the Secretary-General received formal notification from the government of Israel that it would withdraw its forces from Lebanon by July 2000 in 'full accordance with Security Council resolutions 425 (1978) and 426 (1978)'. He was further informed that in so doing the government of Israel intended 'to cooperate fully with the United Nations'. Starting on 16 May, much sooner than anticipated, the IDF began to vacate its positions, amid exchange of fire. Beginning on 21 May, large crowds of Lebanese, accompanied by armed elements, entered villages in the Israeli-controlled area, and the IDF vacated their position in great haste. At the same time, a large number of the pro-Israeli forces, together with their families, crossed into Israel. Others surrendered to the Lebanese authorities. Within a few days, those forces had completely disbanded.

Following the Israeli withdrawal, the Lebanese army refused to take up positions in the south of Lebanon, leaving **Hezbollah** the dominant actor in the region. Although there were fears that conflict would break out along the border, it remained relatively quiet, apart from a few low-level incidents. UNIFIL was gradually reduced in size, and numbered fewer than two thousand troops in 2003, assisted by some fifty military observers of the UN Truce Supervision Organisation (UNTSO) and supported by 115 international civilian personnel and 305 local civilian staff. Military personnel were contributed by France, Ghana, India, Ireland, Italy, Poland and Ukraine.

UN SECURITY COUNCIL RESOLUTIONS

Among the innumerable resolutions passed by the UN on the Israeli–Palestinian conflict, several have left their mark on its history and are worthy of mention:

- Resolution 181 of the General Assembly, which, on 29 November 1947, partitioned Palestine (see **Partition Plan** and Appendix 3).
- Resolution 194 of the General Assembly which, on 11 December 1948, after the first Arab–Israeli war (**1948–49 War**), asserted the right of 'refugees wishing to return to their homes', who 'should be permitted to do so at the earliest practicable date' or, failing this, 'compensation should be paid for the property of those choosing not to return and for loss of or damage to property'. Both of these rights were to be re-stated by 20 UN resolutions between 1949 and 1967.
- Resolution 273 of the General Assembly which, on 11 May 1949, admitted **Israel** as a member of the UN.
- The famous Resolution 242 of the Security Council which, on 22 November 1967, almost six months after the Six Day War (**1967 War**), acknowledged the existence and security of the state of Israel, but also made 'the withdrawal of Israeli armed forces from territories occupied in the recent conflict' the condition of a lasting peace. But, with typical UN ambiguity, the official English text speaks of 'Occupied Territories'

whereas the official French text speaks of 'the territories occupied'. The Palestine question is still treated only as a 'problem of refugees', just as in Resolution 338 of the Security Council which, on 22 October 1973, after the Yom Kippur War (**1973 War**), merely called on the parties in conflict 'to begin immediately after the ceasefire to apply Security Council Resolution 242 (1967) in all of its parts'.

– Resolution 2443 of the General Assembly, which, on 19 December 1968, was concerned about the 'violation of human rights in Arab territories occupied by Israel', a situation taken up again throughout the 1970s and 1980s in numerous texts.

– Resolution 2535 of the General Assembly, which, on 10 December 1969, evoked for the first time since 1948 the 'inalienable rights' of the Palestinian people, confirmed by Resolution 2628, which, on 4 November 1970, claimed that 'respect for the rights of the Palestinians is an indispensable element in the establishment of a just and lasting peace in the Middle East'.

– Resolution 2649 of the General Assembly, which, on 30 November 1970, made explicit mention of the Palestinian people's 'right to self deter-mination'.

– Resolution 2949 of the General Assembly, which, on 8 December 1972, deemed as 'null and void' the 'changes brought about by Israel in the occupied Arab territories', a view that would later be coupled with a condemnation of both the transfers of population and the establish-ment of **settlements**. Thus Resolution 32/5, of 28 October 1977, stipulates that 'the measures and actions taken by the Government of Israel, as the occupying Power, and designed to change the legal status, geo-graphical nature and demographic composition of those territories... taken by Israel in the Palestinian and other Arab territories occupied since 1967 have no legal validity and constitute a serious obstruction of efforts aimed at achieving a just and lasting peace in the Middle East'.

– Resolution 3236 of the General Assembly which, on 22 November 1974 – in the presence of **Yasser Arafat**, who had addressed the UN – recognised the Palestinian people's 'right to national independence and sovereignty', as well as Resolution 3237, which 'invites the Palestine Liberation Organisation to participate in the sessions and the work of the General Assembly in the capacity of observer'.

– Resolution 3379 of the General Assembly, which, on 10 November 1975, classed **Zionism** as a form of racism (this was to be annulled in December 1991).

The Resolutions adopted since then have remained faithful to these ideas, a fundamental contradiction therefore remaining between Security Council Resolutions 242 and 338 and the rest of the texts adopted by the General Assembly. It is this gap that explains on the one hand the insistence of Israel and the **US** on the first two Resolutions and, on the other hand, the stance of the **Palestine Liberation Organisation (PLO)** in accepting only the UN resolutions 'as a whole'. The Palestine National Council of Algiers, recognising on 15 November 1988 Resolutions 181, 242 and 338, overcame this final obstacle – a process which was fully completed almost eight years later when the Palestinian National Charter was modified to recognise Israel's right to exist.

Faced with the outbreak of the **second Intifada**, the Security Council passed several resolutions, notably the three following:

– Resolution 1322, of 7 October 2000, adopted by 14 votes in favour and one abstention (the US), 'deplores the provocation carried out at Al-Haram Al-Sharif in **Jerusalem** on 28 September 2000, and the subsequent violence there and at other Holy Places, as well as in other areas throughout the territories occupied by Israel since 1967, resulting in over 80 Palestinian deaths and many other casualties'.

– Resolution 1397, of 12 March 2002, adopted by 14 votes in favour and one abstention (**Syria**), affirmed, for the first time explicitly since the Partition Plan of 29 November 1947, 'a vision of a region where two States, Israel and Palestine, live side by side within secure and recognized borders' (see Appendix 14).

– On 24 September 2002, Resolution 1435 'reiterates its demand for the complete cessation of all acts of violence, including all acts of terror, provocation, incitement and destruction'.

UNITED STATES OF AMERICA

The most recent of the Western arrivals in the Middle East, where it was never a colonial power, the US has gradually taken over from **Britain** and **France** to become the most influential country in the region.

During the Cold War, Washington saw the Middle East as having a primarily strategic value: the crossroads of three continents, the meeting point of the great trade routes, it was from 1917 onwards the southern border of the Soviet Union. Hence the military imperative: the US needed a chain of bases coupled with regimes which it armed to make them the region's local policeman, as in the case of **Iran** under the Shah. But **oil** also continues to motivate American policy, as well as the petrodollars that result from it, which, for the most part, come to be recycled on the other side of the Atlantic. The last but not the least facet of America's ambitions is the massive market, both civil and military, that the countries of the region represent for the American economy.

These objectives, which underlie all American policy in the Middle East, also determine its basic features, clearly distinguishable in the long term.

First, the desire to eliminate Western competitors, under cover of the 'open door' policy, in order to assure itself an indisputable supremacy over other Western countries. This it has done with growing success, first after World War II, then after the Franco–British Suez fiasco in 1956, and finally with the British retreat from the Gulf at the end of the 1960s. Second, the attempt to form a massive regional alliance directed against the USSR and its local allies, an effort that quickly paid dividends in the north (Greece, Turkey, Iran), but has always been in vain in the south, where any co-operation between Israel and the Arab countries inevitably runs up against the block of the Palestinian question. Under these conditions, the Jewish state remains the White House's strategic priority. Third, the determination to resort to any means, including military, to satisfy these demands, on the one hand by supporting Israel in its conflicts with its neighbours (with the exception of the 1956 War), on the other by intervening against any threat of destabilisation when circumstances require and permit it (such as Iran in 1953, Lebanon in 1958, Jordan in 1970, Lebanon in 1983 and the Gulf War in 1990–91). The aims of the US pro-lsraeli lobby coincide here with the country's strategic aims.

The US had first to gain a foothold in the region, since its involvement with the Ottoman Empire was confined to the cultural level. In the settle-ment following World War I, the 'Fourteen Points' of President Wilson, who had come out against the Europeans' secret agreements, were scarcely taken into account; a similar situation was faced by the commission formed by the Americans King and Crane who, in 1919, criticised the Zionist plan. Lacking a mandate and a sphere of influence, Washington made its first move by getting into the Middle Eastern oil business: in Iraq in 1927, then in Saudi Arabia in 1933 and Kuwait in 1934. Ten years later, American companies controlled 20 per cent of Middle East production and 50 per cent of its reserves.

With World War II the balance of power shifted. While France lost its only bases in Lebanon and Syria, and Britain found itself struggling in Palestine, and consequently in the Arab world as a whole, the US, on the other hand, was becoming established. In 1947 Harry Truman had under-taken to help 'free peoples who are fighting against the attempts of armed minorities to enslave them or against external pressures': in this way Greece, Turkey and Iran found themselves being lent the means to buy American arms. Saudi Arabia was securely tied up by the lend-lease of 1943. On 20 January 1949 a new bill, the Four Point Plan, allowed money to be poured into the Arab countries.

But this proved a more difficult task. During the war, Franklin D. Roosevelt had made several contradictory promises, to Ibn Saud on the one hand, and Zionist leaders on the other. This double game became impossible when decisions were called for: for instance, in face of Arab reactions, Washington went back on its vote in favour of the **Partition Plan** for Palestine, but did not oppose Israel in the **1948–49 War**. Furthermore, America ratified the Jewish state's territorial expansion and the non-creation of the Arab state. On 25 May 1950, the US, Britain and France announced that their countries, 'if they ascertained that any Middle East state was preparing to violate the frontiers of the armistice lines, would not hesitate, in accordance with their obligations as members of the United Nations or outside this framework, to intervene to prevent such a violation'. And the tripartite declaration placed on all arms deliveries the condition that 'the buyer country has no intention of committing an act of aggression against another state'.

One can imagine the reaction of the **Arabs**, thus forced to accept what was for them the catastrophic status quo of the post-war situation and to have to ask for aid with strict conditions attached, whereas it was well known that Israel was granted aid without strings. Their discontent explains the rejection of the Allied Supreme Command in the Middle East set up by London in 1950 and the Middle East Defence Organisation, which London, Washington, Paris and Ankara invited Cairo to join in 1951. **Egypt's 'no'** was all the more resounding when, in July 1952, the Free Officers organised by **Gamal Abdel Nasser** took power. If the US had made advances in the north, with Turkey joining NATO in 1951, and in the east in 1953, by putting an end to the experiment of Iranian Prime Minister Muhammad Mosaddeq, who was trying to regain Iran's control of its oil, it met with failure in the south. A new attempt, called the **Baghdad Pact**, was no more successful: the Turco–Iranian treaty was joined by Britain and Pakistan, but not Lebanon, Jordan, Egypt or Syria. Moreover, opposition to the pact stimulated Egypt's neutralist and nationalist tendencies; in September 1955 Egypt signed an arms contract with the USSR.

Aware of this boomerang effect, Washington held back from the Franco–British operation against the man who had just nationalised the **Suez Canal** Company (see **1956 War**). Staying out of things proved successful on two counts: London and Paris alone footed the fiasco's extremely heavy bill, while the US perceptibly improved its image. The Americans fully intended to fill the gap left by their allies; this was the aim of the Eisenhower Doctrine, outlined on 5 January 1957, as a programme of economic and military aid aimed at combating the USSR's 'power policy'. But it was only accepted by Saudi Arabia, Lebanon and Iraq, where the King and his pro-Western Prime Minister, Nuri Said, perished in the uprising of 14 July 1958. The next day the Marines landed in Beirut and British paratroops in Amman in order to stop things spreading. Baghdad did join Damascus and Cairo in its radical point of view, but this was more a response to the Israeli–Palestinian conflict, a constant source of anti-imperialism.

Paradoxically, the Six Day **1967 War**, which saw Israel quadruple its territory at the expense of Egypt, Jordan and Syria, somewhat reduced the dilemma in which Washington was enmeshed, although it had kept Tel Aviv at arm's length. In the absence of a comprehensive peace settlement that could only be guaranteed by the two superpowers, the Arab defeat of 1967 made the US a possible broker in bilateral peace agreements: the defeat destabilised radical regimes and strengthened the position of moderate elements within them. Already present within the framework of the Rogers Plan and the Jarring mediations of 1970, this logic was to prevail after the **1973 War**. Admittedly, the US took Israel's side, but aside from the International Conference that had come to grief almost as soon as it opened, they were alone in proposing a plan: that of US Secretary of State Henry Kissinger's 'step-by-step' approach, which would lead to the not-so-little steps of the **Camp David Accords**.

To win back these long hostile Arab countries, without in any way having to put at risk the 'special relations' existing between Washington and Tel Aviv, the US employed the carrot and the stick during these decisive years. The carrot was the restitution of the Egyptian and Syrian territories occupied by Israel since 1967, the Palestinian question being treated on the level of vague generalities. It was also the American economic opening in response to the Arab *infitah*. As for the stick, it was the threat of the use of force – already deployed, after Iran in 1953 and Lebanon in 1958, in Jordan to save **King Hussein** in 1970 – against any internal or external attempt at destabilisation. The collapse of the Shah of Iran's regime, which had maintained order in the Gulf, was to reinforce this attitude: 'Any attempt to take control of the Gulf,' Jimmy Carter would declare at the beginning of 1980, 'will be seen as an attack against the interests of the United States, and will be resisted by any means, including military force'. And to back up the threat, the Rapid Deployment Force already dreamed of by the Kennedy administration was formed, and proved its efficiency in the Gulf, against Iran in 1988 and again in 1990–91 against Iraq.

The method was so successful that, immediately after the **1982 War** in Lebanon, Ronald Reagan could feel he held all the trumps: Israel pro-American and stronger than ever, Egypt brought round since Camp David, Jordan soon to be the same, Saudi Arabia and the Gulf in friendly hands, the **Palestine Liberation Organisation (PLO)** bleeding, Lebanon controlled by the Phalangists, Iraq and Iran exhausting themselves in a bloody war. Only distant South **Yemen** and a Syria weakened by the war seemed able to offer any resistance to Washington's projects. Was the strategic consensus embodied by the Reagan Plan of 1 September 1982 finally about to be realised? The negative reply was not long in coming. The defeat of Amin Gemayel and the failure of the Israeli–Lebanese treaty of 17 May 1983 were to rebound on the US, whose troops had to leave Beirut.

After fifteen years of spectacular US ascendancy, revenge for the years of Soviet expansion in the Middle East, the blow incurred in Lebanon and its repercussions appear to have caused Washington some doubts, if not over aims, then certainly over methods. The time seemed ripe for negotiations with Syria, to work out together a settlement taking its trump cards into account and recognising the regional leadership of Damascus. The US forced Iran, mainly by the massive presence of the American fleet in the Gulf, to accept a settlement involving a ceasefire with Iraq and the renewal of contacts with Tehran moderates in the aftermath of the 'Irangate' illegal weapons sales affair. Last and most importantly, detente with the USSR could have implications for the Middle East, by facilitating the convening of a **peace conference**.

Following the Palestine National Council of Algiers, Ronald Reagan, on 15 December 1988, embarked on a new direction before handing over to George Bush Senior. According to the White House, **Yasser Arafat** had finally satisfied the conditions laid down 13 years previously by Kissinger: explicitly recognising Israel and renouncing all forms of **terrorism**. Washington engaged in a 'substantial dialogue' with the PLO. However, following the fall of the Berlin Wall, Bush and his advisors were preoccupied with other matters. The massive changes in the Soviet Union and Central Europe posed a new set of formidable challenges to the US, as well as deflecting attention away from the Middle East. Even if the USSR and its empire, America's main enemy since the Cold War, was in the process of collapsing, the growing strength of the European Economic Community was a direct threat to America's formerly undisputed supremacy. The US was now only responsible for 25 per cent of the world's production, whereas after the Second World War it had supplied 40 per cent.

The Gulf presented ideal conditions for the US to regain lost ground, with its strategic location, its oil wealth, the civil and military market that it provided, the number of possible allies for Washington and the military presence that it already possessed in the region. **Saddam Hussein**'s foray into Kuwait provided an unexpected opportunity. Although it is doubtful that the Iraqi leader fell into a trap – the hesitation of the US in the preceding weeks was a result of the gravity of the pro-Iraqi policy of eight years before – it is nevertheless clear that the US immediately seized its chance.

It did so with considerable success. The Gulf War allowed the US to fulfil five major objectives: a demonstration of massive military power, an unprecedented political and diplomatic force under American control, an exceptional penetration into the regional arms and industrial markets and a severe shake-up in the Middle East, which was now under American leadership. But the crucial factor was undoubtedly the realignment of the European powers that became involved, directly or indirectly, in Operation Desert Storm, which struck a heavy blow to their relations with the Arab world, while the US cemented theirs.

The election of Bill Clinton to the presidency of the US marked a turning point in the history of the Middle East, signalled by the end of the Cold War and the assertion of American hegemony. Initially the new administration treated the PLO with overt hostility, while the Israeli government was locked in secret talks in Oslo. It distanced itself from the traditional positions of American diplomacy: colonies soon became an issue which complicated negotiations but were no longer 'illegal'; Washington withdrew its vote on the **UN Security Council Resolution** 194 on the **right of return** for Palestinian refugees; it no longer considered the **West Bank** and Gaza to be 'Occupied Territories', instead calling them 'disputed territories'. Meanwhile, Clinton's government decreed a policy of 'dual containment' towards Iraq and Iran.

Although surprised by the **Oslo Accords**, Clinton still managed to stage the official signing of the Declaration of Principles at the White House on 13 September 1993. Yet subsequently he left the Israelis and **Palestinians** to their own devices, only intervening when the two sides became obstreperous. The State Department's only involvement in the Middle East was with the **Golan Heights** and the negotiations between the Israelis and the Syrians, and that amounted to nothing. Meanwhile, the war against terrorism had become the central slogan of American strategy, as was witnessed at the Sharm el-Sheikh summit on 13 March 1996, when Washington attempted to isolate **Libya**, **Sudan**, Iran and Iraq. In July 1996, a series of measures was introduced to enforce a 'secondary boycott' against countries that invested in the oil industry in Libya and Iran, causing uproar in Europe.

However, the riots in Jordan, the troubles in Bahrain and the bombings in Saudi Arabia highlighted the fragility of the regimes that are Washington's allies. Although it spared no effort in assisting **Shimon Peres** in May 1996, the US had to come to terms with the victory of the Israeli right and **Benyamin Netanyahu**. But when Netanyahu began to stack up provocations against the **Palestinian Authority**, the White House involved itself increasingly in the Israeli–Palestinian negotiations. After the Wye River summit, in December 1998 Clinton was present at the special session of the Palestinian National Council which abrogated the articles of the Palestinian Charter which spoke of the destruction of the state of Israel. He told them, 'Before you [is] the opportunity to shape a new Palestinian future on your own land'.

General Ehud Barak's victory in May 1999 offered the US a chance to renew friendship links with its privileged partner. This new honeymoon translated into a 30 per cent increase in America's annual military aid to Israel – this would rise to $2.4bn in the following decade. Clinton paid dearly for his alignment with Barak, whose intransigence led to the collapse of negotiations with the Syrians over the Golan Heights. (These negotiations appeared to begin well, but then contributed to the stalemate at Camp

David.) Clinton failed to win the peace that he dreamt of, to crown his two periods in office.

Washington was also pursuing a **sanctions** policy against Baghdad. On 18 December 1998, the US and their British allies took the provocative step of launching a series of raids on Iraq, during the night of 16–17 December. This was a slap in the face for the UN Security Council, which was then in session debating the reports of the UN Special Commission (UNSCOM), for the disarmament of Iraq, and the International Atomic Energy Authority (IAEA).

American foreign policy also took a major turn with the election of George W. Bush in November 2000. As the mouthpiece for the Republican right, the new President was surrounded by hawks intent on imposing US hegemony. They set themselves three priorities, subsequently legitimated by the attacks of 11 September 2001 and the 'crusade' launched against the 'axis of evil': the war against terrorism, of course, but also the search for new oil reserves and the reinforcement of US military superiority.

As regards oil, a report by Vice-President Richard Cheney on 20 May 2001 spelled it out clearly: by 2020, in order to cope with increasing consumption, the US will have to import 60 per cent more oil than in 2002. The Middle East has two thirds of the world's oil resources. Hence the importance of controlling Iraq.

In his electoral campaign, Bush committed himself to 'beginning to build the army of the next century'. The strengthening of US military supremacy would be achieved first by the creation of the famous anti-missile shield supposed to protect US territory, along with Allied zones considered vital, and air and naval bases. It would also imply the development of all the most up-to-date weaponry. But it would require above all that America should have the capacity of projecting its power in order to be able to fight victoriously in every corner of the planet, with more mobile heavy units and more lethal light units. In addition: America has the right to embark on preventive wars against hostile powers liable to make use of **weapons of mass destruction**, which is confirmed in the official document of September 2002, entitled 'The National Security Strategy of the United States of America', where chapter 5 states specifically that

> the United States has long maintained the option of preemptive actions to counter a sufficient threat to our national security. The greater the threat, the greater is the risk of inaction – and the more compelling the case for taking anticipatory action to defend ourselves, even if uncertainty remains as to the time and place of the enemy's attack.

This is the framework for the anti-terrorist war embarked upon by Washington against al-Qaeda, but also against the 'axis of evil'. This 'crusade' requires a redeployment of the presence of the US army in the world, and particularly in the Middle East, where it led directly to the attack on Baghdad in order to get rid of Saddam's regime.

Since his election in February 2001, **Ariel Sharon**'s most signal achievement has been to locate the Israeli–Palestinian conflict within a framework of 'Everyone has their own bin Laden; ours is Arafat'. At first Washington, concerned to build the coalition for its war in Afghanistan and eager to win Arab support for it, gave a degree of backing to Arafat. For instance, on 2 October 2001 Bush stated, 'The idea of a Palestinian state has always been a part of [our] vision, so long as the right of Israel to exist is respected'. On 12 March 2002, the US would even back Resolution 1397 in the Security Council (see Appendix 14), which mentions – for the first time since the Partition Plan for Palestine – 'a vision of a region where two States, Israel and Palestine, live side by side within secure and recognised borders'.

But the increasing number of suicide bombings in spring 2002 enabled Sharon to resume the offensive initiated at the start of December 2001 against the Autonomous Territories and the Palestinian Authority. Bush became increasingly willing to see Israeli operations as a contribution to the war against terrorism. And in his speech of 24 June 2002, he definitively dropped the Palestinian Authority: he made the creation of a Palestinian state conditional on the setting up of a 'new and different Palestinian leadership' and called for 'true reform' which 'will require entirely new political and economic institutions, based on democracy, market economics and action against terrorism'.

The wheel thus came full circle, and Bush returned to the abstentionist position which marked the early months of his presidency in relation to Israeli–Palestinian issues. Ignoring the risks of a new bloodbath, indeed of an explosion in the region, the US administration preferred to devote its energy to the preparation of the second act of its war against terrorism: the offensive against Iraq.

US CENTCOM

A combined force made up of American army, air force, navy and Marine Corps units, **US** Central Command (CENTCOM) and its predecessor the Rapid Deployment Joint Task Force (RDJTF) were designed to intervene in trouble spots with the greatest possible speed, particularly in the Middle East.

Heir to the US Strike Command created in 1962, replaced ten years later by the US Readiness Command, which were both without any specific regional designation, the RDJTF was the result of Presidential Directive 18, issued in August 1977 by Jimmy Carter just after he became President. The RDJTF's mission was spectacularly re-affirmed on 23 January 1980 following the entry of Soviet troops into Afghanistan, on the occasion of the State of the Union address in which Carter affirmed, for the first time, that his country was ready to intervene to protect its 'vital interests' in the Gulf, including **oil**. In March, the Force's unified command was formed, headed by General Paul Kelley of the US Marines.

At the time, American leaders felt, or claimed to feel, threatened by the headway being made in the region by the Soviet Union, which was surrounding the pro-Western regimes and the oilfields from **Libya** to Afghanistan via Ethiopia and South **Yemen**. With the exile of the Shah in 1979 the US had lost its main agent in the region; secure with its elite army, **Iran** had played the very useful role of policeman for Washington in the Middle East and the Gulf. Henceforth, the RDJTF had the task of compensating for this serious loss, which, with the affair of the American embassy hostages in Iran, began to look like a historic humiliation. The force was strengthened by Ronald Reagan soon after he became President, with considerable means and manpower and a growing number of bases and facilities at its disposal. Activated by Reagan on 1 January 1983, US CENTCOM was the permanent successor to the RDJTF.

Headquartered at the huge McDill airbase in Tampa, Florida, CENTCOM is one of nine Unified Combatant Commands assigned operational control of US combat forces. In all CENTCOM has at its disposal 250,000 men, a force that can be increased to half a million, America's biggest contingent. It includes units from the ground forces (one airborne division, one helicopter-borne assault division, one of mechanised infantry, one of light infantry, one of airborne cavalry), the Marines (one unit plus a third of an amphibian unit), the air force (seven tactical air squadrons and two squadrons of strategic bombers) and the navy (three groups of fleet aircraft carriers, one group of surface ships and five navy patrol squadrons). Currently these can be in the field at three or four days' notice for the first units on the spot, and from four to six weeks for the last – the US has close to a thousand military and civil aircraft available for troop transport and around six hundred units in its naval forces. But the speed of intervention depends greatly on the bases available within the region.

The formation of CENTCOM has increased the importance of the chain of bases and facilities which the American army needs as staging posts, sites for stationing troops, arms and supplies, for monitoring stations etc. The bases acquired in Europe since the end of World War II have therefore been augmented over the last two decades: the US now has facilities in Morocco, the Ras Banas base in **Egypt**, the Masirah base in Oman, the port of Mogadishu and the Berbera airport in Somalia, as well as the Kenyan port of Mombasa. It also has, in addition to the Diego Garcia base rented from **Britain**, Israeli military bases that have been put at the disposal of the US, and those that Riyadh agreed to have in **Saudi Arabia**, until US Secretary of State Donald Rumsfeld announced in 2003 that the US would be withdrawing its air force from the kingdom. The **Gulf War** in 1990–91 enabled the US to deploy its forces effectively: 150,000 men, 4 aircraft carriers, 2 command vessels, 1 destroyer, 5 cruisers, 11 frigates, 310 fighter aircraft, 80 bombers, hundreds of tanks, 20 Stealth bombers and an unknown number of Patriot, Hawk, Stinger and Chaparral missiles. Washington did not hide its desire to establish a permanent presence in Saudi Arabia and the Gulf, with air bases and port facilities paid for by its grateful hosts. The insertion of these assets into the Pentagon's military strategy was first seen with Operation Bright Star, during which the US army carried out exercises in conjunction with Egypt, **Sudan** and, up until 1985, Somalia and Oman.

The effectiveness of the American deployment strategy became apparent to the world at the time of the Gulf War. In less than ten months America was able to send 500,000 men, 1000 tanks, 2000 transporters, 1300 aircraft, 1500 helicopters and a fleet of 100 or so ships, of which six were aircraft carriers, into the Persian Gulf. This was the largest military mobilisation in history, and it happened in a very short space of time.

Flushed with the success of its operations during the conflict with **Iraq**, the US was able to extend considerably the network of bases and facilities at its disposal in the Middle East. Besides the ports of Iskenderun and Yumurtalik, it had the advantage of the Incirlik air base in **Turkey**, which served as headquarters for Operation Provide Comfort and from where, following the signature of a co-operation treaty in September 1990 and the approval of a resolution of the Turkish national assembly in January 1991, reconnaissance flights were sent over northern Iraq. It installed military equipment in **Kuwait**, using its ports and airports as laid out in the Defence Pact of September 1991, and also in Qatar, with which a defence pact was signed in 1992 and a more specific agreement completed in March 1995. It gained access to facilities in the bases and ports of the United Arab Emirates (defence agreement in 1991, concluded in July 1994) and in Bahrain (co-operation agreement in October 1991 and a memorandum in January 1994). The irony of the situation was that although Saudi Arabia did not formally sign any treaty with the US, that did not stop more than a thousand American soldiers being posted there, mainly in Riyadh and at the Dhahran base, the headquarters of the 'Peninsula Shield', from where reconnaissance fights over southern Iraq took off during the 1990s. In total, during the summer of 1996, the American army had more than 20,000 men deployed in the Persian Gulf alone. In February 1996, the accords between **Israel** and Turkey coincided with **Jordan**'s decision to open its bases to American aircraft. This meant that the US had cast its net over the length and breadth of the Middle East. The US Fifth Fleet, whose headquarters are in Bahrain, was 'deactivated' in 1947, but went back into service on 1 July 1995. It is made up of 30 warships and 15,000 sailors and marines.

The 2003 US-led war in Iraq once again demonstrated the speed and efficacy of American military planners.

WATER

In 1953, **Israel**'s decision to divert some of the waters of the River Jordan at Lake Tiberias created major tensions in the Middle East. In early 1964, an Arab Summit decided on a counter-project for the exploitation of the Jordan's water. This rivalry was a factor in the escalation which led to the **1967 War. Syria**'s decision, taken in 1973, to fill the Tabqa Dam on the Euphrates also brought Baghdad and Damascus to the edge of war: according to **Iraq**, the livelihoods of three million Iraqi peasants were under threat. In 1990–91, during the **Gulf War**, American experts suggested using water as a weapon against **Saddam Hussein**: it would have been possible to cut off Iraq's water supply by blocking the upstream flows of the Tigris and the Euphrates, both of which originate in **Turkey**.

These examples provide dramatic illustrations of the water issues at stake in the Middle East: in an arid region, where rainfall is scarce, it is a rare resource which all sides have an interest in exploiting. Issues of national security are at stake in the question of how both to exploit and conserve it, particularly since the region suffers from a structural imbalance between its reserves and a consumption which is growing fast as a result of population growth, economic development and urbanisation. According to an **Arab League** report of December 1999, two thirds of the Arab countries have less than 1000 cubic metres of water per inhabitant per year, a level which is technically on the threshold of shortage. The countries of the Gulf, **Jordan**, Israel and the Palestinian areas were all in a critical position, with less than 500 cubic metres.

Conventional water resources in the Middle East consist basically of underground water reserves and the rivers which irrigate the region (the Nile, Jordan, Tigris and Euphrates). They are no longer sufficient to satisfy the needs of agriculture, industry, tourism and basic drinking water.

'Egypt is a gift of the Nile.' Almost 2500 years later, this observation by Herodotus still sums up **Egypt**'s destiny, as illustrated by the events of 1980, when several consecutive years of drought brought the levels of the Nile to their lowest ever. Agriculture suffered, but so did industry, since 28 per cent of the country's electricity is hydro-generated. Although the levels were subsequently restored, it is forecast that Egypt will have a water deficit of 5 billion cubic metres by 2010, mainly as a result of the country's fast-growing population. This accounts for the interest which Cairo has shown in the various countries which control the sources of the Nile, and the territories through which it travels, notably Ethiopia and **Sudan**. Egypt has been particularly worried by the development in southern Sudan of the rebellion led by John Garang, since it led to a stoppage of construction work between Bor and Malakal on the Jonglei Canal, a project intended to make possible a saving of 0.5 billion cubic metres of water. Tension was further heightened by Uganda's project to require Egypt and Sudan to pay for water, and Ethiopia's plan to build two dams on the Blue Nile. By 2002, only Cairo and Khartoum had signed an agreement to plan for the sharing of its waters. In the meantime, the Egyptian authorities had embarked on Operation New Valley to the west of the Nile, which, together with the Toschka Canal, fed by the Aswan Dam, was intended to increase the area of arable land in Egypt from 6 to 25 per cent.

Although it carries only 2 per cent of the amount of water carried by the Nile, and 6 per cent of that of the Euphrates, the River Jordan and its tributaries (in particular the Yarmuk) lie at the heart of occasionally violent confrontations between Israel, Syria – particularly over the **Golan Heights** – and Jordan. The Jewish state intends to maintain control of the water resources of the **West Bank**, 90 per cent of which is used for its own benefit, and of the **Golan**, notably to supply the **settlements**. The **Palestinians** for their part are in a condition of 'hydrological stress', and the water available to them averages a mere 250 cubic metres per inhabitant per year. However, in Appendix B of the **Taba** accord, known as Oslo II, Article 40 stated that Israel recognises the water rights of the Palestinians in the West Bank. The question of water was postponed, together with all the other difficult issues, to final negotiations, which only began in 2000 and then collapsed at the **Camp David** summit. While the world waits for negotiations to be resumed, the increasingly deep well-drilling by the Jewish settlements has led to a drop in the level of the water table, to the frequent incursion of sea water, and thus to a growing salinity, which now exceeds 500mg per litre – the maximum level fixed by the World Health Organisation is 250mg per litre.

Jordan, which at present has a water deficit of almost 300 million cubic metres per year, had hopes of improving its water access as a result of the peace treaty signed with Israel in 1994: under the terms of this treaty its western neighbour was supposed to supply it with 25 billion cubic metres of water per year. But by 2002 no dam project, reservoir or desalination plant had seen the light of day. Meanwhile Amman has pursued other projects to reduce the exploitation of non-renewable underground water resources, mending leaks in the water supply system in its biggest towns and improving the productivity of water and irrigation. The agriculture sector alone consumes 70 per cent of the country's water, although it represents only 3.8 per cent of GNP. Jordan was focusing on the development of non-conventional resources by the re-utilisation of water used for irrigation, and by desalination. One project has already been built, in Hisban south of Amman, enabling the desalination of 30 million cubic metres per year. Two other projects were underway: the development of the Disi underground water resources in the south of the country, which should bring the capital an additional 100 million cubic metres of water per year, and the

Unity Dam project on the Yarmuk, which is expected to be revived as one outcome of Syrian–Jordanian reconciliation.

The waters of the Golan Heights run into Lake Galilee, the Jewish state's largest reservoir, from where they are then distributed to Israel by the National Water Carrier. Following the breakdown of Israeli–Syrian negotiations in spring 2000, positions became irreconcilable: the Syrians demanded sovereignty over the Heights, while the Israelis justified their access to this resource (which supplies one third of their annual consumption) in the name of a usage right acquired by force, and thus in violation of international law. It should be said that Israel has a water deficit of nearly 300 million cubic metres per year, and for several years this has resulted in summertime water cuts in several large towns.

Along with **Lebanon**, Turkey is one of the few countries in the Middle East that does not suffer water shortages. The country controls half the flow of the Tigris and 90 per cent of that of the Euphrates, which has led to confrontations with both Syria and Iraq. Agreements on water sharing have been signed several times, but they have been threatened by Turkey's plans for the development of southeastern Anatolia, known as the GAP project, launched in 1981. With the construction of 21 dams and a dozen power stations on the two rivers over thirty years and at a cost of nearly $50bn, the GAP should make it possible to harness the waters of the two rivers and contribute to the development of one of Turkey's poorest regions, where a Kurdish rebellion is underway – particularly in irrigating 1.7 million hectares, or 25 per cent of the country's arable land. The completion of the huge Atatürk dam on the Euphrates – which, when it is completed, will irrigate some 10,000 sq. km and produce 27 billion kilowatts per year – and its filling in January 1990, which stopped the flow of water for an entire month, created deep anxieties in both Syria and Iraq. Damascus, in particular, fears a reduction of the Euphrates, even though an agreement signed in 1987 guarantees a minimum passage of at least 500 cubic metres per second, in other words, half of the total flow available, to be shared between Syria and Iraq. A major cause of concern has been supplies from the al-Thawra and al-Ba'th dams, which are decisive in the supply of water, the generation of electricity and irrigation in Syria. As for the future, both Syria and Iraq fear that once the GAP dam has been completed Turkey will have a formidable means of not only economic but also political and diplomatic pressure.

In order to resolve the water problems of the Middle East, a two-pronged strategy will be required: on the one hand, a strategy of water conservation, particularly in agriculture, where there is much wastage; on the other, a degree of regional co-operation, which would imply an end to the various states of war in the region. If water is not the object of concerted co-operation by the countries of the Middle East, there is no doubt that it will become a further factor of conflict and destabilisation. Equally, a lasting peace in the region would make it possible for all countries to co-operate in embarking on radically new solutions: the capture and use of solar energy in deserts, which are perfect for such an operation (according to experts from the Egyptian electricity ministry, three ranks of concave mirrors from Casablanca to Rafah could capture four times the electric energy currently consumed by Europe); this energy could make it possible to extend desalination of sea water (in **Kuwait** desalination already produces most of the water consumed); the building of the 'Peace Aqueduct' at the huge cost of $21bn (this would involve Ankara supplying 2.2 million cubic metres of water per day to the whole **Arabian Peninsula**, passing via Syria, Jordan and Iraq) etc.

In short, as Muhammad Sid-Ahmed wrote in *Le Monde diplomatique* (June 1998),

> While water shortages threaten to exacerbate still further the conflicts in the Middle East, they may also have the effect of making people quicker to realise that these are problems that have to be resolved. The advantage of a 'revolutionary environmental policy project worthy of the 21st century' is that it involves thinking big: the very scale of the project should make it possible to write off the cost in the interest of heralding in a new and genuinely global age.

WEAPONS OF MASS DESTRUCTION

Having failed to establish a link between **Iraq** and al-Qaeda (see **Osama bin Laden**), the Bush administration advanced the longer-term danger represented by Baghdad's nuclear, chemical and biological weapons to justify the war that it intended to conduct, with or without the UN, against the Baghdad regime. Leaving aside the threat, real or supposed, of **Saddam Hussein**, this argument shows how much the arms race in weapons of mass destruction (which have been used in the Middle East theatre since the 1980s) has led the region – and the world – to the edge of a precipice.

While awaiting the reports to the UN Security Council by the inspectors who went to Iraq in mid-November 2002, a document published at the end of summer 2002 by the International Institute for Strategic Studies (IISS) in London offered an initial assessment of the Iraqi potential. Using information supplied by former UN inspectors and inspectors from the International Atomic Energy Agency (IAEA), but also from the CIA, the Pentagon and Iraqi exiles, John Chipman stated that 'war, sanctions and inspections have reversed and retarded, but not eliminated Iraq's nuclear, biological and chemical weapons and long range missile capacities'. He stressed, however, that the threat was a lot lower than in 1991. As regards missiles, Iraq apparently had no more than a dozen modified Soviet Scuds, rebaptised al-Hussein (with a range of 600km). But Baghdad 'does not possess facilities to produce fissile material in sufficient amounts for nuclear weapons', and it would need years and extensive foreign aid to equip itself. On the other hand, Iraq 'has probably kept several hundred tons' of mustard gas, sarin and cyclo-sarin, and can 'produce new stocks of bulk BW agent, including botulinum toxin and anthrax with its existing facilities, equipment and materials'.

Today seven Middle East countries possess missiles capable of transporting nuclear warheads over distances ranging between 300 and 2800km. **Israel** has about 50 Jericho I missiles (500km range) and the same number of Jericho 2 (1800km range), which it manufactures domestically. These would be capable of targeting any capital in the Middle East. Both missiles have the capacity to carry nuclear warheads, as do many aircraft owned by the Israeli armed forces, for instance the F-4 Phantom and A-4 Skyhawk, and also the 260 F-16 (1600km range) and F-15 (3500km range) bought from the **US**, which is expected to supply Israel with a further 100 between 2003 and 2008. On the other hand, Washington has refused to equip its ally with the 48 Tomahawk cruise missiles ordered in 2000. For its part, Israel has denied that its Dolphin submarines have a nuclear capacity. Similarly, according to the experts, the small size of the Ofeq satellite precludes direct military usage. For their part, **Egypt**, the United Arab Emirates, Iraq (before the **Gulf War**), **Iran**, **Libya**, **Syria** and **Yemen** have Scud-B and/or Scud-C missiles produced originally in the Soviet Union, China and North Korea, with ranges of 300km and 500km respectively.

Syria has Chinese CSS-6/M-9 missiles with a range of 600km. **Saudi Arabia** also has Chinese missiles, the CSS-2, capable of hitting targets at a distance of up to 2800km, which would bring Greece, India and the former Soviet Union into range. Israel is particularly concerned about the arrival of this missile in the Middle East; it is well aware of its performance specifications, since it was Israeli technicians who secretly assisted China in its conversion from nuclear to conventional warheads, and in perfecting its guidance systems. It is clear that the days are long gone when Washington, Moscow, London and Paris had a monopoly on the manufacture and sale of weapons, and of missiles in particular. New producers have arrived on the scene, notably China and North Korea, and are taking a growing share of the regional market; furthermore, a number of Middle Eastern countries (Israel, Iraq before the Gulf War, Iran, Egypt etc.) are themselves developing independent arms industries. Among the missiles available or currently being developed are the North Korean No-Dong (1000km range), which Libya has acquired, and which Iran has successfully adapted as the Shihab 3, and the Taepo-Dong (2000–3500km range).

The 'war of the cities' embarked on by Iraq and Iran during the protracted hostilities of the **Iran–Iraq War** served as a testbed for this advanced weaponry. For the first time since World War II, missiles were used massively against civilian populations. In the winter of 1987–88 alone, Baghdad and Tehran exchanged 417 Scud-B missiles, which had been revamped to double their range, and which killed over two thousand people. The 1990–91 Gulf War alarmingly escalated the situation even further. With the firing of 93 Iraqi Scud missiles out of the 819 that had been supplied by the USSR against Israel, Saudi Arabia and Bahrain, it appeared that the Middle East was now ripe for a missile war, and that these missiles, instead of carrying conventional payloads, might very soon be used to carry weapons of mass destruction.

The reason why the leaders of the major powers find the escalation of missile technology in the Middle East so disturbing is because it runs parallel with a growing willingness to use weapons of mass destruction – nuclear, chemical and biological – which could one day be employed as warheads in ballistic missiles.

On the nuclear front, Israel led the way by equipping itself first with the atomic bomb, accomplished in 1966 with French assistance, and then the hydrogen bomb, created in co-operation with South Africa and Taiwan at the end of the 1970s. If we are to believe engineer Mordechai Vanunu, who was lifted by the Israeli secret services and sentenced to 18 years of imprisonment on 24 March 1988 for having made defence-related allegations to the *Sunday Times* in 1986, the Israeli nuclear stockpile at that point included 200 bombs. In 1996 the estimated figure was 300.

'We cannot rule out the possibility that the other side is going to do the same, leading the conflict to new levels,' said Yevgeni Primakov, Mikhail Gorbachev's advisor, back in 1987. In fact during the second half of the 1970s, Iraq went to great lengths to ensure that it too was equipped with nuclear weapons. On 'Thanksgiving Day' in November 1990, while George Bush Senior was visiting US troops on the Saudi 'front', he claimed that 'every day Saddam Hussein is getting closer to the realisation of his aim: a nuclear weapons arsenal'. This provided a further justification for the pursuit of war. More cautiously, Israeli sources confirmed that Iraq would already have had the bomb if the Israeli army had not destroyed the Tammuz nuclear reactor in 1981, reactors which were built by **France** and which Paris had always insisted were designed only for civil purposes. Similarly, according to the checks carried out by the IAEA, with which Baghdad was co-operating at the time, there was no way for Iraqi engineers to divert the civilian technology in their possession to military ends. Subsequently, in August 1991, the Iraqi authorities confirmed to the UN inspection team that they had produced 3g of plutonium suitable for use in an atom bomb, a derisory quantity – it takes 6kg to make a bomb, according to UN officials – but a significant step nonetheless. But as we have seen, as a result of the embargo following the Gulf War Baghdad has been obliged to renounce its nuclear ambitions.

This is not the case with Tehran, which is also part of the 'axis of evil' denounced by George W. Bush. Although there is limited information available on Iran's military programme, the development of its civil nuclear programme is public knowledge. Defying the opposition of the US, **Russia** has committed itself to supplying Iran with a 1000 megawatt reactor, which may be followed by two others, of 1000 and 400 megawatts apiece. China has also offered to assist in the construction of future power stations. The country now has three uranium mines, and Beijing has delivered an electromagnetic isotope separator. Thus far the IAEA has found no evidence of the production of nuclear weapons. However, the Israeli and American secret services claim that these could well be developed in the coming period. Be that as it may, Tehran is a signatory to the nuclear Non-Proliferation Treaty (NPT), and in May 1994 arrived at a new agreement with the IAEA, which declared itself happy with the degree of Iranian co-operation. Iran came under pressure to sign the additional protocol to the NPT in 2003, which would allow for a more intrusive inspections regime.

In the absence of nuclear reactors, several countries in the region have taken steps to acquire the 'poor man's atomic bomb': chemical weapons. Iraq appears to have been the first to be so equipped, with the assistance of German companies (subsequently prosecuted by their government), but also, it appears, of companies in Austria, Spain, India, the US and France. Saddam lost no time in moving from theory to practice during the Iran–Iraq War: chemical weapons were used against Iranian troops and the Kurdish population of Halabja.

According to experts, on the battlefield the effect of a chemical bombardment would be more psychological than tactical. It was in this spirit, exploiting the element of fear, that the **Ba'th** regime played its chemical card during the Gulf crisis, threatening to use chemical weapons as a means of warding off impending attack on Iraq. On 1 April 1991, a key Iraqi official promised to 'burn half of Israel' in the event of Israeli offensive action. During the crisis he repeated his warnings, and expanded them to include the use of biological weapons. Iraqi researchers were known to have carried out bacterial warfare experiments during the preceding four years, and the inspection teams found evidence of this at the Salman Pak site, in the form of bacteria capable of generating anthrax, botulism, brucellosis and tularaemia.

Although they failed in their dissuasive role, these threats led to a major escalation in the preparations for the Gulf War. Faced with an Iraqi arsenal which the CIA estimated at 1000 tons of gas (mustard, sarin and tabun) and 500,000 shells, Baghdad's adversaries were obliged to take spectacular precautions. In Saudi Arabia the Americans brought in anti-bacteriological equipment, vaccinated their troops and equipped them with anti-gas outfits. In October 1990, Israel distributed gas masks to the whole of its population – although the **Palestinians** in the Occupied Territories received only a limited number and were required to pay for them. Even though the Israeli leadership had promised Baghdad almost explicitly to inflict nuclear reprisals in the event of a chemical attack, every time a Scud missile landed the Israelis had to face the prospect that it might be chemically armed. On the other hand, military observers thought this an unlikely outcome, given that a missile warhead can hold only small amounts of gas, that the number of Scuds available was limited and that their targeting was rather less than precise.

In the event, during the course of the Gulf War neither Iraq nor the coalition of countries ranged against it ended up using chemical, let alone biological, weapons, although this did not prevent an American report published in 1994 from blaming the 'Gulf syndrome' suffered by large numbers of Gulf War veterans on Iraqi chemical attacks. Whatever the truth of the matter, the spectre which hung over the region for a period of several months prompted other countries in the region into a massive ordering programme for defensive equipment – led by Egypt, Israel, Saudi Arabia, Syria and **Turkey** – as well as accelerating the production of offensive weaponry which they all already possessed.

This accounted for the new efforts made by the major powers towards disarmament, but this time they attempted to take account of the tendency of numerous countries in the Middle East to link nuclear disarmament to the question of chemical weapons. At its meeting in Paris in July 1991, the five members of the UN Security Council called for a 'zone free of weapons of mass destruction in the Middle East', and, to this end, decided to observe 'rules of restraint' in their arms exports. They also called for the countries of the region to embark on a 'global programme of arms control' which would include 'a freeze on, and eventual elimination of, ground-to-ground missiles' and 'the subjection of all their nuclear activities to IAEA control', 'a ban on importation and production of materials capable of use for manufacturing nuclear weapons', and 'an undertaking to become party to the convention on chemical weapons as soon as it is concluded in 1992'.

Thus far these good intentions have only partially and temporarily been translated into reality. The Chemical Weapons Convention, signed on 13 January 1993, came into force on 29 April 1997. By 31 December 2001 it had been ratified by 145 governments, signed by 29 others, and led to 117 inspections, which made possible the destruction of 6374 tons of chemical agents (out of a declared total of 69,869 tons) and 2,098,013 munitions (out of a declared total of 8,624,493). The reinforcement and acceleration of this process was supposed to be the objective of the fifth conference of member states organised in 2001. But Washington reckoned that the proposed text underestimated the danger represented by the **'terrorist** states' and opposed its adoption, as well as forcing the suspension of the conference and the *ad hoc* group, thus blocking the whole process. The US was even successful in perpetrating within the Organisation for the Prohibition of Chemical Weapons (OPCW) what the *Guardian* called a 'chemical coup d'état': the forced resignation on 22 April 2002 of the General Director, Jose Mauricio Bustani, whose crime was to have argued that American factories should also be inspected, but above all of having wanted to persuade Baghdad, Tripoli, Damascus and Pyongyang to sign the Convention. If this had succeeded, it would have deprived George W. Bush of a powerful argument in his 'crusade'.

In the Middle East, in any event, several countries appear to be continuing their efforts to obtain chemical and biological weapons and to build on already existing stockpiles. In the list prepared by the US Secretary of State for Defence, we find among those countries 'seeking to supply themselves with, or having available the necessary infrastructures for beginning a research programme': Iraq, Iran, Libya, **Sudan** and Syria. In the case of Iraq, we know how much this accusation weighed in the preparation of the war planned by Washington; but, since the fall of Saddam, no weapons of mass destruction have yet been found. In the case of Libya, the US went on to accuse it of having 'factories' in Rabta and Semna, which in the 1990s were accused of manufacturing gases, and then the Tarhuna plant which, by virtue of equipment supplied by Germany, Belgium and **Britain**, was allegedly in a position to produce mustard gas, sarin and soman. Finally, in the case of Sudan, in 1998 the US air force bombed a factory which was allegedly producing chemicals for weapons, whereas in fact it was producing pharmaceuticals.

Thus while chemical and biological weapons are used as pretexts to justify operations that may act as cover for entirely different motives, it also remains the case that nobody knows exactly what is going on in the clandestine laboratories of either side – in the Middle East, or in the US and other Western countries.

WEST BANK

The West Bank of the Jordan was part of Palestine under the British Mandate. It was occupied by the armies of King Abdullah of Transjordan during the **1948–49 War**, and officially annexed by Amman on 24 April 1950, thus giving birth to the Kingdom of **Jordan**. Covering an area of 5440 sq. km, the West Bank takes in East **Jerusalem** and the towns of Nablus, **Jenin**, Tulkarem, Qalqiliya, Ramallah, Hebron and Bethlehem.

Occupied by the Israeli army at the time of the **1967 War**, unlike the Arab section of Jerusalem, the West Bank was not annexed to **Israel**. Nevertheless, its inhabitants (660,000 according to the 1967 census, including Jerusalem) experienced an occupation that totally changed their way of life and their political consciousness. Of the 250,000 people who fled to Jordan in June 1967, only a few thousand have been authorised to return home.

While practising a policy referred to as 'open bridge', which allowed certain contacts and commerce between the West Bank and Jordan, after the occupation Israel stepped up the economic integration of the territories. The West Bank became a crucial market for the Jewish state's exports, while tens of thousands of Palestinians began to cross into Israel to sell their manpower at low prices. From 5000 in 1968, their number increased to 25,000 in 1971, to 40,000 in 1979, stabilising at around 45,000 in the 1980s and early 1990s.

The social consequences of this economic policy on a traditionally agrarian society have been enormous. Most significant is the fact that the industrial working class now represents 40 per cent of the active population of the West Bank, while those employed in agriculture constitute no more than 25 per cent. This reversal provoked the disintegration of the traditional peasant rural society. Moral values and the peoples' way of life have been transformed. Relationships based on clientelism, a system of patronage through which the pro-Jordanian elites dominated society before 1967, have been ruptured. The changes have been aggravated by the increasing proportion of young people in the population and the high percentage of children attending school. Within a few years of the occupation a new, more nationalist intellectual elite came to the fore, replacing its more moderate elders and affirming its support for the **Palestine Liberation Organisation (PLO)**.

The political orientation of this new elite was further shaped by Israeli policy, which left little room for 'collaboration'. The establishment of **settlements**, the assertion of historical Jewish rights to what Israel calls Judea and Samaria, the annexation of Jerusalem (a holy city for both Muslims and Christians: a sizeable **minority** of Palestinians are Christian) all constituted obstacles to such a relationship. The repression – exercised equally against pro-Jordanian elements, nationalists favourable to the *fedayeen* and the communists – succeeded in isolating those whom the population saw as occupiers. While from 1967 to 1970 all political tendencies called for the return to the status quo preceding June 1967, **Black September** and the development of Palestinian national consciousness meant that in later years the pro-Jordan elements in the West Bank lost their influence.

In August 1973, the Palestine National Front (PNF) was formed, bringing together nationalists and communists and recognising the PLO as the 'sole legitimate representative of the Palestinians'. The PNF asserted its hegemony in the spring of 1976 during municipal elections in which it obtained 80 per cent of the seats and most of the mayoral appointments. During this period, the PNF made it possible both to affirm a national identity (in contradistinction to Israel, but also to Jordan) and put pressure on the PLO to adopt a realistic position, in other words favouring a political solution and the establishment of a Palestinian state on the West Bank and in Gaza.

It was the Palestinians of the West Bank who most vigorously opposed the Camp David Accords of 1978 and the concept of **autonomy**. This was because they had concrete experience of the policy of colonisation and the expropriation of land, intensified since **Menachem Begin** became Prime Minister of Israel. Political repression was stepped up in 1982 with the dismissal of most of the elected mayors and their replacement by Israeli administrators. This move was accompanied by measures used on a routine basis against the Palestinians: house arrests, deportations to Jordan, administrative detentions. Israel held, immediately prior to the **Intifada**, 4000 political prisoners from the West Bank and Gaza. The only area of relative freedom was the press. Although subject to rigorous censorship, because the newspapers were published in East Jerusalem, the press benefited from Israeli law. The outbreak of the uprising on the West Bank and in Gaza in December 1987 marked the culmination of a growing political consciousness which reflected a strong national identity and confirmed the central role of 'insiders' – Palestinians inside the Occupied Territories as opposed to those in exile – in the Palestinian struggle. On 31 July 1988 **King Hussein** took action by breaking all legal and administrative links between Jordan and the West Bank.

The status and future of the West Bank was at the heart of the **Oslo Accords** and the implementation of Palestinian autonomy. The **Taba** agreement (also known as Oslo II), signed on 28 September 1995 in Washington, set out the terms of the transitional period due to end in May 1999. The agreement stipulated that the West Bank be divided into three zones:

- Zone A, comprising the major Palestinian towns (Jericho, Jenin, Nablus, Tulkarem, Qalqiliya, Ramallah and Bethlehem), which were under Palestinian control and cover 3 per cent of the territory's area. Hebron with its 120,000 Palestinians and 300 Jewish settlers was to remain under Israeli occupation until mid-January 1997.
- Zone B, covering 27 per cent of the West Bank and practically all the 465 smaller Palestinian communities; although the **Palestinian Authority** had municipal powers in this zone, the Israeli army was still responsible for security and could enter the zone at any time.
- Zone C, covering 70 per cent of the West Bank, is where all the Israeli colonies are situated and remains under Israeli control.

At the end of 1995, Israeli troops withdrew from the major Palestinian towns (with the exception of Hebron) the Palestinian Authority took over. Although the elections on 20 January 1996 showed the depth of Palestinian feeling on the issue, **terrorist** attacks in spring 1996 highlighted the fragility of autonomy: the cordon which was systematically set up around the Autonomous Territories prevented Palestinians from going to work in Israel. It became increasingly difficult for supplies and workers to get through, making it impossible to build a viable economy. During the first half of 1996, the number of Israeli raids rose dramatically, particularly in the smaller towns, and led to the re-occupation of the towns situated in Zone B.

Under the Oslo timetable, 4 May 1996 was supposed to see the start of negotiations on the final status of the West Bank, Gaza and Jerusalem. But the context was far from favourable, given the election of **Benyamin Netanyahu**, who provoked two showdowns with the Palestinians: the decision to open the tunnel under the Haram al-Sharif; and the building of the settlement of Abu Ghneim, also known as Har Homa. In January 1997 he did accept, however, the restoration to the Palestinian Authority of four fifths of Hebron – one fifth would remain under Israeli sovereignty, including the part of the centre of town where some 300 extremist settlers were living. This would be the only 'concession' in the period up to the Wye River summit of October 1998 (here additional territorial withdrawals were discussed, but they would only partially be enacted).

The West Bank looks like a patchwork, a territory sliced up into segments by the settlements and their service-roads: According to a study published in 2002 by the Israeli human-rights association B'Tselem, although the settlements themselves cover only 1.7 per cent of the territory, together with their annexed land they control more than 41.9 per cent, not to mention the unilateral modifications of the 'frontiers' of Jerusalem, in 1967, which trebled its area, removing that area from the area of the West Bank.

Ehud Barak, who was elected Prime Minister on 17 May 1999, left it until the Sharm el-Sheikh summit of 4 September 1999 to redeploy the Israeli army as had been decided at Wye River. The Palestinian Authority had to wait until March 2000 before it had 17.2 per cent control of the West Bank under full sovereignty, and 23.8 per cent under shared sovereignty, leaving 59 per cent in the hands solely of Israel. At the time of the Camp David negotiations, the fact that Israel proposed to annex almost 10 per cent of the West Bank in order to group together about 80 per cent of its settlers was to contribute broadly to the failure of the negotiations.

The escalation of the Palestinian Intifada and the accompanying Israeli repression were to reduce Palestinian sovereignty in the West Bank to its simplest expression. In the initial period, through to autumn 2000 and in 2001, the systematic practice of closures enclosed the inhabitants in a multitude of small prisons, stifling economic life and seriously damaging their standard of living. The increasingly violent repressive operations which the Israeli army periodically launched under the guise of responding to terrorist attacks were to transform themselves into full-scale war with Operation Rampart in April 2002: the re-occupation of autonomous towns, the systematic destruction of infrastructures and the arrest of thousands of people. Much more worryingly for the future, is the 'Protective Wall' – a concrete, barb-wired barrier separating Israelis and Palestinians which snakes around the country. It was begun under the Labour party, but the project has been taken up with renewed vigour by **Sharon**. The wall will cut into 40 per cent of the West Bank and make Palestinian ghettos out of several towns. Nine years after Oslo the Palestinians no longer controlled the 17.2 per cent of the West Bank which had been so laboriously allocated to them under full sovereignty, which the Israeli army has since been intent on ruining.

In 2002, the population of the West Bank (East Jerusalem included) was 2.1 million, of whom 626,000 were refugees. Per-capita GNP had fallen from $2245 in 1992 to $1610. Almost half of all Palestinians are now living on less than $2 a day.

YEMEN

The Bab al-Mandeb ('Gate of Lamentations') links the Red Sea and the Indian Ocean. Less well known than the Straits of Hormuz, it is nonetheless of great strategic importance, especially since the reopening of the **Suez Canal** in 1975. Indeed, it is situated in the heart of a region marked by great political upheavals during the final quarter of the twentieth century: the fall of the monarchy in Ethiopia, Djibouti's accession to **independence**, the war between Ethiopia and Somalia, the independence of Eritrea and the many changes undergone by both Yemens. Divided for two centuries, North Yemen having fallen under Ottoman rule and South Yemen under British dominion, the two countries were reunited on 22 May 1990 with Sana'a as the capital. However, the new republic will long remain marked by the divergent past of its two regions.

North Yemen: stability restored

Independent from the end of World War I, North Yemen was ruled for many years by a monarchy which tried to keep the country isolated from the rest of the world. But in September 1962 Colonel Abdullah al-Salal overthrew Imam Muhammad al-Badr, who had just succeeded his father Ahmad Ben Yahya, and proclaimed a republic. There followed a long civil war, fuelled by massive intervention by the Egyptian army on the republican side and **Saudi Arabia**'s active support of the monarchists, which ravaged the country until 1970.

The protagonists finally negotiated an agreement: the continuation of the republican regime, the return of the royal family to Sana'a and the integration of royalists into the machinery of government. But instability persisted, with a series of political assassinations and coups d'état as well as a war with South Yemen in 1972. In June 1978 came the accession to power of Ali Abdullah Salah, who succeeded in restoring stability to his country, despite the many difficulties, including another brief war with the South at the beginning of 1979. Salah instigated a policy that maintained a balance between his powerful Saudi neighbour and South Yemen. He put down left-wing opposition with an iron fist and confirmed his government's authority in the region. Lastly, he developed close links with the Soviet Union (see **Russia**), in particular in the military sphere, while managing to maintain cordial relations with the **US**. It was the weakened position of the Marxist regime in the South that enabled President Salah to unify the two countries under his leadership.

South Yemen: from radicalisation to instability

Since the country's independence at the end of 1967 and the seizure of power by the National Liberation Front (NLF) following an armed struggle against the British, who had occupied Aden in 1839, South Yemen's political life has received many jolts. The country opted for a socialist regime – much more radical than that chosen by **Syria** or **Iraq** – which resembled the Cuban model in some ways and established close links with the USSR.

The main leaders of the NLF were drawn from the ranks of **George Habash**'s Arab Nationalist Movement (ANM), which influenced an entire generation of left-wingers in the Middle East. The victory of the NLF's Left in June 1969 committed the People's Democratic Republic of Yemen to the construction of socialism: the collectivisation of agriculture and the economy as a whole, including small traders; social programmes and the education of women and improvement of their status. Three men symbolised this new course: Abdul Fatah Ismail, the Secretary-General of the party; Ali Nasser Muhammad, the Prime Minister; Salem Rubaya Ali, President. It took twenty years to eliminate them: two were killed, the other exiled.

Involved at the time in an increasingly close alliance with Moscow, these leaders decided to unite the left – in particular the Ba'thist People's Vanguard Party and the communist People's Democratic Union – to create a single progressive party. On 11 October 1978, the first congress of the new Yemeni Socialist Party (YSP) opened, but without Rubaya, executed in June following an attempted coup d'état.

The reign of the new leader, Ismail, was not to last: accused of aggravating the conflict with the North and of isolating the country from its neighbours, he left in April 1980 for a gilded exile in Moscow. He was replaced by Muhammad, who, while retaining special relations with the USSR, sought to normalise relations with neighbouring states, including Saudi Arabia and Oman, with whom Aden established diplomatic relations on 27 October 1983. From the economic point of view, the new regime improved administration and accorded a more active role to the private sector.

But internal divisions remained, fanned more by personal ambition than political differences. The return of Ismail in February 1985 increased tension. On 13 January 1986, a civil war broke out in Aden and throughout the country between partisans of Ismail and those of Muhammad. The toll was dreadful: several thousands killed, among them many party leaders, including Ismail, and hundreds of millions of dollars of damage. Muhammad and 70,000 of his men sought refuge in North Yemen. The new regime, composed of second-rank leaders – including the new Secretary-General of the YSP, Ali Salem al-Bayd – vigorously repressed its opponents. But it was a blow for the socialist regime in light of the changes taking place in the Soviet Union and Eastern Europe. Under such conditions, the unification of Yemen saved the YSP from extinction.

Unification

The unification of North and South was ratified by the parliament of each country on 21 May 1989, and gave life to a long-cherished dream. A presidential council made up of three Northerners and two Southerners, headed by Salah, was elected and the regime was now dominated by the alliance between his Popular General Congress (PGC) and the YSP. The Saudis were particularly worried by this new regional power because, since 1954, they had been involved in a territorial dispute with their Yemeni neighbours. Sana'a had never recognised Riyadh's annexation of the provinces of Jizan, Asir and Najran. Besides, the Saudis had given their support to the royalist groups between 1962 and 1970, and have continued to finance them ever since.

This dispute was to take on an entirely different character during the **Gulf War**. Yemen refused to join the anti-Iraqi coalition and, in response, Saudi Arabia expelled 800,000 Yemenis who had been living there for decades. The expulsions deprived Sana'a of valuable revenue and placed an unbearable strain on one of the poorest countries in the world, which was exacerbated when Riyadh stopped its financial aid. As a result, there was increasing dissatisfaction within the government coalition: the more secular and modernist YSP and the PGC, trying to please the Saudis and the **Islamist** opposition, and al-Islah, founded in September 1990 by representatives from three socio-political forces: the tribes, the middle classes and the **Muslim Brotherhood**, who controlled the organisation.

Although elections were held on 27 April 1993, and were won by the Popular General Congress, the tension between Southerners and Northerners rose, particularly after dozens of YSP workers were murdered. On 5 May 1994, troops from the North crossed the former border between North and South. The civil war lasted until 7 July, when Aden was taken. After the conflict, the YSP disappeared from political life, the regime intensified its authoritarianism, and al-Islah became increasingly influential.

During the civil war, the Saudis supported the communists in the South in order to destabilise its neighbour. After their defeat, the communists fled to Saudi Arabia. The two countries were again on the brink of war at the beginning of 1995, but this was averted when, on 26 February 1995, a 'document of intent' was signed in Mecca. The overall normalisation of relations was accompanied by a recognition by Sana'a of the 'legitimate and constraining' character of the Taif treaty, which allowed the annexation by Saudi Arabia of the North of Yemen, and then, in 2000, by an agreement defining borders.

The President distanced himself from al-Islah after the elections of 1997, which gave him an absolute majority. While he was negotiating a programme of economic reform under the aegis of the World Bank, his Western allies, notably the US, were pushing him to get rid of the Islamist militants of various movements, mostly made up of former Afghan partisans.

There were increasing numbers of arrests and expulsions, but these did not prevent the bomb attacks of August 1999 (which targeted a supermarket in Sana'a, a bank in Aden and the central prison of Zinjibar where Islamists were held), the October 2000 attack on the British embassy, the deaths in the same month of 17 Americans killed in a suicide attack on the USS *Cole* in Aden, and repeated kidnappings of foreign tourists. The main culprit has been the Islamic Army of Aden-Abyan. But Sana'a also has to deal with movements affiliated to the networks of **Osama bin Laden**. Beyond the divisions between North and South and the difficult relations between the government and its former Islamist supporters, the attempt at national unification was also rendered more difficult by the societal weight of some of the major tribes.

Yemen has taken steps to normalise relations with its neighbours: with Eritrea, which finally recognised Yemeni sovereignty, which was confirmed by the Hague's decision, over the island of Greater Hanish in the Red Sea, occupied since the armed conflict between the two states in 1995; and with **Kuwait** and Saudi Arabia. But after the attacks of 11 September 2001 Sana'a made a marked turn towards Washington, fearing a US intervention. Washington offered aid for dismantling the 'Afghan' networks and a military co-operation in the struggle against the al-Qaeda network of Osama bin Laden, and also in improving security at ports and airports (which did not, however, prevent an attack on a French **oil** tanker in October 2002). Sana'a was rewarded for its co-operation with aid in excess of $300m from the IMF.

The money was needed, because apart from the discovery of substantial oil reserves in both the North and South in the 1980s – which enabled an oil production of 438,000 barrels per day – Yemen remains essentially an agricultural country, and one of the poorest on the planet.

Yemen has a surface area of 528,000 sq. km and had around 18.5 million inhabitants in 2001. Most of the population lives in rural areas and is divided, particularly in the North, into 75 tribes allied to the influential confederations. About half the population are Zaidis – a branch of **Shi'ism** – the remaining half are Sunnis.

YISHUV

The name given to the Jewish community of Palestine and the society it constructed there prior to the creation of the state of **Israel**.

The number of **Jews** who made up the Yishuv increased 15-fold between the first Jewish World Congress (1897) and the UN **Partition Plan** (1947): from 40,000 to more than 600,000 in fifty years, and from 10 to more than 39 per cent of the total population of Palestine.

Not only the number of men and women in the Yishuv grew, but also the land which they owned: by means of the Jewish National Fund, which bought from large absentee landlords their dunums (one dunum equals approximately a tenth of a hectare), the community extended its acquisitions from 204,000 to 1,802,000 dunums in fifty years. At the same time, the number of agricultural colonies rose from 27 to 300, many of which were collective farms, either collectively owned *kibbutzim* or co-operative *moshavim*. In 1947, half of Jewish land was cultivated by these two types of structure, the other half being in private ownership. With 7.7 per cent of land at the end of World War II, Jewish peasants supplied 28.3 per cent of Palestine's agricultural produce.

The 'rejuvenation of the Jewish people through work', promised by **Zionism**, was accomplished in this way in the countryside, but it also took place in the towns, in industry and commerce. Starting from 100 in 1920, the industrial production index had reached almost five thousand by 1945. The annual consumption of electricity rose from around 2 million kilowatts per hour to almost 200 million.

Industry, public services and agriculture, and British military camps, provided 160,000 jobs – 90,000 for **Arabs** and 70,000 for Jews, whose incomes were sometimes double those of Arabs, their expenditure even greater.

The disparity thus created between Arabs and Jews did not stem only from the assets – training, technical resources and capital – which the Jews possessed. It was also the result of a deliberate policy adopted by the Yishuv: 'The necessary condition for the fulfilment of Zionism,' one newspaper wrote, 'is the takeover of all the country's jobs by a Jewish work-force'. In the name of this takeover of jobs, *kibbutzim* and *moshavim* vied with one another in using Arab agricultural labourers. On the walls of **Jerusalem** and Tel Aviv (founded in 1909) the posters said, 'Do not buy Arab produce! Buy Hebrew!'

But the Yishuv, which increased its numbers and its role within the economy, was much more: alongside the Palestinian Arab nation, it incarnated the evolving Jewish Palestinian nation, with its own language (Hebrew, as modernised by Eliezer Ben Yehuda), its public services, its embryonic army (the Haganah, the Palmah, and the troops of the Revisionist Irgun), and of course its institutions. Under the British High Commission, the legislative and executive power in Palestine, Jews were represented, as stipulated in Article 4 of the Mandate, by a 'suitable Jewish body' – the Jewish Agency, which, as well as distributing **immigration** permits, gradually took charge of the entire process of colonisation. The community also elected its own National Council, the Vaad Leumi.

Three major tendencies characterised the Yishuv (see **Israeli political parties**). Often of socialist origins, immigrants favoured the left: the Mapai, which united the various socialist tendencies in 1930, and, further to the left, the Hashomer Hatzair and the Poalei Zion Smole, precursors of the present-day Mapam. The Histadrut union, which controlled a large part of the economic machinery, also represented a forum for them. The right comprised a liberal tendency (the General Zionists) and an authoritarian tendency (the Revisionist Party). Lastly, the religious pole was divided between Mizrahi and Hapoel Mizrahi, which participated in the various institutions, and the Orthodox Agudat Yisrael and Poale Agudat Yisrael, which refused to do so. During the elections of 1931, the left, the right and the religious groups won respectively 42.3 per cent, 32 per cent and 7 per cent of votes. The only Judeo–Arab and non-Zionist organisation, the Communist Party, founded in 1922, had difficulty accommodating the contradictions inherent in its composition, aggravated by the directives of the Comintern, and the 'tagging along' policy which stemmed from it regarding the leadership of the Palestinian movement.

Thus, the Yishuv already constituted a sort of state within the state, an Israel before Israel. On 14 May 1948, it gained the one attribute it still lacked: **independence**.

ZIONISM

An ideology named after Zion, the hill of **Jerusalem** and the symbol of the 'Promised Land'. Zionism is a doctrine and a movement which aims to gather **Jews** together in Palestine in their own state. It was first elaborated politically in 1896 in *The Jewish State* by **Theodor Herzl**, received its first coherent expression in 1897 with the Zionist World Congress, and achieved its first historic victory on 14 May 1948 when the state of **Israel** was born.

The original basis of Zionism is the link that, according to its believers, unites the Jews with the Holy Land. The Jewish kingdoms founded in Palestine around 1000BC perished under the successive attacks of the Assyrians, the Babylonians and the Romans. The crushing of the Bar Kokhba Revolt in AD135 led to the departure of most of the Hebrew population. A small **minority** remained in Jerusalem, Safad, Tiberias and Hebron: despite the addition of pilgrims who came to join them, in particular the exiles of the Iberian Peninsula at the end of the fifteenth century, the Jewish community of Palestine still numbered only around 10,000 at the beginning of the nineteenth century. The others, all over the world, formed the diaspora – in Greek, dispersion.

The memory of the 'lost homeland' and the desire to return there were for long fostered by religion alone: 'Next year in Jerusalem,' believers prayed each year. As the eighteenth century gave way to the nineteenth, the idea of the return became more political. Napoleon, for example, while on campaign in **Egypt**, called on Jews to 'rally under his flag to recreate the old Jerusalem'. The cause had defenders as disparate as the Saint-Simonians, Lord Byron, Disraeli and the secretary of Napoleon III. But it was embodied above all in the work of thinkers like the German Moses Hess (*Rome and Jerusalem*, 1862) and the Russian Leon Pinsker (*Auto-Emancipation*, 1882). The Lovers of Zion, inspired by the latter, were responsible for the first *aliya*, which between 1882 and 1903 attracted 20–30,000 Jews from Tsarist **Russia** to Palestine. With these immigrants and the help of Baron Edmond de Rothschild, along with investments from other Jewish entrepreneurs, a mainly agricultural colonisation of the biblical lands began. The Viennese journalist Theodor Herzl supplied the movement with a theory and an organisation as well as diplomacy, while the Zionist Organisation, with its Jewish National Fund, which was responsible for the purchase of Palestinian land, helped the movement's plan to materialise. 'Around 1900,' Maxime Rodinson points out, 'settlement projects were not seen, as they are today, in an unfavourable light'.

Four hypotheses formed the basis of the edifice conceived by Herzl: the existence of a Jewish people; the impossibility of its assimilation into the societies to which it had been dispersed; its right to the Promised Land; the non-existence in this land of another people who also had rights. For defenders of Zionism, such things are as self-evident as they are false for their opponents. Walter Laqueur, author of a monumental *History of Zionism*, very rightly notes at the conclusion of his work, 'This belief can be accepted or rejected: it can only be the object of rational discussion to a very limited extent. Zionism formulated an ideology, but its scientific pretensions are inevitably less than conclusive.' And it is true that the debate over the very idea of what constitutes a **Jew** remains open: aside from the religion, in which not all believe and which is no doubt insufficient in itself as a definition of a people, what would be the unifying criteria of this national presence? Racial? Territorial? Linguistic?

The question of assimilation is equally controversial: though brutally interrupted by the rise of antisemitism at the end of the nineteenth century, then by the Holocaust, it is nonetheless a very real fact. It even recommenced after the Nazi extermination. A Zionist leader like Nahum Goldmann went so far as to allude publicly to the 'danger' of a 'disintegration of Jewish communities' and their 'loss of awareness of being part of the Jewish people' (26 May 1959). To Zionists, who emphasise the continual re-emergence of anti-Jewish sentiments and deeds as proof of the need for the Jewish state, their opponents counter with the choice made by the vast majority of Jews to remain in their countries, and in many cases to assimilate there. Finally, the problem of the right to Palestine has become all the more contradictory in the light of the interminable Arab–Israeli conflict: allusion to the sacred text of a religion (one of three) and to an occupation (one of twelve) has done nothing to legitimise the unilateral claim to the Holy Land, to the exclusion of another people whose very existence is denied.

Rodinson admits that 'Jewish suffering may – perhaps – justify the aspiration of certain Jews to form an independent state. But, to the **Arabs**, this cannot be sufficient reason for this state to be formed at their expense,' especially, he adds, since they themselves had very little to do with the persecution of the Jews.

If its principles have been the subject of debate, Zionism has in any case undergone a certain development, as much in its influence and organisation outside Palestine as in the construction, within Palestine, of a Jewish national home that became the state of Israel. The basis of its success lies both in the abject poverty of the Jewish masses in Central and Eastern Europe and, from 1882, the new wave of horrific antisemitic pogroms, as witnessed in Albert Londres's poignant report *Le Juif errant est arrivé*. The economic exclusion of Jews was thus coupled with a violent political exclusion, by means of massacres which found a distant echo in Western Europe in the 'Dreyfus affair'. The disillusionment was in proportion to the illusions propagated, in the West, by the emancipation of Jews introduced by the French Revolution. 'Zionism,' summed up Abraham Leon (*La Conception materialiste de la question juive*) 'was born in the glare of the flames of the Russian pogroms of 1882 and in the tumult of the Dreyfus Affair, two events that reflect the increasing gravity of the Jewish problem at the end of the 19th century'.

But the progress of Zionism was also due to the fact that the European powers saw in it an instrument of their own interests: **Britain** in order to further entrench itself in the Middle East and protect the **Suez Canal**; Tsarist Russia to halt the spread of the revolution (many of whose leaders were of Jewish origin); Germany, whose leaders dreamed of ridding themselves of a large, influential Jewish community; the Ottoman Sultan, to fill his empty coffers. To each of these potential partners, Theodor Herzl was able to show how much the Zionist project would be in their interest. Especially for London, for, as Herzl wrote in his *Journal* in 1900, 'free and powerful England, whose gaze encompasses the seven seas, will understand us and our aspirations. It is from there, we may be sure, that the Zionist movement will soar towards new and higher summits.' His successors would do just that, above all with London, which, until 1939, remained the Zionists' main ally, even if Britain's anxiety not to compromise itself in Arab eyes meant the alliance was frequently stormy. But its basic foundation was solid: the protection of the Suez Canal. 'England,' exclaimed Chaim Weizmann, 'will have a secure barrier, and we will have a country'.

It was of course from the Holocaust that Zionism gained its main legitimacy and the strength to materialise. After the extermination of six million Jews against a background of almost total indifference, Europe and America, where public opinion had been stunned, agreed on the need to create a Jewish state – and an Arab one – in Palestine. Only the first of these would ever see the light of day, corresponding, moreover, to the initial demands of the Zionist movement. But this only child carried within it the germ of the crisis that Zionism is currently experiencing. The upheavals sparked within the diaspora by the invasion of **Lebanon** in 1982, followed by the **Intifada** in the late 1980s, were forerunners of things to come. Paradoxically, now, at the start of the twenty-first century, no country in the world is more dangerous for Jews than Israel: between 2001 and 2002, 700 of them lost their lives in the **second Intifada**, the repression of which also cost the lives of more than 2000 **Palestinians**.

'Zionism,' declared Marcel Liebman in *Le Juif*, 'runs up against a double objection, which the facts themselves continue to demonstrate. Having established as its aim the creation of a peaceful haven for the Jews, Zionism in fact created a state which has lived in constant insecurity.' The reason, continues the Belgian analyst, is the plundering of the Palestinians and its consequences. And he promptly adds, 'In its attempt to gather together in a single state all the Jews in the world, Zionism has been equally unsuccessful'. He concludes with a remark on the younger generation and its supposed

Jewishness: 'Why should one focus on them the blinding lights that reflect the flames of yesterday? Yes, of yesterday.'

The fact of the matter is that, almost a hundred years after the death of Theodor Herzl, if the Jewish state does exist, it contains only a minority, less than 40 per cent, of the 'people' it was intended to receive. Nor are the Israelis themselves a monolithic bloc, but, as **Henri Curiel** noted (*Pour une paix juste au Proche Orient*), are divided into

> two elements whose aspirations are different, if not downright contradictory. The first of these elements is composed of real Zionists, in other words those who went to Israel with the sole purpose of establishing a Jewish state there. The second element, which forms the majority of the Jewish population in Israel, is composed of Jews who settled there because they had nowhere else to go.

Is this a positive outcome for the Zionist project?

APPENDICES

APPENDIX 1
THE BALFOUR DECLARATION: 1917

Foreign Office, November 2nd, 1917

Dear Lord Rothschild,

I have much pleasure in conveying to you, on behalf of His Majesty's Government, the following declaration of sympathy with Jewish Zionist aspirations which has been submitted to, and approved by, the Cabinet.

'His Majesty's Government view with favour the establishment in Palestine of a national home for the Jewish people, and will use their best endeavours to facilitate the achievement of this object, it being clearly understood that nothing shall be done which may prejudice the civil and religious rights of existing non-Jewish communities in Palestine, or the rights and political status enjoyed by Jews in any other country.'

I should be grateful if you would bring this declaration to the knowledge of the Zionist Federation.

Yours sincerely,

Arthur James Balfour

APPENDIX 2
THE PALESTINE MANDATE: THE COUNCIL OF THE LEAGUE OF NATIONS: 1922 (extracts)

July 24, 1922

Whereas the Principal Allied Powers have agreed, for the purpose of giving effect to the provisions of Article 22 of the Covenant of the League of Nations, to entrust to a Mandatory selected by the said Powers the administration of the territory of Palestine, which formerly belonged to the Turkish Empire, within such boundaries as may be fixed by them; and

Whereas the Principal Allied Powers have also agreed that the Mandatory should be responsible for putting into effect the declaration originally made on November 2nd, 1917, by the Government of His Britannic Majesty, and adopted by the said Powers, in favour of the establishment in Palestine of a national home for the Jewish people, it being clearly understood that nothing should be done which might prejudice the civil and religious rights of existing non-Jewish communities in Palestine, or the rights and political status enjoyed by Jews in any other country; and

Whereas recognition has thereby been given to the historical connection of the Jewish people with Palestine and to the grounds for reconstituting their national home in that country; and

Whereas the Principal Allied Powers have selected His Britannic Majesty as the Mandatory for Palestine; and

Whereas the mandate in respect of Palestine has been formulated in the following terms and submitted to the Council of the League for approval; and

Whereas His Britannic Majesty has accepted the mandate in respect of Palestine and undertaken to exercise it on behalf of the League of Nations in conformity with the following provisions; and

Whereas by the afore-mentioned Article 22 (paragraph 8), it is provided that the degree of authority, control or administration to be exercised by the Mandatory, not having been previously agreed upon by the Members of the League, shall be explicitly defined by the Council of the League Of Nations; confirming the said Mandate, defines its terms as follows:

ARTICLE 1. The Mandatory shall have full powers of legislation and of administration, save as they may be limited by the terms of this mandate.

ARTICLE 2. The Mandatory shall be responsible for placing the country under such political, administrative and economic conditions as will secure the establishment of the Jewish national home, as laid down in the preamble, and the development of self-governing institutions, and also for safeguarding the civil and religious rights of all the inhabitants of Palestine, irrespective of race and religion.

ARTICLE 3. The Mandatory shall, so far as circumstances permit, encourage local autonomy.

ARTICLE 4. An appropriate Jewish agency shall be recognised as a public body for the purpose of advising and co-operating with the Administration of Palestine in such economic, social and other matters as may affect the establishment of the Jewish national home and the interests of the Jewish population in Palestine, and, subject always to the control of the Administration to assist and take part in the development of the country.

The Zionist organization, so long as its organization and constitution are in the opinion of the Mandatory appropriate, shall be recognised as such agency. It shall take steps in consultation with His Britannic Majesty's Government to secure the co-operation of all Jews who are willing to assist in the establishment of the Jewish national home.

APPENDIX 3
UN GENERAL ASSEMBLY RESOLUTION 181: 1947 (extracts)

November 29, 1947
PLAN OF PARTITION WITH ECONOMIC UNION

Part I. – Future Constitution and Government of Palestine

A. TERMINATION OF MANDATE, PARTITION AND INDEPENDENCE

The Mandate for Palestine shall terminate as soon as possible but in any case not later than 1 August 1948.

The armed forces of the mandatory Power shall be progressively withdrawn from Palestine, the withdrawal to be completed as soon as possible but in any case not later than 1 August 1948.

The mandatory Power shall advise the Commission, as far in advance as possible, of its intention to terminate the mandate and to evacuate each area. The mandatory Power shall use its best endeavours to ensure that an area situated in the territory of the Jewish State, including a seaport and hinterland adequate to provide facilities for a substantial immigration, shall be evacuated at the earliest possible date and in any event not later than 1 February 1948.

Independent Arab and Jewish States and the Special International Regime for the City of Jerusalem, set forth in Part III of this Plan, shall come into existence in Palestine two months after the evacuation of the armed forces of the mandatory Power has been completed but in any case not later than 1 October 1948. The boundaries of the Arab State, the Jewish State, and the City of Jerusalem shall be as described in Parts II and III below.

The period between the adoption by the General Assembly of its recommendation on the question of Palestine and the establishment of the independence of the Arab and Jewish States shall be a transitional period.

C. DECLARATION
A declaration shall be made to the United Nations by the Provisional Government of each proposed State before independence. It shall contain, inter alia, the following clauses:

General Provision
The stipulations contained in the Declaration are recognized as fundamental laws of the State and no law, regulation or official action shall conflict or interfere with these stipulations, nor shall any law, regulation or official action prevail over them.

Chapter 1: Holy Places, Religious Buildings and Sites
Existing rights in respect of Holy Places and religious buildings or sites shall not be denied or impaired.

In so far as Holy Places are concerned, the liberty of access, visit, and transit shall be guaranteed, in conformity with existing rights, to all residents and citizens of the other State and of the City of Jerusalem, as well as to aliens, without distinction as to nationality, subject to requirements of national security, public order and decorum.

Similarly, freedom of worship shall be guaranteed in conformity with existing rights, subject to the maintenance of public order and decorum.

Holy Places and religious buildings or sites shall be preserved. No act shall be permitted which may in an way impair their sacred character. If at any time it appears to the Government that any particular Holy Place, religious building or site is in need of urgent repair, the Government may call upon the community or communities concerned to carry out such repair. The Government may carry it out itself at the expense of the community or community concerned if no action is taken within a reasonable time.

No taxation shall be levied in respect of any Holy Place, religious building or site which was exempt from taxation on the date of the creation of the State.

No change in the incidence of such taxation shall be made which would either discriminate between the owners or occupiers of Holy Places, religious buildings or sites, or would place such owners or occupiers in a position less favourable in relation to the general incidence of taxation than existed at the time of the adoption of the Assembly's recommendations.

The Governor of the City of Jerusalem shall have the right to determine whether the provisions of the Constitution of the State in relation to Holy Places, religious buildings and sites within the borders of the State and the religious rights appertaining thereto, are being properly applied and respected, and to make decisions on the basis of existing rights in cases of disputes which may arise between the different religious communities or the rites of a religious community with respect to such places, buildings and sites. He shall receive full co-operation and such privileges and immunities as are necessary for the exercise of his functions in the State.

Chapter 2: Religious and Minority Rights
Freedom of conscience and the free exercise of all forms of worship, subject only to the maintenance of public order and morals, shall be ensured to all.

No discrimination of any kind shall be made between the inhabitants on the ground of race, religion, language or sex.

All persons within the jurisdiction of the State shall be entitled to equal protection of the laws.

The family law and personal status of the various minorities and their religious interests, including endowments, shall be respected.

Except as may be required for the maintenance of public order and good government, no measure shall be taken to obstruct or interfere with the enterprise of religious or charitable bodies of all faiths or to discriminate against any representative or member of these bodies on the ground of his religion or nationality.

The State shall ensure adequate primary and secondary education for the Arab and Jewish minority, respectively, in its own language and its cultural traditions.

The right of each community to maintain its own schools for the education of its own members in its own language, while conforming to such educational requirements of a general nature as the State may impose, shall not be denied or impaired. Foreign educational establishments shall continue their activity on the basis of their existing rights.

No restriction shall be imposed on the free use by any citizen of the State of any language in private intercourse, in commerce, in religion, in the Press or in publications of any kind, or at public meetings.(3)

No expropriation of land owned by an Arab in the Jewish State (by a Jew in the Arab State)(4) shall be allowed except for public purposes. In all cases of expropriation full compensation as fixed by the Supreme Court shall be said previous to dispossession.

Part II. – Boundaries

C. THE CITY OF JERUSALEM
The boundaries of the City of Jerusalem are as defined in the recommendations on the City of Jerusalem. (See Part III, section B, below).

Part III. – City of Jerusalem(5)

A. SPECIAL REGIME
The City of Jerusalem shall be established as a corpus separatum under a special international regime and shall be administered by the United Nations. The Trusteeship Council shall be designated to discharge the responsibilities of the Administering Authority on behalf of the United Nations.

B. BOUNDARIES OF THE CITY
The City of Jerusalem shall include the present municipality of Jerusalem plus the surrounding villages and towns, the most eastern of which shall be Abu Dis; the most southern, Bethlehem; the most western, 'Ein Karim (including also the built-up area of Motsa); and the most northern Shu'fat, as indicated on the attached sketch-map (annex B).

C. STATUTE OF THE CITY

The Trusteeship Council shall, within five months of the approval of the present plan, elaborate and approve a detailed statute of the City which shall contain, inter alia, the substance of the following provisions:

Government machinery; special objectives. The Administering Authority in discharging its administrative obligations shall pursue the following special objectives:

To protect and to preserve the unique spiritual and religious interests located in the city of the three great monotheistic faiths throughout the world, Christian, Jewish and Moslem; to this end to ensure that order and peace, and especially religious peace, reign in Jerusalem;

To foster cooperation among all the inhabitants of the city in their own interests as well as in order to encourage and support the peaceful development of the mutual relations between the two Palestinian peoples throughout the Holy Land; to promote the security, well-being and any constructive measures of development of the residents having regard to the special circumstances and customs of the various peoples and communities.

Governor and Administrative staff. A Governor of the City of Jerusalem shall be appointed by the Trusteeship Council and shall be responsible to it. He shall be selected on the basis of special qualifications and without regard to nationality. He shall not, however, be a citizen of either State in Palestine.

The Governor shall represent the United Nations in the City and shall exercise on their behalf all powers of administration, including the conduct of external affairs. He shall be assisted by an administrative staff classed as international officers in the meaning of Article 100 of the Charter and chosen whenever practicable from the residents of the city and of the rest of Palestine on a non-discriminatory basis. A detailed plan for the organization of the administration of the city shall be submitted by the Governor to the Trusteeship Council and duly approved by it.

3. Local autonomy

The existing local autonomous units in the territory of the city (villages, townships and municipalities) shall enjoy wide powers of local government and administration.

The Governor shall study and submit for the consideration and decision of the Trusteeship Council a plan for the establishment of special town units consisting, respectively, of the Jewish and Arab sections of new Jerusalem.

The new town units shall continue to form part of the present municipality of Jerusalem.

Security measures.
The City of Jerusalem shall be demilitarized; neutrality shall be declared and preserved, and no para-military formations, exercises or activities shall be permitted within its borders.

Should the administration of the City of Jerusalem be seriously obstructed or prevented by the non-cooperation or interference of one or more sections of the population the Governor shall have authority to take such measures as may be necessary to restore the effective functioning of administration.

To assist in the maintenance of internal law and order, especially for the protection of the Holy Places and religious buildings and sites in the city, the Governor shall organize a special police force of adequate strength, the members of which shall be recruited outside of Palestine. The Governor shall be empowered to direct such budgetary provision as may be necessary for the maintenance of this force.

Legislative Organization.
A Legislative Council, elected by adult residents of the city irrespective of nationality on the basis of universal and secret suffrage and proportional representation, shall have powers of legislation and taxation. No legislative measures shall, however, conflict or interfere with the provisions which will be set forth in the Statute of the City, nor shall any law, regulation, or official action prevail over them. The Statute shall grant to the Governor a right of vetoing bills inconsistent with the provisions referred to in the preceding sentence. It shall also empower him to promulgate temporary ordinances in case the Council fails to adopt in time a bill deemed essential to the normal functioning of the administration.

Administration of Justice.
The Statute shall provide for the establishment of an independent judiciary system, including a court of appeal. All the inhabitants of the city shall be subject to it.

Economic Union and Economic Regime.
The City of Jerusalem shall be included in the Economic Union of Palestine and be bound by all stipulations of the undertaking and of any treaties issued therefrom, as well as by the decisions of the Joint Economic Board. The headquarters of the Economic Board shall be established in the territory

City. The Statute shall provide for the regulation of economic matters not falling within the regime of the Economic Union, on the basis of equal treatment and non-discrimination for all members of the United Nations and their nationals.

Freedom of Transit and Visit: Control of Residents.
Subject to considerations of security, and of economic welfare as determined by the Governor under the directions of the Trusteeship Council, freedom of entry into, and residence within the borders of the City shall be guaranteed for the residents or citizens of the Arab and Jewish States. Immigration into, and residence within, the borders of the city for nationals of other States shall be controlled by the Governor under the directions of the Trusteeship Council.

Relations with Arab and Jewish States. Representatives of the Arab and Jewish States shall be accredited to the Governor of the City and charged with the protection of the interests of their States and nationals in connection with the international administration of thc City.

Official languages.
Arabic and Hebrew shall be the official languages of the city. This will not preclude the adoption of one or more additional working languages, as may be required.

Citizenship.
All the residents shall become ipso facto citizens of the City of Jerusalem unless they opt for citizenship of the State of which they have been citizens or, if Arabs or Jews, have filed notice of intention to become citizens of the Arab or Jewish State respectively, according to Part 1, section B, paragraph 9, of this Plan.

The Trusteeship Council shall make arrangements for consular protection of the citizens of the City outside its territory.

Freedoms of citizens.
Subject only to the requirements of public order and morals, the inhabitants of the City shall be ensured the enjoyment of human rights and fundamental freedoms, including freedom of conscience, religion and worship, language, education, speech and press, assembly and association, and petition.

No discrimination of any kind shall be made between the inhabitants on the grounds of race, religion, language or sex.

All persons within the City shall be entitled to equal protection of the laws. The family law and personal status of the various persons and communities and their religious interests, including endowments, shall be respected.

Except as may be required for the maintenance of public order and good government, no measure shall be taken to obstruct or interfere with the enterprise of religious or charitable bodies of all faiths or to discriminate against any representative or member of these bodies on the ground of his religion or nationality.

The City shall ensure adequate primary and secondary education for the Arab and Jewish communities respectively, in their own languages and in accordance with their cultural traditions.

The right of each community to maintain its own schools for the education of its own members in its own language, while conforming to such educational requirements of a general nature as the City may impose, shall not be denied or impaired. Foreign educational establishments shall continue their activity on the basis of their existing rights.

No restriction shall be imposed on the free use by any inhabitant of the City of any language in private intercourse, in commerce, in religion, in the Press or in publications of any kind, or at public meetings.

Holy Places.
Existing rights in respect of Holy Places and religious buildings or sites shall not be denied or impaired.

Free access to the Holy Places and religious buildings or sites and the free exercise of worship shall be secured in conformity with existing rights and subject to the requirements of public order and decorum.

Holy Places and religious buildings or sites shall be preserved. No act shall be permitted which may in any way impair their sacred character. If at any time it appears to the Governor that any particular Holy Place, religious building or site is in need of urgent repair, the Governor may call upon the community or communities concerned to carry out such repair. The Governor may carry it out himself at the expense of the community or communities concerned if no action is taken within a reasonable time.

No taxation shall be levied in respect of any Holy Place, religious building or site which was exempt from taxation on the date of the creation of the City. No change in the incidence of such taxation shall be made which would either discriminate between the owners or occupiers of Holy Places, religious buildings or sites or would place such owners or occupiers in a position less favourable in relation to the general incidence of taxation than existed at the time of the adoption of the Assembly's recommendations.

Special powers of the Governor in respect of the Holy Places, religious buildings and sites in the City and in any part of Palestine.

The protection of the Holy Places, religious buildings and sites located in the City of Jerusalem shall be a special concern of the Governor.

With relation to such places, buildings and sites in Palestine outside the city, the Governor shall determine, on the ground of powers granted to him by the Constitution of both States, whether the provisions of the Constitution of the Arab and Jewish States in Palestine dealing therewith and the religious rights appertaining thereto are being properly applied and respected.

The Governor shall also be empowered to make decisions on the basis of existing rights in cases of disputes which may arise between the different religious communities or the rites of a religious community in respect of the Holy Places, religious buildings and sites in any part of Palestine.

In this task he may be assisted by a consultative council of representatives of different denominations acting in an advisory capacity.

D. DURATION OF THE SPECIAL REGIME

The Statute elaborated by the Trusteeship Council on the aforementioned principles shall come into force not later than 1 October 1948. It shall remain in force in the first instance for a period of ten years, unless the Trusteeship Council finds it necessary to undertake a re-examination of these provisions at an earlier date. After the expiration of this period the whole scheme shall be subject to examination by the Trusteeship Council in the light of experience acquired with its functioning. The residents of the City shall be then free to express by means of a referendum their wishes as to possible modifications of regime of the City.

Part IV. – Capitulations

States whose nationals have in the past enjoyed in Palestine the privileges and immunities of foreigners, including the benefits of consular jurisdiction and protection, as formerly enjoyed by capitulation or usage in the Ottoman Empire, are invited to renounce any right pertaining to them to the re-establishment of such privileges and immunities in the proposed Arab and Jewish States and the City of Jerusalem.

APPENDIX 4
UN SECURITY COUNCIL RESOLUTION 242: 1967

22 November 1967

The Security Council,

Expressing its continuing concern with the grave situation in the Middle East,

Emphasizing the inadmissibility of the acquisition of territory by war and the need to work for a just and lasting peace in which every State in the area can live in security,

Emphasizing further that all Member States in their acceptance of the Charter of the United Nations have undertaken a commitment to act in accordance with Article 2 of the Charter,

1. Affirms that the fulfilment of Charter principles requires the establishment of a just and lasting peace in the Middle East which should include the application of both the following principles:

(i) Withdrawal of Israeli armed forces from territories occupied in the recent conflict;

(ii) Termination of all claims or states of belligerency and respect for and acknowledgment of the sovereignty, territorial integrity and political independence of every State in the area and their right to live in peace within secure and recognized boundaries free from threats or acts of force;

2. Affirms further the necessity

(a) For guaranteeing freedom of navigation through international waterways in the area;

(b) For achieving a just settlement of the refugee problem;

(c) For guaranteeing the territorial inviolability and political independence of every State in the area, through measures including the establishment of demilitarized zones;

3. Requests the Secretary-General to designate a Special Representative to proceed to the Middle East to establish and maintain contacts with the States concerned in order to promote agreement and assist efforts to achieve a peaceful and accepted settlement in accordance with the provisions and principles in this resolution;

4. Requests the Secretary-General to report to the Security Council on the progress of the efforts of the Special Representative as soon as possible. Adopted unanimously at the 1382nd meeting.

APPENDIX 5
SEVENTH ARAB LEAGUE SUMMIT CONFERENCE, RESOLUTION ON PALESTINE: RABAT, MOROCCO: 1974

28 October 1974

The Seventh Arab Summit Conference resolves the following:

1. To affirm the right of the Palestinian people to self-determination and to return to their homeland;

2. To affirm the right of the Palestinian people to establish an independent national authority under the command of the Palestine Liberation Organization, the sole legitimate representative of the Palestinian people in any Palestinian territory that is liberated. This authority, once it is established, shall enjoy the support of the Arab states in all fields and at all levels;

3. To support the Palestine Liberation Organization in the exercise of its responsibility at the national and international levels within the framework of Arab commitment;

4. To call on the Hashemite Kingdom of Jordan, the Syrian Arab Republic, the Arab Republic of Egypt and the Palestine Liberation Organization to devise a formula for the regulation of relations between them in the light of these decisions so as to ensure their implementation;

5. That all the Arab states undertake to defend Palestinian national unity and not to interfere in the internal affairs of Palestinian action.

APPENDIX 6
UN GENERAL ASSEMBLY RESOLUTION 3236: 1974

22 November 1974

The General Assembly

Having considered the question of Palestine,

Having heard the statement of the Palestine Liberation Organization, the representative of the Palestinian people,

Having also heard other statements made during the debate,

Deeply concerned that no just solution to the problem of Palestine has yet been achieved and recognizing that the problem of Palestine continues to endanger international peace and security,

Recognizing that the Palestinian people is entitled to self-determination in accordance with the Charter of the United Nations,

Expressing its grave concern that the Palestinian people has been prevented from enjoying its inalienable rights, in particular its right to self-determination,

Guided by the purposes and principles of the Charter,

Recalling its relevant resolutions which affirm the right of the Palestinian people to self-determination,

1. Reaffirms the inalienable rights of the Palestinian people in Palestine, including:

(a) The right to self-determination without external interference;
(b) The right to national independence and sovereignty;

2. Reaffirms also the inalienable right of the Palestinians to return to their homes and property from which they have been displaced and uprooted, and calls for their return;

3. Emphasizes that full respect for and the realization of these inalienable rights of the Palestinian people are indispensable for the solution of the question of Palestine;

4. Recognizes that the Palestinian people is a principal party in the establishment of a just and lasting peace in the Middle East;

5. Further recognizes the right of the Palestinian people to regain its rights by all means in accordance with the purposes and principles of the Charter of the United Nations;

6. Appeals to all States and international organizations to extend their support to the Palestinian people in its struggle to restore its rights, in accordance with the Charter;

7. Requests the Secretary-General to establish contacts with the Palestine Liberation Organization on all matters concerning the question of Palestine;

8. Requests the Secretary-General to report to the General Assembly at its thirtieth session on the implementation of the present resolution;

9. Decides to include the item entitled 'Question of Palestine' in the provisional agenda of its thirtieth Session.

APPENDIX 7
CAMP DAVID ACCORDS: 1978

September 17, 1978

The Framework for Peace in the Middle East

Muhammad Anwar al-Sadat, President of the Arab Republic of Egypt, and Menachem Begin, Prime Minister of Israel, met with Jimmy Carter, President of the United States of America, at Camp David from September 5 to September 17, 1978, and have agreed on the following framework for peace in the Middle East.
[...]
Taking these factors into account, the parties are determined to reach a just, comprehensive, and durable settlement of the Middle East conflict through the conclusion of peace treaties based on Security Council resolutions 242 and 338 in all their parts. Their purpose is to achieve peace and good neighborly relations. They recognize that for peace to endure, it must involve all those who have been most deeply affected by the conflict. They therefore agree that this framework, as appropriate, is intended by them to constitute a basis for peace not only between Egypt and Israel, but

also between Israel and each of its other neighbors which is prepared to negotiate peace with Israel on this basis.

With that objective in mind, they have agreed to proceed as follows:

A. West Bank and Gaza

1. Egypt, Israel, Jordan and the representatives of the Palestinian people should participate in negotiations on the resolution of the Palestinian problem in all its aspects. To achieve that objective, negotiations relating to the West Bank and Gaza should proceed in three stages:

a. Egypt and Israel agree that, in order to ensure a peaceful and orderly transfer of authority, and taking into account the security concerns of all the parties, there should be transitional arrangements for the West Bank and Gaza for a period not exceeding five years. In order to provide full autonomy to the inhabitants, under these arrangements the Israeli military government and its civilian administration will be withdrawn as soon as a self-governing authority has been freely elected by the inhabitants of these areas to replace the existing military government. To negotiate the details of a transitional arrangement, Jordan will be invited to join the negotiations on the basis of this framework. These new arrangements should give due consideration both to the principle of self-government by the inhabitants of these territories and to the legitimate security concerns of the parties involved.

b. Egypt, Israel, and Jordan will agree on the modalities for establishing elected self-governing authority in the West Bank and Gaza. The delegations of Egypt and Jordan may include Palestinians from the West Bank and Gaza or other Palestinians as mutually agreed. The parties will negotiate an agreement which will define the powers and responsibilities of the self-governing authority to be exercised in the West Bank and Gaza. A withdrawal of Israeli armed forces will take place and there will be a redeployment of the remaining Israeli forces into specified security locations. The agreement will also include arrangements for assuring internal and external security and public order. A strong local police force will be established, which may include Jordanian citizens. In addition, Israeli and Jordanian forces will participate in joint patrols and in the manning of control posts to assure the security of the borders.

c. When the self-governing authority (administrative council) in the West Bank and Gaza is established and inaugurated, the transitional period of five years will begin. As soon as possible, but not later than the third year after the beginning of the transitional period, negotiations will take place to determine the final status of the West Bank and Gaza and its relationship with its neighbors and to conclude a peace treaty between Israel and Jordan by the end of the transitional period. These negotiations will be conducted among Egypt, Israel, Jordan and the elected represent-atives of the inhabitants of the West Bank and Gaza. Two separate but related committees will be convened, one committee, consisting of repre-sentatives of the four parties which will negotiate and agree on the final status of the West Bank and Gaza, and its relationship with its neighbors, and the second committee, consisting of representatives of Israel and representatives of Jordan to be joined by the elected representatives of the inhabitants of the West Bank and Gaza, to negotiate the peace treaty between Israel and Jordan, taking into account the agreement reached in the final status of the West Bank and Gaza. The negotiations shall be based on all the provisions and principles of UN Security Council Resolution 242. The negotiations will resolve, among other matters, the location of the boundaries and the nature of the security arrangements. The solution from the negotiations must also recognize the legitimate right of the Palestinian peoples and their just requirements. In this way, the Palestinians will participate in the determination of their own future through:

i. The negotiations among Egypt, Israel, Jordan and the representatives of the inhabitants of the West Bank and Gaza to agree on the final status of the West Bank and Gaza and other outstanding issues by the end of the transitional period.

ii. Submitting their agreements to a vote by the elected representatives of the inhabitants of the West Bank and Gaza.

iii. Providing for the elected representatives of the inhabitants of the West Bank and Gaza to decide how they shall govern themselves consistent with the provisions of their agreement.

iv. Participating as stated above in the work of the committee negotiating the peace treaty between Israel and Jordan.

d. All necessary measures will be taken and provisions made to assure the security of Israel and its neighbors during the transitional period and beyond. To assist in providing such security, a strong local police force will be constituted by the self-governing authority. It will be composed of inhabitants of the West Bank and Gaza. The police will maintain liaison on internal security matters with the designated Israeli, Jordanian, and Egyptian officers.

e. During the transitional period, representatives of Egypt, Israel, Jordan, and the self-governing authority will constitute a continuing committee to decide by agreement on the modalities of admission of persons displaced from the West Bank and Gaza in 1967, together with necessary measures to prevent disruption and disorder. Other matters of common concern may also be dealt with by this committee.

f. Egypt and Israel will work with each other and with other interested parties to establish agreed procedures for a prompt, just and permanent implementation of the resolution of the refugee problem.

APPENDIX 8
VENICE DECLARATION: 1980

12–13 June 1980

Declaration of the European Council on the Middle East in Venice,

1) The heads of state and government and the Ministers for Foreign Affairs held a comprehensive exchange of views on all aspects of the present situation in the Middle East, including the state of negotiations resulting from the agreements signed between Egypt and Israel in March 1979. They agreed that growing tensions affecting this region constitute a serious danger and render a comprehensive solution to the Israeli–Arab conflict more necessary and pressing than ever.

2) The nine member states of the European Community consider that the traditional ties and common interests which link Europe to the Middle East oblige them to play a special role and now require them to work in a more concrete way towards peace.

3) In this regard, the nine countries of the Community base themselves on Security Council Resolutions 242 and 338 and the positions which they have expressed on several occasions, notably in their declarations of 29 June 1977, 19 September 1978, 26 March and 18 June 1979, as well as in the speech made on their behalf on 25 September 1979 by the Irish Minister for Foreign Affairs at the 34th United Nations General Assembly.

4) On the bases thus set out, the time has come to promote the recognition and implementation of the two principles universally accepted by the international community: the right to existence and to security of all states

in the region, including Israel, and justice for all the peoples, which implies the recognition of the legitimate rights of the Palestinian people.

5) All of the countries in the area are entitled to live in peace within secure, recognized and guaranteed borders. The necessary guarantees for a peace settlement should be provided by the United Nations by a decision of the Security Council and, if necessary, on the basis of other mutually agreed procedures. The Nine declare that they are prepared to participate within the framework of a comprehensive settlement in a system of concrete and binding international guarantees, including on the ground.

6) A just solution must finally be found to the Palestinian problem, which is not simply one of refugees. The Palestinian people, which is conscious of existing as such, must be placed in a position, by an appropriate process defined within the framework of the comprehensive peace settlement, to exercise fully its right to self-determination.

7) The achievement of these objectives requires the involvement and support of all the parties concerned in the peace settlement which the Nine are endeavouring to promote in keeping with the principles formulated in the declaration referred to above. These principles are binding on all the parties concerned, and thus the Palestinian people, and on the PLO, which will have to be associated with the negotiations.

8) The Nine recognize the special importance of the role played by the question of Jerusalem for all the parties concerned. The Nine stress that they will not accept any unilateral initiative designed to change the status of Jerusalem and that any agreement on the city's status should guarantee freedom of access for everyone to the Holy Places.

9) The Nine stress the need for Israel to put an end to the territorial occupation which it has maintained since the conflict of 1967, as it has done for part of Sinai. They are deeply convinced that the Israeli settlements constitutes a serious obstacle to the peace process in the Middle East. The Nine consider that these settlements, as well as modifications in population and property in the occupied Arab territories, are illegal under international law.

10) Concerned as they are to put an end to violence, the Nine consider that only the renunciation of force or the threatened use of force by all the parties can create a climate of confidence in the area, and constitute a basic element for a comprehensive settlement of the conflict in the Middle East.

11) The Nine have decided to make the necessary contacts with all the parties concerned. The objective of these contacts would be to ascertain the position of the various parties with respect to the principles set out in this declaration and in the light of the results of this consultation process to determine the form which an initiative on their part could take.

APPENDIX 9
TWELFTH ARAB LEAGUE SUMMIT CONFERENCE – FINAL STATEMENT

Fez, Morocco – 9 September 1982

[...]
I. The Arab–Israeli Conflict

The conference greeted the steadfastness of the Palestine revolutionary forces, the Lebanese and Palestinian peoples and the Syrian Arab Armed Forces and declared its support for the Palestinian people in their struggle for the retrieval of their established national rights.

Out of the conference's belief in the ability of the Arab nation to achieve its legitimate objectives and eliminate the aggression, and out of the principles and basis laid down by the Arab summit conferences, and out of the Arab countries' determination to continue to work by all means for the establishment of peace based on justice in the Middle East and using the plan of President Habib Bourguiba, which is based on international legitimacy, as the foundation for solving the Palestinian question and the plan of His Majesty King Fahd ibn Abdul Aziz which deals with peace in the Middle East, and in the light of the discussions and notes made by their majesties ... , the conference has decided to adopt the following principles:

1. Israel's withdrawal from all Arab territories occupied in 1967, including Arab Jerusalem.

2. The removal of settlements set up by Israel in the Arab territories after 1967.

3. Guarantees of the freedom of worship and the performance of religious rites for all religions at the holy places.

4. Confirmation of the right of the Palestinian people to self-determination and to exercise their firm and inalienable national rights, under the leadership

of the PLO, its sole legitimate representative, and compensation for those who do not wish to return.

5. The placing of the West Bank and Gaza Strip under UN supervision for a transitional period, not longer than several months.

6. The creation of an independent Palestinian state with Jerusalem as its capital.

7. The drawing up by the Security Council of guarantees for peace for all the states of the region, including the independent Palestinian state.

8. Security Council guarantees for the implementation of these principles. [...]

APPENDIX 10
UN SECURITY COUNCIL RESOLUTION 687: 1991

Adopted by the Security Council at its 2981st meeting, on 3 April 1991

The Security Council,
[...]
C
7. Invites Iraq to reaffirm unconditionally its obligations under the Geneva Protocol for the Prohibition of the Use in War of Asphyxiating, Poisonous or Other Gases, and of Bacteriological Methods of Warfare, signed at Geneva on 17 June 1925, and to ratify the Convention on the Prohibition of the Development, Production and Stockpiling of Bacteriological (Biological) and Toxin Weapons and on Their Destruction, of 10 April 1972;

8. Decides that Iraq shall unconditionally accept the destruction, removal, or rendering harmless, under international supervision, of:

(a) All chemical and biological weapons and all stocks of agents and all related subsystems and components and all research, development, support and manufacturing facilities;

(b) All ballistic missiles with a range greater than 150 kilometres and related major parts, and repair and production facilities;
[...]
12. Decides that Iraq shall unconditionally agree not to acquire or develop nuclear weapons or nuclear-weapons-usable material or any subsystems or

components or any research, development, support or manufacturing facilities related to the above; to submit to the Secretary-General and the Director-General of the International Atomic Energy Agency within fifteen days of the adoption of the present resolution a declaration of the locations, amounts, and types of all items specified above; to place all of its nuclear-weapons-usable materials under the exclusive control, for custody and removal, of the International Atomic Energy Agency, with the assistance and cooperation of the Special Commission as provided for in the plan of the Secretary-General discussed in paragraph 9(b) above; to accept, in accordance with the arrangements provided for in paragraph 13 below, urgent on-site inspection and the destruction, removal or rendering harmless as appropriate of all items specified above; and to accept the plan discussed in paragraph 13 below for the future ongoing monitoring and verification of its compliance with these undertakings;

[...]

D

15. Requests the Secretary-General to report to the Security Council on the steps taken to facilitate the return of all Kuwaiti property seized by Iraq, including a list of any property that Kuwait claims has not been returned or which has not been returned intact;

E

16. Reaffirms that Iraq, without prejudice to the debts and obligations of Iraq arising prior to 2 August 1990, which will be addressed through the normal mechanisms, is liable under international law for any direct loss, damage, including environmental damage and the depletion of natural resources, or injury to foreign Governments, nationals and corporations, as a result of Iraq's unlawful invasion and occupation of Kuwait;

17. Decides that all Iraqi statements made since 2 August 1990 repudiating its foreign debt are null and void, and demands that Iraq adhere scrupulously to all of its obligations concerning servicing and repayment of its foreign debt;

18. Decides also to create a fund to pay compensation for claims that fall within paragraph 16 above and to establish a Commission that will administer the fund;

19. Directs the Secretary-General to develop and present to the Security Council for decision, no later than thirty days following the adoption of the present resolution, recommendations for the fund to meet the requirement for the payment of claims established in accordance with paragraph 18 above and for a programme to implement the decisions in paragraphs

16, 17 and 18 above, including: administration of the fund; mechanisms for determining the appropriate level of Iraq's contribution to the fund based on a percentage of the value of the exports of petroleum and petroleum products from Iraq not to exceed a figure to be suggested to the Council by the Secretary-General, taking into account the requirements of the people of Iraq, Iraq's payment capacity as assessed in conjunction with the international financial institutions taking into consideration external debt service, and the needs of the Iraqi economy; arrangements for ensuring that payments are made to the fund; the process by which funds will be allocated and claims paid; appropriate procedures for evaluating losses, listing claims and verifying their validity and resolving disputed claims in respect of Iraq's liability as specified in paragraph 16 above; and the composition of the Commission designated above;

F

20. Decides, effective immediately, that the prohibitions against the sale or supply to Iraq of commodities or products, other than medicine and health supplies, and prohibitions against financial transactions related thereto contained in resolution 661 (1990) shall not apply to foodstuffs notified to the Security Council Committee established by resolution 661 (1990) concerning the situation between Iraq and Kuwait or, with the approval of that Committee, under the simplified and accelerated 'no-objection' procedure, to materials and supplies for essential civilian needs as identified in the report of the Secretary-General dated 20 March 1991, and in any further findings of humanitarian need by the Committee;
[...]
22. Decides that upon the approval by the Security Council of the programme called for in paragraph 19 above and upon Council agreement that Iraq has completed all actions contemplated in paragraphs 8, 9, 10, 11, 12 and 13 above, the prohibitions against the import of commodities and products originating in Iraq and the prohibitions against financial transactions related thereto contained in resolution 661 (1990) shall have no further force or effect;
[...]
24. Decides that, in accordance with resolution 661 (1990) and subsequent related resolutions and until a further decision is taken by the Security Council, all States shall continue to prevent the sale or supply, or the promotion or facilitation of such sale or supply, to Iraq by their nationals, or from their territories or using their flag vessels or aircraft, of:

(a) Arms and related materiel of all types, specifically including the sale or transfer through other means of all forms of conventional military equipment, including for paramilitary forces, and spare parts and components and their means of production, for such equipment;

[...]

(c) Technology under licensing or other transfer arrangements used in the production, utilization or stockpiling of items specified in subparagraphs (a) and (b) above;

(d) Personnel or materials for training or technical support services relating to the design, development, manufacture, use, maintenance or support of items specified in subparagraphs (a) and (b) above;

25. Calls upon all States and international organizations to act strictly in accordance with paragraph 24 above, notwithstanding the existence of any contracts, agreements, licences or any other arrangements;

[...]

G

30. Decides that, in furtherance of its commitment to facilitate the repatriation of all Kuwaiti and third country nationals, Iraq shall extend all necessary cooperation to the International Committee of the Red Cross, providing lists of such persons, facilitating the access of the International Committee of the Red Cross to all such persons wherever located or detained and facilitating the search by the International Committee of the Red Cross for those Kuwaiti and third country nationals still unaccounted for;

[...]

H

32. Requires Iraq to inform the Security Council that it will not commit or support any act of international terrorism or allow any organization directed towards commission of such acts to operate within its territory and to condemn unequivocally and renounce all acts, methods and practices of terrorism;

I

33. Declares that, upon official notification by Iraq to the Secretary-General and to the Security Council of its acceptance of the provisions above, a formal cease-fire is effective between Iraq and Kuwait and the Member States cooperating with Kuwait in accordance with resolution 678 (1990);

34. Decides to remain seized of the matter and to take such further steps as may be required for the implementation of the present resolution and to secure peace and security in the area.

APPENDIX 11
DECLARATION OF PRINCIPLES ON INTERIM SELF-GOVERNMENT ARRANGEMENTS: 1993

September 13, 1993

The Government of the State of Israel and the P.L.O. team (in the Jordanian–Palestinian delegation to the Middle East Peace Conference) (the 'Palestinian Delegation'), representing the Palestinian people, agree that it is time to put an end to decades of confrontation and conflict, recognize their mutual legitimate and political rights, and strive to live in peaceful coexistence and mutual dignity and security and achieve a just, lasting and comprehensive peace settlement and historic reconciliation through the agreed political process. Accordingly, the, two sides agree to the following principles:

ARTICLE I
AIM OF THE NEGOTIATIONS
The aim of the Israeli–Palestinian negotiations within the current Middle East peace process is, among other things, to establish a Palestinian Interim Self-Government Authority, the elected Council (the 'Council'), for the Palestinian people in the West Bank and the Gaza Strip, for a transitional period not exceeding five years, leading to a permanent settlement based on Security Council Resolutions 242 and 338.

It is understood that the interim arrangements are an integral part of the whole peace process and that the negotiations on the permanent status will lead to the implementation of Security Council Resolutions 242 and 338.

ARTICLE II
FRAMEWORK FOR THE INTERIM PERIOD
The agreed framework for the interim period is set forth in this Declaration of Principles.

ARTICLE III
ELECTIONS
In order that the Palestinian people in the West Bank and Gaza Strip may govern themselves according to democratic principles, direct, free and general political elections will be held for the Council under agreed supervision and international observation, while the Palestinian police will ensure public order.

An agreement will be concluded on the exact mode and conditions of the elections in accordance with the protocol attached as Annex I, with the goal of holding the elections not later than nine months after the entry into force of this Declaration of Principles.

These elections will constitute a significant interim preparatory step toward the realization of the legitimate rights of the Palestinian people and their just requirements.

ARTICLE IV
JURISDICTION
Jurisdiction of the Council will cover West Bank and Gaza Strip territory, except for issues that will be negotiated in the permanent status negotiations. The two sides view the West Bank and the Gaza Strip as a single territorial unit, whose integrity will be preserved during the interim period.

ARTICLE V
TRANSITIONAL PERIOD AND PERMANENT STATUS NEGOTIATIONS
The five-year transitional period will begin upon the withdrawal from the Gaza Strip and Jericho area.

Permanent status negotiations will commence as soon as possible, but not later than the beginning of the third year of the interim period, between the Government of Israel and the Palestinian people representatives.

It is understood that these negotiations shall cover remaining issues, including: Jerusalem, refugees, settlements, security arrangements, borders, relations and cooperation with other neighbors, and other issues of common interest.

The two parties agree that the outcome of the permanent status negotiations should not be prejudiced or preempted by agreements reached for the interim period.

ARTICLE VI
PREPARATORY TRANSFER OF POWERS AND RESPONSIBILITIES
Upon the entry into force of this Declaration of Principles and the withdrawal from the Gaza Strip and the Jericho area, a transfer of authority from the Israeli military government and its Civil Administration to the authorized Palestinians for this task, as detailed herein, will commence. This transfer of authority will be of a preparatory nature until the inauguration of the Council.

Immediately after the entry into force of this Declaration of Principles and the withdrawal from the Gaza Strip and Jericho area, with the view to promoting economic development in the West Bank and Gaza Strip, authority will be transferred to the Palestinians on the following spheres: education and culture, health, social welfare, direct taxation, and tourism. The Palestinian side will commence in building the Palestinian police force, as agreed upon. Pending the inauguration of the Council, the two parties may negotiate the transfer of additional powers and responsibilities, as agreed upon.

ARTICLE VII
INTERIM AGREEMENT
The Israeli and Palestinian delegations will negotiate an agreement on the interim period (the 'Interim Agreement').

The Interim Agreement shall specify, among other things, the structure of the Council, the number of its members, and the transfer of powers and responsibilities from the Israeli military government and its Civil Administration to the Council. The Interim Agreement shall also specify the Council's executive authority, legislative authority in accordance with Article IX below, and the independent Palestinian judicial organs.

The Interim Agreement shall include arrangements, to be implemented upon the inauguration of the Council, for the assumption by the Council of all of the powers and responsibilities transferred previously in accordance with Article VI above.

In order to enable the Council to promote economic growth, upon its inauguration, the Council will establish, among other things, a Palestinian Electricity Authority, a Gaza Sea Port Authority, a Palestinian Development Bank, a Palestinian Export Promotion Board, a Palestinian Environmental Authority, a Palestinian Land Authority and a Palestinian Water Administration Authority, and any other Authorities agreed upon, in accordance with the Interim Agreement that will specify their powers and responsibilities.

After the inauguration of the Council, the Civil Administration will be dissolved, and the Israeli military government will be withdrawn.

ARTICLE VIII
PUBLIC ORDER AND SECURITY
In order to guarantee public order and internal security for the Palestinians of the West Bank and the Gaza Strip, the Council will establish a strong

police force, while Israel will continue to carry the responsibility for defending against external threats, as well as the responsibility for overall security of Israelis for the purpose of safeguarding their internal security and public order.

ARTICLE IX
LAWS AND MILITARY ORDERS
The Council will be empowered to legislate, in accordance with the Interim Agreement, within all authorities transferred to it.

Both parties will review jointly laws and military orders presently in force in remaining spheres.

ARTICLE X
JOINT ISRAELI–PALESTINIAN LIAISON COMMITTEE
In order to provide for a smooth implementation of this Declaration of Principles and any subsequent agreements pertaining to the interim period, upon the entry into force of this Declaration of Principles, a Joint Israeli–Palestinian Liaison Committee will be established in order to deal with issues requiring coordination, other issues of common interest, and disputes.

ARTICLE XI
ISRAELI-PALESTINIAN COOPERATION IN ECONOMIC FIELDS
Recognizing the mutual benefit of cooperation in promoting the development of the West Bank, the Gaza Strip and Israel, upon the entry into force of this Declaration of Principles, an Israeli–Palestinian Economic Cooperation Committee will be established in order to develop and implement in a cooperative manner the programs identified in the protocols attached as Annex iii and Annex iv.

ARTICLE XII
LIAISON AND COOPERATION WITH JORDAN AND EGYPT
The two parties will invite the Governments of Jordan and Egypt to participate in establishing further liaison and cooperation arrangements between the Government of Israel and the Palestinian representatives, on the one hand, and the Governments of Jordan and Egypt, on the other hand, to promote cooperation between them. These arrangements will include the constitution of a Continuing Committee that will decide by agreement on the modalities of admission of persons displaced from the West Bank and Gaza Strip in 1967, together with necessary measures to prevent disruption and disorder. Other matters of common concern will be dealt with by this Committee.

ARTICLE XIII
REDEPLOYMENT OF ISRAELI FORCES
After the entry into force of this Declaration of Principles, and not later than the eve of elections for the Council, a redeployment of Israeli military forces in the West Bank and the Gaza Strip will take place, in addition to withdrawal of Israeli forces carried out in accordance with Article XIV.

In redeploying its military forces, Israel will be guided by the principle that its military forces should be redeployed outside populated areas.

Further redeployments to specified locations will be gradually implemented commensurate with the assumption of responsibility for public order and internal security by the Palestinian police force pursuant to Article VIII above.

ARTICLE XIV
ISRAELI WITHDRAWAL FROM THE GAZA STRIP AND JERICHO AREA
Israel will withdraw from the Gaza Strip and Jericho area, as detailed in the protocol attached as Annex ii.

ARTICLE XV
RESOLUTION OF DISPUTES
Disputes arising out of the application or interpretation of this Declaration of Principles. or any subsequent agreements pertaining to the interim period, shall be resolved by negotiations through the Joint Liaison Committee to be established pursuant to Article X above.

Disputes which cannot be settled by negotiations may be resolved by a mechanism of conciliation to be agreed upon by the parties.

The parties may agree to submit to arbitration disputes relating to the interim period, which cannot be settled through conciliation. To this end, upon the agreement of both parties, the parties will establish an Arbitration Committee.

ARTICLE XVI
ISRAELI–PALESTINIAN COOPERATION CONCERNING REGIONAL PROGRAMS
Both parties view the multilateral working groups as an appropriate instrument for promoting a 'Marshall Plan', the regional programs and other programs, including special programs for the West Bank and Gaza Strip, as indicated in the protocol attached as Annex iv.

ARTICLE XVII
MISCELLANEOUS PROVISIONS
This Declaration of Principles will enter into force one month after its signing.

All protocols annexed to this Declaration of Principles and Agreed Minutes pertaining thereto shall be regarded as an integral part hereof.

APPENDIX 12
THE GRAPES OF WRATH UNDERSTANDING: 1996

The United States understands that after discussions with the governments of Israel and Lebanon and in consultation with Syria, Lebanon and Israel will ensure the following:

1. Armed groups in Lebanon will not carry out attacks by Katyusha rockets or by any kind of weapon into Israel.

2. Israel and those cooperating with it will not fire any kind of weapon at civilians or civilian targets in Lebanon.

3. Beyond this, the two parties commit to ensuring that under no circumstances will civilians be the target of attack and that civilian populated areas and industrial and electrical installations will not be used as launching grounds for attacks.

4. Without violating this understanding, nothing herein shall preclude any party from exercising the right of self-defense.

A Monitoring Group is established consisting of the United States, France, Syria, Lebanon and Israel. Its task will be to monitor the application of the understanding stated above. Complaints will be submitted to the Monitoring Group.

In the event of a claimed violation of the understanding, the party submitting the complaint will do so within 24 hours. Procedures for dealing with the complaints will be set by the Monitoring Group. The United States will also organize a Consultative Group, to consist of France, the European Union, Russia and other interested parties, for the purpose of assisting in the reconstruction needs of Lebanon.

It is recognized that the understanding to bring the current crisis between Lebanon and Israel to an end cannot substitute for a permanent solution.

The United States understands the importance of achieving a comprehensive peace in the region.

Toward this end, the United States proposes the resumption of negotiations between Syria and Israel and between Lebanon and Israel at a time to be agreed upon, with the objective of reaching comprehensive peace.

The United States understands that it is desirable that these negotiations be conducted in a climate of stability and tranquillity.

APPENDIX 13
ISRAELI–PALESTINIAN JOINT STATEMENT: 2001

The following is the official text of the joint statement released at the close of the Taba talks by Israeli and Palestinian negotiators as published in the *Jerusalem Post* (Jan 28, 2001):

'The Israeli and Palestinian delegations conducted during the last six days serious, deep and practical talks with the aim of reaching a permanent and stable agreement between the two parties.

'The Taba talks were unprecedented in their positive atmosphere and expression of mutual willingness to meet the national, security and existential needs of each side.

'Given the circumstances and time constraints, it proved impossible to reach understandings on all issues, despite the substantial progress that was achieved in each of the issues discussed.

'The sides declare that they have never been closer to reaching an agreement and it is thus our shared belief that the remaining gaps could be bridged with the resumption of negotiations following the Israeli elections.

'The two sides take upon themselves to return to normalcy and to establish [a] security situation on the ground through the observation of their mutual commitments in the spirit of the Sharm el-Sheikh memorandum.

'The negotiation teams discussed four main themes: refugees, security, borders and Jerusalem, with a goal to reach a permanent agreement that will bring an end to the conflict between them and provide peace to both people.

'The two sides took into account the ideas suggested by President Clinton together with their respective qualifications and reservations.

'On all these issues there was substantial progress in the understanding of the other side's positions and in some of them the two sides grew closer.

'As stated above, the political timetable prevented reaching an agreement on all the issues.

'However, in light of the significant progress in narrowing the differences between the sides, the two sides are convinced that in a short period of time and given an intensive effort and the acknowledgment of the essential and urgent nature of reaching an agreement, it will be possible to bridge the differences remaining and attain a permanent settlement of peace between them.

'In this respect, the two sides are confident that they can begin and move forward in this process at the earliest practical opportunity.

'The Taba talks conclude an extensive phase in the Israeli–Palestinian permanent status negotiations with a sense of having succeeded in rebuilding trust between the sides and with the notion that they were never closer in reaching an agreement between them than today.

'We leave Taba in a spirit of hope and mutual achievement, acknowledging that the foundations have been laid both in reestablishing mutual confidence and in having progressed in a substantive engagement on all core issues.

'The two sides express their gratitude to President Hosni Mubarak for hosting and facilitating these talks.

'They also express their thanks to the European Union for its role in supporting the talks.'

APPENDIX 14
UN SECURITY COUNCIL RESOLUTION 1397: 2002

Adopted by the Security Council at its 4489th meeting, on 12 March 2002
'The Security Council,

'Recalling all its previous relevant resolutions, in particular resolutions 242 (1967) and 338 (1973),

'Affirming a vision of a region where two States, Israel and Palestine, live side by side within secure and recognized borders,

'Expressing its grave concern at the continuation of the tragic and violent events that have taken place since September 2000, especially the recent attacks and the increased number of casualties,

'Stressing the need for all concerned to ensure the safety of civilians,

'Stressing also the need to respect the universally accepted norms of international humanitarian law,

'Welcoming and encouraging the diplomatic efforts of special envoys from the United States of America, the Russian Federation, the European Union and the United Nations Special Coordinator and others to bring about a comprehensive, just and lasting peace in the Middle East,

'Welcoming the contribution of Saudi Crown Prince Abdullah,

'1. Demands immediate cessation of all acts of violence, including all acts of terror, provocation, incitement and destruction;

'2. Calls upon the Israeli and Palestinian sides and their leaders to co-operate in the implementation of the Tenet work plan and Mitchell Report recommendations with the aim of resuming negotiations on a political settlement;

'3. Expresses support for the efforts of the Secretary-General and others to assist the parties to halt the violence and to resume the peace process;

'4. Decides to remain seized of the matter.'

APPENDIX 15
UN SECURITY COUNCIL RESOLUTION 1441: 2002

Adopted by the Security Council at its 4944th meeting, on 8 November 2002

The Security Council,
[...]
Recognizing the threat Iraq's noncompliance with Council resolutions and proliferation of weapons of mass destruction and long-range missiles poses to international peace and security,

Recalling that its resolution 678 (1990) authorized Member States to use all necessary means to uphold and implement its resolution 660 (1990) of 2 August 1990 and all relevant resolutions subsequent to resolution 660 (1990) and to restore international peace and security in the area,

Further recalling that its resolution 687 (1991) imposed obligations on Iraq as a necessary step for achievement of its stated objective of restoring international peace and security in the area,

Deploring the fact that Iraq has not provided an accurate, full, final, and complete disclosure, as required by resolution 687 (1991), of all aspects of its programmes to develop weapons of mass destruction and ballistic missiles with a range greater than one hundred and fifty kilometres, and of all holdings of such weapons, their components and production facilities and locations, as well as all other nuclear programmes, including any which it claims are for purposes not related to nuclear-weapons-usable material,

Deploring further that Iraq repeatedly obstructed immediate, unconditional, and unrestricted access to sites designated by the United Nations Special Commission (UNSCOM) and the International Atomic Energy Agency (IAEA), failed to cooperate fully and unconditionally with UNSCOM and IAEA weapons inspectors, as required by resolution 687 (1991), and ultimately ceased all cooperation with UNSCOM and the IAEA in 1998,

Deploring the absence, since December 1998, in Iraq of international monitoring, inspection, and verification, as required by relevant resolutions, of weapons of mass destruction and ballistic missiles, in spite of the Council's repeated demands that Iraq provide immediate, unconditional, and unrestricted access to the United Nations Monitoring, Verification and Inspection Commission (UNMOVIC), established in resolution 1284 (1999) as the successor organization to UNSCOM, and the IAEA, and regretting the consequent prolonging of the crisis in the region and the suffering of the Iraqi people,

Deploring also that the Government of Iraq has failed to comply with its commitments pursuant to resolution 687 (1991) with regard to terrorism, pursuant to resolution 688 (1991) to end repression of its civilian population and to provide access by international humanitarian organizations to all those in need of assistance in Iraq, and pursuant to resolutions 686 (1991), 687 (1991), and 1284 (1999) to return or cooperate in accounting for Kuwaiti and third country nationals wrongfully detained by Iraq, or to return Kuwaiti property wrongfully seized by Iraq,

Recalling that in its resolution 687 (1991) the Council declared that a ceasefire would be based on acceptance by Iraq of the provisions of that resolution, including the obligations on Iraq contained therein,

Determined to ensure full and immediate compliance by Iraq without conditions or restrictions with its obligations under resolution 687 (1991) and other relevant resolutions and recalling that the resolutions of the Council constitute the governing standard of Iraqi compliance,

Recalling that the effective operation of UNMOVIC, as the successor organization to the Special Commission, and the IAEA is essential for the implementation of resolution 687 (1991) and other relevant resolutions,

Noting the letter dated 16 September 2002 from the Minister for Foreign Affairs of Iraq addressed to the Secretary-General is a necessary first step toward rectifying Iraq's continued failure to comply with relevant Council resolutions,

Noting further the letter dated 8 October 2002 from the Executive Chairman of UNMOVIC and the Director General of the IAEA to General Al-Saadi of the Government of Iraq laying out the practical arrangements, as a follow-up to their meeting in Vienna, that are prerequisites for the resumption of inspections in Iraq by UNMOVIC and the IAEA, and expressing the gravest concern at the continued failure by the Government of Iraq to provide confirmation of the arrangements as laid out in that letter,

Reaffirming the commitment of all Member States to the sovereignty and territorial integrity of Iraq, Kuwait, and the neighbouring States,

Commending the Secretary General and members of the League of Arab States and its Secretary General for their efforts in this regard,

Determined to secure full compliance with its decisions,

Acting under Chapter VII of the Charter of the United Nations,

1. Decides that Iraq has been and remains in material breach of its obligations under relevant resolutions, including resolution 687 (1991), in particular through Iraq's failure to cooperate with United Nations inspectors and the IAEA, and to complete the actions required under paragraphs 8 to 13 of resolution 687 (1991);

2. Decides, while acknowledging paragraph 1 above, to afford Iraq, by this resolution, a final opportunity to comply with its disarmament obligations under relevant resolutions of the Council; and accordingly decides to set up an enhanced inspection regime with the aim of bringing to full and verified completion the disarmament process established by resolution 687 (1991) and subsequent resolutions of the Council;

3. Decides that, in order to begin to comply with its disarmament obligations, in addition to submitting the required biannual declarations, the Government of Iraq shall provide to UNMOVIC, the IAEA, and the Council, not later than 30 days from the date of this resolution, a currently accurate, full, and complete declaration of all aspects of its programmes to develop chemical, biological, and nuclear weapons, ballistic missiles, and other delivery systems such as unmanned aerial vehicles and dispersal systems designed for use on aircraft, including any holdings and precise locations of such weapons, components, sub-components, stocks of agents, and related material and equipment, the locations and work of its research, development and production facilities, as well as all other chemical, biological, and nuclear programmes, including any which it claims are for purposes not related to weapon production or material;

4. Decides that false statements or omissions in the declarations submitted by Iraq pursuant to this resolution and failure by Iraq at any time to comply with, and cooperate fully in the implementation of, this resolution shall constitute a further material breach of Iraq's obligations and will be reported to the Council for assessment in accordance with paragraphs 11 and 12 below;

5. Decides that Iraq shall provide UNMOVIC and the IAEA immediate, unimpeded, unconditional, and unrestricted access to any and all, including underground, areas, facilities, buildings, equipment, records, and means of transport which they wish to inspect, as well as immediate, unimpeded, unrestricted, and private access to all officials and other persons whom UNMOVIC or the IAEA wish to interview in the mode or location of UNMOVIC's or the IAEA's choice pursuant to any aspect of their mandates; further decides that UNMOVIC and the IAEA may at their discretion conduct interviews inside or outside of Iraq, may facilitate the travel of those interviewed and family members outside of Iraq, and that, at the sole discretion of UNMOVIC and the IAEA, such interviews may occur without the presence of observers from the Iraqi government; and instructs UNMOVIC and requests the IAEA to resume inspections no later than 45 days following adoption of this resolution and to update the Council 60 days thereafter;

6. Endorses the 8 October 2002 letter from the Executive Chairman of UNMOVIC and the Director General of the IAEA to General Al-Saadi of the Government of Iraq, which is annexed hereto, and decides that the contents of the letter shall be binding upon Iraq;

7. Decides further that, in view of the prolonged interruption by Iraq of the presence of UNMOVIC and the IAEA and in order for them to accomplish the tasks set forth in this resolution and all previous relevant resolutions and notwithstanding prior understandings, the Council hereby establishes the following revised or additional authorities, which shall be binding upon Iraq, to facilitate their work in Iraq:

• UNMOVIC and the IAEA shall determine the composition of their inspection teams and ensure that these teams are composed of the most qualified and experienced experts available;

• All UNMOVIC and IAEA personnel shall enjoy the privileges and immunities, corresponding to those of experts on mission, provided in the Convention on Privileges and Immunities of the United Nations and the Agreement on the Privileges and Immunities of the IAEA;

• UNMOVIC and the IAEA shall have unrestricted rights of entry into and out of Iraq, the right to free, unrestricted, and immediate movement to and from inspection sites, and the right to inspect any sites and buildings, including immediate, unimpeded, unconditional, and unrestricted access to Presidential Sites equal to that at other sites, notwithstanding the provisions of resolution 1154 (1998);

• UNMOVIC and the IAEA shall have the right to be provided by Iraq the names of all personnel currently and formerly associated with Iraq's chemical, biological, nuclear, and ballistic missile programmes and the associated research, development, and production facilities;

• Security of UNMOVIC and IAEA facilities shall be ensured by sufficient UN security guards;

• UNMOVIC and the IAEA shall have the right to declare, for the purposes of freezing a site to be inspected, exclusion zones, including surrounding areas and transit corridors, in which Iraq will suspend ground and aerial movement so that nothing is changed in or taken out of a site being inspected;

- UNMOVIC and the IAEA shall have the free and unrestricted use and landing of fixed- and rotary-winged aircraft, including manned and unmanned reconnaissance vehicles;

- UNMOVIC and the IAEA shall have the right at their sole discretion verifiably to remove, destroy, or render harmless all prohibited weapons, subsystems, components, records, materials, and other related items, and the right to impound or close any facilities or equipment for the production thereof; and

- UNMOVIC and the IAEA shall have the right to free import and use of equipment or materials for inspections and to seize and export any equipment, materials, or documents taken during inspections, without search of UNMOVIC or IAEA personnel or official or personal baggage;

8. Decides further that Iraq shall not take or threaten hostile acts directed against any representative or personnel of the United Nations or the IAEA or of any Member State taking action to uphold any Council resolution;

9. Requests the Secretary General immediately to notify Iraq of this resolution, which is binding on Iraq; demands that Iraq confirm within seven days of that notification its intention to comply fully with this resolution; and demands further that Iraq cooperate immediately, unconditionally, and actively with UNMOVIC and the IAEA;

10. Requests all Member States to give full support to UNMOVIC and the IAEA in the discharge of their mandates, including by providing any information related to prohibited programmes or other aspects of their mandates, including on Iraqi attempts since 1998 to acquire prohibited items, and by recommending sites to be inspected, persons to be interviewed, conditions of such interviews, and data to be collected, the results of which shall be reported to the Council by UNMOVIC and the IAEA;

11. Directs the Executive Chairman of UNMOVIC and the Director General of the IAEA to report immediately to the Council any interference by Iraq with inspection activities, as well as any failure by Iraq to comply with its disarmament obligations, including its obligations regarding inspections under this resolution;

12. Decides to convene immediately upon receipt of a report in accordance with paragraphs 4 or 11 above, in order to consider the situation and the need for full compliance with all of the relevant Council resolutions in order to secure international peace and security;

13. Recalls, in that context, that the Council has repeatedly warned Iraq that it will face serious consequences as a result of its continued violations of its obligations;

14. Decides to remain seized of the matter.

SELECT BIBLIOGRAPHY

GENERAL HISTORY

François Burgat, *L'Islam dans le monde*, Paris: La Découverte, 1995.
Juan Cole and Nikki Keddie, eds, *Shi'ism and Social Protest*, London: Yale University Press, 1986.

THE ARAB–ISRAELI CONFLICT

Anthony H. Cordesman, *Perilous Prospects, The Peace Process and the Arab–Israeli Military Balance*, Oxford and Boulder: Westview Press, 1996.
Norman G. Finkelstein, *Image and Reality of the Israel–Palestine Conflict*, London and New York: Verso, 1995.
Simha Flapan, *The Birth of Israel: Myths and Realities*, London and Sydney: Croom Helm, 1987.
Alain Gresh and Dominique Vidal, *Palestine 1947: un partage avorté*, Brussels: Complexe, 1987 and 1994.
Alain Gresh, *Israel–Palestine, Vérités sur un conflit*, Paris: Fayard, 2002.
Jacob Coleman Hurewitz, *The Struggle for Palestine*, New York: Schocken Books, 1976 (First Edition 1950).
Yehuda Lukacs, *The Israeli–Palestinian Conflict. A Documentary Record 1967–1990*, Cambridge: Cambridge University Press, 1992.

PEACE NEGOTIATIONS

Joel Peters, *Pathways to Peace: The Multilateral Arab–Israeli Peace Talks*, London: Royal Institute of International Affairs, 1996.
Graham Usher, *Palestine in Crisis*, London and East Haven: Pluto Press, 1995.

ISRAEL

Benjamin Beit-Hallahmi, *Original Sins: Reflections on the History of Zionism and Israel*, London and Concord: Pluto Press, 1992.
Yehuda Ben Meir, *Civil–Military Relations in Israel*, New York: Columbia University Press, 1995.
Akiva Orr, *Israel, Politics, Myths and Identity Crises*, London and Boulder: Pluto Press, 1994.
Shlomo Swirski, *Israel: The Oriental Majority*, London and New Jersey: Zed Books, 1989.

388   SELECT BIBLIOGRAPHY

PALESTINE

Khaled Hroub, *Hamas: Political Thought and Practice*, Washington: Institute for Palestine Studies, 2000.

Benny Morris, *The Birth of the Palestinian Refugee Problem, 1947–1949*, Cambridge: Cambridge University Press, 1987.

Benny Morris, *1948 and After: Israel and the Palestinians*, Oxford: Clarendon Press, 1990.

Nadine Picaudou, *Les Palestiniens, un siècle d'histoire*, Brussels: Complexe, 1997.

Avi Shlaim, *Collusion Across the Jordan: King Abdullah, the Zionist Movement and the Partition of Palestine*, Oxford: Clarendon Press, 1988.

THE GREAT POWERS AND THE MIDDLE EAST

Michael J. Cohen, *Palestine and the Great Powers 1945–1948*, Princeton: Princeton University Press, 1982.

Alice and Sidney Goldstein, *Jews on the Move: Implications for Jewish Identity*, Albany (New York): State University of New York Press, 1996.

Stephen Green, *Living by the Sword: America and Israel in the Middle East, 1968–1987*, London: Faber and Faber, 1988.

Donald Neff, *Fallen Pillars: U.S. Policy towards Palestine and Israel since 1945*, Washington: Institute for Palestine Studies, 1995.

William B. Quandt, *Camp David: Peacemaking and Politics*, Washington: The Brookings Institution, 1986.

Yaacov Roi, *Soviet Decision Making in Practice: The USSR and Israel 1947–1954*, London: Transaction Books, 1980.

EGYPT

Gilles Kepel, *Le Prophète et pharaon. Les mouvements islamistes dans l'Egypte contemporaine*, Paris: La Découverte, 1984.

John Waterbury, *The Egypt of Nasser and Sadat*, Princeton: Princeton University Press, 1983.

LEBANON

Nadine Picaudou, *La Déchirure libanaise*, Brussels: Complexe, 1989.

Kamal Salibi, *A House of Many Mansions: the History of Lebanon Reconsidered*, London: I.B.Tauris, 1988.

SAUDI ARABIA

Joseph Kechichian, *Succession in Saudi Arabia*, New York: Palgrave, 2001.
William B. Quandt, *Saudi Arabia in the 1990s*, Washington: The Brookings Institution, 1981.

THE GULF

Rosemary Hollis, ed., *Oil and Regional Developments in the Gulf*, London: The Royal Institute for International Affairs, 1998.

IRAQ

Faleh Abdul-Jaber, ed., *Ayatollahs, Sufis and Ideologues: Religion and Social Movements in Iraq*, London: Saqi Books, 2002.
Sarah Graham-Brown, *Sanctioning Saddam*, London: I. B. Tauris, 1999.
Marion Farouk-Sluglett and Peter Sluglett, *Iraq since 1958*, London: KPI, 1987.

SYRIA

Hanna Batatu, *Syria's Peasantry, the Descendants of its Lesser Rural Notables and their Politics*, Princeton: Princeton University Press, 1999.
Patrick Seale, *The Struggle for Syria*, London: I. B. Tauris, 1986.
Patrick Seale, *Assad of Syria*, London: I. B. Tauris, 1988.

LIBYA

Jonathan Bearman, *Qadhafi's Libya*, London: Zed Books, 1986.

THE KURDS

Gérard Chaliand, ed., *Les Kurdes et le Kurdistan*, Maspero: 1978.
Robert Olsen, ed., *The Kurdish Nationalist Movement in the 1990s*, Lexington: The University Press of Kentucky, 1996.

TURKEY

Heinz Kramer, *A Changing Turkey*, Washington: The Brookings Institution, 2000.
Philip Robins, *Turkey and the Middle East*, London: The Royal Institute for International Affairs, 1991.
Richard Tapper, ed., *Islam in Modern Turkey*, London, I. B. Tauris, 1991.

STATISTICAL INFORMATION

Arab Petroleum Research Center, *Arab Oil and Gas Directory* 2002.
Central Bureau of Statistics, *Statistical Abstract of Israel* 2002, Jerusalem.
Stockholm International Peace Research Institute, *SIPRI Yearbook* 2002: *Armaments, Disarmament and International Security*, Oxford: Oxford University Press, 2002.
International Institute for Strategic Studies, *The Military Balance* 2002–2003, London: Oxford University Press, 2002.
US Department of Commerce, *Statistical Abstract of the United States*, 2002, Washington.

THE MIDDLE EAST ON THE WEB

International Sites
United Nations: www.un.org/
The Palestine Issue on the UN website (Unispal): domino.un.org/unispal.nsf
International Atomic Energy Agency (IAEA): www.iaea.or.at/
World Bank: www.worldbank.org
United Nations Development Programme: www.undp.org
Stockholm International Peace Research (Sipri): www.sipri.se/
United Nations Educational Scientific and Cultural Organisation: www.unesco.org
European Union: europa.eu.int/
United Nations Relief and Works Agency for Palestine Refugees in the Near East
    (UNRWA): www.un.org/unrwa

Palestine
Palestinian National Authority: www.pna.net
Palestinian Ministry of Information: www.minfo.gov.ps
Palestinian Archive: www.birzeit.edu/palarc
Palestinian Central Bureau of Statistics: www.pcbs.org
Wafa (the press office of the PLO): www.wafa.pna.net
On everyday life in Palestine: www.palestinereport.org
On Marwan Barghouti: www.freebarghouti.org

Israel
Embassy of Israel, Washington: www.israelemb.org
Embassy of Israel, London: www.israel-embassy.org.uk
Central Bureau of Statistics: www.cbs.gov.il
Adva Centre (on socio-economic problems): www.adva.org
Israeli Government: www.gpo.gov.il
Knesset: www.knesset.gov.il
Israeli Ministry for Foreign Affairs: www.mfa.gov.il/mafa/home.asp

NGOs

Alternative Information Center: www.alternativenews.org
Amnesty International: www.amnesty.org
B'Tselem: www.btselem.org
Human Rights Watch: www.hrw.org
Islamic Association for Palestine: www.iap.org
Jerusalem Link: www.batshalom.org
New Israel Fund: www.newisraelfund.org
Israeli Conscientious Objectors (Seruv): www.seruv.org.il
Palestinian Human Rights Monitoring Group: www.phrmg.org
The Palestinian Society for the Protection of Human Rights and the Environment:
    www.lawsociety.org
PeaceWatch: www.ariga.com/peacewatch
Peace Now: www.peacenow.org.il

Information sites

Arabnet: www.arab.net
Badil Resource Centre (information on refugees): www.badil.org
Carnegie Endowment for International Peace (information on the Iraq Crisis):
    www.ceip.org/files/Iraq/index.htm
Center for Strategic and International Studies: www.csis.org
Columbia University (information on Iraq):
    www.columbia.edu/cu/lweb/indiv/mideast/cuvlm/Iraq.htm
Foundation for Middle East Peace: www.fmep.org
Palestinian links: www.birzeit.edu/links
Israeli links: www.iguide.co.il
Institute for Palestine Studies: www.ipsjps.org
Israel–Palestine Center for Research and Information: www.ip-cri.org/index1.html
Jaffee Center for Strategic Studies: www.tau.ac.il
Jerusalem Media Communication Center: www.ceip.org/files/Iraq/index.htm
Le Monde diplomatique (English language): http://mondediplo.com/
Middle East Research and Information Project: www.mideastinsight.org
Palestinian Refugee Research Net: www.arts.mcgill.ca/MEPP/PRRN/prfront.html
Palestine on the web: www.mom.fr/guides
University of Bir Zeit: www.birzeit.edu
US report on the Middle East: www.usrom.com

Online Publications

The Jerusalem Post: www.jpost.com
Haaretz (Israeli daily newspaper): www.haaretzdaily.com
Infopal: www.infopal.org
Al Ayyam (Palestinian daily newspaper): www.al-ayyam.com
Al Karmel (Palestinian periodical): www.alkarmel.org/index.html
Al-Quds (Palestinian daily newspaper): www.alquds.com
Middle East Insight: www.mideastinsight.org

Middle East Review of International Affairs: meria.biu.ac.il
The Arab Association for Human Rights (online press round up): www.arabhra.org

OTHER SITES

CIA: www.cia.gov
US State Department: www.state.gov
AIPAC: www.aipac.org
UK Foreign Office: www.fco.gov.uk
White House: www.whitehouse.gov
French Ministry of Foreign Affairs: www.france.diplomatie.fr

INDEX

1948–49 War xi, xv, 1–2, 3, 6, 7, 41,
48, 50, 64, 76, 90, 105, 107, 142,
153, 161, 172, 178, 212, 215,
225, 242, 244, 253, 255, 271,
282, 313, 333
1956 War xi, 3–4, 7, 29, 51, 85, 90,
107, 117, 260, 265, 283, 316, 317
1962 Constitution (Kuwait) 187
1967 War xi, 5–7, 12, 28, 43, 54, 58,
68, 78, 80, 85, 94, 105, 111, 117,
129, 153, 161, 169, 172, 178,
196, 198, 199, 207, 210, 216,
221, 232, 234, 248, 253, 255,
271, 274, 278, 292, 294, 301,
313, 317, 325, 333
1973 (Yom Kippur) War xi, xvii,
7–9, 21, 34, 48, 55, 56, 68, 71,
90, 95, 117, 152, 178, 210, 220,
221, 233, 246, 267, 274, 295,
314, 318
1982 War xi, 9–11, 24, 47, 115, 153,
164, 204, 211, 217, 232, 261,
284, 318

A Peace to End All Peace (Frokin) 294
Abadan 135
Abbas, Mahmoud (Abu Mazen)
xxviii, 30, 31, 59, 109, 110, 133,
241
Abbasid Empire 27, 134, 142, 147,
241
Abboud, Ibrahim 288
Abdul Aziz, King (Saudi Arabia) 272,
274
Abdullah, Emir 177
Abdullah I, King (Jordan) xv, xxi, 1,
2, 51, 64, 246, 333
Abdullah II, King (Jordan) xxv, 2
Abdullah, Prince (Saudi Arabia) 17,
123, 272, 273, 276, 277, 380
Abiye region 291
Abu Ala' see Qorei, Ahmed
Abu Ammar see Arafat, Yasser
Abu Dhabi 25, 27
Abu Dis 59, 353
Abu Ghneim 219, 336
Abu Hannoud, Mahmoud xxvi

Abu Iyad see Khalaf, Salah
Abu Jihad see al-Wazir, Khalil
Abu Mazen see Abbas, Mahmoud
Abu Musa 21, 25, 26, 135
Abu Nidal (Sabri al-Banna) 12–13,
200
Achaeminid 134
Action Organisation for the
Liberation of Palestine 271
Acre 42, 97, 271, 293
Adana 84, 293
Aden 6, 98, 230, 339, 341
Addis Ababa 13, 288, 289, 290
Adva Centre 227
Afghanistan/Afghans ix, xii, xxvi,
52, 53, 54, 70, 99, 134, 138, 139,
151, 152, 182, 230, 275, 286,
287, 322, 323, 340, 341
Aflaq, Michel 45, 46
Africa 14, 15, 18, 20, 27, 147, 157,
198, 200, 201, 222, 224, 225,
230, 233, 252, 292
Aga Khan 286
Age of Terrorism and the International
Policy, The (Guelke) 301
Agence France Presse 132
Agudat Yisrael 343
Ahdut (journal) 49, 167
Ain al-Rummaneh 191
Ajman 25
al-Adem 199
al-Afghani, Jamal al-Din 148, 212
al-Ahmad al-Sabah, Emir Jaber
(Kuwait) 188, 189
al-Aqsa (mosque) 2, 133, 154, 177,
178
al-Aqsa Martyrs Brigades 44, 302
al-Arif, Arif 64
al-'Asifa 232
al-Assad, Basel 35
al-Assad, Bashar xi, xxv, 35, 96
al-Assad, Hafez xi, xvii, xxv, 18,
34–35, 46, 96, 104, 120, 127,
196, 197, 206, 294, 295, 296
al-Assad, Rifa'at 34, 35
al-Atasi, Nureddin 46
al-Aziz Rantissi, Abd 110

al-Badr, Imam Muhammad 338
al-Bakr, Hassan 119
al-Banna, Abdul Rahman 107
al-Banna, Hassan 151, 211, 212, 213
al-Banna, Sabri *see* Abu Nidal
al-Bashir, General Omar Hassan xxi,
    289
al-Ba'th (Syrian dam) 327
al-Bayd, Ali Salem 339
al-Darazi (founder of Druze sect) 65
al-Faysaliya (building) 52
al-Haboush, Jalil 12
al-Hakim, Ayatollah Muhammad
    Baqr ix, 146
al-Hakim, Caliph 65
al-Hasa 274, 276
al-Hayat (newspaper) 13
al-Hudaibi, Maamun 214
al-Husseini (family) 29
al-Husseini, Abdel Qader 65
al-Husseini, Hajj Amin 107
al-Islah (political party) 340
al-Islam, Saif 252
al-Ittihad (newspaper) 162
al-Jadid (newspaper) 162
al-Jazeera (TV channel) 25, 29, 69
al-Joulan 94
al-Kailani, Ali 142
al-Khadra (mosque)
al-Khalifa, Isa bin 24
al-Khobar xxiv
al-Khosheh 71
al-Mahdi, Sadiq 289
al-Manar (TV channel) 116
al-Muharraq 23
al-Mukhtar, Omar 199
al-Nimeiri, Jaafar xvii, 39, 288, 289
al-Qaeda ix, 52, 53, 54, 150, 151,
    152, 185, 299, 321, 328, 341
al-Qasim, General Abd al-Karim
    118, 119, 143, 183, 186
al-Quds (newspaper) xxvii
al-Rahman al-Kawakibi, Abd 28
al-Saadi, General 382, 384
al-Sabah (dynasty) 186
al-Sadr, Muhammad Baqr 115, 144
al-Sa'iqa (Palestinian group) 106,
    232, 235
al-Salal, Colonel Abdullah 338
al-Sanussi, Idris (King Idris I [Libya])
    198, 199, 251

al-Shaqaqi, Fathi 108
al-Sharif, Haram 130, 284, 315, 336
al-Sheikh Family 272, 273, 275, 320
al-Sibri, Mustafa 106
al-Tal, Wasfi 55
al-Thani (family) 24
al-Thawra (Syrian dam) 327
al-Turabi, Hassan 289, 290
al-Wasat (political party) 214
al-Wazir, Khalil xxi, 29, 237, 254
al-Zahar, Mahmoud 109, 110
al-Zawahiri, Ayman 54, 70
Alamut 286
Alawi 34, 209
Alawite 84, 125, 208, 209, 287, 294,
    295, 296, 297
Albania/Albanian 67
Aleppo 84, 125, 294
Alexandretta 84, 125, 294, 305, 309
Alexandria 16, 211
Algeria/Algerian xviii, 3, 6, 16, 28,
    73, 83, 85, 102, 140, 141, 196,
    221, 222, 223, 298, 300, 301, 303
Algerian National Liberation Front
    45, 63
Algerian Revolution 30
Algiers xviii, xxi, 104, 106, 112,
    118, 128, 142, 183, 230, 233, 235
Ali, Muhammad 67, 211, 274, 287
aliya/aliyot 13–15, 49, 344
Allenby, General Edmund 190
Allied Supreme Command in the
    Middle East 317
Allies 42, 183, 294, 303, 308
Allon, Yigal 77, 253
Allon Plan 278
Altalena affair 48
Alumot 248
Amal (militia) xx, 114, 192, 195,
    196, 235
Amer, Abdel Hakim 3
American aid 15–16
Amir, Yigal xxiv
Amman xx, xxvi, xxviii, 4, 12, 43,
    54, 69, 82, 83, 105, 116, 118,
    119, 180, 285, 294, 317, 326, 333
Amnesty International 123, 124, 303
Anatolia 183, 293, 294, 305, 308,
    327
ANC 301
Anders, General Wladyslaw 47

Ankara 15, 69, 185, 263, 281, 307,
309, 310, 311, 317, 327
Ankori, Zvi 64
Annan, Kofi 170, 269, 311
Anti-Lebanon mountain range 94
Aoum sect 300
Aoun, General Michel xxi, xxii, 87,
195, 196, 296, 298
Aouzou Strip 200, 201
Aqaba, Gulf of 4, 5, 6, 42, 190
Arab Independence 28
Arab League xviii, xxvi, 2, 16–17,
18, 27, 40, 69, 85, 100, 177, 178,
186, 194, 196, 201, 211, 232,
268, 298, 325, 360
Arab Nationalist Movement 105,
111, 339
Arab Revolt (1916) 28, 142, 177, 190
Arab Socialist Party 45
Arab Socialist Union 68
Arab Summit xviii, xix, xxvi, 17,
117, 128, 169, 189, 273, 276,
325, 367
Arab world 18–19
Arabian Peninsula 6, 20–27, 53, 97,
98, 273, 293, 328
Arabism 28, 30, 46, 47, 98, 199
Arabs 27–29
Arafat, Yasser xvii, xviii, xix, xx, xxi,
xxiii, xxiv, xxv, xxvi, xxvii,
xxviii, 5, 12, 29–31, 37, 38, 43,
45, 54, 58, 59, 60, 68, 80, 81, 86,
90, 106, 109, 112, 129, 132, 154,
200, 211, 219, 227, 228, 232,
233, 234, 235, 236, 237, 238,
239, 240, 247, 249, 254, 255,
271, 272, 301, 314, 319, 322
Arctic Circle 47
Arens, Moshe 217
Argentina 32, 33, 114, 177
Ariel 59
Armenia/Armenians 93, 192, 208,
209, 230, 255, 305, 307
arms trade 31–34
Arnon, Jacob 271, 272
Arslan family 66
Ashkenazi 157, 163, 167, 217, 224,
225, 226, 227
Ashrawi, Hanan 236, 240
Asia/Asian 14, 15, 18, 19, 24, 122,
123, 124, 147, 156, 157, 175,
186, 222, 223, 224, 225, 263,
286, 292, 305, 310
Asia Minor 230, 259, 293
Asir 274, 276, 340
Association Agreement 73, 74, 75
Assyria/Assyrian 208, 255, 344
Aswan Dam 68, 167, 326
Asyut 215
Atarot 173
Atassi, Jamal 295
Atatürk dam 309, 327
Atef, Abu Baqr 13
Atlantic 28, 50
Atlanticist 75, 89
Atta, Muhammad 70
Auschwitz 93
Australia x
Austria/Austrian xix, 92, 231, 331
Austro-Hungary 42, 293
Auto-Emancipation (Pinsker) 344
Autonomous Territories 60, 75, 80,
237, 322, 336
autonomy 35–39
Averroes 149
Avicenna 149
Avnery, Uri xix, 63, 165, 271, 272
Axis 303
Ayash, Yahya xxiv, 109, 249
Azzam, Abdullah Yusuf 52
Azerbaijan 264, 310
Aziz, Tariq 103, 104
Azury, Neguib 28

Bab al-Mandeb 338
Babel 120
Babylonians 175, 344
Baghdad ix, x, xvii, xix, xxviii, 17,
40, 46, 88, 89, 94, 100, 103, 118,
119, 121, 139, 140, 141, 142,
143, 144, 145, 146, 181, 182,
183, 185, 188, 189, 209, 225,
232, 262, 263, 269, 294, 295,
321, 325, 328, 329, 330, 331, 333
Baghdad Pact xv, 40–41, 117, 142,
143, 306, 309, 317, 321
Baha'i 209
Bahr al-Ghazal 287, 288
Bahrain 16, 20, 21, 22, 23, 24, 25,
26, 27, 31, 103, 123, 126, 186,
221, 304, 320, 324, 330
Bahrain Code 82

Baker, James x, xxiii, 103, 104
Baker Plan 154
Baku 264, 310
Baku Congress 260
Balad 164
Balata xxvii
Balfour Agreement 98
Balfour, Arthur James 41
Balfour Declaration 14, 41–43, 49,
    97, 126, 242
Bali 53
Balkans 254
Baluchs 139
Bandung Conference xvi, 3, 216
Bangladesh 53, 147
Bar Kokhba Revolt 13, 175, 344
Bar Lev line 8, 221
Barak, Ehud xxv, 35, 58, 59, 60, 96,
    130, 131, 154, 159, 162, 163,
    164, 197, 219, 226, 229, 258,
    280, 320, 336
Barcelona 73, 75, 197
Barcelona Process 74
Barghouti, Marwan 43–45, 131
Barnea, Nahum 91
Barzani, Massoud 184, 186
Barzani, Mustafa 183
Bar-Zohar, Michel 49
Basel 113, 114, 296
Bashar 296, 297
Bashir II, King (Lebanon) 193
Basque 299
Basra 103, 144
Ba'th party (various countries),
    Ba'thism, Ba'thist xvi, xvii, 6, 12,
    28, 30, 34, 35, 45–47, 100, 115,
    118, 119, 126, 140, 141, 143,
    144, 151, 181, 183, 191, 294,
    295, 296, 297, 331, 339
Battle of the Canal 292
Bauer, Gary 205
Baykal, Deniz 308
Bazargan, Mehdi 136
BBC 99, 266
Beaufort Castle 312
Bechir, Salah 209
Bedouin 178, 187, 190, 251
Begin, Benny 166, 167, 217, 282
Begin, Menachem xviii, xxiii, 1, 5,
    8, 9, 36, 47–49, 56, 57, 64, 65,
    76, 86, 95, 153, 155, 158, 165,

224, 226, 249, 254, 265, 272,
    279, 281, 301, 335, 362
Beijing 101, 331
Beilin, Yossi 30, 59, 255
Beirut xvii, xix, xx, xxi, 10, 17, 62,
    86, 88, 105, 110, 111, 114, 116,
    117, 169, 189, 191, 193, 194,
    195, 196, 197, 198, 234, 242,
    254, 258, 265, 266, 272, 273,
    276, 284, 298, 317, 318
Beirut Summit 17
Beja 291
Belgium/Belgian 74, 89, 231, 266,
    333, 347
Belorussia 248, 282
Belzec 93
Ben Ami, Shlomo 162
Ben Bella, Ahmad 301
Ben Dov, Meir 171
Ben Eliezer, Benyamin xxvi, 164, 280
Ben Gurion, David xvi, 2, 47,
    49–52, 64, 76, 77, 153, 157, 158,
    227, 246, 248, 253, 256, 284
Ben Nitai, Benyamin see Netanyahu,
    Benyamin
Ben Yahya, Ahmed 274, 338
Ben Yehuda, Eliezer 342
Ben Zakai, Yohanan 208
Benghazi xx, 200
Benghazi Military Academy 251
Beni Mor 215
Beni Walid 202
Beqaa 114, 115, 206
Berbera airport
Berlin xxv, 13, 14, 75, 282
Berlin Summit 74
Berlin Wall xi, 319
Berlusconi, Silvio 75
Bernadotte, Count 245, 282
Berri, Nabih 114, 196
Beshair 291
Bet El 59
Bet Horon 253
Betar (colony) 173
Betar (political party) 47, 49
Bethlehem xxvii, 36, 128, 131, 229,
    241, 244, 333, 335, 353
Bevin, Ernest 2
Biltmore Conference 50
bin Abdullah, Muhammad Ahmed
    287

bin Laden, Osama xii, 52–54, 70,
    99, 150, 152, 188, 205, 275, 276,
    290, 299, 322, 328, 341
bin Sultan, Prince Bandar 273
Bir Zeit University 43, 88
Biro, Aryeh 283
*Birth of the Palestinian Refugee
    Problem, The* (Morris) 76
Bitar, Salah al-Din 45
Biton, Charlie 227
Bitter Lakes 291
Black Sea 259, 293, 305
Black September xvii, 34, 54–55,
    233, 242, 285, 301, 334
Blair, Tony 73, 99
Blum, Léon 176
B'nai Brith 203
Bohemia-Moravia 92
Bologne Conference 63
Bolshevik Revolution 259
Bombay 291
Bonaparte, Napoleon 13, 67, 83,
    291, 344
Bor 325
Borujerdi, Muhammad 181
Bosporus 259, 293, 305
Boumedienne, Houari 140
Bourgès-Maunoury, Maurice 248
Bourgey, André 122
Bourguiba, Habib 367
Bourguiba Plan xvi
Brandt, Chancellor Willy xix
Brazil 32, 33, 232
Bremer, Paul 146
Brest-Litovsk 47, 49, 282
Brezhnev, Leonid 7, 264
British Mandate 29, 90, 253, 254,
    278, 285, 333
Broken Dream, The (Enderlin) 58
Brown Shirts 91
Brussels xxvi, 75, 266
B'Tselem 91, 336
Bubian 100
Budapest 113
Bulgaria 230
Buraimi 27
Burgat, François 150, 151, 152, 199
Burundi 201
Bush, George Senior ix, xxii, xxiii,
    101, 172, 203, 204, 236, 247,
    262, 319, 330

Bush, George W. ix, x, xii, xxvi,
    xxvii, xxviii, 20, 89, 99, 121, 138,
    145, 146, 172, 185, 205, 209,
    211, 218, 252, 263, 264, 297,
    298, 321, 322, 328, 330, 333
Bustani, Jose Mauricio 333
Byron, Lord 13, 344
Byzantine Empire 102, 103, 134,
    206, 209, 230

Cairo xv, xviii, 3, 4, 5, 6, 7, 8, 9, 16,
    17, 28, 29, 36, 40, 41, 62, 65, 67,
    68, 69, 70, 87, 89, 90, 111, 119,
    123, 127, 150, 190, 199, 200,
    201, 211, 212, 228, 261, 267,
    268, 272, 287, 290, 292, 317,
    325, 326
Cairo Accord xvii, xxiii
Cairo Agreement 195
California 203, 220
Cambodia/Cambodian 93
Camp David xi, xxv, 30, 36, 49, 56,
    57, 58–61, 71, 79, 229, 257, 280,
    318, 326, 336, 362
Camp David Accords xviii, xix, 9,
    34, 35, 56–58, 68, 106, 117, 130,
    140, 154, 164, 165, 166, 178,
    179, 205, 210, 229, 234, 255,
    266, 296, 318, 321, 335, 362
Canada 20, 60, 258
Canal Zone (Suez) 56, 67, 98, 292
Cannes 73
Canton, Marcel xxi
Cape of Good Hope 292
Capitol Hill 203
Carré, Olivier 212
Carter, Jimmy 22, 36, 56, 318, 322,
    362
Casablanca ix, 53, 83, 328
Caspian Sea 230, 264
Castro, Fidel 201
Catroux, General 85
Caucasus 85, 255, 263
Cave of the Patriarchs xxiii
CENTO *see* Baghdad Pact
Central African Republic 201
Ceyhan river 264, 307, 310
Chabry, Laurent and Annie 208
Chad 200, 201, 252, 289, 291
chador 137
Chalabi, Ahmed 146

Chaldeans 209
Chamoun, Camille 191, 194
Chechen rebels 264
Chechnya 264
Chehab family 193
Chehab, General 194
Chelmno 93
Chemical Weapons Convention
    332
Cheney, Dick 52, 321
China/Chinese 18, 31, 32, 101, 103,
    122, 147, 175, 268, 291, 293,
    299, 329, 331
Chipman, John 328
Chirac, Jacques 87, 88, 89
Christian/Christianity xiii, 10, 27,
    28, 45, 61, 62, 66, 69, 71, 81, 83,
    84, 85, 92, 111, 146, 147, 161,
    171, 172, 173, 174, 180, 190,
    192, 193, 194, 195, 196, 205,
    206, 208, 209, 227, 230, 233,
    241, 251, 288, 290, 291, 297,
    298, 321, 334, 354
Christopher, Warren 96
Church of the Nativity xxvii
CIA (Central Intelligence Agency,
    US) xv, 52, 109, 135, 185, 220,
    290, 328, 331
Cilicia 84, 293
Çiller, Tansu 308, 309
City of Poros 12
Clemenceau, Georges 84, 87, 293
Clinton, Bill x, xxiii, xxiv, xxv, 38,
    58, 59, 145, 172, 203, 204, 218,
    219, 238, 263, 271, 309, 320,
    321, 379
Clinton Plan 60
Cohen, Elie 225
Cold War x, 40, 51, 141, 315, 319,
    320
Communist Party (various
    countries), communist xviii, 3, 6,
    39, 41, 61, 92, 112, 129, 139,
    143, 144, 146, 149, 157, 162,
    164, 182, 184, 191, 215, 235,
    236, 259, 260, 268, 271, 288,
    289, 294, 295, 300, 335, 340,
    341, 344
Comoros 16
Conciliation Commission for
    Palestine 245

confessionalism 61–62
Connecticut 203
Conservative Party (Great Britain)
    21
Constantinople 49, 230, 259, 293
Consultative Council 23, 26
Copenhagen Plan 83
Corfu 73
Corm, George 223
Cox, Sir Percy 125, 190
Crusaders 83
Cuba 103, 271
Cunningham, Sir Allan 126
Curiel, Henri 62–63, 271, 347
Curzon, Lord 43, 293
Cyprus 74, 230, 307, 309, 311
Cyrenaica 198, 199
Cyrus the Great 134
Czechoslovakia 1, 3, 64, 216, 248,
    260, 261

da Silva, Marina 114
D'Amato Act 271
Da'wa party 115, 146
Daguet Division 87
DaimlerChrysler 187
Dalet Plan 77, 78
Damascus xvi, xvii, 6, 12, 30, 34,
    41, 45, 46, 84, 88, 94, 95, 96,
    105, 107, 111, 125, 186, 195,
    197, 198, 232, 247, 294, 295,
    296, 309, 319, 325, 327, 333
Damascus Spring 297
Dar al-Ulum 211, 213
Dar es Salaam 290
Dardanelles 259, 293, 305
Darwish, Mahmoud 243
Davar 266
Dayan, Moshe 7, 85, 248, 253,
    282
d'Estaing, Valéry Giscard 74, 86,
    311
de Charette, Hervé 88
de Gaulle, General 83, 85
de Lesseps, Ferdinand 291
de Rothschild, Baron Edmond 13,
    344
Dead Sea 207
Declaration of Principles on
    Palestinian Autonomy xxiii, 38,
    80, 255, 262, 320

Declaration of the Rights of Man 300
Declaration of Venice 72
Degania 13
Degel Tora 167
Deir Yassin xv, 1, 48, 64–65, 76, 77
Delcorde, Raoul 21
Delta 63
Demirel, President Süleyman 309
Democratic Arab Party 164
Democratic Republic of Congo 201
Democratic Unionist Party 289
Deri, Arie 167
DFLP (Democratic Front for the Liberation of Palestine) (pre-1974 Popular Democratic Front for the Liberation of Palestine [PDFLP]) xi, xxvi, 54, 105, 106, 107, 111, 112, 129, 166, 232, 233, 235, 236, 237, 240, 302
Dhahran xxiv, 324
Dhofar 26, 135
Diaspora 227
Diego Garcia military base 22, 323
Dimona 225, 248
Dinkas 288
Disi 326
Disraeli, Benjamin 344
Diyarbakir 185
Djibouti 16, 338
Draper, Morris 266
Dreyfus, Alfred (Dreyfus affair) 113, 176, 345, 346
Druze (sect) xx, 61, 62, 65–66, 84, 85, 95, 125, 161, 193, 206, 208, 209, 286, 297
Druze Maan (family) 193
Dubai 25, 123
Dulles, John Foster 40
Dumas, Roland 87
Duras, Marguerite 94

Eban, Abba 246
Ecevit, Bülent 308
Economic Union of Palestine 355, 356
Economist 301
Ecuador 33
Eddé, Raymond 192, 209
Eddé family 206
Efrat 173

Egypt/Egyptian x, xv, xvi, xvii, xviii, xix, xxv, 1, 2, 3, 4, 5, 6, 7, 8, 9, 12, 13, 15, 16, 17, 18, 22, 27, 28, 29, 31, 32, 33, 34, 36, 40, 41, 42, 46, 51, 53, 56, 57, 59, 62, 67–71, 73, 74, 80, 83, 84, 85, 86, 87, 90, 95, 97, 101, 104, 107, 112, 117, 118, 122, 123, 124, 126, 127, 140, 142, 143, 151, 152, 153, 154, 194, 198, 199, 200, 209, 210, 211, 212, 213, 214, 215, 216, 221, 230, 232, 234, 235, 244, 246, 247, 248, 256, 257, 259, 260, 261, 263, 267, 268, 270, 274, 283, 286, 287, 288, 289, 291, 292, 295, 296, 297, 303, 305, 317, 318, 323, 324, 325, 326, 328, 329, 332, 338, 344, 360, 362, 363, 364, 365, 375
Egyptian National Liberation Movement (ENLM) 63
Eilat 2, 4
'Ein Karim 353
Einsatzgruppen 92
Eisenhower, Dwight 40
Eisenhower Doctrine xvi, 317
Eitan, Raphael 159, 166, 265, 266, 283
Eitan, Walter 256
Ekeus, Rolf 145
El Al 301
El Shifa Pharmaceutical Company 290
Eleazar 207
Eliav, Arie 271
Enderlin, Charles 58
Enron 26
Entebbe 217
Equatoria 287, 288
Equatoria Corps 288
Erbakan, Necmettin xxiv, 307, 309, 310
Erdogan, Recep Tayyip 310
Eritrea/Eritreans 289, 290, 291, 341
Eshkol, Levy xvi, 49, 51, 153, 253, 278
Eskenazi, Frank 176
Essen 73
Ethiopia/Ethiopian xx, 14, 157, 225, 282, 289, 323, 325, 326, 338
Euphrates 139, 325, 326, 327

Europe/European xx, 8, 13, 15, 18, 27, 42, 61, 67, 71, 72, 73, 74, 87, 89, 92, 94, 234, 236, 241, 252, 271, 281, 282, 293, 296, 300, 305, 311, 319, 320, 323, 328, 339, 345, 346
European Council 74, 300, 310, 365
European Economic Community (EEC) 71, 72, 73, 86, 307, 319
European Investment Bank 74
European Summit xviii
European Union (EU) xi, xxv, xxviii, 8, 39, 61, 71–76, 83, 87, 89, 91, 132, 133, 138, 171, 197, 198, 201, 223, 239, 241, 264, 300, 305, 308, 310, 311, 377, 379, 380
Evian Accords 63
expulsions 76–79

Fadel, Ahmed Ali 292
Fadel, Muhammad 216
Fadlallah, Muhammad Hussein 115
Fahd, King (Saudi Arabia) xxii, 110, 275, 276, 277, 367
Fahd, Prince (Saudi Arabia) xix, 272
Fahd Plan 86
Faisal, King (Syria/Iraq) 84, 124, 142, 190, 210, 274, 294
Faisal II, King (Egypt) 142
Fakhreddin II, King (Lebanon) 66, 193
Falasha (Jews) xx, 157, 225, 282
Falujah, Battle of 215
Faluji, Imad 109
Fanon, Frantz 218
Fao Peninsula 141
Farsi 23, 138
Faruq, King (Egypt) 67, 212, 267
Fasht al-Dibel 27
Fatah xvi, xx, xxviii, 5, 12, 29, 30, 37, 43, 44, 55, 90, 105, 106, 108, 109, 110, 112, 129, 131, 133, 186, 233, 235, 236, 240, 242, 271, 275, 301, 302
Fatah Abu Ghoda, Abdul 295
Fatah Ismail, Abdul
Fatimid dynasty 65, 286
Faurisson, Robert 93
Fayyad, Shafiq 35
Fazilet 310

fedayeen 12, 28, 30, 54, 68, 117, 178, 195, 232, 265, 282, 283, 285, 334
Fez Plan 17, 122, 172
Fez Summit xix
Fezzan 199, 251
Fighters for the Freedom of Israel 281
Fiji 312
'Final Solution' 92
Final Status Negotiations 80–83
Finland 19, 312
First Crusade 73
Fish, John 300
Fontaine, Marcel xxi
Ford, Gerald 95
France/French x, xvi, xx, xxi, xxii, xxviii, 3, 4, 5, 20, 22, 28, 32, 33, 34, 40, 42, 51, 53, 61, 62, 63, 83–90, 93, 97, 99, 102, 110, 113, 115, 116, 125, 126, 133, 136, 138, 153, 176, 177, 181, 190, 193, 194, 199, 206, 208, 215, 217, 230, 231, 248, 252, 253, 258, 260, 265, 267, 270, 275, 288, 290, 292, 293, 294, 301, 303, 305, 309, 312, 313, 314, 315, 316, 330, 331, 341, 345, 377
François I (France) 83, 230
Franjieh, Suleiman 191, 195
Franjieh family 206
Free French forces 85
Free Officers 67, 251, 267, 288
Free Princes 272
French Hill 173
French Mandate 294
French Popular Front 84
French Resistance 300
French Revolution 300
French Somaliland 83
Friedman, Milton 217
Frokin, David 294
Fujairah 25
Fur 291

Gahal 165
Galilee xviii, 2, 94, 161, 234, 313, 328
Gama'a Islamiya movement 70
GAP project 327
Garang, John 288, 325
Garner, Jay 146

Gaulanitide 94
Gaza xv, xvi, xxiii, xxiv, xxv, xxvi,
2, 3, 4, 5, 6, 7, 9, 12, 15, 17, 29,
30, 35, 36, 37, 38, 57, 58, 59, 60,
79, 80, 81, 90, 91, 96, 106, 107,
108, 109, 110, 112, 117, 127,
128, 129, 130, 132, 156, 159,
161, 166, 204, 218, 219, 227,
228, 233, 234, 235, 236, 237,
238, 239, 240, 241, 242, 253,
278, 279, 280, 281, 283, 302,
303, 308, 320, 335, 336, 363,
364, 365, 368, 369, 372, 373,
374, 375, 376, 377
Gaza Strip 90–91
Geagea, Samir 196
Gemayel, Amin xix, xx, 116, 195
Gemayel, Bashir xix, 265, 266
Gemayel, Pierre 191, 318
Geneva xxv, xxviii, 9, 103, 106,
173, 221, 258, 368
Geneva Agreement 61
Geneva Conference 56
Geneva Convention 128, 132, 170,
280
genocide 91–94
Georgia 310
Germany/German x, xix, 14, 32, 33,
42, 47, 48, 67, 85, 89, 92, 97, 99,
101, 113, 135, 142, 154, 187,
230, 231, 248, 281, 282, 292,
299, 305, 306, 331, 333, 346
Gesher party 226
Gestapo 92
Geva kibbutz 248
Ghana 312, 313
Ghassemlou, Abdul Rahman 184
Ghosheh, Ibrahim 109, 110
Gilo 173
Givat Shaul 64
Givat Ze'ev 173
Glaspie, April 100, 101
Glubb, Sir John ('Glubb Pasha') xvi,
117, 177
Goebbels, Joseph 92
Golan Heights xvi, xix, xxiii, 5, 6, 8,
9, 17, 35, 81, 86, 87, 88, 94–96,
161, 192, 197, 278, 279, 280,
295, 296, 320, 326, 327
Goldmann, Nahum 345
Goldstein, Baruch xxiii, 279

Gorbachev, Mikhail xxii, xxiii, 14,
101, 167, 261, 262, 296, 330
Gouraud, General 84
Great Britain/British x, xvi, 1, 2, 3,
4, 6, 14, 21, 23, 28, 29, 32, 33,
40, 41, 42, 43, 47, 48, 50, 51, 61,
67, 83, 84, 85, 88, 96–100, 101,
102, 113, 116, 117, 121, 124,
125, 126, 134, 135, 142, 145,
153, 163, 171, 177, 183, 186,
187, 190, 194, 197, 199, 208,
212, 215, 220, 222, 230, 231,
242, 243, 244, 248, 253, 260,
270, 281, 282, 285, 287, 288,
291, 292, 293, 315, 316, 317,
321, 333, 338, 339, 342, 346
Great Nile Oil Project 291
Greater Tunb 135
Greece/Greek xx, 12, 61, 66, 94, 98,
230, 293, 305, 307, 316, 329, 344
Green Book (Qadhaffi) 251
'Green Line' 81, 161
Grin, David 49
Gromyko, Andrei 56, 246, 247, 260
Grynspan, Herschel 92
Guardian (newspaper) 139, 333
Guatemala 33
Guelke, Adrian 301
Gül, Abdullah 310
Gulf Cooperation Council 22, 23, 24
Gulf War (1990–91) ix, x, xi, xxvi,
16, 17, 19, 23, 24, 28, 31, 33, 46,
53, 58, 69, 72, 86, 88, 100–4,
118, 122, 123, 130, 144, 146,
154, 179, 184, 185, 186, 204,
211, 214, 222, 236, 237, 243,
247, 254, 268, 271, 275, 277,
278, 282, 289, 296, 305, 307,
308, 309, 316, 319, 323, 324,
325, 329, 330, 331, 332, 340
Gulf War (2003) ix, 19, 32, 262, 276
Gush Adumi 173
Gush Emunim 166, 279
Gush Etzion 173
Gush Shalom 165

Haaretz (newspaper) 283
Haas, Richard 20
Habash, George, 54, 105–7, 111,
129, 232, 235, 237, 239
Haber, Eytan 48

Habib, Philip 265
Habibi, Émile 162, 143
Habre, Hissene 200, 289
Hadash 164
Haddad, Saad 312
Haddad, Wadih 106
'Haddadland' 312
Hadramawt 52
Haganah 1, 47, 64, 65, 77, 248, 253, 282, 342
Hague, The 27, 75, 89, 341
Haidar, Abdul Shafi
Haifa xxvi, 1, 13, 42, 77, 97, 126, 224, 244, 248, 293
Haifa University 77
Haiti 33
Halabja 184, 331
Halevi, Ilan 174, 175
Halimi, Gisèle 45
Halutza 60
Hama 295
Hamas xxiii, xxiv, xxvi, xxviii, 28, 38, 75, 90, 91, 107–10, 129, 130, 131, 133, 150, 169, 179, 214, 219, 236, 237, 240, 249, 255
Hammami, Said 12
Hanish 341
Hapoel Mizrahi 344
Har Homa 173, 219, 336
Haram al-Sharif (Dome of the Rock) xxiv, 59, 60
Hariri, Rafiq 110–11, 196, 197
Harkabi, Yehoshafat 159
Harris, David A. 217
Hasbaya 66
Hashemite 2, 16, 117, 118, 125, 172, 177, 178, 180, 190, 208, 210, 293, 294, 360
Hashomer Hatzair 47, 163, 343
Prince Hassan (Jordan) 118, 179, 209, 210
Hatay province 309
Hatikvah 175
Hawar Islands 27
Hawashin 169, 170
Hawatmeh, Nayef 105, 111–13, 129, 232, 237
Hayat
Hebron xxiii, xxiv, xxv, 13, 36, 59, 109, 154, 166, 207, 219, 229, 240, 278, 279, 333, 336, 344

Hejaz 125, 190, 274, 276
Helms-Burton Law 271
Helou, Charles 194
Helsinki xxii, 74, 262, 310
Herod, King 207
Hérodote (journal) 251
Herodotus 325
Herut party 48, 49, 217, 282
Herzl, Theodor 13, 113–14, 155, 156, 157, 159, 160, 344, 346, 347
Hess, Moses 344
Heydrich, Reinhard 92, 93
Hezbollah xxiv, xxv, 86, 88, 114–16, 196, 197, 249, 297, 298, 302, 313
Himmler, Heinrich 92
Hiroshima 303
Hisban 326
Histadrut 65, 156, 159
Histoire des Juifs (Graetz) 175
History of Zionism (Lacquer) 345
Hitler, Adolf 91, 153, 190, 281
Hobeika, Elie 266
Hoechst 187
hojat ol-eslam 136
Holland 220
Holocaust 93, 94, 98, 345, 346
Holy Land 14, 41, 42, 159, 175, 226, 345, 346, 355
Holy Places 53, 60, 72, 256, 275, 326, 352, 353, 358, 359, 367, 368
Homs 34, 295
Honduras 33
Hook, Ian John 171
Hormuz, Straits of 21, 22, 26, 27, 338
Hoss, Selim 111, 196, 197
Hourani, Akram 45
Hoveida, Amir Abbas 135
Hrawi, Elias 196, 197, 298
Human Rights Watch 91, 302
Hungary 230, 231, 260
Hussein, King xvii, xix, xx, xxi, xxv, 18, 54, 55, 116–18, 129, 178, 179, 210, 214, 235, 309, 318, 335
Hussein, Saddam ix, x, xii, xxii, xxviii, 18, 23, 69, 100, 101, 102, 115, 118–21, 130, 140, 142, 143, 144, 145, 183, 184, 185, 187, 201, 205, 235, 236, 262, 263, 296, 319, 321, 325, 328, 330, 331, 333

Hussein, Sherif 2, 43, 97, 125, 142,
177, 190, 274, 294
Hussein, Qusay 120
Hussein, Uday 120
Husseini, Faisal 236

IAEA *see* International Atomic
Energy Agency
Iberian Peninsula 13, 344
Ibn Abdul Wahhab, Muhammad
272, 274
Ibn Ali, Ahmad 24
Ibn Hamad, Khalifa 24
Ibn Khaldun 149
Ibn Khalifa, Hamad 24,25
Ibn Saud, Muhammad 273, 277
Ibn Taimur, Sultan (Oman) 26
Ibrahim, Saad Eddin 70
Idris I, King (Libya) *see* al-Sanussi,
Idris
Ilyushin 263
IMF *see* International Monetary
Fund
immigration 122–24
Incirlik air base 324
independence 124–26
India/Indian 18, 22, 24, 25, 26, 27,
96, 97, 122, 134, 147, 244, 286,
291, 313, 329, 331, 338
Indonesia/Indonesian 27, 147, 300
infitah 6, 68, 126–27, 211, 261, 267,
268, 297, 318
Inönü, Ismet 306
International Atomic Energy
Agency (IAEA) 138, 145, 224,
263, 321, 328, 330, 331, 332,
369, 381, 382, 383, 384, 385
International Committee of the Red
Cross 371
International Court of Justice 24, 27
International Herald Tribune 20
International Institute of Strategic
Studies (IISS) 31, 328
International Monetary Fund (IMF)
69, 127, 179, 268, 289, 291, 310,
342
International Socialist Congress xx
Intifada xxi, xxv, 17, 23, 26, 43, 44,
45, 59, 61, 66, 69, 72, 90, 91, 96,
107, 108, 109, 113, 116, 118,
127–34, 154, 159, 160, 162, 164,

165, 166, 178, 179, 180, 204,
205, 218, 229, 235, 236, 238,
239, 240, 241, 247, 254, 258,
302, 315, 335, 336, 346
IRA (Irish Republican Army) 300
Iran/Iranian xv, xxi, 3, 22, 23, 24,
25, 26, 27, 31, 33, 40, 41, 54, 82,
86, 97, 98, 99, 104, 114, 115,
119, 122, 134–39, 140, 141, 142,
143, 144, 146, 148, 179, 181,
182, 183, 184, 185, 186, 201,
211, 218, 220, 221, 222, 224,
252, 263, 264, 270, 271, 276,
286, 287, 296, 297, 301, 305,
307, 309, 315, 316, 318, 319,
320, 321, 323, 329, 330, 331, 333
Iran–Iraq War x, xi, xix, 19, 22, 23,
24, 86, 89, 119, 136, 137,
139–42, 182, 183, 184, 187, 275,
329, 331
'Irangate' xxi, 319
Iranian Revolution 22, 114, 115,
187
Iraq/Iraqi ix, x, xii, xvi, xix, xxi,
xxii, xxiii, xxiv, xxviii, 1, 2, 4, 5,
6, 12, 16, 17, 18, 22, 23, 24, 25,
26, 27, 32, 33, 35, 39, 40, 46, 47,
52, 54, 68, 69, 70, 72, 75, 82, 85,
86, 87, 88, 89, 97, 98, 99, 100,
101, 102, 103, 104, 105, 106,
111, 115, 119, 120, 121, 122,
123, 124, 125, 126, 127, 130,
136, 139, 140, 141, 142–47, 179,
180, 181, 182, 183, 184, 185,
186, 188, 189, 190, 194, 197,
209, 210, 218, 221, 222, 223,
224, 225, 226, 236, 244, 252,
261, 262, 263, 264, 268, 270,
271, 273, 274, 275, 276, 282,
285, 286, 287, 289, 297, 298,
301, 304, 307, 308, 309, 310,
316, 317, 318, 319, 320, 322,
324, 325, 327, 328, 329, 330,
331, 332, 333, 339, 368, 369,
370, 371, 380, 381, 382, 383,
384, 385, 386
Iraqi Governing Council 39
Ireland/Irish 300, 312, 313, 365
Irgun xv, 47, 48, 50, 64, 65, 76, 77,
244, 342
Isfahan 181

Iskenderun 324
Islam/Islamic ix, xii, 26, 27, 28, 30,
    46, 54, 61, 85, 147–49, 150, 151,
    152, 153, 162, 164, 172, 251,
    262, 263, 273, 274, 275, 276,
    285, 286, 287, 291, 295, 299,
    306, 341
Islamic Jihad xxviii, 54, 75, 91, 108,
    109, 110, 133
Islamic Resistance Movement 90
Islamism/Islamist xii, xxi, xxiii, 12,
    18, 19, 23, 28, 53, 54, 69,
    70, 99, 149–53, 260, 277, 289,
    290, 295, 302, 309, 310, 340, 341
Ismail, Khedive 287
Ismailis 209, 286
Ismailism 286
Ismailiya 4, 212
Israel/Israeli x, xi, xv, xvi, xvii, xviii,
    xix, xx, xxi, xxii, xxiii, xxiv, xxv,
    xxvi, xxvii, xxviii, 1, 2, 3, 4, 5, 6,
    7, 8, 9, 12, 13, 15, 16, 17, 19, 22,
    25, 26, 27, 29, 30, 31, 32, 33, 34,
    35, 36, 37, 38, 40, 41, 42, 43, 44,
    45, 47, 49, 51, 53, 54, 55, 56, 57,
    58, 59, 60, 61, 63, 64, 65, 66, 69,
    72, 73, 74, 75, 76, 77, 78, 80, 81,
    83, 85, 86, 87, 88, 90, 91, 94, 95,
    96, 101, 103, 105, 107, 108, 109,
    110, 111, 112, 113, 114, 115,
    116, 117, 118, 126, 127, 128,
    129, 130, 131, 132, 133, 134,
    141, 153–61, 162, 163, 164, 165,
    166, 167, 168, 169, 171, 172,
    173, 174, 175, 176, 177, 179,
    180, 192, 195, 197, 202, 203,
    204, 205, 209, 210, 216, 217,
    218, 219, 220, 221, 224, 225,
    226, 227, 229, 232, 233, 234,
    236, 237, 238, 239, 241, 242,
    243, 244, 245, 246, 247, 248,
    249, 250, 253, 254, 255, 256,
    257, 258, 260, 261, 262, 263,
    264, 265, 266, 267, 268, 271,
    273, 276, 278, 279, 280, 281,
    282, 283, 284, 285, 288, 292,
    293, 295, 296, 298, 301, 302,
    303, 304, 305, 307, 308, 309,
    310, 312, 313, 314, 315, 316,
    317, 318, 319, 320, 322, 324,
    325, 326, 327, 329, 330, 331,
    332, 334, 335, 336, 337, 341,
    343, 344, 345, 346, 347, 359,
    362, 363, 364, 365, 366, 367,
    372, 373, 374, 375, 377, 378,
    379, 380
Israel Beitenu 167
Israeli Arabs 161–62
Israeli Defence Forces (IDF) 1, 4, 5,
    6, 7, 9, 10, 30, 51, 86, 95, 117,
    159, 169, 170, 195, 265, 310,
    313, 314
Israeli Political Parties 162–68
Istanbul 12, 53, 307, 310, 311
Italy/Italian 33, 102, 113, 198, 199,
    221, 231, 267, 293, 294, 312, 313
Izmir 307
Izzedin al-Qassam Brigades 108

Jaber, Emir (Kuwait) see al-Ahmad
    al-Sabah, Emir Jaber
Jabotinsky, Ze'ev 47, 49, 165, 217,
    281, 284
Jadid, Salah 34, 46, 294
Jaffa 1, 12, 244
Jaffee Center for Strategic Studies 309
Jakarta ix
Jamahiriyya 200, 201, 251
Janissaries 230
Japan 20, 69, 220, 221, 223, 305
Jarring, Gunnar 7
Jaruzelski, General 95
Jbeil Mountain 62
Jebel Druze 294
Jeddah 52, 100, 275
Jenin xxvii, 36, 44, 131, 169–71,
    229, 302, 333, 335
Jericho 36, 228, 229, 335, 373, 374,
    376
Jerusalem xvii, xviii, xix, xxii, xxiv,
    xxvi, 1, 2, 3, 5, 6, 7, 13, 17, 29,
    30, 35, 37, 48, 51, 56, 57, 58, 59,
    60, 64, 65, 68, 72, 76, 80, 81, 88,
    106, 107, 117, 125, 128, 130,
    133, 158, 159, 161, 171–74, 177,
    178, 207, 219, 228, 229, 232,
    234, 236, 237, 240, 241, 244,
    245, 247, 256, 268, 275, 276,
    278, 279, 309, 315, 333, 334,
    335, 336, 337, 342, 344, 351,
    352, 353, 354, 355, 356, 358,
    359, 366, 367, 368, 373, 378

Jerusalem Post 378
Jesuit College 62
Jewish National Fund 342, 344
Jewish State, The (Herzl) 344
Jewish World Congress 114, 342
Jews 174–77
Jheilet 206
Jibril 235
Jibril, Ahmed 106, 232
Jilouwi 272
Jirys, Sabri 271
Jizan 340
Jolo 201, 252
Jonglei Canal 325
Jordan/Jordanian ix, xv, xvi, xvii,
    xviii, xxi, xxiv, xxv, 2, 3, 4, 5, 6,
    9, 15, 16, 17, 18, 30, 31, 32, 34,
    36, 37, 41, 43, 51, 54, 55, 57, 60,
    68, 73, 74, 81, 83, 95, 97, 102,
    105, 107, 109, 111, 116, 117,
    118, 120, 122, 123, 125, 129,
    143, 172, 177–80, 189, 191, 195,
    209, 210, 214, 219, 232, 233,
    235, 242, 246, 247, 254, 271,
    281, 283, 285, 293, 301, 304,
    307, 309, 316, 317, 318, 320,
    324, 325, 326, 327, 328, 333,
    334, 335, 360, 363, 364, 365,
    372, 375
Jordan, River 5, 48, 58, 80, 81, 95,
    111, 117, 125, 177, 178, 246,
    249, 256, 257, 258, 260, 278,
    325, 326, 333
Jordan valley 37, 59, 81, 96, 278,
    279, 280
Jordanian–Palestinian Accord xx
Jordanian–Palestinian
    Confederation xix
Josephus, Flavius 207
Jospin, Lionel 88
Journal of Palestinian Studies 283
Juba 288
Judea 81, 279, 334
Jumblatt, Kamal 66, 191
Jumblatt, Walid xx, 66, 195
Jumblatt family 66
Justice and Development Party
    (AKP) 310

Kabul 52, 53, 138
Kabyles 18

Kach 166
Kadesh 4
Kafr Kubr 43
Kahane, Rabbi 166, 203, 265
Kahane Commission 265
Kalak, Ezzedine 12
Kamel al-Majid, Hussein 120
Kamel, Saddam 120
Kanafani, Ghassan 243
Karameh, Battle of xvii, 30
Karameh, Rashid 195, 196
Karbala 144, 286
Karine A xxvi
Kashani, Abol Qasim 181
Kashmir 299
Kassis, Father 191
Kauffmann, Jean-Paul xxi
Kazakhstan 138, 310
Kebabdjian, Gérard 73
Kedumim 59
Kelly, David 99
Kelley, General Paul 323
Kemal, Mustafa (Atatürk) 147, 183,
    294, 305, 306
Kemalism 306, 311
Kennedy, John F. 318
Kenya 22, 33, 53, 185, 290, 323
Kepel, Gilles 213
Kesruan 206
Kfar Etzion 278
Khaddam, Abdul Halim 35
Khalaf, Salah xxii, 12, 29, 55, 237
Khalid, King (Saudi Arabia) 272
Khamenei, Ali 136, 137, 287
Khan, Reza *see* Reza Shah
Kharijism 147
Khartoum xvii, 12, 53, 268, 289,
    290, 291, 326
Khatami, Muhammad 137, 138
Khatmiyya Brotherhood 287, 288,
    289
Khawr al-Ubayd 27
Khazar 175
Khomeini, Ayatollah Ruhollah xix,
    xxi, 41, 115, 135, 136, 140, 141,
    144, 152, 181–82, 286, 287
Khrushchev, Nikita 68
Khuzistan 140
'Kilometer 101' 56
Kimmerling, Baruch 159
King Abdul Aziz University 52

King David Hotel 48, 244
King's Square 284
Kiryat Arba 59
Kisrawan 62
Kissinger, Henry 8, 34, 56, 95, 192,
    246, 247, 267, 318, 319
Knesset xix, xxviii, 48, 76, 80, 95,
    157, 158, 163, 164, 165, 166,
    167, 168, 172, 226, 266, 271, 282
Koestler, Arthur 41, 175
Kol Hair (newspaper) 283
Koni, Joseph 290
KDPI *see* Kurdish Democratic Party
    of Iran
Korea 122
Korean War (1950) 3, 306
Kreisky, Chancellor Bruno xix
Kremlin 259, 263, 264
'Kristallnacht' 92
Kuala Lumpur 52
Kulturkampf 159
Kurdish Democratic Party of Iran
    (KDPI) 184
Kurdistan xxiv, 39, 142, 146, 183,
    184, 301, 308
Kurdistan Workers' Party (PKK) 307,
    308
Kurds xxiii, 18, 27, 39, 87, 103, 104,
    119, 120, 126, 135, 136, 139,
    140, 143, 144, 182–86, 208, 210,
    230, 255, 257, 297, 305, 306,
    307, 309, 311, 327, 331
Kuwait x, xvi, 8, 16, 20, 22, 23, 26,
    27, 31, 32, 52, 72, 87, 100, 101,
    102, 103, 119, 122, 123, 126,
    127, 142, 144, 151, 179, 186–90,
    214, 221, 224, 232, 242, 243,
    247, 262, 268, 304, 305, 316,
    319, 324, 328, 341, 369, 370,
    371, 381, 382

La Belle discotheque 113
La Conception materialiste de la
    question juive (Leon) 346
La Douleur (Duras) 94
Labour Party (British) 21, 99, 244
Labour party (Israeli) xxv, xxvi,
    xxviii, 37, 48, 51, 56, 60, 80, 81,
    95, 237, 248, 249, 250, 253, 254,
    271, 278, 279, 280, 337
Lahoud, Émile 111, 197, 199

Laoust, Henri 274
Laqueur, Walter 345
Laronde, André 199
Latin America 18, 19, 242
Lattaqieh 34
Lausanne Conference 78, 245, 246,
    256
Lavon, Pinhas 51
Lavon affair 51, 153
Lawrence, T.E. (Lawrence of Arabia)
    28, 97, 98, 190, 210
Le Juif (Liebman) 346
Le Juif errant est arrivé (Londres) 345
Le Monde diplomatique 73,114, 131,
    207, 209, 222, 224, 266, 298, 328
Le Pen, Jean-Marie 93, 176
Le Point (Suffert) 63
League of Arab States 382
League of Nations 125, 142, 294, 349
League of the Arab Fatherland 28
Lebanese Civil War (1958) xi
Lebanese Civil War (1975–89) xi,
    xviii, 111, 114, 160, 190, 191–92,
    195, 234, 295, 296
Lebanese National Movement xviii
Lebanon/Lebanese xv, xvi, xvii,
    xviii, xix, xx, xxi, xxii, xxiii,
    xxiv, xxv, 1, 2, 4, 9, 16, 18, 24,
    27, 31, 34, 35, 41, 46, 47, 49, 57,
    61, 66, 72, 73, 74, 82, 83, 84, 85,
    86, 87, 88, 97, 101, 104, 107,
    108, 110, 111, 114, 115, 116,
    117, 122, 125, 126, 153, 154,
    159, 161, 164, 191, 192, 193–98,
    206, 209, 217, 218, 221, 230,
    233, 234, 235, 242, 243, 249,
    250, 254, 255, 256, 258, 260,
    261, 265, 266, 267, 286, 293,
    294, 295, 296, 297, 298, 299,
    301, 302, 304, 312, 313, 316,
    317, 318, 327, 346, 367, 377, 378
Lebensraum 93
Leclerc (tank)
Lehi xv, 47, 64, 65, 76, 77, 245, 281,
    282
Leibovitz, Professor 160
Leibowitz, Shammai 45
Leibowitz, Yeshayahu 45
Lenin 259
Leon, Abraham 345
Lesser Tunb 135

Levant 85, 227
Levy, David 217, 219, 226
Levy, Moshe 283
L'Huilier, Fernand 97
Liberia 33
Liberman, Avigdor 167
Liberman, Jean 177
Libya xviii, xx, xxiii, 6, 12, 16, 18, 32, 33, 73, 82, 85, 86, 102, 114, 148, 198–202, 218, 221, 251, 252, 270, 271, 304, 305, 320, 323, 329, 333
Liebman, Marcel 346
Likud xi, xxviii, 49, 56, 81, 133, 153, 156, 157, 158, 159, 163, 165, 166, 167, 168, 204, 217, 219, 226, 250, 272, 284
Limburg 53
Lipkin-Shahak, Amnon 159
Litani Valley 312
lobby 202–5
Lockerbie 13, 201, 252, 270
Lomé Summit 201
London xviii, 1, 2, 3, 4, 16, 42, 43, 50, 67, 72, 89, 96, 97, 98, 99, 117, 124, 126, 135, 142, 190, 230, 260, 263, 291, 292, 296, 317, 328, 329, 346
Londres, Albert 345
Lord's Resistance Army (LRA) 290
Lovers of Zion 49, 344
loya jirga 146
Luxor 70
Lydda 77, 253

M1 Abrams (tank)
Ma'ale Adumim 173
Maalot 112
Maarakh 163
Ma'ariv (newspaper) 283
Maastricht Treaty 74
Machakos 290
MacMahon, Sir Henry 190
Madagascar 92
Madrid xiii, 75, 89, 112, 154, 178, 236, 247, 254, 256, 296
Madrid Conference xiii, 34, 81, 82, 87, 95, 109, 130, 154, 217, 245, 256, 262, 282
Mafdal 167
Maghreb 28, 29, 200, 214

Mahabad 135, 183
Mahdiyya Brotherhood 287, 288, 289
Mahjub, Abdel Khaliq 288
Majlis al-Shura 110, 277
Major, John 99
Making of the Arab-Israeli Conflict, 1947–1951, The (Pappé) 77
Maktab, al-Khidmaat 52
Malakal 325
Malaysia/Malaysian 291
Malta 74, 97, 230
Manama 24
Mandela, Nelson 45
Mapai party 49, 50, 51, 163, 248, 284, 342
Mapam 163, 343
Marienstras, Richard 176, 177
Marin, Manuel 73
Marine Corps 322, 323
Marley, Bob 225
Maronites 61, 66, 83, 114, 191, 192, 193, 194, 196, 197, 206, 209, 295, 296
Marseille 201
Marshall Plan 376
Marxism/Marxist 52, 105, 111, 308, 339
Maryland 203
Marzouk, Dr Muhammad Abu 110
Masada 207–8
Mashreq 28, 29
Masirah base 323
Massachusetts 203, 217
Massignon, Louis 285
Massoud, Commander 53
Matzpen 112
Maurienne Agreement
Mauritania 16, 17, 73, 102
Mawdudi 151
McDill Airbase 323
Mecca 52, 53, 142, 147, 148, 172, 177, 182, 274, 275, 340
Medina 52, 53, 172, 274, 275
Mediterranean 73, 74, 94, 264, 291, 293, 305, 310
Mein Kampf (Hitler) 91
Meir, Golda 1, 153, 248, 254, 260
Melchites 209
Menderes, Adnan 306
Mendès-France, Pierre 63

Meretz 164
Meridor, Dan 217, 219
Mesopotamia 125, 139, 230, 293
Metn 62, 66
Mexico 222
Miari, Muhammad 162
Middle East Defence Organisation 317
Middle East Peace Conference 372
MiG (Russian aircraft manufacturer)
Milo, Roni 217
Ministerial Council of the Arab
    League 102
Ministry of Defence 285
minorities 208–10
Mishaal, Khaled 109
Mitchell, George 74
Mitchell Report xxvi, 380
Mutla, Battle of 283
Mutla Pass 283
Mitterrand, François 86, 87
Mitzna, Amram 159, 250
Mizrahi party 166, 167, 344
Mizrahi, Rachel 160
Mizrahi 224
Moawad, René 196, 298
Modim settlement 59
Mogadishu 53, 323
Mojahedin-e Khalq 136, 182
Moledet party 166
Mollet, Guy 248, 301
Mombasa 53, 323
Mombaz, Paulina 49
Monophysites 209
Montazeri, Ayatollah 136
Montreux Convention 306
Moratinos, Miguel Angel 61, 74
Mordechai, Yitzhak 226
Moro National Liberation Front 252
Morocco 16, 17, 20, 22, 60, 73, 74,
    83, 196, 200, 225, 226, 298, 323,
    360, 367
Morris, Benny 76, 77
Mosaddeq, Muhammad xv, 3, 40,
    98, 135, 136, 220, 221
Moscow 1, 32, 41, 57, 82, 101, 135,
    138, 141, 199, 200, 201, 202,
    233, 247, 259, 260, 261, 262,
    263, 264, 267, 296, 299, 305,
    329, 339
Mosley, Sir Oswald 190
Mossad 109

Mosul 121, 142, 183, 220, 293
Motherland Party 307, 308
Motsa 353
Mount Hermon 94
Mount Lebanon xx, 61, 66
Mozambique 114
Mubarak, Gamal 70, 211
Mubarak, Hosni 13, 68, 69, 70, 120,
    210–11, 214, 290, 379
Mubarak, Muhammad 270
Muhammad, Ali Nasser 339
Muhammad Reza Shah (Iran) 135
Mujahedin (Afghanistan) 52, 151
Mukabad 215
Multilateral Group on Refugees 256
Multinational Force xix, xx, 265
Munich Olympic Games 54
Muqata'a 241
Murabitun 191
Musa, Amr 17
Muscat 26
Musharraf, Pervez xii
Muslim Brotherhood 29, 70, 107,
    108, 151, 179, 211–14, 267, 268,
    289, 295, 341
Mussadam Cape 27
Mussolini, Benito 198, 281
Mustafa, Abu Ali xxvi

Nabaa 114
Nablus xix, xxvi, xxvii, 12, 36, 128,
    131, 169, 171, 229, 333, 335
Nabulsi, Suleiman 117
Nagasaki 303
Nahas Pasha 67
Nairobi 290
Najaf 115, 144, 146, 181
Najran 340
Napoleon see Bonaparte, Napoleon
    67, 83, 291, 344
Napoleon III 291, 344
Nasrallah, Hassan 116
Nasser, Gamal Abdel xv, xvi, xvii, 3,
    4, 5, 6, 29, 30, 41, 46, 54, 67, 68,
    105, 107, 117, 124, 126, 142,
    153, 178, 194, 199, 212, 213,
    215–16, 232, 248, 251, 267, 272,
    274, 288, 292, 294
Nasserism/Nasserist 28, 46, 105,
    117, 143, 151, 191, 199, 213,
    216, 251, 271, 273, 296, 317

National Democratic Alliance 290
National Democratic Party (NDP) 70, 268
National Guard 272, 277
National Islamic Front 289
National Liberation Front (NLF) 338, 339
National Reconciliation Charter 298
National Security Council 310
National Security Strategy 321
National Unionist Party 288
Nationalist Action Party (MHP) 309
NATO (North Atlantic Treaty Organisation) 40, 104, 306, 307, 309, 317
Nayef, Prince (Saudi Arabia) 214, 272
Nazareth 77, 162, 241
Nazi/Nazism 14, 91, 93, 244, 265, 299, 303, 345
Nazzal, Muhammad 110
Ne'eman, Amos 283
Negev 2, 51, 60, 161
Neguib 124, 125
Neher, Andre 176
Nejd 125, 272, 273, 274, 276
Nepal 312
Netanya 162, 169, 225
Netanyahu, Benyamin xxiv, 17, 58, 74, 80, 81, 154, 163, 166, 173, 197, 216–19, 250, 266, 279, 280, 284, 320, 336
Netanyahu, Jonathan 217
Neue Freie Presse 113
Neveh Ya'acov 173
New Jersey 203, 220
New York xxvi, 54, 102, 150, 166, 203, 220, 222, 299
New York Times 101, 149, 253
Nicaragua 200
Nicosia 108
Nidal, Abu 235, 272, 301
Niger 252, 270
Nile 287, 288, 325, 326
Nissim, Moshe 171
Nitai, Ben 217
Nixon, Richard 7
Nobel Peace Prize 249
Nokrashi Pasha 2, 212
Non-Proliferation Treaty 138, 331
North Africa 83, 84, 85, 175, 198, 230

North Korea 32, 252, 263, 329
North Yemen xvi, 6, 16, 21, 126, 274, 287, 338, 339, 340
see also South Yemen, Yemen
Northern Ireland 299
Norway 171, 122, 228, 312
Nubians 291
Nuers 288
Nureddin al-Atasi, Dr
Nuremberg Laws 91, 300

Obock 83
Öçalan, Abdullah 185, 307, 310, 311
Occupied Territories xix, xxvii, xxviii, 7, 36, 38, 44, 57, 59, 82, 90, 91, 233, 248, 249, 256, 266, 302, 303, 313, 320, 332, 335
Oil 220–24
Oklahoma 300
Oman 16, 17, 20, 22, 26, 31, 123, 126, 186, 230, 304, 323, 324, 339
Operation Bright Star 324
Operation Desert Fox 73, 88, 145
Operation Desert Shield 102, 103
Operation Desert Storm 31, 104, 123, 319
Operation Firm Voice xxvii
Operation Grapes of Wrath xxiv, 88, 249, 308
Operation Jenin 169
Operation Nahshon 64
Operation New Valley 326
Operation Peace in Galilee 9, 234, 312
Operation Provide Comfort 324
Operation Rampart 44, 132, 169, 336
Operation Season 48
Operation Solomon 282
Oren, Amir 266
Organisation for the Prohibition of Chemical Weapons (OPCW) 333
Organisation of African Unity 252
Organisation of the Islamic Conference 275
Orient House xvi
Oriental Jews 224–27
Orontes Valley 206
Orwell, George 140
Osiraq xix

Oslo 87, 247, 249, 254, 281, 320, 336, 337
Oslo Accords x, xi, xxiii, xxiv, 12, 30, 35, 37, 38, 43, 45, 58, 69, 81, 87, 90, 95, 106, 109, 112, 118, 130, 131, 132, 154, 164, 179, 204, 211, 219, 227–30, 237, 239, 240, 243, 255, 257, 279, 280, 284, 302, 320, 326, 335
Otte, Marc 74
Ottoman Empire/Ottoman 27, 42, 49, 61, 67, 83, 84, 97, 142, 177, 183, 186, 190, 193, 198, 208, 220, 230–31, 241, 259, 263, 274, 278, 293, 305, 316, 338, 346, 358
Our Palestine 29
Oyak 310
Özal, Turgut 307

Pahlavi dynasty 134
Pail, Meir 271, 283
Pakistan/Pakistani xii, 24, 25, 26, 27, 40, 41, 52, 53, 54, 147, 151, 152, 286, 287, 317
Palestine/Palestinian ix, x, xi, xii, xv, xvi, xvii, xviii, xix, xx, xxi, xxii, xxiii, xxiv, xxv, xxvi, xxvii, xxviii, 1, 2, 6, 7, 8, 9, 12, 15, 16, 17, 18, 23, 28, 29, 30, 31, 34, 35, 36, 37, 38, 41, 42, 43, 44, 45, 46, 47, 48, 49, 50, 51, 52, 53, 54, 55, 57, 58, 59, 60, 61, 63, 64, 65, 67, 69, 71, 72, 75, 76, 77, 79, 80, 81, 82, 83, 86, 87, 89, 90, 91, 94, 97, 98, 99, 105, 106, 108, 113, 117, 122, 123, 125, 126, 127, 128, 129, 130, 131, 132, 133, 134, 152, 153, 154, 155, 156, 157, 158, 160, 161, 162, 164, 165, 166, 169, 170, 171, 172, 173, 174, 175, 177, 178, 180, 186, 187, 188, 190, 191, 192, 195, 197, 200, 201, 204, 205, 208, 210, 211, 212, 214, 215, 218, 219, 225, 227, 228, 229, 230, 231, 232, 233, 234, 235, 236, 237, 238, 239, 240, 241–43, 244, 245, 246, 249, 253, 254, 255, 256, 257, 258, 260, 261, 262, 264, 265, 268, 271, 272, 273, 275, 276, 278, 280, 281, 282,
284, 285, 293, 294, 296, 297, 298, 299, 302, 303, 307, 312, 313, 314, 315, 316, 318, 320, 322, 325, 326, 333, 334, 335, 336, 337, 341, 342, 343, 344, 345, 346, 349, 350, 351, 354, 355, 358, 360, 361, 362, 363, 364, 366, 367, 368, 372, 373, 374, 375, 376, 378, 379, 380
Palestine Liberation Organisation (PLO) xvi, xvii, xviii, xix, xx, xxi, xxii, xxv, 5, 9, 12, 13, 16, 17, 20, 29, 30, 36, 43, 54, 55, 57, 68, 71, 86, 87, 90, 102, 105, 106, 107, 108, 109, 112, 114, 117, 128, 129, 130, 150, 178, 186, 189, 191, 192, 195, 200, 204, 227, 228, 229, 232–38, 239, 242, 243, 246, 247, 249, 254, 255, 257, 265, 271, 272, 275, 301, 314, 315, 318, 319, 320, 332, 334, 335, 360, 361, 362, 366, 368, 372
Palestine National Council (PNC) 106, 112, 118, 128, 130, 229, 232, 235, 236, 237, 238, 316, 319, 320
Palestinian Authority 30, 36, 37, 38, 44, 45, 58, 74, 75, 76, 80, 81, 90, 237, 238–41, 243, 257, 284, 303, 320, 322, 335, 336
Palestinian National Charter 80, 106, 112, 229, 232, 315, 320
Palestinian National Salvation Front 235, 334
Palestinian Students Union 29
Palmah 64, 253, 342
Pan-Arab/Pan-Arabism 28, 30, 46, 47, 98, 102, 115, 271
Pappé, Ilan 77
Paris xxi, 4, 63, 72, 75, 83, 84, 86, 89, 92, 97, 141, 145, 194, 201, 229, 230, 256, 261, 263, 271, 317, 329, 330, 332
Paris Accord xxiii, 3, 38
Parti socialiste populaire 191, 195
Partition Plan xv, 1, 50, 63, 76, 98, 129, 161, 172, 235, 243–44, 245, 260, 313, 315, 317, 322, 341, 350
Party of the Democratic Left (DSP) 308, 309
Pasdaran 137

Pasha, Glubb *see* Glubb, Sir John
Pasha, Nahas *see* Nahas Pasha
Pasha, Nokrashi *see* Nokrashi Pasha
Pasuvalyuk, Vladimir 263
'Peace Aqueduct' 328
Peace Conferences 245–47
Péan, Pierre 266
Pearl Harbor x
Peled, Matityahu xix, 5, 63, 159,
    162, 271, 272
Peninsula Shield 325
Pennsylvania 203
Pentagon xxvi, 22, 276, 301, 324,
    328
People's Democratic Union 339
People's Liberation Army 289, 290
Peraea 94
Peres, Shimon xxiv, 80, 81, 153,
    154, 163, 164, 216, 248–50, 253,
    254, 255, 279, 280, 309, 320
Perez de Cuellar, Javier 312
Persepolis 135
Persia 21, 23, 97, 134, 135, 138,
    139, 184, 230, 274
Persian Gulf 22, 325
Persky, Shimon *see* Peres, Shimon
Pesach (Passover) 169
Phalangist 114, 206, 266
Philadelphia, University of 217
Philippines 122, 252
Picard, Elizabeth 62
Picaudou, Nadine 131
Pinsker, Leon 13, 113, 344
'Pirate Coast' 25, 97, 126, 230
Pisgat Ze'ev 173
PLO *see* Palestine Liberation
    Organisation
Plonsk 49
Poale Agudat Yisrael 343
Poalei Zion 49, 163
Poland/Polish xix, 13, 14, 47, 69,
    92, 95, 174, 175, 248, 281, 312,
    313
Pompidou, Georges 86
Popular General Congress (PGC)
    340
Popular Front for the Liberation of
    Oman 26
Popular Democratic Front for the
    Liberation of Palestine (PDFLP)
    see DFLP

Popular Front for the Liberation of
    Palestine (PFLP) xxi, xxiv, 54,
    105, 106, 107, 166, 232, 233,
    235, 236, 237, 240, 301
Poriyat *kibbutz* 248
Portugal xx, 224
Pour une paix juste au Proche Orient
    (Curiel) 347
Prague xviii, 41, 51
Primakov, Yevgeni 262, 330
Progressive National Front (PNF)
    295
Progressive Socialist Party (PSP) 66
Putin, Vladimir 201, 264
Pyongyang 333

Qabus, Sultan (Oman) 26
Qaddoumi, Farouq 237
Qadhaffi, Muammar xvii, 9, 12, 18,
    120, 199, 200, 201, 202, 221,
    251–52, 270
Qadi 273
Qadisiyya 134
Qajar dynasty 134
Qalqiliya 36, 117, 169, 229, 333, 335
Qana xxiv, 312
Qasim, General Abd al-Karim *see* al-
    Qasim, General Abd al-Karim
Qastel 65
Qatar 17, 20, 22, 23, 24, 25, 27, 31,
    32, 123, 126, 186, 221, 290, 324
Qibya 3, 283
Qordaha 34
Qorei, Ahmed xxviii, 133, 241
Quadripartite Committee 257
Quai d'Orsay 88
'Quartet' xi, 39, 75, 89, 133, 134, 264
Quedar 173
Qum 181
Quneitra 94, 95
Qur'an xxii, 215, 251, 274, 277
Qutb, Sayyid 151, 152, 213

Rabat xviii, 117, 233, 301, 360
Rabath, Edmond 28
Rabbani, Burhanuddin 53
Rabin, Yitzhak xi, xxiii, xxiv, 5, 26,
    35, 95, 96, 108, 128, 153, 154,
    164, 165, 204, 227, 228, 248,
    249, 253–54, 255, 271, 279, 280,
    301, 302, 309

Rabta 333
Rafah 42, 328
Rafi party 51, 248
Rafsanjani, Hashemi 136, 141
Rajavi, Massoud 136, 182
Rajoub, Jibril 43
Ramadan 148
Ramadan, Said 107
Ramallah xix, xxvi, xxvii, 36, 43, 131, 132, 229, 240, 241, 333, 335
Ramat Eshkol 173
Ramleh 77, 253
Ramonet, Ignacio 299
Ramot Allon 173
Rapid Deployment Joint Task Force (RDJTF) 22, 318, 322, 323
Ras al-Khaimah 25
Ras Banas base 323
Ras Muhammad 283
Ras Sudar 283
Rashid, Sheikh (Dubai, United Arab Emirates) 25
Ratz 163
Reagan, Ronald xxi, 208, 218, 318, 319, 323
Reagan Peace Plan xix, 318
Red Sea xxvii, 2, 287, 291, 293, 338, 341
Refah (Islamic Welfare Party) xxiv, 307, 308
Refugees 255–58
Reichstag 92
Rejectionist Front xviii, 272
Republican Guard 103, 120
Republican People's Party 306, 308
Revisionist 47, 64, 65, 77, 93, 165, 218, 281, 343, 344
Revolutionary Command Council 119, 289
Reza Shah (Iran) 134
Rhodesia 269
Rida, Rashid 212
Right of Return 255–58
Riyadh ix, xxiv, 51, 53, 186, 192, 272, 273, 274, 277, 323, 324, 340
'Road Map' xi, xiii, xxviii, 39, 76, 96, 133, 241, 264
Rodinson, Maxime 148, 176, 207, 344, 345
Rogers Plan xvii, 7, 54, 68, 318
Roman Empire 13, 41

Rome/Romans 49, 75, 89, 241, 280, 301, 344
Rome and Jerusalem (Hess) 344
Roosevelt, Franklin D. 204, 274, 316
Rothschild, Lord Walter 41
Rouleau, Eric 7
Roy, Olivier 151, 152, 302
Rozyrev, Andrei 262
Rubaya Ali, Salem 339
Rue des Rosiers 12
Rufeisen, Daniel 174
Rumaila oilfield 100
Rumsfeld, Donald ix, x, 276, 323
Russia xi, xxviii, 3, 13, 14, 21, 31, 32, 33, 39, 40, 42, 47, 61, 75, 82, 89, 97, 259–64, 268, 274, 293, 300, 305, 312, 330, 338, 344, 346, 377, 380

Saadabad Pact 183
Saadat, Ahmed 107, 119
Sabha 251
Sabra xix, xx, xxvi, 191, 234, 253, 259, 265–67, 284
Sabri, Ali 267
Sadat, Muhammad Anwar al- xviii, xix, 6, 7, 8, 9, 36, 56, 68, 117, 126, 127, 150, 151, 210, 213, 215, 216, 234, 246, 251, 261, 267–68, 362
Sadr, Bani 136
Sadr, Imam Musa 114
Safad 1, 13, 344
Safavi, Isma'il 134
Safavid Empire/dynasty 134, 139, 286
Sahara 251
Sahel-Saharan 201
Said, Nuri 142, 317
Said, Port 4, 291, 293
Saint Jean-de-Maurienne Agreement 293
Saint Simonians 13, 344
Salah, Ali Abdullah 338, 340
Saleh, Abdel Jawad 240
Saleh, Ali 240
Salem 128
Salman Pak site 331
Salman, Prince (Saudi Arabia) 272
Salonika 49

Salvador 33
Samara, Adel 37
Samaria 81, 279, 334
Samuel, Herbert 42
Samuel, Jacob 113
San Remo Conference 294
Sana'a xxii, 286, 338, 340, 341
Sanbar, Elias 129
sanctions 269–71
Sandinistas 200
Sanussi Brotherhood 198, 199
Sarkis, Nikos 224
Sarrail, General 84
Sartawi, Issam xix, 12, 63, 234,
    271–72
Sartre, Jean-Paul 176, 218
Sassanid dynasty 134
Sasson, Eliahu 246
Saud, Ibn 52, 125, 220, 273
Saud dynasty/family 52, 272–73,
    274, 275, 277
Saudi Arabia/Saudi x, xix, xxi, xxii,
    xxiv, xxvii, 3, 4, 12, 16, 18, 19,
    20, 21, 22, 23, 24, 25, 26, 27, 31,
    32, 33, 52, 53, 54, 86, 89, 98,
    100, 102, 103, 108, 110, 123,
    124, 125, 126, 138, 140, 141,
    148, 151, 152, 169, 179, 186,
    187, 192, 196, 211, 214, 221,
    222, 223, 224, 261, 263, 272,
    273–78, 296, 298, 304, 305, 316,
    317, 323, 324, 329, 330, 331,
    338, 339, 340, 341
Saudi Arabian Oil Company (Saudi
    Aramco) 274
Savak 135
Savir, Uri 96, 255
Sazonov, Sergei 259
Scarcia, Biancamaria 148
Schröder, Gerhardt 89
Schwarzkopf, General Norman 40
Scotland 201, 252
Scud missile (al-Hussein) xxiii, 99,
    103, 282, 329, 330, 331, 333
Sde Boker 51
Sea of Marmara 259, 293
Selim I, Sultan (Ottoman Empire)
    230
Semna 333
Senustret III, Pharaoh 291
Sephardi 163, 224, 225, 226

September 11 ix, xi, xxvi, xxviii, 15,
    31, 53, 54, 70, 75, 99, 120, 148,
    149, 150, 180, 188, 205, 223,
    252, 261, 274, 276, 300, 307,
    311, 322, 342
Serbia 230, 269
Serte 251
Seruv 159, 165
settlements 278–81
Seurat, Michel xxi, 116
Sèvres 4, 183, 231, 248, 294
Seyhan river 307
Shabbat 158
Shabiba 43
Shafi, Haydar Abdel 236, 240
Shahal, Moshe 37
Shahed, Laila 258
Shahine, Tanios 193
Shalit, Benjamin 173
Shalom, Abraham 266
Shalom Achshav 164, 165, 281
Shamir, Yitzhak 64, 76, 153, 154,
    157, 165, 217, 236, 247, 249,
    254, 281–82, 301
Shammar 272
Shanab, Ismail Abu Shatila 110
Shanghai 175
Sharansky, Natan 167
Sharara, Walid 114
Sharett, Moshe 51, 246
Sharjah 25
Sharm el-Sheikh 4, 5, 283, 336, 378
Sharon, Ariel xi, xxv, xxvi, xxviii, 8,
    15, 44, 45, 59, 61, 77, 89, 90, 99,
    130, 131, 132, 133, 154, 159,
    164, 166, 167, 170, 180, 205,
    217, 219, 226, 250, 254, 258,
    265, 266, 280, 282–85, 302, 322,
    337
Shas 166, 167, 226
Shatila xix, xx, xxvi, 234, 258,
    265–67, 284
Shatt al-Arab 26, 100, 139, 140
Shatt al-Basra 100
Sheba'a 116, 197
Shem Tov 225
Shemen Agricultural College 248
Shenuda III (Coptic Pope) 268
Shi'a 285
Shi'ism 22, 23, 65, 66, 115, 134,
    147, 181, 274, 285–87, 311, 341

Shi'ite ix, xx, xxi, xxiii, 22, 23, 24, 34, 61, 62, 66, 103, 104, 114, 115, 120, 135, 139, 140, 142, 144, 146, 181, 187, 188, 189, 192, 196, 206, 209, 276, 286, 287, 298, 302, 311
Shilluk 288
Shilo 59
Shinui party 163, 168
Shuf xx, 62, 66, 195, 206
Shu'fat 353
Shuqairi, Ahmad 5, 117, 232
Siberia 92
Sid-Ahmed, Muhammad 328
Sidon 110, 221
Sierra Leone 201
Silva, Flavius 207
Sinai xvi, xix, 5, 6, 8, 9, 56, 57, 68, 72, 83, 114, 132, 234, 268, 292, 366
Singer, Yoel 255
Sirte 201
Smyrna 293
Sobibor 93
Socialist International 272
Society of Muslim Brothers 107, 108, 151, 152, 179, 188, 211, 212, 213, 214, 215
Solel Boneh 65
Solidere 111
Somalia 16, 18, 22, 54, 201, 323, 324, 338
South Africa/South African 33, 45, 52, 200, 269, 302, 331
South Lebanon Army xx, xxv, 312
South Yemen xviii, xxii, 16, 26, 105, 111, 112, 261, 319, 324, 339, 340
see also North Yemen, Yemen
Spain 121, 145, 147, 187, 224, 255, 331
Special International Regime for the City of Jerusalem 351
Stalin, Joseph 47, 260
Stern Gang 47, 244
Sternhell, Ze'ev 156
Stockholm 61
Stockholm International Peace Research Institute (SIPRI) 31, 32
Sublime Porte 193, 230
Sudairis 272

Sudan xxi, xxiv, 15, 16, 18, 31, 39, 53, 97, 102, 124, 126, 201, 214, 218, 230, 255, 270, 287–91, 320, 323, 325, 326, 333
Sudanese People's Liberation Army 289, 290
Sudanese Socialist Union 289
Suez 3, 4, 8, 29, 42, 51, 85, 98, 117, 126, 291, 292, 293, 316
Suez Canal xvi, 4, 6, 7, 42, 56, 66, 67, 68, 70, 83, 96, 97, 98, 124, 212, 215, 216, 221, 230, 268, 291–93, 317, 338, 346
Suffert, Georges 63
Suleiman, Sultan (the Magnificent) (Ottoman Empire) 230
Sultan, Prince (Saudi Arabia) 52, 272, 273
Sultan, Sheikh (Sharjah, United Arab Emirates) 25
Sultanate of Muscat and Oman 26
Sunday Times xx, 330
Sunna 251, 276
Sunni/Sunnism 24, 34, 45, 61, 62, 66, 71, 110, 118, 119, 121, 142, 147, 148, 180, 182, 187, 188, 191, 193, 194, 196, 209, 274, 285, 286, 287, 294, 297, 298, 302, 311, 341
Sweden/Swedish 61, 282
Switzerland/Swiss 231
Sykes, Mark 293
Sykes–Picot Agreement 42, 84, 94, 97, 231, 259, 293–94
Syria/Syrian x, xi, xv, xvi, xvii, xviii, xx, xxi, xxii, xxv, 1, 2, 3, 4, 5, 6, 7, 8, 9, 12, 16, 17, 18, 23, 27, 28, 30, 31, 32, 33, 34, 41, 45, 46, 47, 58, 60, 61, 65, 66, 68, 73, 82, 83, 84, 85, 86, 87, 88, 94, 95, 96, 101, 104, 105, 107, 110, 111, 112, 115, 116, 117, 118, 119, 122, 125, 126, 127, 142, 154, 161, 183, 186, 190, 192, 194, 196, 197, 198, 200, 206, 207, 209, 214, 218, 221, 230, 232, 234, 235, 242, 246, 247, 251, 254, 256, 258, 259, 260, 261, 272, 275, 278, 287, 293, 294–97, 298, 301, 305, 306, 309, 310, 315, 316, 317, 318, 319, 320, 325, 326, 327, 328, 329, 332, 333, 339, 360, 367, 377, 378

Taayush 165
Taba xi, xxv, 35, 57, 58–61, 74, 80, 228, 257, 258, 281, 325, 335, 378, 379
Taba Negotiations 79, 229
Taba Summit 61
Tabqa Dam 325
Tabriz 134
Taibeh 161
Taif xxi, 62, 110, 115, 116, 192, 196, 197, 198, 206, 298, 340
Taif Accords 66, 87, 298–99
Taiwan 330
Tajikistan 151
Talabani, Jalal 184, 186
Talal 116, 178
Taliban ix, xii, 53, 138
Talpiot 173
Tammuz nuclear reactor xix, 9, 330
Tanzania 53
Tarhuna 201, 333
Tehiya 166
Tehran xix, 32, 40, 86, 88, 115, 138, 139, 140, 141, 142, 146, 181, 183, 185, 221, 263, 319, 330, 331
Tel al-Za'atar xviii, 234
Tel Aviv xxiv, xxvi, 5, 6, 7, 13, 36, 48, 51, 64, 69, 88, 95, 153, 154, 172, 195, 209, 211, 217, 240, 246, 249, 255, 265, 266, 279, 284, 301, 309, 318, 342
Temple Mount xxv
terrorism 299–304
Terzian, Pierre 222
Thatcher, Margaret 99
Third Reich 281, 303
Tiananmen Square 101
Tiberias, Lake 1, 13, 77, 95, 96, 324, 344
Tigris, River 324, 327
Tikrit 118, 119
Tlass, Mustafa 34
Tobruk 199
Tokyo 300
Toschka Canal 326
Toubous 201
Touma 162
trade patterns 304–5
'Transfer Committee' 78
Transjordan xv, 1, 2, 16, 42, 46, 47, 64, 177, 178, 190, 333

Transylvania 230
Treaty of Lausanne 183, 305
Treaty of Sèvres 183, 231, 305, 306
Treblinka 93
Tripoli xvii, xviii, xx, 62, 86, 200, 201, 242, 252, 270, 333
Tripolitania 198, 199
True Path Party (DYP) 308
Truman, Harry 202, 204, 246, 316
Tsahal 1, 51
Tsar Nicholas I (Russia) 230
Tsomet 158, 159, 166
Tuaregs 201
Tulkarem 36, 169, 229, 333, 335
Tunb Islands (Greater and Lesser) 22, 25
Tunis xix, xx, xxi, xxii, 16, 43, 254, 268, 301
Tunisia 16, 28, 73, 74, 83, 102, 200
Turkey/Turkish xxiv, 15, 22, 27, 31, 32, 40, 41, 67, 74, 84, 89, 97, 104, 113, 125, 134, 139, 142, 147, 151, 179, 181, 182, 183, 184, 185, 186, 190, 214, 220, 230, 255, 259, 263, 264, 287, 292, 293, 294, 305–11, 316, 317, 324, 325, 327, 332, 333, 349
Turkish Petroleum Company 84
Tutsis 93
Twin Towers, New York 276

UAE see United Arab Emirates
Uganda 217, 290, 291, 326
Ukraine 313
Umayyad 27, 147, 241, 286
Umm al-Fahm 161, 162
Umm al-Qaywain 25
Umm Qasr 188
Umma party 288, 289
UNESCO (United Nations Educational, Social and Cultural Organisation) 171
Union of Arab and French Banks 304
United Arab Emirates (UAE) x, 16, 20, 22, 23, 25, 26, 27, 31, 32, 89, 123, 126, 186, 224, 304, 305, 324, 329
United Arab Republic (UAR) xvi, 17, 28, 30, 34, 46, 68, 105, 117, 143, 194, 216, 251, 294

United Kingdom *see* Great Britain
United Nations (UN) ix, x, xi, xv,
  xviii, xxii, xxiii, xxiv, xxviii, 1, 2,
  3, 4, 6, 17, 23, 52, 53, 59, 72, 75,
  76, 81, 82, 85, 89, 98, 99, 101,
  102, 103 106, 120, 121, 126, 129,
  141, 144, 145, 146, 153, 171,
  172, 173, 183, 188, 194, 199,
  201, 216, 235, 236, 239, 244,
  246, 247, 250, 256, 260, 264,
  269, 270, 282, 283, 290, 312,
  313, 314, 317, 328, 330, 332,
  351, 353, 354, 356, 359, 361,
  362, 364, 366, 368, 370, 379,
  380, 382, 384, 385
United Nations Charter xxii
United Nations Interim Force in
  Lebanon 312–13
United Nations General Assembly
  78, 86, 95, 233, 245, 256, 257,
  303, 313, 314
United Nations Programme for
  Development xi, 18
United Nations Relief and Works
  Agency for Palestine Refugees
  (UNRWA) 74, 76, 79, 90, 242, 255,
  257
United Nations Resolutions xvii,
  xxi, xxii, xxiii, xxiv, xxvi, xxvii,
  6, 7, 8, 17, 38, 39, 59, 60, 102,
  103, 106, 112, 120, 121, 130,
  133, 136, 144, 145, 153, 170,
  185, 197, 228, 235, 238, 243,
  245, 256, 257, 263, 269, 270,
  280, 312, 313–15, 320, 322, 350,
  359, 361, 264, 365, 368, 371,
  372, 379, 380, 381, 382, 383, 384
United Nations Special Commission
  (UNSCOM) 321, 381
United Nations Truce Supervision
  Organisation (UNTSO) 313
United States Central Command
  (CENTCOM) 322–24
United States of America/American
  ix, x, xi, xii, xiv, xvi, xviii, xxix,
  xxi, xxiv, xxviii, 3, 4, 7, 8, 9, 10,
  14, 15, 20, 21, 22, 23, 25, 26, 27,
  30, 31, 32, 33, 35, 39, 40, 41, 42,
  46, 47, 49, 50, 51, 52, 53, 54, 55,
  57, 58, 59, 61, 68, 69, 70, 72, 73,
  74, 75, 82, 85, 86, 87, 88, 89, 93,
  95, 96, 98, 99, 100, 101, 102, 103,
  104, 105, 115, 116, 118, 119, 120,
  121, 130, 133, 135, 136, 137, 138,
  141, 144, 145, 146, 149, 150, 151,
  152, 154, 155, 158, 160, 171, 176,
  177, 179, 180, 181, 183, 185, 188,
  189, 192, 194, 195, 197, 199, 200,
  201, 202, 203, 204, 205, 209, 210,
  211, 216, 217, 218, 219, 220, 223,
  224, 225, 227, 234, 236, 241, 242,
  243, 246, 247, 248, 249, 252, 253,
  254, 259, 260, 261, 262, 263, 264,
  265, 267, 268, 270, 271, 272, 273,
  274, 275, 276, 277, 285, 288, 289,
  290, 291, 295, 299, 300, 304, 305,
  306, 309, 310, 315–22, 323, 324,
  329, 331, 332, 333, 338, 340, 341,
  346, 362, 377, 378, 380
Unity Dam 327
Universal Company of the Maritime
  Suez Canal 291
Untermenschen 93
Urban II, Pope 73
USS *Cole* 53, 341
USSR/Soviet Union x, 1, 3, 4, 7, 8,
  9, 14, 15, 21, 22, 31, 34, 40, 41,
  47, 51, 52, 56, 57, 58, 68, 85, 86,
  101, 106, 113, 133, 134, 135,
  138, 139, 140, 143, 144, 149,
  154, 157, 160, 167, 175, 183,
  186, 199, 200, 202, 204, 210,
  216, 218, 222, 230, 226, 233,
  234, 235, 243, 246, 247, 248,
  259, 260, 261, 262, 267, 268,
  287, 294, 299, 305, 306, 307,
  310, 315, 316, 317, 319, 322,
  323, 328, 329, 330, 338, 339

Vaad Leumi 342
Vanunu, Mordechai xx, xxi, 330
Vatican xxiii
Védrine, Hubert x, 88
Venezuela 33, 220, 222
Venice 71, 365
Verete, Mayir 42
Vichy 85, 176, 194
Vidal-Naquet, Pierre 93
Vienna/Viennese xix, 113, 184, 230,
  344, 382
Vietnam xxii
Vietnam War 21, 22

Vishneva 248
Voice of Palestine 29
Voice of the Arabs 28, 68
von Rath, Ernest 92

Wadi Salib 224
Wafd 2, 67, 97, 124, 212, 215
Wahhabi/Wahhabism 272, 274, 275
Wailing Wall 60
Waintrop, Edouard 176
Waldheim, Kurt 246
Wannsee, Berlin 92, 93
Warba 100
Warsaw 47
Wasat party
Washington DC ix, x, xi, xii, xix,
    xx, xxv, xxvi, 3, 8, 15, 20, 22, 25,
    32, 40, 41, 53, 59, 69, 72, 75, 80,
    89, 96, 99, 145, 150, 178, 179,
    185, 189, 201, 209, 216, 217,
    222, 228, 236, 246, 247, 252,
    253, 254, 260, 262, 263, 264,
    267, 271, 272, 273, 276, 290,
    299, 305, 309, 315, 316, 317,
    318, 319, 320, 321, 322, 323,
    324, 329, 332, 333, 335, 341
Washington Declaration 35
Washington Post 262
water 325–28
Wazzan government xx
weapons of mass destruction
    328–33
Weitz, Josef 78
Weizmann, Chaim 42, 43, 346
West Bank xv, xvi, xvii, xviii, xxi,
    xxiii, xxiv, xxv, xxvi, xxvii, 2, 5,
    6, 7, 9, 15, 17, 30, 35, 36, 37, 38,
    43, 44, 56, 57, 58, 59, 60, 78, 80,
    81, 88, 90, 91, 96, 106, 107, 108,
    110, 117, 118, 125, 127, 128,
    129, 130, 132, 156, 158, 159,
    161, 166, 169, 171, 173, 177,
    178, 180, 204, 205, 219, 227,
    228, 229, 233, 234, 235, 236,
    238, 239, 241, 242, 243, 278,
    279, 280, 302, 308, 320, 326,
    333–37, 363, 364, 365, 368, 372,
    373, 374, 375, 376
Western Wall 60
Wheelus military base 199
White Guard 277

White House ix, xii, 8, 9, 34, 37, 59,
    73, 95, 316, 319, 320
Wilson, Woodrow 316
Wolf, Danny 283
World Bank 20, 38, 69, 239, 340
World Health Organisation 326
'World Islamic Front for Jihad
    against Jews and Crusaders' 53
World Islamic League 275
World Trade Center xxvi, 299, 300
World Trade Organisation (WTO)
    180, 273, 304
World War I 14, 28, 49, 83, 84, 94,
    97, 124, 134, 142, 147, 177, 183,
    184, 190, 193, 198, 208, 220,
    230, 231, 255, 260, 274, 292,
    293, 294, 305, 316, 338
World War II 9, 16, 28, 50, 63, 85,
    89, 93, 94, 97, 98, 126, 142, 150,
    155, 175, 177, 183, 186, 199,
    203, 204, 260, 270, 281, 292,
    294, 303, 306, 316, 319, 323,
    330, 342
Wye River Memorandum xxv, 219
Wye River Summit 320, 336

Yahad Shivtei Yisrael 167
Yarmuk river 326, 327
Yaron, Arnos 266
Yassin, Sheikh Ahmed 107, 108,
    109, 110, 219
Yazbaki clan 66
Yazid 286
Yediot Aharonot (newspaper) 64, 112,
    171, 265, 283
Yehud 282
Yeltsin, Boris 262, 263
Yemen/Yemeni xvi, xviii, xxii, xxiii,
    3, 4, 6, 13, 16, 20, 21, 22, 25, 26,
    27, 31, 52, 53, 102, 103, 105,
    111, 112, 122, 126, 167, 189,
    214, 225, 274, 276, 286, 329,
    338–41
    see also North Yemen, South
    Yemen
Yemeni Socialist Party (YSP) 339,
    340
Yemeni War (1962–70) xi
Yertsinski, Yitzhak 281
Yerushalayim (newspaper) 283
Yesh Gvul 159, 164

Yezidis 209
Yilmaz, Mesut 308
Yinon, Oded
Yishuv 14, 50, 155, 160, 163, 204,
    245, 282, 341–43
Yugoslavia 230, 268
Yumurtalik 324

Zaghlul, Saad 67
Zaidi/Zaidism 209, 286, 341
Zarka 54
Zatec 1
Zayid, Sheikh (Abu Dhabi, United
    Arab Emirates) 25, 26

Zealots 207
Zeevi, Rehavam xxvi, 107, 166
Zghorta 191, 206
Zimbabwe 198
Zinjibar prison 341
Zionism/Zionist 13, 14, 42, 43,
    47, 48, 49, 50, 65, 86, 97, 98,
    234, 242, 244, 260, 261, 271,
    281, 314, 316, 342, 343,
    344–47
Zionist Organisation 344
Ziv, Saul 283
Ziyyad, Tawfiq 162
Zoroastrian 134